GOVERNMENT AND ECONOMIC DEVELOPMENT

A Publication of the Economic Growth Center, Yale University

GOVERNMENT

AND

ECONOMIC DEVELOPMENT

EDITED BY GUSTAV RANIS

New Haven and London, Yale University Press, 1971

Library of Congress catalog card number: 79–140537
International standard book number: 0–300–01417–1

Designed by Sally Sullivan,
set in Linotype Times Roman type,
and printed in the United States of America by
The Colonial Press Inc., Clinton, Mass.

Distributed in Great Britain, Europe, and Africa by
Yale University Press, Ltd., London; in Canada by
McGill-Queen's University Press, Montreal; in Mexico
by Centro Interamericano de Libros Académicos,
Mexico City; in Central and South America by Kaiman
& Polon, Inc., New York City; in Australasia by
Australia and New Zealand Book Co., Pty., Ltd.,
Artarmon, New South Wales; in India by UBS Publishers'
Distributors Pvt., Ltd., Delhi; in Japan by John
Weatherhill, Inc., Tokyo.

Contents

Foreword

This volume is one in a series of studies supported by the Economic Growth Center, an activity of the Yale Department of Economics since 1961. The Center is a research organization with worldwide activities and interests. Its research interests are defined in terms of both method of approach and subject matter. In terms of method, the Center sponsors studies which are designed to test significant general hypotheses concerning the problem of economic growth and which draw on quantitative information from national economic accounts and other sources. In terms of subject matter, the Center's research interests include theoretical analyses of economic structure and growth, quantitative analyses of a national economy as an integral whole, comparative cross-sectional studies using data from a number of countries, and efforts to improve the techniques of national economic measurement. The research program includes field investigation of recent economic growth in twenty-five developing countries of Asia, Africa, and Latin America.

The Center administers, jointly with the Department of Economics, the Yale training program in International and Foreign Economic Administration. It presents a regular series of seminar and workshop meetings and includes among its publications both book-length studies and journal reprints by staff members, the latter circulated as Center Papers.

Gustav Ranis, Director

Preface

Early versions of most of the papers contained in this volume were originally presented at a 1968 Economic Growth Center conference on "The Role of Government in Economic Development." Most of the contributions emerged as a by-product of the Center's country analysis program, through which we are attempting to analyze growth and structural change in about twenty-five of the major developing countries over substantial historical time periods. A few aim at making comparisons among countries; but all are primarily concerned with shedding some light on the role of government policy in the post–World War II period.

While inflation, the cold war, or urban decay may command a good deal of attention in the rest of the world, developing societies customarily place national economic growth at the top of their public policy agenda. Government can and does affect the course of such development in a number of ways: through the more specific societal goals it sets or permits to be reflected; through its choice concerning the extent of government participation in directly productive activity; through the quantity and quality of its controls over the private sector; and through its role as fiscal agent on both the tax and the expenditure sides. The conference was organized less on functional than on geographical lines, leaving contributors free to range across a number of dimensions of the subject under discussion. Nevertheless, the papers exhibited some tendency to group themselves naturally by focusing on one or the other of the dimensions just cited.

In Part I, papers by Berry and Snodgrass seek to explore the setting of societal goals as a function of the environment as a whole. Berry, in discussing Colombia, presents a rather unusual—by the standards of our profession—case study of the interaction between social structure, the role assigned to the government, and economic growth. Snodgrass traces the economic effects of the largely political acts of first pulling together, and then partly breaking apart, various components of the Malaysian Federation.

The contributions of Part II, by Land and Frank, deal mainly with the question of the relative roles of public and private enterprise and the impact of different mixes on efficiency and overall growth. Land's analysis of the private and social profitability of state enterprises in Turkey, perhaps the most formidable contemporary etatist stronghold outside the socialist bloc, is based on highly original detective work on the relevant enterprise accounts. Caught in a mesh of extraeconomic objectives and constraints, such enterprises exhibit extremely poor cash flows, starve the private sector of resources and opportunities, and retard economic growth. Frank, on the other hand, comparing performance in five differently mixed African economies, is unable to come up with any clearcut findings that show the superiority of private enterprise. Although growth in the more private-oriented industrial sectors of Kenya and Tanzania is found to have been faster than that in the more government-oriented equivalents in Nigeria and Ghana, he reminds us of the existence of somehow successful Ugandan public enterprise and raises the question of whether the usual prescription for achieving sustained profitability and national growth has to be modified when "private" is mainly to be read as "foreign" or "expatriate."

Part III contains four papers that focus mainly on the performance of various individual developing societies in relation to the quantity and quality of selected public sector policies toward their private sectors. Hymer, Mamalakis, and Díaz analyze the history of government policies toward the private sector in the cases of Ghana, Chile, and Argentina over relatively long historical time periods. Hymer attempts to show that during the colonial period the private Ghanaian economy prospered despite rather than because of usually wrongheaded government efforts; while postindependence governments—aside from the excesses of the late Nkrumah period—reversed this process. Mamalakis seeks to highlight, for the case of the nitrate industry in Chile, the possible options open to governments interposing themselves on an essentially colonial pattern of resource flows. As a consequence of a (possibly misapplied) laissez-faire philosophy, the decision was made early not to buy out foreign capitalists who had provided relatively little in exchange for the chance to exploit Chile's monopoly position. Instead the government attempted to intervene indirectly—and, apparently from a long-term growth standpoint,

ineffectually—due to its failure to provide a network of fairly predictable rules by which the game was to be played.

Díaz's analysis of the developmental role of government through
four phases of Argentine history provides a number of interesting
lessons. For one, it reinforces the view that the initial determination
of the size of the public sector—even pre-Peron—may have relatively little to do with economic considerations, but that, once a given
public sector establishment exists, the ability to fix the proper mix of
economic policies becomes severely constrained; secondly we learn
that Argentina, more industrialized than most other developing countries and reacting to the recession of the 1930s as much as to the
developmental pressure of the 1950s, was an early student of Hjalmar
Schacht's; that is, virtually every combination of trade, price controls,
and financial controls over the private sector was tried at one time or
another in the dual effort to achieve a socially desirable change in
income distribution and to encourage growth via a preponderant
emphasis on import substitution.

Pack's paper on Israel starts with an analysis of a somewhat unusual
set of social objectives, including geopolitically motivated agricultural
growth *cum* population dispersal. It moves from there to a consideration of the policy package, including foreign exchange controls, licensing, budget deficits, and fairly high consumption standards, all of
which were considered essential to producing the desired results.
The entire array of policy instruments, largely direct, some indirect,
used to induce certain private sector actions are scrutinized. Yet the
superior dynamic foresight of an omnipresent public sector is viewed
as sufficient to swamp the admittedly considerable static inefficiencies
entailed.

The contributions in Part IV are addressed in the main to what is
still the most traditional dimension in tracing the governmental impact
on economic development, namely that exercised through its fiscal
powers. Ho's paper emphasizes the importance of government exhaustive expenditures in Taiwan, especially during the period of Japanese colonialism. Expenditures on research and, somewhat surprisingly, on the police turn out to have had major nation-building consequences, more so than the attempt to influence private sector actions
through indirect controls or regulations.

The two Latin American papers in this group, one by Clark
Reynolds on Mexico, the other by Hunt on Peru, are concerned, as

one would expect, with the fiscal system's impact on distributional as well as developmental objectives. Reynolds's careful description of the level and composition of Mexican tax and expenditures policies since the late 1930s reveals, inter alia, that in spite of a good deal of socialist rhetoric it is social expenditures, especially on education and health, and not exhaustive expenditures in the directly productive areas, that have kept total government expenditures from declining as a percentage of national income. Reynolds, moreover, puts forward the unorthodox proposition that government controls over the private sector may be intended mainly as a stabilizing device, in the effort to have private expenditures respond to government budgets geared to the rhythm of the six-year presidential term. Hunt sees the budget mechanism as the main tool for accommodating clashes among the various interest groups. With the tax structure dominated by the oligarchy and increasingly regressive—as is typical of many developing countries—the expenditures side is relied on to achieve redistribution at a minimum cost in terms of either efficiency or reinvestment capacity. Hunt's paper also includes a review of the relevant literature on cross-country expenditure and revenue patterns at different levels of per capita income, as well as on the joint incidence of taxation and expenditure across a number of countries.

Finally, in Part V a number of relevant intercountry comparative papers are presented. The Cohen-Ranis contribution attempts to compare the effectiveness of various attempts to restructure colonial resource patterns in the post–World War II period. It seeks to make the point that in the 1950s the governments of the developing countries, unhappy with the objectives and results of the colonial era, by and large attempted to redirect vital resource flows by means of direct controls and a good deal of across-the-board interventionism; and, moreover, that the generally mediocre results of this effort have led to a gradual realization in the 1960s, in at least a number of cases, that the achievement of national economic growth objectives may be more consistent with the hitherto discredited indirect tools of government policy, working through rather than substituting for the market mechanism.

One important component of the tool kit available, namely that of adjustment in the developing economy's exchange rate, is examined more closely in the contribution by Cooper. His paper overcomes substantial data handicaps in making a first attempt to examine a considerable number (two dozen) of recent devaluation cases and in distilling from that experience some generalizations (if still tentative) concerning likely impacts on a number of fronts. Some comfortable shibboleths concerning the effects of exchange rate adjustments on prices, the terms of trade, and political stability—among others—are subjected to question in the course of the inquiry.

The final paper, by Lloyd Reynolds, surveys the state of our knowledge—and ignorance—on government's contribution to saving and capital formation in a substantial number of countries. Not surprisingly, he finds it easier to trace the evolution of the public sector's contribution to total capital formation in the mature economies—it has been rising historically—than to come up with reliable data on the developing world, where public sector saving has been falling somewhat with rising GNP. But it is the composition of that contribution, as it affects not only the quality of the public sector effort, but also the size and quality of private investment, that is rightly recognized as crucial. The author manages to pull together in a clear, coherent fashion what is currently known on this difficult subject, and to propose a road map for our future research effort.

It remains for me only to express my appreciation to the authors and discussants of the papers included in this volume, and to extend special thanks to Albert Berry, who helped to organize the original conference on which the volume is based.

G. R.

PART I: THE GOVERNMENT AS GOAL SETTER

1

Some Implications of Elitist Rule
for Economic Development in Colombia

BY R. ALBERT BERRY

Who controls a nation's political system and dominates its society clearly has many economic and other implications for the various groups that make up that society. In general, the greater a group's social and political power the greater the share of income it receives.[1] But the different implications for the level of economic performance of rule by an oligarchy, by a corporate state with representation of various interested groups (not necessarily through the voting process), by a relatively modern "democratic" state in the sense of the North American and Western European states, or by a military dictatorship, are not clear. The stage of economic development undoubtedly helps to determine the form of government, but again the form and directness of the relationship is unclear.

This paper has the limited goal of outlining some of the economic effects of the concentration of power in a rather small and elite group —a concentration that has characterized Colombia throughout its history (though the degree has waned in recent years). It does not attempt, explicitly, to contrast the policies and implications of rule by the elite with those of a possible alternative form of government. Comments will be made on the size of the government sector, and on the government's historical policies with respect to agriculture, education, and population. Other implications of elitist rule do not

1. This relationship is not necessarily a simple one. As a generalization to be applied across countries it has some but not complete validity. And it does not mean that the overwhelming use of political and social power is to increase wealth, nor that all the wealthy necessarily have great social and political power. In some cases patterns of life associated with the oligarchy are inconsistent with achieving maximum income and wealth positions in a changing economy, e.g. landlords who are not willing to become businessmen. Nevertheless, within a given country and for a given social system, the generalization seems valid.

show themselves specifically through economic policy but follow more directly from the distribution of income and power; for example, distribution of income may affect the savings ratio, distribution of power may affect the degree of competition in the economy, and so on.

Two general cautioning remarks should be made here. First, the discussion that follows confines itself to the effects of the concentration of power and largely ignores broader questions such as the effects of factors that helped to lead to that concentration and had distinct and important economic effects as well. It has been cogently argued that the single factor responsible for Colombia's economic backwardness relative to the United States has been the original distribution of land.[2] This distribution, it is claimed, led directly to retardation of the development of the agricultural sector (and hence the economy as a whole) and also was the basis for the concentration of power, which then had certain economic effects of its own. In this study we disregard the broader (and perhaps more interesting) question of the overall economic effects (direct and indirect, through the political and social system) of land distribution and, in a sense holding that distribution constant, ask how the concentration of power per se affected the course of events.

Second, the discussion here is by no means as fully applicable to the Colombia of 1968 as it was even as late as the 1950s, though the decreasing applicability has, of course, been gradual.[3] The late 1950s and the 1960s have seen fairly rapid changes in the country; in the last few years there has been much more stress on agriculture than before; education has made considerable advances; there are breaks in society's stance on birth control. Hence, tardily but unambiguously, Colombia is moving into the modern world. The issue under discussion here is, Why so late? [4]

2. See, in particular, T. Lynn Smith, *Colombia: Social Structure and the Process of Development* (Gainesville: University of Florida Press, 1967).

3. Certainly President Alfonso López carried out some reforms and executed some policies in the 1930s that are inconsistent with the general tenor of the arguments here.

4. The question might be posed differently. We would argue that the factors discussed in this paper are to a considerable extent responsible for the relatively low standard of living that now prevails in Colombia. But we would not necessarily expect them to be manifested in a slow rate of growth or change. (And, of course, Colombia's growth during the twentieth century has not been particularly slow.) For when the factors we discuss retard progress long enough, it becomes in a sense harder and harder for them to retard it any longer, and growth is almost forced upon the country. When the technological

BACKGROUND ON COLOMBIAN SOCIETY AND GOVERNMENT

With very brief exceptions since the country attained its independence around 1820, Colombia has been ruled by a civilian elite. Only rarely has military government come to the fore, most recently with the dictatorship of General Rojas Pinilla during the years 1953–57; Rojas's dictatorship did not constitute a victory of the military over civilian government, however; civilian strife was so serious that much of the elite favored some form of strong rule for a transitional period. Even weaker have been the challenges from other elements in the society; this is true both for the leftist and the nonleftist opposition. At present the possibility of revolution, or even of a large increase in the political influence of the nonelite groups, is not great. We can cite a number of key elements underlying the elite's unchallenged rule over time:

1. the strength of loyalty on the part of people at all social levels to one or the other of the traditional parties—the Conservatives and the Liberals—an adherence so strong as to lessen the possibility of the creation of class feeling;
2. a very strong Church, which has been closely related to the Conservative party in particular, and which has in general been very traditionalist and a supporter of paternalistic elitist rule and social stability;
3. tight civilian control over the military and a tradition on the part of the military of nonintervention in political affairs;
4. a relative adaptability on the part of the elite to pressures coming from farther down in the system, in order to avoid class or other confrontations. The traditional parties, while distinctly oligarchic, have been the base from which the reformist president Alfonso López developed much of the country's current labor and social legislation in the 1930s, and from which the popular reformer Jorge Eliécer Gaitán made his bid for the presidency in the late 1940s before being assassinated.

Some of the characteristics of the elite in Colombia are undoubtedly found in comparable groups anywhere in the world; others are char-

gap between the country and the modern world gets very wide, then gains from borrowing and the pressure to borrow become correspondingly great. And when the status of the lower class relative to its counterparts in other countries worsens and is coupled with better international communications, the possibilities of continued subservience, lack of education, etc. are reduced.

acteristic of the particular type of oligarchy found in Colombia, and perhaps in some other Latin American countries, but not uniformly throughout the world. We now turn to a consideration of several of the channels through which this form of social organization has affected economic development.

THE SIZE OF THE GOVERNMENT'S ROLE IN THE ECONOMY

The share of the government in total expenditures (GNP) usually rises as an economy grows in per capita income. This increase results to some degree from each of a variety of changes that accompany economic development. Development is usually associated with an increasing democratization in the sense that more and more people are able to exert claims on the government—claims the government cannot afford to disregard. Increasing per capita income leads to economies of scale in tax collection, making a larger government sector feasible. And both the increasing complexity of the economic system and the higher per capita incomes may increase the relative demand for goods and (especially) services usually produced by the government; the growing need for government services associated with urbanization shows the effects of complexity, and increasing demands for education reflect the high income elasticity of demand for this service.

At a given level of income and urbanization, we may hypothesize that the size of the "government share" is likely to be related to the degree of popular participation. Government expenditures range from those that benefit primarily the rich (paved streets in rich residential areas) to those that benefit primarily the poor (public primary education). Other things being equal, one would expect the total government share to be lower where the pressures for income-redistributive spending are smaller. To distinguish the effect of the distribution of power and income on the size of government from such factors as the average income level and the degree of urbanization, we perform a cross-country comparison that implicitly tries to hold these latter factors constant.[5] The share of government expenditures in Colombian GNP is consistent with the independent (albeit impressionistic) evi-

5. Several other factors have, in various cross-country studies, been found to be systematically related to the size of government, and these will be mentioned when appropriate.

dence referred to above of very tight and effective control of the country by the oligarchy in Colombia.

Thorn's cross-country study relating central government expenditures to per capita GNP for many countries indicates that Colombia is well below the trend line.[6] It is not appropriate to draw conclusions directly from this, since the importance of the central government in the public sector as a whole is relatively smaller in Colombia than in many other countries. But even if the whole of the public sector is included, its share of GNP was smaller than that of the central government alone in the typical country in the same income range. (See Table 1.1 for calculations made by the author for Colombia against the framework of Thorn's figures.) With respect to the more appropriate comparison using the total government share of GNP, and possibly including certain semipublic institutions in the public sector,[7] no current comparative study is known to the author. But data from a study done by Lewis and Martin a decade ago, plus some knowledge of subsequent trends, suggest that Colombia again is on the low side.[8] (See Tables 1.2 and 1.3.)

6. See Richard S. Thorn, "The Evolution of Public Finance during Economic Development," *Manchester School of Economic and Social Studies* 35, no. 1 (January 1967). Thorn's seems to be the most complete cross-country study analyzing the evolution of central government finance during economic development. He points out (see Table 1.1) that approximately one-half of the total increase in the ratio of current government expenditures to GNP and 65 percent of the increase of total current civil expenditures between the lowest and the highest per capita income groups are accounted for by current transfer payments to households. Civil consumption expenditures show a much smaller, irregular upward trend (if it is a trend at all), and the share of interest on the public debt also tends to rise. The share of GNP typically used up as central government current expenditure in the income group in which Colombia falls ($200–$500 per capita per year) is 14.8 percent. In Table 1.1 we indicate how the distribution of Colombian revenues and expenditures compare. This comparison is instructive; by itself it is not conclusive since the expenditure of other government levels has not been taken into account, but, as we see later, such inclusion does not alter our results in any important way. The striking fact is that Colombia's current central government expenditure ratio is at most only a little more than half that typical of countries in the $200–$500 per capita range. Current transfers to households are about one-tenth of the average and civil consumption expenditure is probably less than one-half.

7. Although it is frequently said in Colombia that there is an unusually large "semipublic" sector, the figures do not seem to bear this out. There are *many* semipublic organizations, but most of them are relatively small.

8. Table 1.2, taken from that study, summarizes the relevant information. The data for the other countries in this study referred to either 1953 or 1954; for Colombia they referred to 1947. This could conceivably have led to a

Table 1.1: Current Government Revenues and Expenditures: Colombia Compared to Other Countries

	Income in dollars				Differences between highest and lowest income groups	Colombia[c] figures from Thorn's study	Author's figures: central government	Author's figures: public sector (including most semipublic organizations)
	I Above 1200	II 500–1200	III 200–500	IV Under 200				
Number of countries[a]	7	8	10	11				
Revenue								
1. Indirect taxes	10.5	13.1	9.1	8.5	2.0			
2. Direct taxes on corporations	4.1	(7) 2.6	(7)2.2	2.2	1.9			
3. Direct taxes on households	10.9	(7)10.8	(7)3.8	2.0	8.9			
4. Income from property and entrepreneurs	(6)1.8	1.5	1.1	1.6	0.2			
5. Current Revenue (Sum of 1–4)	27.3	28.0	16.2	14.3	13.0			
6. Current Revenue Calculated Directly	27.3	29.1	17.8	15.9	11.4	7.81		
Expenditure								
7. Consumption expenditure	14.1	12.7	10.6	10.9	3.2		3.75	6.38
(a) Civil	8.6	(5)10.1	(2)7.5	(4)6.2	(2.4)		2.13	4.76
(b) Military	5.5	(5) 2.8	(2)4.8	(4)2.8	(2.7)	1.62	1.62	1.62
8. Subsidies	1.0	2.0	0.6	0.2	0.8	0.10	0.10	0.17
9. Interest on Public Debts	2.3	1.3	(8)0.8	(10)0.5	1.8	0.15	0.14	
10. Current transfers to households	6.7[b]	7.9	2.8	1.0	5.7	0.20	0.27	0.84
11. Current Expenditure (Sum 7–10)	24.1	23.9	14.8	12.6	11.5	7.96	4.14	7.59
12. Current Expenditure Calculated Directly	24.3	24.0	14.8	12.7	11.6			
13. Saving Calculated Directly	3.0	5.0	3.0	3.2	–0.2			

[a] Where data was not available for all countries, the number of countries having data is shown in parentheses. As a consequence, totals may not equal sum of parts.

[b] This figure becomes 7.8 when the United States is excluded.

[c] Colombia's average GNP per capita over this ten-year period was $296, according to Thorn's figures.

Sources: The first five columns of Table 1.1 are a direct reproduction of Table 1 in Thorn, while columns 7 and 8 are the author's figures—still for the same set of years, 1950–59. The sources for columns 7 and 8 were the National Accounts (Cuentas Nacionales) of Colombia and unpublished statistics from the Central Bank (Banco de la República) which were used in making up the national accounts.

Thorn's figures appear to have come from the national budget statistics in the *Anuario General de Estadística* published annually by the statistics office (Departamento Administrativo Nacional de Estadística). It seems clear that they include expenditures which in the national accounts are classified as investment. Thorn's estimate of current national government expenditure is greater than mine for current expenditure by all government levels. The figures of column 7 are an underestimate of the influence of the central government as they include only expenditures made directly by that government and exclude all transfers to other government levels; they are taken from the unpublished tables of the Central Bank from which the consolidated expenditures of all government are calculated.

It is possible that the figures for many of the other countries are overestimates relative to those of Colombia (for example, through the inclusion of investment expenditures as consumption, as in the case of Colombia), but the differences are so great as to make it unlikely that such overestimates could come close to wiping out the observed differential.

Table 1.2: Government Current and Capital Expenditure as a Percentage of GNP
at Factor Cost in Selected Countries, 1953 or 1954

Countries (in ascending order of GNP/capita)	Current expenditure as a share of GNP		Capital expenditure as a % of GNP	Current and capital expenditure/GNP
	A	B	C	A + C
Tanganyika	11.91	10.68	3.98	15.89
Uganda	12.26	10.78	6.81	19.07
India	8.84	6.15	2.30	11.14
Nigeria	4.98	4.34	2.40	7.38
Ceylon	14.42	11.59	7.45	21.87
Gold Coast	12.20	10.43	8.24	20.44
Jamaica	13.08	10.38	4.04	17.12
Br. Guiana	14.29	11.44	5.96	20.25
Colombia	11.80	8.42	3.21	15.01
Italy	24.58	12.79	5.55	30.13
Trinidad	15.54	12.42	5.51	21.05
France	25.76	10.79	8.11	33.87
U.K.	34.00	11.52	5.37	39.37
New Zealand	30.12	13.77	8.27	38.39
Sweden	23.49	13.26	13.99	37.48
U.S.A.	27.43	7.24	4.26	31.69

Note: The figures for Colombia were for 1947, while for the other countries they
were for either 1953 or 1954.

Columns *A* and *B* differ in that *A* shows total current expenditure while *B* excludes
social insurance, food or agricultural subsidies, defense, and public debt expenditure.

Source: Alison Martin and W. A. Lewis, "Patterns of Public Revenue and Expenditure," *Manchester School of Economic and Social Studies* 24, no. 3 (September 1956),
Tables I and III.

Experience in developed countries shows that the share of government (either including only exhaustive expenditures or also including
transfers) usually increases as development progresses and average

---

sizable downward bias for Colombia; but Table 1.3 suggests that such is not
the case. The discrepancy between the Martin-Lewis figure (Table 1.2) and
my own (Table 1.3) results in part from the fact that I adjusted pre-1950
GNP figures upward from the original World Bank data used by Martin-Lewis,
on the basis of the more thorough national accounts going back to 1950 and
overlapping with the earlier series.

The sample of countries used by Martin-Lewis is much smaller than the
Thorn sample and thus lacks some credibility on this count. A more serious
difficulty with the Martin-Lewis sample is that among the less developed countries it includes predominately ex-British colonies. These may well have a
higher government share than is typical of the LDC's as a whole.

Table 1.3: Colombian Government Exhaustive Expenditure as a Percentage of Total Purchases of Goods and Services

	(1)	(2)
1925	9.41	
1926	10.15	
1927	13.25	
1928	13.65	
1929	11.64	
1930	12.64	
1931	12.79	
1932	12.43	
1933	12.80	
1934	9.62	
1935	9.22	
1936	9.52	
1937	9.89	
1938	9.92	
1939	10.04	
1940	10.88	
1941	10.01	
1942	11.58	
1943	10.35	
1944	9.01	
1945	8.40	
1946	8.35	
1947	10.37	
1948	9.87	
1949	8.60	
1950	9.02	8.25
1951	10.35	
1952	10.59	
1953	11.14	
1962		12.17

Source: Calculations by the author. Column 1 uses primarily ECLA government and GDP figures, though the latter have been adjusted upward by the author for the years before 1950. Column 2 is from unpublished Central Bank statistics.

income rises.[9] The figures for Colombia (Table 1.3), showing the share of government exhaustive expenditure as a percentage of total production in the economy, reveal no long-run trend up to the 1950s,

9. Simon Kuznets, in "Quantitative Aspects of the Economic Growth of Nations: VII. The Share and Structure of Consumption," *Economic Development and Cultural Change* 10 (January 1962), part 2, found that government consumption expenditures as a proportion of GNP have risen substantially in the twentieth century in all of the countries for which long series were available,

an unusual phenomenon over such a long period in a country with rising income per capita. Since then the ratio does appear to have risen, though the year-to-year changes were not available at time of writing.

A final revealing fact is that social expenditures (i.e. expenditures on health, education, social welfare, and so forth, but excluding housing) are a smaller share of total central government expenditures in Colombia than in most countries at comparable per capita income levels.[10] (This share tends to increase with rising income levels, either cross-country or over time.)

As one might guess after surveying the above evidence, the opposition to higher taxes and tax reform in Colombia is strong; it seems that only in times of apparent crisis can such changes be made. Colombia has usually been fiscally orthodox to a greater degree than many Latin American countries, so that large-scale deficit financing has not been the rule. There is much opposition to a large government establishment as such (as well as to a large military establishment). The preference for a small government sector probably has the effect of curtailing even some public activities that would pay off from the elite's point of view. This provides an interesting parallel to another criticism made of such oligarchies: they may not give high priority to raising their own (private) incomes if this requires some action they feel is demeaning or does not fit into their classic pattern of life. This implies the existence of an inefficient overall investment pattern from any point of view.[11]

AGRICULTURAL DEVELOPMENT, INCOMES, AND POLICY

A striking feature of the Latin American economies during this century has been the slow growth of their agricultural sectors; Colombia,

---

i.e. Canada, Germany, Italy, Norway, Sweden, the United Kingdom, and the United States. It is certain that total government exhaustive expenditures have also shown a rapidly rising trend as well; if transfers were included the upward trend would probably be even more rapid.

10. Of eight countries in the per capita income range $200–$500 in 1960, Thorn's figures indicate that Colombia's social expenditure/total central government expenditure ratio was seventh; the median ratio was 31 percent; Colombia's was 19 percent. There is, of course, still the possibility that the picture would be different if all government levels could be included.

11. The traditional complaint that the government sector is so inefficient that the smaller its size the better is not convincing. The decision to staff the sector with low quality personnel (which is indeed the case) must be con-

with an average annual growth of agricultural output of about 3 percent over the last forty years, is somewhere around the mean for Latin America. One is immediately led to suspect that this may be related to the small, urban-oriented oligarchies which have dominated politics and society in most of these countries and have owned much of the land.[12]

That Spanish cultures have tended to be urban oriented is evidenced in a variety of ways, including the manner in which new settlements were laid out during colonization. While land owning is highly prestigious, many of the traditional *latifundistas* have spent most of their time in the city (or abroad). They do not send their children to school in the rural areas or even the small towns. As they have tended to live in the town, and sometimes have incomes so large that they are relatively unconcerned about increasing them, they have less interest than would otherwise be the case in pressuring the government to build roads, carry out research, and so forth.

The picture painted thus far matches the Colombian scenery; to fill it out several additional aspects should be mentioned. As time went on, some of the large-scale landowners also came to have commercial and industrial interests, leading to an ambivalence in the way they pressured the government to distribute its expenditure between agriculture and other sectors.[13] Meanwhile, the bulk of the agricultural population has been both culturally and physically unable to make serious claims on the government. Culturally this is due to the maintenance in many parts of the country, if in somewhat diminishing degree, of the traditional patron-client relationship whereby the worker and the small-scale farmer often approached a state of serfdom. Physically it is difficult because of the geographic dispersion of the farm population; political action is easier for an

---

sidered either a natural or a deliberate reaction to the fact that little has been asked of the government sector. Inefficiency is not simply an exogenously determined characteristic of government.

12. The continued control of a large share of all agricultural land by a declining number of people attests to the stability of the distribution. This is exemplified in Colombia by the existence of an agrarian reform institute, which does a certain amount of redistribution of private lands, along with a situation in which it is alleged that, with the construction of new highways into government-owned lands, large-scale landowners have easily gained control of large blocks of land in several regions. The latter phenomenon is, of course, much less publicized than the former, and such control may be contested. But the combination of events is indeed ironic and symptomatic.

13. Also, of course, a group of industrialists with no agricultural ties developed and gradually increased its political power.

urban proletariat than for a rural one, especially in a country with Colombia's terrain. There has been rural unrest culminating in the extensive violence of the mid-1940s to the mid-1950s; but although this violence demonstrated that all was not well in the countryside, it was not a class movement but rather a manifestation at the lower levels of society of the traditional hatred between Colombia's two political parties. As such it did not generate then, and has not generated to date, a political force which might vigorously represent the small farmer or the agricultural worker.[14]

The government attitude toward the agricultural sector as a whole has been characterized by a lack of interest and emphasis, though not by the extreme discrimination that was characteristic, for example, of the Perón administration in Argentina. (Moreover, this disinterest has been modified substantially in the last decade, and particularly in the last five years.) Although the general feeling that the government should be responsible for national progress and development, which gained a substantial foothold in the 1930s, did manifest itself in the form of certain institutions created to help the agricultural sector, such as the National Credit Bank, and in the formation of a Ministry of Agriculture in the late 1940s, the serious attention given to the sector has remained relatively small. Indicative of this is the lower than average quality staff the Ministries of Agriculture and related institutions have had, at least until fairly recent years.[15]

The situation, to sum up, is one in which land has been very unequally distributed *and* in which the government has not had an aggressive policy to promote agricultural output. Each of these aspects has implications. Comparisons with other countries suggest

14. Further supporting the lack of government emphasis on agricultural development in the last three or four decades has been the prevailing concept linking modernization and economic progress with industrialization. The strong adherence to this idea probably dates from the depression years, and the industrial sector has been favored since then through tariff policy, exchange policy, and other instruments. The wisdom of such a course of action, at least of the extreme way in which it has been carried out in the last ten years or so, is very doubtful.

15. Taxation of the agricultural sector has admittedly been small, partly because it is difficult, and partly because of the political forces aligned against it. (Coffee is an exception; it is produced primarily by small farmers and is easily taxed since it is an export.) But taxation, if it had been spent on the sector, would more likely have been a spur than a drag. So it is certainly valid to say that the government's agricultural policy has not been one to favor the farmer in comparison with others.

rather convincingly that, if land distribution had been more even from the start, there would have been more widespread rural education, more widespread generation of entrepreneurial talents and acceptance of new modes of farming, and so forth.[16] The lack of initiative, both individual and cooperative, in the rural sector is certainly due in considerable measure to the characteristic patron-client relationship. In the Colombian context it would not even be possible, at present, to argue that the unequal distribution of land leads to a higher average savings rate, since the latifundistas may have rather low savings rates (though there is as yet no data on this).

Even given the present nonoptimal structure of land tenure and ownership, it appears that the government's lack of interest in the agricultural sector has probably led to the loss of some of the potentially most productive investments for the economy. In some cases (agricultural research, extension, etc.) the lack of emphasis has reflected this general disinterest in agriculture; in other cases (feeder roads, credit to small farmers) it has also reflected the lack of bargaining power of the little man, whether he be found in the agricultural sector or elsewhere. Colombia began a serious agricultural research operation only in the early 1950s and to a considerable extent at the instigation of the Rockefeller Foundation. Figures on changes in yields as a result of this research suggest that it may have paid off reasonably well, despite the fact that even today extension work is low in both quality and quantity. The low quality of the extension service reflects in part the general urban orientation of the society and in part the very low levels of rural education, all of which means that few farm boys ever get to the level of agronomist,

16. Despite a general data shortage, there is some evidence that the latifundia-minifundia system is less productive than would be a system involving a more even distribution of land. Data from the Agricultural Census of 1959 strongly suggests that, while small farms are not generally as productive as large ones in terms of the yield per hectare of individual crops, they do tend to use their land much more intensively (i.e. more for crops and less for cattle) than do large farms, thus implying a greater total output. The Colombian data do not lend themselves to the sort of careful analysis that has been carried out by William Cline on this issue (see William R. Cline, "Economic Considerations for a Land Reform in Brazil" [Ph.D. diss., Yale University, 1969]). He finds that, for sugar, cotton, coffee, and several other products, returns to scale are generally constant but that there is a very definite tendency for small farms to cultivate a large share of their land. His data are better and more disaggregated than anything in Colombia and indicate that output per bundle of input (weighted by social cost) is higher on small farms; differences in output per hectare between large and small farms are even greater due to the higher labor/land ratio on small farms.

while few city boys want to. The slow development of an adequate storage system for agricultural products in Colombia is symptomatic of government disinterest and the lack of private entrepreneurial capacity and finance in the rural sector.

With the popularity of an overvalued exchange rate during the last couple of decades, the lack of emphasis on agriculture has been particularly serious and is almost sure to reflect itself in a slower growth rate of the economy at large.[17] In an economy with an overvalued exchange rate, the cost of a policy error that turns a potential export into a nonexport is particularly high. It appears that most of the substantial export potential for products other than coffee and petroleum has characteristically resided within the agricultural sector,[18] with beef probably the most important at the present time.[19]

One characteristic of Colombia's agricultural sector, resulting in part from the nature of past governmental agricultural policy and in part from the original distribution of land, is that a policy aimed at rapid increases in agricultural output runs the risk of worsening the distribution of income within the sector. It either leads to greater rural poverty and misery or forces larger migrations to the city, so that the misery will be located there, possibly constituting a force for social disruption or revolution. This potential conflict of goals has not always been so great; it is especially characteristic of a situation where output increases are likely to come from technological improvements most easily adopted by large farmers, either because of greater

17. An equilibrium exchange rate for agricultural exports would increase their private profitability over that with an overvalued exchange rate; improved social infrastructure, technological gains, and other reflections of greater government attention would have the same effect. The two are thus substitutes for each other, and the absence of one makes the existence of the other more important.

18. This is certainly less true now than it was in the past. But it must also be recognized that the current relative competitiveness of some industrial products may be the result of unwise past emphasis on the industrial sector. This current competitiveness may thus have been bought at a high price.

19. It is possible that simply instituting an equilibrium exchange rate for exports would have substantially increased the beef exports; it is also possible that a nonlatifundia structure of the sector would have had the same result. (Many cattle are produced on large farms whose technical level of operations is low and some of whose owners have such high incomes that they are not very interested in and do not spend much time on the farm.) But more relevant to the present discussion is the point that government policy alone (e.g. vigorous tax and extension policies) could probably have pushed the product into the large export sector some time ago. And other products are close enough to the export margin so that with a policy only slightly more favorable to agriculture they might have been exported, or exported in larger quantities, by now.

literacy, etc., or because the technology (e.g. large machines) is suitable only for large farms. When expansion of land and traditional capital are the sources of growth, the conflict is likely to be much less severe, if present at all.

EDUCATIONAL POLICY

The traditional educational policy of the Colombian government can be most simply classified as restrictive—in other words, public education has not been aimed at the majority of the population. Until fairly recently most children did not receive as much as two years of primary education, and even now a very small proportion finish secondary school.[20] Most of those who do attend secondary school go to private

20. Among the factors most important in determining the educational performance of a country are its average income level and its degree of urbanization (education being cheaper to supply in cities or towns than in rural areas). Table 1.4 presents comparative evidence revealing rather strikingly Colombia's weak performance at the primary and secondary levels, relative to its average income. When educational performance (as defined in Table 1.4) is regressed on average income and level of urbanization (for the set of countries listed in Table 1.4), the resulting equation is:

$$E = 33.71 - 0.012Y + 0.767U \qquad R^2 = 0.40 \qquad (1.1)$$
$$(4.36) \quad (0.019) \quad (0.280)$$

where E is educational performance, Y is income per capita, and U is the share of the population living in urban centers of 20,000 or more people.

(Several alternative income series were used because of the difficulties in cross-country comparisons, but results were little altered.) The fact that income level explained none of the educational performance is interesting and perhaps revealing. But the low R^2, the obvious exclusion of some other relevant variables, and the high multicolinearity between the income and urbanization variables suggest that conclusions from this fact be limited. The important point here is that, regardless of what combination of income and urbanization indexes were used, Colombia's actual performance, 33.6, fell far short of the predicted one, which ranged between 47.4 and 48.6.

There was virtually no improvement in the proportion of the school-age population actually attending schools from 1935 until about 1953; since then the increase has been substantial (see Table 1.5). The share of public education in the total has been decreasing at both the primary level (where it accounts for the bulk of all education) and the secondary level (where the majority of students are in private schools).

As recently as 1964, only about 21 percent of the population were receiving any postprimary education; 15 percent were in academic secondary schools. The corresponding figure for postprimary education in 1951 was 10 percent. (Figures in each case refer to the age group 5–19.)

The educational system fails most notably in the rural areas, where even in 1964 probably about 30 percent never began primary school and perhaps 30 to 40 percent reached the third grade. Comparable figures for other countries

Table 1.4: Percentage of Children Age 5–19 in Primary and Secondary School

Country (ranked by income per capita)

Venezuela	50.5
Argentina	51.4
Uruguay	59.9
Chile	56.6
Japan	70.1
Greece	61.3
Costa Rica	55.9
Mexico	47.8
Colombia	33.6
Peru	54.3
Guatemala	26.8
Brazil	37.8
Turkey	38.1
Ghana	55.7
Honduras	29.5
Tunisia	51.1
Ecuador	44.8
Egypt	41.2
Paraguay	48.3
Taiwan	58.0
South Korea	54.8
India	36.2
Pakistan	25.9

Note: There may be some lack of comparability in the education figures, but not such as to alter the relationships substantially. The ranking by income levels is assuredly open to question, but the conclusion that Colombia, with a per capita income somewhere in the middle of the group, has had an educational performance near the bottom, is not.

Sources: Education figures are from UNESCO, *World Survey of Education*, various issues. Population figures were based on U.N. *Demographic Yearbook*, various issues.

schools. Public expenditures on education are low relative to other countries, as revealed in a comparison with other Latin American countries in 1960.[21] Education is a commodity deeply desired by most Colombian parents for their children. Its shortage directly reflects the fact that large segments of the population have not had

---

are difficult to obtain, but it seems unlikely that many with Colombia's average income perform as badly in the rural areas.

21. See, for example, Charles H. Boehm, *Administration, Organization and Financing of Colombian Education,* vol. 1, U.S. AID, UNESCO, and IBRD (1965), p. 51.

Table 1.5: Percentage of Children Age 5–19 in Primary and Secondary Schools in Colombia

	Primary and academic secondary	*Primary and all forms of secondary*[a]
1935	22.7	24.7
1940	22.1	22.8
1945	22.0	23.9
1950	23.5	25.1
1955	27.5	29.2
1960	31.7	34.1
1962	34.0	

[a] Includes vocational, commercial, etc. Does not include university level work.

Source: Figures compiled by the author, based on adjustments to figures appearing in the *Anuario General de Estadística*.

the power to claim it and that the ruling group has not seen fit to dispense it.

The retarded level of education has probably had two braking effects on economic development, related to the two potential functions of education in an economy. The first function is to increase the stock of human capital; if the rate of return on education is higher than on other investments in the economy, then underinvestment has occurred. While data must be interpreted with great care in a country where education is often a result of the same social and economic position of family that assures that a person gets a good job, the differences in income levels associated with different educational levels are wide indeed. (See Table 1.6.) It is always difficult to know how much of the income differential results from a real increase in ability and how much results from the fact that the employer assumes such an increase; it is my impression that if additional investment along educational lines went toward improving quality as well as toward increasing quantity, its return would be quite high in a real sense.

Education's second major function is to act as a sieve to assure that those people most suited for a given occupation are channeled into it. Education has clearly not performed this function in Colombia; in fact the withholding of more than a year or two of education from the majority of the population has helped to make it impossible for that majority to challenge the domination of the elite, either in the political or the economic sphere. More education might have led to one of two possible sequences of events. If the barriers to a person

Table 1.6: Average Hourly Income by Educational Level
Bogotá, Men, 1963–66
(Pesos of 1966)

Illiterate	1.95
Primary:	
One year	2.45
Two or three years	2.78
Five years	4.12
Academic secondary:	
One or two years	5.05
Three or four years	8.26
Six years	16.18
University:	
One or two years	14.46
Three or four years	21.22
Five or six years	25.48

Note: The above table does not distinguish among age groups; if it did there would be some changes; for example, people with one or two years of university would be above those with completed secondary. For our present purpose such details are not important.

Source: Marcelo Selowsky, "El efecto del desempleo y el crecimiento sobre la rentabilidad de la inversión educacional: una aplicación a Colombia," Versión preliminar, mimeographed (Bogotá, 1968), Table 19-A.

starting from the bottom were not too serious, the educational system would lead to an improved average quality of personnel in the higher economic and political positions in the society.[22] If, even after a person was educated, the barriers were stringent, his education would probably make him more politically aware, more able to challenge the system, and therefore better able to force the system to respond to some of his claims. Under a policy of limited education it has been possible for the elite to avoid such challenges, and Colombia has therefore had the appearance of a relatively mobile society, where

22. It must be recognized that this may be an oversimplified and perhaps even naïve approach to the issue. It has been argued, especially by John E. Turner and Robert T. Holt, *The Political Basis of Economic Development* (Princeton: Van Nostrand, 1965), that rapid economic development is most likely when entrance into the socially elite group is difficult, so that aspirants are diverted to other goals, namely economic power. The lack of native entrepreneurship in Latin America has sometimes been interpreted as resulting from a too easy upward mobility into the elite, which is accompanied by a lack of interest in economic affairs. But such mobility can hardly be so easy when the number of aspirants mushrooms, as it does when education is widespread, so some efficiency-producing shake-up seems almost inevitable.

a number of people who made good were more or less accepted by or into the power groups. This mobility does not imply possible loss of these positions by the power groups, since the challenges to them are eliminated "in the bud." With an uneducated lower class, upper-class attitudes of paternalism and superiority vis-à-vis the lower class are more easily maintained.

INCOME DISTRIBUTION AND THE SAVINGS RATIO

An unequal distribution of income is a natural concomitant of an elitist society; an important argument in favor of such a distribution during the development process is that it generates a higher total amount of savings.[23] In Colombia distribution is very unequal, as suggested in the somewhat illustrative figures of Table 1.7. (Reasonably accurate figures on the distribution of income are notoriously difficult to obtain.) But a comparison of the figures with those presented for other Latin American countries throws some doubt on the hypothesis that the smaller and securer the dominating elite or ruling group in a country is, the more unequal the income distribution of that country will be. Other factors may be just as important.[24] All the Latin American countries have unequal distributions, noticeably more so than many developed countries had around the turn of the century (e.g. Germany, Denmark) but not more so than England apparently had as recently as the late nineteenth century. And, as is true of most underdeveloped countries, their tax systems tend to have very little redistributive impact. In Colombia the tax system itself

23. Kuznets, for example, in "Quantitative Aspects of the Economic Growth of Nations: VIII. Distribution of Income by Size," *Economic Development and Cultural Change* (January 1963), concluded on the basis of a rather small sample of developed and underdeveloped countries that personal income distribution was more uneven in the latter group, and that the positive difference between the savings ratios of high and low income groups was greater in that group. The countries in his underdeveloped country sample included some (Guatemala, El Salvador) with such dubious data as to cast considerable doubt on his conclusions. The issue remains in substantial doubt.

24. It is interesting to note that Mexico's distribution (before taxes at least) is more uneven than Colombia's. It may well be true that rapid growth, which opens up big new sources of income for entrepreneurs as the structure of the economy is modified, implies, *ceteris paribus,* more inequality. The greater inequality in Mexico might then be interpreted to result from the fact that the faster growth ncreases inequality more than the more open social system decreases it. Meanwhile the considerable difference in distribution between India and Colombia is probably traceable to the difference in social structure.

Table 1.7: Income Distribution before Tax in Selected Countries
Percentage of Personal Income Accruing to x Percent of Income Earners

	Colombia[a] 1961	Chile[b] 1960	Ecuador[c] 1957	Mexico[d] 1957	Venezuela[e] 1957	Argentina[f] 1961	India[g] 1953-4	Denmark, Germany, Netherlands, Sweden, U.K.[h] 1957	Weighted average for Mexico, Ecuador, Chile, Venezuela[i]
Top x percent									
2	19	14	21	20.5	18		20	15	19
5	29	24	26	38	31		28		33
10	42	38[i]		45[i]	45	40			
25	65								
50	82	84	76	86	89		70		84
Bottom x percent									
50	18	16	24	16	11		30	30[i]	16
10	2						4		

[a] Joint Tax Program, *Fiscal Survey of Colombia*, Johns Hopkins Press, 1965.
[b,c,d,e,f,h,i] ECLA, *The Economic Development of Latin America in the Postwar Period*, pp. 65–67. For methodologies underlying the various distributions, see this source. Some methodologies are very weak (e.g. Ecuador) and some involve different definitions from others. So the figures for different countries are not fully comparable.
[g] P. D. Ojha and U. U. Bhatt, "Pattern of Income Distribution in an Underdeveloped Country: A Case Study of India," *American Economic Review*, September 1964.
[i] Author's interpolations.

seems to have little redistributive impact,[25] while the direction of government expenditures implies a small one.

That the social structure accounts in part for the skewed income distribution in Colombia (and in most of Latin America) does seem clear, though the extent of the effect is not. In any case it is of interest to ask how this skewness affects the savings rate. Figures in Colombia, unfortunately, do not permit a really adequate test but at least give grounds for reasonable speculation.

The family budget study of 1953 suggested a high marginal savings ratio for incomes above about $250 per month for white collar families and above about $100–$200 for blue collar families (see Table 1.8). Average savings ratios for even moderately high income fami-

Table 1.8: Average Consumption/Income Ratio for White Collar and Blue Collar Workers by Income Groups; Seven Colombian Cities, 1953

Monthly family income in pesos (2.5 pesos = 1 dollar)	*White collar workers*	*Blue collar workers*
100–199	.90	1.12
200–299	1.08	1.01
300–399	.99	.92
400–499	1.00	.91
500–599	1.00	.81
600–699	1.01	.86
700–799	.97	.80
800–899	.91	.72
900–999	.92	.75
1000–1499	.76	.70

Source: Calculated from data presented in Contraloría General de la República, *Economía y Estadística*, no. 85 (Bogotá, 1958).

lies were quite high. It is possible that some expenditures were missed at the high incomes, but the study was for the most part well designed, and it seems unlikely that the general conclusions could have been much affected by this.

The national accounts suggest that savings of families and unincorporated enterprises constitute a very small share of national income. Over the period 1958–62 the estimated average savings ratio for family income was 3.2 percent. Even if only the top quartile of income earners had any savings, their average rate would be about 5

25. Preliminary calculations of the distribution of the tax burden being made by the Musgrave Tax Reform Commssion suggest this.

percent. If only the top decile saved, their average rate would be about 7 percent.

The savings estimate from the national accounts is very weak, in part because it is calculated as a residual and in part because some savings attributed to corporate enterprise are in effect personal savings and should be so considered. It is far below the average savings ratio implied by an application of the ratios in Table 1.8 to the income distribution for the population. (At the same time the ratio derived in the latter fashion is above the range that logic dictates and the overall savings figures suggest.) Many people have guessed on impressionistic evidence that personal savings rates are low in the Latin American middle classes because of their "consumption orientation," but the Colombian evidence does not support this conclusion. And one could not argue from the statistics that the savings rates of the upper income groups were low.[26]

Government-nongovernment income distribution has a definite impact on the overall savings ratio in the economy. The average savings ratio of government current income in 1955–62 was about 36 percent, while that for the private sector was between 10 and 20 percent. When this is taken into account along with the evidence suggesting an increasing marginal propensity to save, with higher incomes, the net impact of the social structure (which creates both income inequalities and a small government sector) remains indeterminate.

POPULATION CONTROL POLICY

On the issue of population control, the attitude of the Colombian government and society has been, until quite recently, more negative than in many other underdeveloped countries. The difference is probably related to the characteristics of the elite.

Until the last two or three years fast population growth was not felt by any politically important group to be one of Colombia's most serious economic problems. But the social structure, and its attendant income distribution and educational system, has affected population growth in several ways. The small size of the middle class probably implied a higher overall birth rate, since it is that class which in

26. It could be argued that the figures in Table 1.8 do not refer to the traditional upper class, whose influence has been so strong for so long in Colombia, since the income levels of its members are far above those referred to. And the members are very difficult to interview.

other countries has most often controlled family size in order to progress economically and which has easier access to information about birth control practices. Low levels of education, in particular for women, have certainly contributed to the high birth rates and family sizes. Finally, the well-enforced preference of the Church against contraceptives may have prevented a desired decrease in family size. Certainly there is now evidence that the typical urban woman from the lower class has more children than she would like,[27] and that a major obstacle to her achieving the desired family size is lack of information as to how to do so. This information might have been more readily available had the attitude of the Church and the upper classes in general been different.

Much of the problem resides in the fact that the large number of children in poor families has not appeared to threaten the welfare, present or future, of the rich families. Rather, the large number of children tends to depress the wages of unskilled labor and raise the remuneration of the factors of production supplied by the wealthier classes, i.e. higher levels of manpower, capital, and land. The poorer people themselves are the ones who suffer. One might expect a different policy in an egalitarian society in which some of the potential beneficiaries of a positive policy had a voice in government. At some point (possibly now) the ruling groups are likely to become conscious of the fact that the population explosion in the lower class, while constituting an economic advantage for them, constitutes a political danger.

For whatever reason, some elements in the government have now awakened to the problem but are constrained in their efforts by the attitudes of other groups, including the Church. For a full understanding of how much damage these attitudes have done and are doing, one has to be aware of the elements that go into a family's planning, or lack of planning, with respect to the number of its children. It has been alleged in Colombia that the very large family size has nothing to do with the conservative attitudes of the Church and society, but results from such factors as *machismo*, the need for a large family in the rural areas to maintain security in one's old age, etc. Recent research has cast considerable doubt on whether machismo is as important a factor as previously believed; in fact all factors

27. See, for example, Rafael Prieto and Roberto Cuca, *Análisis de la encuesta de fecundidad* (Informe preliminar, Centro de Estudios Sobre Desarrollo Económico, Universidad de los Andes, September 1965)

other than the lack of information about birth control techniques lose a considerable amount of their explanatory power in the light of the recent survey showing that Bogotá women want considerably fewer children than they have had. While the survey was restricted to Bogotá, there is some evidence from other parts of the country, including rural areas, that the situation is not very different elsewhere.

We have discussed the implications of oligarchic government and some of its concomitants as they show themselves in government size, agricultural policy, educational policy, savings rates, and population policy. On balance the ledger appears very negative, a result consistent with the fact that a country as well endowed with resources as Colombia does not have a higher per capita income level or growth rate than is presently the case. While it is difficult to quantify the relative effects of these various factors, it seems likely that either a strong educational policy or a strong agricultural policy by itself could have resolved many of Colombia's economic and social problems. Since policy on both these fronts is now improving substantially, developments in the next decade may point to at least a partial answer.

Comments by John Sheahan

This is a surprising paper, for several reasons. One of them is the force with which the data bring out evidence of resistance to economic and social change. It is possible to work for a long time in Colombia without ever quite realizing the strength of the opposition to change, or the multiplicity of directions in which its effects work against the society. The paper provides a healthy corrective to any notion that the main problems of development are simply those created by objective economic restraints. It casts a new light on the common observation that Colombian economists and political leaders are brilliantly able to dissect the difficulties of the country during conversation, but singularly slow about doing anything to correct them.

Granting the significance of social and political factors in explaining why Colombia made so little economic progress for more than a century after obtaining independence, it then becomes surprising that so many changes have begun to be visible in the last decade. As the paper makes clear at many points, change is definitely under way in both agriculture and education. Much of the best farmland, used for little more than extensive pasture ever since the Spaniards took over from the Indians, has been converted in the 1960s to systematic cultivation of commercial crops or production of meat for both domestic and foreign markets. A slowly growing fraction of small farmers is being given a chance to get past subsistence agriculture by a land reform program introduced in 1961 and rescued from political attack every time that it seemed likely to be stopped.

In education the government has failed miserably to do much about widening opportunities at the secondary level but has at least made possible a rapid expansion of university facilities for those whose families can help them through secondary schools. The growth of the National University in particular means that young people from previously excluded social groups are becoming better placed to exert pressure for change.

If real improvements are taking place now that were conspicuously lacking before, what happened to the resistances of the elite? This paper conveys the impression that Colombian society has certain core characteristics, perhaps not immune to evolution but sufficiently durable to account for the main features of behavior through much of the country's history. If the society were dominated by social forces adverse to change, then it would be most unlikely that the developments actually observed during the last decade or so would have occurred.

Two possibilities are evident. One is that I may have overstated the changes. The other is that the social groups adverse to progress really do not run the show any more. They may be in there causing all the difficulties they can, but they are no longer able to stop the system. Either way, I hope that Berry will go on in later work to consider specifically whether or not there has been a real break in trend and, if there has, how the social forces responsible for prior stagnation have altered.

Under the momentary intoxication of being able to suggest what someone else might do, without having to prove anything myself, it is difficult to resist the temptation to offer a hypothesis. It is essentially that Colombia started on a growth process during the 1920s, perhaps without full recognition of it by the country's more conservative forces, and that this process is inexorably going to crack open ancient resistances if it is not stopped by totalitarian methods. Industrialization has created a growing middle class whose income does not come from land ownership but depends rather on ability to make new things, to invest, to find workers with new skills or to train them, and to keep up with change. It is not that the new industrial leaders are particularly farsighted or concerned with social justice. But they and the new economic groups emerging with them are trying to crack educational barriers for their children and to force a modicum of efficiency on the governmental processes that hamper them. While they may not wish to do so, they are also opening the system a little wider for urban workers to exert some pressures of their own.

If there were a social group that wanted to stop all this, it would have to do so by fairly brutal and direct methods. In fact, one might argue that there is such a group, that they did try to block the opening up of the society after the initial reforms of the 1930s and that they succeeded in slowing things up for a decade at the cost of immense suffering and countless violent deaths, but that they lost. They are not to be counted out, but they do not control the society any more.

The people who control Colombian economic policy now are still members of the traditional elite and can by no stretch of the imagination be considered radical reformers. Their concern for preservation of the orderly and familiar often seems greater than their concern for creating more decent lives for the poor, or for widening opportunities for those who are trying to move upward in the system. Their policies over the years should be tested by the types of measures attempted in Berry's paper, and the results when tested will be subject to valid criticism. But they are not trying to reverse history. Their policies cannot be interpreted in terms of positive resistance to change and they do have some important improvements to their credit. The elite is too narrow, but it includes a fairly wide range of positions, including a moderately progressive one. Berry is fundamentally right: the nature of the ruling social group is extremely important for economic progress; when the balance within the group changed, progress became more feasible.

To retreat to economies for one last point, the paper is surprisingly positive about a difficult question, namely the meaning of comparative advantage in Colombia at present. It suggests that the industrial investment of the postwar period has been in general a mistake; that greater emphasis on agriculture would have permitted faster growth. This seems doubtful. Much of the investment that has actually gone into agriculture has been in the form of machinery that adds little to output but rather displaces labor which is already in excess supply.

Such investment has been encouraged by below-average tariffs and preferred import licensing for agricultural machinery, combined with the overvalued exchange rate which Berry properly criticizes. It has come at the cost of tighter restrictions on imports of industrial equipment that could have raised both jobs and output. It is surely true that more favorable exchange rates for exports other than coffee, combined with investment oriented toward raising production possibilities rather than displacing labor, would have permitted a faster rate of growth of national income. Such policies would also have improved markets for manufactured goods and have permitted more imports of industrial equipment. It is at least conceivable that optimal choices would have favored more industrial investment than has actually taken place.

No one could deny that much industrial investment has been misdirected, that the balance has worked out poorly, and that income and employment have grown more slowly than they could have with a more efficient allocation of resources. But this does not mean that industrialization itself is a mistake, or that it should now be dropped in favor of agricultural development. The question is not one of a choice between the two sectors. The actual response of new exports to improvement in exchange rates gives some good clues: the exports that have emerged and grown include beef, tobacco, bananas, and other foods, but they also include textiles, chemicals and drugs, paper and cartons, rubber tires, and dozens of other industrial products. Industrial exports have been growing and diversifying for the last ten years. Comparative advantage should not be identified with a single sector. It consists of the many things that either favorable resources, good management, or good luck have brought to the borderline of international competitiveness.

Conclusion: a fine paper, full of invaluable suggestions, but one that should distinguish more clearly between the factors that accounted for a generally unhappy history and those that are now the central determinants for a society in the process of genuine change.

2

Some Development Implications
of Political Integration
and Disintegration in Malaysia

BY DONALD R. SNODGRASS

The Malaysian Federation was formed in September 1963, embracing the independent eleven-state Federation of Malaya, the internally self-governing colony of Singapore, and the Borneo colonies of North Borneo (renamed Sabah) and Sarawak. In its original form the Federation lasted only until August 1965, when Singapore was expelled and became an independent entity. Despite some uncertainty about its prospects, the rest of Malaysia has hung together and now seems likely to remain united in the future. The intent of this paper is to examine Malaysia's brief history, project its presumably longer future, and try to answer the following question: What is the effect on the economic development prospects of Malaysia's three main components of their integration into a single, federally structured state?

I have posed the question this way so as to isolate the issue of political integration and disintegration (and economic integration and disintegration resulting from them) from other aspects of the government's impact on development. For instance, I will ignore the several types of change in economic policy that typically accompany independence. I will also omit discussion of economic effects of federalism that are internal to West Malaysia.[1]

The substance of this paper was presented orally at the Yale conference. The present version, written subsequently, has benefited from comments by Van Doorn Ooms, who was discussant at the conference. Although the author was an employee of the U.S. Agency for International Development at the time this paper was written, the views expressed are his own, and not necessarily those of AID.

1. I will generally employ current terminology, which is to refer to the former Federation of Malaya as West Malaysia and the Borneo states of Sabah and Sarawak collectively as East Malaysia.

One cannot discuss the developmental effects of integration into an independent federal state without saying what alternative form of organization one assumes would exist in its absence. I will assume that the alternative to independence with integration would have been independence without it, rather than continued dependence (although both Sabah and Sarawak would undoubtedly have taken longer to achieve independence had the Malaysia scheme never been broached).

Later in this paper I will identify actual and potential resource transfers induced by political integration and will try to say something about their effect on the growth of each of Malaysia's three major components. First, however, some political background must be sketched for the benefit of readers not familiar with recent Malaysian history.

Malaysia was conceived by most of the participants in its creation as the solution to a political problem. For the United Kingdom it was a means of disengaging from its responsibilities in Singapore, Sarawak, Brunei, and North Borneo, with reasonable prospect that these areas would remain politically stable after independence. For the Federation of Malaya, independent since 1957, Malaysia was an ingenious constitutional arrangement whereby its neighbor Singapore could be neutralized and guarded from Communist domination through submersion in a state dominated by Malay peoples. The Borneo states[2] played their role in this arrangement by helping to offset Singapore's impact on Malaysia. They did this by limiting the rise in the proportion of the population that would be ethnically Chinese (although together they had a population of only 1,255,000, 72 percent non-Chinese, versus 1,700,000 in Singapore, three-quarters Chinese) and the Chinese role in federal politics (the new constitution gave Sabah 16 seats in the Malaysian Parliament and Sarawak 24, but Singapore only 15).[3] The wishes of the peoples of Singapore, Sarawak, and Sabah to enter Malaysia were at least nominally tested, and the answer was judged to be in the affirmative.[4]

2. In the original conception, there were to have been three Borneo states, with the British protectorate of Brunei also acceding to Malaysia. Negotiations over the terms of Brunei's entry broke down, however, reportedly because of disagreement over the apportionment of Brunei's oil-enriched state treasury and the appropriate position of its sultan in the order of succession to Malaysia's rotating titular kingship.
3. Malaya received 104 seats. See the Federal Constitution (Kuala Lumpur, 1964).
4. Singapore held a referendum giving voters a say on the *terms* under which

Whereas Britain and Malaya found the idea of Malaysia attractive mainly for political reasons, the new states of Singapore, Sarawak, and Sabah stood to gain more in the economic arena. For Singapore, an overcrowded, highly urbanized island dependent for its livelihood on old, stagnant, regional trade flows, Malaysia offered an enhanced home market for the products of the extensive manufacturing sector which it hoped to develop. At its inception Malaysia was a patchwork of separate customs areas, six in all (Malaya, Singapore, Sarawak, Sabah, and the "free ports" of Penang and Labuan). The progressive consolidation of these areas into one had been blueprinted by the Rueff Report in 1963.[5] Sabah and Sarawak had low, colonial-style tariff structures and would therefore have to bear price increases when they were incorporated into a common national market. But they were underdeveloped relative to Malaya and Singapore (GNP per capita in 1963, according to estimates made by the Rueff Mission, was M$801 in Malaya, M$1,304 in Singapore, M$563 in Sarawak, and M$645 in Sabah)[6] and could hope that a federation would result in substantial net transfers of public funds to finance their development.[7]

Considerable furor attended the birth of the new nation.[8] The

the colony should enter the new federation; no legal means were provided for recording a desire not to enter at all. See Willard A. Hanna, *The Formation of Malaysia* (New York: American Universities Field Staff, 1964), pp. 113–25. Popular sentiment in the Borneo territories was sampled by the Cobbold Commission, which reported a general desire to join, despite the obvious difficulties of measuring public opinion in such primitive and heterogeneous areas. See *Report of the Commission of Enquiry, North Borneo and Sarawak* (Kuala Lumpur, 1962).

5. *Report on the Economic Aspects of Malaysia* (Kuala Lumpur, 1963).

6. The Malayan or Straits dollar, the common currency of all territories up to June 1967, exchanged for the U.S. dollar at 3.06 to one. For details of these GNP estimates, see the "Rueff Report" (*Report on the Economic Aspects of Malaysia*), p. 102.

7. A certain volume of such transfers was explicitly guaranteed. Malaya pledged to support higher levels of development expenditure in Sarawak and Sabah (at least M$300 million and M$200 million respectively), while Singapore agreed to a subsidized loan of M$150 million for Borneo development. See Annex J to the *Malaysia Agreement* (Kuala Lumpur, 1963), pp. 226–31; *Malaysia: Report of the Inter-Governmental Committee, 1962* (Kuala Lumpur, 1963), p. 16.

8. The events immediately preceding and following the formation of Malaysia will not be recounted in detail here. Among many references, see Hanna, *Formation of Malaysia*; Donald Hindley, "Indonesia's Confrontation with Malaysia: A Search for Motives," *Asian Survey*, vol. 4, no. 6, June 1964, pp. 904–13; Richard Butwell, "Malaysia and Its Impact on the International Relations of Southeast Asia," *Asian Survey*, vol. 4, no. 7, July 1964, pp. 940–46; George McT. Kahin, "Malaysia and Indonesia," *Pacific Affairs*, vol. 37, no. 3,

Azahari rebellion in Brunei and eastern Sarawak (December 1962) was followed by growing Indonesian and Filipino concern over the new state. Formal creation of Malaysia, set for 31 August 1963, was postponed until September 15 in a last attempt to placate Indonesia. Despite confirmation by a team of United Nations observers that the people of Sabah and Sarawak wished to join Malaysia, Sukarno declared *confrontasi,* a cold war that heated up from time to time and lasted nearly three years. Confrontasi drew to Malaysia in augmented force the very Commonwealth armed forces whose presence Sukarno had feared in the creation of Malaysia. Its main economic effects were to halt (or at least greatly reduce) trade and factor movements between Malaysia (primarily Singapore) and Indonesia.

ECONOMIC ELEMENTS OF FEDERATION

In assessing the economic impact of Malaysia's creation, one must distinguish between political and economic integration. Malaysian experience in this regard does not altogether accord with one's preconceptions, or with experience elsewhere. The normal expectation is that economic integration precedes political integration, which is not even deemed to be a necessary condition for the early stages of economic integration. Only as economic integration is pushed toward total achievement is increasing political integration considered a necessary concomitant of it. Thus Balassa[9] lists the following sequence of steps leading to complete economic integration: (1) removal of barriers to internal trade, (2) adoption of common barriers to external trade, (3) removal of barriers to internal factor movements, (4) harmonization of economic policies to remove discrimination among member countries or regions, and finally, (5) unification of monetary, fiscal, and other economic and social policy making in a single, central authority. Only step (5) necessarily implies political integration. On the other hand, we normally expect that when political integration does occur it brings with it total economic integration, in the sense of all five of Balassa's steps.

Malaysia's sequence of steps toward economic and political union does not accord with Balassa's chronology. On the one hand, signifi-

---

Fall 1964, pp. 253–70; H. B. Jacobini, "Fundamentals of Philippine Policy toward Malaysia," *Asian Survey,* vol. 4, no. 11, November 1964, pp. 1144–51.

9. Bela Balassa, *The Theory of Economic Integration* (Homewood, Ill.: Richard D. Irwin, 1961), p. 2.

cant elements of economic integration, some of them among those usually assumed to be the most difficult to achieve, existed before 1963. On the other hand, the Malaysian constitution specified a complex set of federal, state, and shared powers in the policy areas related to development. In some areas, policy was integrated in federal hands. In others (e.g. internal and external customs) transitional arrangements leading toward integration were specified. In still other areas, powers were left wholly or partly in the hands of the states (the new states received markedly greater powers than the constituent states in the old Federation of Malaya had enjoyed), with no provision made for future centralization or harmonization.

The most important element of economic integration that existed before 1963 was totally free movement of private capital, unfettered by exchange control or other restrictions and promoted by the use of a common currency, a common reliance on Singapore banks, and established financial relationships arising from family and ethnic connections. Substantial, although far from total, freedom of labor movement also existed before the creation of Malaysia. Curiously, one of the least integrated spheres of economic activity was commodity trade. Singapore was an important participant in the external trade of Malaya and Sarawak, but not in that of Sabah. None of the other pairings of territories had significant trading relationships with each other. Although locational and historical factors are primarily responsible for this low volume of intraregional trade, the aforementioned six customs areas did not help. Economic policies for the four political entities were made independently, although within the general framework of the Commonwealth and the British colonial heritage. Only in the defense field was there significant integration.

Steps toward economic integration taken during the 1963–65 period will be discussed below.

POTENTIALS OF THE ORIGINAL FEDERATION

Economic integration, as we all know, both creates and diverts trade. The relative magnitudes of trade that is created and trade that is diverted, through their effects on production and the degree of discrimination between domestic and foreign goods respectively, determine the effect of economic integration on potential welfare (efficiency). Actual welfare is also influenced by effects on the distribution of income within and among participating countries or territories.[10] To the extent that trade is a response to complementarities in resource endowment, Malaysia was fairly well situated at its conception in 1963. Certainly it had much more resource complementarity among its original components than do most groups of less developed countries that have been discussed as possible bases for economic integration.

Table 2.1 illustrates the extent of this complementarity, insofar as data availability permits. Malaya in 1963 was a relatively rich, highly specialized exporter of tropical products to the world market, somewhat overpopulated relative to developed land but also with considerable quantities of uncultivated land remaining for future development. Its main development problem was the fact that its two dominant exports, rubber and tin, both had poor future prospects as earners of foreign exchange. Malayan development plans therefore stressed diversification into new lines of production, both agricultural and industrial. Singapore, as Table 2.1 shows, was still more prosperous (although possibly no richer than the principal cities on the peninsula), crowded, and dependent on the provision of various kinds of services to foreigners. The Singapore government's view of the future, as already noted, stressed industrialization; the output, it was thought, would go primarily to the world market, but an enlarged home market would be a valuable base for this future export trade. Sarawak emerges as the poorest component of the new federation, underpopulated and totally dependent on agriculture and natural resource extraction. Sarawak's economic potential appears to be low; it is hard to conceive any strategy by which it might achieve substantial development, short of really massive applications of capital. Sabah is seen in Table 2.1 to be underpopulated as well, but it is richer and appears to have a high potential for growth based on plantation and extractive industries, provided (especially in the case of the plantations) that an adequate labor supply is somehow made available.

The main past response to (and to some extent the cause of) the complementarities in capital, natural, and human resources hinted at in Table 2.1 had been Singapore's specialized role within the region (which extended, of course, beyond the limits of 1963-vintage Malaysia to Indonesia and, in lesser degree, other Southeast Asian countries). Singapore was the natural financier, shipper, and processor

10. Ibid., p. 11.

Table 2.1: Dimensions of Malaysia, 1964

	W. Malaysia (former Federation)	E. Malaysia		Current Malaysia	Singapore	Original Malaysia
		Sarawak	Sabah			
Population (thousands)	7,810	820	507	9,137	1,820	10,957
Density (Population/sq. mi.)	153	17	17	71	8,125	85
GNP (M$ millions)[a]	7,007	553	410	7,957[b]	2,520	10,477
GNP per capita (M$)	897	674	809	871	1,385	956
GDP by sector (%):						
Primary production	37	48	54	39	9	32
Rubber planting	15	12	8	14	—	11
Other agriculture & forestry	14	28	46	17	9	15
Mining	9	7	—	8	—	6
Industry	17	12	11	13	36	21
Services	46	40	34	47	56	48
Exports by commodity (M$ millions)	2,781	401	260	3,397	2,772	5,101
Rubber	1,303	60	32	1,396	644	c
Tin	728	—	—	728	6	c
Timber	87	62	149	295	41	c
Others	663	279	79	978	2,081	c
Exports by destination (M$ millions)	2,781	401	260	3,397	2,772	5,101
W. Malaysia	d	16	1	d	(225)[e]	d
E. Malaysia	14	9	4	d	(73)	d
Singapore	569[f]	170	31	770	d	d
Rest of world	2,198	206	224	2,627	(2,474)	5,101
Imports by source (M$ millions)	2,521	448	298	3,227	3,479	5,531
W. Malaysia	d	9	12	d	(626)	d
E. Malaysia	16	1	3	d	(221)	d
Singapore	248	43	37	328	d	d
Rest of world	2,257	396	246	2,899	(2,632)	5,531

^a M$3.06 = US$1.00.

^b Because of discrepancies in intra-Malaysian trade figures, component GNP's do not quite add up to the Malaysian total.

^c Not available.

^d Not applicable.

^e Singapore trade data are highly untrustworthy; accordingly, numbers in parentheses are estimates based on data published by trading partners. A 10 percent markup in going from F.O.B. valuation to C.I.F. valuation is assumed.

^f Exports to or via Singapore totaled M$793 million.

Sources: *Annual Bulletins of Statistics*; *External Trade Statistics*; unpublished sources.

of much that was produced in the other territories (North Borneo largely excepted). It also supplied entrepreneurship and skilled labor. The other areas had plentiful land and other natural resources to offer, and these in turn had attracted entrepreneurs and laborers from outside the region.

Continuation of the Malaysian Federation in its original form would have had three principal economic effects. (1) It would have meant free and increasing internal trade, especially in manufactures, which would have been produced primarily in Singapore but also in Malaya; (2) it would have led to a greatly expanded public investment program in both Sabah and Sarawak, intended to gradually bring the level of public services and infrastructure up to the West Malaysian level and financed by net transfers from Malaya and Singapore; and (3) it would probably have led to some transfer of excess labor from Malaya and Singapore to Sabah. The overall result would clearly have been net trade creation and improvements in resource allocation. But it was not to be.

ECONOMIC INTEGRATION, 1963–65

Singapore was unexpectedly expelled from Malaysia in August 1965, largely because the Malay-dominated Alliance party, which controlled the Federal government and twelve of the state governments, was unwilling to let Singapore prime minister Lee Kwan Yew's Chinese-dominated Peoples' Action party play the active role outside Singapore that he insisted it should play. Economic issues are not assigned a major role in the breakup by most analysts of Malaysian affairs, but in fact serious difficulties had been encountered in implementing the original economic scheme for the Federation.

The principal contribution of the Malaysia Agreement and the Malaysian Constitution of 1963 to economic integration had been in the area of trade. The Rueff Mission appointed by the World Bank had proposed creation of a common market (i.e. elimination of internal trade barriers, plus adoption of common barriers to external trade), with safeguards for Singapore's entrepôt trade. Annex J of the Constitution called for gradual realization of this goal through item-by-item negotiations. Some progress was made in these negotiations during the two years Singapore was in Malaysia. However both parties were anxious to protect their own interests as they saw them, and the talks moved slowly. Singapore wanted to preserve what was left of its entrepôt trade, which depended on low duties, from extermination by protective tariffs. Malaya's aims were to protect its existing small manufacturing sector and, increasingly as time went by and the political climate worsened, to insure that a common market would not mean that all new plants would gravitate to Singapore. The Federal government contended that the Singapore state government unfairly biased industrial location decisions through subsidization of plant sites and utility rates. Although many of the same techniques were used to attract industry to Malaya, it was generally conceded that Singapore did it better, besides which it possessed locational and infrastructural advantages that Malaya could not hope to match.

By 1965 the Federal government, increasingly reluctant to see Rueff's proposal implemented in its original form, had adopted the position that if a full common market was to be established, then the Annex J provision on the sharing of income tax revenue—that 60 percent of the revenue from income attributable to Singapore was to go to the Center (i.e. Federal government)—would have to be modified in favor of Kuala Lumpur. A Federal turnover tax was established in lieu of an increase in the income tax, apparently as a means of circumventing the revenue-sharing provisions applicable to the latter. The expulsion of Singapore from Malaysia intervened shortly thereafter to end the debate. However, it was already abundantly clear that allocating the benefits of a common market would have remained a thorny, perhaps insoluble, issue had Singapore remained inside the Federation.

The Borneo states were only minor participants in the common market discussions. With minuscule industrial sectors and very limited industrial prospects, they could not hope to benefit from elimination of internal duties when this was to be combined with common—and for them substantially higher—external tariffs.

The original Federation had little impact on private factor markets. It did nothing to hamper the free capital market which had existed before its creation. With regard to labor, the avowed aim was completely free movement within the Federation, but little was done to increase mobility during the two years Singapore was part of Malaysia.

ECONOMIC INTEGRATION AND DISINTEGRATION, 1965–68

With Singapore out, most of the resource complementarity and development-inducing potential of the Federation was lost. Establishment of a common national market—now of greatly reduced significance—proceeded quickly and smoothly. A common market now exists between West Malaysia and East Malaysia, with minor exceptions. It works almost entirely to the benefit of West Malaysia and the detriment of Sarawak and Sabah, which are compensated through public capital transfers.

Not only did Singapore's departure cost the Federation a large share of its *potential* advantages, but it ultimately also destroyed or threatened to destroy some of the *actual* economic integration that had existed before political integration:

1. Malaysia, Singapore, and Brunei each issued their own currencies in June 1967, thus bringing to an end decades of currency unification. Although the three new currencies are in principle freely convertible, there have already been brief periods in which they were not. Moreover, Malaysia, unlike the other two, has abandoned the currency board system in favor of a central bank issue—although under highly conservative management—and with growing balance of payments deficits the temptation to impose direct controls on capital outflows and other types of external payment may grow. The free capital market, although still intact, has obviously been rendered more precarious.

2. Labor movement between Malaysia and Singapore has actually become less free. Singapore is faced with a serious unemployment problem, which will be severely aggravated as the British withdraw from their bases on the island over the next three years. This has led to talk of imposing sanctions against Malaysian citizens working in Singapore. Malaysia in turn has threatened retaliation with respect to Singaporeans working in the Federation.[11]

3. Malaysia is imposing on itself the cost of building infrastructure, especially ports, to substitute in part for the Singapore facilities upon which it has traditionally relied.

POTENTIAL AND ACTUAL EFFECTS OF THE PRESENT FEDERATION

What is the effect on the development potential of Malaya, Sabah, and Sarawak of their being joined in a Malaysia that now excludes Singapore? West Malaysian industry now has a million and a half

11. However, the *Far Eastern Economic Review* of 18 April 1968, p. 169, reports that plans to act against the employment of each other's nationals have been set aside, at least temporarily.

more home market customers, at the cost of price increases in East Malaysia. At present rather low levels of protection it is doubtful whether trade diversion is serious, but it could become so if import substitution were pushed really hard. There is also the possibility that labor, and probably capital as well, can be allocated more efficiently around the Federation, as will be discussed below.

Turning from potential to actual observed effects, we can see some things already happening in response to the formation of the Federation. As Table 2.2 shows, there has indeed been a trade response. In

Table 2.2: Intra-Malaysian Trade, 1960–65
(M$ millions)

	W. Malaysian imports from		*Sabah imports from*		*Sarawak imports from*	
	Sabah	*Sarawak*	*W. Malaysia*	*Sarawak*	*W. Malaysia*	*Sabah*
1960	0.1	0.1	2.3	0.4	2.4	0.5
1961	0.1	0.2	3.5	0.8	3.4	0.6
1962	0.6	0.2	3.6	1.6	3.9	1.1
1963	0.1	4.7	5.8	2.9	4.9	1.1
1964	0.2	15.9	12.2	3.1	8.6	0.7
1965	0.6	23.2	17.8	2.6	14.3	0.5
1966	0.7	29.6	32.6	4.2	39.2[a]	0.6

[a] The 1967 figure was M$46.8 million, according to the *Far Eastern Economic Review*, 13 June 1968, p. 574.

Sources: States of Malaya External Trade; Sabah: External Trade; Sarawak: Statistics of External Trade; various years.

1960 commodity flows were negligible in all directions. Since then, three of the six flows have shown rapid growth: imports of both Sarawak and Sabah from West Malaysia (mostly manufactures) and West Malaysia's imports from Sarawak (mainly crude oil for the refineries completed in 1963).

The First Malaysia Plan (1966–70) postulates a transfer of 5,000 workers from West Malaysia to Sabah. There has been some actual migration, partly in response to government assistance, but it is unlikely to be really significant in size or effect.

By far the most significant effect of federation to date has been the transfers of public sector resources from West Malaysia to Sarawak and Sabah. There have been antifederation stirrings in both states since August 1965, and these resource transfers can be construed as the price Malaya must pay for continuation of the Federation. The transfers are difficult to measure precisely with the data presently available to me. However, the overall net transfer of public sector resources appears to have been about M$200 million in 1964 and approximately M$230 million in 1965. Figures of about this size can be deduced from West Malaysian balance of payments statistics, when allowance is made for small public sector resource transfers to the rest of the world. The figure for 1966 may be larger, though the advent of serious budgetary pressures seems to have held it well below the level it would otherwise have attained. About two-thirds of the transfer seems to be going to Sarawak and one-third to Sabah. Table 2.3 gives the basis for these rough estimates.

Table 2.3: Indicators of Public Resource Transfer
(M$ millions)

	1964	1965	1966	1967
W. Malaysia balance of payments data				
Gross transfers from general government to rest of world[a]				
Current	233	242	c	c
Capital	61	97	c	c
Central government accounts data[b]				
Current expenditure				
Sabah	75.3	102.5	109.4	133.8
Sarawak	113.2	141.7	171.6	184.6
Revenue				
Sabah	57.6	67.5	79.4	94.6
Sarawak	58.2	68.7	73.7	89.2
Current deficit				
Sabah	17.7	35.0	30.0	39.2
Sarawak	55.0	73.0	97.9	95.4
Development expenditure				
Sabah	15.8	35.6	38.0	54.1
Sarawak	41.7	68.3	72.3	79.7
Overall deficit				
Sabah	33.5	70.6	68.0	93.3
Sarawak	96.7	141.3	170.2	175.1

[a] The current transfers item includes roughly M$25–40 million directed to areas other than Sabah and Sarawak (subscriptions and contributions to international organizations). Capital transfers are entirely for Sabah and Sarawak.
[b] Data for 1964 and 1965 are actual revenues and expenditures, while 1966 data are revised estimates and 1967 data are initial budget estimates.
[c] Not available.

Sources: National Accounts of the States of Malaya; Annual Bulletin of Statistics—Malaysia; various years.

Most of the public sector resource transfer is from the Federal government accounts. Table 2.3 also gives estimates of this component. It is based on actual data for 1964 and 1965, revised budget estimates for 1966, and original budget estimates for 1967. The estimates for the last two years are undoubtedly higher than the realized totals. These estimates can be compared with some made by the 1967 World Bank team. Excluding the substantial transfers for defense and internal security purposes, the Bank economists put the net transfer from the Federal government to the state governments at M$105 million in 1964, M$114 million in 1965, and M$112 million in 1966. Even if one is interested only in resources available for development, however, there is a good case for including transfers to finance defense and police expenditures, since the states would have had to divert from other uses at least part of the sums transferred for these purposes if they had not received them from West Malaysia.

The public sector resource transfer is very large relative to other magnitudes for Sabah and Sarawak. It amounts to about 20 to 25 percent of their combined GNP, or 25 to 30 percent of their imports of goods and services, and is roughly equal to their gross investment, both public and private. If security transfers are excluded, these figures fall to 10 percent of GNP, 10 to 15 percent of imports, and 50 percent of gross investment. On the other hand, the transfer represented only 3 percent of West Malaysian GNP and 17 percent of central government receipts in 1965.

IMPACT OF FEDERATION ON DEVELOPMENT

It would be an impressive model that could formally encompass the various effects of federation discussed above:

1. For West Malaysia, some slight increase in export opportunities, a small reduction in labor supply, most of it redundant, and a relatively small but significant transfer of scarce public sector resources;
2. for Sarawak and Sabah, somewhat higher import costs and a large increase in funds available for public expenditure;
3. for Sabah alone, some slight alleviation of its labor shortage, though at the cost of restricted Filipino and Indonesian immigration.[12]

12. Much plantation and lumbering work in Sabah is done by immigrants from nearby parts of Kalimantan and the Sulu Archipelago. This flow was

In lieu of a formal model, I will simply suggest what may be the principal development effects of the resource flows engendered by federation.

There are fairly well-defined institutional and ideological limits on the uses to which public sector resources can be put in Malaysia. These limits are man-made, but they are real nevertheless and it would take a major change of government to alter them significantly. Basically, they restrict the government to supplying certain kinds of public consumption services and certain kinds of essentially infrastructural development services. Public consumption is generally confined to the traditional public goods, such as defense and justice. Most of the development services are also those that would be likely to be supplied by any government in Western Europe: post office, railroad, power, telephone, education, public health, etc. These services are all infrastructural rather than directly productive, but some—such as agricultural research, land settlement, and the building of industrial estates—are more closely related to directly productive activity than the rest. Many of the public services provided by the government in Malaysia are hybrids, in that they constitute consumption for their own sake but also contribute to development. In such fields (notably education) the impact on development is determined less by the volume of resources than the way in which they are used (for example, the type and quality of education offered). As in other countries, the list of development services is considerably longer than the list of things included in public investment, traditionally defined.

One could, at least in principle, specify a national production function for a country such as Malaysia, in which there were four factors of production: labor, capital, land, and service-yielding public sector capital. This would, I think, accurately express the development role of the Malaysian government. While it does not engage directly in production, except for the traditional public goods, it does supply important development inputs which combine with private sector resources to produce the national product.

Although the permissible area of public development activity is the same in all parts of Malaysia, one would expect equal increments of public sector resources to have different productivities from state to state, depending on (1) the existing stock of public capital, built up

interrupted during Confrontasi, and its future is uncertain in the light of the Malaysian government's desire to settle agricultural laborers from West Malaysia in Sabah.

through past development expenditure, and (2) the existing stock of private sector resources which must combine with it to produce output. Assuming rationality and perfect knowledge in the allocation of public resources, i.e. that the most productive projects are always selected to absorb limited public funds, the productivity of new public development expenditure should be inversely related to the existing stock of public capital. It should, of course, be directly related to the stock of cooperating private capital.

If this rule were assumed to hold, one would expect the productivity of public development expenditure to be highest in Sabah, which is rich in at least some kinds of private resources but relatively low in public capital stock. West Malaysia would be lower, and Sarawak would probably be lowest of all (although this is not certain, since while Sarawak has far fewer present and potential cooperating private resources than West Malaysia it also has far less existing public capital).

If actual differentials in the productivity of public capital conform to the pattern just deduced, then the kind of model just mentioned would obviously show that transfers of public funds from West Malaysia to Sabah would raise Malaysian GNP and its rate of growth, while transfers to Sarawak would lower them. It would be difficult, however, to provide an empirical demonstration of this effect or to measure its quantitative significance.

In attempting to make a welfare judgment regarding these intra-Malaysian transfers, one would have to decide whose welfare one was most interested in: that of Malayans, Sabahans, Sarawakians, or all Malaysians equally. It is also necessary to take into account the scale effect resulting from the fact that the population of West Malaysia is six times greater than that of Sarawak and Sabah together. If there were no interregional differences at all in the productivity of public capital, Malaysia could always raise the aggregate income of East Malaysians by $6 by agreeing to reduce that of West Malaysians by only $1. Thus, whether one values the welfare of the Borneans or whether one—West Malaysian or not—attaches a positive value for its own sake to preservation of the Malaysian Federation, then the interregional resource transfers do succeed in raising welfare.

Finally, some comments on two related points:

1. Racial income distribution: The political stability of the Federation has been portrayed above as hinging in part on an acceptable distribution of income among the regions of Malaysia. An even more

fundamental point is the distribution of income among races, especially between the Malays and the Borneo natives, on the one hand, and the ethnic Chinese, Indians, and other "non-natives," on the other. The politically dominant Malay and Borneo peoples will presumably not acquiesce for long in a federal development policy that does not work to lessen their disadvantage vis-à-vis the others. Statistics on the racial distribution of income, taxation, and other crucial quantities in this equation are scarce. However, it is possible that attempts to improve the regional distribution of income could actually be perverse in racial terms. This could occur if funds intended for rural development in Malaya were diverted to the Borneo states and spent there in a pattern similar to the one that prevailed in Malaya in the late 1950s and early 1960s. This kind of transfer would be egalitarian in regional terms but unegalitarian in racial terms, since it would mean that expenditures to raise the productive capacity of rural Malays were being foregone to provide more residential electricity, better city streets, and improved water supplies for the small, predominantly Chinese, urban populations of Sabah and Sarawak. This pattern of investment allocation would constitute a particularly unfortunate departure from the rationality principle assumed above, since it could widen the racial income gaps in both East and West Malaysia. It can, of course, be avoided through adequate control over the allocation of public sector resources.

2. Public resource transfers as (foreign) aid: Even though they take place within the confines of a single country, the transfers from West Malaysia to Sabah and Sarawak are in many ways similar to foreign aid. The use of this analogy suggests two further comments. One is that the aid is in this case wholly untied. It is several times as large as West Malaysian exports to the Borneo states and in effect goes to help finance the large current account deficits which both Sabah and Sarawak run with the rest of the world. This is not to suggest that Malaysia should start tying aid, since under the circumstances this would enormously reduce its real value. Another point suggested by the aid analogy is that in territories with low levels of skills technical assistance must accompany capital assistance if the latter is to be effective. Flows of public capital to East Malaysia have in fact been accompanied by transfers of technical and administrative skills. The new development push in Borneo is increasing the need for such skills at the same time as the former reliance on expatriates is being reduced for political reasons. These latter transfers may well

have a more serious detrimental effect on West Malaysian development than the capital flows they accompany, since human skills are a crucial bottleneck in West Malaysia as well.

After sorting through the various possible and likely effects of federation on Malaysian development, it seems valid to conclude that:

1. Malaysian GNP and its growth rate are relatively unaffected in either direction by federation. If anything, they are slightly reduced by the fact that two-thirds of the public capital transfers go to Sarawak, where they are relatively unproductive.

2. The welfare judgment—whether economically Malaysia is "a good thing"—is easily answered from the Sabahan or Sarawakian point of view, from which it is positive, or the West Malaysian point of view, from which it is negative. From the "all-Malaysians-are-equal" viewpoint the judgment is much harder to make, but it is probably slightly negative. Only if one values preservation of the Federation for its own sake, as Malaysia's political leaders and many of its people obviously do, is the judgment clearly positive. It is in fact hard to say what price Malaysia's leaders, even though they are predominantly Malay and almost all West Malaysian, would *not* pay to preserve the Federation. They do not, of course, enjoy the option of going back to 1963 and considering anew the question of federation, this time with foreknowledge of the fact that Singapore would not remain a member.

Comments by Van Doorn Ooms

Donald Snodgrass's very interesting paper on Malaysian integration and disintegration quite properly analyzes the problem of regional costs and benefits within the context of the political economy of development. I find myself in agreement with the main lines of his analysis and argument, subject to the differences in emphasis and questions on detail noted below. The major shortcoming of the paper —perhaps unavoidable, given the limited access to Malaysian official sources—is its lack of a firm empirical base. One clearly needs to know in some detail how the transfer of public sector resources has affected the structure of investment in both East and West Malaysia before the effects on national and regional growth and distribution can be analyzed. This is perhaps the best place therefore to inject the conventional plea for further research in an area where the problem of regional development takes on an extreme form with respect to differences in location, income levels, and race.

My more specific criticisms of the paper will focus on (1) the potential for trade creation embodied in the original Federation, (2) the analysis of relative marginal productivities of public investment between regions, and (3) the tentative conclusions with respect to the net growth effects of public resource transfer in the existing Federation.

As Snodgrass notes, the existing Federation has no significant trade-creating effects (as distinct from perhaps a small potential gain resulting from an increase in market size), since neither the new flows of manufactures from West to East Malaysia nor the oil exports from Sarawak to West Malaysia displace less efficient local production. The former, unless we use the infant-industry escape hatch, can be regarded largely as trade diversion from more efficient suppliers. The latter has resulted from a discrete change in industrial structure (the introduction of oil refining in West Malaysia) and would no doubt have emerged in any case.

However, Snodgrass argues that the inclusion of Singapore in the original Federation offered a strong set of complementary relationships (as inferred from the large present flows of goods, capital, and, to a lesser extent, labor between Singapore and the rest of the Federation) and that the "overall result would clearly have been net trade creation." It seems to me that this conclusion, which has often been reached, is overstated, and in any case does not follow from the evidence.

Trade creation, apart from the separate problem of the effects of market size, depends upon either (1) the existence of potential but unexploited gains from the reallocation of existing resources, which would result from the removal of restraints upon regional trade or factor movements, or (2) a more efficient future specialization in production resulting from complementary additions to resources in different parts of the region. The high degree of present integration between Singapore and other parts of the region is in fact testimony to the evolution toward fairly complete actual exploitation of regional specialization during the last century as a result of the virtually free movement of goods and factors. But this *ipso facto* also implies that the unexploited *potential* gains from the reallocation of existing resources are extremely limited.

Trade creation would therefore depend upon a demonstration that integration would lead to a more efficient allocation of incremental resources than would evolve in its absence. Here however, the existing complementarities in production are a poor guide, since the historical pattern of regional specialization in raw material production and entrepôt and finance services seems unlikely to continue as the major source of growth. In any case, it is not evident that further integration would have been required to allow for the efficient allocation of incremental resources in these sectors. In the future both Singapore and West Malaysia will have to rely to an increasing extent on import substitution in manufacturing, and in this sector resource endowments would appear to be far more competitive than complementary. Indeed, the intense competition during the 1963–65 period between the two areas for the location of new industrial investments, to which Snodgrass refers, dramatized this relationship.

This argument should not be taken to minimize either the potential gains from expanded market size, which would have resulted from integration of these small economies as tariffs on manufactured goods increase, or the unquestionably large efficiency losses, with respect to both existing and incremental resource allocation, from the process of disintegration which now seems under way. It merely makes the obvious point that the gains from integration are likely to be small for a region that has already evolved a high degree of integration and efficient specialization, and suggests that future resource growth is unlikely to exhibit the high degree of complementarity observed in the past.

In analyzing theoretically the marginal productivity of public investment in different regions of the Federation, Snodgrass implicitly uses a production function in which the two inputs are public capital and "all other" resources, the latter presumably being understood to include the "level of technology" or other components of the "residual." First of all, one would expect that the parameters of such a function would differ greatly in two economies at extremely different levels of development, such as, for instance, Sarawak and West Malaysia. Under such circumstances the relative volume of the inputs in the two economies will provide little information with respect to their marginal products. Secondly, the degree of aggregation in this formulation makes it of doubtful assistance in dealing with development problems because the assumed declining marginal productivity of public capital neglects the complementarities between specific capital inputs. Assuming, for example, that the building of trunk roads in Sarawak would currently be the most productive public investment, we cannot infer that such an investment would be more productive than an investment in feeder roads, given an adequate system of trunk roads. And we certainly cannot infer that such an investment would be more productive than the extension of feeder roads in West Malaysia, which possesses a larger stock of public capital embodied in a highly developed trunk road system.

Finally, I would tend to be somewhat more pessimistic than the author with respect to the potential detrimental effects of public resource transfers on the Malaysian growth rate and in particular on West Malaysian development. Malaysia has historically been extremely efficient in mobilizing public savings through taxes on the foreign sector, and a transfer of "only" 17 percent of central government revenues may not appear unduly burdensome. However, the traditional sources of public revenue do not hold great promise for the future, and pressures on the government budget are likely to become increasingly severe in the years ahead. Judging by past and current experience, the development budget is likely to bear the main burden of a restricted growth of public expenditure at exactly the time when imaginative public investments in West Malaysia will be required to deal with increasing disparities in regional and racial incomes and urban unemployment. Under such circumstances, the opportunity cost to West Malaysia of these "marginal" public resources may be very great. Unless the transferred resources find extremely productive use in East Malaysia, they may indeed become a type of "foreign aid," in which the resources transfer becomes functionally an international payment designed to purchase political stability under progressively more unfavorable circumstances. It is not clear that West Malaysia, whose needs for nation building will become increasingly urgent, will be able to afford this costly exercise in Federation building.

PART II: THE GOVERNMENT AS PRODUCER

3

The Role of Public Enterprise
in Turkish Economic Development

BY JAMES W. LAND

The role of the public sector in the economic development of Turkey is a prominent one. Established as a new republic in 1923, Turkey's main inheritance from the Ottoman Empire was a devastated agricultural economy. A succession of battles across the western half of Turkey had resulted in ruined farms; the necessity to maintain standing armies meant that many other farms were uncared for and left fallow. The Ottoman Turk's hostility to participation in commerce and industry, together with the Ottoman Empire's granting of important special rights to foreigners, resulted in the commercial activities of the empire being carried on by foreigners or foreign minorities living in Turkey. Hostilities with these groups prior to establishment of the republic during the 1920s caused the Turks to arrange a vast population exchange with Greece that resulted in a depletion of Turkey's already limited supply of entrepreneurs.

In these circumstances, it was perhaps inevitable that the state would need to play an important role in the social and economic development of the country. Since the government was anxious to establish a viable economic order, believing that development of a strong economy was a prerequisite for survival of the new republic, it immediately concerned itself with some basic political and social reforms. These reforms, carried out during the 1920s, included the dismantling of the Muslim hierarchy in Istanbul (Caliphate), the establishment of a secular state, and reform of the language and alphabet. By the 1930s the government was able to turn its attention more to economic affairs.

On the economic front, the government attempted to deal simultaneously with three problem areas: it undertook the task of raising savings and providing the economic and social infrastructure for a backward agricultural economy; to the public enterprises it assigned the job of establishing a modern industrial sector in the absence or scarcity of private entrepreneurship and capital; and to new financial institutions it assigned the task of creating a modern money economy and insuring the financing of government and public enterprise investment programs.

Consequently, Turkey has had a set of government programs to promote rapid economic growth and industrialization for a longer time than most underdeveloped countries. The present paper is a summary analysis of the role public enterprises played in the economic development of Turkey. After a brief introduction to the Turkish economy, we will look at the determinants of growth of the public enterprise sector by examining the growth of output in relationship to the growth of the capital stock and the labor force. This will enable us to look briefly at the changes in productivity and technology that have occurred during the period from 1939 to 1963. We can then push the analysis one step further by examining the determinants of investment in the public enterprise sector. This will be seen to be influenced greatly by the financing ability of individual enterprises, which in turn is influenced by their organizational structure, operating efficiency, and pricing policies. Ultimately, however, we wish to look at the effect of the growth of the public enterprise sector on the growth of the Turkish economy as a whole.

DEVELOPMENT OF THE ECONOMY

Conventionally, modern Turkish history is divided into four periods: the first attempts at economic recovery during the period from 1923 to 1932, the period of etatism from 1933 to 1949, the era of rapid growth during the ostensibly free enterprise period from 1950 to 1960, and the beginning of more comprehensive planning during the period after 1960.

1923–32: Economic and Political Recovery

During the period of recovery from 1923 to 1932, the Turkish government was primarily concerned with establishing a viable national order. Dismantling the trappings of a religious empire and creating institutions suitable for a republic required both skill and time. However, the government took some steps toward encouraging industrialization and growth of agricultural output. The Agricultural Bank was reorganized; a Business Bank was established, with private sponsorship but under the control and influence of the government, to provide capital for private entrepreneurs; and in 1927 a law for the "assistance of industry" was passed. This law sought to encourage the private sector through a system of land grants, tax advantages, direct subsidies, government purchases of domestically produced goods, and the guaranteeing of monopoly rights for certain new private firms.

The new programs resulted in little increase of private industrial activity, with the exception of the textile and cement industries. The lack of success in Turkey's early industrialization efforts can be attributed largely to two causes: a shortage of capital and a shortage of skills. There was no foreign capital coming into Turkey because government officials had bitter memories of the political consequences of heavy borrowing and investment from abroad, and foreign capitalists had little desire to invest in a country that was undergoing radical changes in its political structure. Nationalization of transportation and communication facilities further frightened investors. The population exchanges along with the great casualties among the Armenians seriously depleted the ranks of those in Turkey who had experience in economic activity and who might reasonably be expected to assume the risks of entrepreneurial activity. The lack of regard with which many Turks considered industrial and commercial affairs meant that it would be some time before an indigenous class of managers and skilled workers would develop on its own; and it also meant that the indigenous propertied classes were not likely to develop into entrepreneurs.

Intellectuals and government leaders were persuaded that economic planning and state intervention were necessary to establish an industrial economy without the unemployment and instability that characterized the West during the early 1930s. The high levels of unemployment in all countries except Russia, and the isolationist economic policies followed as each country sought to minimize foreign disturbances on its own economy, tended to reinforce the intellectuals' bias against the private enterpreneurial sector.

Consequently the government eventually adopted a policy of etatism, or government intervention and guidance in the economic affairs of the country, although the government conceded that the dominant role should be played by private initiative and capital. In practice the adoption of etatism meant that the government discontinued its program to develop an indigenous Turkish enterpreneurial system through legislative and financial acts. Instead the government drew up five-year plans with emphasis on government investment in economic and social infrastructure and the creation of a modern public enterprise sector. The plans or, more accurately, the array of industrial projects did not add up to a comprehensive attempt at planning; rather, they constituted a set of ad hoc measures, often contradictory, with the objective of rapidly industrializing Turkey.

1933–50: The War Years and Etatism

Through the public enterprise sector the state became the sole producer in many areas and an important producer in others. Among the new enterprises were special investment and development banks, textile plants, cement factories, paper mills, a glass factory, and an iron and steel works. During the course of the 1930s, government activity in transportation, industry, and finance became increasingly important. Not only did the application of etatism result in the creation of many new enterprises in Turkey, but some privately owned enterprises, especially coal mines and sugar factories, were nationalized.

There were also discriminatory practices in the government sector, including tax exemptions, priority in the allocation of scarce resources, first claim on foreign exchange, and state assistance in training technical personnel. Perhaps more important, some enterprises had access to credit from the government banks and others did not. Concurrent with its increasing commercial and industrial activities, the state developed legal barriers to entry into government spheres and increased regulation of those areas in which the government had no direct interest.

Etatism aimed for a rational attack on Turkey's problems, with due emphasis on transportation, education, and the building up of industry by government in the absence of a large group of entrepreneurs. But the results were poorer than desired. Restricted government receipts and a conservative expenditure policy during the first part of this period meant that government investment and development expenditures were a modest proportion of GNP. As we shall see below, the public enterprise sector grew rapidly but to some extent did so by virtue of nationalization and at the expense of the private sector. During World War II military expenditures again held down government investment, and the reduction of imports and government discrimination continued to restrict the private sector.

1950–60: Economic Growth

In 1949 the Democratic party was elected to power on a platform that favored private enterprise, but in practice the importance of government became even greater.[1] Expenditures in the public sector increased, and since there was a reaction against planning, the ad hoc nature of state enterprise and of government policies became even more pronounced.

This period as a whole was one of growth, particularly from 1948 to 1953. A main cause of growth was expansion of agricultural output, brought about by mechanization and the increase of lands under cultivation. Since there was little increase in land productivity, the increase in production was a once-and-for-all phenomenon, brought to an end as soon as all usable land was under cultivation. Increased agricultural incomes and monetary expansion did not at first result in rapid inflation, largely because of the temporarily expanded agricultural output and excess capacity in the public enterprise sector. After 1955, however, the slower rate of growth in agriculture, more rapid monetary expansion, large military and other government expenditures, and an ambitious crop subsidy program resulted in serious balance of payments difficulties, a large external debt, and rapid inflation (over 15 percent annually). A balance of payments crisis in 1958, government repression of criticism, continued inflation, and loss of confidence in the economic prospects of the country caused the military to intervene in 1960 and to establish a new government.

1960–63: The Era of Planning[2]

At the end of the revolution in 1960 Turkey was still a predominantly agricultural country. The country's high ambitions were not being

1. The reasons for a continued, vigorous, public sector economic policy are complex. At first the Democratic party seemed genuinely anxious to reduce the influence of the government and public enterprises, even to the point of selling off public enterprises to private interests. But there were political outcries at plans to sell the profitable enterprises and no buyers for the unprofitable ones. Furthermore, the private sector was not interested in many of the industries the government wanted to establish, either because they required large capital outlays or because they were thought to be unprofitable. The government also found that the electorate demanded and was pleased by increased expenditures in education, health, infrastructure, and urban development. Moreover, the government was already committed to heavy expenditures —amounting to more than 4 percent of GNP—for national defense.
2. The Turkish government is still committed to planning. The period

realized, and the military government had to deal with the pressure of a rapidly growing population, the lack of growth of the agricultural sector, and the need for an increase in the level of investment to sustain economic growth at the rate envisaged by the government. Shortly after the revolution the State Planning Office was established in order to introduce greater rationality into the allocation of resources. The year 1967 is the last year of the first five-year plan, and only now are sufficient data becoming available to evaluate the results of planning.

Output and Price Changes from 1938 to 1963

From 1933 to 1963, the terminal date of the present study, Turkey enjoyed a moderately high growth rate of net national product[3]— about 3 percent in the period 1933–48, and about 5 percent since 1948. The lower rate in the earlier period—despite impressive growth in the public enterprise sector—was the result of stagnation in the private industrial and agricultural sectors of the economy during the war years. Table 3.1 and Figures 3.1–3.3 show more clearly the change in output and prices during the period 1938–63.[4]

Table 3.1 shows the growth of the major components of net national product, population, and per capita NNP. The population grew at about 1.7 percent from 1938 to 1948 and at rates approaching 3 percent after 1948. The lower rate during the early period was caused by the distorted age and sex distribution of the population brought about by war conditions and deaths during the period 1910–23. If we take population growth into account, Turkey's per capita income grew at an annual rate of about 1.5 percent from 1938 to 1963 and at about 2.5 percent after 1948. While not unusually high, and certainly below the aspirations of the Turkish government, these growth rates are impressive considering the length of time for which they have been sustained.

1960–63 is arbitrary, corresponding to the years for which public enterprise data are available.

3. Estimates of net national product are used in preference to GNP data since NNP estimates are prepared by the State Institute of Statistics first and independent estimates of depreciation allowances and indirect taxes are then added in to obtain the GNP estimates. Since the estimates of depreciation allowances are poor, particularly in the earlier periods, the NNP estimates are more comparable.

4. It is not possible to treat the period 1933–38 in much detail because of the poor quality of the aggregate data available. However, there is a reasonable estimate for national income for 1933, and this is used in the text.

Table 3.1: Net National Product, Population, and Per Capita NNP of Turkey,
1938–63
(1962 prices)

	Values				
	1938	*1948*	*1953*	*1961*	*1963*
Net national product (billions of TL)	21.5	25.8	37.0	48.9	56.1
Population (millions)	17.0	20.1	22.8	28.6	30.3
Per capita NNP (TL)	1,265	1,283	1,623	1,710	1,851

	Annual compound growth rates *(Percentages)*				
	1938–48	*1948–53*	*1953–61*	*1961–63*	*1938–63*
Net national product	1.9	7.5	3.5	7.0	3.8
Population	1.7	2.5	2.8	3.0	2.3
Per capita NNP	0.2	5.0	0.7	4.0	1.5

Sources: Population figures are from Devlet Istatistik Enstitüsü, *Türkiye Istatistik Yilliği, 1964–65,* Publication no. 510 (Ankara), p. 55; national income data are from State Institute of Statistics, *National Income,* Publication no. 536 (Ankara, 1968).

Figure 3.1 shows more clearly the pattern of growth during the post-1938 period. The period as a whole can be subdivided into four main subperiods: stagnation or slow growth from 1938 to 1948, when Turkish military forces were mobilized and critical imports were curtailed; rapid growth from 1949 to 1953; more moderate growth from 1954 to 1960, accompanied by rapid inflation; and improved growth performance from 1960 to 1964 (despite the leveling off of agricultural output in 1958), following the revolution of 1960.[5]

It is apparent from Figure 3.1 that the Turkish economy is very much influenced by the performance of the agricultural sector. Exceptionally bad crop years in 1949 and 1954 resulted in substantial reductions in total output. On the other hand, rapid growth in agricultural output from 1950 to 1953 made possible an impressive expansion of total output without price inflation.[6] Between 1954 and 1961, when

5. Price changes in percentages during the period 1938–63 are summarized below:

	Annual price changes
1938–48	14.8
1948–53	3.5
1953–58	13.0
1958–61	8.0
1961–63	5.0

6. The growth rate of agricultural output from 1950 to 1953 was not

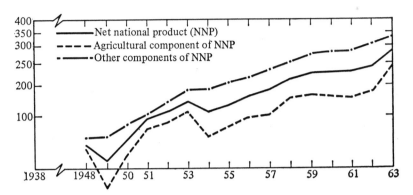

Figure 3.1: Growth of Net National Product of Turkey, 1938, 1948–63

(Indexes with 1938 = 100, 1962 prices)

Source: Republic of Turkey, Prime Ministry, State Institute of Statistics, *National Income: Total Expenditure and Investment of Turkey 1938, 1948–67*, Publication no. 536 (Ankara, 1968), pp. 2–3.

agricultural output grew very slowly, government spending programs, public enterprise investment, and other efforts by the government to encourage industrialization and growth resulted in rapid inflation.

Figure 3.2 shows the relative shares of NNP in current prices by producing sector. The relatively small changes from 1938 to 1963 in the shares of agriculture and industry, as shown in Figure 3.2, are remarkable. The share of agriculture declined from 47.2 percent of NNP in 1938 to 42.1 percent in 1963, and the share of industry increased from 12.5 percent to 15.8 percent. However, there were important fluctuations within the period. From 1938 to 1948 the share of agriculture increased from 47.4 percent to 53.2 percent. Most of this increase was the result of changing terms of trade between agriculture and other sectors of the economy. Agricultural prices increased six times during this ten-year period, whereas prices in most other

matched in succeeding years because most of the expansion was achieved through an increase of land under cultivation and mechanization of large farms. By 1954 there was no longer any easy way to bring additional land under cultivation, and most large farms had been mechanized. In fact, some land had to be returned to inactive use because of severe erosion. Agricultural output, however, continued to grow until 1958; afterward there was a virtual leveling off of agricultural production (in the period 1958–62).

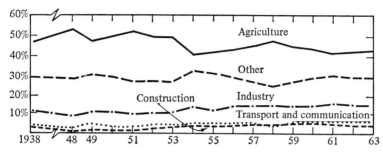

Figure 3.2: Sector Shares of Net National Product of Turkey, 1938, 1948–63

(Percentage of NNP, current prices)

Source: Same as for Figure 3.1.

sectors of the economy increased only three to four times. Agricultural prices advanced because of the severe disruptions of the agricultural sector during the war and a particularly bad crop year in 1948.[7]

Consequently, it is more instructive to look at the changes in relative shares when calculated in constant prices. Figure 3.3 shows the shares for the years 1938–63 in 1962 prices. It is seen that, while the decline of the agricultural sector is more substantial than that in Figure 3.2, the cyclical variations have disappeared. On the other hand, while the agricultural share was declining from 54.6 percent to 40.0 percent, the industrial share increased only slightly—to 16.8 percent in 1963 from its 13.7 percent share in 1938. One of the questions that will concern us later is why the share of industry has changed so slightly despite government efforts to create a modern industrial sector.

THE ROLE OF PUBLIC ENTERPRISES IN THE TURKISH ECONOMY

There are well over a hundred nonfinancial public enterprises in Turkey, and the government participates to a significant extent in some sixty-five others. Around 40 percent of public sector investment is by public enterprises, and they hire 20 percent of all nonagricultural wage earners. Public enterprises exist in many sectors of the Turkish

7. From 1938 to 1948 agricultural prices rose, as indicated in the text, much more rapidly than industrial and other prices. From 1948 to 1954 there was virtual stability in agricultural prices and a rapid increase in industrial prices. After 1954 agricultural and industrial prices moved together, and there were no important changes in the terms of trade.

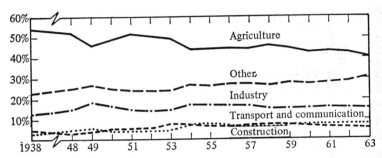

Figure 3.3: Sector Shares of Net National Product of Turkey, 1938,
1948–63

(Percentage of NNP, 1962 prices)

Source: Same as for Figure 3.1.

economy—transportation, communications, manufacturing, mining, electricity, agriculture, construction, wholesale and retail trade, and finance. In addition, there are several enterprises that perform quasi-governmental functions—such as the regulation of agricultural commodity prices. Most of the value added, however, is concentrated in the transportation, communication, and industrial sectors.

Table 3.2 shows the importance of public enterprises in the economy as a whole.[8] In transportation and communication, public enterprises account for about 30 percent of total value added by the sector in 1938. By 1950 this proportion had increased to 41 percent, and by the end of the decade it had declined to 34 percent. Actually the public enterprise share is understated since it excludes municipal transportation systems. In the industrial sector public enterprises account for a rising share of value added; they accounted for only 18 percent of value added in 1938, for 32 percent in 1950, and for 42 percent by the end of the decade. Excluded from the public enterprise figures above is some government enterprise activity—namely that of municipal enterprises (such as electric works, utilities, and slaughter houses)—for which detailed accounts are not available and which have been excluded from the public enterprise study on which the

8. The data used in Table 3.2 and succeeding tables of this paper are newly published by the State Institute of Statistics in Ankara. They are the result of a study conducted by the author on public enterprises in Turkey. See James W. Land, *Economic Accounts of Nonfinancial Public Enterprises in Turkey* (Ankara: State Institute of Statistics, 1969).

Table 3.2: Value Added by Public and Private Enterprises in the Transportation, Communication, and Industrial Sectors, 1938, 1950, 1960, and 1963
(Millions of T.L., 1962 prices)

	1938		1950		1960		1963	
	Value	Percent	Value	Percent	Value	Percent	Value	Percent
1. Transportation and communication	791	21	1,297	23	3,302	30	4,148	32
a. Public enterprise	307	8	646	11	1,303	12	1,274	10
b. Private enterprise[a]	484	13	651	12	1,999	18	2,874	22
2. Industry (incl. monopolies)	2,945	79	4,367	77	7,713	70	8,989	68
a. Public enterprise	612	16	1,606	28	3,732	34	4,139	32
b. Private enterprise[a]	2,333	63	2,761	49	3,981	36	4,850	36
Total	3,736	100	5,664	100	11,015	100	13,137	100

[a] For 1938 and 1950, a breakdown of the private sector is available from Republic of Turkey, Prime Ministry, State Institute of Statistics, *National Income of Turkey, 1938, 1948–1951*, official translation of Publication no. 352 (Ankara, 1967), pp. 261–63, 294–95.

Sources: Republic of Turkey, Prime Ministry, State Institute of Statistics, *National Income: Total Expenditure and Investment of Turkey, 1938, 1948–1951*, Publication no. 536 (Ankara, 1968), pp. 2–3; and from James W. Land, *Public Enterprise Economic Accounts in Turkey, 1939–1963*, Special Project no. 3, Training Center, State Institute of Statistics (Ankara, 1968), pp. 66–67, 107–08, 111–13 (hereafter cited as Land, SP3).

Private Enterprise Value Added in the Transportation, Communication, and Industrial Sectors by Type of Enterprise, 1938 and 1950
(Percentages)

	1938	1950
1. Transportation and communication	100	100
a. Rail & ocean transport	19	10
b. Land & motor vehicle	16	35
c. Animal drawn vehicles, nonmotor vehicles, & porters	61	50
d. Other	4	5
2. Industry (incl. monopolies)	100	100
a. Large-scale	37	42
b. Small-scale	63	58

data in Table 3.2 are based. Consequently, the size of the public enterprise share of the industrial sector is also understated.[9]

Table 3.2 also indicates certain changes in the structure of the private enterprise sector from 1938 to 1950.[10] In transportation and communication, private rail and ocean transport declined (partly the result of government take-overs), and land and motor vehicles more than doubled (the result of road construction and increased use of bus and truck transportation). The increasing share of private enterprise in transportation after 1950 is the result of an enormous increase in privately owned bus and truck usage, made possible through an ambitious highway construction program sponsored by the government.

In the industrial sector there was a slight decline in the importance of small-scale private industry, almost entirely concentrated in mining, as government firms bought up small privately owned mining operations. It is noteworthy, however, that cottage industries and other small-scale privately owned firms did not decrease in importance.

The changing shares of public and private enterprise in the transportation, communication, and industrial sectors indicate that public and private enterprises have not been growing at the same rate. As we have seen, public enterprises in the industrial sector grew much faster than private enterprises. Table 3.3 and 3.4 show in more detail growth and composition of the public enterprise sector.

Table 3.3 classifies value added by public enterprises according to the producing sector of the economy.[11] Most of the categories in Table 3.3 are self-explanatory. The "other" firms include a group of model farms, some construction firms, and a few wholesale and retail outlets for other public enterprises. The importance of the transportation, communication, and industrial sectors is underscored by the fact that ancillary and other firms together account for less than 10 percent of value added by public enterprises.[12] For most purposes items (2)

9. The private enterprise share is calculated residually. Since the public enterprise data used in this study are somewhat different from those used in the calculation of national income by the State Institute of Statistics, the private enterprise estimates are also different. However, the difference is more or less a constant proportion.

10. Unfortunately, comparable data are not available for 1960 and 1963.

11. This section of the paper concentrates on the period after 1939 because it was not until after this date that data were collected on a regular basis and that there were enough firms to make quantitative analysis worthwhile.

12. Although ancillary agencies are not important in terms of value added, their indirect influence on output in other sectors of the economy is substantial, since they are primarily price regulatory agencies.

Table 3.3: Value Added of Public Enterprises by Industrial Sector, 1939, 1945, 1950, 1960, 1963
(Millions of T.L., 1962 prices)

Sector	1939 Value	1939 Percent	1945 Value	1945 Percent	1950 Value	1950 Percent	1960 Value	1960 Percent	1963 Value	1963 Percent
1. Transportation and communication	307	33	589	29	645	28	1,303	25	1,274	23
a. Railways	131	14	231	11	307	13	615	12	617	11
b. Waterways	72	8	101	6	169	7	394	8	349	6
c. Airways	—[a]	—	4	—	13	1	22	—	26	1
d. P.T.T.	104	11	253	12	156	7	272	5	282	5
2. Industry	284	30	721	34	820	36	2,129	41	2,324	43
a. Manufacturing	206	22	548	26	529	23	1,426	28	1,560	29
(1) Heavy industry	—	—	56	3	100	4	325	6	381	7
(2) Food processing	78	8	73	3	111	5	455	9	355	7
(3) Textiles	97	11	340	16	264	11	437	9	448	8
(4) Other	31	3	79	4	54	2	209	4	376	7
b. Mining and quarrying	78	8	173	8	291	13	623	12	613	11
(1) Coal	32	3	137	6	233	10	397	8	448	8
(2) Copper	28	3	23	1	35	2	164	3	115	2
(3) Other	18	2	13	1	23	1	62	1	50	1
c. Electricity	—	—	—	—	—	—	80	1	151	3
3. Monopolies	327	35	571	27	649	28	1,294	24	1,334	24
4. Ancillary	19	2	130	6	101	4	300	6	292	5
5. Other	2	—	81	4	77	3	189	4	232	4
Total public enterprise sector	939	100	2,092	100	2,292	100	5,215	100	5,456	100

[a] Dash indicates negligible value.

Source: Land, SP3.

Table 3.4: Growth Rates of Value Added of Public Enterprises, 1939–63
(Constant 1962 market prices)

Sector	1939–45	1945–50	1939–50	1950–60	1960–63	1939–63
1. Transportation and communication	8.1	1.5	6.9	8.0	-0.7	6.4
a. Railways	5.0	4.4	9.2	8.8	0.2	7.4
b. Waterways	5.7	11.5	7.7	8.2	-4.6	7.8
c. Airways	39.7	31.5	36.0	8.6	6.9	14.9
d. P.T.T.	12.5	-9.8	2.1	6.3	1.7	3.3
2. Industry	16.7	6.0	10.1	10.0	4.7	9.3
a. Manufacturing	18.1	4.3	10.8	9.4	5.0	8.7
(1) Heavy industry	14.5	23.8	18.7	10.7	10.7	14.9
(2) Food processing	-0.2	9.9	4.5	14.1	-9.8	9.2
(3) Textiles	24.7	.1	11.9	4.5	2.4	5.1
(4) Other	16.9	-7.2	4.7	14.5	22.4	9.6
b. Mining	13.4	10.7	8.6	10.1	1.8	9.7
(1) Coal	25.1	11.8	13.3	6.8	4.0	9.5
(2) Copper	-1.5	2.6	0.0	9.9	-9.5	7.7
(3) Other	-3.1	17.4	4.6	30.2	5.6	15.4
c. Electricity						
3. Monopolies	9.5	1.8	5.1	7.2	1.0	5.5
4. Ancillary	32.5	-6.6	14.7	12.2	-1.3	10.7
5. Other	97.9	-6.0	8.2	9.5	7.4	14.3
Total public enterprise sector	13.5	2.6	7.6	8.9	2.4	7.5

Source: Land, SP3

and (3) should be considered together since the State Monopolies Administration is made up of industrial firms. In the table, however, the State Monopolies Administration is separated from other industrial firms because of the administration's role as a major revenue collector for the government. The high mark-up of prices charged by the monopolies over the cost of production results in extraordinary profits which are turned over to the government. These profits, which can be thought of as indirect taxes, inflate the value added by almost three times what it would be if output were valued at competitive market prices.

Table 3.4 looks at the growth of public enterprises during the period 1939–63. For the period as a whole, public enterprises in Turkey grew at a rate of slightly over 7 percent per annum. There is, of course, no absolute criterion by which one can say that such a rate is low or high. However, considering the low base of the industrial sector when Turkey began its industrialization effort and the great ambitions which Turkey had for the public enterprise sector, the rate is disappointing. What is more relevant for our present purposes, however, is the difference in growth rates corresponding to the different political subperiods distinguished earlier in the paper.

Scrutiny of Table 3.4 reveals some surprising results. Public enterprises in Turkey from 1939 to 1950 grew at an annual rate of about 7.6 percent, but from 1950 to 1960, during the supposed free enterprise era, they grew at about 8.9 percent. During the short postrevolution period covered by this study, public enterprises grew at 2.4 percent annually. It is noteworthy that they grew somewhat faster during the 1950s than during the period from 1939 to 1950. To some extent this paradox can be explained by looking at the growth rates of the subperiods 1939–45 and 1945–50. It can be seen in Table 3.3 that public enterprises grew very rapidly during the war, even though the economy as a whole was expanding slowly, and at a very low rate from 1945 until 1950. The faster growth rate during the early period was possible because some public enterprises, which were established during the late 1930s, either did not begin full-scale production until the early 1940s or enjoyed increased demand for their output during the war because of the sharp cutback in imports. After the war, when increased imports became available and domestic demand no longer increased so rapidly, public enterprises grew more slowly until 1950, when vigorous government programs created new enterprises and expanded many of the old ones.

Tables 3.3 and 3.4 also indicate changes in the sectorial composition of value added by the public enterprise sector from 1939 to 1963. The transportation and communication sector grew more slowly than the public enterprise sector as a whole, and its share of the total declined from 33 percent in 1939 to 23 percent in 1963. Industry, including both items (2) and (3), increased only slightly from 65 percent in 1939 to 67 percent in 1963. However, there were substantial changes within industry as the share of the state monopolies declined from 35 to 24 percent, and the share of manufacturing increased from 22 to 29 percent and mining and quarrying from 8 to 11 percent.[13]

Within the industrial sector there was substantial growth in manufacturing, mining, and electricity. The increase in the share of manufacturing is associated with substantial investment in the iron and steel complex and growth of the textile industry. Mining increased mainly as a result of high growth rates of coal and copper production. The relative decline in importance of the state monopolies can be explained partly because these industries were already established in 1939. Their main products are tobacco, matches, alcoholic beverages, ammunition, and salt. Some of the monopoly products have low income elasticity of demand, and the market for others is restricted by the exceptionally high prices charged by the monopoly administration.

It is, of course, one thing to observe that public enterprises in Turkey grew as fast in one political period as another, and another to conclude from that observation that the political changes from one period to another were unimportant. The factors influencing the growth rate of the public enterprise sector surely are diverse, and it might very well be that public enterprises grew slightly faster in the 1950s than in the 1940s *despite,* and not because of, government policy. To shed more light on this complicated issue it is necessary to probe deeper into the determinants of growth of the public enterprise sector.

Because of the restricted output of the state monopolies and the

13. In fact, however, changes in the industrial sector are more important than Table 3.2 indicates. The sector shares in Table 3.2 are greatly influenced by the tax revenue aspect of the state monopolies and a few other enterprises. If we were to subtract indirect taxes collected by the state monopolies from their total revenue, we would find that their value added decreases to almost one-third of its value at market prices. Consequently we can get a better idea of physical production by measuring value added at factor cost rather than at market prices. When measured in this way, value added of public enterprises in the industrial sector increased from 44 percent in 1939 to 57 percent in 1963, and value added in industry, excluding the state monopolies, increased from 32 percent to 47 percent.

relative unimportance of ancillary agencies and other public enterprises in Turkey, it simplifies analysis considerably if we consider in the remaining part of this paper only the public enterprises in the transportation, communication, and industrial sectors. Figure 3.4 shows the growth of value added, capital stock, and labor force of these public enterprises in Turkey for the period since 1939. Table 3.5 indicates the index of value added, capital stock, and employment for the same enterprises for the years 1939, 1950, 1960, and 1963, and Table 3.6 summarizes the relationships between capital and output, capital and labor, output and labor, and the real wage and return to capital for 1939, 1945, 1950, 1960, and 1963.

Data on value added are stated in constant 1962 prices. Capital stock estimates are in 1962 prices, after adjustment for depreciation calculated by the "one-horse shay" method.[14] Real wages per worker are calculated using a cost-of-living index, and rates of return are calculated by dividing profits, deflated by the value added index in terms of 1962 prices, by the value of the capital stock defined earlier.[15]

Over the period from 1939 to 1963, value added increased almost seven times, whereas the capital stock increased over three and a half times and employment somewhat less than four times. As Figure 3.4 makes clear, value added and the labor force moved very nearly together until 1950; after 1950 there was a great increase in the productivity of labor (the value added to labor ratio increased from 9.9 thousand TL in 1950 to 17.1 TL in 1963). There is less variation in the growth rate of the capital stock than for the other two variables, although during the period from 1939 to 1947 the capital stock grew relatively slowly, mainly because of difficulties in importing capital goods. During 1939–45, the period of most rapid growth of public enterprises, there was a dramatic substitution of labor for capital or, more accurately, a dramatic decrease in the capital/labor ratio.

Table 3.6 shows marked declines in the capital/value added and capital/labor ratios from 1939 to 1945. Since 1945 the capital/value added ratio has varied between 5.8 and 4.3. Similarly, the capital/

14. The "one-horse shay" depreciation method assumes the capital stock is maintained in such a way that it is fully productive until retirement; this method of calculating the value of the capital stock in real terms is particularly useful in production-function analysis.

15. Ideally, rates of return ought to be measured by dividing profits in current prices by the capital stock measured in current prices. This definition of the capital stock should not be confused with a measure of the capital stock in nominal prices, which usually is a measure of the stock at original cost, the prices used depending upon the year in which the asset is purchased.

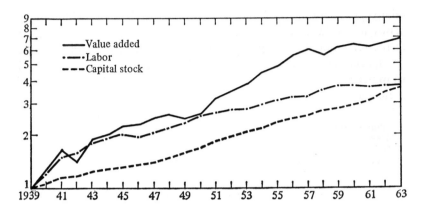

Figure 3.4: Growth of Value Added, Capital Stock, and Labor of
Public Enterprises in the Transportation, Communication, and
Industrial Sectors

(Indexes with 1939 = 100, 1962 prices)

Note: Excluding state monopolies.
Source: Land, SP3.

labor ratio declined from 87,000 TL in 1939 to 56,000 in 1945, after
which the ratio was relatively stable until a sharp increase in the
period after 1960.

Three aspects of the behavior of these ratios need to be explained:
the relatively high capital/value added ratio (K/V), the marked decline in the capital/value added and capital/labor (K/L) ratios from
1939 to 1945, and a sharp increase in the capital/labor ratio after
1960. Changes in any of the above relationships can occur as a result

Table 3.5: Indexes of Value Added, Capital Stock, and Employment of Public
Enterprises in the Transportation, Communication, and Industrial Sectors[a]
(Indexes with 1939 = 100, 1962 prices)

	Value added	Capital stock	Employment
1939	100	100	100
1950	270	167	254
1960	632	288	375
1963	689	362	375

[a] Excluding state monopolies.

Source: Land, SP3.

of changes in the composition of output, say, from a capital-intensive industry to a labor-intensive industry, or because of changes in factor proportions and productivity within given industries. In fact, both sorts of changes were important in the public enterprise sector during 1939–63.

Figure 3.5 shows separately the relationship between value added,

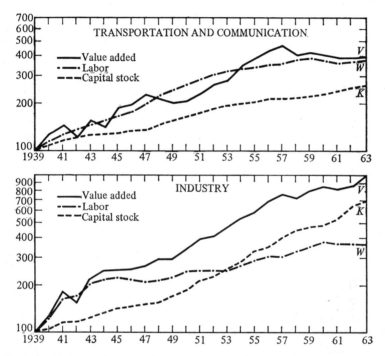

Figure 3.5: Growth of Value Added, Capital Stock, and Labor of Public Enterprises in the Transportation, Communication, and Industrial Sectors

Source: Land, SP3.

employment, and capital stock for the transportation and communication firms and for industrial firms. Over the period as a whole there was no improvement in labor productivity in the transportation and communication sector since value added and employment increased together. Value added per worker (V/L) has remained close to 12,000 TL per worker, a number that reflects relatively high labor productivity in 1939 and relatively low productivity in 1963. (See Table 3.6.)

Table 3.6: Capital/Output Ratios, Capital/Labor Ratios, Output/Labor Ratios, Real Wages and Return to Capital for Public Enterprises in the Transportation, Communication, and Industry Sectors

	K/V	K/L (*1,000 TL/worker*)	V/L (*1,000 TL/worker*)	W (*1,000 TL/worker*)	R (*percentage*)
1939	9.4	87	9.3	5.7	1
1945	5.5	56	10.2	4.1	3
1950	5.8	57	9.9	6.1	1
1960	4.3	66	15.6	8.4	2
1963	4.9	84	17.1	9.3	1

Source: Land, SP3, pp. 14, 16, 31, 52–53.

The K/V ratio and the K/L ratio in the transportation and communication sector are high in comparison with those of the industrial sector. The K/V ratio in 1939 was 13.8, although by 1945 the ratio was fluctuating around 9.0. The K/L ratio in 1939 was 155,000 TL per worker; by 1945 it had declined to 117,000. These data do not indicate that the substitution of labor for capital, while substantial, was as dramatic as that observed for the combined sectors in Figure 3.4.[16]

On the other hand, changes in factor proportions and productivity of the industrial sector are impressive. The K/V ratio for the industrial sector in 1939 was 4.6, and by 1945 it had decreased to only 2.6. These low K/V ratios indicate that the high K/V ratio for the combined sectors is accounted for mainly by the transportation and communication sector. However, changes in the aggregate ratio, particularly from 1939 to 1945, are caused by the declining ratio in both the transportation and communication and the industrial sectors and by the increasing importance of the industrial sector in total value added by the combined sectors. (See Table 3.2.) After the war the K/L ratio for the industrial sector began to increase, and by 1954 it

16. These conclusions must be qualified to take into account the quality of the data for the transportation and communication sector from 1939 to the mid-1950s. Until the mid-1950s the transportation and communication firms published their operating accounts as annexed budgets to the general government budget, since legally they were government agencies rather than enterprises. Annexed budgets do not give as complete information regarding value added, capital stock, and employment as do the accounts for industrial firms. In some cases data are available only for benchmark years and estimates were interpolated for intervening years. Interpolation naturally cannot take account of short-run variations. For this reason variations in the K/V or K/L ratios as shown in Figure 3.5 for transportation and communication firms may be greatly understated for the period 1939–55.

had reached its 1939 level. Subsequent increases in the K/L ratio were caused by production of new commodities using more capital-intensive technology.

In summary, it is seen that the high capital/value added ratio is the result of a large, highly capital-intensive transportation and communication sector. The capital/output ratio for the industrial sector (excluding monopolies) for the most part is close to the traditional 3.0. The decline of both the capital/value added and capital/labor ratios from 1939 to 1945 is partially the result of using up the excess capacity that existed in several public enterprises in 1939 (such as the iron and steel complex). It is also the result of substituting labor for capital during the war years. The unavailability of imports forced some of the public enterprises to increase output through double shifts and other capital-saving devices in order to meet the increased domestic demand. Finally, the increase in the K/L ratio after 1960 is the result of two factors: heavy investment in the transportation industry in the face of declining markets and value added, and a large flow of investment in the capital stock of several public enterprises that had just begun to produce by 1963. If we were to continue the data from 1963 to 1967, the capital/labor ratio undoubtedly would decline from its 1963 level as some of the new firms increased production.

Labor productivity remained remarkably constant for the combined sectors over the period as a whole. Gains in productivity of labor in the industrial sector completely offset losses in the transportation and communication sector. After 1950 the growth of output outpaced that of employment and the capital stock, particularly in the industrial sector, where the V/L ratio doubled from 1950 to 1963. Corresponding to what one might expect when there are important increases in labor productivity, there was, after 1945, rapid growth in real wages of workers employed in the public enterprise sector.

The preceding analysis explains increase in output and labor productivity before 1950 in terms of wartime conditions and excess capacity. After 1950 the rapid increase in labor productivity and a growth rate of output consistently higher than that of either labor or capital strongly suggests the importance of technological change in explaining growth of output since 1950. Before we seek to allocate growth in output among growth of the capital stock, growth of employment, and technological change, we must look briefly at the market structure of the public enterprise sector.

Public enterprises in Turkey operate almost independently of market forces. They are protected from competition at home by virtual monopoly position in most industries and from competition abroad by high tariff levels or embargo on imports.[17] On the other hand, there is heavy government interference in the operating, investment, and pricing decisions of the public enterprises at almost every level. Public enterprise wage rates are determined by law, and ministerial interference in the selection and promotion of managers is common. Sometimes the level and composition of investment are determined by government ministries rather than by the enterprises themselves. Perhaps of most importance, however, is the tendency for the government to set prices of outputs and inputs, often with a view to holding down prices but seldom in a way to maximize profits or growth.

Granted certain assumptions about technology, it is possible in a competitive economy to estimate output elasticities with respect to the factors of production by looking at the factor shares of value added. Such a relationship is remote, however, with regard to the Turkish public enterprise sector with its characteristic elements of monopoly and nonmarket behavior. Further evidence of the lack of the traditionally assumed relationship between output elasticities and factor shares is the coexistence of a high capital/output ratio and low returns to capital (such as are suggested in Table 3.7) in an economy with low savings and a small capital stock. One would normally expect such a high capital/output ratio in the public enterprise sector only if there are high rates of return to capital.

The preceding analysis suggests two reasons for the low return to capital. First of all, the transportation and communication firms collectively have a high K/V ratio, and investment in this sector has been made in terms of creating basic infrastructure rather than of making profits. Secondly, government pricing policies frequently result in below-market prices for output while, at the same time, enterprises are forced to pay wage rates very nearly approximating, and sometimes even exceeding, those of a competitive market. Consequently, profits and the rate of return on capital are low.

Nonetheless it is possible, without independent information on output elasticities, to get some indication of the amount of technological progress from examination of Figure 3.1. From 1939 to 1963 the capital stock grew at about 5.5 percent annually and employment at about 5.0 percent annually. Regardless of the weights used in attribut-

17. The most important exceptions are certain textile firms, but many textile firms produce rather specialized products of which they are the sole producer.

ing growth in output (value added) to growth of the capital stock and the labor force, technological change would not be markedly different from 5.0 percent. If we disregard the period 1939–47 because of the war years and gradual decline in the excess capacity existing in 1939 and look only at the period 1947–60, for which there is a relatively smooth trend in the growth of the capital stock and the labor force, we get a somewhat different measure of technological change. During this period the labor force grew at 4.3 percent and the capital stock grew at 5.4 percent, whereas value added grew at 6.8 percent. If, at one extreme, we assume the output elasticities for capital and labor to be at one-third and two-thirds, the estimate for the "residual" technological change is 2.1 percent. If, on the other hand, we assume that the capital elasticity is understated because of the market conditions described and reverse these proportions, the estimate of technological change becomes 1.8 percent. These two estimates are not sufficiently different from each other to warrant much worry about the "correct" weights.

To some extent the technological progress indicated above is the result of worker-training programs, increased experience, and overall improved educational opportunities for those living in urban Turkey. It is also the result of a change in the composition of investment, because advanced Western technology was introduced along with new products in the 1950s. In present research we are trying to indicate roughly the relative magnitude of these two causes of technological change since 1947.

Although technological change is important in explaining growth of output in the public enterprise sector, the basic explanation of the growth rate of public enterprise, and particularly the composition of output, depends upon the level and composition of investment. Only during the 1930s was skilled and semiskilled labor a serious bottleneck to growth.[18]

Investment expenditures and operating surpluses are shown in Table 3.7 for public enterprises in Turkey for the periods 1939–45, 1946–50, 1951–60, and 1961–63. As Table 3.7 shows, a substantial amount of public enterprise investment is financed by borrowing, mainly from the Central Bank and other public financial institutions.

---

18. Of course, more skilled labor or a greater supply of management to draw on undoubtedly would increase the growth rate, though in the informal calculation performed above this increase would be attributed to technological change.

Table 3.7: Surplus (Profits and Depreciation Allowances) and Investment of Public Enterprises, by Industrial Sector, 1939–44, 1945–49, 1950–59, 1960–63

(Millions of T.L., current prices)

Sector	1939-45 Inv.	Sur-plus	S-I	1946-50 Inv.	Sur-plus	S-I	1951-60 Inv.	Sur-plus	S-I	1961-63 Inv.	Sur-plus	S-I
1. Transportation and communication	199	156	-43	428	78	-350	1,857	1,363	-494	1,137	430	-707
2. Industry	149	174	25	214	233	19	3,814	2,052	-1,762	1,890	1,537	-353
a. Manufacturing	82	134	52	81	204	123	2,308	1,578	-730	1,380	950	-430
b. Mining and quarrying	67	41	-26	133	29	-104	751	466	-285	299	422	123
c. Electricity	—a	—	—	—	—	—	755	8	-747	211	166	-45
3. Monopolies	19	215	196	54	79	25	163	1,101	938	141	432	291
4. Ancillary	32	31	-1	25	66	41	668	562	-106	99	307	208
5. Other	6	85	79	50	28	-22	225	386	161	95	198	103
Transportation, communication and industrial sectors (excl. monopolies)	348	330	-18	642	311	-331	5,671	3,415	-2,256	3,027	1,967	-1,060
Total public enterprise sector, (excluding monopolies)	386	446	60	717	405	-312	6,564	4,363	-2,201	3,221	2,472	-749
Total public enterprise sector	405	661	256	771	484	-287	6,727	5,464	-1,263	3,362	2,904	-458

a Dash indicates negligible amount.

Source: Land, SP3.

For the public enterprise sector as a whole, borrowing to finance investment constituted 37 percent of investment expenditures during 1946–50, 19 percent during 1951–60, and 14 percent during 1961–63. In fact, however, borrowing is more substantial than those figures indicate. The monopolies, as we have noted before, collect substantial amounts of indirect taxes, and their surpluses (which in fact are indirect taxes) are passed on to the central government. When the monopolies are excluded, borrowing as a proportion of investment expenditures is substantially higher. If we also exclude ancillary and other enterprises, as we have in the preceding analysis, and look at the transportation, communication, and industrial sectors (excluding monopolies), borrowing represented the following proportion of investment expenditures: 52 percent during 1946–50, 40 percent during 1951–60, and 35 percent during 1961–63. Until 1950 almost all public enterprise borrowing was done by firms in the transportation and communication sector. During the 1950s, however, industrial firms financed a greater proportion of their investment expenditures by borrowing than did transportation and communication firms.

The above analysis has important implications. During the full bloom of etatism the government of Turkey permitted borrowing by public enterprises in order to finance development of the railways, waterways, and, to a lesser extent, the postal and telephone system. Such is the practice in many countries with or without an important public enterprise sector. Investment by public enterprises in the industrial sector as a whole was financed out of surpluses generated by the enterprises, although coal mining operations were also financed by borrowing. After 1950 the "free enterprise" government continued to borrow to finance extension of transportation and communication facilities but also allowed extensive borrowing to finance investment in the industrial sector. After 1953, despite strong inflationary pressures, the government borrowed from the Central Bank and other public and private financial institutions to finance expanded investment expenditures in the public enterprise sector.

Given the inflationary pressures of the 1950s, if public enterprises in Turkey were to have grown faster they should have done so with higher operating surpluses. They were unable to generate these surpluses because of the financial and pricing policies they pursued. The carefully circumscribed decision making of public enterprises by the government hierarchy, the low quality of management that characterizes most of the enterprises, and the use of enterprises to carry out noneconomic, social policies of the government have all militated against a vigorous public enterprise sector that aggressively seeks to maximize growth by the creation of larger surpluses. Naturally, the high level of public enterprise borrowing diminished potential sources of credit to the private enterprise sector. The low rates of profitability and the high level of borrowing suggest that, had different pricing and operating policies been pursued by the public enterprises, the growth rate of this sector could have been substantially improved, inflationary pressures reduced, and greater financial support extended to the private enterprise sector.[19]

It is difficult on the basis of the evidence presented in this brief paper to evaluate the overall performance of the public enterprise sector in Turkey. Much more needs to be said about the operating efficiency of this sector, as well as about its industrial organization, goals, and noneconomic objectives. Still it is possible to reach some conclusions. The performance turned in by the sector as a whole is not bad. For a long time public transportation, communication, and industrial enterprises sustained a growth rate averaging 8 percent. Furthermore, the industries established within the public enterprise sector had important external economies for private industry. Such enterprises had vigorous training programs, introduced new technology to Turkey, frequently set up modern sales organizations, and in many cases operated first-rate plants that served as models to other firms. Starting from practically nothing in 1933, the public enterprise sector managed to accumulate a large staff of skilled workers and through its training programs supplied workers to other industries.

On the other hand, growth of the public enterprise sector was paid for with a relatively high level of public investment and was probably highly inefficient. Since this investment was, moreover, financed to a large extent by borrowing from other sectors of the economy, and undoubtedly at high opportunity cost to the private sector, the question can be asked whether performance would not have been better

19. Yugoslavia may be a useful example. Value added since World War II has grown at rates varying between 12 and 15 percent. Of course the "social sector" of the Yugoslavian economy is much larger and broader-based than the Turkish public enterprise sector, but the main difference appears to be that in Yugoslavia high rates of return are paid to capital, and the worker-management industrial organization is geared toward growth financed by high profit rates.

had these firms operated as profit- or growth-maximizing enterprises, free of government control in their operating and pricing and more responsive to market pressures.

There is another aspect of public enterprise growth in Turkey that is interesting. Public enterprise investment policies were strangely related to overall government policy. During a time when the government ostensibly sought to encourage the private enterprise sector, public enterprises in the industrial sector grew faster than private ones. Furthermore, the levels of investment needed for their growth required borrowing from government and private financial institutions. During a time of inflation public enterprise borrowing therefore undoubtedly retarded rather than assisted the growth of private enterprise.

Comments by Charles R. Rockwell

James Land has selected a topic that is not only of critical importance to an understanding of the historical development of the Turkish economy, but that also contributes to our understanding of the problems and rewards of direct government formation and control of enterprises in any mixed economy. Initiated during the etatist period (1933–49), the government's industrialization strategy centered upon the public enterprises. With privileged access to markets and resources, these firms were expected not only to play a catalytic role, but also to provide the basic sinews for industrial growth. The extent of their success is Land's topic.

The paper is divided into two parts: the first section is a general introduction to the development of the Turkish economy since 1933; the second analyzes the role of the public enterprises in that development. Actually, the first part does little more than set the stage for the second, but as such it has one distinct weakness. Nowhere are we told the relative sizes of the public and private sectors. This reviewer finds it difficult to reach confident judgments concerning the success of public enterprises in various branches without knowing how well the private enterprises were doing in the same branches.

I would also like to make one substantive criticism of the first part. Within the years 1939–63 covered by the analysis, the period 1950–60 produced the highest growth rates of net national income. The average compound rate for that decade was 6.2 percent. Explaining this, Land states that "a main cause of the growth was expansion of agricultural output." This is puzzling since during this period the share of agriculture in Net National Income declined steadily and at a comparatively rapid rate (Figure 3.3). It is services including transportation and communication, not agriculture, that is the big gainer. Since the public enterprises were disproportionately large in the transportation and communication sector, a more detailed examination of their role in this period of major growth would seem useful. Again, it is impossible for the reader to make such assessments because of the absence of disaggregated statistics on the private sector.

We turn now to part two of Land's paper. The most important arguments of this section focus on two issues. First, were the public enterprises reasonably efficient in both a static and dynamic sense; and second, did they grow at a satisfactory rate, and if not, why not? As we shall discuss below, the evidence and conclusions concerning efficiency are mixed and perhaps unavoidably inconclusive. On the issue of growth, however, Land has quite definite feelings: "The low rates of profitability . . . suggest that, had different pricing and operating policies been pursued by public enterprises, the growth rate of this sector would have been substantially improved."

The approach taken by this review is to look critically at the extent to which Land's data give unambiguous support to his conclusion. Such an admittedly unimaginative endeavor is necessary because of this author's ignorance of the Turkish economy and is possible because Land has kindly provided elsewhere the raw data on which his work rests.[1]

Two pieces of evidence are directed toward the efficiency issue. From a static point of view, the public enterprises exhibit rather high capital/output ratios. Since 1945, capital/output ratios for the aggregate of all public enterprises have fluctuated between 5.0 and 6.0.

1. These raw data are published by James Land as Special Project 3 (hereafter cited as SP3) sponsored jointly by the Economic Growth Center and the State Institute of Statistics, Ankara, and entitled "Public Enterprise Economic Accounts in Turkey, 1933 to 1963." SP3 gives capital and current accounts for twenty industrial aggregations of the Turkish public enterprise sector and describes the constituent firms of each. In addition, fixed price capital stock and employment series are presented for each of the above. The creation of such well-articulated statistics for a most important sector of the Turkish economy is a major achievement. Perhaps the extensive use we make of these statistics is indicative of the importance of Land's work.

For industry alone it is near 3.0.[2] We agree that these magnitudes are in excess of what one is used to seeing. In addition to the inefficient use of capital, however, such magnitudes might be explained by the composition of output or by peculiarities in the definition of the capital stock. Since the relevant fixed price capital stock figures are discussed more fully below, we will note here only that Land's deflation technique and the "one-horse shay" convention he utilizes produce capital stock estimates that, while acceptable, are nevertheless higher than most of the available alternatives. Clearly, not much weight can be placed on the resulting capital/output ratios as a measure of efficiency.

From a dynamic point of view, using the disembodied Solow model, the public enterprises do slightly better. For the 1943–63 period, the aggregate of the transportation and communication and the industrial sectors show a rate of technical progress of 2.3 percent.[3] These aggregate results, however, hide a substantial divergence between the transportation and communication component and the industrial component. The rate for the former is 0.4 and for the latter 3.0. There is an equally large difference in the pattern of capital/labor ratio changes for the two sectors. This is shown in Table 3.8.

Table 3.8: Growth Rates of Inputs, Value Added, and Technical Progress, 1943–63

	Labor	Capital	Value added	Residual technical progress
Transportation and communication	4.9	3.8	5.0	0.4
Industry	2.3	8.1	6.8	3.0
Total	3.3	5.2	6.1	2.3

Note: Capital and value added are in 1962 prices. The labor and capital coefficients used to estimate residual technical progress are .75 and .25 respectively.

Source: Land SP3.

While the capital/labor ratio was decreasing in transportation and communication, the same ratio was increasing rapidly in industry. Capital stock in industry grew three and one-half times as fast as did employment—a very significant divergence. This divergence also raises

2. SP3, p. 20.
3. We discard the years 1939–42 because of the existence of surplus capacity. Quite arbitrarily, we use labor and capital coefficients of .75 and .25, respectively.

the question of whether the residual technical progress measure is independent of the assumed values of the input coefficients, as Land suggests. Changing the coefficients from 75/25 to 66/33 causes the technical progress measure for industry to change from 3.0 to 2.6. In any event, while industry does much better than transportation and communication by this measure, neither shows a very impressive performance. We now consider the issue of the growth of public enterprise.

Perhaps Land's most important conclusion is that bureaucratic interference with the operations of the public enterprises constrained the "natural" growth that could have been expected of these firms. Since these enterprises had a favored, often monopolistic, position in the economy, impediments to their growth did not yield corresponding or offsetting incentives to the private sector; consequently the economy as a whole was bound to suffer.

The most damaging form of this bureaucratic meddling, according to Land, was the imposition of price ceilings on the output of public enterprises. Imposed to placate various special interests, these ceilings are alleged to have reduced the amount of investable surplus at the disposal of the public enterprises, thus hindering their expansion.[4] In what follows we seek to cast some doubt on whether the statistics presented by Land give adequate support to this conclusion.

One measure of the adequacy of selling prices is the return on invested capital. Land cites the low rates of return presented in column 5, Table 3.6, as evidence that the public enterprises are being starved for investable funds. Unfortunately, the measure of rate of return that he uses is not defined, and this author was unable to infer his method from the raw data. Consequently we have had to construct our own measures.

Although annual depreciation charges are available from SP3, the accumulated depreciation fund is not. (The sum of annual depreciation charges differs from the accumulated depreciation fund because of retirements.) For this reason we define the rate of return on capital as the ratio of profits before depreciation to the gross value of the capital stock. Both quantities are measured in nominal values, and the capital stock variable includes "work in progress"

---

4. We are here talking about industry and transportation and communication, not the public monopolies such as salt, tobacco, alcoholic beverages, and so forth. In the latter industries, government price fixing sought to raise prices in a typically monopolistic manner, thereby increasing profits which were ultimately turned over to the government.

but excludes "land." Gross profits are defined as the sum of interest, depreciation, and residual profit less subsidies. A second variant includes, in addition to the above, "indirect taxes" in gross profits. The rationale behind this is that taxes as well as interest and profits are a return on the government's investment. Given the high payoff to imaginative tax avoidance, it is questionable whether the same quantity of taxes would be collected if these firms were in the private sector rather than the public. Also, as with the state monopolies, some of these taxes may be introduced specifically in order to shift profits from the enterprise to the government. While this certainly reduces the free surplus of the enterprises, it is not indicative of arbitrary pricing. In any event, the second profit variant measures the total surplus value added of the firm after the payment of wages.

A number of objections can be raised to the use of the above variables to measure the return on capital. We shall consider only one of these, the effect of inflation. From SP3 (p. 105) we obtain that for the twenty-year period terminating in 1963 the price of investment goods roughly quadrupled. That is, prices increased at a compound rate of approximately 7 percent per annum. In SP3, Land computes a revalued capital stock in 1962 prices. For that year his revalued capital stock is twice as large as the nominal value. Even if we allow that half of the price increases may be due to unmeasured improvements in the quality of capital goods, this still would produce a revalued capital stock about 1.5 times larger than the nominal value. The import of this is that our measure of the rate of return on capital includes significant gains due to the inflation of capital goods prices. A crude rule of thumb would be to reduce our rates by one-third to remove this component.

A related, although slightly digressive, question is whether, under such inflationary conditions, the depreciation allowances are actually adequate to provide firms with the funds necessary to replenish their capital stock as it is retired. This question, for parameters believed to be representative for Turkey, can be answered affirmatively. Assume a twenty-year average life for capital, retirements according to the dictates of the one-horse shay convention, and a capital stock growing at a real rate of 5.6 percent. (This number is derived from Land's Figure 3.4 and Table 3.5.) If there is no inflation, replacement will be only one-half as large as depreciation.[5] The rate of

5. Evsey Domar, "Depreciation Replacement and Growth," *Economic Journal,* March 1953, Chart II, p. 8.

inflation that equates depreciation and replacement is approximately 8 percent.[6] Since we noted earlier that inflation in Turkey was at a rate of 7 percent, and as perhaps half of this represented quality improvements, it would seem safe to conclude that the straight-line depreciation methods used in Turkey provide tax set-asides that are more than equal to replacement needs.

We turn now to a comparison of our rates of return on capital for the years 1939, 1950, and 1963—see Table 3.9—with those of Land.

Table 3.9: Rates of Return on Capital
(Percentage)

	Land	Variant I (Excludes indirect taxes from profits)	Variant II (Includes indirect taxes in profits)
1939			
Transportation and communication	4.0	2.4	2.5
Industry		11.8	24.8
Total	4.0	3.6	5.6
1950			
Transportation and communication		−1.9	−.05
Industry		12.2	44.3
Total	1.0	2.1	12.3
1963			
Transportation and communication		5.5	7.9
Industry		13.7	22.6
Total	5.0	10.0	15.8

Source: Taken from Land, SP3, Table 7.

Land's statistics, which are available only for the sum of transportation and communication plus industry, do not differ importantly from our Variant I. An examination of transportation and communication and industry shows why Land's figures are so low. Our Variant I shows a reasonably consistent 12 percent rate of return for industry but a very low, even negative return for transportation and communication. Clearly, averaging these components hides important information. A closer look at the capital accounts shows that in 1963 half of the capital stock in transportation and communication was in the form of railroad "land improvements," presumably mainly road-beds.

The argument I wish to make is that the maintenance of artificially

6. Ibid., Table II, p. 11.

low charges for rail usage is not unusual and is generally rationalized on the grounds of the external effects of the opening of new areas and so forth. A low rate of return for railroads might more convincingly be taken as an indication that supply had built ahead of demand rather than that the liquidity of the industry was being strained. Unless there is some direct evidence that inadequate rail facilities constitute a bottleneck to growth, it would seem wiser to consider transportation and communication as much a special case as the state monopolies and to restrict our attention to the industrial class of public enterprises. This is done in the remainder of this comment.

Considering only industry, we now ask whether internally generated funds were inadequate for the expansion of these public enterprises. The Variant I return for industry (excluding indirect taxes) is consistently over 12 percent. About one-third of this return is in the form of "interest payments" which are not investable resources of the enterprise. Thus cash flow or internally financed investment expanded the nominal capital stock at a rate of 9 percent. At the same time the nominal rate of growth of the total capital stock was over 19 percent per annum. This 10 percent difference is the amount of external financing required. Industry therefore was dependent on external sources for more than half of its funds. Is this excessive?

There is no simple answer to this question. There are too many institutional unknowns: how difficult is it for enterprises to obtain partial external financing; what is the cost of external financing; are internal funds accumulated by individual firms in large enough amounts to permit the exploitation of large-scale projects without external approval? This last point is quite important when one compares Yugoslav and Turkish performance, as Land does in note 18. For, although the surplus after wages accumulated by Yugoslav firms is somewhat larger than that for Turkish firms (60 percent of value added as opposed to 55 percent in 1963), these funds are by no means all freely available to the Yugoslav enterprise. In fact, since most projects require some external support, probably less than one-third of the above surplus can be invested without the direct support of one or more of the Yugoslav central bureaucracies.

One may also raise the question of whether any rapidly expanding segment of the economy should be required to be self-financing. It is not the proportion of external financing that is critical, but rather the terms of that financing, and on this score Land offers no evidence.

With respect to one conclusion, I find the evidence not simply ambiguous but actually contradictory. Speaking of the high level of investment in the public enterprise sector, Land states that "this investment was to a large extent financed by borrowing from other sectors of the economy, and undoubtedly at high opportunity costs to the private sector." The total investments of all public enterprises from 1939 to 1963 was 11,265 million TL (see Table 3.7). Of this, 8,218 million TL was financed from the internal cash flow of these firms, and 3,047 million or 27 percent from external sources. Not only is 27 percent a relatively small proportion of external financing, but this figure does not include the interest payments of these firms. Over the same twenty-five year period, interest payments were 2,601 million TL (SP3, p. 3). Consequently, it appears that the public enterprises financed their development with almost no reliance on the private sector of the economy. Over the same period these firms paid indirect taxes of 14,602 million TL. This amount is 30 percent greater than their total investment.

On the basis of these statistics, it is hard to find support for the contention that the public enterprises drained funds from the private enterprises at "high opportunity costs" to the latter. If public enterprises advanced at the expense of private ones, it would appear to be because the public monopolies and oligopolies preempted the market by getting there first, but this is a different matter. What did happen is that surpluses earned in the state monopolies and in textile and other miscellaneous branches were used to finance the expansion of transportation, food processing, heavy industry, and other manufacturing (principally intermediate goods and construction materials, i.e. pulp, paper, rubber products, porcelain, cement, etc.). To this author this suggests that bureaucratic price meddling, so far as it is responsible for these outcomes, was principally directed toward reducing investment goods prices and increasing consumer goods prices. As such, these policies are growth-inducing, not growth-inhibiting.

One additional comment may be made to the credit of bureaucratic meddling in the price system. The public enterprises operated in oligopolistic if not monopolistic market structures. Without considerably greater knowledge of the behavior and goals of these firms, we cannot know whether complete pricing freedom would have led to the maximization of short-run profits rather than long-run growth. Under similar circumstances, the Yugoslavs have been unable to eliminate price ceilings. However, there is one indication that the high wages and low interest rates charged to public enterprises in

Turkey may have had a distorting and detrimental effect. This is the increase in the industrial capital/output ratio.

In conclusion, it does not seem to this author that the evidence presented by Land convincingly demonstrates that the lack of internal funds constrained the growth of the public enterprises. The rapid increase of the capital/labor ratio in industry suggests the availability of ample funds. Furthermore, in conflict with Land's assertion that the expansion of the public enterprises was at a high opportunity cost to the private sector, we find that the public enterprises were almost entirely self-financing. Consequently it is difficult to argue that they were a serious financial drain on the resources of the private sector.

4

Public and Private Enterprise in Africa

BY CHARLES R. FRANK, JR.

Most sub-Saharan African countries have some form of mixed economic system. Regardless of the merits or disadvantages of eventual, near complete government ownership and control of the means of production, the African nations lack the manpower capabilities to perform all the functions of the vast existing private sector of the economy. Any African country that attempted a sweeping nationalization of the private sector today would surely experience greatly reduced national income. Thus for most African countries a mixed economic system is probably most desirable and most likely for some time to come.

With this in mind, the first part of this paper is devoted to a comparative historical analysis of public and private enterprise in East Africa, Ghana, and Nigeria. From this analysis, we lead into a discussion of general policy prescriptions regarding the relative roles of public and private enterprise in the process of economic development.

THE NATURE AND SCOPE OF PUBLIC AND PRIVATE ENTERPRISE

Today the former British colonies in Africa have one kind or another of a ministerial form of government, staffed by a civil service. The functions performed by ministries are largely bureaucratic, and

The author wishes to thank Henry Bienen of Princeton, John Harris of M.I.T., Peter Kilby of Wesleyan, and W. Arthur Lewis of Princeton for their helpful comments and suggestions. A special thanks goes to my research assistant, Mrs. Doris Garvey, for her role in compiling bibliographical material and data, performing calculations, and doing a good deal of the background

a ministerial bureaucracy is ill-suited to engage in activities typically associated with any form of productive enterprise. For this reason, most African public enterprises are organized as parastatal (sometimes called quasi-governmental) bodies which are not part of the ministerial structure of government and whose existence is provided for by articles of incorporation, specific legislation, or governmental directive or decree. The degree of government participation in and control of parastatal organizations varies considerably from case to case.[1]

There are three basic types of such organizations:

1. Development Corporations: These government-owned corporations are largely holding companies, having equity in and granting loans to a number of different enterprises or subsidiary companies. Many of the activities of African development corporations are large-scale, joint ventures with foreign-owned companies or local entrepreneurs. In some cases, the development corporations also make loans or grants to public authorities.

2. Public Utility Corporations: In many African countries, the great bulk of electricity generation, distribution, and sale is in the hands of a single, nationwide corporation. The same is true for railways, ports, posts, telecommunications, and air travel. Radio broadcasting and water works are usually ministerial functions at either the national or regional level.

3. Single Nationalized Establishments: In addition, there are examples of independent, state-owned productive establishments that cannot be placed in either of the above two categories.

Industrialization Policies

In the recent past, African countries have pursued three distinct types of industrialization policies. These will be labeled Patterns I, II, and III.

Pattern I: Industrialization mainly through reliance on private enterprise. Kenya is the prime example of this type. Until the Arusha Declaration of 1967, Tanzania followed the same basic policy.[2]

---

research for the case studies discussed in this paper. David Wheeler also assisted in the bibliographical work. The responsibility for the study remains with the author.

1. For a discussion of the basic types of organization of quasi-governmental institutions, see Donald C. Stone et al., *National Organization for the Conduct of Economic Development Programs* (Brussels, 1954), pp. 53–56.

2. The Arusha Declaration of February 1967 was a major policy statement

Pattern II: Industrialization in which private enterprise is encouraged but the role of the national development corporations is conspicuous. Both Uganda and Nigeria fall into this category.

Pattern III: A heavy reliance on public enterprises, some of which are obtained by the government through nationalization. Ghana exhibited a pattern of increasing importance of state-owned enterprises, especially in manufacturing, trade, and commerce, from 1962 through 1965. Nkrumah's overthrow resulted in a reversal of the trend after 1965. Tanzania nationalized a number of enterprises just after the Arusha Declaration of 1967.

Despite considerable differences in the degree to which these African countries rely or have relied on public enterprises, the significance and scope of publicly owned enterprises does not compare with that which one finds in some of the socialist countries. The vast majority of agricultural activity in the African countries is in private hands, and the role of agriculture is considerable. The following table gives the percentage of gross domestic product (GDP) originating in agriculture for four typical African countries:

	1955	1960	1964
Uganda	59.6	61.3	60.0
Kenya	41.5	40.0	42.1
Tanzania	62.6	61.0	58.0
Nigeria	63.9	65.2	64.0 (1963)

These figures include estimates of nonmarketed agricultural production which are, if anything, on the low side. Furthermore, the percentage of the economically active population engaged in agriculture can be presumed to be considerably higher than the percentage of agriculture in total GDP. Thus the latter measure tends to understate the relative significance of private activity in the agricultural sector.

The impact of public enterprise is felt, if at all, most significantly in the nonagricultural sectors of the economy (such as mining, manufacturing, public utilities, trade, and commerce), which account only for about one-half of total production and probably considerably less than one-half of the total work force. Even within these sectors, a

---

by President Julius Nyrere of Tanzania calling for "nationalization of key financial and foreign trade institutions combined with an expansion of the public sector's share in large-scale food processing and manufacturing." For a discussion see United Republic of Tanzania, *Background to the Budget, 1967–68* (Dar es Salaam: Government Printer, 1967), pp. 6–7.

great deal of activity is carried out on a small-scale or cottage basis by indigenous, private entrepreneurs or by large-scale, foreign-owned enterprises. Public corporations, operating on a relatively large-scale basis and using modern methods of production, accounted for considerably less than half of total production in Ghana in all nonagricultural sectors (with the exception of public utilities) even in 1965, as Table 4.1 indicates. In Tanzania, the nationalization decrees were

Table 4.1: Percentage of Total Gross Output by State-Owned and Partially State-Owned Enterprises in the Nonagricultural Sectors of Ghana

	1962	1963	1964	1965
Mining and quarrying				
State-owned	26.3	25.6	20.3	17.2
Partially state-owned	0.0	0.0	0.0	0.0
Total	26.3	25.6	20.3	17.2
Manufacturing				
State-owned	11.8	14.3	13.9	17.2
Partially state-owned	7.1	7.4	7.3	10.0
Total	18.9	21.7	21.2	27.2
Electricity				
State-owned	100.0	100.0	100.0	100.0
Partially state-owned	0.0	0.0	0.0	0.0
Total	100.0	100.0	100.0	100.0
All secondary industry				
State-owned	22.1	23.0	21.5	24.2
Partially state-owned	4.1	4.7	4.8	6.8
Total	26.2	27.7	26.3	31.0

Source: Ghana, *Economic Survey, 1965* (Accra, Government Printer), p. 71.

limited to specific industries and the largest part of the private sector was untouched.[3]

The Indirect Influence of Government

While the quantitative significance of direct government ownership and control is relatively small, the role of government is considerable in providing the economic, political, and social milieu in which pro-

3. Tanzania completely nationalized a number of firms in the banking, insurance, and flour milling industries. In addition, majority control was acquired in a number of trading companies, food processing firms, the sisal estates, and miscellaneous manufacturing firms. For a discussion of the nature and extent of the Tanzanian nationalization which took place in 1967 see: *East African Reporter,* 10 Feb. 1967, p. 11, 24 Feb. 1967, p. 11, and 2 June 1967, pp. 13–14;

ductive enterprises operate. Investments by African governments and quasi-governmental organizations in economic and social overhead facilities such as roads, railways, communications, health, and education are an important component of total investment activity and lay the foundation for the growth of more directly productive economic activity. In East Africa, investment by governments and the East African Common Services Organization[4] comprised from 32 to 44 percent of total identifiable investment activity during the period from 1957 to 1963.[5] In Nigeria the percentage ranged from 46 percent in 1958 to 36 percent in 1963.[6] In addition, a whole range of governmental administrative and legal activities profoundly affect the profitability of private enterprise and the ability and willingness of private entrepreneurs to make risky investment decisions in various sectors of the economy. Some of the most important government activities and policy decisions in this regard are:

1. prices paid to growers of cash crops by government-controlled marketing boards;
2. the degree and type of tariff protection and tax relief offered to new industries;
3. the granting of licenses and quotas to import;
4. licensing and controls of various sorts on private entrepreneurs in certain specified industries such as trade, transport, insurance, banking, crop processing and grading, etc.;
5. investment guarantees and repatriation terms offered to foreign firms; and

Economist Intelligence Unit, *Quarterly Reports* (March 1967), pp. 5–6 (June 1967), p. 6, and (August 1967), p. 7; Bank of Tanzania, *Economic and Operations Report* (Dar es Salaam, June 1967), pp. 14–16.

4. The East African Common Services Organization (EACSO) is a quasi-governmental organization set up and controlled jointly by the three East African governments, Kenya, Uganda, and Tanzania. EACSO has basic responsibility for providing coordinated services such as posts, telecommunications, railways, harbors, airlines, weather forecasting, etc. EACSO will be discussed at greater length below.

5. See EACSO, *Economic and Statistical Review* (December 1964), p. 105. These investment figures are derived mainly from cement production and imports and from import data on other building materials and capital equipment. They include only notional estimates of agricultural investment activity, especially of that done on a subsistence basis. Thus these percentages probably tend to overstate the relative significance of government investments.

6. Government of Nigeria, *Economic Indicators* (Lagos: Office of Statistics, March 1966), p. 43.

6. the manner in which nationalization of industries takes place and the amount and method of compensation offered.

PATTERNS OF INDUSTRIALIZATION

Kenya and Tanzania

The industrialization processes of Kenya and Tanzania (prior to 1967) provide the archetypes for Pattern I—heavy reliance on private enterprise. While the Kenyan and Tanzanian governments participated, through the East African Common Services Organization, in the ownership of East Africa railways, harbors, airways, posts, and telecommunications, the extent of government ownership and control beyond this was minimal. Even in the area of the generation and sale of electricity, the government's role has been limited.[7]

A move toward increased government participation in productive enterprise in Kenya was made in 1964 with the establishment of the Development Finance Company, which was authorized to provide share capital (and loans) for productive enterprises. The scope of this company was limited, however, "to fill marginal gaps in private project finance." [8]

In Tanzania a number of more notable policy shifts in relation to the relative roles of public and private enterprise preceded the 1967 nationalization decrees. In 1964 two government trading companies were founded with a view toward increased government participation and control in the marketing of export crops and imports at both

7. The hydroelectric scheme at Seven Forks on the Tana River, which will satisfy Kenya's power needs for some time to come, represents a significant increase in government participation in power generation but is a joint venture by the Kenyan government, East African Power and Lighting, and Power Securities Corporation. Total control will revert to the Kenyan government when it is able to repay the other two participants for their investments. See Government of Kenya, *Development Plan, 1964–1970* (Nairobi: Government Printer, 1964), pp. 96–97.

8. Ibid., p. 81. The Kenyan government's attitude toward the role of public and private sectors is summarized in the development plan as follows:

The limited capital resources of Government will be used to develop needed social services, such as health, housing, and education; to provide security and defense for the nation; and to expand those basic services and complementary facilities, such as roads, rail networks, communications and agricultural extension and research services, which are needed to lay the foundations for growth in the private sector. It is hoped that private capital will thereby be encouraged to stimulate growth in farming, manufacturing, tourism and other fields (pp. 37–38).

the wholesale and the retail levels. In 1965 the Tanzanian National Development Corporation was founded. By early 1967, however, most of its projects (aside from those taken over from the Tanganyika Agricultural Corporation, the remnant successor of the notorious Tanganyika Groundnut Scheme) were in the planning or construction stage.[9]

If we measure success in terms of growth rates, the Kenya experience with private enterprise has been fairly satisfactory. Value added in manufacturing more than doubled between 1954 and 1965 from £14.1 to £32.0 million. This corresponds to a growth rate of nearly 8.0 percent per annum, with a good part of this growth occurring in the last two years—20.5 percent in 1964 and 9.0 percent in 1965.[10] The growth of manufacturing also provided some of the impetus to the growth of the service industries, which has also been substantial, as indicated below:

	1954 (£ million)	1965 (£ million)	Annual rate of growth (percentage)
Electricity and water	1.24	3.56	10.1
Transport, storage, and communication	11.84	29.60	8.7
Trade	21.59	35.37	4.6
Banking, insurance, and real estate	1.38	4.63	11.6
Other services	7.90	18.37	8.0

The key to a substantial part of this impressive growth performance, however, is found in the rapid growth in exports of manufactured products to Kenya's partners, Uganda and Tanzania, in the East African Common Market. Between 1954 and 1964 Kenya's manufactured exports increased more than four and one-half times, from £5.2 million to £23.7 million, at a rate of 16.4 percent per annum.[11] The common market gives substantial tariff protection to

9. See Tanzania, *Background to the Budget, 1967–68*, pp. 36–37.
10. Sources for these figures and for table below are Government of Kenya, *Statistical Abstract, 1964* (Nairobi: Government Printer), p. 100; and *Economic Survey, 1966* (Nairobi: Government Printer), p. 2.
11. Paul G. Clark, *Development Planning in East Africa* (Nairobi: East African Publishing House, 1965), Table 2-C, p. 34. See also Dharam P. Ghai, "Territorial Distribution of Benefits and Costs of the East African Common Market," *East African Economics Review* 11, no. 1 (June 1964), 29–40, for a discussion of Kenya's growth in exports to its common market partners.

Kenya's manufacturing industry against imports from outside East Africa[12] and allows free entry into the common market countries. Without the common market, it is hardly conceivable that the high rate of growth in manufacturing and related industries could have been achieved. Although precise figures are not available, Kenya's commercial and manufacturing centers, Nairobi and Mombasa, undoubtedly attracted substantial capital investment, both from outside East Africa and from Kenya's partners in the common market.

Tanzania exhibited even more rapid growth in manufacturing than Kenya, although the secondary industries were not stimulated to the same extent. Manufacturing grew at a rate of 11.3 percent per annum between 1955 and 1962 [13] and 16.4 percent per annum between 1960 and 1966.[14]

Some of Tanzania's growth in manufacturing was for export but not nearly to the same extent as in Kenya. Although Tanzania's manufactured exports grew at an annual rate of 9.8 percent between 1954 and 1964,[15] production for domestic markets grew much faster.

The considerable growth in private enterprise manufacturing production in both Kenya and Tanzania has had one very important defect, at least as far as the African governments are concerned. Nearly all the growth can be attributed to European and Asian entrepreneurship. Very little of manufacturing, trade, or commerce is in the hands of Africans.[16] This has two important consequences. First, income distribution is highly skewed, with per capita incomes of Africans substantially below that of the European and Asian ethnic groups.[17] Second, their lack of experience in responsible positions,

12. See Ghai, pp. 36–37, for a discussion of protection levels received by Kenyan exports to Uganda and Tanzania.

13. Government of Tanganyika, *Statistical Abstract, 1963* (Dar es Salaam: Government Printer), p. 146.

14. Tanzania, *Background to the Budget, 1967–68*, p. 10. The Tanzanian national accounts were revised after 1962, and a consistent set of revised estimates is provided back to 1960.

15. P. G. Clark, Table 2-B, p. 32.

16. A. Bharati, "Political Pressures and Reactions in the Asian Minority in East Africa" (Occasional Paper no. 12, Maxwell Graduate School of Public Affairs, Syracuse, N.Y., October 1964), estimates that "in urban East Africa more than 75 percent of all buildings and real estate, and about an equal proportion of investments belonged to Asians" (p. 1). For what it is worth, Bharati conducted an experiment in which he stood on a downtown street corner in Nairobi and in Dar es Salaam and counted the proportion of automobiles driven by Asians. "Eighty out of 100 cars are driven by Asians in Dar es Salaam [and] 85 in Nairobi" (p. 1).

17. D. Ghai, "Some Aspects of Income Distribution in East Africa," East

in running efficient business enterprise, and in evaluating investment opportunities places Africans at a serious disadvantage in competing with non-Africans. The operation of a completely free economic system will not alleviate these disadvantages and tends in many cases to reinforce existing patterns of economic inequality.[18]

Nigeria and Uganda

Nigeria and Uganda provide a very interesting comparison of the second pattern of industrialization—emphasis on private enterprise combined with the use of national development corporations and other quasi-governmental bodies. Both these countries were especially favored by the boom in world prices for primary product exports that accompanied and followed World War II and the Korean War. Both were able to siphon off a good part of the windfall gains caused by favorable export prices through the device of government-sponsored marketing boards that had virtual monopoly control over the purchase and export of primary commodities produced by African peasants. The prices paid by marketing boards to African growers were substantially below prices received on the world market. As a consequence, the marketing boards accumulated large surpluses which enabled the Nigerian and Ugandan governments to finance investments by the newly founded national development corporations and other quasi-governmental organizations.[19] Here, however, the com-

---

African Institute of Social Research, Paper EDRP, no. 52 (Kampala, November 1964), estimates that approximately 60 percent of total monetary income in Kenya in 1962 was received by Europeans and Asians, who comprise about 3 percent of the total population (p. 12). In Tanzania, Europeans and Asians comprise about 1.5 percent of the population and earned close to 40 percent of monetary income in 1962 (p. 16).

18. See D. and Y. Ghai, eds., *Portrait of a Minority* (Nairobi: Oxford University Press, 1966).

19. Walter Elkan, *The Economic Development of Uganda* (London: Oxford University Press, 1961), notes that at one point in 1954 the accumulated surpluses of the cotton and coffee marketing boards reached the sum of £37 million. By 1955 "some £18 million had been transferred to an African Development Fund which was used for general purposes of development" (p. 38). See also David Walker and Cyril Ehrlich, "Stabilization and Development Policy in Uganda: An Appraisal," *Kyklos* 12 (1959), fasc. 2, for a critical evaluation of the role of marketing boards in providing funds for investment in development projects.

Gerald K. Helleiner, "The Fiscal Role of Marketing Boards in Nigerian Economic Development, 1947–61," *Economic Journal* 74, no. 295 (September 1964), discusses the role of marketing boards in financing development in general and the regional development corporations in particular. From 1947/48 to 1953/54, accumulated marketing board surpluses were more than £100

parison ends, because the success and growth of quasi-governmental organizations in Nigeria and Uganda were vastly different.

Nigerian development corporations

In Nigeria three regional development production boards were organized in 1949, one each for the Northern, Eastern, and Western Regions. The newly formed boards were financed by allocating the assets of the Nigerian Local Development Board which formerly serviced the whole country and by subventions from the surpluses of the four marketing boards, cocoa, palm oil and kernels, groundnuts, and cotton. After 1954 the regional development boards were reorganized and renamed, the Western Nigeria, Northern Nigeria, and Eastern Nigeria Development Corporations. Helleiner estimates that by 1962 the total amount of capital allocated to these corporations exceeded £40 million.[20]

Prior to 1954 the emphasis of the production boards was on providing loans and grants to public authorities, on direct investment in social overhead projects (education, roads, market construction, etc.), and on experimental or pilot schemes relating to crop production and processing. From 1955 onward, however, the policy shifted to investment in commercially viable, large-scale manufacturing and agricultural establishments, often in conjunction with private capital. Furthermore, the greatest amount of the development corporations' total investment activity occurred after the 1955 shift in policy.

It is evident that the record of development corporations in Nigeria is hardly short of disastrous. Two main criticisms can be made. First, many of the presumably commercially viable enterprises have not been profitable and many show large accumulated losses. Second, many of the investments of the development corporations have been made with poor planning and without proper estimates of economic viability. Very often they are made with political patronage in mind and to the benefit primarily of powerful political figures.[21]

---

million (p. 586), of which over £23 million were allocated to regional production development boards, the institutional predecessors to the regional development corporations which were founded in 1954.

20. G. Helleiner, "A Wide-Ranging Development Institution: The Northern Nigeria Development Corporation, 1949–62," *Nigerian Journal of Economic and Social Studies* 6, no. 2 (July 1964): 239.

21. Well-documented and careful appraisals of the activities of the Nigerian development corporations are G. Helleiner, "The Eastern Nigeria Development Corporation: A Study in Sources and Uses of Public Development Funds, 1949–62," *Nigerian Journal of Economic and Social Studies* 6, no. 1 (March

Up to 1962 the Western Nigeria Development Corporation (W.N.D.C.) invested substantial sums in three different types of operations: (1) £5.8 million in large-scale commercial agricultural schemes (oil palm, rubber, cocoa, citrus, coffee, cashew nuts, and pineapple), (2) £2.3 million in industrial establishments wholly owned and managed by W.N.D.C., and (3) £5.5 million (£1.3 million in equity and £4.2 million in loans) in associated industrial enterprises.

With regard to the agricultural schemes, Teriba notes:

[They] were, for the most, undertaken haphazardly. . . . The heavy and sometimes excessive burden of overhead and infrastructural services expenditure imposed on most agricultural projects seems to suggest inadequate weighing of costs and benefits of investments in terms of alternative location. Some of these projects are still to emerge into the "directly productive" stage from the "development" stage in spite of 14 years of continuous investment in them. Their ability to cover capital amortization during their economic life, let alone yield dividends matching even the rate of interest usually earned on very safe investments like bank deposits or government securities, is very much in doubt. This might not have been a serious criticism if there were significant and compensating indirect benefits.[22]

Of the seven wholly owned and managed industrial enterprises invested in by the W.N.D.C., not one had accumulated profits by 1962. Accumulated losses totaled £1.2 million, and a £.6 million investment in the Pioneer Oil and Rice Mills scheme and a canning factory had to be written off as an almost total loss. Thus losses and capital write-offs had eaten up 78 percent of the original investment of £2.3 million. Teriba attributes these losses to "errors of management and [over-large capacity], and as well [to] defective and poor

1964): 98–123; and O. Teriba, "Development Strategy, Investment Decisions and Expenditure Patterns of a Public Development Institution: The Case of the Western Nigeria Development Corporation, 1949–1962," *Nigerian Journal of Economic and Social Studies* 8, no. 2 (July 1966): 235–58. A more detailed and specific analysis of the activities of the Western Nigeria Development Corporation appears in the Government of Nigeria, *Report of the Coker Commission of Inquiry into the Affairs of Certain Statutory Corporations* (Lagos, Federal Ministry of Information: Printing Division, 1962). The Coker Commission of Inquiry arose out of a political crisis in the Western Region in 1961 involving allegations of misuse of funds and conflicts of interest in the management and policies of the statutory corporations.

22. Teriba, p. 257.

management. Almost without exception, their central problem lay in unsteadiness or inaccessibility of required inputs from economic sources, and, hence, in under-capacity utilization." [23]

Only three of the W.N.D.C. associated companies were in full operation by 1961. Accumulated losses were only £63.5 thousand, and Teriba is optimistic about their financial future. There are several things to note, however, with regard to the £4.2 million in loans to associated companies. First, many of these loans were unsecured and some were made without interest.[24] Second, two of the firms, Nigeria Construction Company Limited and Nigerian Water Resources Development, Ltd., were able to obtain from the Western Region government a guarantee of £30 million in construction contracts without being required to compete with other contractors on a bid basis and despite evidence that other contractors and the government itself could have performed a substantial proportion of this work. Finally, the Western Nigerian Development Corporation made a loan of £3 million to Nigersol and Nigerian Water Resources Development, £2.2 million of which was then loaned by the two companies to National Investment and Properties Company. This latter company was a front for the Action Group political party in the Western Region. By 1962 the company was insolvent, mainly because of subventions by one means or another of £4 million to the Action Group. Only a small portion of the loan has been paid back.[25]

The experience of the Eastern Nigeria Development Corporation (E.N.D.C.) has been roughly similar to that of the W.N.D.C. Of a total capital expenditure of £10.7 million between 1949 and 1962, nearly half (£4.9 million) was invested in wholly owned and managed commercial schemes. Only one, an oil palm estate, had accumulated any profits by 1962. Net accumulated losses by 1962 on wholly owned enterprises were £1.1 million.[26]

Equity investments by the E.N.D.C. in associated companies were largely in the Oban Rubber Estates, the Nigeria Cement Company, and the African Continental Bank. The first two of these were probably well advised.[27] The latter, however, involving an equity invest-

---

23. Ibid., pp. 252–54.
24. Ibid., p. 255.
25. See *Report of the Coker Commission* 1: 41–73; 2: 31–40; and 4: 1–4.
26. Helleiner, "The Eastern Nigeria Development Corporation," pp. 122–23.
27. Ibid., p. 122. See also S. U. Ugoh, "The Nigerian Cement Company," *Nigerian Journal of Economic and Social Studies* 6, no. 1 (March 1964): 72–91.

ment of £1 million, was primarily a "bailing out operation designed to extricate the bank from the consequences of its ill-advised lending policies." [28] It is also known that the African Continental Bank was closely linked with the governing National Council of Nigeria and the Cameroons party in the Eastern Region.[29]

The E.N.D.C. had over £2 million in loans outstanding in 1962. The largest loan was £1 million to the African Real Estate and Insurance Company. The E.N.D.C. denied the existence of this loan after it was made, and Helleiner asserts that the loan was made "under circumstances which look suspiciously similar to those in which the NIPC (National Investment and Properties Company) operated in the Western Region." [30] Although a few of the companies receiving loans were successful, most "were, in the main, disasters as far as the Loans Department was concerned." [31] Over 32 percent of total payments were in arrears by 1962, while for loans to manufacturing firms, nearly 60 percent of repayments were in arrears.[32]

Since 1962 and prior to the outbreak of hostilities in the Eastern Region in 1967 (although the pattern of losses of E.N.D.C. companies continued), corporation and government officials became increasingly concerned with the seriousness of the continued pattern of E.N.D.C. company losses. Several of the companies were reorganized to increase profitability.[33] In order to help overcome the problems of faulty management, a School of Management Development and Productivity began operations in 1964 at the Institute of Administration in Enugu. The school worked closely with E.N.D.C. officials to train managers and consulted with the E.N.D.C. on reorganization plans.[34]

28. Helleiner, "The Eastern Nigeria Development Corporation," p. 107. See also *Report of the Tribunal Appointed to Inquire into Allegations Reflecting in the Official Conduct of the Premier of, and Certain Persons Holding Ministerial and Other Public Offices in the Eastern Region of Nigeria* (London: H.M.S.O., 1957).

29. Ibid.

30. Helleiner, "The Eastern Nigeria Development Corporation," p. 123.

31. Ibid., p. 118.

32. Ibid.

33. See Eastern Nigeria Printing Corporation, *Annual Report and Accounts for the Years 1961–62, 1962–63, and 1963–64*, pp. 7, 9 and 11–16. Also E.N.D.C. Bottling Project (Pepsi Cola), "Interim Report of the E.N.D.C. Management," mimeographed (November 8, 1964).

34. See E.N.D.C. Bottling Project (Pepsi Cola), "Interim Report," and School of Management Development and Productivity Institute of Administration, Enugu, "Proposed Activities for Second Year of Operation (1965–66)," mimeographed.

Between 1955 and 1962 the Northern Nigeria Development Corporation (N.N.D.C.) received nearly £10 million in allocations from the marketing boards, the Northern Region government, and its predecessor, the Northern Region Development Board. A good part of this (£2.2 million) was used for grants to support social overhead projects, research, and pilot schemes in agriculture and industry. Only a small investment (£0.6 million) was made in wholly owned commercial schemes. One of these, the dairy scheme at Vom, was very successful and was later sold to a private dairy company. A much larger amount (£3.7 million) was invested in associated manufacturing companies and financial institutions, including an investment bank, Northern Developments (Nigeria), Ltd. Finally, the N.N.D.C. used its capital to make loans to small businesses and local government authorities. Loans outstanding in 1962 totaled £1.8 million.[35]

Although Helleiner's 1963 article about the Northern Nigeria Development Corporation was optimistic about its financial prospects,[36] by 1966 it was clear that the N.N.D.C. was following rather closely in the footsteps of its western and eastern counterparts. A 1966 government White Paper came to the following conclusions:

1. Of twelve wholly owned enterprises only one, the Jema Fibre Estate, could be considered successful.
2. Of twenty-seven joint ventures, only six were financially viable. The failures included:
   a. the cement works near Sokoto, a joint venture with a West German firm (the local limestone was too wet for the machinery and the plant was abandoned);
   b. an office building built by Arab Bros., which was sold to the N.N.D.C. for a significantly higher price than its valuation (by July 1966, eighteen months after purchase, there were no rentals);
   c. the Nortex Textile Mill in Kaduna, which accumulated losses from its inception in 1963 of £327,000 (the White Paper noted that some of the mill's machinery dated from 1896); and
   d. Kaduna Hotels, Ltd., which was run at a loss by Leventis

35. Helleiner, "Northern Nigeria Development Corporation," pp. 248–52.
36. Ibid., p. 257. Helleiner states that although "it is too soon to say whether all of its enterprises were successful . . . there does seem to have been a remarkable absence of glaring errors."

(White Paper noted that the hotels made purchases from Leventis retail outlets at no discount).

3. Of loans to individuals, which totaled £1.8 million in March 1966, about £1.4 million were outstanding and £0.8 million were overdue.

4. Many loans and joint ventures were made under extremely questionable circumstances, including absurdly low rates of interest.

By December 1967 the N.N.D.C.'s future was in doubt, with various proposals made for its reorganization.[37]

The other important public corporations in Nigeria are the Nigerian Railway Corporation, the Electricity Corporation of Nigeria, and the Nigeria Airways. The Railway Corporation has been running an overall deficit for a number of years. In addition, in recent years the railways have failed to cover even their operating costs.[38] The major problem of the railways has been high operating costs due to poor management and overstaffing of workers, while freight traffic has met increasingly serious competition from road transport.[39]

The Electricity Corporation of Nigeria (E.C.N.) has been a very profitable enterprise. Electricity output increased fivefold between 1951 and 1961 and is expected to have tripled between 1962 and 1968. The company has been able to finance the necessary capital expansion from federal government loans and borrowings from abroad.[40] The profitability of the E.C.N. is clouded by persistent evidence of faulty service and frequent interruptions of power. This sporadic power has forced Nigerian enterprises that depend on continual service to incur higher capital costs in order to establish standby generating capacity.[41]

Overall, the record of public enterprise in Nigeria has been rather

37. For discussions of the White Paper's findings and the various proposals for reorganizing the N.N.D.C. see *West Africa*, 26 November 1966, pp. 1360–61, 2 December 1967, p. 1537, 9 December 1967, p. 1569, 16 December 1967, pp. 1603 and 1609–11.

38. Helleiner, *Peasant Agriculture, Government and Economic Growth in Nigeria* (Homewood, Ill.: Richard D. Irwin, 1966), p. 271.

39. See A. O. Hirschman, *Development Projects Observed* (Washington: Brookings Institution, 1967), pp. 46, 109, 139–48.

40. Helleiner, *Economic Growth in Nigeria*, p. 271.

41. See Sayre P. Schatz, "Economic Environment and Private Enterprise in West Africa," *Economic Bulletin of Ghana* 7, no. 4 (April 1963): 49–56; and Peter Kilby, *Industrialization in an Open Economy: Nigeria 1965–1966* (London: Cambridge University Press, 1969).

abysmal, especially when the three development corporations are considered.[42] This record contrasts very strikingly with the progress of Uganda, especially in the case of the major public corporations— the Uganda Development Corporation and the Uganda Electricity Board.

Uganda's development corporations

The Uganda Development Corporation (U.D.C.), in which the government of Uganda is the sole shareholder, was created in 1952 with a share capital of £5 million which was immediately allotted to and fully paid by the government. The corporation acquired government interests in a number of enterprises which included a cement plant and the Lake Victoria Hotel. In 1955 the share capital was increased to £8 million and by the end of 1958 the government took up and paid for further shares amounting to £1.4 million, bringing the paid-up capital of the corporation to the present level of £6.4 million. Thereafter, the U.D.C. has raised funds by investing into commercially viable projects that attract foreign investment participation and by reinvesting its net profits, coupled with sale of some of the corporation's shares held in its profit-making subsidiary companies.[43] The consolidated profit and loss account of the U.D.C. has shown an overall profit ever since its first full year of operation. Profits were £69,432 in 1953, reached £307,211 in 1957, and reached an all-time high of £1,706,389 in 1965 (about 19 percent of paid-up capital). Accumulated profits by 1966 totaled more than £8 million[44] and were a significant source of investment funds.

The two most profitable enterprises owned by the U.D.C. in 1966 were Nyanza Textiles (£1,027,000) and Uganda Cement (£542,-000). Nyanza Textiles was purchased from the Ugandan government, which bought it from Calico Printers Association. Calico Printers was retained as a managing agent. The fully paid, authorized capital in 1961 was £1.5 million. Accumulated losses through 1958 were

42. Kilby has an excellent and extensive discussion of public enterprise in Nigeria and comes up with similar conclusions on the basis of a much more detailed analysis than could be attempted in this short paper. Kilby attributes the failure of Nigerian public enterprise to structural impediments to competent management performance.

43. Personal correspondence with S. Nyanzi, chairman, Uganda Development Corporation.

44. Uganda Development Corporation, *Annual Reports and Accounts, 1953–66.*

£394,000 but a profit has been made every year since then.[45] Profits reached £225,000 in 1959, increased every year, and more than quintupled by 1966. The basic reason for this growing success was an ever increasing rate of capacity utilization. By 1964 the mills were operating on three shifts, and a further expansion of capacity was completed in 1965. Nyanza Textiles has specialized in inexpensive, durable, cotton yard goods which have a large market in East Africa. The company seems to be tautly managed. Labor productivity has increased very rapidly, and the company has been successful, after several false starts, in training and holding middle-level supervisory personnel.[46]

Uganda Cement also owes its high profit return in 1966 to near full-capacity operation, although the company made profits every year since its inception. Between 1956 and 1964 annual profits were between £100,000 and £300,000, even though, during most of those years, production was running at less than 50 percent of capacity.[47]

Other profitable enterprises of the Uganda Development Corporation include Agricultural Enterprises, Uganda Hotels, and Uganda Consolidated Properties. Agricultural Enterprises is itself a holding corporation for subsidiaries operating commercial schemes in agriculture. Agricultural Enterprises' largest interests are in tea, owning tea-processing factories that have planted a total of over 7,600 acres of estate tea. Most of the tea leaves, however, are soon to be obtained from peasant outgrowers. The outgrower scheme expanded very rapidly between 1962 and 1966; the number of stumps given to outgrowers increased more than twelvefold from 307,000 to 3.7 million.[48] Although only mildly profitable to Agricultural Enterprises, the tea scheme has been immensely profitable for the peasant outgrowers

45. Part of the profits of Nyanza Textiles may be attributed to a tariff of about 33 percent on imported textiles during most of its operation. Even without such subsidies, however, Nyanza Textiles would still be very profitable at the present time although it would have sustained losses for a longer period in the early stages.

46. Azarias Baryaruha, "Factors Affecting Industrial Employment, Case Study No. 1, Nyanza Textiles," East African Institute of Social Research, Paper EDRP, no. 69 (Kampala, March 1965). Baryaruha estimates that between 1960 and 1964 labor productivity increased at a phenomenal rate of 12.2 percent per annum.

47. Uganda Development Corporation, *Annual Reports and Accounts, 1956–64*.

48. Ibid., 1966, p. 2.

(whose accounts, of course, are not consolidated with those of the U.D.C.). Many of these peasants receive financing from Agricultural Enterprises during the three-year waiting period in which tea plants do not yet bear a significant amount of leaves.[49]

In 1964 Uganda had a total of 26,000 acres planted in tea, much of which was not fully mature. Production in 1966 was 23 million pounds (valued at £3.4 million), a fifteenfold increase over 1946. Tea production is expected to reach 42 million pounds by 1971, most of the increase resulting from U.D.C.'s Agricultural Enterprises. Between 1958 and 1964 the value of tea exports more than doubled, from £1.0 million to £2.2 million. The value of exports in 1971 should be about £6 million if current prices hold.[50] Thus tea will probably become one of Uganda's major export crops, providing some welcome diversification for a country in which 75 percent of export earnings are attributable to cotton and coffee alone.[51]

Agricultural Enterprises' other main operation is a 100,000-acre cattle-ranching scheme begun in 1956. This scheme has been unsuccessful to date because of reinfestation of the area by the tsetse fly,[52] but it is being resuscitated along with plans for an integrated meat industry.

Uganda Hotels and Uganda Consolidated Properties have been consistent profit makers for the U.D.C. Uganda Hotels runs a chain of hotels throughout Uganda, catering to the tourist trade and traveling businessmen and government officials. The standard of service is quite high and the operation has been consistently, albeit modestly (£10,000 to £40,000 per year), profitable, with the exception of a single year, 1959.[53] Another indicator of the success of the hotel services is the rapid rise in the number of tourists in Uganda.[54]

Uganda Consolidated Properties had a record of consistently rising

49. Tea plants do not reach their maximum productivity until they are about ten years old. See IBRD, *The Economic Development of Tanganyika* (Baltimore: Johns Hopkins Press, 1961), p. 379.

50. Government of Uganda, *Work for Progress, Uganda's Second Five-Year Plan* (Kampala: Government Printer, 1966), pp. 1, 66, 67, and 76.

51. Total exports in 1965 were £62.7 million, of which £30.4 million were coffee and 16.8 million were cotton. Ibid., p. 1.

52. IBRD, *The Economic Development of Uganda* (Baltimore: Johns Hopkins Press, 1963), p. 217.

53. Uganda Development Corporation, *Annual Reports and Accounts, 1956–65*.

54. Government of Uganda, *Work for Progress*, p. 116.

profits, from £23.2 thousand in 1956 to £103.1 thousand in 1965, although profits dropped slightly in 1966.[55] "Its assets consist of long term lease-hold properties," which it leases mainly to U.D.C. subsidiary companies. Its "financial position appears sound." [56]

The only notable failure of the U.D.C., other than the cattle-ranching scheme, seems to be the Uganda Metal Products and Enameling Company, which has found it difficult to compete with imports of cheap enamelware from the Far East.[57] After some initial losses in the early years (£34,000 in 1958), Uganda Metal Products made a large profit in 1959 (over £30,000) because the imposition of stiff import duties enabled the company to raise its prices. The profit has been declining ever since 1959, however, and turned into a small loss in 1965. In 1966 the company was drastically reorganized in an attempt to reduce its high costs of production, and a small profit appeared.[58]

Some more recent U.D.C. enterprises include a meat-packing factory, a dairy scheme, and cattle-feed production in conjunction with plans for extension of cattle ranching. Tororo Industrial Chemicals and Fertilizers produces high quality single-phosphate fertilizer and will begin producing triple-superphosphate fertilizer as well as sulphuric acid and other chemicals as by-products, using as raw materials the high-grade phosphate ores found in the Tororo area. Other new enterprises include a garment factory, a distillery, expansion of tourist facilities in the new national park in Northern Uganda, and a steel-rolling mill that uses scrap as raw material.[59] The steel mill has been in production for a few years but has been operating at a very low level of capacity due to technical problems, difficulties in training labor, and the low level of demand for construction materials in recent years. The management claimed to have solved the technical problems by late 1965,[60] and the level of demand began picking up considerably as the result of the export boom in 1964 and 1965.

The other main public corporation in East Africa is the Uganda Electricity Board (U.E.B.), which was established in 1947. In 1954

55. Uganda Development Corporation, *Annual Reports and Accounts, 1956–66.*
56. Quotes from IBRD, *Economic Development of Uganda,* p. 276.
57. Ibid.
58. Uganda Development Corporation, *Annual Reports and Accounts, 1958–66.*
59. Ibid., *1965,* pp. 1–2.
60. Ibid.

the Owen Falls hydroelectric scheme became the U.E.B.'s main source of energy. The Owen Falls scheme had a potential capacity of 150,000 kilowatts, but initially only two generators were installed with a total capacity of 30,000 kilowatts. In 1966 the ninth generating unit was installed, bringing capacity up to 135,000 kilowatts, and plans were being made for a second hydro scheme that would increase total capacity significantly.[61]

Unfortunately, the demand for electricity did not rise as rapidly as had been expected in the beginning (although revenue more than tripled between 1954 and 1962, from £0.7 million to £2.4 million). Substantial losses were made because of the low rate of potential capacity utilization. Capital charges in 1960 (interest and depreciation) were £1.66 million, and revenue (£1.67 million) was barely large enough to cover these charges, much less the operating expenditures. Furthermore, capital charges were rising since much of the original financing was in short-term or medium-term loans which had to be refinanced at higher rates of interest.[62]

The problem of unexpectedly slow growth in demand coupled with high capital charges was attacked in two ways. In 1955 a fifty-year agreement was concluded with Kenya to purchase bulk supplies of electricity. The bulk supplies were purchased at a much lower per unit price than other consumers paid,[63] but Kenya contracted to pay for a minimum number of units (the equivalent of 30,000 kilowatts of capacity). Furthermore, Kenya agreed to pay three times the base price for units generated above 26,000 kilowatts. Uganda was required to supply 45,000 kilowatts to Kenya on demand, but this was to be reduced to 30,000 in 1968 when Kenya's large hydroelectric scheme at Seven Forks came into operation. This agreement with Kenya eased the U.E.B.'s financial position. As long as Uganda's demand was under potential capacity, the cost of generating these bulk supplies was considerably below the revenue obtained from Kenya. As the Uganda demand nears capacity, however, the low price paid

61. Uganda Electricity Board, *Annual Reports and Accounts, 1956, 1965.*

62. IBRD, *Economic Development of Uganda,* p. 340. Part of the losses prior to 1960 were hidden in the accounts of the UEB through an accounting device in which a portion (22 percent in 1960) of the interest charges were charged to the capital account. One of the conditions under which the World Bank and the United Kingdom Treasury loaned £5.5 million to the UEB was that this accounting practice be dropped. The result was that a small surplus in 1961 was converted to a deficit of £359.4 thousand. See UEB, *Annual Report and Accounts, 1961,* p. 61.

63. Ibid., p. 341.

by Kenya reduces the revenue the U.E.B. might obtain from supplying Uganda consumers at higher prices. Furthermore, the provision of bulk supplies to Kenya will probably force the U.E.B. to engage in a second hydroelectric scheme at an earlier date than would otherwise be the case. This would involve additional capital expenditures of at least £10 million and add to the U.E.B.'s capital charges.

The second approach to U.E.B.'s financial problems was to obtain a loan in 1961 of £5.5 million from the World Bank and the United Kingdom Treasury. This was to enable the U.E.B. to pay off the capital charges not met out of current revenues and to engage in some needed capital expansion, especially of transmission facilities. In conjunction with this loan, tariff charges were raised an average of 18 percent in the hope that the U.E.B. would soon be able to carry the capital charges on its own and eventually build up a fund for capital expansion out of its profits. By 1963 accumulated losses were £781,000. In 1964 a small profit was made and in 1965 profits totaled £377,000. By 1968, the annual profit was nearly £1.5 million. Accumulated losses were eliminated in 1966, and by 1968 had turned into an accumulated surplus of nearly £3.0 million.[64] The much more favorable profit picture since 1964 has been to a large extent the result of a boom in Uganda's economy. Export revenue, which had been falling from 1958, rose from £37.6 million in 1962 to £51.5 million in 1963 and £64.4 million in 1964.[65] U.E.B. revenues increased by 12.6 percent in 1963, 9.5 percent in 1964, and 14.2 percent in 1965. Peak demand as a percentage of capacity increased substantially.[66]

Most of the U.E.B.'s troubles can be attributed to the fact that its major hydroelectric installation came into operation at the peak of a booming export economy and suffered a fairly severe period of economic stagnation in its first eight years. This made it difficult to cover the high fixed charges. The U.E.B.'s more recent financial success is probably more indicative of its viability. There are relatively few complaints about the company's services, and it is generally agreed that the U.E.B. is well managed.

The Uganda government, in addition to the U.D.C. and the U.E.B., has interests in three other major public enterprises, namely, the East African railways and harbors, the airways, and posts and telecom-

64. Ibid., *1968*, p. 8.
65. Government of Uganda, *Work for Progress*, p. 1.
66. UEB, *Annual Reports and Accounts, 1965*.

munications, all of them self-contained services of the East African Common Services Organization.

The railways, as in Nigeria, have suffered from severe competition from road transport firms, although various licensing regulations have protected the railways from some of this competition.[67] Railway officials claim, however, that if road transporters were charged fully for the services of the road network and the railways were allowed more flexibility in setting tariffs to meet competition, then road transport licensing would not be necessary.[68]

The railways have run an operating surplus every year from their beginning in 1948 when the Kenya-Uganda Railways and Harbours and the Tanganyika Railways and Ports merged to form the East African Railways and Harbours Administration. Operating surpluses have averaged about £3.7 million between 1948 and 1963, enough to cover an annual contribution for depreciation that has averaged about £2.5 million.[69] Unfortunately, however, much of the railways' rolling stock and locomotives, purchased in the 1920s, were in need of replacement in 1963, and the railways found it difficult to raise the capital and expand quickly enough to meet growing traffic demands.[70] In addition, the railways embarked on a massive training and promotion scheme to Africanize its staff.[71] The heavy costs of Africanization and the needs for rolling stock replacement put the railways' future financial success in some doubt.

The East African Airways has been one of the few profit-making national airlines. It has run an operating surplus since 1955 and an overall profit from 1959 through 1963 (despite a very rapid write-off on four Comet jets purchased in 1960). Accumulated profits between 1959 and 1965 were £1.5 million.[72]

All three of the Common Services Organizations have demonstrated remarkable growth in the recent past. Revenues of the Railways and

67. See Arthur Hazlewood, *Rail and Road in East Africa* (Oxford: Basil Blackwell, 1964).

68. Hazlewood, chapter 6, pp. 58–81.

69. East African Railways and Harbours, *Annual Reports and Accounts, 1948–1963.*

70. See East African Railways and Harbours, "Memorandum to the International Bank for Reconstruction and Development, Rolling Stock Requirements, Phases II and III" (Nairobi, General Manager's Office, November 1963).

71. See J. H. Proctor and K. G. V. Krishna, "The East African Common Services Organization: An Assessment," *South Atlantic Quarterly* 64, no. 4 (Autumn 1965): 545.

72. East African Airways, *Annual Reports and Accounts, 1949–63.*

Harbours nearly tripled between 1948 and 1963, from £9.4 million to £27.3 million.[73] The East African Airways flew 0.6 million aircraft miles in 1946 and 7.7 million in 1963, and total revenues rose from £86,000 to £7.6 million.[74] The East African Posts and Telecommunications serviced 14,839 telephones in 1948 and 83,234 in 1963. The postal services handled 62.3 million pieces of mail in 1948 and 140.1 million in 1963.[75]

"Perhaps the most significant achievement of the transport and communications services is to be found in their successful borrowing program. The interest-bearing capital of the EARH (East African Railways and Harbours) has been raised from a variety of sources including the World Bank (£6.3 million)."[76] The financial soundness of these organizations has been a major factor in enabling them to raise such significant amounts of capital.

Uganda's public corporations and those of the East African Common Services stand as a model of successful use of public enterprises in pursuing economic development objectives. Their efforts were supplemented by a few Asian entrepreneurs who made large profits in sugar estates and sugar refining (most notably Muljibhai Madhvani & Sons) which they used to invest in a wide range of industrial and commercial agriculture schemes, some in conjunction with the Uganda Development Corporation. The African private entrepreneur, however, has been singularly absent as a major factor in Uganda's growth and development. This is not the case in Nigeria. Where public enterprise failed, private entrepreneurs of all sorts—European, residents of Near Eastern origin, and Africans (albeit on a smaller scale than the others)—expanded their activities extremely rapidly. Between 1958 and 1963 value added (in 1957 prices) in the manufacturing and public utilities sector of the Nigerian economy increased from £25.4 million to £49.1 million, an impressive average annual rate of 14.1 percent per annum.[77]

Ghana

Prior to 1960 the scope of government enterprise in Ghana was quite limited. Government activity was confined to public utility undertak-

73. East African Railways and Harbours, *Annual Reports and Accounts, 1949, 1963.*
74. Proctor and Krishna, p. 532.
75. Ibid.
76. Ibid., p. 533.
77. Nigeria, *Economic Indicators* (March 1966), p. 40.

ings, the export of cocoa, a few industrial schemes under the aegis of the Ghana Industrial Development Corporation, and several commercial agriculture schemes by the Agricultural Development Corporation. With the launching of the second five-year development plan in March 1959, government activity in directly productive enterprises began to increase substantially. By mid-1964 the government had set up thirty-seven state-owned establishments and obtained ownership shares in nine others.[78] By 1966 the number of state enterprises had grown to fifty-four and there were twelve joint state/private establishments.[79] The gross output of state-owned firms increased from £13.6 million in 1962 to £21.4 million in 1965, an increase of 58 percent. Gross output of joint enterprises more than doubled, from £2.5 million to £6.0 million.[80]

By the end of 1964 thirty-two of Ghana's thirty-five state enterprises, representing an investment of £39.7 million, had accumulated losses of £15.1 million (three had not reported). There were only three profitable ventures: the Bank of Ghana, Ghana Commercial Bank, and Ghana National Trading Corporation. The three heaviest losers, accounting for £13.5 million in losses, were the State Mining Corporation, Ghana Airways, and the State Farms Corporation.[81] The state enterprises also proved a significant drain on foreign exchange, accounting for £53 million of the £80 million foreign debt as of June 1964.[82]

The eight joint state/private enterprises did not do so badly. Only one, the Ghana Bottling Company, lost money in 1964. Total profits for the eight companies were £586,000.[83]

Concern over the lack of financial viability led to the establishment of a State Enterprises Secretariat in April 1964. The secretariat was empowered to supervise the state corporations closely in order to increase their profitability and to look after the government's interests in joint enterprises. By 1966 some twenty-two state corporations were under the aegis of the secretariat.

78. E. N. Omaboe, "The Process of Planning," in W. Birmingham, I. Neustadt and E. N. Omaboe, eds., *A Study of Contemporary Ghana*, vol. 1 (London: George Allen & Unwin, 1966), p. 449.

79. The Economist Intelligence Unit, *Quarterly Economic Review*, January 1967, p. 5.

80. Ghana, *Economic Survey, 1965*, p. 71.

81. *West Africa*, 6 February 1965, p. 143.

82. Ibid., 20 March 1965, p. 419.

83. Ghana, Budget Speech, 1967, as quoted in *West Africa*, 2 July 1966, p. 735.

In order to help overcome the problem of poor management, the secretariat instituted a series of courses and seminars for management and supervisory staff. For some establishments, especially those with severe technical problems, special managing agents were hired. Many of the state enterprises responsible to the secretariat began to make some profits. Many others were able to reduce losses or about break even. Of the fifteen companies reporting in 1963, eleven made losses of £254,000 and four made profits of £219,000, for a net loss of £35,000. In 1965, of these same fifteen companies (1964 in the case of two that were late in reporting for 1965), nine made profits of £425,000 and six made losses of £286,000, for a net profit of £139,000.

It is easy to exaggerate the poor record of state enterprises in Ghana. One of the reasons for large accumulated losses in the last few years is that a large proportion of the state firms had just begun operations. Losses in the development stage are typical of most new enterprises. Many of the early losers are now showing an encouraging trend toward profitability. What is evident, however, is that Ghana's emphasis on state enterprise has produced no big winners to date and a number of outstanding big losers. The Ghana Airways (which made a loss of £7 million by 1965),[84] the State Mining Corporation (a loss of over £6 million by 1963),[85] and the State Farms Corporation perennially made such large losses that they overshadow the relative success of a number of the smaller enterprises. Other relatively large losers include the Fibre Bag Manufacturing Corporation (losses of £438,000 between 1963 and 1965), the Furniture and Joinery Corporation (accumulated losses of £53,000 by 1964), the Cannery Corporation (£95,000 by December 1965), the Boatyards Corporation (£70,000 through 1965), the Bakery Corporation (£35,000 through 1965), and the Marble Works Corporation (about £55,000 accumulated losses).

Some of the companies reporting profits have been called into question regarding the accuracy of the accounts, bribes, and possible fraud. The Ghana National Trading Corporation reported a profit of £1.3 million in 1965 but was in arrears for a large proportion of its outstanding debt and was under investigation by a Commission of Inquiry for alleged illegalities involving the sale of the Leventis Company to the corporation. The Ghana National Construction Company

84. *West Africa,* 9 July 1966, p. 772.
85. Ibid.

showed a net profit in 1963 of £176,000 but was substantially in arrears on debt repayment.[86]

The National Liberation Council which succeeded Nkrumah in 1966 has taken steps to reverse the policies of the former regime. First, a number of the state enterprises are to be sold to private firms.[87] Second, to correct some of the more blatant overstaffing problems, workers are being laid off at a rapid pace. Between February and December of 1966 approximately 47,000 workers were laid off, about one-seventh of all recorded employment. Most of the layoffs occurred in the public sector, for example:

1. 16,000 in National Construction,
2. 9,600 in Workers' Brigade,
3. 9,000 in State Farms,
4. 2,300 in State Housing Corporation, and
5. 1,200 in Cocoa Division of Ministry of Agriculture.[88]

Finally, the control of state enterprises through the State Enterprises Secretariat is expected to tighten. Eventually the secretariat may be converted into a holding company much like the Industrial Development Corporation which was liquidated in 1962.

POLICY IMPLICATIONS

Profitability as a Criterion

Up to this point we have implicitly assumed that profitability is a measure of the success of a public enterprise. This needs some justification since there is a wide diversion of opinion as to whether profitability is a meaningful criterion of success for a state enterprise.

There are several arguments against the use of profitability as a criterion. First, the nonmeasurable social benefits of a scheme must be taken into account. This argument is particularly cogent for projects such as roads, hospitals, education, for which it is either impossible or repugnant to specify and charge a price for the services of the project that will reflect their social usefulness. For industrial and commercial projects, however, the problem is not as acute. Although some nonmeasurable benefits may exist, it is often difficult to

86. *West Africa,* 25 March 1967, pp. 409–10.
87. *West Africa,* 2 July 1966, p. 735, lists the firms originally intended for private sale. The NLC made revisions in the list, as noted in *West Africa,* 4 February 1967, p. 179, 15 July 1967, p. 919.
88. *West Africa,* 25 February 1967, pp. 261–62.

identify them adequately. Furthermore, the case for choosing a non-profitable project rests on a demonstration that the nonmeasurable benefits of a less profitable project are considerably greater than those of a profitable one. The mere existence of nonmeasurable benefits is not enough.

Second, the prices paid for certain inputs often are not a reflection of their true scarcity value. Wages may be higher than the true scarcity value of unskilled labor because of union demands, minimum wage legislation, or government pressures for wage increases. The cost of imported goods is often too low because of an undervalued foreign exchange rate, the symptom of which is a chronic tendency toward balance of payments deficits. In these cases use of the profitability criterion may lead to an uneconomic allocation of resources. Labor is used less abundantly than is desirable since, although labor is in plentiful supply, its price is high and profitability can be enhanced by conserving on labor inputs. Imported materials and capital equipment may be used when it would be more economical to use domestic supplies. In some instances, however, attempts to take into account these divergencies between actual prices and scarcity values have resulted in very marginal changes or no changes at all in the ranking of projects.[89]

Finally, there is a set of arguments related to the time required for an enterprise or group of enterprises to enter the profit-making stage. First, current market prices of the products and inputs of an enterprise do not necessarily reflect future profitability. The future prices of goods and services depend on how rapidly demand is rising and how rapidly increased supplies are available from all sources. An enterprise that is initially unprofitable may become profitable later. The natural question that arises is: Why not wait to make the investment until profitability is assured? This may not be feasible if some investments are very "lumpy." The success of an investment may be dependent on other investments being made. It may not be possible to make them all at one time because of the limited availability of capital.[90] Thus some enterprises will be forced to make losses until the entire investment program is implemented. This argument is crucially dependent on the degree of lumpiness of investment (returns to

89. Wolfgang Stolper, *Planning without Facts* (Cambridge: Harvard University Press, 1966), pp. 195–97.

90. Cf. P. P. Streeten, "Unbalanced Growth," *Oxford Economic Papers,* n.s. 11 (June 1959): 167–90.

scale), and while it may make sense for some small countries, its application is limited in large countries with extensive markets for final goods and a sizable absolute capacity for mobilizing investment funds.

The most cogent justification for losses in the early stages of an enterprise's development is that the enterprise requires an initial testing and learning stage. Both management and labor have to become familiar with their roles, learn the consequences of their actions and decisions, experiment with different forms of organization, and adapt to unforeseen difficulties that could not possibly be predicted beforehand. This argument can be applied to groups of enterprises, particularly those in a given industry. A labor force must be trained, entrepreneurial and managerial abilities given a chance to grow, and experience accumulated, before an industry can hope to be profitable.

While one may reasonably expect some enterprises to make losses for a time, especially those that are subject to economies of scale or those for which a trained labor force and entrepreneurial experience is necessary, this factor can be taken into account by a reasonable method of discounting the future stream of expected losses and profits. Persistent and significant losses, however, can have an extremely deleterious effect on the prospects for development. It is not easy or costless for the government to raise funds (and to achieve the command over real resources they represent) for purposes of investment. Private savings rates in less developed countries are low. Government's taxing and borrowing capabilities are limited. Taxation is administratively difficult, costly, and politically sensitive.

The use of inflation as a means of raising investment funds is limited either because continuing inflation defeats its own purposes as those whose real incomes are being reduced by inflation are able to raise money incomes and reduce savings, or because balance of payments difficulties emerge.

When state enterprises incur losses, they must obtain government loans and subsidies, the funds for which are diverted from other uses. When state enterprises realize profits they are able either to expand on their own, without government funds, or to make contributions to government revenues. Even if state enterprises draw profits merely because of their monopoly powers or high protective tariffs, these profits can add to the total availability of investable funds. Such funds are not costless, of course, since the consumers and users of the product are, in effect, being taxed through high prices, and resources probably are not being allocated most efficiently. Provided, however, that the return on investments financed in this manner are higher than the costs, the profits are justified.[91]

Causes of Lack of Profitability

A perusal of the literature cited in this paper indicates that the basic cause of lack of success of state enterprise is poor management and administration. This is evidenced in several ways. First, many enterprises fail because of inadequate planning and feasibility studies. Demand for the product is overestimated. Improper machinery and equipment is ordered. Plant layout is inadequate. The wrong location is chosen. An even, adequate supply of raw materials of sufficient quality is not forthcoming.

Second, the operating managers and supervisors often lack organizational talent. They tend to overstaff. They sometimes do not have the proper technical competence.

Third, at times lack of success may be attributed to the inefficiency of a government bureaucracy and elected officials. Restrictions may be placed on the prices of products and conditions of sale. Licenses for crucial imported materials may be delayed or not granted because of organizational inefficiency or failure to realize the implications of such delays and refusals. The same delay may be true for permits to hire expatriate technical help.

Although one can identify lack of managerial, administrative, and supervisory talent as the cause of inefficiency of government enterprise, it is important to go beyond this and inquire about the factors that are responsible for this lack of ability in state enterprises. Otherwise one might jump immediately to a simplistic policy conclusion that the only way to overcome this deficiency is to embark immediately on large-scale, massive training and educational programs. The degree of success of state enterprise in Uganda, where the overall supply of people with the necessary abilities is certainly more limited than in Nigeria or Ghana, indicates that a crash program is neither necessary

91. This discussion of profitability as a criterion owes much to Stolper, especially pp. 138–218. I am perhaps less concerned than he with the static resource allocation aspects of the problem. Thus I would place more emphasis on the time profile of profits and losses and am less bothered by profits obtained by monopolistic advantages or through high protective tariffs. Cf. A. H. Hanson, *Public Enterprise and Economic Development* (London: Routledge and Kegan Paul, 1959), pp. 434–37; and Brian Van Arkadie and Charles R. Frank, Jr., *Economic Accounting and Development Planning* (Nairobi: Oxford University Press, 1966), pp. 325–30.

nor sufficient. The political milieu in which state enterprises operate is probably far more important.

The three cases of Ghana, Nigeria, and Uganda have to be dealt with separately since different political factors were operating in each. In Ghana Nkrumah was able to build and maintain power for some time by an appeal to mass popular support. In this process he more or less disenfranchised and alienated a significant number of sophisticated, once powerful, political and intellectual elites. This made it even more imperative for him to consolidate and strengthen his mass support. The impact of this political necessity on policies toward public enterprise was twofold. First, projects tended to be visible and impressive and to reflect nationalistic aspirations. Thus the Ghana Airways were to be "the Great Airline of Africa" and the State Farm Corporation was to serve as a demonstration of the government's attempt to spur an agricultural revolution.[92] Second, state enterprises were intended to generate mass employment opportunities. This was particularly true of the State Mining Corporation.[93] The concern with project visibility and employment generation conflicted with the desire for profitable operation of state enterprises.

In Uganda public enterprise grew and reached a high degree of prestige and importance before independence from Britain and before political awareness and competition reached its zenith.[94] The colonial regime was able to operate the enterprises on the basis of "sound business principles" and could hire managers and skilled manpower regardless of their nationality, tribe, or political viewpoint without fear of vast political repercussions. Although Uganda attained self-government in the early 1960s, the public enterprise pattern of success, autonomy, and exclusion from the political arena had been set. There is little recent indication that public enterprises have come under control of the government and politicians to the same extent as in Ghana and Nigeria. If this pattern continues, then Ugandan public enterprises have a reasonable prospect of continued successful operation.

Nigeria began to move toward self-government in 1953 and had a plethora of able politicians. Alliances and coalitions of individuals and groups have shifted frequently. Internal political struggles have

92. See *West Africa,* 6 February 1965, p. 143.
93. Ibid.
94. Uganda attained independence in 1963. In contrast Nigeria and Ghana began moving toward political self-government early, roughly after 1951 in Ghana and 1953 in Nigeria.

been complicated by political rivalries among the regions which cul-
minated in the Nigerian Civil War in 1967. Individual Nigerian politicians have not been able to consolidate power for any long period of
time.[95]

In such a milieu of vigorous political competition, political power
may reward allies or buy off potential rivals with sinecures in government enterprises. Honesty and managerial competence often have little
correlation with political perspicacity. A politician in an executive
capacity has control over funds for the party or his wing of the party
and may use them as an instrument for political patronage; hence the
tendency for corruption and overstaffing. He may interpret the national interest in his own interest. He may be reluctant to enhance
the success of the enterprise by employing managing consultants from
abroad, if this subjects him to charges by his opponents that he is
abandoning nationalistic principles. He may view joint ventures with
other firms, foreign or domestic, as a method of making political allies
rather than as a means of injecting needed resources and talents into
a state enterprise.[96]

The Role of Public Enterprise

If political rivalry is fierce, it may be desirable to limit the role of
public enterprise, unless its political autonomy can be assured in some
way.[97] There are certain industries, however, such as electricity, water
supplies, rail transport, communications, and heavy industry, where
large-scale operations are clearly more efficient. One of the salient
features of indigenously run enterprises in Africa is their small scale
and the reluctance and inability of entrepreneurs to extend their
operations beyond that which they or their extended family can

95. For an excellent discussion of West African politics, see W. Arthur
Lewis, *Politics in West Africa* (London: George Allen & Unwin, 1965), especially pp. 13–36.
96. This is not to deny the possible necessity for patronage of various kinds
(possibly including graft and corruption) in order to maintain reasonably
stable political structures. The relevant question is whether patronage in a
form that destroys the economic effectiveness of directly productive government enterprises is not too costly a way to build political structures when
alternative forms of patronage may exist.
97. It may or may not be possible to protect public enterprise from being
used excessively as a device for political patronage. This is a question that
has been debated quite extensively in the literature on state enterprises in
developed as well as in less developed countries, and there does not seem to
be any easy answer.

exercise close control.[98] Thus when large-scale, modern establishments are substantially more economical, the role of public corporations may be dominant. The problem remains, however, of determining which institutional forms effectively insulate the management and administration from the political arena.

In those countries where indigenous entrepreneurs are lacking and/or where political control is more certain, the role of the public corporation can be more considerable. The state enterprise can be a vehicle for the training of indigenous managers, administrators, and entrepreneurs. The public corporation, if it is profitable, can be a means of accumulating investable funds which are less likely to be sent abroad than is the case with profits of foreign firms or those run by nonindigenous entrepreneurs. If profitable, the public enterprise can secure loan capital from foreign governments, multilateral aid-giving organizations, and private investors. In its response to profitable investment opportunities, the public enterprise can mitigate the degree of dependence on foreign-owned firms and increase the role of indigenously controlled institutions in the economy of the country.

The role of the public corporations in training indigenous managerial personnel should not be underemphasized. This training function, however, is not performed without costs in terms of possible losses or lowered profitability. The judicious use of foreign managing agents or joint ventures can often reduce these costs.

One of the main implications of the case studies above is that joint state/private enterprises are profitable more often than wholly owned state enterprises. This may be because the private investors provide some managerial abilities. More important, however, is the fact that private entrepreneurs are less likely to invest in potentially nonprofitable projects. Thus, ability to attract private investors may be one criterion to aid public corporations in choosing profitable investment opportunities.

The Role of Indigenous, Private Enterprise

The indigenous private sector in African economies performs several functions. First, its contribution to total output is substantial. Nationalization of the thousands of small-scale enterprises would

98. See Helleiner, *Economic Growth in Nigeria*, pp. 321–25; and Kilby, *The Development of Small Industry in Eastern Nigeria* (Eastern Nigeria Ministry of Commerce and U.S. Agency for International Development, 1962).

significantly reduce this contribution, since African governments lack the ability to administer and manage such a wide range of activities.

Second, a thriving private sector is able to mobilize significant entrepreneurial talent which governments could not hope to identify by any other means. Those who respond most vigorously to economic opportunities in the private sector are often the most motivated and capable managers and entrepreneurs. Reinvested profits enable the successful entrepreneurs to expand rapidly and increase their control of economic activities.

Third, a vigorous private sector is a training ground for entrepreneurs and managers. The profits or losses of an operation provide important learning feedbacks. If certain measures increase efficiency and raise profits, then the private entrepreneur has an incentive to continue along the same line of action; losses act as a signal and an incentive to try something different. The profit motive is also an important stimulator of innovation.

Finally, the small-scale, indigenous entrepreneur generally pays lower wages than a large-scale modern firm,[99] and he can be more flexible in his hiring practices and in adjusting working hours to the needs of his enterprise. He also pays a higher price for his capital.[100] This makes it profitable for him to use more labor-intensive and fewer capital-intensive techniques of production than the large-scale modern establishment.[101] In view of the increasing problem of urban unemployment in African countries, the further encouragement of a labor-

99. See Kilby, "Industrial Relations and Wage Determination in Nigeria: Failure of the Anglo-Saxon Model," *Journal of Developing Area Studies* 1 (July 1967): 489–519 (to be part of a forthcoming book on industrialization in Nigeria).

100. Schatz, "Economic Environment and Private Enterprise in West Africa," *Economic Bulletin of Ghana* 7, no. 4 (1963): 42–56.

101. Estimates by Kilby (*Development of Small Industry*, p. 5) for Eastern Nigeria, and by the National Manpower Board for other areas of Nigeria, indicate that investment per worker in small-scale indigenous firms is in the range of £100 to £200. In large-scale establishments, the average ratio is £2000 to £3000 per worker. For example, analysis of the data in *Industrial Survey of Nigeria, 1963* (Lagos: Federal Office of Statistics, 1966), indicates that paid-up capital alone (excluding debt-financed investment) amounts to about £1700 per worker in manufacturing. A forthcoming study by T. M. Yesufu reveals that the investment per worker in selected current and prospective development projects in Nigeria ranges from £1700 to £34,000. A survey conducted by the East African Manufacturers Association with thirty-eight responses indicated a total paid-up capital of £44 million and 19,626 workers (an average of over £2200 per worker with a range of £1000 to £50,000 over the thirty-eight establishments).

absorbing, small-scale, indigenous sector seems particularly attractive.[102]

What then are the ways to encourage the growth of the small-scale private sector? The proposals made most often are (1) loan schemes for small-scale entrepreneurs; (2) technical aid and advice, possibly in conjunction with loans; and (3) managerial training schemes. Loan schemes are often unsuccessful because of the high cost of identifying worthwhile loan applicants and the high administrative costs of small-loan schemes.[103]

Technical aid to small-scale producers is often ineffective because, in many cases, aid recipients are not willing to take the advice offered them, since the particular type of advice given is "not what they most need." [104] Technical aid to small producers is also extremely costly. If the aid specialist is to be effective, he must become very familiar with the firm's operations and problems. This requires a significant investment of the specialist's time, and the specialist's annual salary frequently may be several times the annual net output of the enterprise.

Training people to become competent managers is not simple, but training schemes can be and have been effective. Experience on the job, temperament, and character, however, are probably just as important as learning management tricks and techniques, if not more so.[105]

Training, loan schemes, and technical aid, despite their costliness, can and should play some role at least in the development of indigenous entrepreneurs. The simplest and most effective way to train small-scale entrepreneurs, however, is to provide profitable opportunities for investment. Although social and cultural factors play a role in inhibiting response to economic opportunities, there always seem

102. See C. R. Frank, Jr., "Urban Unemployment and Economic Growth in Africa," *Oxford Economic Papers* 20, no. 2 (July 1968). The discussion in the text on the functions of the private sector agrees with that in Theodore Geiger and Winifred Armstrong, *The Development of African Private Enterprise*, National Planning Association, Pamphlet no. 120 (Washington, 1964), pp. 7–10.

103. See Sayre P. Schatz, "The High Cost of Aiding Business in Developing Economies: Nigeria's Loans Programs," *Oxford Economic Papers* 20, no. 3 (November 1968): 277.

104. Schatz, "Aiding Nigerian Business: The Yaba Industrial Estate," *Nigerian Journal of Economic and Social Studies, 6,* no. 2 (July 1964), 210.

105. Cf. W. A. Lewis, *The Theory of Economic Growth* (London: George Allen & Unwin, 1955), pp. 196–200.

to be some aberrant individuals, tribes, or social groups, perhaps a very small minority, who do invest when profitable economic opportunities arise.[106] The rapid growth of cash crop agriculture in Africa and the emergence of a vigorous small-scale manufacturing sector in Nigeria (especially after the introduction of protective tariffs which greatly increased the profitability of many lines of activity) testify to the existence of a latent response that manifested itself when profitable opportunities arose. Papanek and others have noted a similar phenomenon in Pakistan, where the imposition of high tariffs after partition eventually induced phenomenal growth in the indigenous private sector,[107] and where the introduction of tube wells into agriculture spread rapidly and stimulated the industries that could manufacture and service the tube-well equipment.

Those who make the initial response to economic opportunities will, if their efforts are rewarded by profits, expand their operations and inspire imitators.[108] The imitators often are closely related by social and cultural ties to the successful entrepreneurs. (Thus the tendency for certain social and ethnic groups to have an undue proportion of successful entrepreneurs.) As long as profitable opportunities remain or others arise, the growth process is maintained and tends to accelerate. Entrepreneurial and managerial experience widens. Social and cultural inhibitions diminish with repeated exposure to profitable opportunities. Social norms and attitudes may change in response to the needs of successful operation of business. At some point, the choice of socialism or free enterprise becomes more meaningful as the society acquires a significant number of able entrepreneurs, man-

---

106. A notable example of differential response to economic opportunity is the contrast between the Chagga and the Masai, neighboring tribes in the Kilimanjaro region of Tanganyika (now Tanzania). The pastoral Masai changed very little under the impact of modernizing influences introduced in the last half century. The Chagga, on the other hand, have invested heavily in the growing of Arabica coffees on the slopes of the mountain. The Chagga also formed, on their own initiative, a successful cooperative for purchasing, grading, processing, distributing, and selling the coffee. See Kathleen M. Stahl, *The History of the Chagga People of Kilimanjaro* (London: Mouton, 1964).

107. See Gustav F. Papanek, "The Development of Entrepreneurship," and discussion by F. C. Shorter, *American Economic Review* 52, no. 2 (May 1962): 46–58 and 64–66.

108. Schumpeter's emphasis on the pathological nature of original entrepreneurship and the importance of imitators is as applicable to the less developed areas of Africa as he meant it to be to the Western world. See J. A. Schumpeter, *The Theory of Economic Development* (Cambridge: Harvard University Press, 1934), pp. 74–94 and 228–30.

agers, and administrators. In the meantime, however, the dictates of growth may require a significant role for private enterprise.

Comments by Stephen H. Hymer

"Is the industrialization of the Gold Coast to be done by the Government, by African businessmen, by foreigners, or by these three in combination? This issue has still to be settled." [1] Arthur Lewis raised this question in the early 1950s; Frank's paper shows it is still far from resolved.

Lewis's own answer was that the government ought not to participate directly in industry but should concentrate on providing support services to private enterprises (infrastructure, research, pioneering, etc.) and leave the productive sector in private hands. Since the local private sector was weak, this meant that the main instrument for industrialization would have to be foreign capital, at least initially. But, Lewis stressed, "the role of the foreigner is that of the tutor; a sometimes likeable but usually tiresome fellow, from dependence on whom one wishes to escape at the earliest possible moment." Thus the goal of the industrialization program was not merely growth but the development of African capitalists: "the crucial test of an industrialization policy is not how rapidly it increases employment or output, but how rapidly it builds up African enterprise."

Frank's paper is a heroic attempt to examine the experience of Ghana and four other former British colonies during the fifteen years following the Lewis report. Several lessons about the role of public and private enterprise emerge from his survey. In Kenya, Tanzania, and Uganda, a rapid industrialization program by outsiders failed to build up African enterprise, showing how weak the tutelage effects of foreign enterprise can be. Tanzania has already changed its strategy because of this, and it would not be surprising if others will follow soon.

In Nigeria and Ghana the initial conditions were very different, for both had a stronger African business sector to begin with and far fewer foreigners. Nigeria chose a strategy of private enterprise and greatly enlarged its indigenous sector despite the abysmal record of

1. This and subsequent quotes are from W. Arthur Lewis, *Report on Industrialization and the Gold Coast* (Accra: Government Printer, 1953).

public enterprise (or perhaps because of it; note that public enterprise was most "successful" in the northern region where the private sector was weakest). But the political development accompanying this economic decision was disastrous. To what extent this result was a fulfillment of the prophecy made in Ghana in 1948 by the Watson Commission that "unbridled private enterprise would at best lay the foundations of future social strife" is still to be determined.

In Ghana the state sector was strengthened at the expense of the private sector. This led to many transition difficulties because of the unsuitability of the colonial bureaucratic structure for commercial activity. (This was no doubt one of the major reasons Lewis had cautioned the government against entering into the productive sector.) It is still too early to fully evaluate the costs and benefits of this strategy. A few years ago it was widely viewed as a disaster, but Frank points out that the poor record has been exaggerated; that the early losers are "now showing an encouraging trend toward profitability"; and that the large losses are concentrated in a few activities that were consciously associated with nonpecuniary goals.

The overall impression one gets in reading Frank's paper is that development theory has a long way to go before it can offer professional advice on the questions posed by Lewis. Opinions abound since the subject is highly political, but that is not the same thing as a scientific analysis of the costs and benefits of expanding state enterprise, creating a private African business sector, or inviting foreign enterprise. One is struck in reading through the footnotes to Frank's paper by the great dearth of empirical and theoretical work on the subject. Frank had to rely mainly on original sources such as annual reports, economic bulletins, and other official publications because so few scholarly monographs were available analyzing in depth the experience of the various sectors over a long stretch of time.

Moreover the existing sources approach the problem essentially on a micro level, while Frank's concern is the process of development, which requires a macro analysis. The three strategies for industrialization outlined by Frank involve a whole gamut of policies with regard to taxes, subsidies, and economic controls, not just policies toward enterprise. Only limited results can be obtained from a detailed examination of the internal operations of public enterprises. The whole economy must be looked at, for the question is not only how public enterprises function, but also how they affect the performance of other sectors.

Unfortunately we do not have much theory on which to base a macro approach. Our theory relating the performance of an economy to the organization of its industry—the share controlled by foreigners, the share controlled by the state, the share controlled by large firms—is extremely weak, especially when we consider the great prominence given to these ratios in political debate and in development plans. The lack of a theory made it very difficult for Frank to organize and evaluate the material he gathered, and the frustrations he surely felt on this account should indicate, at least in my view, an important avenue for further research. The countries examined in this essay, like most countries in the underdeveloped world, want to increase the size of their industrial sector and to decrease their dependency on foreign capital. Some want a large portion of the economy in the hands of the state; others want to restrict the scope of the government. Each country starts with a given structure of enterprise that differs from the one it desires, and a limited number of instruments with which it can try to influence the course of events. A major economic problem is to choose the best path to the desired target. The advice we can offer as economists is limited at present. We know in general that the limits of an enterprise, its ability to organize capital and absorb technologies, its propensity to learn to innovate and to diversify, will differ according to whether it is large or small, foreign or local, private or public; but we have had very little systematic investigation and empirical estimation of how these various behavioral patterns are related to type and size of enterprise and still less investigation on the macro level relating overall technology levels and consumption patterns to the degree of foreign capital involvement and of state ownership. These important areas of economic policy, i.e. the question of organization, Marshall's fourth factor, fell into a state of neglect with the passing of the classical school. They cannot however be safely ignored in the field of development economics, where a change in institutions is often at the heart of the problem. Perhaps we ought to go back and start again with the masters. A good place to begin might be with Marshall's "Principles," especially his appendices A and B on "The Growth of Free Industry and Enterprise" and "The Growth of Economic Science." And with Marx's *Capital,* especially Chapter 25 on "Capitalist Accumulation" and the sections of Part VIII on primitive accumulation.

PART III: THE GOVERNMENT AS REGULATOR

5

The Political Economy of
the Gold Coast and Ghana

BY STEPHEN H. HYMER

The government of Ghana has made three major efforts at "development" in this century (see Table 5.1, especially data on extraordinary expenditure and development expenditure). The first (1900–20) may be referred to as the opening-up or early colonial period. The second (1920–30) is usually called the Guggisberg Plan after the governor who was its major driving force. Little was done during the depression and war. The third (1945–65) consisted of two phases: a British late colonial or preindependence round centered upon the Development Plan of 1951, and the Nkrumah round beginning after 1960.

This essay examines the strategies and results of each of these efforts with particular emphasis on the colonial period.[1] In essence its main conclusion is that the colonial government's efforts were unproductive to a surprising degree and that its policies, taken as a whole, probably retarded the growth rate of the economy. The government extracted a large surplus from the Ghanaian private sector, the main driving

This essay is a brief summary of a larger book on the development of the Ghanaian economy. Its themes, like those of the book, are the result of collaboration and discussion with a large number of people. At the very minimum I would like to acknowledge the contributions of Reginald Green, Geoffrey Kay, and Stephen Resnick.

Note: Until the Independence of 1957, Ghana was known as the Gold Coast. For simplicity we shall use the name Ghana throughout the text except in direct quotations.

1. The theoretical framework underlying the analysis is spelled out in S. Hymer and S. Resnick, "Interactions between the Government and the Private Sector, an Analysis of Government Expenditure Policy and the Reflection Ratio," in Ian Stewart, ed., *Economic Developement and Structural Change* (Edinburgh: University of Edinburgh Press, 1969); and S. Hymer and S. Resnick, "Capital and Wealth in the Development Process," Economic Growth Center, Yale University, Center Discussion Paper no. 63, mimeographed (New Haven, 1969).

Table 5.1: The Government Sector 1900–60

	Government expenditure in constant (1953) prices			Percentage distribution of government expenditure		Index of government expenditure per capita (1953 = 100)	Government revenue as a percentage of exports
	Total	Ordinary, including public debt changes	Extraordinary and development expenditure	Extraordinary and development	Public debt changes		
				(% of total expenditure)			
	(1)	(2)	(3)	(4)	(5)	(6)	(7)
1900	8.2	2.3	5.9	72	0	46	44
1901	6.6	2.6	4.0	61	2	38	90
1902	9.1	3.4	5.7	63	2	52	67
1903	8.4	4.6	3.9	46	5	47	58
1904	5.0	4.5	0.5	9	10	27	48
1905	4.3	4.0	0.3	7	10	24	35
1906	4.6	3.9	0.7	15	10	25	32
1907	4.2	3.7	0.5	11	10	23	25
1908	5.1	4.0	1.1	22	8	28	30
1909	7.6	4.5	3.1	46	7	41	29
1910	6.8	4.3	2.5	37	7	34	36
1911	6.0	4.3	1.7	29	7	31	29
1912	6.2	4.5	1.7	28	7	32	28
1913	7.1	4.5	2.7	37	5	34	23
1914	8.2	4.9	3.4	41	6	40	27
1915	7.8	5.4	2.5	32	8	37	23
1916	5.1	3.7	1.4	27	8	24	30
1917	4.6	3.7	1.0	21	9	20	26
1918	3.3	2.8	0.5	15	9	15	28
1919	3.9	3.3	0.6	14	7	17	22
1920/21	7.0	4.0	2.9	42	7	30	28
1921/22	13.6	6.8	6.8	50	6	58	39
1922/23	15.5	10.9	4.7	30	7	65	39
1923/24	10.7	5.5	5.2	48	8	43	39
1924/25	12.5	5.9	6.6	53	7	49	36
1925/26	11.5	6.5	5.0	43	7	44	34
1926/27	13.4	7.5	5.9	44	11	52	33
1927/28	11.7	6.6	5.1	44	10	43	33
1928/29	14.4	8.8	5.6	39	10	52	33
1929/30	12.6	9.2	3.4	27	11	45	33
1930/31	13.5	10.6	3.0	22	11	47	38

Table 5.1: *continued*

	Government expenditure in constant (1953) prices			Percentage distribution of government expenditure		Index of government expenditure per capita (1953 = 100)	Government revenue as a percentage of exports
Total	Ordinary, including public debt changes	Extraordinary and development expenditure	Extraordinary and development	Public debt changes		
			(% of total expenditure)			
	(1)	(2)	(3)	(4)	(5)	(6)	(7)
1931/32	11.8	11.3	0.5	4	15	40	36
1932/33	11.9	11.8	0.1	1	18	40	39
1933/34	10.1	10.1	a	a	19	33	42
1934/35	11.8	11.7	0.1	1	17	38	42
1935/36	12.8	12.1	0.7	6	16	40	43
1936/37	14.7	13.1	1.6	11	14	44	37
1937/38	13.7	12.0	1.7	13	12	40	28
1938/39	14.8	12.7	2.1	14	11	42	40
1939/40	15.7	13.6	2.1	14	10	43	34
1940/41	13.2	12.6	0.7	5	9	35	33
1941	10.7	10.4	0.4	3	10	28	39
1942	10.1	9.6	0.5	4	9	26	42
1943	9.2	8.4	0.8	9	8	23	43
1944	8.8	7.5	1.3	14	9	22	53
1945/46	11.0	8.3	2.7	25	5	26	54
1946	11.5	9.2	2.4	20	4	27	43
1947	15.0	10.9	4.2	28	2	33	18
1948	15.9	12.0	3.9	25	2	34	22
1949	20.1	14.6	5.4	27	1	43	75
1950/51	22.2	16.1	6.1	28	1	47	54
1951	25.0	15.5	9.5	38	1	51	47
1952	40.0	22.6	17.4	44	1	80	55
1953	52.2	30.0	22.2	43	1	100	65
1954	64.3	36.8	27.4	43	2	121	76
1955/56	89.3	50.4	38.9	44	1	162	67
1956	77.6	47.6	29.9	39	1	139	50
1957	77.3	49.6	27.7	36	1	134	72
1958	98.6	58.9	39.7	40	1	166	72
1959/60	116.3	74.2	42.0	36	1	192	62

a Less than .05%.

force in the economy, but gave it little in return and often acted to frustrate the development of Ghanaian capital. It devoted most of its efforts to expanding the government sector and promoting foreign capital, neither of which contributed proportionate returns to Ghanaians. The result was a highly undesirable economic structure, i.e. an inefficient (from the point of view of economic growth) state bureaucracy, a sluggish and reluctant foreign business sector, and an underdeveloped Ghanaian business sector.

If this conclusion seems surprising, it should be noted that the primary goal of the colonial administrators was not economic growth but the maintenance of a certain political structure, a task they had to carry out without any political base in Ghana itself and with only limited access to manpower and money from Great Britain.[2] Because they lacked the strength to handle the tensions of economic growth, they feared the development of local bases of power and often acted as a brake rather than an accelerator in an attempt to slow down the growth of specialization, exchange, and the accumulation of capital.[3] After World War II, when the problems became too acute to be handled in this way, the administrators left. That they so with a certain amount of grace and dignity was a question of style rather than substance. The problem of underdevelopment remained.

1900–20

Colonial administrators in 1900 did not view development with the same sense of urgency as we do now, but they did see the Gold Coast

2. Geoffrey Kay spells out this argument in detail in his introduction to a collection of historical documents and statistics on the economy of Ghana, in *The Underdevelopment of Ghana* (Cambridge: Cambridge University Press, forthcoming).

3. "It is probable that the nation is advancing faster than may seem good to the government who actually has had occasion to act as a brake rather than an accelerating force." A. W. Cardinall, *The Gold Coast, 1931* (Accra: Government Printer, 1932). Cardinall was a senior colonial civil servant and head of the census. This quote is taken from his review of the developments during the Guggisberg decade. See also the conclusion reached by D. Walker and Cyril Ehrlich, "Stabilization and Development Policy in Uganda: An Appraisal," *Kyklos* 12 (1959), fasc. 3: "the British administrator often sees himself as a paternal protector rather than a revolutionary; taking pride to maintaining peace and order among primitive people rather than taking pride in those people who are thrusting forward in an economic or political direction"; and that of C. L. R. James, *The Black Jacobins* (New York: Vintage Books, 1963), p. 377: "Colonialism strangles the real wealth of the continent—the creative genius of the African people."

as an underdeveloped country ("the soil is everywhere fertile and the needs of the people being few there is little incentive to work") and had a plan for bringing about "improved methods and new manners." [4] Their strategy was outward looking with regard to capital, enterprise, and markets. In their view, Africa had a plentiful (though not always willing) supply of labor and rich natural resources; capital and enterprise were, however, lacking and these would have to be obtained from abroad. The colonies were regarded as "underdeveloped estates and estates which can never be developed without imperial assistance." [5] The Gold Coast and Great Britain were thus complementary: the one being for land- and labor abundant and the other capital-abundant; the role of the state was to break down barriers between the colony and mother country, to provide infrastructure and basic services in the colony, and to maintain a favorable climate there for foreign investment. This approach led the British to overstress foreign markets and foreign capital and to neglect internal markets and indigenous enterprise.

The first development "plan" for the Gold Coast was put into effect around 1900. Its strategy was to develop the country by following the three R's: "Rule of the British, the Railways, and Ross' medical achievements." [6] The program was short, modest, and, by appearances at least, highly successful. The main thrust of the plan lay in the construction of a railway and the pacification of the country. The government did not have sufficient revenue at the time to finance the entire program and made up the deficit by issuing bonds in the London capital market. The construction of a railway from Sekondi to Kumasi was begun in 1898 and completed in 1903. The Ashanti were "paci-

4. On the changing economic structure during the "opening up phase" see R. Szereszewski, *Structural Changes in the Economy of Ghana, 1891–1911* (London: Weidenfield and Nicholson, 1965); and Polly Hill's review in *Economic Development and Cultural Change*, October 1967. For a contemporary view see *Précis of Information concerning the Colony of the Gold Coast and Ashanti,* General Staff (1904) (cited hereafter as *Précis*).

5. Joseph Chamberlain, Secretary of State for the Colonies, the House of Commons, 22 August 1895. The theory of trade was an obvious application of the Recurdian law of diminishing returns. The protection of British capital from Ghanaian capital had strong overlays of mercantilism. It might be noted, as Douglas Rimmer points out in his analysis of "Schumpeter and the Underdeveloped Countries," *Economic Bulletin of Ghana* 2, no. 5 (May 1958), that Ghana was colonized not by British capitalism in its dynamic phase but by capitalism in decline.

6. The phrase is taken from A. McPhee, *The Economic Revolution in British West Africa* (London: Oxford University Press, 1926).

fied" in 1901. A beginning was made toward enlarging the administrative structure. In 1904 the public debt stood at over £2 million.

The decades that followed were marked by a rapid expansion of exports and, along with them, the rest of the economy (Table 5.2). Government revenue rose *pari passu:* the government could easily pay interest and amortization on its debt and still have a large surplus at its disposal for the steady and continuous expansion of its services and infrastructure. The government's satisfaction with the prosperity of the Gold Coast was not, however, justified; its own contribution to the growth process was not the decisive factor, nor even an important one. Many of its policies were misguided and perhaps counterproductive: much was done to encourage foreign investment in the gold industry, which was dominated by Europeans; but the African enterprise in cocoa, which accounted for the prosperity of the colony, received scant help and even some hindrance. It could be said that in a sense the cocoa industry grew in spite of, rather than because of, government policy.

Foreign Capital in Gold

Ghana has a long history as a gold producer;[7] travelers and soldiers visiting Ashanti had brought back visions of fabulous wealth. The gold mines had been in operation since at least the early sixteenth century, but since African methods were inadequate for working deep mines, modern machinery was necessary for further development. This was a classic example of the colonial model: here was a rich raw material, much in demand in world markets, but requiring mechanization and capital which the colonial administration felt only the Europeans could bring. The annual report of the Gold Coast in 1898 predicted that £40 million of gold would be extracted in ten years.

The aid of the government was essential for getting the gold industry on its feet. Even though some rich mines were located relatively near the coast, it was exceedingly difficult and costly to transport machinery by the traditional means of head loading, and the absence of a railroad had thwarted the efforts of Europeans to establish a gold-mining industry in the late 1870s and early 1880s. The European industry

7. On the establishment of the gold industry see: H. Bevin, "M. J. Bonnat: Trader and Mining Promoter," *Economic Bulletin of Ghana* 4, no. 7 (July 1960); Gold Coast Chamber of Mines, *Gold from the Gold Coast* (Ghana, 1950); D. Kimble, *A Political History of Ghana* (Oxford: Oxford University Press, 1963).

became successful only after the construction of the railroad had provided it with cheap transportation.

The government also helped foreign capital to obtain adequate supplies of labor, though not to the extent that was usual in colonial Africa. Most colonial governments, far from believing in laissez faire where labor was concerned, regarded it an essential government function to interfere with the labor market and assure an adequate labor supply for the export sector of the economy.[8] The colonial government of the Gold Coast began with the usual premise that "one of the most serious problems connected with the Gold Coast is the dearth of labour to which the character of the inhabitants largely contributes";[9]

8. See Elliot Berg, "The Development of a Labor Force in Sub-Saharan Africa," *Economic Development and Cultural Change,* n.d., pp. 394–412; and idem, "Backward-Sloping Labor Supply Functions in Dual Economies: The African Case," *Quarterly Journal of Economics,* August 1961, pp. 468–92. The economic rationale for this policy was the theory of the backward-bending supply curve of labor. It was argued that because of the economic backwardness and limited horizons of the indigenous population the supply curve of labor was highly inelastic and probably negatively rather than positively sloped (at least until new tastes were acquired). An outward shift of demand, it was felt, caused both a rise in wages and a decline in the amount of labor available. To overcome this problem, a policy was advocated that would hold wages down to "reasonable" levels and shift the supply curve outward. In many parts of Africa poll taxes, land appropriation, and other coercive measures were used to force the indigenous population to leave the traditional sectors and to work in the new European sectors of China to keep wages from rising. It almost goes without saying that the welfare of the labor force played virtually no role at all in colonial political economy. It was only at the end of the 1930s that a labor department was established. Its investigation revealed that the circumstances under which migrant laborers came south searching for jobs were frequently appalling. The government had done nothing to help.

As Orde Browne, labor adviser to the Secretary of State for the Colonies, noted in his analysis of the development of a Ghanaian labor force, because of the ample supply of labor

> the usual accompaniment of such development in the shape of recruiting, organized transport, a written contract, etc. did not appear . . . the innovation was consequently unobtrusive and the Colonial Government remained hardly aware of its implications.
>
> . . . the position is therefore, theoretically admirable with a flow of entirely free labour, unrecruited and untrammeled by any sort of contract. In practise, however, the worker is at great disadvantage and in a far worse position than his brother in a country where adequate arrangements exist for the collection, transport, care and subsequent repatriation of the worker.

G. St. Orde Browne, *Report on Labour Conditions in West Africa* (London: H.M.S.O., Cmd. 6277, 1941).

9. *Précis.*

Table 5.2: Foreign Trade Indices of Ghana
(1953 = 100)

Exports

	Volume	*Value (in constant purchasing power)*	*Terms of trade*
1886	2	3	129
1887	2	3	127
1888	3	3	112
1889	3	3	130
1890	3	5	184
1891	3	5	169
1892	3	5	162
1893	3	6	186
1894	4	7	179
1895	4	7	186
1896	3	6	222
1897	3	7	243
1898	3	8	291
1899	4	9	260

	Exports			*Imports*	
	Volume	*Value (in constant purchasing power)*	*Terms of trade*	*Volume*	*Per capita*
1900	4	7	202	9	27
1901	3	4	138	13	39
1902	4	7	165	14	42
1903	4	8	202	15	44
1904	5	11	196	13	37
1905	6	12	220	11	31
1906	8	16	208	13	37
1907	9	21	222	13	37
1908	10	20	195	14	38
1909	12	21	180	13	37
1910	12	21	181	17	46
1911	18	30	170	19	50
1912	19	33	170	21	55
1913	23	40	173	21	53
1914	23	29	124	18	47
1915	30	42	142	18	43
1916	27	34	127	23	55
1917	37	27	72	14	34
1918	26	10	40	10	23
1919	59	28	46	19	43
1920	42	30	71	32	73
1921	43	19	43	26	58

Table 5.2: *continued*

	Volume	Exports Value (in constant purchasing power)	Terms of trade	Imports Volume	Per capita
1922	60	37	71	30	65
1923	65	35	55	37	76
1924	73	40	56	34	71
1925	72	43	60	41	82
1926	77	47	62	38	77
1927	70	59	84	52	100
1928	75	57	77	54	100
1929	80	51	64	46	86
1930	67	45	66	43	78
1931	81	37	46	25	44
1932	76	43	57	32	56
1933	78	40	51	30	50
1934	82	46	56	32	52
1935	93	54	59	53	85
1936	106	72	67	61	94
1937	88	82	93	75	114
1938	100	57	57	46	69
1939	100	65	65	45	65
1940	85	55	64	32	45
1941	84	43	51	25	34
1942	56	30	52	28	37
1943	74	25	34	23	31
1944	77	24	30	23	29
1945	86	36	42	31	38
1946	91	44	49	36	43
1947	72	45	63	45	53
1948	85	82	98	53	61
1949	105	70	66	77	87
1950	104	107	104	79	86
1951	95	103	108	85	90
1952	91	91	101	86	89
1953	100	100	100	100	100
1954	92	152	166	97	95
1955	92	130	142	119	113
1956	102	120	119	124	116
1957	115	125	109	129	116
1958	98	143	146	115	96
1959	114	159	140	162	139
1960	131	162	124	178	149
1961	157	139	88	183	148
1962	174	145	84	156	125
1963	164	144	88	179	139
1964	162	148	92	160	122

but it did not in fact take as strong measures to increase the supply as did many other colonial governments. At the turn of the century, when the simultaneous demands for labor in mining, railroad construction, and cocoa caused a labor shortage in Ghana, the government established a Transport Department with the object of alleviating the conditions under which "exorbitant rates had for some time been demanded by the carriers and paid to them by the mining agents." [10] This effort, however, was short-lived, and the Transport Department was disbanded in 1909. At one time the government also considered importing Asian laborers to the Gold Coast, but only a small number were brought in. The government helped the gold industry in its inland recruiting ventures by arranging meetings between recruiters and chiefs, but it did not use coercion or compulsion.

One reason the government did not do more to help foreign enterprise obtain labor in later years was that it had a limited political base in the colony and thus lacked the power to control the labor market. The administrators of Ghana were not ambitious and had a dual attitude toward foreign capital, welcoming and encouraging it, but resenting the difficulties it created for the smooth administration of the colony. In the nineteenth century, the government's attempt to institute a poll tax had met with stiff resistance from the population, and it had no wish to raise the issue again unless forced to do so. The colony was prospering due to the rapid expansion of cocoa, and the labor problems of the Ghanaian sector of the economy were beyond the government's horizons. The colonial administration was quite happy to be relieved of pressure to act on labor problems in this period.

With regard to land, the government was not able to help European investors by seizing mineral rights, but it allowed the negotiations of concessions to be a private matter to be settled between prospectors and local chiefs. Its neutrality, however, was more apparent than real, since the British conquest of Ashanti and colonization of the country had weakened the bargaining cohesiveness of Ghanaians and

10. In this report the head of the department described his functions as follows:

The object of the department in its original conception was to obtain control of the labour market so as to keep down the rate of wages, and for this reason the department has not failed in its object. This has not, however, been accomplished without great difficulty, and at one moment I feared could not be successfully carried through, the chief obstacle having been the indiscriminate way in which mining agents have raised wages. (*Report of the Transport Department*, Accra, 1901).

made it possible for British enterprise to come freely to Ghana. It is now impossible to know what would have happened had there been no colonization, and therefore it is exceedingly difficult to analyze the effects of British colonization on the rapidity with which the gold industry was developed, and the terms and conditions on which capital and technology were introduced into Ghana. However, three points should be noted:

1. The best gold fields had been discovered and worked by Africans. Europeans played only a small role in the discovery of the gold mines, which were originally brought to their attention by African middlemen who knew the potential of the mines and recognized the need to modernize production.[11]

2. Europeans acquired mineral rights very cheaply since they negotiated directly with local chiefs whose bargaining power was weak. This would not have been possible had the Ashanti empire remained intact. The empire had guarded its source of wealth so closely that no foreigner had been allowed to see a gold mine, and the gold industry was dominated by an elite which appropriated its surplus.[12]

3. Uninhibited free enterprise was extraordinarily inefficient in raising capital for the gold-mining industry. The mad scramble for gold concessions during the Jungle Boom was stimulated not by careful rational evaluation, but by something bordering on hysteria. This was the age of Cecil Rhodes and J. Rider Haggard, of the White Man's Destiny and the Dream of King Solomon's Mines. The California gold rush was still remembered, and the discoveries of the South African gold fields were a recent experience. (The Boer War helped to divert capital from South Africa to Ghana.) Consequently the rush for gold was extremely wasteful, although the burden, in the beginning at least, fell mainly on Britain and not on Ghana.[13]

11. For example, the most lucrative strike of all, the Ashanti gold fields, which has produced about one-third of total gold output, was secured by E. A. Cade in 1895 from a group of African concessionaries (Kimble, p. 23). See Bevin for other information on the role of the African middlemen.

12. On the amounts paid for concessions see H. Belfield, *Report on the Legislation Governing the Alienation of Native Lands in the Gold Coast Colony and Ashanti* (London: H.M.S.O., Cmd. 6278, 1912). Because of the system of private sale the chief beneficiaries on the Ghanaian side were frequently not the people as a whole but the lawyers who negotiated the concessions and the chiefs and headmen, who, as Belfield notes, frequently arrogated for themselves the profits from the concessions.

13. S. Herbert Frankel, *Capital Investment in Africa* (London: Oxford University Press, 1938), gives a graphic description of the period:

The potentialities of the field were introduced to Europe in the usual

The returns over the years which the colony obtained by supporting the gold industry were comparatively small. The rapid expansion of production was short-lived, and it took thirty years, three times the period predicted by the government, to produce 10 million ounces. In the 1920s the industry began to decline. There was, however, a revival in the 1930s, when the price of gold rose, which helped to maintain the value of total exports at a time when the value of cocoa exports had fallen. Still the industry was not, all in all, a dynamic factor in Ghana's export economy.

More important, the *returned value* to Ghana of the gold industry (i.e. the share of output after payment for imported raw materials and machinery goods, deduction of dividends, and payment of salaries to European officials) was quite low.[14] Local purchases were and are insignificant, and wages paid to Africans are a small fraction (less than 20 percent) of total value of output. Until the 1930s income taxes were paid to the British and not to the Ghanaian treasury, and in the 1940s and 1950s taxes paid to Ghana were from 10 to 15 percent of output. Tariffs on fuel oil used by the mining industry have been kept low. The gold industry has few links with the rest of the economy, and the spill-over effect is small. The work is unpleasant and dangerous, and the maintenance of an adequate labor supply depends upon the backwardness and ignorance prevailing in the northern territories of Ghana. The industry traditionally used a cheap labor policy; wages were kept low, turnover was high, and little effort was made to develop a skilled labor force. Profits not reinvested in gold itself were sent back to England and no local decision-making center was established

---

fashion, that is, by an exaggerated, quite unwarranted, and soon exploded boom in the shares of innumerable companies whose prospectuses portrayed a new Witwatersrand. It has been estimated that 321 companies were registered up to June 1901, with a total nominal capital of over 25 million, of which possibly 15 million was issued.

There is no clear indication of the exact purpose for which, or the exact geographical area in which, these companies were intended to, or did in fact, operate. There is no doubt that much of the issued capital was never spent anywhere near West Africa in general or the Gold Coast in particular. In fact, notwithstanding the repeated West African mining booms and the considerable speculation in the shares of these companies, it is highly significant that in 1904 there were only some thirteen companies that could report any gold production at all, and of these thirteen only four returned an output worth more than £10,000.

14. See the information contained in the *Award of the Arbitrator in the Matter of a Trade Dispute between the Gold Coast Mines Employees Union and the Gold Coast Chamber of Mines* (Accra: Government Printer, 1946) and the *Mines Board of Inquiry* (Accra: Government Printer, 1957).

to search the local environment and utilize capital in new industries. In nearly all these respects the gold industry contrasts sharply with the cocoa industry, where linkages and externalities were much higher and would have been still higher had the gold industry not absorbed a disproportionate share of the government's help.

The Cocoa Industry

Cocoa, not gold, was the *pôle de croissance* of the Gold Coast economy.[15] The industry was developed by Ghanaian capital, Ghanaian enterprise, and Ghanaian technology, with little help from the colonial government.[16] The cocoa industry had begun on its own to a considerable extent before 1900 and was well developed by 1910. Only when the industry was past the "take-off" point did the government begin to pay it some attention and to plough back some of its surplus into it. The contribution of cocoa to the government, in the form of expanded trade and increased revenue, was completely out of proportion to the contribution made to it by the government.

The early public transport system was of little help to cocoa farmers.[17] The administration chose to begin its railroad to Kumasi in the west at Sekondi, where it could serve the needs of the gold industry, rather than in the east where the capital city of Accra was located and where the cocoa industry was developing, or in the center at Cape Coast which was the major port at the time in terms of volume of trade. Only after 1911 when the first part of the eastern route, from Accra to Kumasi, was built did the share of cocoa exports carried by the railway become significant (see Table 5.3).[18] This link was

15. On the development of the cocoa industry see Polly Hill, *The Migrant Cocoa Farmers of Southern Ghana, a Study in Rural Capitalism* (Cambridge, Cambridge University Press, 1963); and R. H. Green and S. Hymer, "Cocoa in the Gold Coast: A Study in the Relations between African Farmers and Agricultural Experts," *Journal of Economic History* 26, no. 3 (September 1966): 299–319.

16. Neither were European merchants of much help. They had little direct contact with producers and "merely sat on (or near) the port receiving the produce." They neither encouraged nor influenced the growing of cocoa. Polly Hill, "Some Characteristics of Indigenous West African Enterprise," *Economic Bulletin of Ghana* 6, no. 2 (1962).

17. Colonial transport policy will be examined in detail in S. Hymer and G. Kay, "The Political Economy of Transport in the Gold Coast" (forthcoming).

18. According to P. R. Gould, *The Development of the Transportation Pattern in Ghana* (Evanston, Ill.: Northwestern University Press, 1960), p. 23, in 1900 surveys were made for three lines centering upon Accra, one extending eastward into the Volta region, one extending westward, and one

Table 5.3: Cocoa and Railways

| | | | Cocoa carried by rail | | |
	Value of capital (million pounds)	*Track miles open*	*Tons*	*Index of tons per track mile (1921/22 = 100)*	*Percentage of total cocoa exports carried by rail*
1900	—	—	—	—	—
1901	—	—	—	—	—
1902	a	39	0	0	0
1903	1.8	124	0	0	0
1904	1.8	168	.1	b	2
1905	1.8	168	.1	b	2
1906	1.8	168	.1	b	1
1907	1.8	168	.6	1	6
1908	1.8	168	.8	1	6
1909	1.8	168	1.8	3	9
1910	1.8	168	1.9	3	8
1911	2.0	188	5.1	7	13
1912	2.4	222	20.8	24	53
1913	2.6	227	37.4	42	73
1914	2.9	227	41.1	46	78
1915	3.0	245	60.3	62	78
1916	3.2	248	57.4	59	80
1917	3.2	268	79.7	75	88
1918	3.3	269	73.8	69	112
1919	3.4	269	111.9	105	64
1920	4.2	269	95.5	90	74
1921/22	6.1	276	109.1	100	82
1922/23	7.0	334	173.1	108	90
1923/24	6.7	379	164.3	110	82
1924/25	7.4	394	156.1	100	60
1925/26	8.0	394	150.3	96	69
1926/27	8.3	457	149.2	83	64
1927/28	8.4	480	131.2	69	62
1928/29	9.1	500	165.6	84	74
1929/30	9.2	500	139.5	71	59
1930/31	9.3	500	132.5	67	69
1931/32	9.3	500	123.5	62	51
1932/33	9.3	500	122.0	62	52
1933/34	9.2	500	125.9	64	53
1934/35	9.2	500	122.4	62	53
1935/36	9.2	500	130.6	66	45
1936/37	9.4	500	140.1	71	45
1937/38	9.3	500	34.6	18	15
1938/39	8.7	500	207.8	105	79
1939/40	a	500	115.5	58	41
1940/41	a	a	141.7	—	64
1941/42	—	—	131.7	—	60

Table 5.3: *continued*

Cocoa carried by rail

	Value of capital (million pounds)	Track miles open	Tons	Index of tons per track mile (1921/22 = 100)	Percentage of total cocoa exports carried by rail
1942/43	—	—	103.6	—	84
1943/44	—	—	184.3	—	99
1944/45	—	—	—	—	a
1945/46	a	a	—	—	a
1946/47	8.7	635	182.3	73	77
1947/48	8.9	636	129.2	52	72
1948/49	9.0	639	177.4	70	83
1949/50	10.0	641	201.8	80	77
1950/51	10.0	642	193.0	76	72
1951/52	11.7	643	168.5	66	74
1952/53	12.6	646	164.1	64	77
1953/54	14.3	654	141.3	55	60
1954/55	17.1	675	159.9	60	75
1955/56	18.9	749	186.6	63	91
1956/57	19.8	727	180.2	63	77
1957/58	20.3	750	155.9	53	60
1958/59	22.4	750	176.6	60	90
1959/60	29.8	750	225.5	76	90

[a] Data not available.
[b] Less than .05.

Note: The percentage of cocoa exports carried by rail was obtained by dividing cocoa carried by rail by value of exports recorded for that year. Note that cocoa carried by rail one year may not be exported until the following year.

of great value to Ghanaian development, but it must be emphasized that it was built after the cocoa industry was well past the take-off point.

In the early years Ghanaian farmers had to develop their own system of transport by widening roads and building bridges. Even after the railroads were completed, a major part of the journey from the farm to the port took place by means of a costly head-loading system, on paths and roads built with little government help or knowledge.[19]

---

extending inland to Kumasi via Oda. It is interesting to speculate what would have happened if the government had decided to build along these routes. Ashanti would have been unaffected, the mining industry would have failed to develop, the rich agricultural Eastern Region would have been served far better, and Accra would have been a much larger urban complex.

19. Governor Clifford reports that when he arrived in the Gold Coast in

Nor did the government provide any valuable assistance in developing agricultural techniques for growing cocoa in Ghana. On the contrary, its efforts in this direction were counterproductive, and if its recommendations had been followed, the growth of the industry would have been retarded. As the industry developed, the colonial officers, especially those concerned with agriculture, far from being pleased, tended to deplore the tendencies to "overextension," "imprudence," and the "neglect of other crops." Instead of applauding the rapid growth of the industry, they were worried about the "grave danger of farms being extended beyond what might be reckoned reasonable limits" [20] and the "positive danger that irrational development of cocoa planting is taking place." [21] Reports from various parts of the Gold Coast and the Department of Agriculture continually carried complaints of the small farmer who did not "fully realize his responsibility," who only "dimly understands the measures he has been advised to adopt," and who was "more concerned with the money to be made out of his farm than the quality of his produce." The reports repeatedly describe the "dangerous tendencies," "wanton neglect," and "dilatory habits" of the African cocoa farmer and express the hope that "doubtless experience will teach the cultivator that the most profitable farm is that which is cultivated by himself and his family." [22] So strong were the feelings of the agricultural officers that some welcomed the sharp fall in the price of cocoa occasioned by World War I, hoping this would halt further expansion.[23]

1912 he was shocked by the costly head-loading system. "My earliest preoccupation, therefore, on my assumption of the government of the Colony was to endeavour to find some means of relieving the crippling transport disabilities, the continuance of which threatened to render rapid progress quite impossible." Quoted in R. E. Wraith, *Guggisberg* (London: Oxford University Press, 1967).

20. *Annual Report of the Department of Agriculture, 1912* (Accra: Government Printer).

21. *Blue Book, 1914* (Accra: Government Printer).

22. *Annual Report on the Eastern Province, 1912* (Accra: Government Printer).

23. *Annual Report of the Department of Agriculture, 1916* (Accra: Government Printer), said the crisis "may not be unmixed blessing as it will no doubt temporarily, at least, check further planting of cocoa and may have the result of aiding development or resuscitation of other products and be the cause of a more rational system of farming." In 1917 the report said "it is hoped that the temporary adversity occasioned by the fall of the market will more or less remedy what the lack of regulations has permitted, that the area under cocoa will be reduced to a rational basis, the dangers of overproduction minimized and, possibly, that the people will be brought to realize the necessity of personal application to work."

To remedy alleged deficiencies in quality and production techniques, the Department of Agriculture wanted to forbid planting when farms were not kept up to "standards" and to introduce European plantations to demonstrate the proper use of soils.[24] But the government was quite mistaken in its view of what constituted an appropriate technique for planting in Ghana; to this day no method has been found that is economically superior to the one developed by the Ghanaians. The European plantations, using methods advocated by the agricultural officers, found themselves unable to compete with local producers and failed; most of the department's advice went unheeded, and fortunately the department was not given the power to enforce its views.

In objecting to the Ghanaian system the colonial officers were committing two fundamental errors. First, on the technological side, they made the assumption that Ghanaian techniques were inferior to European ones; they did no research on local problems but instead preferred to disseminate imported techniques. The department advocated methods suitable to land-scarce countries in temperate climates; Ghanaian farmers operated in an environment where land was plentiful, labor was scarce, and scientific knowledge was lacking both on the part of the farmers themselves and on the part of the officers who advised them.[25] To save labor, Ghanaian farmers did no extensive

24. The department's analysis of the "problems" of the cocoa industry and its suggested remedies are spelled out in *Papers Relating to the Cocoa Industry,* Gold Coast Sessional Paper no. 2 of 1916–17; W. S. D. Tudhope, *Enquiry into the Gold Coast Cocoa Industry, Interim and Final Reports,* Gold Coast Sessional Papers nos. 2 and 4 of 1918–19. These sessional papers show that the department was actually inhibiting the development of Ghanaian enterprise, though it thought it was helping.

> West Indian cocoa producers are either Europeans, or of European extraction, or are sufficiently intelligent to accept European methods; the producers of cocoa in this colony and Ashanti are natives in a most elementary state of civilization whose sole aim, as yet, appears to be the attainment of a maximum amount of money with a minimum expenditure of energy, however uneconomical the system, and whose lack of foresight for the future welfare of the industry—and consequently of themselves—has not yet been compensated by adequate legislative measures . . . At St. Thome cocoa is better than Gold Coast cocoa with the same labour . . . but these decided measures of coercion obtain under European control. ("Papers Relating to the Cocoa Industry," Sessional Paper no. 2 of 1916–17).

25. See Green and Hymer for a detailed discussion of this issue. For the moment we might take note of the comments of the authoritative and independent report in 1937.

> [It is] extraordinary that until 1937 there was no single agricultural station in the cocoa belt proper at which research could be carried out on

weeding, cleaning, or care of the land. It was also common practice
to grow several crops on a given plot of land, partly to maintain the
fertility of the soil and partly to provide cover crops that would protect
the cocoa from sunlight. These practices gave the farms an "unkempt"
appearance which shocked the European agricultural officers who
were used to European methods. The agricultural officers were particularly distressed by what they thought was a lack of proper disease
control, because it was a practice of Ghanaians to allow a diseased
farm to lie fallow rather than try to eliminate the disease. This worked
reasonably well, as the department's officers noted, since the farms
usually recovered by themselves, but they still felt it was not in accord
with "sound" agricultural principles. However, no superior method
was known.

The second fundamental error of the colonial officers was in their
economic analysis. They did not understand the capitalist nature of
cocoa production, which they continually referred to as peasant agriculture. They failed to see the drive to accumulate farms as the main
dynamic force in the industry. To the Department of Agriculture the
development of cocoa was a result of nature ("the local conditions of
soil and climate are peculiarly favourable"), not human skill ("no
ingenuity and a minimum of exertion is required"),[26] and there was
no

> argument against the fact that the system is wasteful in the ex-
> treme. . . . The cost of establishing new cocoa crops is nil since
> they are obliged to use fresh forest land for food. Cocoa is planted
> amongst food. Food is taken for a few years and then land given
> to cocoa. This means that the farmer has several farms and as
> labour is by no means abundant and the majority of the farmers
> cannot or will not employ sufficient labour to help them to keep
> the farms in order, they become neglected and disease comes
> over.[27]

---

the requirements of the crop. It is difficult to see how any officer of the
Department could be expected to offer correct advice on cultural or other
treatment, as he had no opportunity to acquire knowledge under the local
conditions.

H. C. Simpson and E. M. Crowther, *Report on Crop Production and Soil
Fertility Problems,* West African Commission, 1938–39, Technical Reports
(London: The Leverhulm Trust, Waterlow and Sons, 1943).

26. *Annual Report of the Department of Agriculture, 1916.*
27. *Annual Report of the Department of Agriculture, 1913.*

But Polly Hill has shown, in her study of the migrant cocoa farmers of Southern Ghana, that it was neither easy nor costless to establish a cocoa farm, and that it was precisely the desire of certain Ghanaian cocoa farmers "to plant far more than he and his family can look after" [28]—the major fault in the Department's eyes—and to hire labor that accounted for the rapid growth of the industry. Though there are numerous small cocoa farmers in Ghana who work only their own land, sell only the cocoa produced by their family, and who might be called peasants, the major part of the cocoa crop and the major credit for establishing the industry stems from a much smaller group of cocoa farmers who expanded their operations beyond the family farm by buying extra land and employing outside labor and who, as Polly Hill stresses, should properly be called rural capitalists. Had the expansion of the cocoa industry depended simply on large numbers of individual proprietors switching from other crops to cocoa, the rate of growth would have been much slower than it was. The successful farmer, by accumulating wealth, evolved from a peasant to a rural capitalist, managing farms in several areas at different stages of development, supervising labor and investing in land to satisfy his future needs. This system led to a rapid rate of growth because it used the labor of large numbers of Ghanaians who lacked starting capital of their own, as well as the labor of migrants from the French territories to the north of Ghana.

The accumulation of capital in cocoa also helped start other industries as successful farmers invested in other business or lent money to others. The concentration of capital in the hands of the lucky and the enterprising, who then spread out into new industries is a fundamental feature of the growth process in free enterprise economies. In Ghana it was slowed down by the colonial government's tendency to neglect and frustrate the development of Ghanaian capitalists.[29]

1920–45

The Guggisberg period (1920–30) was in many ways the finest hour of British colonial administration in the Gold Coast.[30] Sir Gordon

---

28. *Annual Report of the Department of Agriculture, 1915.*
29. We might note in passing Polly Hill's comment that "the farmers as businessmen were unimpressed by the colonial administration," in "Ghanaian Capitalist Cocoa Farmers," *Ghanaian Bulletin of Agricultural Economics* 2, no. 1 (March 1962): 26–30.
30. D. K. Greenstreet, "The Guggisberg Ten-Year Development Plan,"

Guggisberg was an exceptional man. His Ten-Year Development Plan was atypically well conceived and based on a highly articulated strategy of development.[31]

In 1919, when Guggisberg took office, the colony had just experienced twenty years of extraordinary growth, interrupted only briefly by World War I. The country was prosperous and the government, thanks to its large revenues from cocoa, was financially sound with a good credit rating in London. Guggisberg's aim was to secure the economic structure built in the first quarter of the century and to provide a more solid foundation for withstanding any future adversity.[32]

Economic Bulletin of Ghana 8, no. 1 (1964): 18–26 and Wraith, *Guggisberg,* are useful introductions to the Guggisberg period. (Neither of these takes the negative view presented here.)

For contemporary statements see: Gordon Guggisberg, *The Gold Coast: A Review of the Events, 1920–27* (Accra: Government Printer, 1928); H. O. Newland, *West Africa: A Handbook of Practical Information for the Official, Planter, Miner, Financer, and Trader* (London, 1922); W. G. Ormsby Gore, *Report by the Hon. W. G. Ormsby Gore on His Visit to West Africa during the Year 1926* (London: H.M.S.O., Cmd. 2744, 1926); A. McPhee, *Economic Revolution in British West Africa*; L. C. A. Knowles, *The Economic Development of the British Overseas Empire* (London, 1928); A. W. Cardinall, *Gold Coast, 1931.*

31. In 1919 Guggisberg had returned to the Gold Coast deeply influenced by the trauma of his experience in World War I, having "made a solemn vow to dedicate the rest of his life to the service of his fellow men" (Ronald E. Wraith, *Guggisberg* [London: Oxford University Press, 1967]). He knew the country better than most for, first as assistant director and later as Director of Surveys between 1902 and 1914, he had explored the interior intensively. By profession a military engineer rather than an administrator, he thought in terms of getting things done and applying science to nature rather than of simply maintaining order and authority.

> Whatever decisions I may be called upon to make I promise the people of the Gold Coast that I will always be guided by the fact that I am an Engineer, sent out here to superintend the construction of a broad Highway of Progress along which the races of the Gold Coast may advance, by gentle gradients over the Ridges of Difficulty and by easy curves around the Swamps of Doubt and Superstition to those far-off Cities of Promise— the Cities of Final Development, Wealth and Happiness.

(Guggisberg's first address to the Legislative Council quoted in Wraith, *Guggisberg,* p. 102.)

32. The severe shocks of World War I and its aftermath left an indelible mark on colonial thinking. In 1917 and 1918 trade fell sharply. ("It may be counted as a blessing that the war was not postponed for another decade when the Gold Coast peoples might have been so far weaned from their old dependencies on the soil as to make the conditions which existed in the early part of 1917 a source of real hardship." *Colonial Report, 1919* [Accra: Government Printer]). In 1919–20 the value of exports rose to unprecedented

The economic principles behind the development plan were the following:

1. Long-run economic growth and development of the colony would require a large expenditure by the government on health, education, and other forms of what we now describe as human capital formation.
2. The government's resources, though substantial at the time, were small in relation to the country's needs, and the first priority was to raise its revenues.
3. The bulk of the plan was therefore to be devoted initially to improving infrastructure in order to increase exports and thereby augment government revenue and overall prosperity.
4. To prepare for the time when more ample resources would be available, a beginning was to be made on a new program of education and health. Major efforts were to be postponed until the second stage of the plan, when it was hoped that increased revenue would be available.

Guggisberg stated these principles succinctly:

> For progress we must have education; for education of the right type we must have a bigger revenue. To get bigger revenue we must have bigger trade, and to get bigger trade we must have more agriculture and far better systems of transportation than at present exist.[33]

In practice the Guggisberg plan faced several obstacles and was never fully implemented. In the first place the shortages of skilled labor held up the construction of infrastructure. Thus the government failures in technical training in the previous decades proved a check on its ability to expand in the 1920s.[34] Equally serious was the financial

---

heights only to fall sharply the following year when the price of cocoa dropped. Guggisberg was extremely perturbed by the boom and bust of 1919–20. ("It was indeed apparent that a large part of the Gold Coast people had lost their head. . . . Motor cars were purchased right and left, champagne flowed freely, smoke of expensive cigars scented the air. . . . If instead of squandering their money they had put some by, the majority of those who took part in the boom would have been comfortably off," *Legislative Council Debates, 1920–21* [Accra: Government Printer]).

33. Guggisberg, in *Legislative Council Debates, 1920–21*, p. 6.
34. For example, Guggisberg, in his 1921–22 address to the Legislative Council, noted that the government was only able to obtain 20 percent of the

constraint; the raising of revenue for the plan was a matter of great concern and Guggisberg had to contend with severe criticism from government officials and the mercantile community. (The Ghanaian sector, however, pressed for more government expenditure.)[35] Still, Guggisberg was able to accomplish a great deal, and the 1920s saw a major expansion of infrastructure and an important beginning in providing more adequate education and health services to Ghanaians.

The achievements of Guggisberg are symbolized by three names: Takoradi, the new deep-water port; Achimota, a first-rate secondary school which became the cornerstone of higher education in Ghana and the training ground for many of the country's future teachers and political leaders; and Korle Bu, the new modern hospital built in Accra for Ghanaians. But in a sense these accomplishments were the trappings of economic growth and not the foundation. The physical hardware of the country expanded, but not the ability to use resources efficiently or to cope with the exigencies of a changing world.

Guggisberg's great leap forward was followed not by the development he expected but by stagnation and retrenchment. Exports failed to rise and indeed fell in real value as a result of falling prices in the 1930s and rising import prices in the 1940s. New industries failed to appear. The plan itself was never completely fulfilled through lack of revenue and was cut short in the late 1920s. In the 1930s even current expenditure had to be retrenched, and during World War II imports fell to an unprecedented low level.

There is a certain irony in the events of this period. The plan was conceived and executed by foreigners who assumed that the best interests of Ghana required it to become integrated into the world economy and "more and more one cog in the world economic machine."[36] Their efforts were directed at turning the Ghanaian economy outward; but as they did so, the world economy collapsed and

carpenters, 15 percent of the masons, and 15 percent of the painters it required. *Legislative Council Debates, 1921–22.*

The government also exercised a certain degree of restraint in hiring labor in deference to the fears of the mine companies, who argued that the government program would aggravate their labor shortage. See *Report of the Committee Appointed to Advise the Government on the Question of Providing a Deep Water Harbour for the Gold Coast,* Sessional Paper no. 8 of 1920–21.

35. See for example the *Report of the Committee on Trade and Taxation of the West African Colonies* (1921), which concluded that the postwar reconstruction was undertaken "on too lavish a scale and with too great rapidity" and argued against export taxes since they would discourage production.

36. McPhee, *Economic Revolution in West Africa,* p. 69.

the Ghanaian economy faltered with it. Their crucial mistake was not that they exaggerated Ghana's potential (they seriously underestimated it), but that they misjudged the potentiality of the British trading network.[37]

The depression of the 1930s illustrated that the British trading network was unable to achieve international cooperation even within its own domain. If the United Kingdom had chosen to expand rather than to contract during the depression, by increasing investment in the colonies it could have solved both its own problem of employment and the colonies' problem of growth. However it was not organized to take the necessary steps and merely transmitted the full impact of its crisis to its empire. The British economic system was not adaptive; it resembled a man who stands irresolutely before a barrier instead of trying to find a way round it.

It is interesting to note that the failure of the Guggisberg plan did not result in a political upheaval in Ghana. There were crises (the cocoa boycott, for example), but political control was maintained throughout the depression and during the great stresses of the war. It was the genius of the British colonial system, as a system for maintaining political power, to react to a crisis by doing nothing.[38]

The failure of the international economy was not the only fault in Guggisberg's strategy; his plan itself was seriously deficient. The health program was an important breakthrough but still a meager achievement in the light of the very low health and nutrition standards in the country and the resulting drain on productivity.[39] The education program was heavily biased toward elitism and failed to provide the kind of scientific and economic training necessary for develop-

37. To round out the irony, Guggisberg himself, after his brief period of glory, ended as a failure. He served for a short period as governor of Guyana but took sick and had to leave after seven months. He never received another job, and because he was a few months short of ten years' service he never received a pension from the civil service and only one month's sick pay. See Wraith, *Guggisberg*, pp. 327–37. He lived out the rest of his life in stringent circumstances (he died in 1930), remembered and honored only in Ghana.

38. For some members of the colonial civil service the retrenchment beginning in the late 1920s may have come as a relief. "The past decade has witnessed a rate of progress which might be even considered dangerous" (A. W. Cardinall, *Gold Coast, 1931*), since many felt that Guggisberg's building plans and his plans for African advancement were too ambitious. Guggisberg was a progressive man in contrast to the rest of the colonial civil service who, as Wraith has put it, "believed in progress only when it was inevitable."

39. D. K. Greenstreet, "Ten-Year Development Plan," p. 25, points out that Korle Bu cost £254,000, Achimota cost £607,000 whereas the expenditure on government bungalows was £420,118.

ment.[40] More important, the agricultural and transportation programs were fraught with error. These must be discussed in greater detail.

Agriculture

Diversification was the major theme of agricultural policy in the Guggisberg period. In part, the decision not to encourage cocoa was based on the feeling that the country could not safely expand cocoa production.[41] The major reason for encouraging other crops was that world demand for cocoa was unpredictable, and it was thought to be a better policy not to have all of the colony's eggs in one basket. The basis for this concern was reasonable, but the conclusion that Ghana should diversify into other tropical export products does not follow from it. In the first place, one would have to know the cost of growing other crops. The experience of Ghanaian cocoa farmers gave Ghana a special advantage in cocoa production that was not

40. Education was, of course, linked with politics since it was the educated classes that articulated the opposition to colonialism, and there had been a long-running battle between Ghanaian intellectuals and colonial administrators over what government policy should be and how it should be decided. The colonial administrators were unsympathetic to politics:

> most people who know the Coast will agree that the African's interest in politics requires no awakening. . . . Many are of the opinion that if less attention had been paid to politics and more to the material improvement of their resources, the Gold Coast would have been in a much higher position today . . . political disputes have led to most disastrous facts which resulted in actual loss of life and increased bitterness (*Report of the Eastern Province, 1923–24*)

but they recognized its importance and knew that it had to be dealt with. In the colonial view the wise and practical path to independence was to train a small educated elite who could eventually take over the administrative structure and run it as "efficiently" as European colonial officers. The new education program was therefore designed more to this end than with any idea of improving economic productivity. The elitist policy led predictably to a continuous excess of demand for education over supply.

41. It is doubtful, however, if it would be wise policy to extend the already large area under this crop necessitating the destruction of more jungle or bush when already the danger of extensive clearings are becoming apparent in a reduced humidity affecting the health of the cocoa trees, and the rainfall in this country is so near the minimum necessary for the successful growth of cocoa. It is, however, recommended that the surplus energy of the people should rather be devoted to the development of other products" (*Agricultural Department,* n.d.).

In fact, the country has since expanded cocoa acreage enormously, without serious consequences to the natural environment as far as has been scientifically ascertained.

easily transferable to other crops. A thousand pounds spent on improving cocoa production might well have had a higher payoff than a thousand pounds spent on other crops, even with the assumption that the price of cocoa might fall. In the second place, it is not clear that diversification would improve stability. The suggested alternative crops faced much the same future as cocoa, since the trends and cycles in demand for various tropical agricultural products share many common causal factors and tend to be highly correlated.[42] Better solutions were available but were not tried because they involved instruments beyond the pale of British colonial political economy. For example, one possible solution to the problem of a declining cocoa price might have been to form a cartel with other African producers (and perhaps Brazil) to control supply, and to promote the demand for chocolate by advertising and other devices. These instruments of market control, in common use by private corporations (including the expatriate merchants and shippers operating in West Africa), were not, however, part of colonial political economy; neither was an industrialization policy to increase the range of goods produced in Ghana. Both of these measures were advocated by Ghanaians in representations to the government but were never seriously considered.[43]

Another creative alternative would have been to promote specialization throughout the empire in order to increase productivity and lower costs; this would have been highly risky for any individual colony but not for the empire as a whole. The solution to the problems of uncertainty and instability that is most compatible with growth is an insurance scheme that encourages specialization by protecting the specialized subcomponents of the economy against the risk of

42. For example, H. W. Ord, "Agricultural Commodity Projections, Real Growth and Gains from Trade," in J. G. Stewart and H. W. Ord, eds. *International African Primary Products and International Trade* (Edinburgh: The University Press, 1965), p. 111, concludes: "Ghana seems to have done better from her heavy dependence on cocoa . . . than Uganda, with a more diverse range of agricultural commodities."

43. *Papers Relating to the Petition of the Delegation from the Gold Coast Colony and Ashanti,* Sessional Paper no. 11 of 1934. These submissions argued for, among other things, an agricultural bank for the benefit of farmers, a cocoa advertisement fund, a world cocoa conference with "full direct representation," encouragement of agriculture and the teaching of it as a special subject in trade and technical Schools, and the introduction of manufacturing. These papers serve as yet another demonstration that the colonial administration in fact had several known alternatives before it and that its policies were the result of a deliberate choice.

price declines. One such device is the federal budget, which redistributes income in the economy in such a way as to make sure that no
sector suffers too greatly from participating in a wider system of
division of labor. To achieve this type of harmonization, political
cooperation among the specialized units is necessary, and it was
precisely this advantage that the British had at their disposal in the
imperial system. They could have used their political power to achieve
diversification on an imperial scale while assuring security to each
participant. Ironically, however, the main potential advantage of the
British imperial trading system was never utilized. The empire remained decentralized, no attempt at coordinated specialization was
made, and each colony was responsible mainly for itself. In addition,
colonial administrators encouraged diversification with some curious
results: in the Gold Coast, for example, the government attempted to
curtail the production of cocoa, as we have shown, and encouraged
the production of rubber in its place; while in Malaya the British administration attempted to expand the production of cocoa. In their
attempt to ensure diversified sources of supply to the mother country,
the British sacrificed the opportunity to increase the size of the total
income and welfare of the commonwealth.

It is of great importance to stress that the strategy of diversification
pursued in the 1920s was not concerned merely with introducing new
crops, but also emphasized changing the mode of production. The
new strategy was not designed to help the emerging cocoa capitalists
to diversify into new crops or new industries; it tried instead to replace
the Ghanaian system with plantation agriculture. The attempt failed
miserably, as had earlier attempts from 1900 to 1920, for none of
the new plantations or new forms of capital ever got beyond the infant
entrepreneurial stage.

The Department of Agriculture had always believed in the need to
introduce estate agriculture into Ghana, and their development attempts of the 1920s must be viewed in the light of their previous
efforts to attract European capital to Gold Coast agriculture. A
number of Europeans did in fact come to the Gold Coast from about
1906 onward, and they acquired concessions of land on which to
establish plantation agriculture; but these ventures were not in fact
successful and encountered numerous difficulties in paying the going
wage and producing at a cost below the going price. By 1920 the
Department of Agriculture reported that "all European plantation

companies established in the colony have in the meantime suspended operations due to low price." By and large this ended the experiment in European agriculture, though a very few plantations lingered on.[44]

The colonial administration, having failed to attract foreign capitalists and being wholly negative in its attitude to Ghanaian capitalists, set out to establish plantations of its own. While Guggisberg told Ghanaians to "Make Your Farms Smaller," the Agriculture Department devoted most of its efforts to establishing large-scale agriculture. Despite the optimism and considerable expenditure of the department, its ventures in coconut and sisal failed to fulfill its objectives, as did the attempts to build a rice mill, subsidize a palm oil mill, and develop sugar, shea nuts, and cotton. Meanwhile it neglected research, and its legacy in terms of scientific knowledge was almost nil.[45]

44. In other colonies in West Africa the colonial administration discouraged European plantations, contrary to the situation in Ghana. At the turn of the century the colonial administration felt that the European enterprise could play an important role in the development of agriculture there, and in 1904 the government amended the Concessions Ordinance so as not to apply to agriculture, thus removing the need for government to approve alienation of land to Europeans in this sector. At the same time the agricultural officers conducted experiments to demonstrate to Europeans the profitable opportunities available in the country. The exact details of the number of European plantations established and their activities are not known, but in all about sixteen or seventeen European plantations are referred to in the reports of the Department of Agriculture between 1906 and 1920.

The epitaph of this strategy of relying on foreign capital in agriculture is found in the following paragraph repeated in each colonial report from 1932 until 1939: "There have been but a few plantation ventures in the Gold Coast and they have, in general, not been sufficiently successful to encourage further development. The fall in price of raw products has now rendered such propositions unattractive."

The reasons why Europeans were unable to introduce new crops and modern methods in the Gold Coast have not been fully explored. Among the likely factors are inadequate help from the government in experimentation and finance and the comparatively high wage rate prevailing in Ghana as a result of the demand for labor by cocoa farmers. Plantations in other parts of Africa did not usually face such competition and were further helped by poll taxes and land expropriation, which drove wages below the opportunity cost of subsistence farming under precolonial conditions.

45. It would take too much space to document these assertions here since the basic material is contained in numerous sessional papers and departmental reports and there do not yet exist adequate monographs analyzing the available information. An attempt to describe these various schemes, from their early optimism—"Seven years after planting we should have a great copra enterprise" (Guggisberg, *Report on Communal Coconut Plantation,* Sessional Paper no. 10 of 1921–22—to their ultimate demise—"on the whole it is unlikely that a large coconut industry can be founded locally" (*Annual Report of the De-*

Lastly, we might briefly note the government's attitude to the continuous conflict between the farmer and the merchant to whom he sold his cocoa. The farmers suspected they were at a disadvantage in their bargaining, as indeed they were, because the buyers were small in number and frequently colluded to keep the terms of trade in their favor. The main bargaining instrument used by the Ghanaian cocoa farmer to counteract the oligopolist powers of the foreign merchant companies was the holdup or the boycott. Periodically the farmers would withhold the sale of their cocoa when they felt the price was low; this occurred a number of times over the years. The government's policy was to discourage these boycotts since they interfered with trade; but they took no steps to counteract the oligopolist collusion of expatriate firms and in fact reinforced it by diverting attention away from the larger expatriate firms and toward the small middlemen who, they argued, were responsible for the difficulties. The cooperative movement which they fostered, instead of tackling the monopoly problem, wasted its time on the spurious issue of the quality of cocoa. When the government established a marketing agency during World War II, it kept the price of cocoa low and gave the force of law to the collusive market-sharing agreement of the ex-

---

partment of Agriculture, 1931–32)—will be undertaken in the larger book of which this essay is a summary. For the present the reader is referred to *Report of the Committee on Agricultural Policy and Organization,* Sessional Paper no. 17 of 1927–28; O. T. Faulkner and J. R. Mackie, *West African Agriculture* (Cambridge: Cambridge University Press, 1933), a textbook for colonial agricultural officers written in the early 1930s which in presenting the new approach to agriculture in the colonies contains a penetrating critique of the old; and the Simpson and Crowther report referred to earlier. We might also note the following statement, written in 1954, with its implied criticism of agricultural policy. According to its source, Albert Smith, "Farms and Gardens to Supplement Rural Science Syllabus for Middle Schools," *Gold Coast Education,* no. 1 (1954), pp. 41–47, in 1954 it was impossible to teach improved agricultural practices in schools because there were no improved techniques to teach.

Some of the keener teachers have followed the recommendations made some twenty years ago by the Department of Agriculture. At that time the Department of Agriculture was active in its work among schools. It was confident that the senior classes of a primary school could keep a small farm in continuous cultivation, provided that the rotation used included certain cover crops, then called green manures.

. . . In the course of time further research on basic problems of soil fertility revealed that permanent fertility could not be maintained solely by the use of short-term shallow and rooted crops.

. . . Until systems of food farming which are an improvement on traditional systems have been recommended for general adoption, there is very little schools can do about teaching or popularizing improved agriculture.

patriate firms (since shares were allotted to firms on the basis of past performance).[46]

Transportation

Transportation was to Guggisberg "without any doubt whatever, by far the most important subject in this country," and by transportation Guggisberg meant railways. "With more railways we shall be safe for all time—without them our future is not only imperilled: it is doomed." [47] The major items of expenditure in the development program of the 1920s were the improvement and expansion of the railway and the construction of the deep-water harbor at Takoradi, the railway's terminus in the western part of the country.

There is no doubt that a deep-water harbor was badly needed; Ghana does not have a natural harbor and the artificial one at Takoradi, opened in 1926, enabled ships to dock on Ghana's coast for the first time.[48] Previously they had had to anchor a safe distance from the shore, the goods being brought ashore by small surf boats and head loading. This system relied heavily on human energy and was costly and wasteful, particularly when heavy cargo was involved. The new harbor made it easier to unload heavy machinery and to load bulky commodities. But by choosing Takoradi or some other Eastern port rather than Accra as the site for the harbor, Guggisberg reinforced the Western bias of the transport system and greatly reduced the productivity of his very large expenditure on infrastructure. Takoradi was crucial to the manganese industry (a low value, high bulk commodity), but since the returned value to the community from this industry is low, the social productivity of the harbor has been much lower than is indicated by the tonnage figures or the value of exports. Takoradi's contribution to the cocoa industry was more limited; much cocoa continued to be shipped from Accra using

46. See *Report of the Commission on the Marketing of West African Cocoa* (the Nowell Report) (London: H.M.S.O., Cmd. 5845, 1938); C. Y. Shepherd, *Report on the Economics of Peasant Agriculture in the Gold Coast* (Accra: Government Printer, 1936); P. T. Bauer, *West African Trade: A Study of Competition, Oligopoly and Monopoly in a Changing Economy* (Cambridge: Cambridge University Press, 1954); R. H. Green, "The West African Shipping Conferences and Ghana: Some Aspects of Colonial Oligopoly and National Policy," *Economic Bulletin of Ghana* 8, no. 3 (1964).

47. Guggisberg, *Legislative Council Debates, 1923–24.*

48. At the time there was much discussion in Central Ghana of closing these other ports in order to protect Takoradi. Because of political opposition this was not done until World War II, and during the 1920s and 1930s the Central Province Railway simply operated far below capacity.

the surf boat system and a large amount of the imported goods destined for cocoa farmers continued to come through Accra. It was only when Tema Harbour was opened in 1962 that the eastern part of the country was provided with a modern form of unloading.

This was not what Guggisberg had planned. By building the Central Province Railway which extended eastward from Takoradi, he hoped to reach the central part of the country and thus to serve agricultural as well as mining needs. In fact, the Central Province Railroad went through sparsely inhabited regions with few commercial crops. It failed to generate traffic since Ghanaian producers found it cheaper to send their products south and to load them by surf boat at Cape Coast and Saltpond rather than via the long route by train to Takoradi.

Guggisberg made a second mistake with regard to the problem of transportation in the country in failing to appreciate the importance of the lorry. The worldwide revolution in transport occasioned by the introduction of motor vehicles spread quickly to Ghana as the Ford truck introduced the "age of the lorry." African businessmen quickly grasped the possibilities of the new technological innovation and the road transport industry grew with amazing rapidity. The flexibility of motor transport, its ability to penetrate deeply and to create an elaborate set of links, made it a revolutionary force. The growing volume of motor transport and the spread of the network throughout the country enabled outlying farmers to obtain better prices and extended the margin of cultivation of cocoa and food. Villages eagerly awaited roads that would make commercial agriculture profitable.[49]

49. The 1920 *Annual Report of the Eastern Region* noted that "during the year mechanical transport has become extremely popular." In 1922–23 it reported that "a minor industry has sprung up and assumed considerable proportions," in referring to "the running of passenger and luggage carrying motor lorries between various ports." The next year it noted that the industry had grown rapidly and that it was "possible to travel practically all over the province"; and in 1924–25 it told of "regular organized routes which run on schedule," covering the whole province. Meanwhile, Guggisberg, *Legislative Council Debates, 1923–24,* thought "it is obvious that motor lorries can only be regarded as temporary and inadequate measures in meeting the general demands of trade in this country."

His view may be contrasted with that of Lieut. Col. Watherson, a Chief Commissioner of the Northern Territories who in 1899 observed that the recent improvements in motor cars suggest

these vehicles as a means of transport vastly superior to carriers, and as providing some at least of the advantages of railways without any of their

Road transport quickly cut into railway revenue and led to the crucial road versus rail dispute. (Table 5.3 shows how the volume of cocoa, which was carried by the railroad, fell as the Guggisberg plan reached fulfillment.) To the colonial administration, the new technology was not a blessing but a problem threatening their plans, and they took a very jaundiced view of the "unfair" competition between state enterprise and Ghanaian enterprise.[50] As they saw it, the problem stemmed not from their own errors but from the inadequate organization of the Ghanaian sector. Railroads, in their view, were properly organized and had a good pedigree because of their strategic role in nineteenth-century development; motor transport, in contrast, was run by Ghanaians without a proper system.[51]

This conflict between road and rail shows the defects and biases in government planning. Given the railway, the appropriate economic policy would have been to set railroad prices equal to marginal cost and to subsidize the deficit out of general revenue. However, the colonial government aimed at covering the railway's operating expenses from its operating revenue, and hence it charged what the traffic would bear. It decided, without analysis, that manganese and

---

drawbacks. Roads suitable for them can easily be constructed . . . No ambitious bridging schemes need to be thought out, for culverts can easily be made locally to bear the weight of a motor car and its load. (Quoted in Cardinall, *Gold Coast*, pp. 36–37.)

In making his assessment Guggisberg was guided by data obtained with difficulty from a few large European transport companies. Their method of operations and costs bore little relation to those of the Ghanaian sector. As late as 1928/29, when the average rate charged for lorry transport by Ghanaians was about 7 pence a ton and there were reports of charges as low as 5 pence, the representatives of the major transport firms "speaking from intimate knowledge of the conditions on the road" said it could not be done for less than 10 pence. *Report of the Central Province Trade Routes Committee, Appointed by His Excellency the Governor, to Consider and Make Recommendations Regarding: (1) Central Province Railway Rates; (2) The Treatment of the Ports of Cape Coast and Saltpond on the Opening of Takoradi,* Sessional Paper no. 6 of 1928–29.

50. "The African lorry owner is becoming a problem on account of his successful competition with the railway . . . Road transport of the Gold Coast is excessively cheap and is actually run on an uneconomic basis" (*Colonial Report, 1931–32*).

51. "The whole system of motor transport in the Gold Coast . . . if, indeed, one can be said to exist . . . rests at present on such an uneconomic basis that it is impossible for the railway or other properly organized or regulated transport system to compete successfully." *Report of the Railway Revenue Committee, Road vs. Rail,* Sessional Paper no. 11 of 1932–33.

Table 5.4: Railway Finance, 1921–39

	Share of freight receipts derived from cocoa (*percentages*)	Freight charges for cocoa as a percentage of the value of cocoa carried by rail
1920	50	4
1921/22	57	8
1922/23	56	7
1923/24	55	8
1924/25	49	8
1925/26	46	7
1926/27	47	7
1927/28	39	5
1928/29	43	5
1929/30	40	6
1930/31	47	7
1931/32	56	12
1932/33	56	12
1933/34	57	14
1934/35	44	13
1935/36	40	13
1936/37	40	10
1937/38	12	5
1938/39	54	14

gold could bear only low rates and that cocoa could bear high rates.[52] (Table 5.4 indicates that cocoa rates were raised in order to maintain revenue.) This was possible only where cocoa had no alternative form of transportation, such as in Ashanti. In other places the high prices, charged to cocoa by the railway in order to recoup the losses suffered

52. See for example the elaborate discussion on the Railway Retrenchment Committee, *Report and Recommendations*, Sessional Paper no. 13 of 1931–32. The committee argued, with respect to the request for lower rates by the African Manganese Committee, that "the importance to the Gold Coast of the continuance of this industry is, in the opinion of the Committee, too obvious to require to be stressed by them: a very considerable revenue must flow into the treasury as a result of the Company's wage payments and the money spent on its employees." However, with regard to cocoa,

He [Mr. Lewis] assented that at existing rates all Ashanti traffic to and from the port of Takoradi would travel by rail if that form of transportation were possible . . . The General Manager did not deny that as a rate on raw products exported in bulk, the rate of cocoa from Kumasi to Takoradi (81s. 9d.) was high. He stated, however, that he would be unable to replace by railway earnings the loss which would accrue from even a small reduction of railway rates on cocoa from Ashanti. In the circumstances, the Committee can make no recommendation for such a reduction at the present time.

because of the low prices charged to mining, drove cocoa traffic onto the road.[53]

Various methods were considered to protect the new infrastructure from the "force of competition from motor lorries and cheaper ports," including increased license fees for motor lorries, the periodic closing of certain roads to heavy traffic, taxation of heavy traffic on roads competing with railways, licensing of routes, the establishment of toll gates, the closing of certain ports, the enforcement of regulations on safety and carrying capacity to avoid the "persistent overloading" that "allowed" the motor lorries to charge low rates. A full account of all the steps taken and their impact is not available. However, in 1934 the Carriage of Goods Road Ordinance prohibited the carriage of specified goods over certain selected roads (called "scheduled roads").[54] Equally important, road construction was held back in the 1930s and "gaps were deliberately left in the system of road com-

53. See the analysis of the *Railway Revenue Committee* (1932–33) on price discrimination. "On studying the map of the colony it will be seen that the road system in Ashanti and the Western Province was developed with due regard for the interests of the Railway which there preceded the roads. In both these Administrations the roads are complementary to, and not competitive with, the Railway; and the result of this system which does not provide direct access to Takoradi by road, is that of a total revenue of £756,548 obtained from goods traffic; in 1930–31 no less than £487,766 or 64.4 percent was derived from traffic either forwarded from or received at stations on the section of line between Kwahu Pahsu and Bunkwa where, as has been indicated, there is little competition between road and rail.

In the Eastern and Central Provinces, on the other hand, the history of road and railway construction is different. For various reasons the Accra-Kumasi railway was built in comparatively short sections, a considerable period elapsing between the completion of one section and the commencement of another. Nsawan, Mangoase, Koforidua, Tafo, and Ansinam became in their turn rail heads, and from each of these towns were constructed feeder roads. In many cases (i.e., the Koforidua-Nkawkaw road) these roads run parallel to the railway and, not having been abandoned with the extension of the line but on the contrary improved, they now provide for the transport by road direct to and from Accra of cocoa and other freight which were formerly carried by the railway."

54. "It has been applied so as to prohibit the carriage of cocoa to the coast by road and the carriage of imported goods and beer by road from the coast to Ashanti. There are 16 sections of road to which these prohibitions apply. These are equipped with barriers at which vehicles passing through are inspected and recorded by the Police. This system has now been in use for nearly ten years and in spite of the objections that can be raised to it in principle, in fact it works and is generally understood—and for that reason accepted" (*Report of the Road-Rail Transport Committee*, Sessional Paper no. 6 of 1945).

munications so as to prevent competition with the railway." [55] Other steps that, directly or indirectly, deliberately or otherwise, restricted road transport were the strict control of the importation of vehicles, tires, and gasoline during World War II and the policy of the West African Produce Control Board of paying the same price for cocoa at all rail points, thus absorbing freight costs and removing the inducement to send it by road to the coast.

In summary, the inability of the authorities to coordinate roads and railways illustrates the inadequacy of colonial planning. The administrators concentrated on certain facets of the problem and neglected others; they lacked the instruments and the information needed to make appropriate decisions. Given the crucial role of transport in development, their errors had the most serious consequences. Internal exchange of local produce depended upon the motor lorry. By slowing down the expansion of the road network in order to divert cocoa to the railroad, the government inhibited the development of regional specialization and exchange of food and closed off business opportunities for Ghanaians in cocoa, transport, distribution, and food.[56]

The neglect of internal trade provides one of the most serious indictments of colonial political economy. Its glaring symbol is the northern part of the country, where for many reasons Ghanaians were unable to create economic growth by themselves and the state did little to help them.[57] The climate of the North differs sharply from

55. Ibid. Also, John H. Dalton, "Gold Coast Economic Development: Problems and Policies" (Ph.D. diss., University of California, 1955), p. 48, reports he learned this from interviews with officials in the road division of the public works department. See too the United Africa Company, *Statistical and Economic Review*, no. 2 (Sept. 1948), p. 39, which claims there "were even instances of the removal of road bridges over roads . . . whether this was the intention or not it effectively discouraged the use of roads for the transport of goods." Gould, *Transportation Pattern in Ghana*, pp. 70–71, details some of these restrictions.

56. The gains from trade within Ghana is one of the most sadly neglected areas of research and policy. Until recently, few attempts were made to measure this exchange (no census of agriculture was taken before 1960), and the national accounts assume that per capita production of "traditional" goods (including food) remains constant through time—one of the most patently absurd and profoundly misleading representations of the economic development in Ghana that one could imagine. In fact, the growth of the cocoa economy wrought a profound change in the structure of production in rural areas by opening up opportunities for internal specialization and exchange in food and other commodities.

57. The attitude toward Northerners is bitterly summed up in the *Report of the Northern Territory of the Gold Coast, 1937–38*: "They were regarded as an amiable but backward people, useful as soldiers, policemen and labourers in the

that of the South and there is a natural basis for division of labor in agriculture. For example, the North could produce cattle and cereals for the South in return for its forest and sea products. But when proposals were made to build a railroad to the North, the discussion was conducted almost entirely in terms of the possibilities of promoting export crops, e.g. shea nuts and groundnuts, and not the stimulation of trade between the North and the South. Moreover, a railroad is not required since the terrain is ideally suited for roads. Furthermore, much more than transportation would have been needed since increased production in the North required irrigation, disease control, and agricultural research. Colonial policy, however, gave the North less than a proportionate share of infrastructure, education, and health and agricultural research, even though its needs were greatest. The colonial government thus ignored the opportunity to promote trade within Ghana. The North remained the most backward and impoverished region in the country, with the lowest educational standards and the most serious problems of malnutrition and disease—a testament to the uneven development promoted under colonialism.[58]

In 1930 a conference was held in the Gold Coast "to find out if a country run by peasant farmers was economically sound." [59] It would have been more relevant to ask whether a country run by British colonialists was economically sound.

---

mines and cocoa farms; in short, fit only to be hewers of wood and drawers of water for their brothers in the Colony of Ashanti."

On the neglect of the North see also J. R. Raeburn, *Report on a Preliminary Economic Survey of the Northern Territories of the Gold Coast* (London, Colonial Office, 1951); J. M. Hunter, "Seasonal Hunger in a Part of the West African Savannah: A Survey of Body Weights in Nangodi, N.E. Ghana," *Transactions of the Institute of British Geographers*, no. 41 (June 1967); Hunter, "Population Pressure in a Part of the West African Savannah: A Study of Nangodi, Northeast Ghana," *Annals of the Association of American Geographers* 57 (March 1967).

58. Similarly, the western part of the country has remained far less prosperous than the eastern, probably due to inadequate roads. The Western Province had the port of Takoradi, the railway, and the mines, but these did not promote development. The 1920 *Report of the Western Province* noted that with the end of railway construction and the mining boom "the energies of the province had come to an abrupt termination and the native has since been content to sink back into a state of complete lethargy." See also Guggisberg's comments. "As regards transportation, the Western Province of the Colony is still far less developed than any other part of the Gold Coast, and this in spite of its having had for nearly twenty years a railway with a terminal port." *Legislative Council Debates 1920–21.*

59. *Bulletin of the Gold Coast Department of Agriculture,* no. 19 (Accra: Government Printer, 1930), p. 9.

1945–65

The years after 1945 were ones of rapid and continuous change. The depression revealed the inadequacies of the colonial system and World War II weakened Great Britain's ability to control the empire. A new strategy was needed. Before we discuss it we may briefly summarize the main conclusions that emerge from our condensed and simplified examination of British colonial policy and its effects in Ghana between 1900 and 1939.[60]

1. Foreign investment proved to be a poor instrument of growth. Although foreign investment was encouraged, its contribution to the economy was very limited.

2. The major dynamics for growth came from the African sector of the economy, and it achieved its success with little help from the government or from foreign capital.

3. Despite the great success of the African sector in establishing Ghana as the leading producer of cocoa in the world and successfully maintaining its share in the face of competition from equally fertile areas elsewhere (including some in which cocoa is grown on a European plantation basis), African businessmen were not able to diversify into manufacturing or large-scale modern farming. Ghana remained a nation of small farmers and traders selling unfinished products on the international market.[61]

60. In the 1930s and 1940s, as the mystique of the early years was destroyed by the breakdown of the old international economic system, colonialism was subjected to a searching review by numerous committees, commissions, and independent scholars. In addition to the reports referring specifically to Ghana cited above, the reader is referred to the following important evaluations of the experience under colonialism from 1900 to 1939: W. K. Hancock, *A Survey of British Commonwealth Affairs,* part 2 of vol. 11, *Problems of Economic Policy 1918–1939* (London; Oxford University Press, 1942); Alan Pim, *The Financial and Economic History of the African Tropical Territories* (Oxford: Oxford University Press, 1940); S. H. Frankel, *Capital Investment in Africa* (New York: Oxford University Press, 1938); W. M. MacMillan, *Africa Emergent,* rev. ed. (New Orleans, La.: Pelican Books, 1949); Rita Hinden, *Plan for Africa* (London: Allen and Unwin, 1941); Kwame Nkrumah, *Towards Colonial Freedom* (London: Heinemann, 1962).

61. A major part of the country's private capital stock is held by Ghanaians in cocoa, transport, etc. However, large-scale organizations and concentration of capital are nearly all European, and middle-scale business is heavily dominated by Levantines. Though there are some fairly large Ghanaian capitalists, they are still few in number and provide only a slender base for further development. See *Industrial Statistics, 1958–1959* and *Industrial Statistics, 1965–66* issued by the Central Bureau of Statistics (Accra); Peter C. Garlich, *African Traders in Kumasi* (Accra: University College of Ghana, 1959); A. Ngpan,

4. The international economy proved highly unreliable and unstable as a foundation on which to build the economy.[62]

5. The productivity of the government sector was low. It made important errors in planning the transport system; it failed to do adequate research; it underestimated the strengths and needs of the Ghanaian sector; and it overstressed the importance of foreign trade and foreign capital. The government created linkages with the mother country, decreased linkages with neighboring African countries, and failed to improve internal linkages within the economy.

6. The government also proved to be rigid and inflexible rather than enterprising. It was one-dimensional in outlook and because of its hegemonic position was able to exclude many reasonable policy alternatives. It was a reluctant and gradual modernizer, bringing some of the benefits of the industrial revolution to Ghana, but also using Ghana as an outlet for the tensions and problems of British society. Contrary to what is often claimed, only limited credit can be given to the British colonial administration for opening up the country, and when it departed in 1957, it left behind a meager heritage.

Development Planning: From the Gold Coast to Ghana

The main ingredient of the postwar strategy to deal with the tensions of the colonial export economy was an expansion of the government sector under the rubric of development planning.[63] In part this in-

---

Market Trade: A Sample Survey of Market Traders in Accra (Accra: University of Ghana, 1960); and Polly Hill, "Some Characteristics of Indigenous West African Enterprise." Polly Hill also has a number of other unpublished papers on Ghanaian capitalists in fishing, cattle, trading, and lorry transport.

62. It should be noted that Ghana was not in fact integrated into the international economy but was tied to the British colonial trading network. After 1930 this network restricted the trade of the colonies considerably.

63. It must be stressed that the use of the words "development planning" to describe the economic policy of the government in this period is a gross misnomer. There was no plan in the sense that a choice was made to achieve desired ends. The plans were for the most part little more than a capital budget for the government sector constructed by asking each department to submit its plans for the next year. These were then summed up with almost no centralized coordination or choices made. Moreover, little attention was paid to targets, and the ones alluded to in government statements—diversification, industrialization, stabilization, development, welfare—were rhetorical ones, entirely remote from the immediate and practical problems facing the country and impossible to approach let alone achieve in the time periods under consideration. It is significant that, as Omaboe points out, the government did not even use the available statistics on the economy in making decisions, let alone call for more.

volved an expansion of social and community services to satisfy the growing pressures for health, education, and urbanization; in part it involved an expansion of infrastructure to provide support services for private enterprise in the productive sector of the economy.

In the first round, the British tried to introduce the new programs within the colonial structure. As a result of the political uprisings in the 1930s, London in 1940–41 sent a circular to each colonial administration asking it to prepare a plan of development for the colony in connection with funds available from the Colonial Development and Welfare Act. The result in Ghana was the Ten-Year Development Plan published in 1946 calling for an expenditure of a little over a million pounds.[64] About one-third of the plan was to be financed through Colonial Development and Welfare grants, another third from loans in the London market, and the remainder out of surplus balances. With hindsight the plan appears overly modest, but it contained a large number of the projects used in the larger plans that came later.

This initial foray into development planning was quickly outpaced by the course of events. Mass dissatisfaction among the young, coupled with postwar inflation and unemployment among returning veterans, led to the boycotts and riots of 1948 and completely upset the slow process of political development planned by the colonial administration.[65] A new plan, seven times as large (in money terms),

E. N. Omaboe, "Some Observations on the Statistical Requirements of Development Planning in the Less Developed Countries," *Economic Bulletin of Ghana* 7, no. 2 (1963). This made it extremely difficult for planners after 1960, when the government began a concerted effort to gain some control over the economy, for they had to begin almost from scratch in obtaining data on agriculture, industry, employment, national accounting, etc.

64. The background of the plan is contained in a number of Sessional Papers produced during World War II under the authorship of the governor, Sir Alan Burns. See *Development Schemes,* Sessional Paper no. 1 of 1943; *A General Plan for Development of the Gold Coast,* Sessional Paper no. 2 of 1944, and the associated Sessional Papers, nos. 3, 4, 5, 7, and 8 of 1944, dealing with specific schemes. The plan was based on the assumption that the annual revenue of the colony would rise to £7,750,000 by 1956–57. This was a conservative estimate and allowed for surplus funds so that contingencies could be met without breaking the plan.

It is interesting to note that in the postwar period the French government called for similar development plans from its colonies. The parallel action is perhaps explained by wartime collaboration in London. See Robert F. Meagher, "Bilateral Aid to Africa," mimeographed (New York: Columbia Law School).

65. See David Apter, *Ghana in Transition* (New York: Atheneum, 1963) and Dennis Austin, *Politics in Ghana, 1946–1960* (London: Oxford University

was prepared for the decade of the 1950s and introduced in 1951, just before Nkrumah became leader of government. Even this estimate, however, turned out to be conservative; the plan was completed in five years instead of ten,[66] yet so great were the funds at the disposal of the government that at independence, in 1957, the government still had international reserves of about £250 million with which to continue the expansion of infrastructure and basic services. Over the years 1950–65 the government spent a total of about £1 billion (an annual average of $200 million, or $30 per head), a level unprecedented in Ghana's history and far higher per capita than has been or will be possible in most African countries. The government of Nigeria, for example, during the same period was able to spend only about £2 billion, or less than $10 per head annually.

This large expansion of the government was only possible because of the crucial fiscal policy decision taken in the early 1950s by the colonial administration. When the price of cocoa rose in the world market after 1945 and especially between 1950 and 1954, the government had to choose an appropriate way of dividing up the windfall. The bounty in foreign exchange could have been given to the private sector if the government had lowered tax rates or raised the price it paid cocoa producers to the level of prices prevailing in the world market. Instead, the government appropriated for its own use a large share of the increased income, justifying the policy in part as an anti-inflationary measure.[67] It was argued that imports could not be increased because of inadequate transportation and harbor facilities, and that if taxes were not raised the high level of aggregate demand acting on the inelastic supply of imports would lead to a rise in prices. It was assumed that the cocoa farmer would not save and that therefore wealth would accumulate in the distribution sector —a large part of which was foreign. To avoid the inflationary pres-

Press, 1964) for an analysis of the politics of this period. The *Report of the Commission of Enquiry into Disturbances in the Gold Coast 1948* (the Watson Report), investigating the riots, contains an extensive analysis of the country's economic problems. See also Immanuel Wallerstein, *The Road to Independence* (Paris: Mouton & Co., 1964).

66. Expenditure for the 1951 plan was set at £76 million. When changed to a five-year plan in 1954, the figure was revised to £81 million.

67. The arguments were first put forth in the Watson Report and then developed with greater rigor by D. Seers and C. R. Ross, *Report on the Financial and Physical Problems of Development of the Gold Coast* (Accra: Office of the Government Statistician, 1952).

sure and maldistribution of income, the government accumulated the windfall itself and invested the funds in Britain.

The argument used to defend the policy, it should be noted, rested on a lack of confidence in the Ghanaian middle class. It assumed that Ghanaian farmers and traders would fail to recognize the transient nature of the rise in income and prices and that all the gains would go to foreigners. A contrary view held that at least some Ghanaians would have taken advantage of boom conditions and that capital would have accumulated in the hands of these enterprising Ghanaians. This would have laid the basis for an entrepreneurial class. Whatever the merits of the case, this avenue of development was not opened. The British colonial administration captured the windfall for the government sector, in one blow sealing the fate of the Ghanaian middle class, providing the British government with a large, low-cost dollar loan during the 1950s,[68] and setting the stage for Nkrumah's socialist strategy.[69]

The results of the massive expansion by the government were not those hoped for. Income did not grow proportionately to capital formation,[70] and the economy, which had appeared buoyant during

68. See Arthur Hazelwood, "Colonial External Finance Since the War," *Review of Economic Studies* 21 (1953–54).

69. The decision to accumulate reserves in government hands was, and continues to be, the subject of an intense debate on the behavior propensities of African capitalists and governments and the appropriate balance between the two. See P. T. Bauer, and R. W. Paish, "The Reduction of Fluctuations in the Incomes of Primary Producers," *Economic Journal*, December 1952, pp. 750–80; Polly Hill, "Fluctuations in Incomes of Primary Producers," *Economic Journal*, June 1953, pp. 468–71, and "Fluctuation in Incomes of Primary Producers: A Comment," *Economic Journal*, September 1953, pp. 594–607; M. Friedman, "The Reduction of Fluctuations in the Incomes of Primary Producers: A Critical Comment," *Economic Journal*, December 1954, pp. 698–703; B. M. Niculescu, "Fluctuations in Incomes of Primary Producers: Further Comment," *Economic Journal*, December 1954, pp. 730–43; P. T. Bauer, "The Reductions of Fluctuations in the Incomes of Primary Producers Further Considered," *Economic Journal*, December 1954, pp. 704–29; E. K. Hawkins, "Marketing Boards and Economic Development in Nigeria and Ghana," *Review of Economic Studies*, October 1958, pp. 51–62; David Walker and Cyril Ehrlich, "Stabilization and Development Policy in Uganda: An Appraisal," *Kyklos* 12 (1959), fasc. 3; R. H. Green, "Some Current Problems in the Cocoa Industry," *Economic Bulletin*, May 1961, pp. 16–32; J. Williams, "The Economy of Ghana," in Calvin B. Hoover, ed., *Economic Systems of the Commonwealth* (Cambridge: Cambridge University Press, 1962); G. K. Helleiner, "The Fiscal Role of the Marketing Boards in Nigeria Economic Development, 1947–61," *Economic Journal*, September 1964, pp. 582–610.

70. R. Szereszewski, "Capital and Output in Ghana, 1955–1961," *Economic*

the 1950s, seemed suddenly, a few short years after independence, to transform itself into a state of stagnation, punctuated by crises. Within a short time the political system erected by the British crumbled, and the country's economic difficulties increased until they reached crisis proportions. The government was in a state of continuous deficit, international reserves were depleted with time, and an alarming foreign debt accumulated; imports were restricted; prices rose sharply, black markets appeared, and parts of the capital stock were forced into idleness as production in some industries came to a standstill. Early in 1966 the military, declaring that "the economic situation of the country is in such a chaotic condition that unless something is done about it now the whole economic system will collapse," [71] overthrew Nkrumah and brought to an end his particular experiment in development strategy.[72]

So great was the imprint of Kwame Nkrumah on Ghana's development policy that it is all too easy to attribute Ghana's economic difficulties to the "unrealistic, stubborn one man rule that has mismanaged and squandered the nation's resources." [73] Until independence, Nkrumah had closely followed traditional colonial development strategy, and the major government programs were planned and implemented by a civil service still largely staffed by British colonial administrators. The premise of these programs was that the government was building a framework to attract foreign capital and mobilize local capital. The state provided infrastructure and other "support" services needed by the private sector, while the task of providing final goods for consumption, investment, or export was left to private enterprise. By improving roads, railways, and harbors, expanding health and educational services, and providing agricultural extension and other such services, the government hoped to stimulate the private

---

Bulletin of Ghana 7, no. 4 (1963), estimates that capital grew at 8 percent, output at 5 percent, and labor at 2 percent.

71. Statement by the new military government on Radio Ghana shortly following the coup.

72. The most comprehensive survey of the structure of the economy during this period is found in the essays by Szereszewski and Killick in W. Birmingham, I. Neustadt, and E. N. Omaboe, eds., *A Study of Contemporary Ghana* (Evanston, Ill.: Northwestern University Press, 1966). A contemporaneous account of these difficulties can be found in the official government publications, particularly the annual *Economic Surveys* which each year documented, criticized, and questioned the problems of the country with extraordinary candor.

73. *New York Times*, 6 March 1966.

sector to expand and diversify exports and to produce new goods for local consumption and investment.[74]

This strategy changed after independence and especially after 1961.[75] A new strategy was initiated based on the large-scale entry of the state into the productive sector. Its premise was that Ghanaian businessmen were not capable of the task of modernization, and that it was therefore more efficient, as well as more desirable on general socialist principles, to rely on the state sector rather than the private sector as the major source of growth. As Nkrumah put it, "colonial rule precluded that accumulation of capital among our citizens which would have assisted thorough-going private investment in industrial construction. It has therefore been left to the government, as the holder of the means, to play the role of main entrepreneur in laying the basis of the national economic and social advancement." [76] A large role was still allotted to foreign capital from both the West and the East, but in partnership with the state sector, not with private enterprises (so as to preclude the formation of a local private sector allied with, and dependent upon, foreign capital). Particular emphasis was placed on cooperation between the state and the very large for-

74. On the question of the division of labor in capital formation between the government and the private sector, see W. A. Lewis, *Report on Industrialization in the Gold Coast* (Accra: Government Printer, 1953), for an extensive analysis and the view that "there is no doubt in the writer's mind that the Gold Coast Government can do more for development by spending its money on expanding the public services, which are woefully inadequate, and on quadrupling that part of its agricultural services which relate to food production for the local market." Lewis foresaw that if the government did its job properly it would attract foreign capital which in turn would create Ghanaian capital via a demonstration effect. We might note as an incidental fact that the Watson Report felt that emphasis should be placed on cooperatives since "unbridled private enterprise would, at best, lay the foundation of future social strife."

75. The new strategy is contained in *Program of the Convention People's Party for Work and Happiness* (Accra: Government Printer, 1962) and in the plan itself, *The Seven-Year Development Plan, 1963/64 to 1969/70,* Office of the Planning Commission (Accra: Government Printer, 1964). See also Omaboe, "The Process of Planning," in *Contemporary Ghana.*

For an analysis of the major economic and political factors behind the change in strategy see B. Fitch and Mary Oppenheimer, *Ghana: End of an Illusion* (New York: Monthly Review Press, 1966); St. Clair Drake and Leslie Alexander Lacy, "Government versus the Unions: The Sekondi Takoradi Strike, 1961," in Givendalen M. Canter, ed., *Politics in Africa* (New York: Harcourt, Brace & World, 1966); Ann Seidman, *Economic Development in Ghana, 1951–65* (Ph.D. diss., University of Wisconsin, 1968); R. Geroud, *Nationalism and Development in Ghana* (New York: Praeger, 1969).

76. Kwame Nkrumah, *Africa Must Unite* (London: Heinemann, 1963), pp. 119–20.

eign corporations such as Kaiser, Parkinson Howard, and Unilever along the lines established in the Volta River Project. Since there were definite limits on the speed with which the government could expand, a transition period was envisaged, involving the coexistence of the public and private sectors. The state sector was to come to the fore, not through nationalization, but through more rapid growth.

After 1961 the government also inaugurated new systems of planning and control and began an all-out effort to develop manufacturing, to modernize agriculture, and to change the direction of trade away from Great Britain and toward other countries, particularly those of the socialist world. The private Ghanaian sector was no longer encouraged to enter medium- and large-scale manufacturing; instead, a number of state enterprises were created in industry, mining distribution, and shipping, to act as a "control" on foreign firms and to stimulate the growth of Ghanaian industrialization. Similarly, in agriculture a major emphasis was placed on state farms, youth farms, cooperatives, etc., as vehicles for modernization and mechanization.

It was because of this change in strategy that Nkrumah was blamed for the "sorry plight of the country that began independence from Britain in 1957 with large financial reserves, abundant resources and the brightest prospects of any new African nation." [77] Critics of the state enterprise approach argued that Nkrumah's new policies frustrated Ghanaian businessmen and frightened away foreign capital, thus killing the goose that laid the golden egg. They felt that private capital, both local and foreign, had far more potential than Nkrumah allowed for. We shall not try to evaluate the strength and weaknesses of Nkrumah's strategy of primary reliance on the state sector here. The issues are too current and too complex to allow brief summary. What we shall try to do instead is to set straight certain key elements of the period and to clear up some of the confusion surrounding Nkrumah's experiment. We merely wish to point out the obvious fact that there is a long gestation period between action and effect, and that many of the troubles during the second round were due to mistaken policies of the first round, just as the performance of the economy after Nkrumah is and will in large part be determined by what was done under his leadership. [78]

77. *New York Times,* 6 March 1966.
78. Geroud places great emphasis on the time factor in interpreting Nkrumah's "grandiose" schemes. He argues that the problem of national independence is neither to keep the colonial system going nor to improve it, but to change it. Nkrumah went slowly at first in order to win independence and

Stabilization Policy

The cycle of expansion and contraction after World War II can usefully be viewed in terms of the following simple relationship which emphasizes the import constraint on economic growth:

$$Y = \frac{1}{m}(X + F),$$

where Y is national income, X is exports, F is foreign borrowing, and m is the average propensity to import. The equation simply states that, for income to grow, one of three things must happen: the propensity to import must fall, exports must grow, or foreign borrowing must increase. The stylized facts of Ghana's postwar experience are that the propensity to import did not fall significantly, if at all, from 1950 to 1965, while the value of exports, which grew rapidly between 1945 and 1954, stagnated thereafter and in 1965 stood at its 1954 level (see Table 5.2). In other words, the economy failed during this period to create new industries or to expand its export earnings.[79] Major growth took place in the production of traditional exports; but the virtual doubling of the quantity exported between 1950 and 1964 was offset by a fall in the terms of trade, and the value of exports remained unchanged.

The path of income deviated significantly from the path of exports as a result of the government's countercyclical policy. The government ran surpluses from 1950 to 1954 and deficits from 1960 on (see

consolidate power. He then devoted all the resources he could command to changing the framework of the country by starting projects on all fronts, creating a new physical infrastructure, and introducing new ideas about where Ghana should go. This strategy involves the high risk that it will not bear fruit before the slack of the old system is exhausted. In fact this happened in Ghana partly because of the falling cocoa prices and partly because a structural change in an underdeveloped country is inherently wasteful and inefficient. Nonetheless the strategy was partially successful from Nkrumah's point of view because his incompleted projects provided the framework for the next round. The post-Nkrumah government has started from the structure Nkrumah created rather than from the colonial structure he inherited. To put this another way, no one would deny that because of Nkrumah Ghana is radically different from the Gold Coast or from other former British colonies in Africa.

79. We cannot go into the reasons for this failure here. We might note, however, that the government expenditure in the 1950s was often characterized by errors and misdirections similar to those described for the pre-1940 era. Agricultural policy was especially deficient. On industrial policy see Stanley Nicholson, *The Economy of Ghana with Special Reference to Government Strategy for Economic Development* (Ph.D. diss., Duke University, 1964).

Table 5.5: Government Revenue, Expenditure, Surplus, and Deficit in Constant (1953) Prices, 1945/46 to 1963/64

	Consolidated		Surplus/Deficit	
			Central government	
	Revenue	*Expenditure*	*only*	*Consolidated govt.*[a]
1945/46	15.0	11.1	2.1	3.9
1946/47	14.9	11.5	1.7	3.4
1947/48	46.4	15.1	0.4	31.4
1948/49	15.6	15.9	0.2	0.3
1949/50	45.9	20.0	4.9	25.9
1950/51	49.2	22.1	4.3	27.0
1951/52	41.2	25.0	15.1	16.3
1952/53	44.5	40.0	4.1	4.5
1953/54	58.0	52.2	2.3	5.8
1954/55	102.2	69.2	41.3	37.9
1955/56	72.4	89.3	5.4	−16.9
1956/57	50.8	77.5	−6.9	−26.7
1957/58	76.6	76.4	8.4	0.2
1958/59	89.3	101.0	5.6	−11.7
1959/60	81.4	112.3	−6.8	−30.9
1960/61	92.1	129.0	−28.2	−36.9
1961/62[b]	104.6	177.6	−60.8	−72.9
1962/63	88.9	157.7	−57.7	−68.8
1963/64[b]	131.4	170.9	−24.9	−37.4

[a] Consolidated equals central government plus Cocoa Marketing Board, plus railways and harbors, plus local government.
[b] Fifteen-month period.

Table 5.5). And F was large and negative in the initial period, dwindled to zero, and became large and positive in the later period. Imports therefore rose steadily through the 1950s and reached their turning point only after 1960. The government's countercyclical policy to some extent confused the underlying trends in the economy and made it appear that the economic difficulties began after 1960, whereas in fact the trouble began in 1954. The rapid expansion of the government sector during the 1950s created an atmosphere of dynamism and progress that was in a sense unrealistic. The government stretched a four-year boom (1950–54) in cocoa prices out to a ten-year boom, but the development thrust did not prepare the economy for the fall in cocoa prices and was instead the prelude to a crisis. The growth of the national income and the seeming prosperity reflected the multiplier effect of the growth in government spending, not an increase in the productive capacity of the economy.

In fact, much of the capital formation of the period had low productivity, at least in the short run.

By 1961 the shortcomings of the "decade of development" were evident. The government was running a continuous deficit, exports were stagnating, international reserves were falling, and little progress had been made toward the introduction of new economic activities or new methods. One possible approach to the problem would have been to trim down the state sector and to allow the private sector more room for maneuvering and more funds for expansion. Nkrumah chose to move in the opposite direction. Instead of retrenching, he plunged ahead, creating new instruments of planning and control and initiating numerous state enterprises. This further squeezed the private sector and strained the economy as a whole. To critics, even those who agreed with Nkrumah's emphasis on the state sector, the initiation of ambitious new programs at the very time when the slack had been used up and exports and revenue were stagnating, represented an unwillingness to face up to economic realities. To supporters it was the very difficulty of the times, representing as they did the effect of past errors, that induced a sense of urgency and impatience and the conviction that it was necessary to bring about a radical change as quickly and as forcefully as possible.[80]

80. Omaboe, *Contemporary Ghana,* p. 460, expressed the view of the planners on the necessity for choice:

> The objective of rapid economic development, as interpreted by the Government, has on a number of occasions been in conflict with the principle of foregoing less important alternatives which form the basis of all planning decisions . . . In Ghana the politicians are always ahead of the civil servants and the planners in the general consideration and implementation of economic and social projects. This has meant that almost all important projects have had to be initiated by the politicians who, on many occasions, have taken their decisions and committed the nation to a certain course of action before the technicians were consulted.

For the other side, Nkrumah in the Dawn Broadcast, 8 April 1961 (Accra: Government Printer, 1961) argued:

> It amazes me that up to the present many civil servants do not realize that we are living in a revolutionary era. This Ghana, which has lost so much time serving colonial masters, cannot afford to be tied down to archaic snailpace methods of work which obstruct expeditious progress. We have lost so much time that we need to do in ten years what has taken others a hundred years to accomplish. Civil servants, therefore, must develop a new orientation, a sense of mission and urgency, to enable them to eliminate all tendencies towards red tapeism, bureaucracy and waste. Civil servants must use their initiative to make the civil service an effective instrument in the rapid development of Ghana.

There was also the conflict on the nature of "socialist" development in

In the ensuing crisis, the problems stemming from the new strategy and the problems stemming from stagnant export conditions became hopelessly entangled. To finance the new program the government increased taxes, increased borrowings from abroad, and imposed import controls. Each of these tactics created its own difficulties.[81] Attempts to raise revenue met with very stiff resistance from all sectors. In the early 1950s it had been possible for the government to increase its revenue enormously by holding down the price paid to cocoa farmers. This was politically feasible (though not without its difficulties) because at that time the gross national product was expanding and it was possible for everyone to benefit. In the 1960s the economy was stagnating, and the increase of the government and associated sectors had to take place at the price of a decline in standards for other sectors of the community. In addition, and predictably, the new forms of taxation were ineffectively administered and at times actually reduced rather than increased revenue.

In short, there was great political pressure to increase private income and not to reduce it. The expansion of consumption in the 1950s created expectations that it would continue. These expectations could only be fulfilled if the new government program had a very quick payoff or if the government could have borrowed abroad for their gestation period. For a time the government was given a certain amount of room to maneuver by the accumulated foreign exchange reserves that had resulted from the very conservative monetary and fiscal policy of the colonial administration of earlier years. It was also able to do considerable borrowing abroad, though much was in the form of suppliers' credit, carrying high interest charges and short repayment periods. These sources were quickly used up; by 1965 the foreign exchange reserves were depleted, and the sums needed to repay the debts stood at alarming heights.

To meet the balance of payments problem, the government made the crucial mistake of instituting a system of import quotas while still running the deficits that stimulated purchasing power in the

Ghana. See J. H. Mensah's presidential address to the Economic Society in 1964 and the reaction to it in *The Spark*.

81. A. Killick, "The Possibilities of Economic Control," in *Contemporary Ghana*; David Dinon, "Fiscal and Monetary Policies in Relation to the Seven-Year Development Plan of Ghana," *Economic Bulletin of Ghana* 7, no. 4 (1963); Robert W. Norris, "On Inflation in Ghana," and Douglas A. Scott, "External Debt Management in a Developing Country," in Tom J. Faner, ed., *Financing African Development* (Cambridge: M.I.T. Press, 1965).

economy. The predictable results of this attempt to keep supply constant, while shifting demand outward, were shortages and price increases. The government then responded by instituting a system of price controls, while continuing to run deficits. It thus continued to generate demand pressure while trying to prevent an increase in prices. Leaving aside the fact that both import and price controls were administered inefficiently through lack of experience, the situation was impossible and was bound to break down eventually. Black markets, corruption, and an erosion of the import control system resulted.[82] Clearly there was no way of closing the deficit in the balance of payments without closing the deficit in the government account. It was the failure to realize this fact, more than anything else, that led to the great wastes and failures of the 1960s and the end of the new strategy.

THE FUTURE

No sooner had Nkrumah gone, when the *Economist* was prepared to revive the myth of the "model" colony and to view Ghana again as a hopeful experiment.

> Their program is hopeful because it is not grandiose, and Ghana has now acquired a new, if different, kind of importance. It could just conceivably emerge as a model among developing nations with a genuine, working democracy, rooted in a balanced economy.

Such a view is superficial and tends to obscure the basic issues of Ghana's economic predicament. The development program did not create the weaknesses of the Ghanaian economy; it merely exposed them. Whatever one's judgment about the errors in Nkrumah's strategy, one should not allow the frenzied and frantic nature of his last years in power to obscure the fundamental fact that colonialism created not a model economy but a distorted and retarded one. If the experience of the last twenty years shows the difficulties of changing the colonial economic structure, the experience of the last seventy shows the necessity for so doing.

What of the future? The issue of the role of the state is still to be

---

82. The system of import controls seems to have been especially severe on small-scale African businessmen, who had great difficulty complying with bureaucratic restrictions.

resolved. The first post-Nkrumah steps went toward dismantling the state enterprises, but the overall direction of the present government's policy is far from fully determined. The private sector is still weak, foreign business is still suspect, and the state sector, greatly enlarged and strengthened during the last fifteen years, contains a number of pressures for growth, not the least of which are the young men who entered the service in the independence period and agreed with large parts of Nkrumah's program. Given these conditions, one can foresee three possibilities for Ghana.

First, the economy may collapse and alternate between civil war and military dictatorship.

Second, and more hopefully, it may be possible to create a viable economy on the present base. Though Ghana has many financial problems, its "real" base is very sound, and if its international financial problems can be resolved, there is considerable potential for growth. It has a relatively well-developed infrastructure and a well-trained and educated labor force. The cocoa industry still provides a strong underpinning, and the Volta Dam complex forms a growing point for industrial development. With foreign aid and investment and an outward-looking policy, Ghana could probably develop into a thriving "model" economy. Development, however, would be largely in the coastal regions. Even under very optimistic projections, the modern sector could not absorb the increases in population, and the majority of the population would be excluded. A growing dualism within the country and between Ghana and her neighbors would develop.

A third alternative would be an attempt to develop the economy as a whole. This would require the mobilization of the entire population and the direction of a high proportion of effort to the rural areas and to the bottom two-thirds of urban society.[83] Throughout Ghana's history the rural areas have provided the surplus for the mostly unproductive efforts of the government and urban sector. Considerable reserves of energy still exist in the population at large, which could be mobilized for increased production, especially if the revenues were directed toward them rather than away from them. However this path is a highly unlikely one to be chosen because it would in-

---

83. Statistics on the income distribution of Ghana are not yet available. But statistics from other countries suggest that the top 10 percent of households receive about one-third of the total income and the top 40 percent about two-thirds.

volve radical changes in the administrative and political structure of the country.

The crucial question is how the new generation will view the alternatives. The Seven-Year Development Plan noted that "the young people for whom jobs must be found every year for the next fifteen years have already been born. Every year a given number of them will come forward to join the labour force. This cannot be postponed by any law or policy." The generations that created the political economy of Ghanaian independence and are now in positions of leadership were formed by the depression, World War II, and the cold war. The coming generation has had an entirely different experience. Its political economy will also be different. Hopefully, it will not place much value on the development planning from *above* that has characterized most of Ghana's experience up until now.

Comments by Gustav Ranis

Hymer's interesting and perceptive foray into the economic history of Ghana focuses on the role of government in three major periods of development: the period of initial exposure to international trade (1900–20), the 1920–26 period under the Guggisberg Plan, and the "late colonial" *cum* Nkrumah period between 1945 and 1965.

The oft-repeated theme that dominates Hymer's analysis of each of the three phases is essentially that whatever development occurred took place in spite of, rather than because of, government action. To whit, in the first period, the government supported gold (and rubber) while cocoa turned out to be the real winner. In the second period, when cocoa was (finally) supported, the technical advice provided the farmers turned out to be bad. In both periods the allocation of overhead capital was directed to the facilitation of specific exports, not the generation of internal production and trade. Finally, in the early postwar years of the third period, the effort to make some last minute amends via increased, if helter-skelter, government development spending proved to be a case of too little, much too late.

Hymer's case for greater faith in the inherent wisdom and the productive and innovative capacities of the indigenous capitalist class, so often "sat upon" and thwarted by a combination of government malfeasance and nonfeasance, is ably demonstrated here. And the point is well taken. Development theorists and practitioners are increasingly coming to the conclusion that the mainsprings of sustained growth are to be found only in the unleashing of these same private energies Hymer refers to.

Unfortunately, however, the analysis of the specific Ghanaian experience becomes clouded, at least in this reviewer's eyes, by the author's apparent need to introduce a second—and, it turns out, really dominant—theme, namely that intervention by colonial governments is invariably bad, while that of postcolonial governments is likely to be constructive.

On the first of these propositions, one can argue, at least as effectively as Hymer, that colonial investment policy has been badly misdirected relative to what might have been, but not necessarily relative to the total absence of such investments being deployed in Ghana. The impact of a mineral export-oriented colonial railroad network, for example, was undoubtedly extremely limited; but the existence of such infrastructure at the time of independence was just as undoubtedly a considerable plus, both in terms of its direct developmental contribution and in terms of the further foreign and domestic investment it attracted; and similarly with respect to health and educational investments, the creation of an unusually competent civil service, etc. There was, after all, more in the balance that made the "dignified" departure of 1951 possible—and contributed to the postindependence links between Ghana and the United Kingdom—than the vaunted British "stiff upper lip."

On the second proposition, the postindependence Nkrumah regime gets off very lightly, especially in terms of any examination of its treatment of those same indigenous African capitalists about whom Hymer is rightly so concerned. The much more pervasive interventionism of this period—first in terms of the mushrooming size of the public sector financed out of the wartime sterling balances and good cocoa years, and then in terms of ever tighter controls on the entire economy, when these balances ran out and cocoa prices declined—is hardly touched upon. Ghana's mediocre development performance since independence is attributed not to poor public policies but to forces outside of the country, mainly the delayed impact of colonialism. In other words, the real culprit continues to be the heavy hand of colonial history rather than the substantial suffocation of indigenous private initiative, especially in agriculture, by the Nkrumah regime, even before 1965.

It is of the utmost importance, it seems to me, for the analyst to try to distinguish between colonial and postcolonial development goals, on the one hand, and the tools—both public/private sector ownership mixes and government policies toward the private sector —that may be deployed to achieve those goals, on the other. One can rightly be critical of the colonial pattern of investment, production, and trade from the vantage point of a postindependence welfare function; and one can equally rightly be impressed with the postcolonial government's efforts to restructure this pattern and reallocate the resources being generated. But this is a long way from asserting that colonial governments were more willing to disregard the limits of their own capabilities in moving the system toward their particular goals than were postcolonial governments. It might, in fact, be considerably easier to document the very opposite case—even if we acknowledge Hymer's interesting point that colonial laissez faire was combined with a pronounced anticommercialism among colonial civil servants.

All in all, this is an instructive and provocative paper. It suffers from too much polemics on colonialism and from inadequate use of the empirical materials, which are (loosely) appended, for a serious comparison of the efficiency and size of the development effort in the various phases of Ghanaian development.

6

The Role of Government in the Resource Transfer and Resource Allocation Processes: The Chilean Nitrate Sector, 1880–1930

BY MARKOS MAMALAKIS

*If the arguments for "key industries" are worth anything
they apply with immense force to the nitrate industry.*[1]

*Nitrate has . . . permitted the inscription of
the word* waste *. . . into the growing list of national vices.*[2]

The addition of the North's nitrate sector to Chile after 1882 revolutionized the structure of the economy, the society, and the political system. The War of the Pacific, which involved a confrontation between Chile on one side and Peru and Bolivia on the other, led to the transfer of the desert provinces of Tarapacá and Antofagasta—the Great North, as it was known after 1882—to Chile. Chilean ownership of the world's single source of natural sodium nitrate, an event almost equally important as the achievement of independence, marked the beginning of a new era. Nitrate and the North dominated economic life for half a century by becoming the primary, if not the single, source of government revenues; by generating a vast resource surplus; and by contributing most, if not all, of the country's exports.[3]

1. J. R. Partington, and L. H. Parker, *The Nitrogen Industry* (London: Constable and Co., 1922), p. 19. This is a highly informative and technical analysis of the nitrogen industry viewed from the English standpoint immediately after World War I.

2. Jorge Vidal, *Veinte años después la tragedia del salitre* (Santiago, Chile: Imprenta Universo, 1933), p. 13. This and all subsequent translations from the Spanish are mine.

3. Export proceeds more than quintupled between 1880 and 1916 with nitrate revenues increasing more than tenfold. See Markos Mamalakis, "Historical Statistics of Chile, 1840–1967," mimeographed (New Haven, Economic Growth Center, 1967). Table II Ela2, pp. A542–43.

Chile had an important export sector even before 1880. The acquisition of the North, however, meant a radical change in the size and structure of the export sector. The size multiplied,[4] and the structure changed from one that included agricultural products, silver, and copper, to one both dominated by and dependent upon nitrate.[5] Furthermore, the relationship of Central Chile to the North was reversed. Chile before 1880 was a talent exporter, as its entrepreneurs —Ossa, Puelma, and others—discovered and developed the nitrate riches in what were then Peruvian and Bolivian territories; after 1880 it was a talent importer, as control of an increasing share of nitrate *oficinas* was taken over by British, German, Yugoslav, and, later, American capitalists. Also, before 1880 Chile exported capital and received large repatriated profits from the Peruvian and Bolivian nitrate sectors. Before 1880 the national product exceeded the domestic product. After 1880 the situation was reversed and has remained unchanged ever since: domestic product has exceeded national product and Chile, instead of having a positive net balance, has had a vast negative net balance in its payments to factors of production Abroad.

The bonanza in the natural nitrate industry resulted from two technological revolutions. Alfred Nobel's discoveries, which made nitrate the key input for explosives and nitrogen an indispensable ingredient of war, started the first technological revolution and the rising demand for Chilean nitrate. Natural sodium nitrate entered its golden age, however, as a result of the second revolution, which, following Justus Liebig's theories, demonstrated the efficiency of cer-

4. Nitrate exports contributed more than 70 percent of export proceeds almost every year between 1891 and 1916, ibid.

5. The literature concerning the nitrate sector and its relation to government is vast. The following publications, however, provide almost all the basic information needed to understand and analyze the "nitrate issue" in Chile. This essay does not cover the "nitrogen problem," which refers to the separate and more general issue of the global demand and supply of both synthetic and natural nitrogen. Ministerio de Hacienda, Sección Salitre, *Antecedentes sobre la industria salitrera* (Santiago: Imprenta Universo, 1925), pp. 1–34—this is an excellent collection of statistics on nitrate and iodine covering the period 1880–1924; Enrique Kaempffer, *La industria del salitre y del yodo 1907–1914* (Santiago: Imprenta Cervantes, 1914), pp. 1–1230; Miguel Cruchaga, *Salitre y guano* (Madrid: Editorial Reus, S.A., 1929); Santiago Marin Vicuña, *El salitre de Chile 1830–1930* (Santiago: Editorial Nascimiento, 1931), pp. 1–15 —this publication contains useful statistical information; Vidal, *Veinte años después la tragedia del salitre*; José Gassiot Llorens, *La lucha por los nitratos,* (Barcelona: I. G. Seix y Barral Hnos, S.A., 1944), pp. 1–60—this monograph explains the beginnings of the War of the Pacific.

tain minerals as fertilizers and, by determining the fertilizer content of sodium nitrate, turned nitrogen into the most important instrument of increasing food supplies and thus of maintaining peace.[6]

Within Chile, nitrate permitted a massive transformation of the economic structure through its unparalleled income size and extensive linkages. Internationally, nitrate revolutionized the supply of food by transforming the world's capacity to produce it. Thus, "if the arguments for 'key industries' are worth anything they apply with immense force to the nitrate industry." [7] The same source held that without nitrogen starvation of the human race would be imminent[8] and "without . . . Chile the Allies would speedily have been reduced to impotence" during World War I.[9] The new dimensions of war and peace led to a century-long nitrate bonanza. The last fifty years, 1880–1930, cover the apogee as well as the demise of natural sodium nitrate.

The end of the Chilean nitrate boom was almost as swift as the beginning, and technical progress was again the force behind it. The prospects of starvation and defeat in war, should the Chilean deposits be depleted or inaccessible, forced the Western powers, beginning with Germany, to develop a cheap synthetic nitrate. By the time of the Great Depression, the West's quest for efficient functioning in war and in peace had made it independent of the exhaustible and diminishing Chilean nitrate supplies.

The generally accepted view is that the nitrate sector's most important impact came from its massive government revenue contribution. As Table 6.1 shows, the percentage of ordinary revenues originating in nitrate and iodine production increased from 4.7 percent in 1880 to 28.21 percent in 1885, 48.90 percent in 1900, and an all-time high of 60.16 percent in the war year of 1915.[10]

6. See Llorens, p. 17.

7. Partington and Parker, *The Nitrogen Industry,* p. viii. The authors go on to say, "Without nitric acid everything else is utterly useless. Even aeroplanes are futile without bombs."

8. "Varying estimates of the possible life of the Chilean nitre-beds have been given. The most reliable put this at from one to three hundred years. When the nitre-beds are worked out, and no other sources of combined nitrogen become available in the meantime, the outlook, as the late Sir William Grookes pointed out, is simply starvation for the human race." Ibid., p. 18.

9. "Still another claim for winning the war might be advanced on behalf of Chile." This and the quotation in the text are from ibid., p. 19.

10. For a detailed breakdown of government revenues for the 1857–1924 period the reader is referred to Markos Mamalakis, "Historical Statistics of Chile," Table II G2a2, pp. A698–700.

Table 6.1: Historical Statistics Concerning Nitrate
(Calculations in gold pesos of 18 pence)

	Nitrate exports (thous. of Q.M.)	Iodine exports (thous. of klg.)	Duties paid by nitrate & iodine (in thous. of pesos)	Ordinary revenues of nation (in thous. of pesos)	Percentage contributed by nitrate & iodine
	(1)	(2)	(3)	(4)	(5)
1880	2,261	87.9	2,293.0	48,736.8	4.71
1881	3,581	200.1	9,759.7	66,991.0	15.25
1882	4,893	263.9	16,306.6	80,592.6	20.23
1883	5,848	220.9	19,806.6	86,653.7	22.86
1884	5,497	218.2	19,104.2	67,765.1	28.19
1885	4,297	256.8	14,386.8	50,984.8	28.21
1886	4,528	175.7	11,700.6	49,424.3	23.67
1887	7,128	76.2	17,893.5	62,459.9	28.64
1888	7,842	91.4	26,129.4	73,182.0	35.70
1889	9,214	201.4	31,705.6	80,871.3	39.21
1890	10,263	219.7	35,048.7	72,784.0	48.15
1891	8,917	424.0	14,727.4	58,237.1	25.28
1892	7,978	513.8	25,554.8	64,311.7	39.73
1893	9,454	597.0	32,065.4	63,876.9	50.19
1894	10,940	326.3	37,349.8	63,611.7	58.71
1895	12,372	180.2	43,959.9	78,331.5	56.12
1896	11,047	207.2	31,394.7	78,784.8	39.84
1897	11,763	229.5	36,459.2	77,352.3	47.13
1898	12,916	241.0	44,450.9	76,715.7	57.94
1899	13,958	307.6	47,387.0	93,885.0	50.47
1900	14,521	326.4	50,142.8	102,532.3	48.90
1901	12,585	283.3	44,158.8	92,914.0	47.53
1902	13,829	258.8	45,330.2	90,886.1	49.87
1903	14,563	399.5	49,549.0	111,689.0	44.36
1904	14,988	465.6	50,886.6	107,716.1	47.24
1905	16,991	572.1	57,333.1	119,476.0	47.99
1906	17,274	409.5	60,164.0	135,123.1	44.53
1907	16,538	259.8	56,139.0	142,911.6	39.28
1908	20,502	358.8	69,120.9	126,450.9	54.66
1909	21,336	499.6	71,876.2	135,909.1	52.89
1910	23,339	589.9	80,392.5	156,654.3	51.32
1911	24,460	460.2	83,519.1	167,062.5	49.99
1912	24,907	466.1	85,040.8	177,445.4	47.91
1913	27,351	436.9	90,683.6	186,099.9	48.73
1914	18,452	489.0	65,694.3	124,167.6	52.91
1915	20,204	708.9	68,199.2	113,355.2	60.16
1916	29,756	1,323.1	101,954.1	169,545.3	60.13
1917	27,711	759.5	107,660.9	213,470.2	50.43
1918	29,835	907.7	111,745.4	248,772.5	44.84
1919	9,372	243.2	30,488.3	124,699.2	24.37
1920	27,725	350.1	105,618.4	212,724.2	40.97
1921	11,286	534.1	42,197.6	125,893.9	33.54
1922	13,008	244.8	39,185.9	125,706.4	31.35
1923	22,843	471.1	76,411.3	187,180.1	40.61
1924	24,204	597.8	79,621.3	200,952.4	39.80
Total	661,884	17,850	2,240,517.9	5,191,928.9	41.85

Table 6.1: *continued*

	No. of oficinas functioning (6)	Number of employees (7)	Product in metric tons (8)	Price of nitrate at Chilean port (excluding export duty) (9)
1880				12.38
1881				11.02
1882				9.76
1883				8.39
1884				7.55
1885				7.14
1886		4,534		7.67
1887				6.99
1888				6.30
1889				6.93
1890		13,060		6.10
1891				6.13
1892				5.80
1893				6.75
1894	51	18,092	1,093.802	6.50
1895	53	22,495	1,307.706	6.79
1896	53	19,345	1,138.919	6.24
1897	42	16,727	1,186.730	6.52
1898	46	15,955	1,314.355	4.48
1899	48	19,914	1,440.391	3.46
1900	51	19,672	1,507.788	5.28
1901	66	20,264	1,328.664	5.84
1902	80	24,538	1,349.300	5.94
1903	72	24,445	1,485.279	6.30
1904	76		1,559.091	6.48
1905	90		1,854.605	7.05
1906	96		1,822.144	7.21
1907	110	39,653	1,846.036	8.44
1908	113	40,825	1,970.974	7.82
1909	102	37,792	2,110.961	7.33
1910	102	43,533	2,465.415	6.30
1911	107	43,876	2,421.023	6.44
1912	118	47,800	2,585.850	6.58
1913	127	53,161	2,772.254	7.24
1914	137	43,979	2,403.356	6.55
1915	116	45,506	1,755.291	5.82
1916	123	53,470	2,912.893	6.15
1917	129	56,981	2,859.303	7.20
1918	125	46,245	1,703.240	8.96
1919	97		2,523.458	10.40
1920	101	33,876	1,309.685	
1921	53	25,462	1,071.041	
1922				
1923				
1924				

Note: Production and export figures for any particular year differ, often significantly. Accumulation or decumulation of stocks is the primary cause accounting for the difference.

Sources: Column 1, Ministerio de Hacienda, Sección Salitre, *Antecedentes sobre la industria salitrera* (Santiago, Imprenta Universo, 1925), pp. 1–118. This column's

In a way, however, the impact was far more profound than that reflected by the increased export-import tax revenues, higher social overhead investment, and a reduced tax burden on agriculture. By forcing Chile into the mainstream of modern capitalism and placing it in direct contact with Europe and the United States, the North's nitrate sector brought to Chile most of the advantages and problems of modern growth. Central Chile, henceforth to be referred to as the Center, acquired not only a veritable gold mine but also all the hazards of defending it and the responsibility of making proper use of the flow of riches. The spectacular technological change experienced in the nitrate and, later, copper sectors, the unprecedented penetration of foreign capital into Chile, and the responsibilities of using vast fortunes created more problems than the Chilean government could handle.

To summarize, then, Chileans had to fight against neighboring Bolivia and Peru to obtain control of nitrate; they had to fight against nature to conquer the inhospitable desert and pampas and extract their "gold"; they had to fight against the foreign capitalists who wanted to reap most of the gains; and, finally, they had to fight against the "Norwegian," "German," and other varieties of synthetic nitrogen. The first was a military, the second a human, the third an economico-political, and the last a technological battle. Chile won the first two but lost the others either partially or completely. Insofar as this experience could serve as a lesson for the future, it would as a "learning by suffering" process.

The aim of the present essay is to illustrate some facets of the role of government in the process of economic development by combining a detailed examination of the nitrate sector with selected, key aspects of the resource transfer and resource allocation processes. The essay is divided into two parts. In the first we present and deal with those aspects of the resource transfer and allocation processes that are considered relevant to the examination of the Chilean nitrate era. In the second part we present the statistical and historical in-

information for the 1880–1924 period was obtained from p. 13. Columns 2–5, ibid., p. 21. Columns 6–8, ibid., p. 57. Column 9, J. R. Partington and L. H. Parker, *The Nitrogen Industry* (London, Constable and Co., 1922), p. 77. This column provides the average value or price of nitrate (pounds per long ton) at Chilean ports, excluding export duty, ocean freight, insurance commission, etc. The level and percentage change of nitrate prices in European ports have varied significantly from the Chilean port prices, depending on the magnitude of freight costs. The spectacular rise of nitrate prices in Europe during World War I was largely the result of the rise in freight and insurance rates.

formation needed to measure, analyze, and understand the resource flows described in the first part, discussing throughout the specific issues relating to the role of government in the historical context of the 1880–1930 period. In view of the strong emphasis on the nitrate sector, the reader can expect a larger than normal dosage of discussion of nitrate and related issues.

GOVERNMENT AND THE RESOURCE TRANSFER AND RESOURCE ALLOCATION PROCESSES

It is frequently argued that the economist's knowledge of the growth process is incomplete because too many noneconomic variables are not or cannot be considered. This section has the limited objective of attempting to improve our knowledge of the economic aspects of the growth process by presenting an analytical framework that is related to the theory of capital accumulation and is pertinent to the examination of Chilean growth in general and the nitrate sector in particular.

Growth depends in part on capital accumulation which, in turn, is determined by the resource transfer and resource allocation processes. The resource transfer process, which encompasses the actions required to generate and transfer a surplus of resources out of a sector, is thus comprised of a resource surplus generation and a resource surplus appropriation (or division) process. A surplus is generated (or exists) in a sector if output exceeds the subsistence wage bill.[11]

The average resource surplus per worker in a sector is defined as the excess of output over subsistence consumption. It has two components. One component is generated because workers receive a wage rate equal to the marginal physical product (MPP) of labor as determined on an economywide basis,[12] rather than a wage rate equaling the higher MPP in the sector where they are employed. This component is equal to that part of wage income which labor does not receive because the wage rate is below the MPP in the sector. The second component of the surplus is equal to the combined income

---

11. This surplus can exist even in absence of disguised unemployment.

12. A surplus would arise automatically if the wage rate were equal to the institutional one and, for technological or other reasons, the MPP exceeded it. See John C. H. Fei and Gustav Ranis, *Development of the Labor Surplus Economy: Theory and Policy* (Homewood, Ill.: Richard D. Irwin, 1964), pp. 7–110, for an analysis of related concepts connected with the notion of disguised unemployment.

shares of capital, land, and factors of production earning quasi rents.

The resource appropriation process encompasses the actions leading to the division of the surplus between national and foreign factors of production and is one facet of the resource distribution process. The resource distribution process has three facets depending on whether gross revenues, value added, or the resource surplus are to be divided. The gross-revenues distribution aspect, which relates to the division of gross proceeds between Chile and the rest of the world, is important because it largely determines the country's gross foreign-exchange proceeds. The value-added distribution aspect, which relates to the division of income between national and foreign factors of production, involves primarily the division of income between foreign capitalists and Chilean labor and government. Finally, the resource-surplus distribution aspect involves a confrontation between Chilean and foreign capitalists in nitrate on the one side and the Chilean government on the other.

The following three identity equations define the three facets of the distribution problem:

$$R = R_F + R_N \tag{6.1}$$

where R stands for gross revenue or expenditures and the subscripts F and N stand for foreign and national respectively;

$$Y = Y_F + Y_N \tag{6.2}$$

where Y stands for value added; and finally,

$$S = S_F + S_N \tag{6.3}$$

where S stands for the surplus generated in the nitrate sector. The third facet stated in equation 6.3 describes the resource appropriation problem. The national surplus equals the surplus accruing to government as well as to Chilean capitalists, once the resource transfer has taken place.[13]

The resource transfer problem can be appropriately identified with the saving problem of conventional theory. However, there are some basic differences. Our notion refers to sectors, which are impersonal agents, while conventional saving theory is concerned with the volition of a personal agent, namely the income group or factor of production. Furthermore, the resource transfer problem aims to break down the process by which sectorial savings are generated into a

13. That is, how surplus is transferred from a sector to national factors of production.

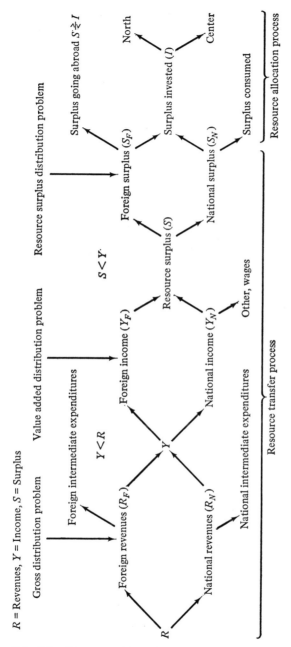

Figure 6.1: The Resource Transfer and Allocation Processes

series of interrelated steps and to identify the factors shaping the process of surplus generation and allocation. It is very difficult to say whether the saving or the resource transfer problem is the more general one; it can only be stated here that our present analysis is essential to an understanding of the growth process in Chile. Figure 6.1 shows the various steps involved in the resource transfer problem.

As Figure 6.1 indicates, even though a sector, such as mining, is able and willing to release an investable surplus, only part will accrue to Chileans. Furthermore, once this first decision to save is made, a second decision to invest or consume has to be made by the recipient of the surplus, be it the government or others.

For purposes of the present essay it is assumed that the primary function of the government is to promote growth. Within this growth-promoting role the key subfunctions of the government are the resource generation, division, and allocation functions. These are presented in greater detail below.

1. The resource generation function has three major aspects: the discovery of resources, the utilization of resources, and the most efficient exploitation of resources. As regards the nitrate sector, the responsibilities of government could range from locating nitrate fields to pursuing research that leads to new uses or new sources of nitrate or mineral wealth.

2. The revenue, income, and surplus division function has the following component functions of: (a) dividing these three magnitudes between Chile and Abroad equitably and profitably; (b) dividing these magnitudes between three regions, i.e. the North, the Center, and Abroad, equitably and profitably; and (c) dividing nitrate income between land, labor, capital, quasi-rent recipients, and the government equitably and profitably.

Function (a) refers to the intercountry distribution of resources, function (b) reflects the interregional distribution, and function (c) pertains to the factor income distribution. The term "profitably" is used here to mean establishment of maximum production incentives. These incentives have an international, regional, and factor-of-production component. They are interrelated and interdependent but distinct. The term "equitably" is used in an attempt to introduce the intangible, social aspect of growth that, in an economy with imperfect markets such as that of Chile, is an indispensable complement to the strict profitability or incentive aspect.

In the present framework, the stabilization role of governmental policy is an integral part of the intertemporal component of all three aspects of resource distribution.

The revenue-raising role of government, in this framework, is part of the overall income distribution function. The resource division directly affects the relative importance of the private versus the public sector, foreign versus national resource shares, the income shares of factors of production, and the relative earnings of the developed West, the North, and the Center.

3. The allocation function has two components.

a. The regional allocation component. The resource division function determines *who* receives the three magnitudes described under (2) above but not *how* or *where* they will be spent. The regional allocation function concerns itself with the direct allocation of government expenditures on a regional basis and with setting up the rules to be followed by noncentral government and private entities in allocating their resources on a regional basis.

b. The investment-consumption allocation function deals with the direct division of government expenditures between consumption and investment, and with establishing an institutional framework within which the noncentral government and private entities are free and able to divide their income between saving and consumption and to convert saving into investment.

The solution of the resource allocation problem is determined by the presence of investment opportunities and the availability of capital goods.

The resource allocation process involves examination of the following alternatives for the use of surplus: (1) for government investment, (2) to increase the income and consumption of persons in subaverage productivity sectors, (3) to augment income of particular sectors above their own marginal productivity and to raise economywide marginal productivity standards, and (4) to finance private investment.

The contribution of government to economic growth within the present framework can be judged in terms of its policies affecting all three angles of the transfer process and the allocation process. It is the basic theme of this essay that the government's most important role in connection with the crucial nitrate sector is to discover, develop, introduce, and apply equitably those rules of the game that lead to an optimum use of nitrate resources for Chilean economic development. Keeping the above concepts in mind, we turn to the

measurement and analysis of the resource flow generated by the
nitrate sector.

The nitrate output in the North was divided, if the regional destina-
tion of the gross nitrate revenues is used as a criterion, into three
parts: one accruing to the North, another to the Center of Chile,
and a third going Abroad. This nitrate revenue partition was almost
identical to a parallel one involving a division of the North's income
among foreign capitalists, labor in the North, and the government in
Chile's Center.

Nitrate revenues can also be subdivided into those that covered
expenditures Abroad, which consisted primarily of payments for intermediate products and to foreign factors, and those that covered national expenditures, which were composed of payments for intermediate products and labor, and the nitrate resource surplus appropriated
by the Chilean government and capitalists.

The government's de jure nitrate growth policy can be only conjectured in retrospect. From a narrow point of view the government's
de facto nitrate taxation policy seemed to have had as its primary
objective the acquisition by the government of the lion's share of
the nitrate-generated resource surplus. From a broader point of view
the government's taxation policy and other actions suggest that its
primary objective was, within our framework and terminology, to
increase, as much as possible, the Center's share in the North's revenues, and that its secondary objective was to increase the joint share
of the North and the Center of Chile. In this and the following sections an attempt will be made to measure these different flows.

Total revenues from nitrate exports between 1880 and 1924 were
in the neighborhood of 6,900 million gold pesos of 18 pence. Total
nitrate and iodine export duties during the same period amounted
to 2,241 million gold pesos of 18 pence. According to these figures
government revenues absorbed an average of 33 percent of the value
of nitrate exports.[14]

14. Export proceeds refer strictly to nitrate, while tax revenues refer to
both nitrate and iodine export duties. To make the two figures more comparable, the value of iodine exports would have to be added to the nitrate
exports. As a result, the ratio of tax revenues to export proceeds should be
slightly below the 33 percent value listed here.

The remaining 66–67 percent of nitrate export revenues was divided between the posttax cost of production and the profit share. A cost estimate presented in *Antecedentes sobre la industria salitrera*[15] suggests that the export duty was approximately equal to 50 percent of the total cost of production, defined to include the export tax, or, in other words, that it had the same value as the posttax cost of production.[16] It can be deduced from this information[17] that another 33 percent of nitrate export revenues, i.e. the same share as that of taxes, was allocated for the cost of production. It also follows that the remaining one-third of export revenues was the posttax income share of foreign and Chilean capitalists.

Although the total nitrate product can be rather neatly divided into three equal shares, i.e. taxes, net profits, and cost of production, it is not possible to divide it as easily into the three flows accruing to the Center, the North, and Abroad.

The Resource Flow Abroad and the Share of Foreign Capital

We start with a more detailed examination of the flow Abroad, which has been the single most important source of controversy concerning nitrate, the North, and the role of government.[18]

Since only part of the capital invested in nitrate was foreign, the share of nitrate revenues that left Chile in the form of profits must have been less than the 33 percent share of nitrate profits in these revenues. Table 6.2 gives the export share of the nitrate companies by nationality of the producer in 1901. A rather conservative estimate would place repatriated profits and capital at approximately 22 percent of nitrate revenues, or about two-thirds of the share of profits.

15. Ministerio de Hacienda, *Antecedentes sobre la industria salitrera,* p. 30, with no reference to particular year. It is likely that the estimate was for some time around 1925, the date of publication of the document.

16. The cost of production per metric quintal of nitrate was 119.8623d, which included 61.1520 pence in export tax. Ibid.

17. This estimate of the relationship between the export duty and the cost of production is consistent with numerous but fragmented data found in the various publications cited in this essay.

18. In the present discussion of the nitrate sector we do not make use of the enclave sector concept which has been rather popular. Rather than talk about an enclave economy we refer to the links between the export sector and the rest of the economy and the links between the North and the Center. As a whole I prefer to deal with the framework of a resource-rich sector and the rest of the economy instead of trying to fit the Chilean experience into a not necessarily relevant jacket.

Table 6.2: Nitrate Export Shares by Nationality of Producer, 1901

	Percentage of shares
English, 48 oficinas	55
Chilean, 11 oficinas	15
German, 12 oficinas	14
Spanish, 8 oficinas	10
Other nationalities, 6 oficinas	6

Note: In the late 1920s, ownership of oficinas by the Americans increased substantially.

Source: Antecedentes sobre la industria salitrera, p. 9.

This estimate is made by assuming, on the basis of the figures given in Table 6.2, that a minimum of 66 percent of exports was produced by foreign-owned companies. The Chilean share of exports was 36 percent in 1884, fell to as little as 15 percent in 1901, and amounted to 25 percent in 1925.[19]

For a variety of reasons, however, the actual share of repatriated profits and capital is likely to have been closer to 30 percent of nitrate revenues between 1880 and 1924. First, some of the foreign and especially the British nitrate mines were the most efficient ones and were therefore receiving a disproportionate share of profits.[20] Second,

19. Ibid., p. 9. In 1884 the share of English-owned oficinas was 20 percent, oficinas under English influence 14 percent, the German share 17.5 percent, and the remaining nationalities 12.5 percent.

20. Detailed statistics concerning capital, output, and profit in British-domiciled companies are given in A. F. Brodie James, *Nitrate Facts and Figures* (London: Fred C. Mathieson & Sons, 1922), pp. 1–15 and appendix. Yearly dividends paid by some of these companies exceeded 100 percent of capital. Others, however, paid no dividends at all during 1920 and 1921. Profit margins varied substantially. Thus for 1923, a typical low-cost producer earned a profit equal to 38 percent of the sales price, while the average for the sixty-five or seventy plants in operation was 24 percent, and the profit margin of a typical high-cost producer was 12 percent of the sales price. Average capacity of plants utilized was 60 percent during the period under consideration. See George A. Makinson, American consul in Valparaiso, Chile, "The Cost of Producing Nitrate in Chile," Records of the Department of State Relating to Internal Affairs of Chile, 1910–1929, Microcopy no. M-487, Roll no. 35 (National Archives, Washington), p. 0588, which provides highly informative and detailed data concerning nitrate costs and profits. Comparison of the long-run government revenue data presented earlier in this essay with the various cost estimates covering a year in the 1920s suggests that at the beginning of the 1880–1930 period the share of government must have exceeded the average figure of one-third of nitrate revenues and that in the 1920s it had fallen to approximately 25 to 27 percent of nitrate revenues. The rising cost of production was the primary factor responsible for this trend. The share of profits also seems to have declined secularly.

part of the cost of production was profits accruing to the foreign-owned traversal railroads and other foreign-owned companies catering to the nitrate sector, which in turn were to a substantial degree repatriated. Third, part of the cost of production—between 10 and 20 percent—reflected amortization of capital and was repatriated. Since no net capital inflow to the nitrate sector from England or elsewhere had occurred to any substantial degree, these repatriated depreciation funds were tantamount to income.[21] However, there exists one reason suggesting lower rather than higher repatriated profits and capital outflows: some of the German and Yugoslav nitrate owners were permanently settled in Chile, or, even if their companies were domiciled in Europe, they did not have the same strong inducement to repatriate profits as the British companies.[22] During the 1880–1930 period the share of profits as a whole and the portion repatriated Abroad increased during the cyclical booms but declined mildly and secularly as both the absolute and the relative demand for natural nitrate declined due to competition from synthetic nitrate.[23]

Before we continue with the discussion of the two other shares in nitrate production, some of the issues that this resource outflow created for Chile should be presented. There is no doubt that with complete Chilean ownership of the nitrate sector Chile would have had no balance of payments problem or at least not as severe a problem as it had throughout the 1880–1930 period. The outflow of the resource surplus was enormous by any standard—50 percent of the surplus generated and also 50 percent of the government's total revenues or expenditures. Since nitrate exports were equal to approximately 24 percent of the gross domestic product and the surplus going to developed nations was in the neighborhood of 30 percent of these exports, the share of repatriated profits to the gross domestic product must have been close to 7 percent. All evidence suggests that this resource outflow was achieved through the contribution of foreign entrepreneurship and skills and not by an influx of foreign investment.

The loss of such riches to Chile led to demands for nationalization

21. It is well known that the famous nitrate pioneer and speculator, John T. North, borrowed the funds to purchase the nitrate titles from the Chilean Bank of Valparaiso.

22. During the years of World War I it was impossible to repatriate profits to these countries.

23. A secular profit squeeze also developed as a result of the rising costs due to the declining quality of caliche.

almost as soon as the War of the Pacific was over. Not so surprisingly, the term nationalization meant ownership by Chileans, not ownership by government, and was used as a synonym to the term Chileanization, equally popular both then and now. One of the key spokesmen of this group, Enrique Kaempffer, argued in 1914:

> *Chilean capital and labor must be favored in the industrial complex of the country at any cost* [because only in this way] *shall we secure the nationalization of the extractive industries, principally that of nitrate, EXCLUSIVE SOURCE, it can be said, of the economic welfare of Chile.* With that we would also obtain *the complete economic independence of the Nation.*[24]

Chileanization or nationalization was also advocated as early as 1908 on grounds that the natural nitrate industry was seriously in danger due to competition from synthetic nitrate, that this source of wealth was directed by industrialists whose interests were not necessarily in harmony with those of the country,[25] and that it would strengthen the currency.[26]

The battle over the North was an event previously unparalleled in Chilean history. In 1879 the Chilean armies sought to achieve by force, in the name of freedom and capitalism, what Chilean individuals had failed to do: to capture the nitrate riches. After 1883 the battle was converted from one of arms, which gave superiority to the Chilean government over Peru and Bolivia, to an economic battle, as superior European imperialism came face to face with Chilean imperialism. And though Chile won the battle in the field, its enforced respect for the currently prevailing capitalist rules of the game led[27] to economic subordination and the substantial loss of resources described earlier.

24. See Kaempffer, *La industria del salitre,* p. 7. Italics are in original, p. 7.
25. See Nicolás Palácios, *Decadencia del espíritu de nacionalidad* (Santiago: Salón Central de la Universidad, 1908), pp. 3–4.
26. Enrique Zañartu Prieto argued that "the nationalization of nitrate is also dictated as a cardinal measure to improve our foreign exchange rate and for the economic prosperity of all Chileans." Quoted in Palácios, *Nacionalización de la industria salitrera* (Santiago: Salón Central de la Universidad, 1908), p. 3.
27. The theme appearing in the literature is that Chile had to placate Bismarck and the other European powers in order not to lose on the diplomatic table what it had gained in the field. According to Palácios, "the regime of industrial liberty declared by Chile as a result of the conquest of those territories influenced Bismarck to leave to our country the prize of its victories." See Palácios, ibid., p. 5.

Most of the outcries and attacks against the role of the various Chilean governments, with the exception of President Balmaceda's, that were expressed before and after 1930 are hardly justified even with the benefits of hindsight. The alleged lack of foresight of the Chilean government in relinquishing control of nitrate to foreign capitalists is an example of misinterpreting history. It is not argued here that Chile would not have been better off with a nationally owned nitrate sector or that it should not have Chileanized nitrate. I argue that Chile *could not* have nationalized the industry, in part for temporary and in part for lasting reasons. Though the "potential" financial resources existed, the current budgetary situation of the Chilean government hardly ever permitted it to acquire the nitrate titles: during and after the War of the Pacific, when the titles were cheap, it was heavily in debt, and later on any purchase in the open market would have required astronomical resources.[28] Furthermore, Chile had conquered the North in the name of capitalism, even though it had in mind at that time exclusively Chilean capitalism and imperialism. The Chilean people and their government could not reverse their views and violate their own principles overnight. Even more important, however, was the Chilean pursuance of an "open door" policy. Chile was trying to attract both human and monetary foreign capital with the hope that it would remain permanently. During the nitrate bonanza it was too early to close the doors with a nationalization policy. And as the assimilation of the Germans, Yugoslavs, and French had shown, this open door policy was frequently successful. It is, however, true that the government neglected its role of establishing rules of the game that would lead both to an optimum nitrate production and to a division of the nitrate output and nitrate-generated resource surplus most attractive to Chile.

Economic nationalism was stimulated, if not initiated, by the annexation of the North, a territory that produced, according to Palácios, a "foreign product"—a Chilean product produced by foreigners.[29] The North also created the first massive and well-organized labor movement that clashed with foreign capitalists, and its extractive social and economic structure generated a new middle class and a new breed of fiery politicians who were as much opposed to the

28. A qualification should be made here, however. As Table 6.3 shows, government received sufficient revenues from nitrate to permit purchase of at least some oficinas, had such investment been given a high priority.

29. Palácios, *Nacionalización,* p. 4. Zañartu, quoted by Palácios, refers to nitrate as a "foreign merchandise."

Center's paternalistic *latifundio* aristocracy as they were to British imperialism.

In the North Chile lost the decisive battle between national and foreign capital and entrepreneurship. Increasing competition from synthetic nitrate, the declining quality of caliche (the sodium nitrate content in the caliche declined from 50 percent in 1880 to 18 percent in 1925), and direct participation in international progress combined to produce a technological change that was rapid by any standard. Although this progress was indispensable for the survival of the North and the maintenance of competitiveness in the mining sector, it brought the demise of most of the Chilean-owned segment of production, which was unable to survive the transition. Unlike the Center, where successful foreign capital and entrepreneurial talent were assimilated and became Chilean, the desolate North had no attraction for the foreign element other than mere exploitation of its natural resources.

It would be an inaccurate tribute to foreign entrepreneurship to credit it with the boom of the North. Its success in controlling the boom was to a very large extent the result of its access to superior banking, marketing, organizational, diplomatic, and technological facilities rather than of superior human qualities. Even if Chile had tried, it is very unlikely that it could have succeeded in either controlling or nationalizing the nitrate industry.

We argued earlier that Chile could not have taken over nitrate; we add now that it *would probably not have been allowed* to take it over. As simple as they are, the reasons are in a way incredible.

The first was that nitrate was too important to be left to the Chileans. World War I made the need for nitrate control all too obvious.

> Those who were in a position to know the facts during the late war realized that the sea transport of nitre which was used in prodigious amounts for the manufacture of explosives, was exposed to great dangers of submarine attack . . . The position at one critical period . . . was of the gravest character: the stock of nitrates was to be reckoned in weeks, not months.[30]

Since nitrate was a strategic product, ownership of the oficinas was part of the war effort to secure continuous supplies. The British, under Churchill's command, cut off the natural sodium nitrate sup-

30. Partington and Parker, *The Nitrogen Industry*, p. 19.

plies to Germany and took all measures to prevent sabotage by Germans in the nitrate fields. After the war, with the Germans defeated, the competition over nitrate control was between the United States and Britain.

> Since the termination of the war, these nitrate companies have shown a strong tendency to divide themselves up on purely national lines, and to-day it is very difficult for American firms to get an "even break" from any but American nitrate companies, and these at present represent possibly only 2% of the nitrate plants in Chile.[31]

The desire of foreign capital to control trade, to enter the most lucrative production activities, and to compete successfully with capital from other countries was the second factor inhibiting Chilean takeover.

The following excerpt from an American consul's report is typical of the atmosphere prevailing before 1930. In a way it matters very little that the views of the consul, C. Innes Brown, were based on outdated information and that they never probably became official policy of the United States government.

> Every experienced exporter knows what nitrate is to the business on this coast. Let us once own our share of it and the influence gained thereby *will be felt all the way from Panama to Punta Arenas; let us invest, and not only will trade be opened up to us that we little dreamed of before,* but it will give our nationals that influence necessary to secure other concessions in this rich country . . .
>
> We must hew a new path, for to continue on the old would be to find that the underbush of foreign competition had become so thick that entry would be impossible: nitrate is the control lever of Chilean trade.[32]

Outside pressures, the Chilean government's commercial philosophy (or lack of it), and the perennial budget deficit largely prevented Chileanization of nitrate. Even though the nationalization

---

31. Report of C. Innes Brown, 21 January 1920, "An American Opportunity," Records of the Department of State Relating to Internal Affairs of Chile, 1910–1929, Microcopy no. M-487, roll no. 33 (National Archives, Washington), p. 3 of report or p. 0476 of microfilm.
32. Ibid., p. 17 of consular report, or pp. 0589–90 of microfilm.

ideology was articulate, popular, and in many respects sound, it was the quasi–laissez faire ideology that was turned into reality.

The Resource Flow to the Center and the Share of Government

We turn at this moment to a more specific analysis of the government's role in determining its own share in nitrate output and to the various problems arising from its policy. We have already seen that government received a third of the nitrate output and half of the nitrate-generated resource surplus and that after 1900 more than 50 percent of total government expenditures was financed out of nitrate and iodine export taxes. Again, according to any standard, the contribution of the nitrate sector to government revenue was spectacular and as vast as its resource contribution to the developed nations. There is an additional similarity in the relationship of the North to Central Chile and Abroad: both gave the North very little and received a fortune. James North, the British adventurer who almost overnight gained control of the nitrate industry and was generally acclaimed both as the "Nitrate King" and the "King of the Pampas," was the foreign counterpart of the Chilean government in the North.

While the North was the playground for the competition between Peru or Bolivia and foreign capitalists—including Chileans—before 1879, it became the battleground for Central Chile and foreign capitalists after the War of the Pacific. The tensions inherited were as important a feature as the wealth.

According to Santiago Marin Vicuña,[33] total government revenues during the half century between 1880 and 1930 can be globally estimated to be equal to £207 million, or 8,250 million Chilean gold pesos. The detailed breakdown of these revenues appears in Table 6.3.

Approximately 97 percent of government revenues come from export duties. Iodine also provided 80 million pesos in revenues.[34] As Table 6.1 shows, fiscal revenues originating from export duties on nitrate increased almost parallel with the size of the budget of public expenditures from 1890 to 1924. The share of ordinary government revenues originating in nitrate export duties rose from a meager 4.7 percent in 1880, when the country started its nitrate policy and ex-

33. See Santiago Marin Vicuña, *El salitre de Chile, 1830–1930* (Santiago: Editorial Nascimiento, 1931), pp. 1–15. This publication contains useful statistical information.

34. 3.80 pesos per kilogram multiplied by 12 million kilograms exported during 1880–1930.

Table 6.3: Government Revenues Originating in Nitrate Sector, 1880–1930
(in thousands of gold pesos of 18 pence)

Export duties	$7,983,500,000
Sales of land	210,000,000
Direct nitrate sales	30,000,000
Rental on land	1,500,000
	$8,250,000,000

Source: Santiago Marín Vicuña, *El salitre de Chile 1830–1930* (Santiago, Editorial Nascimiento, 1931), p. 9.

penditures were only 48.7 million pesos, to 48.15 percent ten years later. This coefficient of almost 50 percent was maintained for four decades until by the time of the Great Depression various forces had completely destroyed this equilibrium.

The effective nitrate tax policy started on 12 September, 1879, when government managed to establish the first tax on nitrate exports to meet its war expenditures. The tax was fixed at 0.40 gold pesos of 18 pence per metric quintal to the north of parallel 24, leaving free for two years the nitrate to the south of the parallel.

After a few intermediate steps, a definite nitrate tax policy was introduced by Law 980 of 23 December, 1899, which established the export duty at 3.38 gold pesos of 18 pence per metric quintal of nitrate.[35] This duty was rigidly maintained for a number of decades. In numerous periods, however, the method of payment was changed in a way that meant an additional tax or surcharge.[36] Thus, by a law of 27 January, 1917, the method of payment of nitrate and iodine export duties was altered appreciably. The letters of credit in London were eliminated and the duties had to be paid in part in gold currency and in part in paper currency in a proportion fixed by the President. With the limited availability of gold during that epoch, an occasionally high surcharge in terms of paper currency had to be paid, which meant an additional variable burden for the nitrate industry.

After some further minor changes and the early turbulent years of the Great Depression,[37] all export duties on nitrate and iodine were

35. This export duty was almost identical with the previous rate of 1.60 gold pesos of 18 pence.

36. Law 980 also modified the tax on iodine from 0.60 gold pesos of 38 pence to its almost exact equivalent of 1.27 gold pesos of 18 pence per kilogram of iodine.

37. During the years 1927/28 to 1929/30 the government ordered the payment of fiscal subsidies to the nitrate producers because of the pressures on the

completely eliminated as a result of the establishment of the government nitrate iodine monopoly which was, in turn, rented for thirty-five years to the Corporación de Ventas de Salitre y Yodo de Chile. This corporation was established in 1934,[38] and the elimination of export taxes was replaced by a 25 percent participation of the State in the profits of the corporation.

The government's nitrate policy was heavily criticized throughout this period. Before we enter into a discussion of some of these criticisms and related issues it has to be conceded that the policy succeeded in transferring resources from the nitrate sector and the North to the Chilean government and the Center.

One of the first criticisms leveled against the relationship between government and the nitrate sector was the excessive dependence of the public sector on nitrate:

> The fiscal and private sectors have lived for a quarter of a century as if nitrate were an inexhaustible vein whose paralysis or extinction were not subject to the contingencies of time and to the always possible exhaustion of extractive wealth.[39]

The first major shock that revealed the excessive economic reliance on nitrate was World War I. It also prompted the recommendation of policies designed to defend Chilean nitrate. These included the joint advertising by nitrate producers of its advantages as a fertilizer, the establishment of a better price by suppressing intermediaries, and the prompt delivery of nitrate by means of direct shipments.[40]

The government, it was agreed, while becoming financially less dependent on the nitrate sector, should also accept major responsibility for formulating and implementing a viable nitrate policy. The role of the State should be extended to include not only the functions

---

industry as a result of the world crisis and the competition from synthetic fertilizers. In its attempt to preserve its policy of rigid export duties, the government argued that these bonuses, which meant a reduction in export duties, would have to be calculated as a compensation for the decline in the sales price of nitrate in the principal markets. With the formation of the Compania de Salitres de Chile (COSACH) in July 1930, all nitrate and iodine export duties had to be eliminated in exchange for the fiscal participation in the profits of COSACH as a stockholder. However the State reestablished the duties in a way such that the payments made by the industry in the years 1930–33 meant practically the same taxes as those in effect before COSACH.

38. By Law 5350 of 8 January 1934, retroactive to 1 July 1933.

39. Vidal, *La tragedia del salitre*, p. 13.

40. Ibid., p. 15. Intermediaries, often speculators, were regarded as major pests.

described in the previous paragraph but also such activities as diplomatic pressure on Germany to terminate its alleged boycott of Chilean nitrate in the early 1920s.

> We are far from committing the sin of *Estatolatria,* the adoration of the State. Visible are its failures as an administrator of industries and of the means of transportation. But it is only just that it should acquire a powerful influence for the best guardianship of the mother industry of this country without reaching the point of strangling constitutionally guaranteed private initiative.[41]

Government should have as a primary responsibility the establishment of institutions conducive to nitrate growth, the introduction of adequate rules of the game, and the creation of a framework within which private initiative can flourish and Chile can reap maximum benefits. The economic literature between 1880 and 1930 criticizing the government for failing to assume adequately its role of introducing continuous institutional change is vast and only partly cited here.

Stated differently, the Chilean government was being accused of pursuing a nitrate policy that possibly maximized the State's share in nitrate revenues and the nitrate-generated surplus but did not maximize the welfare of Chile or the welfare or growth of the nitrate sector. There is again a symmetry in the relationship between foreign capitalists and the "Nitrate North" on the one hand, and the government and the Nitrate North on the other hand. The welfare function foreign capitalists maximized was not necessarily the same as that of Chile or the nitrate sector. In the same fashion, the welfare function of the Chilean government was not necessarily the same as that of the Chilean nation, the nitrate sector, or the Chilean nitrate capitalists.

There exists no evidence that the Chilean government had a clear policy, or was interested in establishing a policy, that would be best for Chile's acquisition of nitrate revenues, nitrate income, or a nitrate-generated resource surplus. The objective of the present comments is not to accuse but to describe government policy; to show that the government has different roles and different functions; and to show that each step in the resource transfer process must ideally be considered.

The third criticism of the relationship between the Chilean government and the nitrate sector is related to the first and is connected with the resource allocation process. The government, it is argued,

41. Ibid., pp. 35–36.

succeeded in appropriating half of the resource surplus generated in nitrate but failed to use it in a way contributing to Chilean growth. Instead of using the surplus for investment, it spent it primarily for consumption. It cannot be denied, however, that social overhead investment in railroads, roads, canals, ports, schools, and other public works of importance during 1880–1930 was substantial. However, it fell considerably short of the maximum possible, and it failed to bring Chile into a stage of sustained growth. Had the expenditure of nitrate revenues been directed toward extraordinary productive items, in symmetry with the extraordinary nature of these revenues and their exhaustible source, the benefits would have been substantially greater.[42]

The government's role in determining growth was severely tested. Although the nitrate sector had brought the issue of public versus private ownership of capital into the foreground, the real controversy was primarily with respect to government intervention and involvement in determining the rules of the game.

It was always agreed that the government should attempt to maximize both nitrate output and the share of this output accruing to Chile. After all, in the pursuit of this goal Chile had gone as far as declaring war on Bolivia and Peru and conquering the disputed areas. Since the war erupted in part around the issue of type of ownership, with Chile favoring the private choice, the debate concerning public and private ownership turned into a seminationalistic comparison of the pre-1880 state of affairs, when Peru was the advocate of public ownership and heavy government intervention—with its policies having some disastrous effects on production—with the post-1883 era, when Chilean liberalism led to spectacular but temporary spurts in output. Government ownership was originally excluded. There can be observed, according to Edwards,

> the enormous contrast between the Peruvian and the Chilean mentality . . . While Peru seeks the complicated and annoying path of fiscal intrusion and of the marriage of State interests with private interests, Chile, as soon as it starts to exercise its authority in the areas of guano and nitrate, parts from that path and emphasizes its intentions of limiting State intervention to a discreet superior vigilance and to the collection of fiscal taxes.[43]

42. Vicuña, *El salitre de Chile*, p. 9.
43. See Augustín Edwards in his introduction to Cruchaga's *Salitre y guano*, p. viii.

Liberalism, however, was not associated exclusively with prosperity. As the Chileans soon found out, free market forces could lead to overproduction, oversupply, and even a crisis with output reductions. And liberalism provided no guarantee against technological innovation detrimental to Chilean interests, or against temporary, market-dictated price increases high enough to lead to replacement of natural by synthetic nitrate.

The Chilean government had to choose among three alternative strategies. First, it could proceed and nationalize the nitrate concerns and exploit the nitrate riches through its own entrepreneurial, capital, and labor resources. The second alternative involved preservation of the old rules of the game, as they were established before the War of the Pacific, and as they were being transformed by the violent forces operating in the 1880s and 1890s. Third, the Chilean government had an opportunity to establish a new set of laissez faire rules of the game which, even though permitting foreign entrepreneurs to operate in Chile, would provide maximum rather than minimum benefits to the Chilean economy. It was feasible during this period to change the laws to allow foreign capital to remit only what can be referred to as a fair return on its invested capital in Chile. It seems that Chile, not only with respect to nitrate but also later on with respect to copper, proceeded to adopt the second rule, that of maintaining an arbitrary status quo. The choice of this alternative has cost the economy millions of dollars and has also invited the wrath of the post-1930 reform groups.

The Resource Flow to the North and the Share of Labor

We turn next to an analysis of the remaining two resource flows, namely, the share of nitrate revenues flowing to the North and the income share of labor. We remind the reader that the cost of production absorbed approximately 33 percent of the nitrate revenues. In order to determine more precisely the two aforementioned flows, we shall take a closer look at the various components of the cost of production.[44]

The best possible insight into the size of these flows can be gained from analyzing Table 6.4, which gives a detailed breakdown of the

44. Prices differed substantially during the period analyzed, and costs varied greatly between oficinas. Information on costs is also found in the Records of the Department of State Relating to Internal Affairs of Chile, 1910–1929, 825.6374/207–417, Microcopy no. M-487, Roll no. 32 (National Archives, Washington), pp. 0195–96.

Table 6.4: Price of a Short Ton of Nitrate and Its Components
(in U.S. dollars, 1922–23)

	Doll.	*U.S.($)*	*%*
Extraction	4.08	13.00	25.8
Transport	1.28		
Elaboration	4.40		
Amortization	2.16		
General costs	1.04		
	———		
	12.96		
Bags, fare to coast, commissions, etc.		4.80	9.5
Minor port costs		1.40	2.8
Export duty		10.40	20.6
Margin of producers		12.00	23.8
Sea fare		4.80	9.5
Margin of importers		3.80	8.0
		———	———
		50.20	100.0

Sources: Harry A. Curtis, *Investigaciones sobre el nitrógeno* (Santiago, Imprenta Universitaria, 1924), p. 35; and idem, *Nitrogen Survey*, U.S. Dept. of Commerce, Trade Information Bulletin no. 226 (Washington, Government Printing Office, 1924), pp. 46–51.

price of nitrate per short ton in the Gulf ports and the ports of the Atlantic coast of the United States during the fiscal year 1922–23.

Prima facie, the share of nitrate price staying in the North would be equal to the cost of extraction, amortization, etc., which is 25 percent of the price, plus some part of items two and three, referring to the cost of bags, fare to the coast, and commissions, reflecting 9.5 percent of the price; and minor port costs, which are 2.8 percent of the price. If we exclude the sea fare and margin to the importers, we can see that the cost of production, according to this table, is close to 50 percent of the nitrate export price, with the export duty being close to 23 percent of the price, and the profit margin being close to 27 percent of the price.[45]

45. The following cost information lends support to these estimates of the resource flows.

According to the authoritative data supplied to the Nitrogen Products Committee. . . . The pre-war cost of production at a medium-sized modern nitrate factory, including all factory expenses in Chile—such as labour, fuel, repairs, bagging, freight to a port, shipping charges, and commission, amortization of the cost of the nitrate grounds and plant, interest on capital at the rate of 5 percent, and Chilean export duty at 2s.4d. per Spanish quintal (101.8 pounds)—amounted to 7s.4d. per quintal of nitrate F.O.B.

A substantial fraction of the cost of production refers to imported intermediate products, such as bags, and expenditures for such inputs as insurance, transportation, and amortization. Value added by labor is likely to be a little below the U.S.$11 figure obtained by excluding the cost of amortization ($2.16) from the total extraction cost ($13.00). If we use the information of Table 6.4 as a criterion, the value added by labor could be as much as 25 percent of the nitrate export price. Since the share flowing to the North was earlier estimated as being close to 33 percent of the nitrate export revenue, the remaining 8 percent in the cost of production would include such costs as amortization, which we cannot at this moment relate either to intermediate product expenditures or to the value added by capital. It is interesting to note that according to the table the share received by government falls appreciably short of the 33 percent figure obtained by comparing total nitrate export revenues and total nitrate government revenues for the 1880–1924 period. Since the table is obtained from figures covering one year only, it can be considered less reliable than the long-term statistics in providing a correct estimate for the shares of government, the North, and Abroad.[46]

The ephemeral prosperity created in the coast towns of the North by the nitrate boom is legendary. The following quotation from a report by Iquique's American consul, C. Inness Brown, is representative of the literature:

Go to any of the coast towns of northern Chile and what

---

in Chile, or £8 1s.4d. (£8.07) per long ton of nitrate (95 percent purity).

Partington and Parker, *The Nitrogen Industry*, p. 76. Although according to these figures the export duty accounted for about one-third of the F.O.B. nitrate price in Chile, which conforms with our earlier estimate, the cost breakdown given on p. 77 shows a cost of production figure close to 50 percent of the F.O.B. price. This figure is rather close to the estimate derived from the information given in Curtis, *Investigaciones*, p. 35. The Partington-Parker cost breakdown allows for no profits and, since it is based on engineering cost data, is not necessarily as accurate as the actual total cost figure presented on p. 76.

46. According to the cost calculation per metric quintal from the office until it reaches the side of the ship given in Ministerio de Hacienda, *La industria salitrera*, p. 9, the major components per metric quintal embarked were the following: loading at the office, including bags, 13.0000 pence; railroad freight from office to Iquique, 15.0528 pence; embarkment in Iquique 3.6413 pence; export duties, 61.1520 pence; amortization of land, 6.5000 pence; and amortization of construction and improvements, 6.5000 pence; etc.; total cost 119.8623 pence.

supports them? . . . nitrate, and in fact what supports the Chilean Government? . . . again nitrate. It is an actual fact, unbelievable as it may seem to be, that nitrate provides 98% of the fiscal income of Chile. Take for instance, Iquique, Antofagasta, or any of a score of other in-between towns, and every one of them, and every business in them, owes its very existence to nitrate. Any visitor to the northern coast knows what a vast number of lucrative businesses one finds in these towns. What sends the price of Chilean money up or down, but nitrate, and one can attribute practically every oscillation of business in Chile to the price or production of this valuable commodity.[47]

In spite of the tremendous wealth generated in the North, the living conditions for local labor in the nitrate fields were far from desirable. Vidal correctly described the North as the "Chilean Siberia" [48] and advocated greater concern of the State for the welfare of those brave Chileans who turned the North into the "Country's bank of funds. . . . We ask for pity for the inhabitants of the North who give everything and who do not receive anything." [49] The main beneficiary, the State, was accused of having an insatiable appetite and of devouring the North's resources at such an excessive rate that it was destroying the very tree that grew the golden apples. Unless methods of exploitation were improved, it was argued, the industry's ability to meet the danger of synthetic nitrate was apt to be wanting.

Both the Chilean government and the nitrate capitalists made investments in the North which increased the latter's share in nitrate revenues. However, the interest of both of these groups in developing the arid nitrate areas was minimal, and any long-term economic justification for developing the areas around the nitrate oficinas through industrial diversification was absent. The nitrate rush was like a gold rush, with uninhabited ghost towns left behind as synthetic nitrate slowly but steadily corroded the markets for natural nitrate.

The "Nitrate North" became the periphery in a dual sense. It was the periphery to the European and the North American industrial centers, providing them with both raw materials and vast riches.

47. C. Innes Brown, "An American Opportunity," p. 3, or p. 0476 of the microfilm. The reader is reminded that Brown's figure of 98 percent for the fiscal revenues generated in the nitrate sector is inaccurate. In a later report Brown himself adjusted the figure downward.
48. Vidal, pp. 7 and 9.
49. Ibid., p. 9.

Exploitation of sodium nitrate deposits was dictated more by technological conditions and the presence of a natural monopoly than by a declining rate of return in the mother countries and the presence of high profit rates in the satellite regions. Distance and location mattered little, except during World War I, since the combination of a natural resource monopoly and improving transportation originally gave the North an absolute advantage which was subsequently converted into a comparative one.

We may now return to the structuralist center-periphery, mother-satellite argument. The link between the capitalist West and the Chilean North was dual, involving the exported product and ownership of the industry's capital. It was during 1880–1930 no matter of dispute that nitrate exports were beneficial to Chile. The crux of controversy centered around the division of the resources generated between the developed West and the underdeveloped Center. In a way, the North was as much a periphery to the center of Chile as it was to Europe. Both regions were dependent on its product, even though to a substantially different degree, and both regions had sent capitalists to exploit the North's natural resources. Furthermore, both regions were, in a way, and to a different degree, dependent upon the resource surplus generated in the North. There existed both in Europe and around Santiago an industrial nucleus whose fortunes were dependent upon the growth pattern of the Chilean North.

If the North, therefore, as a periphery, was a major source of wealth to the Developed Center composed of Europe and the United States, so was it to the Chilean Center. If Europe and the United States were more industrialized and growing more rapidly than the Chilean North, this was also true for the Central part of Chile. The collapse of the nitrate boom meant almost as much, if not more, to Great Britain than to Central Chile. In both instances, the Great Depression exposed and terminated the dependence on the natural nitrate sector.[50]

It was in the North that the low-savings argument found a clear test. Nitrate mining generated, during 1880–1930, as vast a resource surplus as Kuwait's petroleum industry does today. There was hardly ever any idea of industrializing the North on a grand scale com-

50. There was, however, a fundamental difference. Since for the developed nations nitrogen was an essential needed for both peacetime and wartime survival, its interest in the product vastly exceeded its interests in the riches of the North. Chile was interested in the product, however, only insofar as it generated the desperately needed resource surplus.

mensurate with the potentially reinvestable capital resources. Thus, although *ex ante* savings existed, neither mining itself nor the other sectors in the North could ever absorb them.[51] The dilemma then was transferred from one relating to the saving process—how much to save—to one relating to the resource distribution process—how revenues and the net resource surplus should be divided, on the one hand, between Chile and the Developed West (Abroad), and among the Developed West, the mining North, and Central Chile, on the other. Central Chile had a claim emanating from territorial grounds, the West was supporting its adventurous capitalists, and the North was caught in the middle. Thus the low-savings argument was not applicable either to the North or to Chile as a whole, since the nitrate sector generated an enormous surplus.

During the nitrate era there existed no market-dictated rules that could guarantee an optimum division of the nitrate revenues, income, or surplus between Chile and Abroad. Neither did there exist any rules preventing excessive competition or misuse of the nitrate deposits. Government should not follow the principle that "any rules" of the game are optimum, or that "no rules" are optimum. Chaotic liberalism can be as bad as chaotic government intervention. The primary lesson of the Chilean nitrate case is that government should not accept elaborate roles when it has not yet fulfilled its primary responsibilities, that of establishing law and order and appropriate rules of the game. Since the resource transfer, resource appropriation, and even resource allocation problems discussed in this essay can rarely be solved unilaterally, resource allocation on an international level cannot be optimum unless government assumes greater responsibility not only in setting up rules affecting the *Ordo der Wirtschaft* but also in establishing an *Ordo der Weltwirtschaft*. Fulfilling the apparently simple function of setting up appropriate national and international rules of the game may still prove to be the government's most formidable and promising challenge.

Comments by Shane Hunt

With this paper, Markos Mamalakis has drawn our attention to a most interesting episode in development history. It illustrates two of

51. The adverse climatic conditions and limited long-term investment opportunities permitted only partial development of the North.

the problems that most concern development economists and policy makers today.

One problem concerns the beneficence of export-led growth. Critics have argued that too often export sectors are enclaves, devoid of economic connections to the domestic economy and contributing nothing to national development. So described, the export enclave is more an ideal type than a historical reality, but Jonathan Levin, in his study of the Peruvian guano industry, presented a historical example virtually as unproductive.[1] Now Mamalakis gives us another example almost as unhappy in its effects, one that neatly complements Levin's earlier work, since nitrates were extracted from the same desert region that had given the world Peruvian guano, and constituted the successor to guano as the world's principal source of fertilizer.

Unlike Levin, however, Mamalakis traces the resource flows with the object of arguing not that Chile got nothing out of her export sector, but that she should have gotten much more than she did. With regard to the wage bill, for example, Levin argued that it was virtually nonexistent in Peru, since labor demands were not particularly great and labor immobility in the domestic economy obliged guano administrators to rely on convicts and coolies.[2] By contrast, the more detailed data of Mamalakis show a sizable labor force and a share to labor that, while low by standards of modern industry, is nevertheless an important part of factor payments. It is worth noting that the mobilization of so large a labor force in the middle of a thinly settled desert region shows either that conditions of labor mobility were vastly different in Chile and Peru or that Levin greatly underestimated the potential mobility of Peruvian labor. The latter seems to me the more probable explanation.

Chile also gained greatly from tax revenues, which by Mamalakis' Table 6.4 amounted to some 25 percent of F.O.B. value. As Levin quite rightly pointed out, such flows cannot be counted a benefit to the nation until one has an idea of what the government did with the revenue thus acquired. In the case of Peruvian guano Levin minimizes the benefit which such revenues produced for Peru by arguing that the additional expenditure thus permitted ran heavily to unproductive transfer payments and imports of luxury consumer goods,

1. Jonathan Levin, *The Export Economies* (Cambridge: Harvard University Press, 1960), pp. 27–123.
2. Ibid., pp. 41, 85–90.

and that excessive reliance on guano caused the domestic tax-collecting system to fall into decay.[3]

In the Chilean case, Mamalakis argues that government expenditure tended to be unproductive, but he tempers his criticism by pointing out that government expenditure for development was by no means negligible during the nitrate era. His assessment, like Levin's, is couched in most general terms, but quantitative standards of what constitutes acceptable government expenditure performance are very difficult to come by. More interesting, and more practicable, would be the further effort of explaining the process by which Chilean public finances adjusted to the blow of losing an income source producing fully 60 percent of government revenue in 1916, only some fifteen years before the roof fell in.

A second problem besetting policy makers today concerns the beneficence of direct foreign investment, and here Mamalakis's study contributes to a line of inquiry originally pointed out by Edith Penrose.[4] Against the conventional arguments justifying customary profit rates on direct foreign investment in small open economies, Mrs. Penrose offered an Australian example that challenged conventional wisdom. She suggested that profit repatriations could be so great, and indeed were so great in Australian automobile industry, that one could not argue with any confidence that the capital-receiving country had paid a reasonable price for the foreign capital thus obtained.

Mamalakis presents a new example which appears far more extraordinary, however, because he reports that profit repatriations were enormous, amounting to 7 percent of GDP, and suggests that these outflows were made as payment for an initial capital inflow that was insignificantly small. The profit rate of foreign investors was, consequently, approaching infinity.

It is, however, not entirely fair to evaluate a nation's wisdom in striking bargains with foreign companies solely by looking at profit rates. Foreign companies must quite properly be credited with importing technology as well as capital. Viewed in its broadest sense, technological knowledge involves the capability not only of producing given outputs from given inputs, but also of establishing an organizational structure, and of having access to financial resources such that large plants can be established and economies of scale realized. If

3. Ibid., pp. 114, 117.
4. Edith Tilton Penrose, "Foreign Investment and the Growth of the Firm," *Economic Journal,* June 1956, pp. 220–35.

access is limited to patents, or engineering knowledge, or large financial resources, those possessing such attributes exact a rent, and it could very well be in a country's best interest to pay the rent and obtain the technology rather than do without.

This line of reasoning may justify Australia's policy of permitting high "profits" to be enjoyed by the General Motors subsidiary, but it does not appear to justify the profits of the foreign nitrate companies in Chile. There seems to have been no great technological gap. The enormous scale and complicated technology which ensured the dominance of foreigners in copper mining were not present in nitrates. The entrepreneurs were frequently individuals rather than established, impersonal companies, and, as Mamalakis shows in Table 6.2, the nationalities represented were numerous.

One can not help but wonder how on earth the foreigners managed to pull off so successful a financial coup. The brief answer given in the paper, that it was "access to superior banking, marketing, organizational, diplomatic, and technological facilities," does not really satisfy but merely whets the appetite. The question is in fact a very difficult one, and has perplexed a number of Chilean historians.[5] A part of the answer apparently lies in the extraordinary machinations of John North, that extraordinary Englishman; a part in the alleged decline of Chilean entrepreneurial spirit; and a part in the unwillingness or inability of the Chilean government to take more decisive action against a foreign takeover. These factors need much more careful evaluation; it is a bit ungracious of me to ask for more when so much effort is already evident in the paper, but one hopes that Mamalakis or someone else will have time to do further research in this area.

It is of course not enough merely to say that Chile struck a bad bargain with the foreign nitrate companies; we must also bring our hindsight vision into perfect focus and say that other alternatives, either national capitalism or state enterprise, were feasible. In this issue Mamalakis is quite pessimistic; he suggests that there really was little else Chile could have done, and he mounts a number of supporting arguments. Prices of nitrate properties escalated so rapidly that nationalization became prohibitively expensive after only a few years. An antiforeign policy could not have been entertained at a time when Chile desired greatly to attract European immigrants. The pressure

5. See, for example, Anibal Pinto, *Chile; un caso de desarrollo frustrado* (Santiago: Editorial Universitaria, 1959), pp. 52–58.

of European imperialism, both British and German, was too great to withstand.

In a sense one feels these arguments must be right simply because Chile did not nationalize nitrates despite considerable popular agitation. And yet they do not convince me entirely. Granted that the problem of nationalization became more complicated as prices rose, surely prices were still not too high for a truly determined government. Prices of land and of copper properties continued rising throughout the twentieth century, but in recent years Chile has made efforts to buy land for agrarian reform and to Chileanize the copper industry. A determined government probably would not have paid market prices for expropriated properties anyway, and would thus have avoided helping speculators to realize quick capital gains. As for deterrence to immigration, if a different policy brought greater prosperity to Chile and greater opportunity to entrepreneurs who were Chilean citizens, then surely nitrate policy and immigration policy would have been complementary.

As for the pressure of foreign imperialism, I cannot reject this argument so quickly, but I do wish to see more evidence of direct pressure brought to bear by European powers against a Chilean government truly desirous of beginning nationalization. Mamalakis has given us some interesting instances of imperialist bluster but has not tackled the thorny question of British influence behind the revolution, which overthrew President Balmaceda in 1891. If ever imperialism was at work in Chile, that was the moment. The British were extending both moral and financial support to revolutionary forces bent on overthrowing a president who was committed to putting the nitrate industry back into Chilean hands.[6] Yet, while there is no question but that British and other foreign groups directly influenced the outcome of the civil war of 1891, it is not clear how decisive that influence was. Certainly many segments of Chilean society, particularly wealthy segments, also opposed Balmaceda.

These wealthy groups might be dismissed as mere intermediaries for foreign interests, since their wealth was generally built on commercial contact with metropolitan powers, but we must also remember that they were the potential beneficiaries of Balmaceda's nitrate policy.

It is not clear to me why the wealthy classes of Chile were so firmly

6. A review of this episode is in André Gunder Frank, *Capitalism and Underdevelopment in Latin America* (New York: Monthly Review Press, 1967), pp. 73–85.

opposed to a policy from which they could have profited so greatly. Perhaps it is a question best left to those who know a good deal more about Chilean history than I do, but it does seem to me that Mamalakis has pointed to the answers, and that they have to do with the fact that imperialism was not merely a system of economic relationships but was closely wedded to a system of ideas, the ideology of laissez faire. The European influence which beset Chile was intellectual as well as economic, and it was much heavier on the Manchester school than on Friedrich List. Moreover, as Mamalakis shows, this ideological influence was particularly powerful in its application to nitrates, since Chileans justified their conquest of the nitrate provinces by arguing that development had been stunted under the inefficiency of the earlier state-controlled Peruvian administration.

If these suggestions are correct, the foreigners reaped their desert harvest partly by the strength of imperial economic power and partly because the Chilean nation was locked into an ideology that was not in its national self-interest.

7

The Argentine State
and Economic Growth:
A Historical Review

BY CARLOS F. DÍAZ ALEJANDRO

This paper will review the historical record of the Argentine public sector in promoting economic growth. Four major periods will be considered: (1) 1860–1930, (2) 1930–43, (3) 1943–55, and (4) 1955 until the present. Before going into the historical review, a recent snapshot of the public sector will be presented, to provide an idea of the size and influence of the Argentine government today. The paper will close with a few comments on lessons that may be derived from the historical perspective.

THE ARGENTINE PUBLIC SECTOR IN RECENT YEARS

It may be well to start with a description of the public sector in years as recent as detailed data allow. Following Bator, public expenditures will be subdivided into "exhaustive" and "nonexhaustive." [1] During 1955–59 exhaustive expenditures averaged 13.8 percent of the gross national product, measured at market prices; 4.2 percent of GNP corresponds to gross fixed investment of general

This paper was written in part while I held a J. S. Guggenheim Fellowship, for which I am grateful. Donna Brand, David Felix, Lola Fredrickson, and George Perry helped me in its preparation.

1. Francis M. Bator, *The Question of Government Spending* (New York, Harper and Row, 1960), chapter 2. Exhaustive expenditure consists of purchases by the general government of currently produced goods and services from business and households; nonexhaustive expenditure is spending that simply redistributes income or assets. The public sector includes both general government and public enterprises; general government includes national, provincial, and local institutions.

government and public enterprises, and 9.5 percent corresponds to consumption expenditures of the general government.[2] Nonexhaustive general government *current* expenditures, including interest payments on the national debt, social security payments, subsidies to enterprises, including public ones, etc., amounted to 7.2 percent of GNP during the same period. No complete estimates are available on public sector nonexhaustive capital expenditures (purchases of existing assets, subsidies on capital account, etc.); for 1955–59 they may be estimated at between 0.5 and 1.0 percent of GNP. The total for general government expenditures, plus capital account expenditures of public enterprises, would then come to about 21 or 22 percent of GNP.[3]

Similar conclusions regarding the relative size of public expenditures can be reached by considering all public revenues. During 1955–59 general government indirect taxes averaged 9.4 percent of GNP; direct taxes on incorporated enterprises, 0.9 percent; direct taxes on families, 1.9 percent; social security contributions, 5.6 percent; and other nontax current revenues, 0.3 percent. This gives a total of current revenues amounting to 18.2 percent of GNP. During the same period net public borrowing from the banking sector averaged 2.3 percent of GNP.[4] Exact data on other public sector

2. These percentages have been calculated from data at current prices found in Consejo Nacional de Desarrollo (hereafter, CONADE), *Cuentas nacionales de la República Argentina* (Buenos Aires, 1964). Other sources yield slightly different results. Rounding errors account for discrepancies between totals and subtotals.

3. These data may be compared with corresponding percentages for the following industrialized countries:

	Exhaustive expenditures as percentages of GNP	Nonexhaustive expenditures as percentages of GNP
United States (1957)	20	6
West Germany (1953)	19	12
Belgium (1952)	17	14
United Kingdom (1953)	23	13
Canada (1953)	18	8
Sweden (1952)	18	8
Argentina (1955–60)	14	8

Even allowing for different accounting practices in the countries shown, all of them appear to have a larger share of public expenditures in GNP than Argentina. Data taken from Bator, Table 13, p. 157.

4. Net public borrowing from the banking sector is defined as increases in public sector debt to the banking sector (including the Central Bank), minus increases in public sector deposits with the banking sector. Data obtained from Banco Central de la República Argentina (hereafter, BCRA), *Estadísticas*

Table 7.1: Argentine Public Sector Expenditures Expressed as Percentages of the
Gross National Product, 1955–59

Exhaustive expenditures	*13.8*
Consumption expenditures of general government	*9.5*
National	6.1
States	2.4
Municipalities	1.1
Consumption expenditures: national and states	*8.4*
General administration	1.2
Defense	2.6
Justice and internal security	1.1
Roads and waterways	0.4
Education and culture	2.2
Public health	0.7
Agriculture and livestock	0.4
Other	0.8
Minus: Sales of goods and services	−1.0
Consumption expenditures	*9.5*
Wages and salaries	7.9
Purchases of goods and nonpersonal services	2.7
Minus: Sales of goods and services	−1.0
Gross fixed investment of general government and public enterprises	*4.2*
Construction	3.0
New machinery and equipment	1.3
Nonexhaustive current expenditures	*7.2*
Subsidies	3.0
Interest on the public debt	0.3
Current transfers to families	4.0

Note: Percentages were taken from yearly figures at current prices; averages were
then taken of yearly percentages. Rounding errors explain the discrepancies between
totals and the sum of their components.

Sources: Basic data obtained from CONADE, *Cuentas nacionales de la República
Argentina* (Buenos Aires, 1964), Tables 1, 3, 66, and 70.

foreign and domestic borrowing are not available, but it is doubtful
that it exceeded 1 percent of GNP, on the average.

Table 7.1 summarizes public expenditure data expressed as percentages of GNP, and including expenditure breakdown. *Non-*

Monetarias y Bancarias: Años 1940–1960 (Buenos Aires, June 1962), and the
monthly *Boletín Estadístico* of the same institution.

defense exhaustive expenditures amounted to 11.2 percent of GNP, higher than for the United States (9.7 percent in 1957) and Canada (9.7 percent in 1953), although lower than for West Germany (14.3 percent in 1953), the United Kingdom (13.1 percent in 1953), and Sweden (13.6 percent in 1952).[5] Three other points are worth noting in Table 7.1. Current exhaustive expenditures on education and culture by the national government and states (no expenditure breakdown is available for municipalities) reach a proportion of GNP not very different from that corresponding to U.S. total education expenditures in 1952 (2.5 percent of GNP). *Subsidies,* primarily covering public enterprise deficits such as those of railroads, reached a remarkable 3 percent of GNP. Finally, *current transfers to families,* representing mainly social security payments, were lower than social security revenues during 1955–59 and even more so in earlier years. In more recent years, however, this situation has been reversed.

These figures give only a partial view of public sector influence on the economy. It is more revealing to note that during 1955–59 general government wages and salaries amounted to 18.6 percent of all wages and salaries paid in the country.[6] But this is not all. Following international conventions, we have excluded from expenditures the current outlays of public enterprises. Yet for some purposes, such as measuring the public role in the labor market, those current outlays are of interest. (Hiring practices in both the general government and public enterprises have followed criteria different from those of Argentine private enterprises.) Wages and salaries paid by the nationalized railroads during 1955–59 amounted to another 3.9 percent of the total wage bill. No detailed data are available for other public enterprises, but it is reasonable to suppose that at least one-fourth of all Argentine wages and salaries are paid by the public sector.[7]

All these quantitative measures are still insufficient and, by themselves, may be misleading when analyzing the economic role of a public sector. To give an extreme example, the importance of the armed forces in Argentine society and their direct and indirect effects

5. Bator, Table 14, p. 157. Neutral Sweden's defense purchases of goods and services (4.8 percent of GNP in 1952) exceeded those of Argentina.

6. CONADE, p. 81. "Wages and salaries" excludes the labor income of the self-employed.

7. The proportion of the labor force, including the self-employed, working in the public sector is, of course, smaller than one-fourth. The general government employed 10 percent of the labor force during 1955–59; public enterprises probably hired an additional 4 percent.

on growth are hardly reflected in Table 7.1. During at least part of the post–World War II period, the Argentine government also had at its disposal the following instruments to affect economic life.

The Public Enterprises

Public enterprises have controlled all or part of the production and distribution of oil, gas, electricity, and several manufactured goods. According to the 1954 census, public enterprises accounted for 55 percent of all gross output of mining, 10 percent of all gross output of manufacturing, and 21 percent of all gross output of gas and electricity.[8] The state has also taken a keen interest in the steel industry, and SOMISA, the major steel company, which started production in 1961, is a state enterprise under the tutelage of the armed forces.[9] In the service sectors public enterprises have total control over railroads and telephones; there is a public airline for domestic and international flights, and there are public fluvial and oceanic fleets.

Direct and Indirect Control over Banking and Financial Transactions

Besides the rules and regulations most states have over interest rates and banking activities—rules whose leverage is greatly increased when, as in postwar Argentina, the rate of inflation is usually higher than the maximum permissible interest rates—the national government directly owns four commercial financial institutions,[10] which in 1966 accounted for 36 percent of all commercial banks assets. Provincial governments totally owned banks holding 18 percent of all commercial banks assets.[11]

8. República Argentina, Dirección Nacional de Estadística y Censos (hereafter, DNEC), *Censo Industrial, 1954*, p. 40. Within manufacturing, 76 percent of petroleum refining was in public hands and so was 31 percent of the gross output of nonelectric machinery and equipment, where the armed forces managed several plants.

9. In spite of SOMISA, it is probable that the share of public sector enterprises in manufacturing output has declined since 1954. After the overthrow of General Perón in 1955, many state enterprises were sold to private groups, and the expansion of manufacturing (except of steel) took place in branches controlled by private (often foreign) firms. See the helpful paper by David Felix, "Some Notes on the Implementation of Argentine Industrialization Policy," mimeographed (St. Louis, Mo., 1967).

10. Banco de la Nación Argentina, Banco Hipotecario Nacional, Banco Industrial de la República Argentina, and Caja Nacional de Ahorro Postal. The Central Bank does not engage in direct dealings with the public.

11. Data obtained from BCRA, *Boletín Estadístico*, October 1966, p. 59. In

Foreign Trade Controls

Since the nineteenth century the national government has had the power to levy both import and export taxes (the United States government is constitutionally barred from the latter). It can also establish other controls over imports, exports, capital flows, and all types of foreign exchange transactions. Since the creation of the Central Bank, which establishes exchange rates, in 1935, few years have been free of one form or another of exchange control.

Price Controls

Besides controlling rates of public utilities and transportation facilities, the public sector often establishes maximum and minimum prices for rural and industrial commodities, and during the Perón years it totally controlled, through a marketing board, the commercialization of most exportable rural products.

This list could be extended. But what is already included demonstrates that, *at least on paper,* postwar Argentine governments have had at their disposal a formidable array of tools. A mechanical counting of policy instruments and objectives would show that the former exceed the latter, at least when only conventional economic policy objectives are considered. Furthermore, the national executive seldom has had to worry about being thwarted or delayed by Congress or local governments, and has had great *formal* freedom in matters such as tax rates and exemptions, import and export duties, budget expenditures, etc., which in many countries are subject to lengthy and complicated negotiations between the executive and the legislature. Under these circumstances it appears harder to carry out a laissez faire revolution than a socialist one.

We now turn to how and why the public sector evolved historically, and to the use of its policy instruments made at different times to stimulate economic growth.

THE ARGENTINE STATE AND GROWTH BEFORE 1930

Confronted by the vast postwar enlargement of public sector formal powers, some authors have regarded pre-1930 years, especially 1860–1930, as characterized by extreme laissez faire and an inactive public

September 1966, purely private banks accounted for only 42 percent of all assets of commercial banks; foreign private banks had 14 percent of all assets.

sector. This view is not accurate. Although policy instruments were less numerous and more limited, even then the government had at its disposal important mechanisms to influence the economy and its growth. Furthermore, state intervention in economic matters is considered legitimate in the Latin and Spanish traditions, and while some of the "liberals" who dominated the Argentine government fought this ancient custom, attachment to laissez faire was neither very deep nor widespread, even in the pre-1930 halcyon days. For example, as early as 1915–19, the government-owned Banco de la Nación Argentina, founded in 1891, accounted for 45 percent of all commercial banks assets in Argentina.[12] The Banco Hipotecario Nacional, also government-owned and founded in 1886, handled 37 percent of the total mortgage debt in 1925.[13] The public sector oil enterprise, Yacimientos Petrolíferos Fiscales, which started operating in 1907, accounted for 60 percent of all crude oil extraction during 1925–29 and operated refineries. About one-fifth of the railroad network was in public hands during 1925–29.[14]

It remains true that the public sector was a good deal smaller then than it was during postwar years. Only 4 percent of the labor force was employed by the general government in 1900–04; by 1925–29 this had risen to slightly above 5 percent.[15] But in determining public influence on growth, this is not too important. The impact of pre-1930 government policies on growth may be summarized under the following categories.

Growth Rate of the Labor Force

A major, if not *the* major, post-1860 public policy was to encourage European immigration to the empty pampean spaces to build a labor force. "To govern is to populate" became a favored slogan, liberal immigration laws were adopted, and government agents toured Eu-

12. *Anuario de la Sociedad Rural Argentina* (Buenos Aires, 1928), pp. 82–84; and Comité Nacional de Geografía, *Anuario Geográfico Argentino* (Buenos Aires, 1941), pp. 425–36.
13. See my *Essays on the Economic History of the Argentine Republic* (New Haven: Yale University Press, 1970), Table 20, chapter 1, and sources listed in note 12.
14. Oil data obtained from Oficina de Estudios para la Colaboración Económica Internacional, *Importaciones, industrialización, desarrollo económico en la Argentina* (Buenos Aires, 1963): 2, 316; railroad data obtained from *Anuario Geográfico Argentino*, p. 449.
15. U.N. Economic Commission for Latin America (hereafter, ECLA), *El desarrollo económico de la Argentina*, Statistical Appendix, mimeographed, p. 401.

rope "selling" Argentina to potential migrants. As a result, between 1857 and 1930 *net* immigration amounted to nearly 3.5 million persons; total population, which in 1869 was 1.7 million, reached 11.6 million.[16] Immigration, together with proportional increases in land under cultivation and capital stock, was expected to result in more than proportional output increments, as the size of the country in 1860 was deemed too small. Immigration influenced not only the rate of economic growth, but the whole Argentine social fabric.[17] For our purposes it is enough that there was a deliberate public policy to encourage massive immigration and that such policy was a major pillar of what today would be called the development plan.

Growth Rate of Capital Stock

The other major pillar of the pre-1930 development plan was the encouragement of foreign investment in Argentina, especially British. The encouragement ranged from guarantees on minimum rates of return and land grants, e.g. for railroads, to the maintenance of a political climate favorable to foreign investors. The government also issued bonds in foreign markets to finance *its* investments in social overhead capital, as well as other less productive expenditures.

Little more was done to deliberately influence the growth rate of capital. Global tax and monetary investment incentives were not known; public banks followed commercial standards on the whole and, excepting mortgage operations, did not deal usually with long-term credit.

Improvements in the Quality of the Labor Force

The major policy for improving the quality of the labor force was a rapid extension, after 1860, of primary education. The illiteracy rate,

16. See my *Essays,* chapter 1.
17. Factor proportions, especially the land/labor ratio, including under land all potentially usable areas, also changed substantially. Landowners, who controlled the relatively abundant factor of production and had considerable influence in the public sector in those days, stood to gain much from immigration of the scarce factors of production, labor and capital, and from free trade. Growth and urbanization led to a diversification of the social structure and a greater voice for the middle classes in government, especially after 1917, but rural landowners kept a good share of their political power. I have argued elsewhere that the fact that the most fertile Argentine lands are those relatively close to the seaboard and the urban center of Buenos Aires explains why, while the expanding frontier meant the near elimination of the eastern landlord in the United States as a significant economic and political agent, it was accompanied by the opposite effect in Argentina. The social and political status of

calculated as a percentage of the population fourteen years of age and older, dropped from 77 percent according to the 1869 census to 36 percent in the 1914 census, and it was probably around 25 percent in 1929. Many immigrants, although often unlettered, contributed an above-average spirit of entrepreneurship. But besides emphasizing European immigration, little was done to select immigrants on the basis of their skills.

Improvement in the Allocation of Resources

Foreign trade policies during 1860–1930, while not favoring completely free trade, sought to encourage exports. Argentine natural resources, mainly fertile land near ocean transportation, are not as specific as those in several countries for which staple theories of growth have been developed. But it remains true that during the last half of the nineteenth century encouragement of exports, together with complementary policies toward immigration and investment in social overhead facilities, brought into production lands whose value under autarky would have been very low.

During 1860–1930 public policy interfered relatively little with a resource allocation responding to signals originating in *world* markets, to which Argentine markets, for both goods and factors, were closely bound. Although parts of the economy were characterized by concentration of considerable economic power, the climate was on the whole more competitive than in post-1929 Argentina.

How did the pre-1930 development strategy perform? Although no aggregate output data are available before 1900, one may guess[18] that during 1860–1900 both total and per capita output grew at impressive rates. Between 1900–04 and 1910–14 population grew at 4.2 percent per annum, and gross domestic output expanded at an average annual rate of 6.3 percent. However, between 1910–14 and 1925–29, population grew at 2.8 percent and output at only 3.5 percent per year. If the 1860–1930 period is seen as a whole, there is little doubt that the development strategy achieved its objective of transforming Argentina from a backward and underpopulated pastoral country to one whose 1929 GNP per capita could be estimated at around 660 U.S. dollars, at 1964 prices.[19]

landowners was also reinforced by the fact that, in contrast with the rising urban classes, their families had usually been in Argentina for several generations.

18. See my *Essays,* chapter 1, for some supporting evidence.

19. For population and output data see ECLA 1: 15, and my *Essays,* chap-

By these measures the selective pre-1930 strategy performed well, even if we cannot allocate growth points to each of its main policies. But the key to its success also shows, in retrospect, its fragility. The strategy, concentrating on stimulating immigration, capital inflows, and exports, was linked to economic circumstances in Western Europe. When rapid European expansion of output and trade came to an end during 1914–29, stopped first by World War I and then by domestic economic difficulties and protectionism, Argentine growth sagged.

In common with most observers at the time, the authorities considered war and postwar economic difficulties temporary—and indeed the Argentine recovery from the sharp 1914–17 depression was rapid—so little was done to change the development strategy. It was assumed that changes in long-run demand and supply conditions, including variations in Argentine capital/land and labor/land ratios, would take place gradually, allowing for signaling by the price mechanism, thus permitting the desired modifications in the productive structure to proceed smoothly.

PUBLIC POLICY AND GROWTH, 1930–43

The spread of protection and trade controls in industrial countries, the Great Depression, and World War II had a profound cumulative effect on the Argentine public sector and on its view of optimum economic policy. The sector grew and its instruments multiplied.

During the first five years of the 1930s the government created exchange and trade controls, devalued the peso, increased tariffs, established regulatory agencies to supervise the production and marketing of rural products, imposed an income tax, and established a

---

ter 1. Data on factor payments abroad before 1935 are incomplete, but those available suggest that their share in GDP did not change much during 1900–29. Backward "guesstimates" of per capita GNP in 1860 are as follows:

Assumption: 1.5 percent per capita GNP growth, 1860–1929; $236.
Assumption: 2.0 percent per capita GNP growth, 1860–1929; $168.

Truth probably falls between these two estimates. Population expansion, which in resource-rich, labor poor countries could be taken as an index of "progress", was larger in Argentina than in Canada and Australia between 1869 and 1929. In Argentina, population in 1929 was 5.2 times what it had been in 1869, while for Canada and Australia the corresponding figures were 2.8 and 4.0 respectively. In most relevant senses, Argentina "developed" as well as "grew" between 1869 and 1929. It may be noted that the manufacturing growth rate was higher during 1900–29 than during 1930–65.

Central Bank. Large public works programs, especially in road building, were started. Public expenditure, which relative to gross domestic product (GDP) had remained rather stable during 1900–30, increased at a faster rate than GDP during this period.[20]

The discredit of the world liberal system, and particularly the
breakdown of pre-1930 patterns of international trade and finance,
led to a more aggressive use of policy instruments, but the first preoccupation was not so much with long-term growth as with the maintenance of exports, output, and employment, and with shielding the
Argentine economy from disturbances emanating from an erratic
world economy. Before 1930, in contrast, public policy had made
few attempts to offset cyclical fluctuations, although often gold convertibility had been suspended and the exchange rate allowed to
depreciate when exports or the capital inflow decreased. It was then
expected that world economic expansion would sooner or later re-
sume, and that immigration, exports, and capital inflows would follow. After 1929, however, the validity of the pre-1930 development
plan began to be questioned and, increasingly, rejected.

At first, most policy makers were solely preoccupied with Key-
nesian-type problems,[21] but soon it was noticed that the only sector
of the economy showing significant dynamism was that part of manufacturing that produced import-competing goods. (Quantitatively less
important for the country as a whole was the expansion of rural
import-competing activities, which had a strong impact on several
regional economies.) The good performance of import-competing activities arose to some extent spontaneously from changes in world
relative prices brought about by the Great Depression, but primarily
from government efforts to maintain *both* balance of payments equi-

20. In ECLA 1: 79, it is estimated, using data expressed at 1950 prices,
that all public expenditures represented 16 percent of GDP in 1900–04 and
1925–29; by 1935–39 this figure had risen to 21 percent. No breakdown of
these figures is available, and they may not be directly comparable to the
public expenditure percentages presented for 1955–59. However, they clearly
indicate an expansion in the relative role of public expenditure after 1930; between 1925–29 and 1935–39 both current and capital public expenditures increased as percentages of GDP, from 11 to 15 percent for the former, and
from 5 to 7 percent for the latter.

21. "Keynesian" is here used in a slightly different sense than when referring
to fully industrialized countries. While Argentine authorities were worried about
general unemployment and excess capacity, their policies also had *sectorial*
targets, as the Great Depression thrust upon Argentina the need to reallocate
resources to maintain balance of payments equilibrium even with low growth
rates of overall output.

librium and a high level of employment and economic stability. The balance of payments was under severe pressure owing to the fall in export values and capital inflow, and to large foreign debt amortizations, whose real burden was increased by the fall in the world price level. Drastic cuts in merchandise imports were required. Exchange rate devaluation, higher tariffs and import restrictions, and increasingly Keynesian monetary and public expenditure policies were used to achieve these short-term goals.

What started as a reaction to cyclical problems began, in the late 1930s, to be regarded as the cornerstone of a new long-run growth policy. The 1939 outbreak of hostilities further encouraged a school of thought that regarded import-substituting industrialization not as a spontaneous *consequence* of economic growth, but as its *cause*. Export values, on the other hand, were vieved as *exogenously* determined by world conditions. Furthermore, a country which before 1930 was a net importer of labor began to regard labor as a potentially surplus input, whose full employment could present policy problems.

But before 1943 this view was not yet official policy, although it had influential spokesmen, such as Dr. Raúl Prebisch, within government. So 1930–43 public economic policy should be judged using mainly its own Keynesian criteria and bearing in mind the state of economic knowledge at that time. Given world conditions, the Argentine economic performance must be regarded as good. Between 1927–29 and 1941–43, real GDP and the hard-pressed rural sector managed to grow at an annual rate of 1.8 and 1.5 percent, respectively, while manufacturing expanded at 3.4 percent. This growth did not depend on the outbreak of war;[22] by 1939 real Argentine GDP was nearly 15 percent above that of 1929, while the U.S. real GNP advanced by only 4 percent between 1929 and 1939. After dropping 14 percent between 1929 and 1932, the Argentine GDP expanded

22. Contrary to widespread opinion, the war had a net negative effect on Argentine growth. Real GDP rose by 27 percent during 1933–39 (ECLA), and by only 13 percent from 1939 to 1945 (BCRA). In spite of lack of foreign competition, manufacturing output rose by only 23 percent during 1939–45 (BCRA), while it had risen by 43 percent from 1933 to 1939 (ECLA). The war-induced leftward shift in the supply curve of new machinery and equipment led to an absolute fall in real investment in these capital goods, while all real capital formation fell as a percentage of GDP. Neutral Argentina had an especially difficult time in finding foreign supplies of key industrial inputs during and even immediately after the war, in spite of late support to the Allied cause.

every year until 1940. After 1934 open urban unemployment was not a serious problem (precise data on unemployment are lacking), although increased migration from rural to urban zones kept the fear of it alive.

Not all credit for this relatively good performance should be given to post-1930 policies. The ability of the economy to respond favorably to a changed international economic environment was influenced positively by what had been accomplished *before* 1930. As a result of the old development plan, the Argentine economy in 1929 was well provided with social overhead capital, a modern labor force, including managers, and a mass urban market for manufactured products. In short, its capacity to transform and industrialize was high relative to other Latin American countries.[23]

The 1930–45 period witnessed intellectual ferment, not only regarding optimum development policy, but also regarding wider goals of public policy and their relation to economic objectives and instruments. In particular, conflicts among different national objectives, which had been smothered by the 1860–1930 expansion whose dominant philosophy was the belief that economic growth cured all social ills, became easier to see during 1940–43. The coup of June 1943 burst onto this confused scene.

THE PUBLIC SECTOR AND GROWTH, 1943–55

The public sector was dominated during 1943–55 by the charismatic figure of General Juan Domingo Perón. Perón and his group explicitly gave priority to the following goals:

1. a greater degree of national autonomy;
2. a more equal distribution of political power, income, and wealth, not only among families, but also among different regions of the country. Greater security of income and employment for the urban masses was an important aspect of this goal.

These goals should be borne in mind when discussing Peronist policies toward growth, which otherwise often appear as a collection of incomprehensible economic blunders.

23. Whether it should have been made higher by greater diversification before 1930 is a question whose answer very much depends on one's view as to whether policy makers should have been able to forecast the Great Depression, and on one's faith in the allocative efficiency of an undistorted price mechanism.

Even before 1930 Argentine nationalism was aroused by the large share of the capital stock owned by foreigners. Furthermore, many urban groups resented the wealth and influence of landowners producing exportable goods. Contrary to English experience, free trade, which benefited owners of land, the relatively abundant factor of production, came to be regarded as a reactionary policy. As Argentine exportables account for a large fraction of wage earners' budgets, the clash of short-run interests between the urban masses and rural producers is highly visible.[24]

The Great Depression took away the main defense of the pre-1930 liberal system, namely that it generated growth, and the resentment against foreign investors, exporters, and large landowners increased in bitterness. Nonpampean provinces, which had benefited relatively little from the 1860–1930 expansion, also renewed, in a milder form, their pre-1860 quarrels with the city of Buenos Aires and pampean exporters. Politically, the 1930s were dominated by conservative regimes, which abandoned the liberal rules of the game and indulged in repression and massive electoral frauds, as well as notorious corruption.[25] Scandals involving foreign investors plus harsh British terms in the Roca-Runciman commercial treaty of 1933 further aroused Argentine nationalism during the 1930s.[26]

24. The gap between average labor and capital productivities in the Argentine export sector and those for the rest of the economy was not as wide as in countries exporting oil and minerals. Also in contrast with the latter, the natural resources generating pure rents were in the hands of local citizens. As a result, pressures on the government to spread rents of the export sector to the rest of society were weaker, delaying the emergence of the redistributive powers of the state (among families as well as among regions). National defense traditionally has been the strongest argument in favor of regional redistribution of income due to Argentine fears of Chile and Brazil, but the amounts involved have been relatively minor.

25. Paradoxically, these corrupt and dictatorial regimes placed a high quality team of economists and civil servants in key government positions. That team, including such names as Prebisch, Pinedo, and Malaccorto, was responsible for the successful weathering of the Great Depression by Argentina. It is tempting to draw a parallel between this paradox and more recent experiences in countries like Brazil, where talented economists have reached high government positions in regimes dominated by the armed forces.

26. In 1934 a British meat-packing company attempted to smuggle out of the country (marked as corned beef) records of its Argentine activities, which had been subpoenaed by the Senate under a law upheld by the Argentine Supreme Court. A foreign-owned electric company in Buenos Aires was charged a few years later with bribing public officials to obtain a renewal of its concession under favorable terms. In the Roca-Runciman treaty the United Kingdom, holding the threat of Commonwealth preferences over Argentine meat exports, was able to obtain substantial concessions regarding British exports

This background explains why Peronist emphasis on greater national autonomy and redistribution of power and income, even at the expense of economic growth and efficiency, met with massive popular support during its early stages. Before examining the post-1943 expansion of the public sector and its influence on growth, the world economic outlook, as viewed during the war and immediate postwar period, should also be noted. Forecasts for world trade among economists and other observers were then far from encouraging. They foresaw either a new depression or a war between the United States and the Soviet Union. Policy makers already leaning toward autarky, of course, were further encouraged in their views by these predictions, as well as by the unsettled conditions in world trade and finance from 1929 until the Korean truce.

The trend, already visible during the 1930s, toward a larger share of public expenditures in national output gained new momentum after 1943 and reached its high point during 1945–49. Table 7.2

Table 7.2: Argentine Public Sector Expenditures Expressed as Percentages of the Gross Domestic Product, 1935–39 and 1945–49

	1935–39	*1945–49*
Exhaustive expenditures	*15.1*	*20.1*
Consumption expenditures	*9.1*	*11.4*
Wages and salaries	6.9	7.9
Purchases of goods	2.2	3.5
Gross fixed investment	6.0	8.7
Nonexhaustive expenditures	*6.2*	*9.3*
Transfers	5.7	5.1
Other capital expenditures	0.5	4.2

Note: The percentages are calculated on the basis of the old series of national accounts expressed at 1950 prices. Because of this, and of probable differences in accounting methods, the figures in Tables 7.1 and 7.2 are not directly comparable.

Source: ECLA, *El desarrollo económico de la Argentina*, vol. 1, p. 80.

presents comparable data for 1935–39 and 1945–49; while during the 1930s the government share grew in the midst of weakness in

---

and investments in exchange for just a promise not to cut imports of Argentine meat below certain levels. One may speculate that the clash of interests between the beef-raising Argentine "oligarchy" and British meat packers, importers, and Commonwealth producers, accentuated by the Great Depression, was an important reason why profascist sentiment spread so rapidly among the Argentine upper classes after 1930.

several other sectors of the economy, the expansion between 1935–39 and 1945–49 took place mostly while world circumstances created favorable conditions for the Argentine economy (although no one was sure of how long that windfall would last).

The Peronist expansion of public policy instruments is not fully reflected in Table 7.2. The number and importance of public enterprises were sharply increased by the purchase of foreign-owned railroads and public utilities.[27] Using property confiscated from the Germans late in the war, new public manufacturing enterprises were also set up. Enterprises for oceanic, fluvial, and air transportation were either established or received new impetus.[28]

Control over financial institutions became nearly airtight. All bank deposits were "nationalized" in the sense that, on paper, they were redeposited at the Central Bank, which then lent them back to the commercial banks under certain conditions as to the allocation and terms of loans. Insurance companies and the stock and bond markets also came under close supervision. A new public bank, the Banco Industrial, was created to provide long-term credit to manufacturing, and old public banks expanded their operations considerably.[29]

27. It may be recalled that nationalization of railroads and public utilities was also fashionable in postwar Western Europe. The increase in the percentage corresponding to "other capital expenditures" in Table 7.2 for 1945–49 reflects the direct costs of nationalization.

28. In this, as in other matters. Peronist policies carried to extremes trends already noticeable before 1943. For example, in 1938 the government purchased three private railroad companies, and early in the war plans were made to use part of the Argentine blocked sterling balances to buy more railroads (these balances were also used before June 1943 to redeem part of the foreign debt held in England). The share of government railroads in the total network, measured as percentages of railways, rose from 14 percent in 1914 to 23 percent in 1934 and 31 percent in 1940. See *Anuario Geográfico Argentino*, p. 449. Perón took over, and probably overpaid for, a railroad network that had deteriorated badly during the war. A private headache became a public one, at a stiff price.

29. Of all banking loans and advances to industry, the Banco Industrial share rose from 22 percent in 1946 to 78 percent in 1949. During 1951–55 its share was 53 percent. See O. Altimir, H. Santamaría, and J. Sourrouille, "Los instrumentos de promoción industrial en la posguerra," *Desarrollo Económico*, 6, no. 24 (January-March 1967): 723. Hugh Schwartz has estimated a smaller but still substantial share for the Banco Industrial in all industrial loans during these years. *All* banking loans outstanding to manufacturing tripled (in real terms) between 1945 and 1948. See Hugh H. Schwartz, "The Argentine Experience with Industrial Credit and Protection Incentives, 1943–1958" (Ph.D. diss., Yale University, 1967), vol. 1, p. 78. The National Mortgage Bank came to finance directly a large share, in some years more than half, of private investment in housing, while the popular *cédulas hipotecarias* (mortgage pa-

The exchange control inherited by Perón was tightened and converted into still another instrument of an ultraprotectionist system. Multiple exchange rates, import licenses, and exchange permits had a clear protectionist purpose, besides maintaining their balance of payments role. A super marketing board (I.A.P.I.) became the only authorized exporter of most rural exportables; this institution also bought in bulk some foreign industrial raw materials. Although many of these controls over foreign trade were established, as during the 1930s, in response to Western European and U.S. trade policies, they were used for many other purposes besides bargaining with powerful foreign consumers and suppliers.

The creation of a vast social security system provided the public sector with a new source of revenue; until late in the 1950s this system generated a net surplus of funds, which was used to finance other government activities.

Prices and wages were often controlled, and this control was usually effective, in the sense that it was not easy to escape in the short run. Labor laws were changed, giving government and unions a greater voice in factory affairs.

Public policy instruments were clearly formidable during 1945–49, especially after 1946. Although during 1950–54 a partial retreat took place in the size and influence of the public sector, it was to remain more powerful than it had been before 1943. How did this "new" public sector influence economic growth?

Growth Rate of the Labor Force

During the postwar prosperity large immigration was again allowed. In five years, 1947–51, net registered immigration of 460,000 persons took place. There was also substantial unregistered immigration from neighboring countries. Although data are lacking, it appears that the average quality of overseas immigrants was somewhat superior to that of earlier ones, in part due to a more selective public policy. By 1947 the total labor force reached nearly 7 millions, so that the quantitative contribution of postwar immigration to growth was probably not great. This immigration again showed that in no economically relevant sense could Argentina be said to have been a "labor surplus" country. This is an important point to bear in mind when discussing the impact of Peronist policies on resource allocation.

pers) were withdrawn from circulation, after many years of useful service in mortgage markets.

Growth Rate of the Physical Capital Stock

Table 7.2 showed that public gross fixed investment increased from 6.0 percent to 8.7 percent of GDP between 1935–39 and 1945–49.[30] During 1950–54 this percentage declined to a level which, at 1950 prices, may be estimated at around 7 percent.[31] The direct impact of the public sector on capital formation, as it is usually defined, could then be said to have been positive. But note that, reflecting the postwar expansion of public enterprises, the increase in the public investment share in GDP came from public enterprise construction, repairs, and purchases of new machinery and equipment, rather than from general government construction. The latter's share, in fact, fell from 5.8 percent during 1935–39 to 4.5 percent during 1945–49, and to around the same level for 1950–54.[32]

Increasing the rate of public investment by transferring enterprises, such as the railroads, from the private to the public sector does not by itself do much for the overall growth rate. Because of this, and also because of government influence on private capital formation through policies regarding foreign investment, trade, credit, taxes, etc., it is better to look at overall investment figures. Table 7.3 presents investments in different types of capital goods as shares of

30. The reader should be warned that postwar relative prices for capital goods in Argentina were exceedingly high compared with those of other countries; they peaked precisely in 1950, which is the base year used in the estimates, at constant prices, of the investment rates shown in Table 7.2. Even the 1960 price structure, which influences the results shown in Table 7.1, is out of line with that of most other countries. As a result, Argentine rates of capital formation, measured at postwar prices, exaggerate the *real* amount of investment carried out, although they of course measure the effort, in terms of foregone consumption opportunities, involved in savings. The rise in the relative prices of capital goods, only marginally explained by changes in world prices, reflects the postwar deterioration of Argentina's capacity to transform savings decision into tangible machinery and equipment. On this see chapter 6 of my *Essays*.

31. According to the source for Table 7.2 the 1950–54 figure, at 1950 prices, was 8.0 percent. However this calculation uses GDP figures which are now known to have underestimated the level and growth of GDP. The new CONADE GDP series yields, for 1950–54, figures that on average are nearly 13 percent above the old series. According to the National Development Plan published in 1965, gross fixed public investment during 1950–54, *measured at 1960 prices,* was 5.2 percent of GDP. See CONADE, *Plan nacional de desarrollo, 1965–1969* (Buenos Aires, 1965), Table 9, p. 33.

32. These percentages come from data in 1950 prices found in the old series, Secretaría de Asuntos Económicos, *Producto e ingreso de la República Argentina en el período 1935–54* (Buenos Aires, 1955). The GDP percentage given in this source for 1950–54 general government construction is 5.0 percent.

Table 7.3: Total Gross Fixed Capital Formation and Its Composition Expressed as Percentages of Total Apparent Domestic Absorption, (at 1935 prices)

	1935–38	1939–45	1946–48	1949–51	1952–55
All gross fixed capital formation	11.2	9.0	12.1	11.8	12.3
General government construction	3.0	2.2	2.1	3.1	2.8
Other construction	2.5	3.1	3.7	3.8	3.7
Transport equipment	0.9	0.3	1.2	0.4	0.4
Other new machinery and equipment	3.4	1.8	3.7	3.2	3.4
Repairs	1.4	1.6	1.4	1.3	2.0

Source: Díaz Alejandro, *Essays*, Statistical Appendix, Table 116.

total domestic absorption (defined as consumption plus fixed investment plus government exhaustive expenditures). These percentages have been computed from series expressed at 1935 prices, which were closer to "normal" world prices than those of the postwar period.

In spite of postwar world economic conditions which, proving gloomy forecasts wrong, turned out to be better for Argentina than those of 1935–38, and in spite of large exchange reserves accumulated during the war, the rate of capital formation during the postwar Perón years was not much higher than during 1935–38. Furthermore, gross investment in new machinery and equipment, which represented 4.3 percent of absorption before the war, fell below that level once the favorable external circumstances of 1946–48 had passed. (Much of the 1946–48 investment simply replaced capital worn out during the war.) New credit and protection policies, often defended as leading to higher capital formation, showed meager net results in this respect, outside of housing and other construction.[33]

Improvements in the Quality of the Labor Force

The 1947 census showed that illiteracy had fallen to 14 percent of persons fourteen years of age and older. The growing complexity of the economy and pre-1943 achievements in primary education indicated the need for a policy that would concentrate on higher edu-

33. During 1943–53 Perón followed a hostile line toward foreign investment. But in 1935–38 foreign investment was contributing a very small share of capital formation, so that a comparison between prewar and postwar capital formation is not much affected by this switch in policy. In 1953 a new law established a more friendly attitude toward foreign investment. During the early postwar years capital formation was hampered in some branches of production by specific foreign supply shortages (e.g. oil-field equipment, according to David Felix). But after 1947 such difficulties lost importance.

cation and on education more directly linked to economic activity.

The Peronist record is mixed on this issue. There was a large expansion in the number of students attending intermediate and university centers.[34] Impetus was given to government-sponsored industrial apprenticeship programs; technical education was also expanded for older workers. The number of students attending industrial schools for technical education grew from 18,000 in 1945 to 38,000 in 1955.[35] Although a good part of this expansion was dictated by the momentum of previous educational achievements, the Perón regime accelerated the trend and took special interest in the technical education of workers. The expansion in the percentage of public consumption expenditures in GDP between 1935–39 and 1945–49, shown in Table 7.2, came to a large extent from increased expenditures not only on education, but also on new health and recreation facilities. Unfortunately, pre-1955 expenditure breakdowns comparable to those shown in Table 7.1 are not yet available.

This regime, however, also exerted negative influences on the quality of the labor force. The quality of education, especially in universities and high schools, declined as a result of friction between the regime and intellectuals and professionals.[36] Not even primary schools escaped heavy political propaganda. It was at that time that a "brain drain" from Argentina, often motivated by political persecution, was first noticed. Even as labor quality was being improved by technical education, declines in management efficiency, brought about by new labor legislation, often offset its favorable impact on productivity. This legislation and other Peronist policies also discouraged private interest in apprenticeship programs.

34. The following rough data may be given on this point:

Students Attending Educational Institutions in Argentina
(thousands)

	1939	1953	1955
Primary education	1,944	2,625	2,803
Secondary education (including vocational)	135	650	769
Universities	29	125	151

Data for 1939, the closest to 1943 that could be found, are taken from *Anuario Geográfico Argentino,* p. 498; later data are from DNEC, *Boletín de Estadística* (3rd quarter of 1963), pp. 18–22.

35. ECLA 2:247. Not much was done in the field of technical education in agriculture and livestock, however.

36. Peronism had a dark anti-intellectual streak, shared by both its populist and military wings, summarized in the slogan: "Alpargatas sí, libros no."

On the assumption that labor laws, propaganda, and government excesses are transient, while exposure to some form of education leaves a permanent favorable effect, it may be concluded that the *net* effect of Peronist policies on the quality of labor was positive. But it is not clear whether the *rate* of net improvement during 1943–55 was superior to that of earlier years.

Technological Change

A good case can be made that Peronist policies kept Argentina from taking full advantage of postwar world technological change. At least until 1953, many policies showing elements of xenophobic nationalism isolated Argentina from advances in knowledge taking place in the rest of the world.

The policy toward foreign investment, until 1953, deprived the country not so much of investable funds but primarily of access to new foreign technology and production methods. Licensing, patent agreements, and other contacts between domestic and foreign firms were also hampered by Peronist policies and attitudes.

Table 7.3 shows that expenditures on new machinery and equipment during 1946–55 were in fact lower, expressed as percentages of total absorption, than in 1935–38. The fraction of absorption devoted to new *imported* machinery and equipment fell even further between 1935–38 and 1946–55. It is generally accepted that new machinery and equipment embodies a good part of the technological change taking place in industrial centers. Policies leading to the decrease of this type of investment may then be blamed for obstructing technological change in the Argentine economy.

Perhaps the most dramatic example of a technological lag developed under Perón is provided by the rural sector. While temperate zone rural technologies were being revolutionized in North America and Western Europe, thanks to a large extent to public research and extension services, Argentine rural technological change continued at a snail's pace, with the government showing little interest in its promotion.[37] Ironically, while the government neglected local researchers who had developed new hybrid corn varieties as early as 1947, it was "bamboozled" by a European pseudo scientist into trying to create an atomic bomb. At that time the public sector also

37. For the sad story of the neglect, until 1956, of rural research and extension by the Argentine public sector, see chapter 3 of my *Essays*.

financed efforts to develop new types of airplanes and other military equipment domestically.

The Peronist economic climate was in other ways not conducive to rapid technological change. The friction between universities and government and the resulting brain drain have already been noted. Perón, incidentally, was neither the first nor the last strongman whose modernizing intentions were in conflict with his university policies. Protectionist and corporate-state policies also led to tacit market-sharing agreements among entrepreneurs, reducing pressures to cut costs by technological change and improvements in management techniques.

Improvements in the Allocation of Resources

The worst direct and indirect effects of Peronist policies on economic growth came from their negative influence on resource allocation, often difficult to reverse or correct, and creating severe bottlenecks. These structural imbalances neutralized positive influences on growth resulting from other policies.

The major misallocation involved a withdrawal of resources from production of exportable-type goods. Exchange rate and protectionist policies led to a worsening in domestic relative prices and the rates of return of activities, actual or potential, producing exportable goods. Especially hit were traditional rural activities, which also had to face shortages of labor and modern inputs. The decline in exportable output, together with an increase in domestic absorption of these goods, most of which may be regarded as wage goods, led to a fall in the export quantum of 20 percent between 1935–39 and 1945–49; by 1950–54 it was 37 percent below the 1935–39 level! [38]

If all or a major share of resources withdrawn from exportables had been directed to import-competing activities, the negative influence of the export drop could have been offset to some degree,

38. During 1950–54 unusually bad weather also affected rural output. Quantum data obtained from ECLA 1:115. For many rural activities the reallocation of resources implied not only a level of output below what it would have been under more neutral public policies, but also an *absolute* decline in output. In this respect, the drop of around two-thirds in the output of corn and linseed between 1940–44 and 1950–54 is noteworthy. Contrary to what happened during the 1930s, postwar Argentina's shares in world trade of her major export staples plummeted. Neither price inelasticity nor income inelasticity of world demand can be seriously blamed for Argentina's disastrous postwar export performance.

although the efficiency of the economy would still have suffered. But only a small fraction of those resources found their way to import-competing activities. CONADE data indicate that, of the sum formed by the increase in active population *plus* the reduction in the rural labor force between 1947 and 1955, only 26 percent went into oil, mining, and manufacturing, not all of which was truly import-competing, while 13 percent went into construction, another 13 percent into transport, communications, and public utilities, and 48 percent into commerce and other services.[39] According to ECLA data, housing, government, and other services obtained a huge chunk of net capital formation during 1945–55—nearly 70 percent.[40] Between 1941–43 and 1953–55 output of the commodity-producing sectors (agriculture, livestock, fisheries, oil, mining, and manufacturing) grew at an average annual rate far inferior to that for services.

On balance, resources were reallocated from internationally tradeable goods toward nontradeable services. Once the wartime reserves and the very favorable postwar terms of trade disappeared in 1949, a shortage in the foreign exchange required by a steady aggregate growth of, say, 4 or 5 percent per year appeared.

Stop-go cycles and output recessions accompanied by inflation became a feature of Argentine postwar economic history. Output fell in 1949 and in 1952, while the Buenos Aires cost of living rose by 31 percent in 1949 and by 39 percent in 1952. Lack of exchange triggered restrictive domestic policies and tighter import controls, leading to less than full utilization of installed capacity and labor, which often could not be run without imported inputs, difficult to replace on short notice. The importation of new machinery and equipment was assigned a marginal role. Imports needed to run established capacity, even in factories turning out goods of doubtful quality and social value, were given priority over those for expanding capacity. The budding domestic capital goods industry, which had *not* been singled out for special help, could not always fill the gap, while import substitution in intermediate goods was not fast

39. See my *Essays,* Table 19, chapter 2. The general government by itself captured 17 percent of this labor pool.

40. See *Essays,* Table 18, chapter 2. This figure probably exaggerates the share of these sectors, but not by much. An indirect effect of the rural policy was that, by inducing greater migration to cities, it put further pressure on the government to provide more social services and overhead capital, which are costlier in urban than in rural zones. See Andrés Bianchi, "Notas sobre la teoría del desarrollo latinoamericano", in *América Latina: Ensayos de Interpretación Económica* (Santiago: Editorial Universitaria, 1969), pp. 11–40.

enough to free a larger share of exchange for capital goods imports. The exchange bottleneck thus especially hit capital formation in the form of new machinery and equipment and associated technological changes.[41]

Besides the major misallocation leading to post-1948 payments difficulties and the uncertainties generated by stop-go cycles, other public policies also contributed to decreases in the capacity to transform and in the efficiency of the economy. The manner of allocating subsidized banking credit, foreign exchange, and import licenses among entrepreneurs, for example, discouraged competition and the entry of new firms. Labor productivity suffered from new work rules and labor legislation; in public enterprises and many government services the drop was spectacular due to overstaffing and poor management. Sectorial imbalances and bottlenecks after 1948 added cost-push elements to the postwar inflation, which in its early stages had received impetus from increases in world prices and the overexpansive expenditure and credit policies of the regime. This inflation, in turn, together with a policy of controlling and sporadically freezing selected prices, including exchange and interest rates, induced inefficient trends and fluctuations in relative prices. The microinefficiencies accumulated during the Perón regime were so large that they led Dr. Raúl Prebisch late in 1955 to expect a 10 percent increase in average labor

---

41. Under these conditions, a Chenery-McKinnon model appears more appropriate to measure the cost of resource misallocation than the neoclassical model employed by Arnold Harberger, among others. While in the latter model waste boils down to the difference between social marginal productivities in different sectors, in the former it is assumed that if one sector is not "right," *all other* sectors of the economy will work at less than their full efficiency. In terms of a growing economy, the former allows trade-offs among growth-promoting inputs, even if distortions exist, while in the latter if one growth constraint is binding (say the exchange constraint), it will do no good to expand other growth-promoting inputs. On this see the several writings of Celso Furtado, Osvaldo Sunkel and Aníbal Pinto, among others, for the United Nations Economic Commission for Latin America in the *Análisis y Proyecciones del Desarrollo Económico* series; see also *Essays,* chapter 6; Markos Mamalakis, "El sector exportador; etapas del desarrollo económico y el proceso ahorro-inversión en América latina," *El Trimestre Económico,* no. 134 (April-June 1967), pp. 319–41; and Hugh H. Schwartz, "Concerning the Contention that Efficiency in the Allocation of Resources Really Doesn't Matter Very Much After All," *Economic Development and Cultural Change,* vol. 18, no. 1, part 1 (October 1969), pp. 44–50. Note that even without stop-go cycles the exchange bottleneck would have lowered the post-1948 Argentine growth rate. The sporadic fashion in which authorities devalued the exchange rate and tackled inflationary and balance of payments problems led to stop-go cycles and *additional* inefficiencies.

productivity in industry during 1956 simply as a result of changes in work rules.[42]

Besides inducing exchange bottlenecks, stop-go cycles, and substantial microinefficiencies, public policy during 1943–55 failed to give enough attention to an area where government is generally expected to play a key role: social overhead capital linked to commodity production. Electricity shortages plagued industry throughout the Peronist years, often leading to shutdowns and the use of private generating facilities. Rural and industrial production also had to put up with worsening services from railroads and harbors. And public communication services, such as telephones and the mail, deteriorated.

An Evaluation of Peronist Economic Policies

It is difficult to quantify the net effect on growth of all Peronist policies, especially because the relevant comparison is not one contrasting Argentina's growth rates actually achieved in different periods, but one comparing what was achieved during 1943–55 with "what could have been," given the generally favorable world economic conditions for Argentina.[43] Furthermore, the influence of

42. See his "Sound Money or Uncontrolled Inflation," and "Final Report and Economic Recovery Programme," *Review of the River Plate*, 11 November 1955 and 20 January 1956. The fact that such an increase did not take place reveals the political difficulties involved in changing work rules, rather than the lack of inefficiency. The rate of inflation, however, was lower during the Perón years than after 1955; the average rate of annual price increase was 33 percent during 1955–64 and 16 percent during 1943–55.

43. Available data on historical growth rates, expressed as percentages per annum, are as follows:

	Real GDP	Population
1900–04/1910–14 (ECLA)	6.3	4.2
1910–14/1925–29 (ECLA)	3.5	2.8
1927–29/1941–43 (ECLA/CONADE)	1.8	1.9
1927–29/1941–43 (ECLA/BCRA)	1.8	1.9
1941–43/1953–55 (ECLA)	3.2	2.0
1941–43/1953–55 (CONADE)	3.3	2.0
1941–43/1953–55 (BCRA)	2.9	2.0
1953–55/1963–65 (BCRA)	3.1	1.7
1953–55/1964–66 (BCRA)	3.3	1.7

The initials in parentheses refer to the sources; ECLA refers to the old series of the Economic Commission for Latin America; CONADE to the revised series of the Consejo Nacional de Desarrollo for 1935–63; BCRA refers to the revised series of the Central Bank for 1935–66. See *Essays*, chapter 2 and the notes to the Statistical Appendix, for a discussion of these data and sources.

When post–World War II years are taken as a whole, the following results emerge:

Peronist policies on post-1955 growth should also be taken into account.

At first glance, the growth achieved during 1943–55, although not spectacularly high, does not seem unusually low either.[44] A closer look, however, shows how dependent that growth was on the unusually favorable exogenous conditions of the immediate postwar period. Of the total *increase* in real GDP between 1941–43 and 1953–55, 77 percent took place between 1941–43 and 1947.[45]

	Real GDP	Real GNP	Population
1945–49/1962–66 (BCRA)	2.7	2.4	1.9
1947/1966 (BCRA; most unfavorable result)	2.4	1.9	1.9

Postwar cycles have been so marked that, even when estimating growth rates for long periods, averages for several years should be taken as end points, or trend lines should be fitted to *all* annual points.

It is interesting that the secular growth rate is little changed whether data expressed at constant 1960 or 1935–39 prices are used. Employing BCRA time series at 1960 prices, one obtains a GDP growth rate of 3.0 percent per annum between 1935–39 and 1964–68. When the same BCRA sectorial quantum series are weighted (somewhat roughly) using 1935–39 prices, one surprisingly obtains the slightly higher growth rate of 3.2 percent per annum. By concentrating on the manufacturing vs. rural sector debate, one can forget that not all sectors growing faster than GDP saw their relative prices increase during the period under discussion; important counterexamples in Argentina are mining, transport and communications, public utilities and housing and government services. These relatively fast growing sectors experienced declines in their relative prices only partly due to faster than average productivity gains; most suffered from the combination of inflation and price controls. It is a moot point whether similar results would be obtained using "world" prices, which at any rate present conceptual difficulties for non-traded goods.

44. Between 1941–43 and 1953–55 another "country of recent settlement," Canada, had an average annual growth rate in its real GNP of 3.3 percent, while its population expanded at a rate of 2.3 percent per annum. Data from M. C. Urquhart and K. A. H. Buckley, eds., *Historical Statistics of Canada* (Toronto: Macmillan Co. of Canada, 1965), pp. 14 and 132.

45. According to BCRA data. The same source indicates that the 1955 per capita GDP was 4.4 percent *below* that reached in 1947. CONADE figures show that 61 percent of the GDP increase took place between 1941–43 and 1947, and 75 percent took place between 1941–43 and 1948. Using different weights Hugh Schwartz has obtained higher manufacturing growth rates than those of official sources; see his "Argentine Experience," vol. 1, Table 10, p. 130. Most debatable are manufacturing growth rates for 1943–50; different sources yield the following annual average percentage growth rates for manufacturing output in those seven years:

Schwartz	7.6
Old ECLA (1950 weights)	5.9
New CONADE (1960 weights)	5.8
New BCRA (1960 weights)	2.9

Viewed in this light, the Peronist growth record and its post-1955 legacy are far from satisfactory.

Economic growth was not the only policy goal during 1943–55. It could be argued that a mediocre growth performance was a price willingly and consciously paid to achieve greater national autonomy and a redistribution of income, security, and power in favor of urban masses and the nonpampean provinces. To some extent this is true. But this argument is weakened by Peronist inconsistencies and inefficiencies, now defined more broadly, with respect to minimum-cost ways of obtaining social as well as economic goals.

Some examples may be given. Consider the policy toward railroads; presumably it was desired to achieve a certain degree of national control over them at a minimum cost to other targets, including growth. Their purchase, all at once and using convertible reserves as well as blocked sterling balances, does not appear in retrospect as the minimum-cost method of obtaining a given degree of national control, measuring cost as the opportunity foregone to obtain other targets.

Debt policy provides an example of inconsistency, probably due to bad forecasting. In the immediate postwar period the foreign debt was wholly "repatriated"; a few years later the government had to borrow from abroad to meet exchange difficulties, and the terms of the new loans were far less favorable to Argentina than the old. Bad forecasting, resulting from superficial economic views, also explains why Peronist industrialization policies, motivated by a desire for greater national autonomy, resulted in a heavy dependence on imported inputs.

Ironically, it is very likely that, if greater attention had been given to exports, both manufacturing growth and national autonomy would have been greater than those actually achieved. An explicit but misguided industrialization policy can be a lot worse for industrial expansion than a policy that encourages growth across the board.

An industrialization program for greater autonomy should presumably give priority to capital goods industries and to activities producing their intermediate inputs. In fact, Peronist policies mainly favored, at least until around 1953, "light" industries whose growth rate before 1943 was already high (e.g. textiles and clothing). Between 1939–43 and 1952–55 domestic output of new machinery and equipment grew at a slower rate than between 1952–55 and 1962–

64, even though the earlier period started from a lower base.[46] Production of "heavy" industrial inputs of general use also did not receive as much attention as might have been expected. Much was said and little done about steel and petrochemical production, while the annual growth rate of oil output in Y.P.F. (the state-owned company) from 1943 to 1955 was only 3.7 percent, compared with 8.2 percent during 1929–43. In short, while foreign trade policies yielded a sharp cut in the capacity to import, especially new machinery and equipment, industrialization policies did little to provide a large domestic flow of these goods and of other heavy industrial products. From both a nationalistic and a growth point of view, this policy combination presented serious deficiencies and inconsistencies.

Perhaps the best defense of Peronist policies is that they represented a pioneering effort to combine and reconcile different social goals, using the power of the state within a mixed semi-industrialized society. In 1946 Perón's independent foreign policy, his preoccupation with national autonomy and social welfare, his interest in industrialization, etc., were relatively new phenomena in semideveloped countries.[47] At least part of the Peronist mistakes may be blamed on the lack of experience and knowledge on which the regime could draw to chart its pioneering path.

THE ARGENTINE STATE AND ECONOMIC GROWTH SINCE 1955

Both the relative size and the policies of the public sector were being modified, during the last years of the Perón regime, away from what had been done before 1951–52. This trend became more marked after 1955.

The snapshot presented earlier of the 1955–59 public sector could not reveal this decline in the relative size and influence of govern-

46. The annual rates of growth are 7 percent and 13 percent, respectively. See *Essays,* Table 11, chapter 6.

47. Many years before the Alliance for Progress made economic planning fashionable in Latin America, the Peronist regime produced two development plans. However, they added little to the rationalization of public policy, with the exception of some aspects of the second plan. Building on research that had been carried out in the Central Bank before 1943, the Peronist regime was one of the first governments in Latin America to prepare a detailed estimation of national income, output, and expenditure. The Peronist regime should also be credited with other accomplishments difficult to quantify, such as generating in the working class a feeling of self-respect and participation in national life.

ment. But other evidence shows that in spite of the still formidable array of instruments at government disposal they have become less numerous and effective. A basic reason for this loss of effectiveness is that to talk about "the" public sector after 1955 requires considerable abstraction. Between September 1955 and 1967 five national political regimes can be distinguished.[48] Each underwent frequent cabinet crises and policy changes, so that it is difficult to generalize about any one of them. The political stalemate between Peronist and anti-Peronist groups often paralyzed the state; furthermore, different parts of the public sector were controlled by non-Peronist groups warring with each other. Within the armed forces, certainly no monolith, opposing factions have led the country to the brink of civil war more than once.

The revenue machinery has reflected the gradual loosening and disintegration of the public sector. With all variables expressed in constant 1960 prices, current general government revenues, including social security, declined from 21.7 percent of GNP during 1950–55 to 19.6 percent during 1956–63. In fact, the *level* of real current revenues fell slightly between 1956–58 and 1959–61 and fell again, more sharply, between 1959–61 and 1962–63.[49]

Policies have changed with bewildering rapidity. President Frondizi followed, starting in December 1958, an open-arms policy toward foreign investment; in particular, he changed traditional policy regarding foreign investment in oil. A few years later the Illia govern-

48. They are: (1) the Provisional Government of September 1955 to May 1958, with two presidents; (2) the constitutional regime of A. Frondizi, from May 1958 to March 1962; (3) the Provisional Government of March 1962 to October 1963; (4) the constitutional regime of A. Illia, from October 1963 to June 1966; and (5) a military regime, from June 1966 to June 1970. Often these changes of government have been greeted with a sickly euphoria, while public opinion expects new ministers to perform economic miracles in a few months.

49. CONADE, *Plan nacional de desarrollo*, p. 35, Table 10. Tax evasion has become a more serious problem since 1955, especially with respect to the income tax and social security contributions. Since 1955 the public sector has also sold some of its smaller public enterprises to private groups. According to BCRA, public consumption and construction expressed as percentages of GNP (variables expressed in 1960 pesos) have evolved as follows:

	General government consumption	Public construction
1950–54	9.3	3.3
1955–59	8.8	2.6
1960–64	8.5	3.2
1965–66	7.4	2.0

ment annulled the concessions that had been granted to foreign oil companies, thus incurring the wrath of foreign investors. Tax and tariff concessions and exemptions have been given to stimulate different types of investments, but the rules have been changed frequently. Most post-1955 regimes have made efforts to remedy the exchange bottleneck, but exchange rate and foreign trade policies have been highly unstable; coupled with the continuance of inflation, this has led to severe gyrations in the relative prices of exportable and importable goods. The incentive effects of the higher (on the average) relative prices for exportables registered since 1955 have been offset to a large extent by their fluctuations. Instability in economic policies has continued to be reflected in widely divergent year-to-year changes in aggregate output; according to BCRA data, during 1956–66 four years showed negative growth rates, while growth rates larger than 7.0 percent were registered in five other years.

Even though post-1955 economic ministers, and even planners, have had little time to worry about the long-term impact of their policies (as they have been concerned mainly with short-run exchange or output crises and political survival), a few generalizations about the effect of post-1955 public policies on growth can be made.

The most encouraging change has taken place in public rural research and extension services. Since 1956 an autonomous public body (INTA), fortunately somewhat isolated from political vagaries, has expanded its activities, whose pay-off is just beginning to be seen in higher rural yields. Industrial technological change has also been encouraged by the possibility of greater contacts with foreign industrial centers, not all of which involve direct foreign investment, and some changes in work rules and labor legislation.[50]

Public policy has tended to correct some misallocations induced

50. On the other hand, political and economic instability have led to an increase in emigration, whether temporary or permanent no one knows, of skilled manpower and professionals. Besides lowering the average quality of the labor force, this outflow has affected universities and other centers of research. Net capital inflow has been on the whole larger after 1955 than during 1943–55, but Argentine gains from it are not obvious in all cases. Much of this foreign capital has gone into protected, import-substituting activities (e.g. automobile production), while part has gone toward purchasing existing assets from Argentines whose private liquidity preference may be socially harmful. Argentina also contracted a large foreign debt in a mostly unplanned fashion. As counterpart to the greater use of foreign capital since 1955, the external debt has become more of a policy problem than it was during the Perón years. During 1963 through 1967, partly to pay off debt, cumulative Argentine current account surpluses in the Balance of Payments reached nearly $1 billion.

by the Peronist regime. Exports have increased, especially since 1962. Electricity bottlenecks have been eliminated, at least temporarily. With the help of direct foreign investment and a larger domestic output of capital goods, gross investment in new machinery and equipment expressed as a percentage of total absorption (all variables in 1935 prices) rose from 3.8 percent during 1952–55 to 5.6 percent during 1956–64.[51] In contrast to the years between 1941–43 and 1953–55, the total output of the commodity producing sectors has expanded at a faster rate than services between 1953–55 and 1963–65. Yet in 1966 per capita GNP, according to BCRA, was only fractionally higher than that reached in 1947 (49.9 thousand pesos at 1960 prices).

Although many policies were improved after 1955, it is not yet clear whether the net effect of the public sector on Argentina's growth is positive. Protection and credit policies continue to maintain and induce fresh misallocations of resources, including widespread excess capacity. Public services still leave much to be desired, and many public investment projects appear to have a social rate of return inferior to those that could be obtained in private activities.

A major difficulty hampering resource reallocation has been the curious fashion in which the existing structures of production and of labor allocation tend to promote a level and structure of demand that make reallocation unnecessary. That demand has been promoted by politically pressuring the public sector into using its policy instruments (tariffs, credits, subsidies, etc.) so as to generate the revenues needed to keep existing capacity functioning normally and, in some cases, to expand it. Typically, governments have been weak and have yielded, helping supply to create its own demand, regardless of social opportunity costs. Many entrepreneurs have found influencing public policy more profitable than reducing costs and seeking new markets and investment opportunities.

PUBLIC POLICY AND ECONOMIC GROWTH

If one conducts a mental experiment comparing actual Argentine postwar growth with what it would have been had the public sector

51. Sources as in Table 7.3. During 1956–64 all gross fixed capital formation averaged 13.6 percent of total absorption, at 1935 prices. For a more detailed discussion of post-1955 policies, especially toward the balance of payments, see my *Exchange-Rate Devaluation in a Semi-industrialized Country: The Experience of Argentina, 1955–1961* (Cambridge: M.I.T. Press, 1965).

limited its role to that assigned by a neoclassicist, laissez faire economist (flexible exchange rates, zero or low protection, steady and "neutral" fiscal and monetary policies, few or no public enterprises, free capital flows, concentration of public expenditures on health and education, etc.), it is not hard to conclude that the net effect of actual government policies on growth has been negative. Reference to pre-1930 experience, after taking into account the crudity of policy instruments then available and the weaknesses of pre-1930 economic knowledge, reinforces a presumption in favor of a highly selective and restrictive set of government policies toward growth. Even granting that *theoretically* the government could increase growth rates, should we not conclude in the light of economic history that to further growth the Argentine state should return to a neoliberal, laissez faire role?

An initial problem, although relatively unimportant for our purposes, is the difficulty of implementing that resolve when one starts with a public sector as large and a political situation as complex as Argentina's. Since 1955 many economic ministers have espoused laissez faire views, and yet they have been able to accomplish relatively little in reducing the public sector role in an efficient manner. (As in the case of stopping inflation, the remedy can become worse than the disease.) Furthermore, there is always the difficulty of defining what a "neutral" policy toward growth really is.

More fundamentally, the trivial but true fact remains that the public sector has other targets besides fast economic growth. And to achieve these other goals, such as national autonomy and a desired regional and personal distribution of income and security, the old-fashioned liberal state is usually not enough. Even knowing that the net effect of policy may be detrimental to growth, many countries will still prefer having a strong interventionist state for the sake of obtaining other goals. In semi-industrialized countries this will typically be the case, and no amount of preaching against nationalism and social reform is likely to diminish their appeal. And although the point can be argued, it is doubtful that this appeal is limited to elites in those countries.

Accepting a variety of goals, however, does not justify every public measure. Enlightened policy involves a recognition of trade-offs and priorities among targets, a careful assessment of the costs involved in using each policy instrument, and a realistic knowledge of what each instrument can hope to achieve. (Clearly, the less certain one is about the effect of using a given tool, the less it should be used.) Unfortunately, in Argentina, as in other countries, in the heat of political battles it is often argued, even at the highest levels of policy making and by people who know better, that such and such policy can be cheaply implemented *and* will increase the growth rate *and* will improve income distribution *and* will expand national autonomy. Policies for which this is true are, alas, few.

As in the case of other Latin American governments, the Argentine public sector has by now accumulated a wide array of policy instruments driven by the need to achieve long-run national goals, as well as by short-run and myopic political motivations. A reformist government of a mixed economy in this situation should worry less about extending the size of the public sector than about perfecting instruments already at its disposal and deciding what goals should receive which priority.[52] Even as it increases the effective public role in economic and social life, that process could lead to a small quantitative weight for the public sector in GNP, as many instruments now available are not being used in an efficient, minimum-cost fashion. A reexamination of goals and instruments should lead to discarding many old shibboleths about which public actions are labeled progressive or reactionary.[53] It should also produce a clearer sense of priorities for the public sector, which has often started actions on a hopelessly overextended front.

To conclude, some concrete examples of important areas where public sector actions could be considerably improved, but which often involve thorny trade-offs among goals, can be given.

Argentine public enterprises leave much to be desired. A temptation, stimulated by many frustrated efforts to improve their economic efficiency, is to turn them over to private enterprise. Although that

52. In this context, discussions as to whether one more key sector should be nationalized appear, at this stage of the game, of low priority. Although it has been shown that in an uncertain world it is desirable to have as many policy instruments as possible, that analysis assumes that the instrument variables being manipulated do not use up resources during the process either of decision making or of implementation. See William Brainard, "Uncertainty and the Effectiveness of Economic Policy," *American Economic Review* 57, no. 2 (May 1967): 411–25.

53. For example, one may wonder whether protection serves nationalist goals when it increasingly benefits foreign investors. Preoccupation with infant local entrepreneurs, rather than with infant industries, seems much more relevant. See Osvaldo Sunkel's stimulating "Política nacional de desarrollo y dependencia externa," *Revista del Instituto de Estudios Internacionales de la Universidad de Chile,* Año 1, no. 1 (April 1967).

policy may not be necessarily optimal for efficiency (private managers in many of these enterprises could not afford prices equal to marginal costs), it may minimize the maximum harm that those enterprises can do to efficiency and the growth rate. In view of history, it could be argued, this would be a wise course to follow. If Argentina could count on a vigorously expanding class of *local* entrepreneurs who could take over those enterprises and who would be willing to submit to broad public regulations, that solution would have great appeal. But in fields such as oil, railroads, telephones, electricity, and steel, withdrawal by the public sector would almost surely be followed by the entrance of foreign investors. In view of the frictions that even developed countries have had with foreign capital, and assuming that Argentina does not wish to follow the Puerto Rican development model, that outcome, even admitting that it would improve economic efficiency, cannot be said to be socially desirable. The only practical way to reconcile nationalistic and efficiency goals is to keep on trying to turn the public enterprises into modern concerns; greater *effective* decentralization, especially in financial matters, may be a way to achieve this end.[54] In some areas, such as oil, the creation of pan-Latin American public enterprises may lead not only to greater efficiency, but also to a sharp increase in their bargaining power vis-à-vis foreign concerns which may be allowed to cooperate, for the sake of their technological knowledge, in "sensitive" areas of production.

The record of formal economic planning in Argentina is far from brilliant. (The last two plans were published, after months of laborious preparation, not long before the governments sponsoring them were overthrown by military coups.) Yet it is hard not to conclude

54. Some public enterprises have been run as private playthings of powerful political chiefs, while their financing remained closely linked to the national budget. Writing on Argentina, David Felix has pointed out:

Public enterprises have tended to partition off from effective central control to become semi-independent feudal principalities with coteries of trade unions and private supplier and user firms jointly milking the public enterprise through high input prices and low prices for the output, while acting as a strong political force to protect the symbiotic arrangement.

While central authorities have lost control over these enterprises, they are expected to passively foot the bill for their deficits. See Felix, "On Gapsmanship and the Prospects for Less Developed Countries," mimeographed (St. Louis, Mo., 1967), p. 65. Much research remains to be done on Argentine and Latin American public enterprises as well as on other parts of the public sector, including possible differences in the behavioral characteristics of different agencies.

that some central planning under a stable government could improve public sector effectiveness. Much can be done in such areas as research and educational policy, public investment allocation, the improvement of traditional public services (statistics, the post office, etc.), and other pedestrian areas covered by budget expenditures. Credit, tax, social security, and protectionist policies could be improved, and the promotion of technological change could be studied systematically. A planning unit looking at these matters from a long-run perspective could, by the weight of its knowledge, keep short-lived ministers from taking hasty, inefficient actions. Policies could not only be improved, but could be made more steady, something that in the light of recent Argentine history would be no small improvement.[55]

Tax policy could be made to play a larger role in reconciling economic efficiency with desired income distribution. For example, many Argentines have traditionally objected to the use of a free exchange rate to regulate the balance of payments because that policy, compared with one of overvalued rates and import controls, yielded an income distribution favorable to landowners producing exportables. Larger taxes on rural land, not on its output, could free exchange rate policy for allocative rather than distributional ends. Rational study of bids presented by foreign investors would also form an important part of an integrated planning system, which would thus look not only after growth targets, but also after other national priorities.

Comments by Erik Thorbecke

Díaz is one of the most perceptive students of the Argentine economy. His paper provides a very good description of the role of the government in the economic development of Argentina over the last century. The discussion is sound, well documented, and generally

55. For Argentina, no less than for other economies, this dictum of J.E. Meade applies: "In fact, planning *and* the price mechanism not planning *or* the price mechanism should be a central theme of every modern economist's work." See Meade, "Is the New Industrial State Inevitable?" *Economic Journal* 78, no. 310 (June 1968): 392. Argentina certainly needs better planning while giving a freer, undistorted price mechanism a greater role in allocating resources.

convincing. At the same time the analytical framework underlying the study is more implicit than explicit. I shall therefore succumb to the temptation of suggesting ways of improving and specifying more concretely the methodological framework.

It is clear that any examination and evaluation of the role of the government in fostering economic development requires the specification of the major economic and social goals sought by the policy maker as well as of the policy means and instruments available to him. Conceptually, one can view the goal of government as trying to maximize a social welfare function whose major elements are such policy objectives as output (static economic efficiency), income distribution, employment, balance of payments, and price stability. It is obvious that any set of policy objectives can be mutually complementary or conflicting. In the latter case, policy means directed toward the attainment of one or more of the goals may be in conflict with the attainment of others. It is therefore essential to try to specify as well as possible—preferably in a quantitative way—the relative weights to be assigned to the various policy objectives. Such a specification of the welfare function makes it possible to compare *ex ante* goals with *ex post* performance and to test thereby the efficiency of the public sector in attaining its objectives. It is of course true that uncontrollable factors might have interfered with what would otherwise have been successful performance (e.g. an unanticipated drop in export receipts). These extenuating circumstances have to be taken in consideration in evaluating the role of the government.

There are at least two ways to evaluate the efficiency of the government in attaining its goals. First, the outcome of alternative sets of policies on developmental and other goals could be estimated to ascertain how performance resulting from actual policies compares with that estimated to result from alternative sets. Second, the actual performance of the economy as judged by specific indicators, such as the growth rate of GNP, the distribution of income, and the degree of price stability, can be compared to that of other relatively similar countries. In the case of Argentina the relevant set for comparative purposes would appear to be the regions of recent settlement: Australia, Canada, New Zealand, and the Union of South Africa.

In the first case the actual performance of the Argentine economy in terms of goal achievement would be compared to what it might have been under alternative policies. This procedure may have to rely on judgments of an essentially qualitative nature. Such a procedure could, however, be helpful in suggesting orders of magnitude of the opportunity cost of having achieved certain goals as opposed to others. In the second case the international comparison could be useful in illustrating the very high cost of certain Argentine policies in terms of foregone economic development. Likewise, a comparison of the experience of recently settled countries could help identify policies that were conducive to their development and that could have been (or may still be) implemented in Argentina. Neither of these two approaches is explicitly followed in the paper.

Granted that the emphasis of the paper is on the role of government in furthering economic development, it still does not justify the lack of analysis of price stability as an objective. One gathers that Argentine policy was often procyclical rather than countercyclical (indicating perhaps a low welfare weight attached to price stability). It would have been interesting to have analyzed how monetary tools were used to achieve certain goals and the resulting opportunity cost in terms of a high rate of inflation.

The paper does not contain any sectorial breakdown of government expenditures. Yet it is claimed, and probably correctly so, that one of the high costs of import substitution policy was the retardation of the adoption of new technologies in agriculture. A breakdown and analysis of current and capital expenditures by sectors and categories (e.g. how much went into agricultural research, extension, and credit) would have been very instructive in measuring the social payoff of different programs. Such a sectorial analysis of public expenditures would undoubtedly have thrown more light on the "unbalanced growth" development strategy followed by the Argentine government until fairly recently, favoring the domestic production of consumer goods and discriminating against agricultural output and consequently exports.

Finally, it would have been helpful to have analyzed the sources of public investment. For instance, to what extent was public investment over time financed from savings on current account as opposed to foreign investment?

My suspicion is that adoption of the above suggestions to strengthen the methodological and analytical framework underlying the study would not have altered the conclusions. Indeed it appears likely that it would have refined these conclusions and provided greater support for them.

8

Government Objectives and Achievements in Fostering Economic Development in Israel

BY HOWARD PACK

The functioning of the economy of Israel is paradoxical. The dominant political parties and the most powerful economic institutions are avowedly socialist in ideology, yet the importance of government and quasi-government ownership of the means of production is limited. Nevertheless, government management of the economy is so pervasive that it is impossible to explain the country's economic development within the framework of traditional categories such as comparative advantage and income elasticities of demand. Rather, the changing structure of the productive sectors must be viewed largely as the result of the adaptation of decision makers in these sectors to economic circumstances determined by public policy. Among the instruments determining these conditions were foreign trade restrictions (quotas, high tariffs), subsidies, investment allocations, and special tax benefits. The value and mix of these instruments were decided upon in response to the objectives that the government felt were of greatest importance to the economy, namely, labor absorption, elimination of a large import surplus, and the geographic dispersal of the population. This is not meant to imply that a detailed economic plan was followed in which instruments were adjusted in a consistent manner to attain given targets. We choose to analyze the policies that were adopted in terms of the instrument-target framework, however, since this permits an evaluation of the consistency and efficiency of economic policy. Accordingly, the plan of this paper is first to discuss the basic problems that the economy faced, and suggest a policy model

Janet R. Pack offered many helpful suggestions on an earlier draft. The usual disclaimer is in order.

for analyzing them; we then describe the main instruments employed, and finally evaluate their impact on the desired goals.

Labor Absorption

Between 1950 and 1965 both the population and the labor force increased one and a half times, a compound growth rate of 5 percent per annum. As a result of the mass immigration between 1948 and 1950, the unemployment rate had already reached 11 percent by 1950, with at least an additional 5 percent of the labor force employed only part time and seeking more work.[1] Thus between 1950 and 1965 new employment opportunities had to be generated at a rate of 5.2 percent per annum if full employment was to be attained by the end of the period. The rate of job creation was, to a large extent, dependent upon government policies; given the overall rate of capital accumulation, its employment-generating effect depended upon the levels of capital intensity in specific branches, which in turn were a function of governmentally determined relative factor prices and the sectorial distribution of investment funds, which was also decisively influenced by public policy.

The Balance of Payments

Since the beginning of statehood, Israel's balance of payments on current account has been unfavorable, the import surplus often exceeding 15 percent of gross national product. As a large proportion of this deficit was covered by unilateral transfers in every year, the problem posed by the deficit was not so much the need to plan repayment of borrowed funds as that of preventing the implantation of anticipation of levels and rates of growth of private consumption exceeding the economy's resources. As long as continued (costless) financing of the import surplus was available, it was possible to maintain a high rate of consumption increase as well as to sustain high investment levels. It was recognized, however, that, with the diminution of these flows over time, continued development would require the gradual elimination of the payments deficit and a move

1. This estimate is based on the actual underemployment rates obtained from the labor force surveys for 1956, when underemployment was 3.6 percent. We assume that it would have been at least one-third higher in 1950, and even this is probably an underestimate.

toward a higher national savings rate. If these were not realized, foreign exchange shortages would eventually act as a constraint upon the rate of growth of output,[2] given the need to import substantial amounts of raw and semifinished materials that either were absent or for which the domestic market was too small to permit reasonably efficient production.

Population Dispersal

When independence was achieved in 1948, much of the population of Israel was located in a narrow coastal strip between the two major cities of Haifa and Tel Aviv. The southern area, the Negev, contained two-thirds of the total land area but less than 1 percent of the total population.[3] A program of dispersal was begun and new immigrants were settled in the southern region, as well as in underpopulated districts in the rest of the country. Large numbers of new agricultural settlements as well as "development towns" were established in these areas and received special treatment in the provision of both social overhead facilities and economic privileges. By the end of 1954, 4.1 percent of a vastly increased population resided in the Negev, rising to 6.9 percent by the end of 1957;[4] moreover, these percentages do not reflect the additional dispersal resulting from the rapid population increase in development towns in other parts of the country.

On purely economic grounds the dispersal program may not have been justified, since the cost of augmenting the existing social overhead facilities in the major population centers and agricultural settlements would almost certainly have been lower than the erection of completely new facilities in outlying areas. Similarly, locating new factories and farms away from the majority of plants and population as well as from major ports led to increased transportation costs for both inputs and outputs. Although these negative aspects of the dispersion policy were known beforehand, they were overlooked on social, political, and military grounds.

2. Although it might be useful to also explicitly consider the maximization of the rate of growth of income as a policy goal, in view of the oft-predicted foreign exchange bottleneck, it seems more convenient to subsume this goal under the balance of payments target.

3. *Statistical Abstract of Israel, 1965* (Jerusalem: Central Bureau of Statistics, 1966), p. 27.

4. *Statistical Abstract of Israel, 1961* (Jerusalem: Central Bureau of Statistics, 1962), p. 32.

POLICY FRAMEWORK

In pursuing the goals of economic policy, it is well known that the number of instruments utilized must at least equal the number of objectives to be attained. Usually it is implicitly assumed that the measures taken by the authorities will be macroeconomic. However, in Israel it is evident that at least one objective, population dispersal, is not easily amenable to such measures, and this would lead to the expectation of the use of at least one microeconomic instrument. The surprising feature of the policies adopted is that almost *all* measures were microeconomic, i.e. there was only a limited effort to use conventional tax and monetary policies to achieve desired goals. Most attempts at controlling the economy were implemented through such micro devices as investment allocations, quantitative import restrictions, high tariffs, and special tax exemptions. Unfortunately, these measures are likely to be inefficient in the sense of requiring larger percentage changes in the value of the instruments to achieve a given objective than would alternative macro instruments; indeed, it may be impossible to meet policy targets regardless of the level at which these instruments are set. Before discussing this further, we will consider the formal structure of the problem in a simple Tinbergian framework.[5] Since the goal of dispersal is flexible, and inasmuch as its achievement can be accomplished with instruments independent of those affecting employment or the trade deficit, we consider only the latter two problems.

In an economy in which rigid real wages (in terms of product price) are enforced by the major economic institutions and the price of capital is maintained at a stipulated (low) level to encourage investment, the rate of employment growth, $\dot{N}$, is primarily a function of the growth rate of total investment, $\dot{I}$, and its sectorial distribution, a, or

$$\dot{N} = f(\dot{I}, \alpha). \tag{8.1}$$

Given the level of GNP, the current account deficit, B, depends upon the level of domestic absorption, H, and the import component of GNP, m, or

$$B = g(H, m). \tag{8.2}$$

The level and rate of growth of investment were primarily a function

5. J. Tinbergen, *On the Theory of Economic Policy* (North Holland Publishing Co., 1952).

of current inflows of foreign aid, as net national saving during most of this period was close to zero. We thus take i as dependent on the exogenous level of aid, although in principle it would be more accurate to consider it to also be dependent upon policy measures affecting national saving. Taking i as exogenous, Equations 8.1 and 8.2 can thus be rewritten in terms of the underlying policy variables as

$$\dot{N} = \bar{f}(Z, \alpha) \tag{8.1'}$$

$$B = \bar{g}(Z, \alpha, t_p) \tag{8.2'}$$

where Z represents the protective tariff-subsidy-quota system, α the sectorial distribution of investment funds, and t_p the level of personal taxation. The first two instruments are policy vectors, rather than a single average value, and jointly determine the distribution of investment by sector, which in turn determines both the extent of employment creation (given differential labor intensities) and the degree of import substitution (m in equation 8.2). Given the level of investment (determined exogenously) and assuming full utilization of capacity, B will depend on the level of exports; but the main flexibility in domestic absorption is consumption, as investment is already determined (and public expenditures are assumed to be exogenous). Thus t_p becomes the instrument that determines whether the balance of payments current account equilibrium will be achieved.

The structure of Israeli policy may be viewed as having used Z and α, mainly with a view toward decreasing the import coefficient and thus the trade deficit with little systematic concern for employment generation.[6] Even disregarding the employment objective, there appear to have been two instruments to achieve desired levels of B, even if personal taxation was not used. However, these instruments

---

6. The relatively low level of taxation, to be discussed below, might be interpreted as an effort to stimulate employment by establishing a higher equilibrium income level for any given level of exogenous expenditures. However, in view of the absence of Keynesian excess capacity and the rigidity of relative factor prices, a high multiplier would not, in the absence of new investment, itself generate additional employment.

It might be argued that in view of the continuing decline in unemployment rates between 1951 and 1960 there was no need to direct special attention to employment generation. However, throughout most of this period the open unemployment rate remained over 6 percent, and underemployment, manifested mainly in the form of part-time work despite preferences for full-time jobs, was substantial. Unless a conflict existed between output and employment, allocation decisions increasing the rate of job creation (for a given level of investment) would have been desirable.

were not inherently strong enough to achieve balance of payments equilibrium. Given the unavailability of many raw materials, there was a physical minimum to which m, the import coefficient, could fall. Once this was achieved, further improvements in the balance of payments could arise only from increases in the share of exports in GNP. Although investment allocations (a) and tax subsidy schemes (Z) might initially improve the relation profitability of exporting, unless domestic absorption—particularly private consumption—could be limited, a sustained improvement in the share of exports could not be realized. And this required increased levels of personal taxation.

The following section will be devoted to a detailed analysis of the major instruments used by the government in order to provide a factual basis for the preceding policy framework.

POLICY INSTRUMENTS

Macroeconomic Policies

Given the desire to maintain growth and simultaneously achieve an increasing export share in GNP, fiscal and monetary policy should have been directed toward reducing the ratio of consumption to personal income. One measure of the restrictive effect of fiscal policy upon private consumption is the ratio of direct personal taxes plus indirect taxes to national income. Between 1952 and 1965 this ratio rose from 17.6 to 25.9 percent, and since the increase was achieved almost completely through personal income and social security taxes, equity considerations were not neglected. By 1965 this ratio was comparable to that of most advanced nations. By international performance standards the transformation of the tax system had been remarkable, and yet in terms of the goals to be achieved it was inadequate. This is not particularly paradoxical once the enormous initial trade deficit is recalled. While an increase in the tax ratio of 50 percent is likely to be more than adequate for restoring the trade balance when beginning with a situation where the import surplus is, say, 10 percent of GNP, the same is not true when the percentage is 25.

A simple numerical example is illuminating. In 1963 the trade deficit was I£1,156 million. To have eliminated it by restricting consumption and expanding exports by an equal amount[7] would have

_____

7. We assume both consumption and exports have the same import component.

necessitated an increase in personal income taxes of I£ 1,300 million, assuming an (unchanged) marginal propensity to consume of 0.9. This additional taxation represents 22 percent of national income at factor cost, which, added to the existing rates, yields an overall ratio of almost 50 percent of national income. This calculation suggests the difficulty faced by a government that may have realized the need for substantial tax increases but which felt politically constrained by the resistance to any additions to high existing rates.

Two observations on tax policy can be made which are salient for other less developed countries as well as for Israel. First, there is a tendency to attempt to transform tax structures from reliance on indirect (usually import) taxes to direct (usually income) taxes. Although such a change may result in equity gains, it is well to remember that a comparison of a proportional income tax and an equal yield expenditure tax shows that the latter will reduce consumption by a greater amount, assuming a positive marginal propensity to save.[8] Although the magnitude of the additional decrease in consumption may be only a small percentage, it can constitute a considerable percentage of existing saving.

A second point of particular importance in Israel is the dubious value of frequent revisions of the exemption, bracket width, and the rate structure of the personal income tax. Such revisions have usually been designed to rectify the alleged adverse impact of inflation upon the tax structure, specifically, the shrinking real value of the basic exemption and the decreasing real width of the existing tax brackets. The net effect of these inflation-induced changes is to increase both the average and the marginal tax rate, the latter arising as a result of the increase in money incomes pushing taxpayers into higher tax brackets. The case for revision of the structure lies in "equity" considerations (i.e. low income families subjected to high average rates) and possibly in adverse incentive effects. While these may constitute a legitimate basis for change in the presence of prolonged, severe inflation, it is far from clear that in a fairly gradual inflation, say 5 to 8 percent per year, such as Israel experienced, the increased rates are not actually desirable. The maintenance of a fixed tax structure[9] might indeed have been one of the only methods of achieving an

8. See E. C. Brown, "Analysis of Consumption Taxes in Terms of the Theory of Income Determination," *American Economic Review* 40, no. 1 (March 1950): 74–89. For a more elaborate analysis see A. Morag, *Taxes and Inflation* (New York: Random House, 1965).

9. Exemptions, bracket widths, and rates.

increased tax ratio, as its maintenance draws virtually no public attention whereas proposed *upward* revisions inevitably encounter widespread opposition. This basically reflects a political judgment that,
even when taxpayers suffer from no "tax illusion," they are less likely
to transform unhappiness about that part of decreased real incomes
attributable to taxation into political opposition if rates are constant
(unless the marginal rates become prohibitive, as they may during a
period of hyperinflation). A dominant concern with equity and a fear
of reduced work effort may be more appropriate for advanced countries not faced with a severe shortage of domestic saving, but it
constitutes something of a luxury for less-developed countries.[10]

Table 8.1: Ratio of Net Income to Gross Income Based on Tax Rates in Effect
in Different Years

Net income as a percentage of gross income

Basic wage per month (I£)	At 1957/58 rates	At 1959/60 rates	At 1961/62 rates	At 1963/64 rates
200	97.6	98.6	98.3	98.3
400	86.4	88.4	88.4	87.3
600	78.8	81.7	82.0	80.0
800	70.5	74.6	75.8	73.1
1000	64.0	68.7	71.3	68.1

Note: Net income = Gross income minus tax and other compulsory payments.

Source: Bank of Israel, *Annual Report, 1963*, pp. 188–89.

The relevance of these considerations may be seen in Table 8.1,
which shows the effect on disposable income of structural changes

10. Implicitly we are assuming no significant incentive effects, for otherwise
the level of national income could be lower than it would be without these
revisions, and then so might the rate of saving. This seems reasonable to us
in view of the relatively low absolute incomes, the general absence of even
remotely adequate private or public pensions, and the small (relative to desired
levels) stock of consumer durables. Moreover, it does not appear that individual
workers have any significant control over their hours of work, so that it would
be difficult to transform a desire for reduced hours into actual reductions,
although it is conceivable that unions could accomplish this if there were
substantial agreement among members. Although the theoretical possibility of
the substitution effect outweighing the income effect exists, it is unlikely to be
realized given existing marginal tax rates; of course, in cases of hyperinflation
where many taxpayers become subject to marginal rates of 80 percent, a situation which existed in Israel in 1950–51, these strictures are obviously less likely
to be valid, although even then there does not seem to have been any significant
reduction in work effort.

undertaken between 1957 and 1964, a period of frequent revisions in the tax structure implemented for equity and "incentive" purposes. For all the wage groups considered, the ratio of disposable to gross income rose between 1957 and 1964. While this might seem to be attributable solely to a desire to avoid increasing burdens on families as a result of rising prices, it must be emphasized that the basic wage is *exclusive* of cost of living adjustments, although for the bulk of income recipients (those below I£500 per month), the basic wage was *fully* tied to the cost of living index. One interpretation of the process underlying the changes is that it represented an effort to maintain the real incomes of those who were not thus fully tied (incomes over I£500 per month) and that political pressures then led to across-the-board revisions. Had tax rates remained fixed in money terms, the aggregate personal tax/income ratio would have grown, whereas, in fact, it remained constant from 1957 to 1960, though rising somewhat thereafter. In view of this it might well have been better to continue the existing system with high taxation of the upper income groups rather than to reduce the revenue-yielding power of the entire system.

We have considered the income tax system in some detail as this was the primary source of increasing government revenue during the period considered. Although increased indirect taxes might have played an important anti-inflationary role, there was no systematic effort to utilize them. However, recently interest has been aroused in a value-added tax, both for its efficiency properties and for its potential effect on the restriction of consumption.

There is relatively little information to be derived from an analysis of the role of monetary policy in limiting private consumption as it was decidedly expansionary, the money supply often increasing at 20 percent per annum or more, with no selective instruments used to discourage consumption. However, one aspect of monetary policy is of interest, namely, the lack of incentives toward saving.

In the hope of stimulating investment, the authorities limited the interest rate on savings accounts so that negative real rates of interest[11] were the rule, and the principal was of course also depreciating. Eventually savings accounts were tied to the cost of living index, but only the principal was protected, so that the real rate of return remained close to zero. Thus little incentive to save was provided, and

11. The nominal rate deflated by the rate of price increase of either the implicit consumption or investment price deflator.

this is particularly unfortunate as the offer of positive, low yields seems to have been capable of eliciting a significant saving response.[12] While it is not clear whether this would have stimulated a higher level of saving or merely led to a realignment of portfolios, as in other inflationary underdeveloped countries higher rates were not explored as a possible inducement to saving.

The major consequence of the failure of tax and monetary policy to discourage private spending was the continued growth of consumption at almost the same rate as GNP. Table 8.2 shows the disposition

Table 8.2: Resources: Sources and Uses (Percentages, 1955 prices)

	1950	1954	1958	1962	1965
Private consumption	49.5	54.7	53.3	50.0	51.3
Public consumption	14.6	14.2	14.3	13.4	12.9
Investment	32.2	21.5	22.1	21.8	20.3
Exports	3.7	9.6	10.3	14.8	15.5
Total uses	100.0	100.0	100.0	100.0	100.0
Gross domestic product	61.7	71.0	72.0	68.6	70.1
Imports	38.3	29.0	28.0	31.4	29.9

Sources: 1950–62: *Israel's National Income and Expenditure, 1950–1962,* Central Bureau of Statistics (Jerusalem, 1963); 1965: *Statistical Abstract of Israel, 1966.*

of total resources (GNP + imports) between 1950 and 1965. The share of private consumption declined by only 3.4 percentage points and its share of GNP by less,[13] between 1954 (the first "normal" year after the huge immigration) and 1965. Public policy was designed primarily to increase the relative importance of domestically produced products in GNP rather than to increase the share of exports in GNP. We turn now to an examination of the microeconomic devices utilized to achieve this end.

Microeconomic Policies

The development budget

The Development Budget is a special budget which supplements the ordinary one, its main functions being to channel funds, obtained primarily from transfers from abroad, to the private sector; and to

12. For details, see *Bank of Israel Bulletin,* no. 16 (March 1962).
13. This was made possible by the increased share of imports in total resources.

finance social overhead facilities.[14] Outlays from the budget include both loans and direct investment in privately owned corporations as well as the financing of research expenditures. In the early 1950s a large percentage of the budget was devoted to residential construction, but this type of expenditure has diminished in relative importance with the slowing of immigration. Table 8.3 shows the percentage

Table 8.3: Sectorial Distribution of Development Budget Expenditures (Percentages)

	Agriculture and national water project	Mines & quarries	Electricity	Industry & crafts	Communication & transport	Total
1952/53	41	7	3	8	14	73
1953/54	47	5	10	10	9	81
1954/55	35	6	8	8	12	69
1955/56	37	6	16	9	10	78
1956/57	37	7	7	16	12	79
1957/58	40	10	8	16	10	84
1958/59	40	5	10	20	8	83
1959/60	41	5	4	19	9	78
1960/61	40	2	6	21	10	79
1961/62	40	2	2	21	16	81
1962/63	30	5	3	17	22	77

Note: Data indicate distribution after subtraction of outlays on housing and debt redemption.

Source: Unpublished data, Central Bureau of Statistics.

distribution of the Development Budget after housing expenditures and bond redemption allocations are subtracted. During the years through 1962, agriculture (defined to include the national irrigation project) received 35 percent or more of total outlays. Manufacturing, on the other hand, received 10 percent or less of total budget allocations until 1957; the rapidly rising percentage thereafter presumably reflected an increasing awareness by the government of the reliance that would eventually have to be placed upon this sector if the import surplus was to be reduced. Outlays for electricity and transportation were concomitants of the general growth process as the growth of both agriculture and industry required increasing availability of elec-

14. The Development Budget is not a capital budget as many of the expenditures financed by it are on current account, for example agricultural research. However, under a broadly interpreted definition of capital formation, most of the expenditures could be interpreted as such.

tricity (particularly in irrigation) as well as improved internal transport facilities. In addition both a commercial airline system and an extensive merchant marine were developed.

The Development Budget had two major effects. First, it was an important determinant of the relative availability of funds to the various sectors. For all sectors except industry, the government has been a major source of financing and the Development Budget its main component. Table 8.4 shows the share of government financing in

Table 8.4: Percentage of Sectorial Fixed Investment Financed by the Public Sector

	1958	1959
Agriculture (including irrigation)	74	72
Manufacturing and construction	42	32
Mining and quarrying	75	71
Electric power	69	54
Transport and communication	59	68
Services	48	56
Housing	44	44
All sectors	54	52

Source: Bank of Israel Annual Report, 1965, p. 102.

the major sectors for 1958 and 1959, these figures being typical of those for much of the period since 1956. Although these percentages are quite high, even they underestimate the importance of public sector influence as these funds were usually accompanied by matching private investment.[15]

The distribution of capital to the major sectors was not determined on a competitive basis in which interest rates were set by the supply and demand for capital and only those projects whose internal rate of return was greater than or equal to the equilibrium rate would receive funds. Rather, the government set sectorial priorities and then allocated a fixed amount of resources to each sector in accordance with these preferences. Excess demand for investment funds existed at the fixed interest rate, and the marginal productivity of investment in each sector was determined by the size of its allocation rather than by the competitive mechanism. The interest rate thus played no role in intersectorial resource allocation and, along with a wage rate set

15. Moreover, because of its ability to determine the financial policies of commercial banks and other financial intermediaries, including the branches to which they could lend, the government's control of overall investment financing was further increased.

outside the competitive framework, implied unequal marginal rates of factor transformation among the sectors, indicating a static loss in output as well as a sectorial distribution of output deviating from one that would have existed under a free market system. In fact, nominal interest rates were set at such low levels that the real rate (after allowing for price increases) was often negative. The nominal interest rate on all loans from the Development Budget ranged between 5.0 and 5.7 percent between 1950 and 1962.[16] However, through 1957 borrowers using a naïve model of extrapolating recent increases in the GNP price deflator would have anticipated a very low (often negative) real rate of interest as the implicit price deflator increased in most years by more than 10 percent. Even after 1957 when the rate of inflation slowed, the real rate on most loans was quite low since the nominal rate remained between 5 and 6 percent.

The practice adopted in the late 1950s of tying both the principal and the interest of loans to either the consumer price index or the dollar probably had little impact on the *ex ante* cost as viewed by borrowers. First, only part of each loan was linked—50 percent of two to five year loans and 70 percent of loans for eight or more years. Thus, even when price increases were anticipated, only a fraction of the existing liability was affected since devaluation was, in most years, correctly assumed to be unlikely. Moreover, choice was usually granted as to the form of tying, and the dollar was most often chosen since loans obtained and repaid before the devaluation were never subject to increased liability, despite the existence of considerable domestic inflation.[17]

In summary, then, the Development Budget had two major effects on the economy. First, it influenced the sectorial allocation of funds, in particular by neglecting the growth of manufacturing while encouraging the expansion of agriculture. Second, the low interest rates combined with the high price of labor set by the unions and the low price of imported machinery encouraged excessive capital intensity (from the social viewpoint) in all sectors. This will be discussed in

16. H. Ben-Shahar, *Interest Rates and the Cost of Capital in Israel, 1950–1962* (Basel: Kyklos Verlag, 1965), p. 39.

17. Ben-Shahar has calculated the *ex post* real rate of interest, which includes the effect of the actual increases in liability due to the tying agreements. This rate (for all sectors) increased from −6.7 on loans granted in 1950–53 to 4.2 on loans granted in 1960–61. Even this latter figure was clearly below the marginal cost of funds to the economy, as measured by the cost of borrowing abroad. See *ibid.*, pp. 82–84.

more detail under each of the sectorial headings in the concluding section.

Tariffs and quotas

Until the late 1950s quantitative restrictions were placed on all imports, both agricultural and manufactured, that were competitive with domestically produced goods, regardless of the domestic cost of production. Although liberalization has occurred during the period since 1959, restrictions have been removed relatively slowly. Moreover, tariffs on those goods whose import is permitted have been extremely high. As is often the case in LDC's, the only major branch of industry that received neither tariff nor quota benefits was machinery, in the hope of lowering the price and inducing greater investment. The primary impact of this was the reduction of the domestic price of imported machinery to levels considerably below their scarcity value, given the overvaluation of the exchange rate.

The general impact of the tariffs and quotas was to prevent either import substitution or export growth from developing along lines that would have been dictated by comparative advantage in a more competitive economy. Resources flowed into all branches, often in disregard of the current (and in many cases potential) efficiency of the industry vis-à-vis international competitors. Moreover, the protection offered by quotas, combined with cartel practices, encouraged more firms to enter particular branches than could be supported by the limited size of the domestic market.

Approved investment status

While the Development Budget was used to channel funds to all sectors and was the main instrument available to the government for affecting the level and composition of investment in most sectors, an important instrument used mainly to influence the composition of industrial investment was the Law for the Encouragement of Investment. This law was initially designed to stimulate direct foreign investment, although domestic investors could also benefit from its provisions. The first law, passed in 1950 and continued with slight modifications until the present, contained the following benefits for approved investments:

1. foreign investors could annually repatriate 10 percent of their initial investment in the same currency they brought in;

2. imported capital goods and raw materials were excluded from customs duty;
3. exemption from property tax for five years with possible extension was granted;
4. accelerated depreciation which made it possible to write off the initial cost of a machine in four and a half years was granted;
5. a 25 percent maximum tax on business income was set;
6. foreign-owned companies could have their Israeli tax liabilities refunded if the same income was being taxed in the home country of the company and if the Israel tax liability was not deductible.[18]

Such laws have become familiar in the LDC's, differing only in detail. It is impossible to evaluate the additional investment they generate, as recorded data on the number of new firms or the amount of investment benefiting from their provisions does not yield information on how much of this investment would have occurred in any case; this would require knowledge of the *ex ante* investment plans of firms. A substantial fraction of investments receiving approved status might well not have occurred without official encouragement, as the government did not simply choose among a given set of projects suggested by the private sector. Rather it was often responsible for conceiving industrial needs (usually designed to fill lacunae in the existing production structure), finding entrepreneurs, and inducing them to undertake the project by offering approved status and substantial financing from the Development Budget. In view of these activities, an examination of actual approvals may provide at least a partial explanation of the evolution of the branch structure of the industrial sector as well as some indication of the government's sectorial preferences.

We turn now to an analysis of the impact of the various micro-economic instruments upon the major sectors.

SECTORIAL IMPACT OF GOVERNMENT POLICY

Agriculture

The massive investment program in agriculture was intended to lead to self-sufficiency, the constraints on autarky being those of climate and resource scarcities rather than economic desiderata, while quotas

---

18. *Israel Economic Bulletin* 2, no. 14 (1957).

and tariffs provided a useful adjunct weapon for maintaining agricultural incomes by preventing declines in product prices.

One measure of the achievement of the autarkic development scheme is provided by the balance of payments in food (processed and unprocessed) and cotton (the only major traded nonfood good). The trade deficit in these categories was $62.3 million in 1952 and $49.4 million in 1964, although the doubling of GNP and a population increase of 50 percent over this period led to enormously increased consumption of these goods. Although this calculation can be taken only as a rough approximation of the total balance of payments effect since it omits industrial imports used in agricultural production, as well as domestic agricultural output embodied in nonfood exports (particularly clothing and textiles), it is suggestive of the success of the government in utilizing agriculture to reduce the trade deficit. The efficiency of this program is, however, open to question.

In evaluating the efficiency of production, assuming the only variable in the social welfare function to be the elimination of the balance of payments deficit, the criterion for deciding on whether a commodity is to be produced (or its production expanded) is its efficiency vis-à-vis world competition. An operational measure is provided by "the cost of a dollar added" (CDA), the total domestic resource costs (at shadow prices) necessary to earn a net dollar of foreign exchange[19] through import substitution or export promotion. If all projects were ranked by this measure, the ones with the lowest CDA should have been chosen until investment funds were exhausted.

CDA estimates, based upon the 1958 input-output table, indicate that existing efficiency in several agricultural branches—citrus, vegetables and fruit, industrial crops, and poultry—was comparable to or lower than that in many branches of manufacturing.[20] Thus the direct allocation mechanism functioned well in allocating resources to these subsectors.[21]

19. F.O.B. price of exports (or C.I.F. price of imports) minus the total import component. A derivation of the CDA as an investment criterion is given in Michael Bruno, "The Optimal Selection of Export Promoting and Import Substituting Projects," in *Planning the External Sector: Techniques, Problems and Policies* (New York: United Nations, 1967).

20. Estimates of the CDA are given in M. Bruno, *Interdependence, Resource Use and Structural Change in Israel* (Jerusalem: Bank of Israel, 1962), chapter 4.

21. Of course an accurate assessment of the optimality of allocation should compare agriculture to foregone manufacturing opportunities rather than existing ones.

However, the expanded output of meat and livestock feeds may be considered misguided. Planners in the early 1950s had to choose between importation and domestic production of meat. A main desideratum should have been the fact that the fodder needed for feed had resource intensities (especially in the limiting factors of land and water) very similar to more profitable industrial crops (groundnuts, cotton, and sugar beet) and would require a high percentage of the total availability of these resources. Nevertheless, partly for ideological reasons (a desire to foster self-sufficient individual farm units), expansion of cattle raising occurred, accompanied by an enormous expansion of the land devoted to fodder production.

In order to demonstrate that this pattern of allocation was undesirable, and to assess its quantitative importance would require an explicit linear programming formulation that allowed for an import activity for meat and export activities for industrial crops. Although such a calculation has not been carried out, it is generally believed that the use of fodder area for industrial crops that could be exported together with the importation of meat would have resulted in substantial foreign exchange savings. The failure of the private economy to develop this socially desirable alternative pattern of resource allocation is attributable to the extensive quantitative restrictions and fiscal distortions introduced by the government in order to bring about self-sufficiency.

The overall impact, then, of government measures on the agricultural sector seems to have been not so much an excessive expansion of the entire sector as a distortion of the allocation of resources that prevented the sector from making its maximum contribution to growth and the balance of payments. However, in considering the sector's overall contribution to national goals, it is also necessary to consider its impact on the absorption of population and the provision of employment.

Between 1948 and 1957, the Jewish rural population increased almost fourfold while total population roughly doubled[22] the growth in the labor force, though substantial, was slower. Despite the rapid growth of the agricultural labor force, it would seem that the government failed to make maximum use of the sector in achieving its employment objectives as output growth was accompanied by a rapidly

22. *Statistical Abstract of Israel, 1957/58,* pp. 13–15. The Arab rural population increased by a much smaller percentage.

increasing capital-labor ratio, with much of the capital increase consisting of advanced machinery and farm structures. This capital intensive mode of growth was encouraged by the negative real interest rate
on loans as well as the absence of tariffs on machinery. How much
added employment would have been possible, had relative factor prices
reflected social scarcities depends upon the (partial) elasticity of
factor substitution in the agricultural sector between the types of investment that could have been cut back (primarily machinery and
structures) and labor. Unfortunately, we are unable to estimate production functions that would permit an empirical estimate. However,
comparisons between techniques on farms with differing ownership
patterns suggest that substantial substitution possibilities did exist,
particularly in the dairy and poultry branches, the most capital-intensive subsectors.[23]

While the capital-intensive expansion process appears incorrect in
terms of resource allocation, it could be argued that such a path might
be desirable in a dynamic sense, i.e. that the returns to capital would
constitute a higher share of value added than if labor-intensive processes were used and that potential saving would be increased.[24] For
actual saving to be greater, an additional assumption is required—a
higher propensity to save out of nonwage income than out of wage
income.[25] In Israel it appears that farm owners save a relatively low
proportion of their income since almost all investment is publicly financed and the structure of ownership is such that any saving that did
occur would be reflected in internal financing. While this may in part
have been attributable to the absence of a need for saving as a result
of the low real rate of interest on loans, it was also probably due in
good part simply to the example set by rising urban consumption patterns. Whatever the reason, owners exhibited an extremely high mar-

23. See E. Kanovsky, *The Economy of the Israeli Kibbutz* (Cambridge: Harvard University Press, 1966). It has also been suggested that the irrigation
system was another area in which considerable funds could have been saved
by adopting alternate techniques. See Albert C. Black, "Reflections Upon
Israel's Recent Agricultural Development and Its Relationship to General Development," in *The Challenge of Development* (Jerusalem: Hebrew University,
1958).

24. This proposition constitutes part of the Galenson-Liebenstein hypothesis.
Although these authors did not postulate a specific production function, it
should be noted that a higher capital-labor ratio will increase the capital share
only if the elasticity of substitution is greater than unity.

25. It should be noted that wage labor is not utilized in a substantial fraction
of the agricultural sector, viz. kibbutzim, and the saving argument could be
relevant only for the remainder of the sector.

ginal propensity to consume and thus provided little justification, from the saving side, for a capital-intensive agricultural development policy.

In summary, then, it appears that the entire constellation of policy measures was quite successful in leading to a reduction in the agricultural balance of payments as well as to population absorption. Yet it would appear that, had the same resources been made available with fewer government-induced distortions, the contribution of the agricultural sector toward both goals would have been greater. However, it is important to note that important subsidiary objectives were achieved by these government measures, particularly the fostering of a large number of mixed family farms as well as the establishment of farm units in strategically important areas. While these might have been achieved more efficiently by an outright income maintenance policy, there may have been strong social and political reasons for avoiding these. Ultimately, the "optimality" of government policies affecting agriculture depends on one's weighing of these other objectives against the more strictly economic ones.

Manufacturing

The impact of the government on the manufacturing sector is most easily comprehended by considering some major aspects of the sector's development. There have been two fairly distinct phases in the evolution of this sector. The first, from 1950 to roughly 1958, was a period of significant import substitution,[26] while in the years from 1958 until 1964 the vital source of the continued growth of the sector was export growth. In both periods domestic demand provided the major part of total final demand, but its growth rate was considerably less than that of total output, the difference being attributable to import substitution and rapid export growth.

Table 8.5 provides two measures of import substitution. Columns 1 and 2 show the import coefficients M_i/Z_i for 1950 and 1958. Although changes in this magnitude are frequently used as an index of import substitution, they fail to supply information on either the relative size of the sectors involved or the absolute amounts of imports "saved." Of the several ways of incorporating these considerations, we use the measure $[M_{i_{58}} - \left(\dfrac{M_i}{Z_i}\right)_{50} Z_{i_{58}}]$ i.e. the actual imports of good i

---

26. Here defined as an increase of the share of domestic supply (X_i) in the total availability of a good, Z_i $(= X_i + M_i)$ where M_i denotes imports originating in branch i.

Table 8.5: Measures of Import Substitution

	$(M_i/Z_i)1950$	$(M_i/Z_i)1958$	CDA[a]	Absolute import substitution[a]
Chemicals	62.1	25.0	9.94	69,630
Metals and metal products	45.2	31.1	1.80	36,752
Food	21.2[b]	17.0	3.18	33,113
Leather	33.5	.8	2.40	26,809
Machinery	71.4	57.8	2.46	17,302
Textiles	19.9	13.0	4.06	13,302
Nonmetallic minerals	15.9	2.6	3.21	9,197
Woodworking	10.6	5.8	2.50	7,658
Paper and printing	20.1	15.2	2.06	6,475
Electrical appliances	45.9	43.4	1.85	2,412
Clothing	2.3	1.8	4.56	1,718

Source: Bruno, *Interdependence, Resource Use and Structural Change,* unpublished Ministry of Finance data and H. Lubell, *Israel's National Expenditure, 1950-54* (Jerusalem, Folk Project for Economic Research, 1958).
[a] For definition see text.
[b] 1951.

in 1958 minus the expected level had the 1950 import coefficient been unchanged and the 1958 total supply required. For the purpose of obtaining a rough indication of the total (primary) inputs committed to import substitution, this latter measure is more useful than the simple M_i/Z_i ratio, as a large percentage decline in M_i/Z_i may occur with only a small commitment of resources in a relatively unimportant branch. Also shown in the table is a measure of the production efficiency of each sector in 1958 as measured by the CDA. The data suggest that there was relatively little agreement between the efficiency measure (CDA) and the extent of import substitution. While it is not necessarily optimal to allocate resources to branches in strict order of CDA, e.g. because of risk of international price fluctuations, one would nevertheless expect some correlation between the extent of import substitution and the efficiency of particular branches. As is readily evident in the table, there is little systematic relation between the two (the rank correlation coefficient being .05), and several egregious violations of the dictates of static comparative advantage appear, e.g. the chemicals and textiles expansion and the failure to substitute in electric appliances. If it is assumed that, in a more competitive economy, private profitability would have led to decisions that conformed to the CDA ranking, it is necessary to seek a nonmarket mechanism to explain the observed evolution of the sector.

The use of quantitative restrictions and tariffs cannot explain the *differential* in the degree of import substitution since they were essentially nondiscriminating, in effect completely protecting any branch in which output was physically feasible.[27] Rather, the explanation of the sectorial growth patterns seems to have been decisively influenced by the offer of Development Budget loans and approved status for new investment.

The overall importance of government policy in the development of the manufacturing sector can be seen in the following data. The total amount of investment in industry as a whole in 1950–58 in current prices was I£956 million. Although a complete breakdown between manufacturing, on the one hand, and construction, mines and quarries, and electricity, on the other, does not exist, available data suggest that about 40 percent of this investment was not in manufacturing. Thus about I£574 million was invested in manufacturing. In the same period loans from the Development Budget to manufacturing totaled about I£140 million. However, since private participation in projects was usually at least equal to the government's contribution, the total amount of investment coming under direct government influence was of the order of I£280 million or about 50 percent of total investment. In the period since 1958, public sector financing has been about 40 percent of total manufacturing investment, and matching private participation probably brings the percentage subject to immediate government influence up to perhaps 60 to 75 percent.[28]

Of the investment financed directly by the government through 1958, about 70 percent went to four major import-substituting branches (textiles, food, metals, and chemicals), the remaining funds being divided in small amounts among the other industries. Not surprisingly the distribution of approved investment by branch (shown in Table 8.6) is similar, with textiles, food, metals, and chemicals receiving the largest approvals, although nonmetallic minerals were also a major recipient of approved status. Thus, for at least four of the main import-substituting industries, the government's lending and approval policies provide an adequate explanation of the process and

27. For a review of the policy along with rather startling case studies see A. Rubner, *The Economy of Israel* (London: Frank Cass and Co., 1960), particularly chapters 7 and 20.

28. In the period since 1958 private participation relative to that of government apparently declined somewhat, primarily as a result of the government's willingness to finance almost the entire capital of firms in some development areas.

Table 8.6: Loans to Approved Enterprises Reaching Production
by December 31, 1957

Branch	Capitalization in Millions	
	I£	Dollars
Food production	9,194	5,399
Food storage facilities	4,607	2,950
Spinning, weaving, knitting	12,612	8,811
Wearing apparel	138	1,246
Wood and wood products	1,188	2,036
Paper and printing	4,628	4,686
Metals and metalworking	12,437	8,730
Machinery and cars	1,879	2,999
Electrical appliances and precision equipment	3,518	5,304
Quarries	95	957
Building materials (including cement)	5,565	8,867
Glass	1,115	1,464
Chemicals	11,735	6,932
Rubber and plastic	3,157	6,865
Miscellaneous	5,344	4,511

Source: Israel Economic Bulletin vol. 3, no. 3 (1958).

undoubtedly accounted for the rapid growth of three high-cost branches (textiles, food processing, chemicals) which if left to private devices would presumably have expanded by much smaller amounts.[29]

Since 1958 the government has relied heavily on Development Budget loans, and approved status has become much less important than in the earlier years. Loans are still concentrated in textiles, chemicals, and nonmetallic minerals, although in some years other branches have also received sizable loans. For all three branches, the continuation of loans represents an effort to insure rapid growth of exports; indeed, the industrial development plan proposed in 1962 envisioned these sectors as providing a major source of future export growth. Although there is some evidence that the efficiency of these branches has improved, it is still doubtful whether textiles and chemicals should have been chosen for continued expansion.

Having seen that the government was instrumental in determining the sectorial structure of manufacturing, it is of interest to identify more carefully the factors that may have determined the size of loans

29. It is again worth emphasizing the fact that the government was not a passive agent in the loan approval process. Rather, it was often a prime instigator in the entrepreneurial process, perceiving areas of possible investment opportunities, seeking private entrepreneurs, and using the lure of loans and tax benefits to encourage the proposed enterprise.

to particular branches or, in a rough sense, the relative weight of the government's preferences among the three major objectives: a priori one would expect the labor intensity of a branch, its potential for achieving population dispersal, and its international competitiveness to be determining factors. To evaluate the validity of this hypothesis we have analyzed detailed data on the branch distribution of Development Budget loans to manufacturing. Regression equations were estimated in which the dependent variable in each year was the percentage of total loans going to each branch (I_i/I) and the independent variables are the labor/capital ratio (l), the CDA, and a measure of the dispersal effect (D). Presumably the proportion of total loans made available to a sector (I_i/I) would, if the authorities followed their stated goals, exhibit a negative correlation with the cost of a dollar added (CDA_i), and positive ones with (D_i) and (l_i). As the empirical equivalent of each of these measures we have used the labor/capital ratio estimates from the 1958 input-output table, the CDA estimates from the same table, and the percentage of loans in each branch actually made to firms in development areas.

As usual, in trying to approximate theoretical variables with empirical ones, there are several points of divergence. The only available labor/capital ratio is the average for 1958, whereas for investment allocation decisions the marginal is the relevant magnitude. It is thus implicitly assumed that the marginal can be approximated by the average. Moreover, it is assumed that the relative labor/capital ratios remained constant between 1955 and 1964. These assumptions are imposed by the availability of only one set of capital/labor ratios.

The cost of a dollar added is available for only thirteen branches. In these there was no significant correlation between a branch's share in investment funds and its CDA in any year. The lack of importance of this variable may not mean that balance of payments considerations were ignored; rather it may indicate that the process of import substitution and export promotion was not efficient.

Table 8.7 shows the results of the regression of I_i/I on D_i and I_i. Until the 1958–60 period the two variables explain little of the variation in I_i/I. However, after 1959 the coefficient of determination becomes considerably higher and the coefficient of each variable becomes significant, usually at the .05 level. The coefficient of l_i is initially not significantly different from zero and after 1959 becomes significantly negative. This pattern might be interpreted as indicating no specific government interest in employment generation even during the period

Table 8.7: Regression of Sectorial Share of Investment on D_i and l_i

	D_i	l_i	R^2
1955/56–1956/57	.0302	−5.978[a]	.1223
	(.0370)	(4.073)	
1956/57–1957/58	.0478	−7.189	.1248
	(.0496)	(6.216)	
1957/58–1958/59	.0582	−11.64[a]	.1573
	(.0472)	(7.130)	
1958/59–1959/60	.1272[b]	−16.09[b]	.4121
	(.0385)	(6.034)	
1959/60–1960/61	.1315[b]	−16.09[c]	.3527
	(.0437)	(6.895)	
1960/61–1961/62	.1534[c]	−17.56[c]	.2464
	(.0662)	(9.440)	
1961/62–1962/63	.0865[c]	−14.05[c]	.2724
	(.0412)	(7.011)	
1962/63–1963/64	.0858[b]	−16.05[b]	.4384
	(.0312)	(4.938)	
1963/64–1964/65	.0850[c]	−14.69[c]	.2860
	(.0424)	(6.129)	

Note: Numbers in parentheses indicate standard deviation.
[a] Significant at .10.
[b] Significant at .05.
[c] Significant at .01.

of high unemployment.[30] However, the increasing negative sign after 1959 might imply that, although the government may always have believed that the capital-intensive branches were the ones to be expanded, until 1959 employment considerations led to the favoring of industries offering substantial employment possibilities. However, examination of detailed project evaluations as well as the plans of the Ministry of Commerce and Industry suggests that, although perfunctory attention was given to the employment potential of a given project, other project characteristics were more heavily weighted. The changing coefficient of l_i is, moreover, readily interpretable in terms of the development of the industrial sector. Before 1958 or 1959 there were sufficient unmet needs in the economy so that investment opportunities existed in most industries, including the ones that produce primarily for consumers and that were relatively labor in-

30. The interpretations of policy based on the regressions discussed in this and the following paragraph must be considered as tentative, as covariance tests of significance of the differences in the coefficients between groups of years do not show statistically significant changes.

tensive (important parts of the food processing branch, clothing, and leather). However, by 1959 industrial policy became oriented toward production for export and filling the interstices of the existing production structure. Thus it was not as a result of an explicit response to the improving employment picture that a switch toward capital-intensive branches occurred, but rather as the outcome of the desired evolution of the industrial structure. Hence the negative sign of l_i occurs because l_i serves roughly as a proxy variable for important sectors, e.g. rubber, plastics, chemicals, and nonmetallic minerals, all branches in which either substantial import substitution or export possibilities were present; all received increasingly large loans and had much higher than average capital/labor ratios.[31]

The interpretation of the dispersal coefficient is relatively simple. It is readily admitted by government officials that until 1959 or 1960 relatively little effort was devoted to insuring the location of new firms in development areas. Since 1960, once a desirable industry has been agreed upon, an attempt has been made to induce location in the development areas, using as lures both tax incentives and a very high ratio of loans to equity capital.[32] This implies that the truly independent variable is the branch allocation of investment, and the dependent one the percentage of loans going to development areas, while the form of the regression suggests the opposite, i.e. that the government faced a set of investment proposals and systematically favored those that, regardless of branch, proposed location in development towns. Whichever way one interprets the causality, it is clear that the government evinced more concern with dispersal after 1959, a finding that corroborates official statements.

It appears, then, that the attempt to improve the balance of payments rapidly, through micro measures alone, led to attempts at rapid import substitution and export promotion that seemed to have no clear foundation in current or potential comparative advantage. Had there been less haste, it is possible that fewer errors in the choice of industries would have been made and that a more suitable industrial

31. Even textiles had a higher than average capital/labor ratio.
32. Much of the recent literature on capital budgeting suggests that a high leverage ratio may be undesirable because the impact of fluctuations in earnings upon earnings per share of common stock will be amplified as a result of fixed interest charges. However, the high loan/equity ratio was attractive to owners for several reasons. First, interest payments did not begin immediately after the business was begun but were delayed for a considerable time. Second, it was usually anticipated that, even when such payments became due, if earnings were still low (or fluctuating), they would be further deferred.

structure would have been established, relying to a greater extent on the production of machinery, metal products, and electronics, branches in which it was recognized that costs would be low. On the other hand, to a large extent the machinery and metal products industries depend, for their advantage, on low cost, skilled labor, and many of the workers who were absorbed in textiles and perhaps building materials would not have possessed adequate skills. However, from a long-range viewpoint, it might well have been better to have used investment resources (which were virtually completely financed by unilateral transfers) to provide training for new workers, whether in the form of further vocational and remedial education or subsidies to firms providing on-the-job training. Had this policy been followed, along with liberalization of trade restrictions and of the capital market, higher future per capita real income could have been expected, although this would have had to be weighed against current income losses.

Thus one may fairly characterize the government's view of the manufacturing sector as primarily an instrument for enabling the economy to eliminate the trade deficit. Not only was there an absence of any systematic effort to encourage employment, but the low interest rate charged on Development Budget loans along with the low tariffs on machinery led to a more capital-intensive mode of production than would have prevailed had prices reflected social scarcities.

Home Goods Sectors and Employment Strategy

Our analyses of agriculture and manufacturing suggest that the main goal which the government pursued in these sectors was the reduction of the foreign trade deficit. There was no discernible employment policy as relative factor prices, decisively influenced by government policies, led to capital-intensive production choices while the branch distribution of investment funds did not reflect a clear effort to encourage the growth of labor-intensive branches. Nevertheless, these facts alone do not provide sufficient information for an evaluation of the consistency of the overall policy package. Such an assessment must explicitly consider the employment performance of the home goods industries[33] and the government's role in them, as it is possible that the capital-intensive policy in the traded goods sectors may have been consonant with a full employment policy, if home goods output were expected to expand rapidly and be "sufficiently" labor intensive.

33. Construction, utilities, transport, and services.

Between 1954 and 1959, years of continued unemployment, the sectorial distribution of employment remained relatively constant, whereas, had a "home goods employment strategy" been followed, it might be expected that this would have been based on some objective indication of the absorption possibilities in this sector as revealed by a faster than average employment growth rate. It may be true, however, that the growth in home goods employment which did occur was in fact greater than it would have been in the absence of government measures to encourage it. However, there is little evidence of conscious government stimulation of employment in construction and services, the major components of these sectors. The maintenance of a relatively high share of construction employment in these years (over 9 percent) was attributable to continued immigration and the upgrading of dwellings, the latter financed by unilateral transfers from abroad to individuals (mainly German restitutions) and capital gains on previous dwellings. Although the continued growth of service employment was attributable in large measure to the increasing improtance of direct goverment employment, this seems to have been a response to desired health and educational objectives requiring the employment of skilled manpower, rather than an effort to offer low productivity jobs to unskilled workers.[34] There is thus no evidence to indicate that the government attempted to separate the roles of the trade and home sectors, using the former for balance of payments contributions and the latter for employment absorption. When full employment finally was achieved it was a result not of particular government policies, but of the sustained high investment level. Although this level might itself be interpreted as being determined by public policy, as indicated in the discussion on the policy framework, it was to a large extent independent of it, as most was financed by the import surplus, only a small fraction of investment being financed by domestic saving.

One aspect of employment policy is of particular interest. Assuming that labor/capital substitution was feasible and that it had occurred, what might (or should) have been done with the released investment funds, in particular the foreign exchange component?[35] The simplest answer would be to invest them in socially profitable export activities.

34. For a detailed study see G. Ofer, *The Service Industries in a Developing Economy: The Case of Israel* (New York: Praeger, 1967).

35. On the assumption that foreign exchange reserves would not have been augmented.

Another possibility would have been the use of the freed exchange to cover the costs of import liberalization. It might be argued that the existence of unemployment forced the government to continue a large investment program, whereas the actual achievement of full employment via higher labor intensities would have allowed some consideration of liberalization. Whether this would in fact have been carried out is debatable, as significant internal pressures existed for the continuation of administrative protection (quotas), but at least it would have provided the alternative, and as should be clear from our earlier discussion of resource allocation, import liberalization could have provided substantial benefits to the economy.

The Israeli government played an active and major role in the development process of the country. However, its primary economic objectives of reducing the import surplus and achieving full employment were pursued with insufficiently powerful instruments: in particular the failure to restrain aggregate demand with macro instruments placed all of the burden of adjustment on micro measures such as trade restrictions and investment allocation. In turn these were occasionally used in an insufficiently discriminating way, inadequate attention being given to economic efficiency, and with little systematic attention to employment. Although some major allocation errors resulted, e.g. the large investments in textiles and an overly capital-intensive production structure, an evaluation of government performance must also acknowledge the positive contributions—which constituted an improvement over what could have been expected from the private economy. Specifically, the shortage of skilled entrepreneurs and business managers makes it unlikely that many of the (socially) profitable investments undertaken by the private sector at the instigation of the government would have been independently perceived as desirable ventures. In this sense the government may be viewed as having engaged in a type of indicative planning, foreseeing future requirements and encouraging investment in these projects. While the actual implementation and the incentives offered may have occasionally led to inefficiencies of one type or another, in the absence of government prodding the private sector might well have delayed many of these projects. Insofar as most evidence suggests that businesses expected the domestic market to provide almost all of their sales, the feedback effect of this government-stimulated investment may indeed have been catalytic in maintaining the rapid growth rates in domestic output. The added growth thus engendered would have to be weighed against the output losses incurred through static resource misallocation. This paper has mainly emphasized the latter aspects, as they are more readily identified, simpler to quantify, and amenable to fairly straightforward policy recommendations. Dynamic questions are much more intractable, yet a balanced evaluation of government policies should really consider them as well, especially in the case of a rapidly developing economy such as Israel's.

Comments by Charles R. Frank, Jr.

Israel's experience with economic development provides a very important case study because of the very large role government has played in the development process. Howard Pack's paper is a very useful summary and critique of Israel's efforts to deal with problems of growth, balance of payments, employment, and population dispersal. Pack concludes that tax and monetary policies were not pursued energetically enough to deal with the problems that arose in the process of development. The use of microinstruments is heavily criticized as he concludes that the policy mix was very inefficient in achieving the desired economic objectives. Since the paper is a weighty and well-argued indictment of Israel's postwar economic policies, I think it is appropriate to point to some mitigating factors and suggest some noneconomic goals that might provide some rationale for Israel's policies.

Between 1953 and 1964 Israeli GNP in constant prices grew at a rate of more than 11 percent per annum. Although the economy was the recipient of very large capital inflows and experienced a high rate of increase of the labor force through immigration (much of it highly educated and skilled in the postwar period), such a rate of economic growth is a considerable achievement. Inflation occurred but did not get out of hand. As one might expect in such a rapidly growing economy, balance of payments difficulties arose quite frequently, but the crises were never so severe that financial collapse was imminent. Defense expenditures were a heavy burden on the economy for a very long time, but tax revenues increased from 17.6 percent to 25.9 percent of national income between 1962 and 1965. The large influx of labor was absorbed at a rapid rate, and although unemployment has continued as a problem, its severity has been mitigated through time. Despite a large proportion of investment funds passing through the government, political corruption was never a major problem and the integrity and honesty of government officials did not seriously deteriorate. Viewed against the achievements of the rest of the world, both developed and underdeveloped, the Israeli performance is quite remarkable.

Certainly it is true that, despite a very heavy increase in the tax burden, fiscal policy was not sufficient to completely alleviate balance of payments pressures. Pack's criterion of a successful policy, however, is very stringent (pp. 254–55). Israel did not need to eliminate its trade deficit, as implied by Pack's calculations. It would have been sufficient to maintain the deficit at a level consistent with the falling off of the relative importance of capital inflows, which remained fairly constant in absolute terms in the few years prior to 1967 but fell as a proportion of commodity imports. Fiscal policy may not have been too far off the mark. Monetary policy seems to be the real culprit in this case. A 20 percent rate of increase in the money supply, an 8 percent inflation, and a reluctance to let interest rates rise surely is a negative contribution to balance of payments stability. In this connection it is interesting to note that Pack makes no mention of exchange rate policy. Surely a more flexible attitude toward exchange rates could have alleviated some of Israel's balance of payments problems.

On the micropolicy side, Pack's evidence of considerable inefficiency in pursuing policy objectives is strikingly well documented. It is difficult, however, to assess whether this stems from a fundamental weakness in economic policy making or whether military and strategic considerations were of overriding importance. For example, the attempt to achieve self-sufficiency in certain food products, while saving little in foreign exchange, may have been dictated by a fear of being cut off from supplies of these products during wartime or in periods of crisis.

The relatively modest resort to labor-intensive projects to foster employment is not evidence of a complete lack of concern for full employment objectives as the author implies. Rather it may reflect a judgment that the use of microinstruments is not a very effective way to foster employment and that microinstruments might better serve other policy objectives such as population dispersal or self-sufficiency in specific lines of production. The indirect effects of a project often far outweigh the primary initial effect in terms of labor absorption.

Thus, relative differences in primary effects may be quite small and not a very important consideration. The very rapid induced expansion of the service and construction sectors was very important in absorbing a large part of the increase in Israel's labor force. The heavy emphasis on the expansion of government services and government expenditures on construction was also important in absorbing labor. Despite the fact that expansion of government services and construction served objectives other than employment absorption, the employment effect is still very real and served Israel's employment goals.

There are a few minor technical and theoretical points on which the paper is not very clear. In the section on the policy framework the parameters Z (the protective tariff-subsidy-quota scheme), and α (the sectorial distribution of investment funds) are viewed as influencing the level and composition of imports, while t_p (personal taxation) is seen as determining the level of exports. An increase in personal taxes, however, would surely affect import levels in addition to reducing demand for domestically produced goods and releasing them for export.

Another problem arises in the discussion of the effect of sectorial investment allocations on the goals of balance of payments, population dispersal, and employment. Pack cites a negative correlation between CDA and investment allocations presumably as justification for leaving out the balance of payments in the regression results reported in Table 8.7. In a multivariate regression analysis, the relationship conceivably could be reversed. If the author in fact performed a multivariate analysis with the same negative results, it would be useful to have these presented.

Finally, the regression results in Table 8.7 can be interpreted somewhat differently than the author proposes. If industrial sector A contributes to both population dispersal and employment objectives, but sector B contributes relatively more to employment but very little or not at all to population dispersal, an optimal policy may be to concentrate on activity A. A regression analysis would show a positive relation to population dispersal but a negative relation to employment; yet the policies followed would be consistent and optimal. Furthermore, the tendency for both the positive association with population dispersal and the negative association with employment to increase through time may reflect a shifting relative emphasis on the two goals and the consequent shift in the optimal policy mix.

Aside from these minor points, the paper is a very well-argued and useful critique of Israel's economic policy. Israel's policies must be viewed, however, in the general context of a rather successful overall development effort and the preoccupation by Israeli leaders with military and strategic problems.

PART IV: THE GOVERNMENT AS FISCAL AGENT

9

The Development Policy of
the Japanese Colonial Government
in Taiwan, 1895–1945

BY SAMUEL P. S. HO

At the conclusion of the Sino-Japanese War in 1895, Japan assumed control of Taiwan. During the fifty years that Japan governed Taiwan (1895–1945), the island experienced profound economic changes. Since these were largely achieved as a result of government policy, a study of the government's activities is of interest, not only because of what it may reveal about the role of government in economic development, but also because of what it may reveal about a relatively unknown subject, Japanese colonialism.

The immediate concerns of the colonial government were three: (1) to bring order and stability to the island, (2) to establish an effective administrative structure, and (3) to achieve financial independence.[1] The accomplishment of these immediate objectives enabled the government to give thought to its long-run goals in Taiwan. The Kodama-Gotō administration (1898–1906), perhaps more than any other factor, was responsible for formulating Japan's objectives and setting the general tone of colonial policy in Taiwan.[2] Both of these unusually imaginative administrators believed that, in an economically

---

I am indebted to Hugh Patrick and Gustav Ranis for their helpful comments on an earlier draft of this paper.

1. Interesting discussions of early Japanese policy in Taiwan can be found in Han-yu Chang and Ramon Myers, "Japanese Colonial Development Policy, 1895–1906: A Case of Bureaucratic Entrepreneurship," *Journal of Asian Studies* 22 (August 1963): 433–49; and E. Patricia Tsurumi, "Taiwan under Kodama Gentarō and Gotō Shimpei," Harvard University East Asian Research Center Papers on Japan 4 (Cambridge, 1967): 95–137.

2. Gentarō Kodama and Shimpei Gotō were respectively Governor-General and Chief Civil Administrator of Taiwan from 1898 to 1906. For a synopsis of their lives see Tsurumi, ibid., pp. 102–03.

competitive world, only the fittest can survive. The urgency of making Taiwan economically viable led Kodama to say in 1902, "Today's most urgent task is to develop the resources of Taiwan." [3] Events later showed this to mean the development of an economy in Taiwan to complement that of Japan. In fact the long-run objective of the government was to develop Taiwan as an agricultural appendage of Japan. In this capacity, the colony served two functions: it supplied Japan with sugar and rice, and it became a market for Japan's manufactured goods. Thus Taiwan was developed primarily for the benefit of the Japanese. There is nothing unusual about this, since the customary reason for acquiring colonies is supposed to be to have them serve the mother country.

What is perhaps different in the case of Taiwan is the great care with which the government planned and directed the island's development. Gotō was largely responsible for giving the colonial government this image of a systematic planner. He described his philosophy of colonial administration as "biological politics," subscribing to the belief that to survive one must adapt to one's environment, which implies a knowledge of one's environment as well as the taking of measures to adjust to the environment.[4] His adherence to this concept and his ability to convince Kodama, his superior, of its validity were responsible for the introduction of a more scientific approach to policy making, in the sense that it encouraged the policy maker to base his decision more on research and investigation of the problem and less on the bureaucratic method of precedent. It was not by chance that among the first things done by the colonial government were an investigation of the traditional laws and customs of the island, a land survey, and a population census. Perhaps the fact that Japan had no previous experience as a colonial power also allowed it greater flexibility for experimentation.

Out of the years of the Kodama-Gotō administration, the colonial government emerged committed to the following tenets: (1) the government was to be an active force on the island, (2) the island was to be developed under government leadership and guidance for the purpose of serving Japanese interests, and (3) in pursuing its objectives, the government was not to depend solely on Japanese institu-

3. From his only major policy speech, delivered in 1901 at a conference of ranking officials of the Government-General, see Moshiji Rokusaburo, ed., *Colonial Policy in Taiwan* (Tokyo: Fuzambo, 1912), p. 173.

4. For a fuller discussion of Gotō's "biological politics" see Tsurumi, pp. 107–09, and Chang and Myers, pp. 438–39.

tions or practices but also to give consideration to methods based on the indigenous conditions in Taiwan. It is clear that under the Japanese the government would not play a laissez faire role. Indeed, the driving force behind Taiwan's economic growth and development during the colonial period was none other than the government and its bureaucratic entrepreneurs.

The purpose of this essay is to study the colonial government's policy and, in particular, to appraise its effects on Taiwan's economic development and growth. Primarily this will be done by examining the government's expenditures, but a few of the other instruments available to the government will also be touched upon. We will begin with a brief discussion of the constraint, if any, imposed on the government by its ability to generate revenue. Next, we will discuss the size of the government relative to the economy and evaluate the extent of government involvement in the economy. Finally, we shall turn to the government's expenditures in detail, with particular emphasis on those areas that have the greatest effect on economic development: social infrastructure, human resources, investment, and production.

REVENUE CONSTRAINT

The initial years of Japanese colonialism were unhappy ones. The resistance of the indigenous population, the unhealthy environment, and the general backwardness of the island were all more difficult to overcome than the Japanese had first anticipated. Furthermore, Taiwan in these early years proved to be a financial liability to Japan. Large cash subsidies had to be provided for the colonial government: 6.98 million yen in 1896 and 5.96 million yen in 1897. This was 6.6 percent of Japan's total regular revenue in 1896 and 4.8 percent in 1897.[5] For the colonial government, in these two years the cash subsidies provided over 50 percent of its total receipts. In absolute amount the cash subsidies may not seem large, but they were provided at a time when Japan was engaged in its own industrialization and they represented more than just a small sacrifice.

The cash subsidies proved sufficiently burdensome to Japan to make the development of a financially independent Taiwan a matter of great urgency for the colonial government. Considering the chaotic

5. T. Huang, T. H. Chang, and C. C. Lee, *Government Financing in Taiwan under the Japanese Regime,* Joint Commission on Rural Reconstruction Publication no. 1 (Taipei, 1951), p. 20.

state of the fiscal system left behind by the Manchu government, this independence was attained relatively rapidly. In Table 9.1 the extent of Japan's financial assistance to the colonial government is shown. Of the 30.5 million yen that Japan provided out of its budget to

Table 9.1: Japan's Financial Contribution to the Taiwan Government-General
(Million yen)

	Cash subsidies		Estimated "transfer" of sugar consumption tax to the Government-General
	Earmarked	Actual transfer	
1896	6.9	6.9	—ᵃ
1897	5.9	5.9	—
1898	4.0	4.0	—
1899	3.0	3.0	—
1900	2.6	2.6	—
1901	2.4	2.4	0.3
1902	3.4	2.4	0.7
1903	2.5	2.4	0.7
1904	1.5	0.7	1.3
1905	1.5	—	1.7
1906	1.4	—	2.2
1907	1.2	—	1.8
1908	1.0	—	3.3
1909	1.0	—	5.2
1910	—	—	11.8
1911	—	—	10.3
1912	—	—	7.0
1913	—	—	5.0
1914	—	—	4.6
Total	37.5	30.5	55.9

ᵃ Dash means zero.

Sources: The figures in the first two columns are from Takabashi Kamekichi, *Taiwan Economy in Modern Times* (Chikewa, 1937). The figures in the last column are from Fukujirō Kitayama, "Adequate Financing in Taiwan," *Taihoku Imperial University Political Science Research Yearbook* 1 (Taipei, Taihoku Imperial University, 1934), Table 21.

finance the colonial government, 42 percent was allocated during 1896–97. Cash subsidy stopped in 1904, five years before the Japanese anticipated its end. But in a more subtle manner, Japan continued to contribute financially to the colonial government until 1914. In 1901, when the sugar consumption tax was established, Taiwan was allowed to keep all the tax collected on sugar originating in

Taiwan, even though a large portion of this tax was paid by Japanese consumers. Only after 1911 did Japan begin to retain a portion of the sugar consumption tax; it waited until 1915 to claim its complete share. Kitayama estimated that through this device Japan subsidized the colonial government by nearly 56 million yen between 1901 and 1914 (see Table 9.1). Thus between 1898 and 1914 a total of 86.5 million yen was transferred to the colonial government. As a share of the colonial government's total current receipts, Japanese subsidies averaged 34.1 percent during 1898–04, 18.1 percent during 1905–09, and 29.4 percent during 1910–14. After 1914, the colonial government was financially independent of Japan.

In the early years, the lack of revenue from domestic sources and the unwillingness or the inability of Japan to continue its large cash subsidies to Taiwan served as an effective constraint on government expenditures. During the difficult years of 1898–1904, nearly 90 percent of the budget went for current expenditures, leaving only 10 percent for capital projects. Yet the need for capital expenditures must have been at its height during these early years. To finance the numerous capital projects, the government consequently resorted to deficit financing. The plan, devised by Gotō, was to have the Japanese government invest in Taiwan by absorbing the debt issues of the colonial government.[6] Within a fixed period of time, the colonial government would refund the debt with interest. Originally Gotō called for a bond issue of 100 to 150 million yen. On the advice of Kodama, this was scaled down to 60 million yen. The colonial government, however, was able to persuade the Japanese cabinet to accept a debt issue of only 40 million yen, further reduced by the Japanese Diet to 35 million yen. Quite obviously, many of the projects thought necessary by the colonial government in these early years had to be postponed or discarded.

After 1910, government revenue was much less of a serious constraint on expenditure. The colonial government structured its revenue system to rely heavily on the profits of government monopolies and on various other kinds of property income. By the mid-1920s, monopoly profits and government property income together accounted for over 50 percent of the government's total current receipts. The reorganized fiscal system was able to generate for the government

6. For a fuller discussion, see Chang and Myers, pp. 446–48, and Tsurumi, pp. 122–24.

large amounts of revenue from within the island. This and the fact that the government was not burdened by military expenditures allowed it to channel a major portion of its current receipts into savings. The government, except for a brief period in the early 1920s, saved on the average about one-third of its current receipts. As Table

Table 9.2: Current Receipts, Current Expenditures, and Savings of the Taiwan
Government-General
(Annual averages in million yen)

	Current receipts (A)	Current expenditures (B)	Savings (A − B)	Government savings/ Government fixed investment (percentages)
1898–1904	8.8	7.6	1.2	26.7
1905–09	15.5	10.1	5.4	103.9
1910–14	26.2	20.6	5.6	63.6
1915–19	29.6	19.5	10.1	132.8
1920–24	40.0	33.1	6.9	43.4
1925–29	53.7	35.7	18.0	112.8
1930–34	55.7	41.9	13.8	92.0
1935–39	93.8	63.6	30.2	137.0

Notes and Sources: These figures are obtained after reclassifying and reorganizing the receipts and outlays of the Taiwan Government-General. The reclassification used as its primary source the Government-General's final account of receipts and expenditures, which appears annually in Taiwan, Government-General, *Taiwan Government Statistical Book*. The detailed results of the reclassification, as well as information giving the basis for the reclassification, are to be included in a larger study by Samuel P. S. Ho on the economic development of Taiwan. The results may, however, be obtained from him on request.

9.2 indicates, the savings of the government were usually more than adequate to finance all its investment projects.

GOVERNMENT SIZE AND ECONOMIC INVOLVEMENT

Before discussing the specific roles played by the government in promoting economic growth, it may be well to establish the relative importance of the government in the economy. One measurement of the government's impact on the economy is the extent of its command over the availability of goods and services as reflected by the size of its expenditures. In such analysis, government expenditures are normally categorized as exhaustive or nonexhaustive and the subdivisions are then compared with estimates of GNP. The importance of making a distinction between exhaustive and nonexhaustive expenditures are that the latter are government transfer payments, over the final disposal of which the government exercises no direct control. Such comparisons, however, cannot be easily made in the case of Taiwan because (1) there exists no estimate of GNP, except for a crude and most probably underestimated figure for 1937,[7] and (2) satisfactory estimates of exhaustive and nonexhaustive expenditures are not easily obtainable. Consequently, we must be satisfied with cruder comparative measurements.

In Table 9.3, total government expenditures are shown for selected years. While attempts to separate the exhaustive from the nonexhaustive expenditures have not been entirely successful, the major nonexhaustive expenditures can be identified: interest payments on the debts incurred by the Government-General, the pension payments of the Government-General, and the transfer payments to the private sector on capital account of the Government-General. It is believed that, by excluding these items from government expenditures, the residual would serve reasonably well as a crude estimate of exhaustive expenditures. Except for the early years, when interest payments were not important, this residual as a percentage of total government expenditure remained at approximately 90 percent.

The lack of GNP estimates forces us to accept a cruder and much inferior measure of available goods and services—the gross value of production of goods. This substitute measurement is marred by statistical weaknesses as well as by conceptual problems. In particular, the reliability of production data during the first quarter of the century, before a comprehensive statistical reporting system was firmly established, is questionable. Most probably the early estimates are biased downward. Nevertheless, for lack of better data we attempt to measure the government's impact on the economy by comparing our estimate of exhaustive expenditures and the gross value of production. The results are shown in Table 9.3.

Since we suspect the early production data to be underestimated, it may be well to disregard the results of the earlier years, when exhaustive expenditures as a percentage of gross value of production were relatively high in comparison with later years. In the years after 1920, for example, when the production data are presumably more reliable, exhaustive expenditures of the government absorbed a fairly

7. See China, Executive Yuan, DGBAS, *Taiwan's Gross National Product and Income* (Taipei, 1955), pp. 129–74.

Table 9.3: Government Expenditure as a Share of Gross Value of Production

	Total government expenditures[a] (million yen) (A)	Government exhaustive expenditures[b] (million yen) (B)	Gross value of production[c] (million yen) (C)	B/A (percentage)	B/C (percentage)
1900	16.6	16.2	—	97.6	—
1905	13.6	12.0	80.0	88.2	15.0
1910	30.5	25.9	145.8	84.9	17.7
1915	26.8	21.8	156.8	81.3	13.9
1920	51.8	47.5	454.4	91.7	10.4
1925	65.0	58.5	601.3	90.0	9.7
1930	91.1	81.7	593.4	89.7	13.8
1935	110.4	95.1	760.5	86.1	12.5
1937	144.3	130.3	902.4	90.3	14.4
1939	177.5	162.3	1,326.1	91.4	12.2

[a] The sum of current expenditures, fixed investment, and capital transfers of the Government-General, and the total outlays of all local governments minus intra-government transfers.
[b] Estimated as total government expenditures minus the interest payments, current transfer payments, and capital transfer payments of the Government-General.
[c] The gross value of production of agriculture, forestry, fishing, mining, manufacturing, and government monopolies.

Sources: For the source of the Government-General's expenditures see Table 9.2; the local government's expenditures are from *Taiwan Government-General Statistical Book*, various issues. The gross values of production, except of that of the government monopolies, are from Taiwan, Provincial Government, Department of Agriculture and Forestry, *Taiwan Agricultural Yearbook, 1948*, Table 4-A. The gross value of production of the government monopolies is not available. As a substitute, we use the value of sale by the government monopolies to wholesale and retail outlets. This, of course, assumes that sales closely approximate production or that the changes in inventory are small. The sales figures are taken from Taiwan, Government-general, *Taiwan Government Monopoly Yearbook*, various issues.

constant share of the gross value of production, fluctuating between 10 and 13 percent. This is quite impressive considering that, except for agriculture, which accounted for approximately 50 percent of the gross value of production during the 1920s and the 1930s, the other important industries were primarily agricultural processing industries whose contributions to value added were relatively small compared to their contributions to the gross value of production. In 1937, for instance, when estimates of both gross value of production and GNP were available, government exhaustive expenditures were found to have absorbed 14.4 percent of the gross value of production and nearly 18 percent of GNP.[8] Admittedly, the 1937 GNP measurement may be underestimated, but even if the GNP measurement is increased by 20 percent, government exhaustive expenditures would still account for 15 percent of GNP. If the relationship between gross value of production and GNP in 1937 can be extrapolated to other years, then the data would suggest that during the 1920s and 1930s government exhaustive expenditures as a share of GNP would be in the neighborhood of 15 to 20 percent. This tentative measurement of aggregate demand in Taiwan would suggest that the government's position in the economy was an important one, particularly for an underdeveloped economy. Further, the data suggest that the colonial government participated in the island's economy from the very beginning of the twentieth century and that the level of direct participation remained high throughout the colonial period.

The expenditure figures cited so far give but a partial view of the government's impact on the economy. For one thing, the current expenditures of government enterprises and government monopolies, which in the 1930s fluctuated between 50 to 90 million yen, are excluded from government expenditures. The government monopolies controlled the production and distribution of important commodities, e.g. tobacco and tobacco products, camphor, wine, and liquor. In the service industry, the public enterprises dominated railroads, telegraph, and telephones. The government also exerted strong influence over such important industries as electric power and sugar through part ownership of the industry and/or government regulation. Similarly, the government's impact on the labor market was substantial. In the 1930s the government directly employed nearly 10 percent of the occupied males in the nonagricultural sector; in fact, it was the third largest employer outside of agriculture, following trade and manufacturing.[9] It was also involved in the economy through such semiofficial institutions as the Bank of Taiwan, the Farmers' Association, and the Irrigation Association.

GOVERNMENT EXPENDITURES AND ECONOMIC DEVELOPMENT

In examining government expenditures, emphasis will be placed on the central government, the Taiwan Government-General.[10] This

8. DGBAS estimated that in 1937 Taiwan's GNP was 724 million Taiwan yen. See ibid., p. 129.

9. Census Bureau, *Census of 1930, Statistical Tables, Total Island* (Taipei, 1934), p. 232.

10. Hereafter, unless stated otherwise, central government, colonial govern-

decision is made not only because the central government was the main policy maker, but also because the quantifiable evidence of government expenditures is available for the central government in greater abundance and detail than for the local government. The primary source of government data is the final accounts of the Taiwan Government-General, which contain a massive amount of detailed information, unfortunately organized in a manner not suitable for economic analysis.[11] In order to be useful, these accounts had to be extensively reorganized. Efforts are made to distinguish between capital and current transactions, and these have been reorganized into separate accounts. Furthermore, current expenditures have been reorganized according to a functional classification scheme, allowing distinctions to be made between general expenditures and developmental expenditures. Needless to say, the reorganization is not without errors. Some of the items from the original accounts would probably be treated differently in the reorganization if more were known about them. The results discussed in the following pages, therefore, must be considered as tentative. They do, however, provide a more revealing picture, even though only an approximate one, of the nature and significance of the central government's activities.

It should also be pointed out that although documents of government expenditures and receipts are available until 1942, only those through 1939 have been reorganized. It became apparent, while working with the original documents, that for the war years 1940–42, the accounts of the central government are too complex for this purpose. The exclusion of these years, while regrettable, does not represent a serious loss of information. They were abnormal years, and for the type of problem we are concerned with here it is the normal years that are of interest.

It is helpful to start by taking an overall view of the pattern of government expenditures, from the point of view of the changing share of total expenditures for each of the major functional categories (see Table 9.4). Not surprisingly, current expenditures account for a major share of the government's expenditures, averaging about 70 percent of the total. Capital formation accounts for another 25

---

ment, and government are used interchangeably, and they all refer to the Taiwan Government-General.

11. For a sample of the Government-General Account of Receipts and Expenditures, see any issue of the *Taiwan Government-General Statistical Book.*

Table 9.4: Functional Distribution of Total Expenditures of the Taiwan Government-General, Selected Years
(Percentage of total)

	1900	1905	1910	1915	1920	1925	1930	1935	1939
Total expenditures (million yen)	14.8	10.7	26.6	21.2	51.5	41.8	63.4	65.1	116.5
Percentage distribution	100.0	100.0	100.0	100.0	100.0	100.0	100.0	100.0	100.0
Current expenditures	*47.6*	*75.7*	*73.9*	*81.5*	*64.9*	*74.5*	*65.7*	*74.4*	*72.5*
General	27.9	43.0	32.5	33.2	38.7	43.3	32.8	32.3	38.8
Development	17.0	17.8	23.5	19.9	16.1	17.9	20.3	18.7	20.1
Transfer payment	0.7	0.9	0.4	a	a	a	a	11.8	4.7
Interest on public debt	2.0	14.0	16.8	23.7	5.4	9.5	8.8	9.2	4.3
Unallocable expenditure	a	a	0.7	4.7	4.7	3.8	3.8	2.4	4.6
Capital expenditures	*52.4*	*24.3*	*26.1*	*18.5*	*35.1*	*25.5*	*34.3*	*25.6*	*27.5*
Fixed capital formation	52.4	25.2	26.5	19.4	34.1	20.5	26.9	24.4	24.4
Transfer to capital account of domestic sectors	—b	—	—	—	2.9	5.9	6.0	2.4	4.0
Direct loans and advances	—	—	—	—	—	—	2.3	—	—
Purchase less sales of property	a	−0.9	−0.4	−0.9	−1.9	−0.9	−0.9	−1.2	−0.9

a Less than 0.05 percent.
b Dash means zero.

Source: See Table 9.2.

percent of total expenditures, although in the early years it reached over 50 percent. About half of the current expenditures are related to administration and police. Perhaps the most notable thing revealed by the general expenditures is that the government did not directly concern itself with the defense of the island until the late 1930s (see Table 9.5). This made it possible for the government to direct its entire attention to the internal affairs and development of the island. The fact that developmental expenditures as a whole consistently

Table 9.5: General Expenditures of the Government-General
(Annual averages in million yen and as percentages of total current expenditures)

	1898–1904	1905–09	1910–14	1915–19	1920–24	1925–29	1930–34	1935–39
Government-General								
expenditures	4.1	5.5	8.9	10.0	19.8	19.3	20.0	33.0
(percentage)	54.0	54.4	43.2	51.3	59.8	54.0	47.7	51.9
A. Administration	2.7	4.3	4.2	8.9	17.2	16.5	16.7	19.5
(percentage)	35.6	42.5	20.4	45.6	52.0	46.2	39.8	30.6
B. Defense	—a	—	—	—	—	—	—	9.7
(percentage)	—	—	—	—	—	—	—	15.3
C. Justice & police	1.4	1.2	4.7	1.1	2.5	2.7	3.2	3.7
(percentage)	18.4	11.9	22.8	5.7	7.5	7.5	7.6	5.8
D. Other	b	b	b	b	.1	.1	.1	.1
(percentage)	b	b	b	b	.3	.3	.3	.2

a Dash means zero.
b Less than one-half the unit.

Source: See Table 9.2.

absorbed a large share of total current expenditures (about 25 percent) is evidence of this. Within this category, the government placed greater emphasis on those services closely related to economic development than on those only indirectly related to development; greater attention was paid to the development of agriculture, transport, and communication than to health and education. When these current developmental expenditures are combined with government fixed investments, they account for over 40 percent of total government expenditures. The direct effort of the government to develop the island was indeed impressive.

Welfare and transfer payments to individuals were insignificant until the 1930s, when the government initiated a pension program for its employees, most of whom were Japanese. The government's lack of interest in this area can in part be explained by the fact that as a colonial power it could be less responsive to the claims of its subjects. On the other hand, the need for government assistance was also probably not urgent because the government did not attempt to alter the basic social structure of the island, and traditional private channels for solving social problems (e.g. the extended family, the clan, and the guild) continued to operate throughout the colonial period. Finally, because the government incurred sizable debts during its first decade of administration, interest on public debt as a share of total government expenditures was high, particularly before 1920. These and other government activities are amplified in the following sections.

The Development of Social Infrastructure

The problems faced by underdeveloped economies are very different from those faced by the more developed ones. Things that are taken for granted in the more developed countries cannot be assumed in the less developed countries, for example, an orderly society. Consequently, in an economy such as Taiwan's at the beginning of the twentieth century, the most important contribution of the government to economic development may very well be the establishment of social order and stability. It is therefore necessary to have more than a perfunctory discussion of the government's efforts to create a social infrastructure for Taiwan.

The society that Japan inherited in Taiwan was disorganized politically and economically. In part, this was because Taiwan was not brought into the Chinese imperial administrative system until the seventeenth century, when it received little attention and continued to remain backward. Although in 1887 the island was elevated to the status of province, it was still very much a "frontier territory." Lawlessness was the rule rather than the exception. Local historical records report a continuous series of rebellions against the government, which led to the saying, "Every three years a small revolt, every five years a big one" (*San-nien hsiao p'an wu-nien ta-luan*). Contributing to the confusion was the fact that by the nineteenth century the political administration system in Taiwan, as was generally the case in mainland China, was thoroughly demoralized and unfit to cope with a modern world. Centuries of government misrule and apathy resulted in an atmosphere in which the state and its subjects could neither communicate nor cooperate with each other.

When the colonial government was established in Taiwan, it found itself in the midst of a hostile population. In the cities and in the countryside, the government had to deal with a rebellious Chinese population, and in the mountains the aborigines remained to be pacified. When the news of Taiwan's cession to Japan reached the island, the local Chinese leaders quickly declared Taiwan a republic and made known their intention to resist Japanese occupation. The aborigines, on the other hand, had never accepted the authority of any central government, and the Japanese represented just another force to be resisted. Thus before anything could be accomplished in the economic sphere, authority and order first had to be established and a structure of government developed by the Japanese. Much of the colonial government's early effort was therefore devoted to the consolidation of its power and to the development of an organizational structure throughout the island. It is understandable, under these conditions, that government general expenditures would be high (see Table 9.5). On the average, general expenditures absorbed a bit over one-half of total current expenditures, much of it going to administrative and police expenses.

Police expenses in the early years were especially high. During 1898–1904 they absorbed, on the average, about 18 percent of the annual total current expenditures. By the 1900s, the police had eliminated organized resistance among the Chinese and had established order over the western half of the island. The aborigines, though never more than 3 percent of the population, proved to be more stubborn. Unable to subdue the aborigines at first, the police adopted a containment policy, isolating them in the central mountain ranges. In 1910, after the government was firmly established, the police initiated a five-year pacification campaign. The extra expenses of this campaign increased the average share of legal and police expenses in total current expenditures to nearly 23 percent. By the end of the fifth year the government had spent over 16 million yen, but the aborigines had been subdued and placed on reservations. The government finally had gained firm control over the entire island.

By 1915–19 the problem of government was no longer one of pacification and control. One manifestation of this was the appointment of Taiwan's first civilian governor-general, Baron Kenjiro Den, in 1919. Another was the sharp decline (relatively as well as in absolute amounts) of police expenditures and the concurrent increase in administrative expenditures. To enable the government to become more than just an instrument of pacification, Kenjiro Den's administration (1919–23) drastically reorganized the government structure, de-emphasizing the police, enlarging the administrative network, and greatly extending the prestige and authority of prefectural and local governments. In no way, however, should this be construed as a shift of power from the central to the local government. In fact, the administrative reorganization of 1920 greatly enhanced the central government's influence over the population because it provided it with the organization and the personnel to implement its policies.

The effect of the 1920 reorganization on government expenditures was a sharp increase in the administrative expenses of the central government. From an annual average of 8.9 million yen in 1915–19, administrative expenses increased to an average of over 17 million yen in 1920–24. As a share of total current expenditures, it increased from approximately 40–45 percent from 1915 to 1919 to over 50 percent in the early 1920s, even though during this period total current expenditures increased by over 30 percent.

The 1920 reorganization was the last major change in government structure. Because government administration after 1920 became more routine, its annual cost also stabilized at around 16–17 million yen. Administrative costs increased somewhat in the late 1930s as the government, in preparation for war, increased its control over the economy and the population. As a share of total current expenditures, however, government administrative expenditures declined steadily throughout the 1920s and the 1930s, from a peak of over 50 percent in the early 1920s to approximately 30 percent in the late 1930s. The share of total current expenditures absorbed by general expenditures also declined, reflecting the stabilized administrative expenses, but the introduction of defense expenses in the late 1930s once again brought the share of general expenditures to over one-half of total current expenditures.

Theoretically the island was ruled through its district and subdistrict government, but in fact, it was primarily the police who ruled and administered it.[12] This was true during most of the colonial period, but particularly before 1920 and in the late 1930s. Besides performing its usual duties, the police also supervised tax collection, enforced sanitary measures, and even occasionally performed agricultural extension services. The special role of the police in the government of Taiwan makes the distinction between administrative expenses and police expenses, especially before the 1920 administrative reorganization, somewhat arbitrary. Considering the multiple functions performed by the police, some of these expenses probably belong rightfully in the category of developmental expenditures. Lack of data unfortunately prevents this type of refinement.

12. For a discussion of the police during the colonial period, see Chin-hih Chen, "The Police and *Hokō* Systems in Taiwan under Japanese Administration," Harvard East Asian Research Center Papers on Japan 4 (Cambridge, 1967); and Shunji Shiomi, "The Police and Taiwan's Economy during the Japanese Period," translated into Chinese by Hsien-wen Chou, *Bank of Taiwan Quarterly* 5 (March 1953): 253–73.

Another interesting feature of the colonial administrative structure is the *pao-chia* system, a mutual responsibility scheme.[13] Gotō discovered the pao-chia system from a government survey of Taiwan's social customs, convinced Kodama of its usefulness, and the two of them developed a plan whereby the traditional pao-chia system was reestablished and connected to a modern police system. The pao-chia system arranges households into groups and assigns joint responsibility to the groups for the conduct of their members. A *chia* is a group of about ten households. Ten chia, or approximately a hundred households, form a *pao*. During the colonial period, the head of each chia was elected by the member households, but the choice had to be approved by the local government. The head of each pao was also elected, but the choice had to be approved not only by the local government but also by the police and the district or prefectural government. Under close police supervision, the pao-chia is an extremely effective administrative device.

By the beginning of the twentieth century, all Taiwanese households in the rural areas outside of the aborigines' territory were incorporated into the pao-chia system. Population in the cities was also organized in a roughly similar manner. The heads of the pao and the chia were responsible for maintaining peace and order as well as for carrying out administrative duties, e.g. disseminating information and taking local censuses. Under the auspices of the pao, associations were formed to perform certain defensive and community services, such as guarding against banditry and providing assistance during floods and fires. The heads of the pao and chia served without remuneration, and the miscellaneous operating expenses connected with the pao-chia system were defrayed by compulsory contributions, independent of the regular tax system, collected from the participating households. The pao-chia system enabled the government to greatly enhance its influence and authority; in fact, it allowed the government and the police to reach literally every household, without creating a huge bureaucracy at the same time. Furthermore the system was self-supporting, adding little or no fiscal burden to the government. The adoption of the pao-chia system provides one important example of the colonial government using traditional institutions to its ad-

13. For discussions of the *pao-chia* (Japanese, *hokō*) system, see Chen; George Barclay, *Colonial Development and Population in Taiwan* (Princeton: Princeton University Press, 1954), pp. 50–51; and U.S. Navy Department, Office of the Chief of Naval Operations, *Civil Affairs Handbook: Taiwan*, OPNAV 50E-12 (June 1944), pp. 77–79 (hereafter cited as *Handbook*).

vantage. Had the pao-chia system not been made an integral part of the government administrative framework during the Kodama administration, a greater share of the government's current expenditures would have been absorbed by administrative and police expenditures.

The general expenditures of the central government had profound and far-reaching effects on the economy. Most importantly it established order and political stability on the island without which economic progress would have been impossible. It helped to transform a disorganized society into a somewhat orderly one in which events were more predictable, making it easier for entrepreneurs to operate. The administrative structure provided the Japanese with a channel to the indigenous population through which the government could introduce innovations as well as influence individual decisions and behavior. To the extent that general expenditures created the social infrastructure needed for economic growth and development they take on aspects of an investment outlay that paid rich dividends for the Japanese.

The Development of Human Resources

Public health and population policy

Nineteenth-century Taiwan was renowned for its unhealthy environment and its epidemics. The most significant achievement of the early colonial administrations was in public health. Measures adopted by the government in this area, however, relied more on administrative devices than on large government spending to control epidemics and improve sanitation. The annual government expenditures on public health very rarely exceeded one million yen, in most years falling below half a million (Table 9.6). As a share of total current expenditures, the central government's outlay on public health varied between 2 and 3 percent. Local governments also allocated a part of their expenditures to public health, but in absolute as well as relative magnitude, this portion was exceedingly small.

The approach of the government to the health problem would seem primitive by today's standards. Only a limited amount of medical equipment and medically trained personnel were made available to combat this problem. Although the number of hospitals in Taiwan during the late 1930s reached several hundred, only twenty had a capacity greater than eighty beds.[14] The number of doctors in Taiwan

14. U.S. Navy, ibid., p. 13.

Table 9.6: Development Expenditures on Current Account
of the Government-General
(Annual averages in million yen and as percentages of total current expenditure)

	1898–1904	1905–09	1910–14	1915–19	1920–24	1925–29	1930–34	1935–39
Developmental expenditure	2.8	2.3	6.0	4.6	7.8	9.8	11.7	16.3
(percentage)	36.8	22.8	29.1	23.6	23.6	27.4	27.9	25.6
A. Education	0.2	0.2	0.4	0.6	2.0	3.8	4.4	6.2
(percentage)	2.6	2.0	1.9	3.1	6.0	10.6	10.5	9.7
B. Health	0.2	0.2	0.3	0.4	0.7	0.8	1.1	0.7
(percentage)	2.6	2.0	1.4	2.1	2.1	2.3	2.6	1.1
C. Other social	0.1	0.1	0.2	0.3	0.3	0.1	0.2	0.6
(percentage)	1.3	1.0	1.0	1.5	1.0	0.3	0.5	0.9
D. Agriculture	1.0	1.2	4.0	2.1	2.9	3.4	4.1	5.7
(percentage)	13.2	11.9	19.4	10.8	8.8	9.5	9.8	9.0
E. Transportation and communication	1.3	0.6	1.0	1.0	1.5	1.5	1.7	2.1
(percentage)	17.1	5.9	4.9	5.1	4.5	4.2	4.0	3.3
F. Other industry	—[a]	[b]	0.1	0.2	0.4	0.2	0.2	1.0
(percentage)	—	[b]	0.5	1.0	1.2	0.6	0.5	1.6

[a] Dash means zero.
[b] Less than one-half the unit.

Source: See Table 9.2.

in 1937, including those without diplomas from a recognized medical school but who had passed the government examination, was 1,845, or about one doctor for every 3,040 persons.[15] As most doctors worked in Taipei or other large cities, the patient/doctor ratio was probably much less favorable in the countryside where most Taiwanese resided.

The Japanese made up for a lack of medical facilities by relying heavily on administrative measures and direct controls to counter the unhealthy environment. It is interesting to note that the public health program was administered by the police department, often operating through the pao-chia system. Through strict quarantine regulations and an incessant search for afflicted persons, infectious diseases were eradicated or brought under control. In 1906, the first year for which we have data, death from plague numbered 2,534 (presumably for early years the number would be even greater),

15. Taiwan, Provincial Government, Bureau of Accounting and Statistics, *Taiwan Province: Statistical Summary of the Past 51 Years* (Taipei, 1946), pp. 1249–50.

while a decade later only two deaths from plague were reported.[16] Cholera was also brought under control quickly. In later years, innoculation became the main deterrent against these diseases. For all its successes in curbing infectious diseases, however, the colonial government was unable to eliminate malaria. As late as the 1930s and the 1940s, 4,000–5,000 deaths from malaria were reported annually. Until DDT became available after World War II there was no cost-effective way to destroy mosquitoes. The government tried draining swamps, but the need to flood the rice fields for production purposes frustrated these attempts. Through a policy of compulsory blood tests and immediate quinine treatment, however, the government was able to contain malaria and to prevent it from assuming epidemic proportions.[17]

The public health programs also attempted to improve the general sanitary condition of the island, again relying primarily on administrative devices. Adequate facilities for sewage disposal were not provided, although Taipei and some of the other larger cities had open concrete drainage systems. Regular collection of night soil was carried out by fertilizer brokers or farmers' associations under police supervision and stored in "reservoirs" on the outskirts of cities.[18] In some towns simple septic tanks were required. Farmers, however, purchased night soil for use as fertilizer. Consequently outbreaks of enteric diseases frequently resulted. Through the pao-chia system, numerous sanitary measures were enforced. Compulsory house cleaning is one example.[19] Twice a year people in the rural areas were organized for house cleaning. Objects were removed from buildings for airing and the insides of the dwellings were swept and cleaned. The cleaned premises were inspected by the police. Only those that met with police approval received certificates, which were posted at the doors of the dwellings.

These simple administrative measures rigorously enforced, combined with small government expenditures brought about significant improvements in public health which in turn affected the rates of increase, as well as the quality, of the population and the labor force. Between 1906 and 1936–40 the mean life expectancy of Taiwanese

16. The number of deaths includes only Japanese and Taiwanese. See ibid., pp. 269–85.
17. Barclay, p. 137.
18. Leonard Chang, *Collection, Disposal and Utilization of Night Soil in Taiwan,* Food and Fertilizer Series no. 6 (Taipei: JCRR, 1956), pp. 6–7.
19. U.S. Navy, *Handbook,* p. 28.

males at birth increased by 13.4 years to 41.1 and that of Taiwanese females by 16.7 years to 45.7.[20] The decline of the death rate is perhaps even more dramatic (Table 9.7). Between 1906 and 1943, the death rate was cut by nearly one-half, from 31.3 to 17.6 deaths

Table 9.7: Vital Statistics, 1906–43
(Annual averages)

	Births per thousand of population	Deaths per thousand of population	Natural increase (percentage)
1906–10	39.5	31.3	0.82
1911–15	41.1	27.1	1.40
1916–20	39.2	29.7	0.95
1921–25	41.2	23.7	1.75
1926–30	43.9	21.5	2.24
1931–35	44.7	20.4	2.43
1936–40	43.6	19.7	2.39
1941–43	40.5	17.6	2.29

Sources: Calculated from Taiwan Population Studies Center, *Demographic Reference: Taiwan Republic of China, 1965,* vol. 1 and vol. 2, Table 12, pp. 1–3.

per thousand. The decline was steady and continuous with the exception of a short period in 1915–20, when a series of near epidemic attacks of influenza interrupted the decline. The official vital statistics also reveal a slight rise in the birth rate, from about forty to forty-four births per thousand. The divergent movement of the birth and death rates caused the rate of natural increases to move rapidly upward, from about 0.8 to over 2.4 percent per annum.

The total population and its composition by nationality for the census years appear in Table 9.8. The effect of a decline in the death rate on the size of the population is evident. There are some differences in coverage among the censuses, but they are sufficiently minor for comparisons of population size to be made. Total population in Taiwan between 1905 and 1944 more than doubled. Population did not grow at a constant rate; it grew slowly in the early years and then accelerated, reflecting the downward trend in the death rate.

While the rapid rate of natural increase was the primary cause of population growth, a secondary cause was a sizable influx of Japanese into Taiwan. The Japanese population in Taiwan between 1905 and

20. Barclay, p. 154. Also see his chapter 6, "Public Health and the Risk of Death," for detailed documentation of the changing public health conditions in Taiwan during the first quarter of the twentieth century.

Table 9.8: Population in Taiwan, Census Years

Time of census or survey	Total	Taiwanese	Japanese	Other[a]	Exponential rate of growth Total	Taiwanese
10/1/1905[b]	3,039,751	2,973,280	57,335	9,136		
10/1/1915[b]	3,479,922	3,325,755	135,401	18,766	1.35	1.14
10/1/1920[b]	3,655,308	3,466,507	164,266	24,535	1.07	0.82
10/1/1925[b]	3,993,408	3,775,288	183,722	34,398	1.78	1.71
						2.20
10/1/1930[b]	—[c]	4,218,663	—	—		
10/1/1930[d]	4,592,537	4,313,681	228,281	50,575		
10/1/1935[d]	5,212,426	4,882,945	270,584	58,897	2.53	2.48
10/1/1940[d]	5,872,084	5,510,259	312,386	49,439	2.39	2.43
7/15/1944[d,e]	6,269,949	5,900,391	319,808	49,750	1.65	1.71

[a] Includes mainland Chinese and all foreigners other than Japanese.
[b] Excluding Aborigine District.
[c] Dash means zero.
[d] Including Aborigine District.
[e] These figures are based on surveys rather than on a complete census and are probably less reliable than the census figures.

Sources: The figures for 1905–40 are census figures. The 1944 figures are from a special survey conducted on 15 July 1944, and published in Taiwan, Provincial Government, Bureau of Accounting and Statistics, *Results of the Seventh Population Census of Taiwan, 1940* (Taipei, 1953), pp. 157–69.

1944 increased by more than fivefold. The colonial government encouraged this migration and in certain periods actively recruited Japanese. Because it was a selective migration it had immense significance for the development of Taiwan, for it provided the island with a stock of human capital that otherwise would have taken several decades to obtain. The annual statistics on the net movement of Japanese to Taiwan during 1900–39 indicate that, on the average, 32 percent of those who declared an occupation were government administrators or professionals and 41 percent were engaged in commerce or services.[21] It was from these migrants that Taiwan obtained the technicians, entrepreneurs, administrators, professionals, and skilled workers to develop its economy.

A rapidly growing population caused by a high rate of natural increase has uncertain effects on economic development. On the one hand, it enlarges the labor force and thus the productive capacity of

21. Calculated from data taken from *Taiwan Province: Statistical Summary,* pp. 322–23.

the economy. On the other hand, it usually results in a fundamental structural change in the age composition of the population, causing the share of the dependent population to total population to increase, thus increasing the burdens to the economy. Between 1905 and 1940, Taiwan's dependency ratio increased from 40.7 to 48.9 percent.[22] The improved sanitary and health conditions that brought about this condition, however, also improved the quality and productivity of the working population and thus had a positive effect on development. Whether an increasing population will have a similar effect on development depends to a large extent on how other factors in the economy behave. More specifically, it depends on the existing resource endowment of the economy and on how well capital and technological change keep pace with population growth. Since at that time uncultivated land still existed in Taiwan and the colonial government was willing to serve as a channel for investment and for the transfer of technology to Taiwan, the possibility that the increasing population may have been a net stimulus to economic development should not be ruled out.

Educational policy

The colonial government adopted a restrictive education policy until the late 1920s, when, for political and economic reasons, the policy was liberalized. The early policy was restrictive in terms of both the size of the government program and the type of education provided. As in other countries, education was primarily the responsibility of the local government, although policy matters remained very much in the hands of the central government. Only the normal schools, senior high schools, and institutes of higher education were operated and financed directly by the central government. Expenditures on education, therefore, only reflect the costs of operating these educational institutions and of subsidies earmarked for lower government levels. In Table 9.9 expenditures on education by all levels of government are compiled and totaled. The sum is a combined rather than a consolidated figure, therefore overstating government expenditure on education by an indeterminate but probably small amount.

Educational expenditures, whether viewed in total or disaggregated by levels of government, show two major jumps during the colonial

22. Dependent population as a percentage of total population. Dependent population is defined as the sum of those under the age of fourteen and those above fifty-nine. Calculations are based on figures from the censuses.

Table 9.9: Combined Government Expenditures on Education
(Thousand yen)

	Government-general	Local government	Total
1900	203	201	404
1905	190	326	516
1910	327	597	924
1915	526	1,056	1,582
1920	1,331	2,770	4,101
1925	2,745	9,781	12,526
1930	4,805	10,977	15,782
1935	4,792	13,478	18,270
1939	8,076	22,275	30,351

Sources: The sources of the expenditure figures of the Government-General are explained in Table 9.2. The expenditure figures of the local governments are from *Taiwan Government-General Statistical Book*, various issues.

period. Before 1920 the central government spent less than 2–3 percent of its current expenditures and the local government no more than 10–12 percent of its total outlays on education. In absolute amounts, the combined expenditure on education by all levels of government during this early period seldom exceeded 1.5 million yen. The first jump came in the early 1920s, following the administrative reorganization, which provided the local government with an independent financial system and enabled a limited extension of primary education. The enrollment in primary schools tripled between 1915 and 1925, going from 81,879 to 244,902 students.[23] The second jump, which occurred in the 1930s, came as the result of the government's decision to Japanize the population, with primary education as its chief instrument. In this later period the central government diverted 10 percent of its current expenditures and the local government one-third of its total outlay, to education. The increased expenditure enabled the school system to increase its absorption of school-age (6–14) Taiwanese children from 33 percent in 1930–31 to 71 percent in 1943–44.[24]

The government's policy toward education remained restrictive in the sense that it limited the Taiwanese to certain quality, types, and levels of education. In 1936, for instance, the expenditure per

23. *Taiwan Province: Statistical Summary,* p. 1212.
24. Ibid., pp. 1241–42. In 1920, 98 percent of the school-age Japanese children in Taiwan were in school. Such high attendance rates existed in Japan as early as the late 1900s.

student in schools primarily for Japanese children was twice that of schools for Chinese children. In the same year the minimum monthly salary for teachers in schools for Japanese children was 40 yen for men and 30 yen for women; in schools for Chinese children, the minimum monthly salary for teachers was 10 yen.[25] With few exceptions Taiwanese who were allowed to continue their education beyond primary school attended vocational schools. The regular middle and senior high schools were the prerogative of the Japanese and a select number of privileged Taiwanese children.[26] In fact, Taiwanese youths were subjected to restrictive quotas at all levels of educational institutions. One restrictive device used was the requirement that students of middle and senior high schools have a fluent command of Japanese. The stringency of this regulation can be gauged by the fact that as late as 1930, after thirty-five years of Japanese occupation, only 8.5 percent of the Taiwanese population spoke Japanese. Since private schools were expensive and limited in number, they did not serve as an alternative to public education for the Taiwanese.[27]

Institutes of higher education, in particular the one university in Taiwan, existed more for research than for instruction. In the 1930s, Taihoku Imperial University had an enrollment of several hundred students and could boast a faculty/student ratio of approximately 1.2:1.0.[28] University professors were retained not so much to teach as to advise the government on matters such as tropical diseases, agricultural science, economics, and conditions in South China and Southeast Asia. The latter area of research reflects the role Taiwan played in Japan's design to control this part of Asia. A limited number of Taiwanese were admitted to these institutions of higher education, but they were largely confined to the study of medicine, the one profession where Taiwanese had relative ease of entry. Government educational policy allowed the middle and higher levels of education to serve only a few specific purposes: to provide an adequate education for the Japanese children in Taiwan, to train a very limited num-

25. Andrew J. Grajdanzev, *Formosa Today* (New York: Institute of Pacific Relations, 1942), p. 167.
26. In 1930, of the 10,507 students enrolled in the public middle and senior schools, 7,063 were Japanese.
27. During the colonial period the total enrollment of formal private schools exceeded 5,000 students in only one year.
28. For example, in 1935 the faculty numbered 105 and students 114, of whom 89 were Japanese. See *Taiwan Province: Statistical Summary*, pp. 1214–15.

ber of Taiwanese as technicians in areas where the Japanese were unable or unwilling to staff themselves, and to provide the proper environment for government-directed research. There is evidence which suggests that in the late 1930s the government, in an attempt to increase the supply of skilled workers and technicians, eased some of its restrictions and allowed a greater number of Taiwanese to participate in the higher education system.

The demand for education has always been high in Chinese society. Taiwan was no exception. During the first two decades of the century, before the government extended its education program, this demand was largely satisfied in the traditional manner through training in the Chinese classics in informal private tutorials. At the beginning of the twentieth century, enrollment in these traditional institutions was nearly 30,000, but it declined rapidly once public education was introduced.[29] Even after the government expanded its educational system in the late 1920s and in the 1930s, the demand for education exceeded supply and more than 10,000 applicants for primary school were turned down annually.[30]

The reason for the government's early restrictive educational policy as well as its later reversal was largely political. The government was reluctant to provide education to a large segment of the population because it was aware of the inherent danger to its own existence of a discontented, educated population. Its decision to limit higher education to a small select group of Taiwanese was a device to keep the political and economic control of the island in Japanese hands. Only as tension between China and Japan grew in the 1930s and the government felt the need to assimilate the Taiwanese did it reverse its educational policy.

In view of its significant impact on labor productivity, the level of income, and general welfare of the population, the government underinvested in education, in the sense that the return on education was probably higher than on other investments in the economy. One constant complaint of Japanese industrialists operating in Taiwan during the colonial period was the shortage and the low quality of industrial laborers, a condition that may have dissuaded some Japanese capitalists from investing in Taiwan.[31] From such complaints

29. Ibid., p. 1213.
30. U.S. Navy *Handbook,* p. 35.
31. The government itself commented on the low quality of Taiwanese

the impression arises that any additional investment to enlarge, as
well as to improve the quality of, the educational system would have
had a high rate of return. The government policy of restricting Taiwanese to certain levels and types of education prevented the Taiwanese from entering many occupations for which some of them were
well suited. Labor markets in less developed countries are well known
for their imperfections, and these artificial barriers merely made them
more imperfect in Taiwan. From the standpoint of growth or efficient
resource allocation, the education policy of the government must be
judged as suboptimal. From the standpoint of Japan, the policy was
also inefficient because it resulted in the transfer of the very types
of human resources from Japan to Taiwan during the 1930s and the
early 1940s that Japan could ill afford to lose.

The Development of the Agriculture and Industry

Throughout the colonial period, the government consistently adhered
to its philosophy of active participation in the economy. It was, without question, the island's most important entrepreneur and investor.
Because of Taiwan's colonial status, the economic strategy followed
by the government was largely dictated by Japan's economic needs.
The objective was to develop the island to complement Japan; thus
emphasis was placed on the economic integration of the two regions.
Under these conditions, as Japan's needs altered, so Taiwan's economic role in the empire altered. The government's economic policy
can be conveniently divided into two periods, with the early 1930s as
the line of demarcation. In the first period, the government was primarily concerned with the development of agriculture. In the second
period, for political and to a lesser extent economic reasons, it shifted
its emphasis somewhat toward industry.

Considering Taiwan's natural endowment and Japan's economic
needs, it is understandable that the objective of the government was
the development of agriculture, in particular the sugar industry. Taiwan was the only area in the empire climatically suited for growing
sugar cane, and Japan traditionally had been a sugar importer. From
1896 to 1904, before Taiwan became a significant sugar producer,
Japan on the average used 22 million yen of its foreign exchange
earnings annually to finance its sugar imports, an amount that was

laborers. See Ryūzō Kusui, *The Economy of Taiwan during the War* (Taipei:
Nanpō Jinmon Kenkyū Jo, 1944), pp. 173–74, 191, and 200–01.

greater than 50 percent of Japan's trade deficit during this same period.[32] The acquisition of Taiwan therefore made it possible for Japan to develop a source of sugar within the yen bloc and thus ease the pressure on its balance of payments. Although it was sugar that initially occupied the government's attention, the appearance of an increasingly large food deficit in Japan soon broadened the government's interest in the general development of agriculture, which in Taiwan meant rice.

To realize these objectives, the government (1) allocated its expenditures and used its authority to license and regulate in favor of what it wished to promote; (2) used tax incentives and subsidies to influence the behavior of producers; (3) manipulated indigenous institutions to serve as disseminators of innovations; and (4) claimed a limited but important segment of the economy for government ownership and control. The last measure was taken for three reasons: (1) the government needed additional sources of revenue to avoid becoming a budgetary drain on Japan; (2) the government had to develop and maintain that part of the island's infrastructure that was too risky or too costly for any one group of private entrepreneurs to finance; and (3) by controlling the strategic sectors, the government hoped to control the rest of the economy. The government monopolies were created for the first reason, and the development and operation of the railroads and the electric power industry were done primarily for the second and third reasons. We turn now to a more detailed discussion of how these instruments were applied to the economy and then to an appraisal of the results.

The successful development and commercialization of agriculture requires as a minimum the existence of an inexpensive mode of transportation. At the turn of the century, Taiwan was devoid of a modern transport system, which among other things hindered the development of an efficient internal market. For military as well as for economic reasons, the development of a transport system both within Taiwan and connecting Taiwan to Japan was given the highest priority. Immediately after Japan occupied the island, railroad and harbor construction was pushed forward with enthusiasm. Over the years the central government showed its concern for the development

32. Calculated from statistics taken from the Bank of Japan, Statistics Department, *Hundred-Year Statistics of the Japanese Economy* (1966), pp. 278–79 and 282–89.

of the transport and communication sector by consistently allocating
to it over 50 percent of its annual fixed investment (Table 9.10). By
1908 the two most important harbors, Keelung in the North and
Kaohsiung in the South, were connected by rail, with the completion

Table 9.10: Fixed Capital Formation of the Government-General Distributed
by Use
(Annual averages as percentages of total)

	1898–1904	1905–09	1910–14	1915–19	1920–24	1925–29	1930–34	1935–39
Total (million yen)	4.5	5.2	8.9	8.2	15.9	14.1	15.0	22.0
Percentage distribution	100	100	100	100	100	100	100	100
A. Agriculture	*4.4*	*11.8*	*15.5*	*16.9*	*15.1*	*12.0*	*25.3*	*19.5*
1. Irrigation	4.4	11.8	8.9	7.2	6.9	1.4	2.7	a
2. Flood control	—b	—	4.4	9.6	8.2	10.6	22.6	19.1
3. Other	a	a	2.2	a	—	a	—	0.4
B. Transport & communication	*71.1*	*62.7*	*47.8*	*55.4*	*67.9*	*68.1*	*60.0*	*65.9*
1. Harbor	11.1	17.6	20.0	13.2	15.7	21.3	22.0	20.5
2. Rail	55.6	41.2	18.8	27.7	40.3	29.8	20.7	24.1
3. Road	a	—	2.2	7.2	8.8	10.6	11.3	9.5
4. Other	4.4	3.9	6.7	7.2	3.1	6.4	6.0	11.8
C. Other	*24.5*	*25.5*	*36.7*	*27.7*	*17.0*	*19.9*	*14.7*	*14.6*

a Less than 0.05%.
b Dash means zero.

Source: See Table 9.2.

of the North-South trunk line at a cost of over 27 million yen. By
the 1920s all major trunk lines were completed and inexpensive transportation became accessible to most parts of the island.

Besides direct investment, the government also assumed a share of
the operating costs of the transport and communication enterprises.
Item E in Table 9.6 shows the magnitude of this support in absolute
terms and in relation to the central government's current expenditures.
This item includes subsidies to private and public transport and communication enterprises and a small amount of survey costs. At first
the government railroads operated at a level substantially below
capacity. Large operating deficits were incurred which the government covered, causing its expenditures on transport and communications as a share of total current expenditure to reach the very high
average level of 17 percent during the years 1898–1904. After 1905

the government's annual current expenditures on transport and communication remained at about the same absolute level as its spending during 1898–1904, but as a share of total current expenditure it declined and remained at a low level of 4 to 5 percent. Much of this later expenditure represented subsidies to Japanese shipping companies and, after 1935, to the air transport industry. From 1899 to 1935 the central government provided the Japanese shipping companies with sizable subsidies for the dual purpose of maintaining the frequency of voyages between Taiwan and Japan at a level that initially exceeded the commercial needs of the island, and of diverting the shipping business from Western to Japanese firms. These efforts not only kept Taiwan closely tied to Japan but also helped to remove foreign interests from Taiwan.

As the above figures indicate, the government assumed a large share of the responsibility of providing the island with a modern infrastructure. This was done at considerable expense at a time of very limited revenue. Furthermore, for a long period of time the infrastructure was not fully utilized, which meant that operating and maintenance costs had to be subsidized. Until the 1930s, when war preparations greatly intensified economic activity, the freight carried by the government railroads increased at a slower rate than the operating length of the rail system. It is clear that for a period of time the government maintained an infrastructure larger than the needs of the island. By doing this it provided forward linkages which may have quickened the commercialization and development of agriculture and the sugar industry.

The build-up of capital around the periphery of agriculture can only stimulate its growth indirectly. For more dramatic results, actions directed at agriculture itself are needed. The central government can be considered the main catalytic agent accelerating Taiwan's agricultural growth.[33] Certainly the available evidence indicates that the government devoted large amounts of its energy and money to transform agriculture.

Perhaps in no other area did the government conduct such thorough research before formulating its policies as in agriculture. At least one-third of the central government's development expenditures,

33. For a fuller discussion of agricultural development during the colonial period see my article "Agricultural Transformation Under Colonialism: The Case of Taiwan," *Journal of Economic History,* 28 (September 1968); and Ramon H. Myers and Adrienne Ching, "Agricultural Development in Taiwan under Japanese Colonial Rule," *Journal of Asian Studies,* 23 (August 1964).

or 10 percent of its total current expenditures, were spent on promoting agriculture through research, extension, and subsidies (Table 9.6). A considerable number of Japanese technicians and agronomists were brought to Taiwan to help transform its agriculture. Agricultural experiment stations and research institutions were established, some even before the end of the nineteenth century. Agricultural policies were largely based on the results of these surveys and research efforts.

The rural conditions revealed by government surveys were tackled by reforms aimed at establishing a more stable rural society. For example, at the beginning of the twentieth century, much of rural Taiwan operated under an archaic three-level tenancy system composed of the *ta-tsu hu* (the great landlords), the *hsiao-tsu hu* (the tenant landlords), and the cultivators (the subtenants). The ta-tsu hu were descendants of the wealthy Chinese who originally financed or sponsored many of the settlement attempts during the Ch'ing dynasty. The hsiao-tsu hu were descendants of the original settlers who cleared the land for the ta-tsu hu and received for their efforts the perpetual right to use the land at a fixed rent. As more immigrants came to the island from mainland China, the hsiao-tsu hu leased a part or all of their holdings to the newcomers and also became landlords of a sort.[34] Under this system, property rights were unclear, making land transactions and tax collection exceedingly difficult. To increase its yield from land tax and to eliminate a major cause of dispute from rural Taiwan, in 1905 the government, after completing an extensive cadastral survey, introduced a land reform program that simplified the tenancy system. It exchanged 3.78 million yen, of which 3.67 million were in the form of government bonds, for the property rights of some 40,000 ta-tsu hu.[35] In this fashion the hsiao-tsu hu became the legal owners of the land and were directly responsible for the land tax.

The conditions of tenant farmers were also improved when the government introduced and enforced regulations that extended the term of tenancy from one to five years; provided automatic renewal of contracts between landlord and tenant unless one party announced a change in intent six months before the termination of contract; sug-

34. For a fuller description of this complex system, see Santaro Okamatsu, *Provisional Report on Investigation of Laws and Customs in the Island of Formosa* (English ed., Kyoto: Provisional Commission for Research on Customs in Formosa, 1903), pp. 26–75.
35. Myers and Ching, p. 561.

gested the reduction of rent in case of crop failures; and required the landlord to share the expense of land improvement undertaken by the tenants. Arbitration committees, sponsored by the government, were established to settle disputes. Although the membership of the arbitration committee was weighted heavily in favor of the landlord, its establishment was a step in the right direction. By the late 1930s it was reported that three-quarters of the tenure arrangements in Taiwan were governed by written leases.

It is clear that the government, through these actions, did not intend to alter the existing social structure in rural Taiwan but rather to correct, in some instances only marginally, the worst abuses of the traditional Chinese tenure system. But since two-thirds of the agricultural population were tenants or part tenants, such improvements had far-reaching effects, for example, in lessening the possibility of rural unrest. Most importantly, however, the reforms gave the tenant farmers that minimum amount of stability and security without which it would have been unprofitable to participate in the development of the agricultural sector.

The Japanese administrators did not attempt to eliminate indigenous rural institutions, but modified them and used them within the government administrative framework to channel new technology and other nontraditional inputs into agriculture to make it more efficient and productive. For an underdeveloped and colonial economy, the government was unusually research oriented. New techniques of cultivation, new varieties of seeds, and new methods of applying nontraditional agricultural inputs such as chemical fertilizer were developed, experimented with, and made available to the farmers. The success of the government's extension program relied heavily on the Farmers' Associations and the pao-chia system. The pao-chia system was a particularly useful instrument for disseminating agricultural information. The Farmers' Associations, which began at the initiative of Taiwanese farmers in 1900, were seized and reorganized by the government in 1909 to become the major extension agent in Taiwan.[36] By controlling rural organizations such as the Farmers' Associations, most of which were financially independent, the government created a network that enabled it to establish a highly effective extension system at a relatively low cost to itself. In the late 1920s and 1930s,

36. For a fuller description of the development of the Farmers' Associations, see Taiwan, Provincial Department of Agriculture and Forestry, *The Reorganization of Farmers' Associations in Taiwan* (Taipei, 1950), pp. 1–28.

some 10,000 to 13,000 agricultural extension workers and technicians were employed by these government-controlled or government-regulated, but not completely government-financed, rural agencies.[37] It was the combination of its practical knowledge of local institutions, its attention to details, and its painstaking supervision of research and extension work, that made the government so influential in guiding Taiwan's agricultural development.

Government investments also helped to modify agriculture, both by altering its relationship with the rest of the economy and by improving its productivity. While estimates of total investment are not available for the colonial period, there is little doubt that the government was probably the island's most important investor. Its annual investment in fixed capital distributed by use is given in Table 9.10. On the average, the central government annually invested an amount equivalent to approximately 40 percent of its total current expenditures, or about 20 percent of the exhaustive expenditures of all levels of government.

When the central government's investment is disaggregated by use, its effects on the economy, in particular on agriculture, can be better appraised. Overwhelmingly, government investment was in overhead capital, with transport and communication consistently receiving the major share, usually about 60 percent. The stimulating effects of this type of investment, especially in terms of the forward linkages it provided, have already been suggested. Another 15 to 30 percent of the government's annual investment went to construct government buildings, schools, and hospitals, and to increase the capital stock of the government monopolies. Of these, only the latter directly increased the productive capacity of the economy.

The government investment that affected production most directly was in agriculture, particularly in irrigation facilities. In a rice economy such as Taiwan's, irrigation is the most important capital input in the production process. For Taiwan the significance of irrigation is further magnified by the prominence of agriculture in the economy. Only when these factors are realized can one fully comprehend the strategic importance of public investments in agriculture. Besides direct investment, the amount of which is indicated in Table 9.10, the government also provided grants and loans to finance the construction of those irrigation projects that had its approval but were

37. Ibid., p. 20.

not under its direct supervision. The latter forms of aid became particularly important after 1920 when the Irrigation Association, a semi-official organization, became firmly established throughout the island.

The combined sum of direct government investments in irrigation and government grants for irrigation construction as a share of total investment in irrigation is presented in Table 9.11. Between 1906

Table 9.11: Total Investment in Irrigation Facilities
(Million yen)

	Government[a]		*Irrigation association*		*Total*	
1900–04	0.3	100%	—[b]	—	0.3	100%
1905–09	2.9	94	0.2	6%	3.1	100
1910–14	2.9	100	—	—	2.9	100
1915–19	3.0	79	0.8	21	3.8	100
1920–24	12.9	48	14.0	52	26.9	100
1925–29	16.1	29	39.4	71	55.5	100
1930–34	6.5	36	11.7	64	18.2	100
1935–39	—	—	6.4	100	6.4	100
1940–44	32.7	69	14.9	31	47.6	100
1900–44	77.3	47	87.4	53	164.7	100

[a] Includes the direct investment in and the grants for irrigation construction provided by the Government-General.
[b] Dash means zero.

Sources: For the sources of the data on government investment, see Table 9.2. The figures on investments of the irrigation associations are taken from Bank of Taiwan, *On the Problem of Taiwan's Irrigation* (Taipei, 1950), p. 95.

and 1942, the total area under irrigation increased from 200,000 to 545,000 hectares, and the percentage of irrigated land to cultivated land increased from 32 to 64 percent.[38] It is evident that until 1920 the central government directly financed out of its budget practically all irrigation investments. After 1920, through the Irrigation Association, the government was able to supplement its expenditure by mobilizing and channeling a part of rural savings to investment in irrigation facilities. Even during this latter period, however, the government still directly financed between 30 to 50 percent of the total investment in irrigation. For the period 1900–44, 47 percent of the cost of irrigation construction was paid directly by the government

38. *Taiwan Province: Statistical Summary,* p. 594.

and the rest by the Irrigation Association.[39] Between 1926 and 1930 the Irrigation Association also borrowed 18.7 million yen from the government for irrigation construction. Because World War II interrupted the repayment of these loans, they essentially became government grants. When these loans are included with the other government investments in irrigation, the government met 58.2 percent of the total cost of irrigation development in Taiwan for the period 1900–44.

The promotion of agriculture was of course intimately related to the government's desire to establish a sugar industry. Its involvement in the development of this industry probably provides the best illustration of how the government, by cooperating with private Japanese capital, created a corporate business structure through which it at last virtually eliminated the Taiwanese capitalists from the industry. The government's program was devised to induce Japanese investment in Taiwan and to persuade Taiwanese farmers to cultivate more sugar cane. Investments in infrastructure were of course made to make the island a more attractive place to invest, but more direct inducements were needed. At first, the government directly negotiated with groups of Japanese capitalists and used as bait the promise of a guaranteed dividend of 6 percent of their investment for the first six years.[40] This initial overture resulted in the formation of the Taiwan Sugar Company in 1900; the major investors were the Japanese Imperial Household, and the Mitsui and the Mori families. A more general promotional scheme was launched in 1902 with the establishment of the Sugar Bureau and the promulgation of the Regulation for the Encouragement of the Sugar Industry.

The 1902 regulation clarified the government's intention to favor the sugar industry. Its major features were:

1. Anyone who cultivated five acres or more of sugar cane could apply for fertilizer subsidies of 5 yen and sugar cane shoot

39. For the ten major irrigation projects completed during the colonial period, supplying water to 177,297 hectares of land, the Government-General provided nearly 60 percent of the total construction costs of 65 million yen. See Shigeto Kawano, *A Study of Taiwan's Rice Economy* (Tokyo: Yukikaku Ltd., 1941), p. 40.

40. Chang and Myers, "Japanese Colonial Development Policy," p. 443. In James W. Davidson's *The Island of Formosa, Past and Present* (London: Macmillan & Co., 1903), p. 453, the impression is given that the government support was in the form of an annual subsidy of a 6 percent of the invested capital. That the support was in the form of a guaranteed dividend seems, however, more likely, and this interpretation is adopted here.

subsidies of 3.4 yen for every 0.25 acre of land under sugar cane;

2. the government could subsidize up to 50 percent of the construction costs of irrigation and drainage projects that benefited sugar cane cultivation, if the total cost exceeded 1,000 yen;
3. sugar manufacturers using government-approved machinery could be subsidized up to 20 percent of its cost;
4. sugar companies with grinding capacity above a government-determined limit would be entitled to subsidies;
5. government land could be cleared and used for cane cultivation without rent, and if the settlement proved successful, the land could be transferred to private ownership; and
6. government land could be used without cost for irrigation construction.[41]

The purpose of this regulation, obviously, was to promote the planting of sugar cane and the greater utilization of fertilizer and irrigation. It also aimed at eliminating the nearly 1,500 primitive mills owned by the Taiwanese capitalists at the end of the nineteenth century by encouraging the construction of modern refineries.

Besides the explicit inducements stated in the regulation, the government also offered prospective investors the possibility of special legal privileges, trifling taxes, and its willingness to maintain a most cordial and cooperative relationship. Furthermore, government railroads gave preferential freight rates to the sugar companies. By 1944 the government had subsidized the sugar industry to the tune of 12.9 million yen and had provided over 700 million free sugar cane shoots.[42] Of the 12.9 million yen, 31.9 percent went to subsidize the purchase of fertilizer, 14.4 percent to irrigation, 9.7 percent to seedlings, and the rest to the sugar-refining firms. In other words, approximately 56 percent of the subsidies went to promote cane cultivation and 44 percent to the modernization of sugar refineries. Over 70 percent of these cash subsidies were distributed during the decade immediately following the promulgation of the 1902 regulation. Because improved cane varieties were periodically introduced by the government experimental stations,

41. Yosaburo Takekoshi, *Japanese Rule in Formosa*, trans. George Braithwaite (London: Longmans, Green, and Co., 1907), p. 244. Also see Cheng-siang Chen, *The Utilization of Land in Taiwan* (Taipei: National Taiwan University, 1950), pp. 163–64.

42. These and the following figures are derived from Taiwan, Provincial Government, Department of Agriculture and Forestry, *Taiwan Sugar Statistics*, no. 2 (1948), pp. 140–41.

the free distribution of cane shoots continued unabated throughout the colonial period.

Under such favorable terms, the sugar industry expanded rapidly. Large amounts of Japanese capital moved to Taiwan. In a decade, sugar production increased more than sixfold, from 30,000 metric tons in 1902 to 204,000 in 1910; of the 1910 production more than 75 percent was produced by newly improved or modern mills. In fact, the expansion of the industry was too rapid, and as demand fluctuated, a series of crises developed. Fearful that the industry could not survive unless some order was imposed, the government became the regulator as well as the promoter of the industry. To maintain stability in the industry, the government took measures to regulate the output as well as the supply of raw cane.

In 1905 the government issued a regulation to ensure that adequate supplies of cane were available to each of the existing refineries: (1) sugar-producing areas were divided into supply regions, with each region assigned to a refinery; (2) without the permission of the government, cane produced in one supply region could not be moved to another or be used for purposes other than sugar manufacturing; (3) without government permission new mills could not be established; and (4) sugar companies were responsible for the purchase of the total harvest of cane at appropriate prices.[43] This regulation in essence made the sugar companies monopsonists, with immense power to influence the price of raw cane. Persuasive measures were also devised to attract landowners to cane production. Sugar cane fields were classified as "upland field," which was taxed at a considerably lower rate than rice fields, which were classified as "paddy land."[44] By this discriminatory measure, landowners were induced to remain in cane production or to switch from rice to cane. Perhaps the most influential device was the ability of the government, through its control of the Irrigation Association, to withhold irrigation from rice fields and thus force the cultivation of cane.

To stabilize the price and the output of sugar, the government took several measures to protect and govern the industry. Starting in 1906, Japan enforced a highly discriminatory tariff on sugar not produced

43. Cheng-siang Chen, *Taiwan: An Economic and Social Geography* (Taipei: Fu-Min Geographical Institute of Economic Development, 1963), p. 312.

44. Depending on the grade, the differences in tax rates between upland and paddy land may be as much as 20 percent. See S. M. Yeh and T. S. Kuo, *Rural Land Taxation in Taiwan,* Economic Digest Series no. 2 (Taipei: JCRR, 1952), Table 1.

in Taiwan, which eliminated all of Taiwan's competitors from the Japanese market. In 1909–10 the government allowed and in fact encouraged the formation of a cartel among the sugar producers, later known as the Taiwan Sugar Association, which was given the power to regulate, with government guidance, such matters as the level of output, price, and export. The government supported this arrangement by assuming the responsibility of regulating the capacity of sugar refineries and restricting the expansion of existing factories and the construction of new refineries. With these privileges, the monopolistic structure of the industry was ensured. The cartel arrangement suited both the sugar companies and the government. The sugar companies were able to maximize their profit jointly, and the government, by allowing the cartel to exist, was in a strong position to influence and control the industry. Even such internal financial decisions as the magnitude of dividend payments could not be made without government approval.[45] In effect, through the monopolistic industrial structure it helped to create, the government was able to influence the savings ratio.

During the colonial period, the government relied primarily on its own savings and the savings of the Japanese corporate business structures it helped create to provide the capital for industry. It never encouraged the emergence of an indigenous industrialist class; in fact, its whole policy was directed toward preventing the emergence of such a class. Until 1924 Taiwanese were not allowed to organize or operate corporations unless there was Japanese participation.[46] Thus the modern sector became a monopoly of the Japanese capitalists. Even after this restrictive rule against Taiwanese participation was rescinded, Taiwanese were reluctant to seek entry to the modern sector because of its domination by Japanese capitalists. Through its power to regulate, and license, and by granting exclusive privileges to Japanese capitalists, the government successfully kept the Taiwanese from acquiring any economic power.

Once its agricultural and sugar policies were developed and had proven reasonably effective, the colonial government became somewhat relaxed and allowed itself to be trapped by its own image of Taiwan as an agricultural appendage to Japan. Little effort was made

45. U.S. Navy *Handbook, Economic Supplement,* OPNAV 50E-13 (June 1944), p. 6.

46. Han-yu Chang, "Evolution of Taiwan's Economy during the Period of Japanese Rule," Series Two of Taiwan's Economic History (Taipei: Bank of Taiwan, 1956), p. 96.

to prepare the foundation for a more diversified economy. Therefore it was not until the 1930s, when Japan turned to war preparations, that the government altered its concept of the island as a two-commodity agricultural economy. The impetus for change came from Japan, when its war preparations made it more difficult to satisfy Taiwan's needs for manufacturers and Taiwan needed to depend more on its own industrial capacity. Consequently a new government attitude toward industry emerged. Prior to the 1930s, except for the sugar industry, the government was indifferent toward this sector although it did not discriminate against it. But now, reflecting the changes in the political atmosphere and in Japan's economic needs, the colonial government began to partake directly in more industrial activity.[47] The changed political atmosphere also allowed the government to assume even greater control over the economy, and by the late 1930s very little remained outside its control.[48]

Two government conferences were held, one in 1930 and the other in 1935, to investigate the island's resources and to determine the most appropriate manner of developing the economy.[49] Objectives and conditions, however, changed so rapidly during this decade that most suggestions made at these conferences soon became dated or irrelevant. Unlike the earlier period, the policy makers in the 1930s operated in a much more uncertain environment, and decisions were based more on short-term than on long-term considerations.

By its actions, it is apparent that by the mid-1930s the government had added two new objectives to its economic program: (1) the expansion of Taiwan's industrial capacity to produce goods previously imported from Japan and to supply industrial raw materials such as aluminum ingots and chemicals needed by Japan's heavy industry;

47. The most detailed study of the post-1930 period is Kusui, *Economy of Taiwan.*

48. The economic controls introduced during the late 1930s and the early 1940s were extensive. An economic division was added to the police system in 1938 to enforce the new regulations governing the economy. The government directly collected and distributed rice, the staple food for the island. Labor bureaus were established at all levels of government to "adjust demand to supply" and to control wage rates. The labor shortages eventually led to the conscription of labor. Prices of essential goods were put under control and the goods rationed. Firms in existing industries were merged, better enabling the government to control their operation. These and other controls introduced by the government are discussed in great detail in Kusui, ibid.

49. For the program adopted by the 1930 conference, see *Production Planning in Taiwan* (Taipei: Taiwan Nōyō Kai, 1931). The program of the 1935 conference is discussed in Kusui, pp. 49–57.

and (2) the reorientation of Taiwan's external economic relationships by increasing its ties with South China and Southeast Asia. The first objective was largely dictated by the desire to reduce some of the demands made on the hard-pressed Japanese industry. The second objective was designed to further strengthen Japan's position in South China and Southeast Asia. Japan had always considered Taiwan the natural base for extending its influence in these two areas. Economically, it was hoped that, at a minimum, more of Taiwan's exports could be directed toward them. With its growing productive capacity, the government realized that Taiwan had to broaden its market, and it had visions of transforming Taiwan into an industrial center, with South China and Southeast Asia as its markets as well as its sources of raw materials.

The main instrument of industrialization selected by the government was the semiofficial enterprise. This was but a refinement of earlier devices used to promote the sugar industry. The two semiofficial enterprises that spearheaded the industrialization program were the Taiwan Electric Power Company (TEPC) and the Taiwan Development Company (TDC). TEPC was formed in 1919 with the original purpose of developing the island's electric power resources. Besides the government, major investors in TEPC included Mitsui and the Japan Life Insurance Company. As a result of the government's decision to industrialize the island, TEPC expanded its operations and became the entrepreneur-investor for the government in heavy industry. In 1935, TEPC, with Mitsui and Mitsubishi, established the Japan Aluminum Company, with plants in Kaoshiung and Hualien. Power for the aluminum plants was provided by the TEPC at reduced rates and bauxite was supplied from Indonesia. The Japan Aluminum Company became the most important metal producer in Taiwan; by 1940 it supplied approximately one-sixth of the total aluminum produced in the Japanese Empire. In the late 1930s, TEPC also helped to create in Taiwan such metal industries as iron, steel, and ferromagnesium.

The Taiwan Development Company was established by the government in 1936 specifically to coordinate the development of Taiwan with that of South China and Southeast Asia. While it did operate in South China and in Southeast Asia, TDC's major interests remained in Taiwan.[50] It was authorized to invest and operate enter-

50. TDC had mining interests in Malaya and Indochina and operated numerous enterprises in Thailand, South China, and the Philippines.

prises in mining, agriculture, forestry, trade, and light manufacturing. In the few years of its existence, TDC initiated numerous projects, including the extraction of oil from cotton seed, the extraction of butyl alcohol from sweet potatoes, the manufacture of pulp, the raising of livestock, and the assembly of motor vehicles.

Despite these vigorous efforts, Taiwan was able to make only extremely limited progress in expanding its industrial capacity. Ironically it was the early policies of the government that frustrated its later designs for the economy. Human resources needed for industrialization, unlike material capital, cannot be developed quickly, and in the 1930s the government was to regret its earlier reluctance to invest in education for the Taiwanese. Moreover the transport system, developed primarily to support agricultural development, was unable to meet the combined demand of the new industries and the military, and became a major bottleneck in the late 1930s. The light rails and the steep grades and curves of the tracks limited the speed and length of trains. Furthermore, the capacity of the freight cars (10-12 tons) was small. There were few highways, and many rivers had to be crossed by ferry. Harbor facilities, developed only in Keelung and Kaoshiung, were inadequate. The government made frantic efforts to correct these weaknesses but could not overcome them in a short period of time.[51] For Japan, the broadening of economic objectives in Taiwan came too late.

The colonial government's record, viewed in the light of its own objectives, was a successful one. The island was pacified and brought under tight Japanese control. The material resources of the island were successfully developed and systematically exploited for the benefit of Japan. The government and private Japanese capitalists owned and operated much of the nonagricultural sector and retained a firm control over agriculture. The achievements in agriculture and the sugar industry were the most impressive of all the sectors in the economy and they were gained largely through the efforts of the government. The stagnant agricultural sector began to grow at around 2-2.5 percent per year and increased after 1920 at an annual compound rate of 3.8 percent. The five-year average yield of all crops increased by over 55 percent between 1910–15 and 1936–40. Between 1901–10 and 1931–40 the ten-year average yield for Taiwan's

---

51. For a discussion of these last-minute efforts to develop Taiwan, see U.S. Navy, *Handbook, Economic Supplement,* chapters 6–9; and Kusui, chapters 3–5.

three major crops—rice, sugar cane, and sweet potatoes—increased by 69, 46, and 59 percent respectively. Sugar production rose from 30,000 metric tons in 1903 to 1.4 million metric tons in 1939, an increase of almost fiftyfold. By the 1930s Taiwan was supplying 6 to 7 percent of Japan's rice requirement. As for sugar, Taiwan accounted for nearly 10 percent of world export in the 1930s, supplying the empire with 90 percent of its sugar requirement.[52] These figures leave no doubt that the colonial government successfully achieved the objectives initially set for it by Japan.

Although its late efforts to industrialize the island were less successful, the colonial government laid the beginnings of the foundation on which current Taiwanese industrialization is based. In the 1930s and the early 1940s, the transport bottleneck that was constraining the island's industrial growth was partially eliminated. Moreover, the belated efforts in the 1930s to educate the Taiwanese greatly increased the number of children in school, and by the 1940s Taiwan had one of the more literate populations among the less developed countries. While the colonial government reaped little benefit from these efforts to remove two of the most serious obstacles to development, the future benefit to Taiwan was immense.

The success of the Japanese colonial program can largely be attributed to two factors: (1) in most instances, the Japanese planned their programs with care, paying an unusual amount of attention to research; and (2) the presence of large groups of Japanese in the colonial administration and in the modern industries made it possible for the government to supervise closely the enactment of its programs. For the most part, the colonial administrators were pragmatists in the fashion of Kodama and Gotō who followed "a consistent pattern of study, planning, enactment, further study, further planning, and revision"[53] in their dealings with the island's problems. Detailed planning alone does not, however, ensure success. The successful execution of programs also depends on competent and careful supervision. Unlike such colonial powers as Great Britain, which relied heavily on native administrators, Japan carried out its colonial program in Taiwan primarily with Japanese. According to the censuses, some 25,000 Japanese males, approximately 30 percent of the total

52. U.N. Food and Agriculture Organization, *The World Sugar Economy in Figures, 1880–1959*, Commodity Reference Series no. 1 (1961), pp. 46–48 and 100.
53. Tsurumi, "Taiwan," p. 136.

Japanese employed males in Taiwan, were government employees. In 1940 nearly 70 percent of the technicians in agriculture, industry, mining, transport, etc., were Japanese.[54] Because the colonial government was willing and able to draw talent from Japan, competent personnel could be placed at all levels of the colonial establishment. The competence of the lower echelons of the colonial administration as well as of the modern semipublic enterprises is a major reason for Japan's success in Taiwan.

When viewed in a broader context the government's program becomes less successful. Because policy was oriented toward keeping economic power and control out of the hands of the native population, education for Taiwanese was largely neglected, industrial skilled labor and technicians were recruited as needed from Japan, and the emergence of an indigenous entrepreneur-capitalist class was discouraged. The elements needed for sustained economic growth were therefore never created in Taiwan. Had Japan suddenly withdrawn from Taiwan at any time, economic growth would probably have been seriously retarded. In fact, when Japan did withdraw in 1945 and the island was left without Japanese entrepreneurs and capitalists, much economic dislocation resulted. The government's policy, which introduced large segments of the Taiwanese population to modern agricultural techniques and inputs, restricted most Taiwanese from participating in the industrialization of the island. Indeed, any industry or sector not sponsored by the government was left undeveloped or underdeveloped. Thus policies that the Japanese believed were needed to achieve its objectives of controlling and exploiting the economy wasted resources and eventually became a constraint to further growth.

Comments by Hugh T. Patrick

Samuel Ho provides a useful survey and appraisal of the role of Japanese colonial policy in Taiwan's economic development from accession in 1895 until World War II. That he has assiduously mined basic sources in order to provide a coherent quantitative base in a well-organized framework for analysis is evident; this clearly involved

54. George Barclay, *A Report on Taiwan's Population* (Princeton: Office of Population Research, Princeton University, 1954), p. 63.

great effort and the quantitative estimates themselves are a major contribution to our understanding of Taiwanese development. But Ho goes far beyond "number grubbing"; his analysis of the overwhelming role of government is on the whole comprehensive and persuasive.

Precolonial Taiwan is presented as a rather backward, fragmented, agrarian economy, with serious law and order problems, attendant lack of domestic administrative control, fairly rampant disease, and relatively high death rates—but with some (considerable?) degree of Chinese traditional education and Taiwanese entrepreneurship (at least in sugar refining). I have the suspicion that Ho somewhat underestimates the heritage and perhaps overestimates local security problems (which may be different from the need of a colonial government to establish control in its version of "domestic tranquility").

At any rate, the colonial government's economic objectives are clear: to develop Taiwan, but as a tropical agrarian producer—of sugar and rice notably—complementing the Japanese economy; at minimum cost to Japan's governmental budget (if not to the Japanese consumer); and with much of the benefits of growth appropriated by Japanese ownership in Taiwan. Japanization of the Taiwanese apparently did not become an important objective until the 1930s. Government policy was successful in that the growth of output was substantial and a social overhead infrastructure was built up, particularly in transportation and communications, substantially in public health, but only somewhat in education.

The implementation of government policy through its expenditure pattern is well delineated in this paper. Development expenditures constitute a large proportion of government expenditures—three-quarters of investment, more than a quarter of current expenditures, and most of the nonexhaustive expenditures (notably transfers to the railroads and subsidies to sugar producers). Ho readily admits the difficulties of separating out developmental from general or welfare expenditures, not just statistically but in a causal sense. For example, establishment of law and order is an important precondition for economic development, though it by no means guarantees that development will occur. Yet expenditures for such purposes are not usually classified as developmental. I find I tend to agree with his approach: to take a fairly narrow classification of developmental expenditures and to note exceptions or areas of wider implication for development.

The welfare benefits of Taiwan's growth for the native Taiwanese population are presented as limited. Taiwanese were systematically excluded from opportunities for higher education and thus from higher government or business positions; their entrepreneurial activities were repressed; even the goods they produced were purchased at monopolistically low prices by Japanese-owned firms; the tax system was regressive. Yet some of the benefits must have trickled down, in higher real wages or agrarian real incomes. No doubt Ho will treat this matter more fully in his larger study of Taiwanese economic development. And of course he points out that public health and related measures substantially improved the health and life expectancy of the Taiwanese.

Ho suggests that an increasing rate of population growth was a net stimulus to the economy, because of the availability of uncultivated land and the government's active role. Perhaps in terms of total output the effect of population growth was positive, but surely in terms of output per person (the more relevant welfare criterion—though probably not that of the Japanese colonial administration) population growth was a hindrance. The government would have been active anyway. Land farmed per family was very small; I suspect that the availability of uncultivated land reflected more a lack of transport, irrigation, and other (capital-using) facilities than lack of labor. Even if labor was not in surplus in the Fei-Ranis sense, its productivity was low.[1] Population growth diluted the (presumably scarce) capital stock available.

One of Ho's objectives is to describe the nature of Japanese colonialism. In its economic aspects it appears similar to other ventures: development of the colony as a docile producer of raw materials for the colonial power and a market for its manufacturers, with much of the benefits going to the colonialists (though probably the exploited local population were in absolute terms better off economically than before). What distinguishes the Japanese is perhaps not the greater priority of economic growth but the assiduous detail and pragmatism of their effort. Government supervision, encouragement, and other forms of intervention were regarded as natural and desirable. Technological change in agriculture and processing was emphasized and widely disseminated through a major agricultural extension program.

Though outside the scope of Ho's paper, one might well ask whether Taiwan paid off economically as a colony for Japan. The fact that a discriminatory tariff against other producers was necessary

1. Gustav Ranis and John C. H. Fei, "A Theory of Economic Development," *The American Economic Review* 51 (September 1961): 533–58.

to assure Taiwan of Japan's sugar market suggests that Taiwan was not a notably low-cost producer (or maybe it was, but this was more than offset by monopsony and monopoly profits to the Japanese-owned sugar refiners and traders). In addition, for a long period the Japanese consumer excise tax on sugar went to Taiwan.

Taiwan was a relatively low-cost producer of rice, and, following the rice riots of 1918 in Japan, the Japanese government undertook to import substantial amounts from Taiwan. While this might have been efficient in terms of the long-run reallocation of labor in Japan from agriculture to industry, in fact in the 1920s (and until the mid-1930s) Japan's industrial sector was not absorbing labor very rapidly. In part because of import competition from Taiwan, Japanese agricultural output and incomes stagnated. The worsening agrarian conditions in Japan are related, though in a way not yet fully understood, to the resurgent militarism of the 1930s. In this broad sense it is not clear that rice imports from Taiwan were to Japan's net benefit.

Thus the picture of costs and benefits to Japan is mixed: the benefits of one group were often the costs of another. Consumers had to pay relatively high prices for sugar, but somewhat lower prices for rice. Japanese farmers faced lower prices for their rice than otherwise would have been the case. Japanese investors in Taiwan did well. No doubt Ho's larger study will provide further insights into the question whether Japan's colonial administration of Taiwan was an economic success and which group really benefited.

10

Public Finance in
Postrevolutionary Mexico

BY CLARK W. REYNOLDS

Mexico illustrates as well as any country in Latin America that the role of government in economic development must be regarded as part of a broader process of social equilibration in which material, psychological, social, and political factors interact to bring about growth and structural change. (Economic relationships merely represent a subsystem conditioning and being conditioned by these other factors.) In Mexico a number of basic institutions have been drastically altered during the past century, carrying traditional economic structures with them. As a result the analysis of public finance in contemporary Mexican development might best be regarded as a study in political and economic evolution. The following material, however, is more conventional, confining itself to a primarily descriptive treatment of the level and composition of public expenditures and taxation in Mexico since the late 1930s.[1]

The modern economic history of Mexico may be separated for convenience into three major epochs: (1) the years of dictatorship

This essay draws upon material from a broader study by the same author, *The Mexican Economy: Twentieth-Century Structure and Growth* (New Haven: Yale University Press, 1970). There the role of the public sector is analyzed as part of the general process of Mexican development since 1900. Taxation and expenditures are presented in greater statistical detail and there is a far greater discussion of the indirect role of public policy on growth especially in agriculture, industry, and foreign trade. The author wishes to thank R. Albert Berry, Shane Hunt, Donald Keesing, and James Wilkie, among others, for their valuable comments and criticisms, a number of which were impossible to satisfy within the limits of time, information, and technical competence.

1. For a convincing presentation of a similar analytical perspective, see Richard S. Thorn, "The Evolution of Public Finances during Economic Development," *Manchester School of Economic and Social Studies*, 35, no. 1 (January 1967): 20.

under Porfirio Díaz from 1876 to 1910, during which laissez faire policies and large-scale foreign investments combined to bring about rapid expansion of primary production, (2) the interim decades of revolution, recovery, and reform from 1910 to 1940, and (3) the period from 1940 to the present, during which the rate of growth not only recovered but surpassed the best prerevolutionary years. The cumulative annual rates of growth during each of these periods were 4 percent before 1910, 2 percent between 1910 and 1940, and 6 percent from 1940 to the mid-1960s. Only during the three decades of revolution and reform did the rate of economic expansion fail to keep pace with the natural rate of increase in population.

The present essay focuses on the role of public finance since the late 1930s. Hence it ignores a crucial period in Mexican economic history during which (1) large numbers of the population were killed through war, famine, and disease; (2) traditional mineral-based export industries were either taxed virtually to extinction or expropriated; (3) political power shifted from a foreign and domestic oligarchy to revolutionary leaders from the lower and middle classes; (4) Indians and those with mixed blood finally achieved full social equality; (5) the vast majority of arable landholdings were expropriated and given out in small parcels to landless peasants; (6) the educational system was greatly expanded, secularized, and utilized as an instrument to forge a national self-consciousness and sense of social identity.

As a result of these and other factors, the demands placed upon the government in 1940 were quite different from those facing prerevolutionary administrations, calling for more emphasis on social infrastructure and income equality than is customarily true for the rest of Latin America, even today. On the other hand, the capacity of the Mexican government to intervene in banking, commerce, agriculture, and manufacturing was much greater after the Revolution than is true for most developing countries today. With greater demands upon it, but with correspondingly greater freedom to act, the Mexican government was uniquely challenged in 1940 to provide both economic growth and rapid improvements in social welfare. This essay deals with the response to this challenge within the narrow framework of tax and expenditure policies as reflected in the best statistical evidence presently available. Some of the statistical series go as far back as 1935; few extend beyond 1962. The analysis covers over two decades of growth under the mixed enterprise system, revealing both its strengths and its weaknesses from a fiscal point of view. The interpretation of the data suffers from a number of difficulties in addition to incomplete specification of the social and political aspects of fiscal performance. These include:

1. Discrepancies between *ex post* and *ex ante* tax and expenditure policies as revealed by the growing gap between planned and actual budget levels. These discrepancies make both quantitative and qualitative imputations of fiscal intent extremely difficult to determine.[2]
2. The steady increase in licensing and other forms of indirect controls as instruments of indicative planning governing private expenditure, which may well have played a more important role than direct public expenditures in altering the pattern of resource allocation and growth since 1940.
3. Ambiguities in the value of economic indicators, including gross and net investment and the functional and personal distribution of income, which are essential to determining both the incidence and the effects of taxation and government expenditure on the level of output and the distribution of income.
4. The growing relative importance of monetary policy in Mexico, which, while making fiscal policy more effective through stabilizing the price level, also increasingly acts as a substitute for taxation by permitting the government deficit to be increasingly financed through the transfer of private savings to public investment.[3]

As is characteristic of so many developing countries, the Mexican

2. A detailed analysis of planned and actual budgets by economic and social category since the Revolution is presented by historian James Wilkie in *The Mexican Revolution: Federal Expenditure and Social Change since 1910* (Berkeley: University of California Press, 1967), part 1.

3. A number of works deal with the history of Mexican financial institutions and monetary policy. These include Dwight Brothers and Leopoldo Solís, *Mexican Financial Development* (Austin: University of Texas Press, 1966); Antonio Campos Andapia, "Teoría de la intermediación financiera y las sociedades financieras privadas Mexicanas" (thesis for Licenciatura, U.N.A.M., Mexico, 1962), part of which appeared as *Obstáculos al desarrollo económico* (C.E.M.L.A., Mexico); Robert L. Bennett, *The Financial Sector and Economic Development: The Mexican Case* (Baltimore: Johns Hopkins Press, 1965); David H. Shelton, "The Banking System: Money and the Goal of Growth," in Vernon, ed., *Public Policy and Private Enterprise in Mexico*, pp. 111–90; Raymond W. Goldsmith, *The Financial Development of Mexico* (Paris: OECD, 1966).

economy may be regarded as a dynamic disequilibrium system in which markets in excess demand coexist with those in excess supply for prolonged periods of time. As a result, the use of traditional neoclassical analysis, relying as it does on assumptions of relatively instantaneous adjustment of markets to marginal changes in the conditions of supply and demand, is not entirely appropriate. Nor is it very meaningful to introduce Keynesian assumptions of underemployment in all factor markets associated with the general excess demand for liquidity. In a disequilibrium system such as has characterized Mexico since 1940, a number of markets are already in excess demand (such as the market for investable funds due to the fixed interest rate policy of the Central Bank), so that changes in public expenditure tend to produce an asymmetrical response among goods and factor markets. While some markets experience changes in real output and factor employment, others face increased excess demand, producing shortages, pressure on the price level, and the need for rationing in the short run. This means that the real impact of public policy on employment, resource allocation, and growth is analytically difficult, if not impossible, to determine. Nevertheless it is useful to measure the injections and leakages from the public sector, using the best indicators available, as a precondition for further analysis of the functional impact of public expenditure.

THE HISTORICAL TREND IN MEXICAN PUBLIC EXPENDITURE

The most direct impact of the public sector on the national economy is in terms of its demand for goods and services as shown by the level and distribution of public expenditure. In this section government expenditures are divided into two major categories: those that make direct demands upon the productive capacity of the economy (exhaustive expenditures), and those that redistribute purchasing power within the private sector (nonexhaustive expenditures).[4] Government exhaustive expenditures are those that can best be associated with other

4. The methodology employed in this section, including the distinction between exhaustive and nonexhaustive expenditures, is described in Francis Bator, *The Question of Government Spending; Public Needs and Private Wants* (New York: Harper & Brothers, 1960). Calculations for Mexico were prepared with the assistance of Bosco A. Muro at El Colegio de México in 1964 and were presented in Muro, "Estructura y evolución del gasto público en México," typescript (Mexico, 1964). Detailed information as to the basis for these calculations is available on request.

value-added components of gross national product. They include government purchases of goods and services on current and capital account. Government consumption is confined for the most part to administrative expenditures essential to its day-to-day operations. Government investment, on the other hand, represents the increase in the stock of physical capital brought about directly through public expenditures.

Government nonexhaustive expenditures represent transfer payments on both current and capital account. Since the eventual disposition of these payments in terms of consumption or investment is under the control of private decision makers, nonexhaustive expenditures are separated from direct government purchases of goods and services for analytical purposes. The assumption is made in such a separation that, even though the social welfare function underlying public expenditure may be identical to that for private expenditure, the former represent collective purchases of public goods and services on current and capital account that would not be demanded in the same proportion if left up to individuals in the economy, owing to externalities in both production and consumption. In the case of government expenditure on social infrastructure such as public health, education, and welfare, and on economic infrastructure such as roads, dams, and irrigation systems, this has clearly been true for Mexico. While in some cases transfer payments such as investment subsidies serve a similar purpose in allocating resources toward the creation of public goods, in general they are used for private consumption and investment in response to individual demand.

A classification of total government spending in Mexico from 1935 to 1962 in terms of exhaustive and nonexhaustive expenditures is presented in Table 10.1. The percentage relationships including the share of public expenditure in GDP are found in Table 12.2. The figures in Table 12.2 reveal that the proportion of federal, state, and local government expenditures in domestic product has not increased since the late 1930s.[5] Meanwhile, exhaustive expenditures as a share of total government expenditures have declined from an average of 93 percent in the 1930s to 67 percent in the last half of the 1950s.

5. The share of total government spending in GDP in 1900 was between 5 and 6 percent, compared to 11 percent in 1939. (The earlier calculation is based on government expenditure data from El Colegio de México, *Estadísticas económicas del porfiriato: fuerza de trabajo y actividad económica por sectores* (1965), and GDP estimates for 1900 as described in C. Reynolds, *The Mexican Economy*, Appendix C.

Table 10.1: Economic Classification of Total Federal, State, and Local Government Budgeted Expenditures, 1935–62 (Millions of current pesos)

	(1) Consumption	(2) Investment	(3) Total exhaustive (3) = (1) + (2)	(4) Nonexhaustive expenditures	(5) Total federal, state, and local expenditures (5 = 3 + 4)	(6) Gross domestic product
	Exhaustive expenditures					
1935	345	72	418	26	444	
1936	442	89	531	34	565	
1937	511	87	598	46	644	
1938	498	144	642	53	695	
1939	513	159	672	53	725	6,559
1940	538	189	767	64	791	7,108
1941	485	262	747	62	809	8,413
1942	604	275	879	100	979	10,332
1943	787	322	1,109	110	1,219	12,989
1944	801	487	1,288	194	1,483	16,895
1945	1,073	561	1,634	190	1,824	19,666
1946	1,136	569	1,705	170	1,875	25,329
1947	1,265	820	2,085	176	2,261	27,798
1948	1,647	1,050	2,696	250	2,947	29,997
1949	2,517	1,141	3,658	255	3,913	33,482
1950	1,722	1,392	3,114	262	3,376	41,060
1951	1,842	1,561	3,403	374	3,777	53,026
1952	2,169	1,870	4,040	517	4,556	59,384
1953	2,340	1,642	3,982	1,548	5,530	58,926
1954	2,782	2,156	4,937	1,850	6,787	72,205
1955	3,431	2,189	5,620	2,619	8,238	88,218
1956	3,955	2,344	6,299	3,447	9,746	100,600
1957	4,668	2,946	7,613	3,676	11,289	115,542
1958	5,506	2,933	8,439	4,139	12,578	128,570
1959	5,924	3,207	9,130	4,414	13,544	137,676
1960	7,085	3,175	10,260	4,591	14,851	155,867
1961	7,591	3,178	10,769	6,079	16,848	165,672
1962	8,358	3,496	11,854	7,193	19,047	179,874

Note: Rows may not sum to totals due to rounding. The official exchange rate in pesos per dollar was: 1940, 5.40; 1941, 4.86; 1942–47, 4.85; 1948, 5.76; 1949, 8.02; 1950–53, 8.65; 1954, 11.34; 1955–present, 12.50. Mexico maintains free convertibility with the dollar at a fixed rate of exchange.

Source: Bosco A. Muro, "Estructura y evolución del gasto público en México."

The government's command over resources in the economy has lagged accordingly during the most rapid period of Mexican growth, the very period when the economy was developing its strongest central controls and declaring itself "socialist within the Constitution."

Table 10.2: The Composition of Public Expenditures and Their Share of Gross
Domestic Product (Percentages)

Share of gov't.							
exhaustive		*Share of total*					
expenditures		*government expenditures*		*Share of gross domestic product*			
						Total	*Total gov't*
						gov't. ex-	*exhaustive*
						haustive	*& nonex-*
						expendi-	*haustive*
						tures plus	*expendi-*
Gov't.	*Gov't.*		*Non-*	*Gov't. ex-*	*investment*	*tures (not*	
con-	*in-*	*Exhaustive*	*exhaustive*	*haustive*	*of gov't.*	*including*	
sump-	*vest-*	*expendi-*	*expendi-*	*expendi-*	*enter-*	*investment*	
tion	*ment*	*tures*	*tures*	*tures*	*prises*	*of gov't.*	
						enterprises)	
(1)	(2)	(3)	(4)	(5)	(6)	(7)	
1935–40	80	20	93	7	10.2	—[a]	11.0
1941–45	66	34	90	10	8.4	10.4	9.3
1946–50	62	38	92	8	8.3	10.8	9.0
1951–55	57	43	78	22	6.6	9.4	8.6
1956–60	65	35	67	33	6.5	9.4	9.7
1961–62	70	30	63	37	6.5	10.5	10.4

[a] Dash indicates zero.

Source: Columns 1–5, 7: All percentages are the averages of the percentages for
each year in the period from the figures in Table 10.1. The percentages for each year
are in C. W. Reynolds, *Mexican Economy,* chapter 7. Column 6: From Table 10.4.

Concurrent with this downtrend in the share of government purchases of goods and services, a rising share of public revenues was
being disbursed in the form of transfer payments to the private sector.
The share of exhaustive expenditures in GDP has fallen steadily from
10.2 percent in the last half of the 1930s to 6.5 percent from 1956–62
(Table 10.2). Although most developing countries experience a secular rise in the share of total government expenditures in GDP, this
has not been true for Mexico since the 1930s. Normally the proportion
of government expenditures devoted to transfer payments to households (included in our figures under nonexhaustive expenditures)
rises steadily as a share of GDP, while other expenditures remain
fairly proportional.[6] In Mexico, however, a comparison of the columns

6. Thorn, Table 1, p. 21, and context.
Briefly the hypothesis that is set forth . . . is that the social and political
tendencies that are inherent in the process of economic development result in a rate of growth of public social expenditures substantially in

in Table 12.2 shows that, while nonexhaustive expenditures have risen from less than 1 percent of GDP to almost 4 percent over the period 1935–62, exhaustive expenditures have fallen by the same proportion, so that total government expenditures have failed to increase their share of gross domestic product. We shall see later that this is partly due to fiscal constraints arising from the desire for price stability and a low capacity to tax, and partly because investments of private and mixed enterprise were sufficient to sustain a high rate of economic growth. Most of the increase in the share of government transfer payments occurred *after* 1950 and particularly during the administrations of Ruiz Cortines (1952–58) and López Mateos (1958–64). But before 1952, government exhaustive expenditures, including investment in economic and social infrastructure, maintained an important share of both total government expenditure and GDP (Table 12.2, column 2).

Among the three branches of government the federal share of exhaustive expenditures has not changed significantly since 1940. It was 67 percent in that year, 71 percent in 1950, and 67 percent in 1960.[7] This reflects the high degree of concentration of political power in the hands of the federal government. The regional allocation of public expenditures is subject to a high degree of control by the president and his ministers. There is evidence that considerable regional reallocation of resources through the maintenance of net surpluses or deficits on public account by the federal government has taken place since 1940. For example, a large share of public investment in rural infrastructure was concentrated in the North and Northwest during the 1940s. In recent years a greater balance of regional investment has been maintained. Meanwhile the share of the Federal District[8] in total exhaustive expenditures has risen sharply from 6.8 percent in 1940 to 10.5 percent in 1950 and 11.3 percent in 1960. Since the Federal District does not customarily run a deficit, the rela-

---

excess of the rate of growth of national product while other public expenditures taken together tend to grow at a substantially lesser rate than social expenditures but not at a low enough rate to offset the growth in social expenditures so that the ratio of total public expenditures to GNP tends to rise historically. (pp. 22 f.)

The author supports this hypothesis with cross-sectional data for thirty-six countries for the period 1950–59.

7. These figures are taken from Muro, "Estructura y Evolución," and are reproduced in Reynolds, *The Mexican Economy*, chapter 7.

8. The government of the Federal District has pursued its tax and expenditure policy independently of the federal government.

tive increase in spending reflects a growing concentration of industry and population in the capital city. It is probable that total taxes exceeded expenditures in the Federal District. If so, then a net outflow of public expenditure to the rest of Mexico partly compensated for government subsidies to industry and labor which contributed to what many observers regard as overconcentration of manufacturing and commerce in the center of the country.

Although exhaustive expenditures have declined as a share of total government outlays since the late 1930s, this is by no means true of public investment expenditures. From 1940 to 1960 there was a sharp rise in the share of direct investment expenditures in both exhaustive and total government expenditures. Government direct investment has steadily increased, particularly during the last years of the Alemán administration. Alemán's public works projects involved the large-scale construction of roads, dams, and irrigation systems. These expenditures were widely criticized at the time as being grandiose, extravagant, and inflationary, but subsequent analysis has revealed their true importance. By uniting both domestic and foreign markets and permitting the opening of new land for cultivation, economies of scale and a more efficient allocation of resources have been facilitated by these infrastructure expenditures. While it is not possible to do justice here to the way in which government investment expenditures served to open up and raise the level of both industry and commercial agricultural production, it is important to note that they did, especially since large-scale public investment in rural infrastructure has been conspicuously absent elsewhere in Latin America.[9]

Tax revenues were insufficient to cover the cost of this upswing in government investment between 1947 and 1952. Because it was impossible before the mid-1950s to attract a large amount of private savings to sustain the desired level of government investment, government deficits progressively increased. These deficits were offset by unsupported credits from the Central Bank resulting in a severe postwar inflation. Two major devaluations were necessary (1954 and 1958) before it became possible for the government to ultilize increased private savings to finance public investment. The relative price stability presently enjoyed by Mexico was only possible after more than a decade of rapid growth under inflation, during which

9. The author's broader study (*The Mexican Economy*) provides detailed evidence substantiating the role of public investment in the development of both agriculture and industry since World War II.

the rate of savings was virtually doubled through a rise in the profit share of GDP as prices rose faster than wages. Time has tended to erase the memory of Mexico's postwar inflation, yet the problems of those years were cited at the time as a prime example of the difficulty of sustaining high rates of savings and investment without large, inflationary government deficits and aggregate excess demand.

Commentators are mixed in their interpretation of the necessity and wisdom of inflationary fiscal policy during the 1940s and early 1950s. Barry Siegel used Mexico's performance from 1939 to 1955 to argue hypothetically that although developing countries are extremely susceptible to inflation in times of rapid growth, growth and inflation might not have to coexist in Latin America.[10] His contention was that if the public sector had pursued a balanced budget policy by increasing the rate of taxation, factor mobility and profit rates in Mexico would have been even higher. Inflationary financing of government expenditures, according to Siegel, was dictated not by necessity but by unwise government policies that served to force savings from the masses indirectly through inflation rather than by channeling savings from industry and commerce directly into public investment through a high effective rate of taxation.[11] His argument was based on the assumption that higher tax rates could have been absorbed by the economy without substantially lowering the rate of private savings and investment. Most Mexican officials of the period were convinced, on the other hand, that sharp tax increases would have been abortive and that private investment would have been so reduced by this policy that these declines would have offset any gains from increased government investment.

An analysis that illustrates the official position was presented in 1949 by Alfredo Navarrete, who noted the existence of supply inelasticities in the domestic economy necessitating a high degree of protection and internal price rises so as to stimulate private investment in manufacturing.[12] Wartime and postwar inflation were regarded as essential to permit rising rates of return on capital in the private sector.

10. Barry Siegel, *Inflación y desarrollo: las experiencias de México* (C.E.M.L.A., 1960).
11. Ibid., pp. 179–87.
12. Navarrete, "Exchange Stability, Business Cycles, and Economic Development: An Inquiry into Mexico's Balance of Payments Problems, 1929–1946," later published as *Estabilidad de cambios, el ciclo, y el desarrollo económico. Una investigación sobre los problemas de la balanza de pagos de México, 1929–1946* (Mexico, 1951).

This author predicted that, although excess demand and balance of payments disequilibria were certain to result in the short run, in the long run the investments would bear fruit in expanded production, eventually eliminating excess demand. Inflation would be overcome by the process of development itself.[13] This prophecy was fulfilled in the following decade, but this was partly owing to substantial increases in tourism revenues that could not readily have been predicted in the late 1940s.

The debate over the necessity for inflation in the early stage of Mexican growth remains open. Its resolution depends to a large extent on the scholar's interpretation of two imponderables: (1) the ability of the government to have substantially increased the incidence of taxation during those early years of rapid growth without causing political instability or offsetting reductions in private investment expenditure, and (2) the effectiveness with which public investment might have been substituted for the high, sustained rate of private investment that actually took place. In fairness to those who took a position similar to that of Siegel, the earlier statistical evidence on which he relied was eventually superseded by data that indicated a far greater rate of increase in both private investment and GDP than had been known at the time. In retrospect it is likely that political, administrative, and institutional constraints during the years before 1954 would have placed serious limits on the rate of growth of public investment, while increased taxes would probably have more than retarded the growth of the private sector of the economy. The government's strategy did in fact work to bring about rapid and sustained growth with eventual price stability and a high rate of public investment. As a result one is inclined to accept this as *ex post facto* evidence favoring the Navarrete postion. A more detailed examination of the nature of the fiscal constraints of the period is presented below. The entire episode illustrates the atmosphere of uncertainty and risk within which major public policies were being pursued during times of rapid growth. It is important to emphasize, as a qualification to those who would have urged even more government investment in earlier years, that the actual rate of growth of GDP, as well as the level and rate of private investment, were unknown to policy makers until long after the fact.

Recent trends in public expenditure suggest that the market mechanism and private decision making are more important than ever in

13. Navarrete, p. 158.

the allocation of goods and services in Mexico. Not only has the share of total government expenditure in gross domestic product remained at approximately the same level since the late 1930s, but the share of direct consumption expenditures has fallen sharply. Only government investment expenditures have increased their share of gross domestic product, with the greatest rise occurring in the early 1950s.

AN INTERNATIONAL COMPARISON OF PUBLIC EXPENDITURE AS A SHARE OF GNP

The share of direct government expenditure in gross domestic product in Mexico as of the mid-1960s was much below that of other countries for which comparable figures are available. Among countries of a similar level of per capita income, Mexico's share of both exhaustive and total government expenditure in GNP was only slightly more than half of the average (see Table 10.3). Recent exhaustive expenditures of government in a representative country with per capita income between $200 and $500 averaged 10.6 percent of

Table 10.3: Percentage of Government Expenditures as Share of Gross National Product: Mexico and Rest of World

	Per capita product ($)			
	I *under* *200*	*II* *201–* *500*	*III* *501–* *1200*	*IV* *over* *1200*
A. Rest of world (1950–59)				
1. Current exhaustive expenditures/GNP	10.9	10.6	12.7	14.1
2. Total current expenditures/GNP	12.7	14.8	24.0	24.3
3. Total current expenditures & gov't. saving/ GNP	15.9	17.8	29.0	27.3
B. Mexico (1941–50)				
4. Current exhaustive expenditures/GDP		5.3		
5. Total current expenditures/GDP		6.1		
6. Total government expenditures/GDP		9.2		
C. Mexico (1951–60)				
7. Current exhaustive expenditures/GDP		4.0		
8. Total current expenditures/GDP		5.3		
9. Total government expenditures/GDP		9.2		

Sources: Rows 1–3: Thorn, "Evolution of Public Finances," Table 1, p. 21, based upon data for thirty-six countries. Rows 4, 6, 7, and 9: From Tables 10.1 and 10.2, averaging the annual percentages by five-year intervals. Rows 5 and 8: From Table 10.6, again averaging the percentages by five-year intervals.

GNP, but in Mexico the figure was only 5.3 percent of GDP in the 1940s. Furthermore, although cross-sectional data suggest that this percentage rises with the level of per capita output, the Mexican share declined from 5.3 percent in the 1940s to 4.0 percent in the 1950s. Total Mexican current expenditures as a share of GDP fell from 6.1 percent to 5.3 percent over the two decades, although the corresponding world average was well over twice that figure, or 14.8 percent for countries in the same income class as Mexico. Furthermore, cross-sectional evidence suggests a *rise* in the share of current expenditures in GNP, though the Mexican share *declines* during its period of rapid growth. It should be noted that this decline is due completely to a fall in the share of current exhaustive expenditures in GDP. Current transfer payments actually rose as a share of GDP from 0.8 percent to 1.3 percent (compare rows 4 and 5 with 7 and 8 in Table 12.3). Total government expenditures in Mexico were only 9.2 percent of GDP in each decade, while similar countries showed an average of 17.8 percent for total government consumption plus savings. Note that the discrepancy between the Mexican performance and that of the average underdeveloped country included in the sample would be still greater had total government investment and consumption expenditures been taken into consideration in the sample for the rest of the world. Estimates of government exhaustive expenditures similar to those employed here are available for more developed countries during the 1950s. For example, government exhaustive expenditures as a share of GNP were 16.8 percent in Belgium (1952), 18.4 percent in Sweden (1952), 22.9 percent in the United Kingdom (1953), and 18.2 percent in the United States (1957).[14] The similar figure for Mexico averaged only 8.3 percent in the 1940s and 6.5 percent in the 1950s (Table 12.2).

A comparison of Mexican budgeted expenditures as a share of GNP with comparable figures for other Latin American countries shows Mexico's to have been among the lowest in the hemisphere as of 1966 (see Table 10.4). Furthermore, Mexico is the only country that has shown a decline in the share of budgeted expenditures in GNP between 1950 and 1966, with the possible exception of Argentina. Those countries, such as Bolivia, Chile, and Venezuela, that are export monocultures show high and rising shares of government expenditures, averaging over 20 percent of GNP. Argentina, Brazil, and Colombia, on the other hand, have a much lower government share, averaging

14. Bator, p. 158.

Table 10.4: Comparative Government Expenditures as a Percentage of Gross National Product, 1950, 1960, 1966

	1950	1960	1966
Mexico	9.1	9.0	7.2
Argentina	12.9	13.2	12.8
Bolivia	a	39.8	43.0[b]
Brazil	9.4	11.0	14.0
Chile	15.5[c]	22.1	22.8
Colombia	6.7	8.4	8.0[d]
Ecuador	6.0	13.1	15.8
Peru	12.3	15.1	16.7[d]
Venezuela	20.1	25.9	21.4

[a] Data not available.
[b] 1963.
[c] 1953.
[d] 1965.

Sources: U.N., *Statistical Yearbook, 1967*, pp. 550–59, 631, 635–41; *Statistical Year book, 1963*, pp. 577, 581–87; *Statistical Yearbook, 1952*, pp. 447, 450–54.

under 12 percent. But only Colombia has maintained a comparably low share throughout the period 1950–66, and Colombia's share rose from 6.7 to 8.0 percent while Mexico's declined. Since actual expenditures have tended to outstrip budgeted outlays in Mexico, the decline in the share of the latter is somewhat exaggerated. Nevertheless, the figures are sufficient to illustrate that Mexico has been able to experience a rapid and sustained rate of growth with an absolute minimum of public expenditure, even compared with the poorest countries of Latin America.

INVESTMENT EXPENDITURES OF PUBLIC ENTERPRISES

Offsetting the low and falling share of direct government expenditures in GDP, those of public and mixed public-private enterprise have accounted for an increasing share of aggregate demand. The investment expenditures of wholly and partially government-owned enterprises have been added to total exhaustive expenditures of government in Table 10.5. The figures show that in recent years investment of public enterprises has amounted to as much as one-third to one-half of total exhaustive expenditures of government. Direct government expenditure including the investment of government enterprises averaged 10.6 percent of GDP in the 1940s, falling to 9.4 percent in the 1950s, and rising to 10.5 percent in 1961–62 (Table 10.2).

Table 10.5: Total Direct Expenditures of Government and Government Enterprise
(Millions of current pesos)

	(1)	(2)	(3)
	Total exhaustive expenditures of government	*Investment of wholly or partially owned government enterprises*	*Total direct government expenditures* (1 + 2 = 3)
1935	418	41	459
1936	531	48	579
1937	598	56	654
1938	642	57	699
1939	672	106	778
1940	737	148	874
1941	747	121	869
1942	879	217	1,096
1943	1,325	200	1,525
1944	1,288	236	1,525
1945	1,634	388	2,023
1946	1,705	561	2,266
1947	2,085	609	2,694
1948	2,696	591	3,288
1949	3,658	823	4,481
1950	3,114	1,132	4,446
1951	3,403	1,466	5,869
1952	4,040	1,630	5,670
1953	3,982	1,627	5,608
1954	4,937	2,232	7,160
1955	5,620	2,488	8,008
1956	6,299	2,567	8,866
1957	7,613	3,043	10,556
1958	8,439	3,594	12,033
1959	9,130	3,673	12,803
1960	10,260	5,604	15,864
1961	10,769	6,715	17,484
1962	11,854	7,077	18,931

Sources: Column 1: Table 10.1, column 3. Columns 2 and 3 are from Muro, "Estructura y Evolución," Table 7.

Since the investment decisions of government-owned industry appear, until recently, to have been largely independent of the federal budget, and since public corporations have drawn heavily on retained earnings and nongovernmental sources of financing for new investment, one might expect their relationship to the level and rate of growth of output to be more analogous to that of private investment than to other forms of government investment. Nevertheless, the investment expenditures of public enterprises have proven to be negatively correlated with private investment outlays, suggesting that the government does exercise some indirect influence over its semiautonomous enterprises. This causes them to register investment expenditures that are more closely related to total government spending than to private investment (the latter being negatively correlated with direct government investment).

No matter how inclusive one makes the definition of direct government expenditures, Table 10.2 shows that the total has not risen as a share of gross domestic product in Mexico since 1940. Yet one should not suppose that the relative influence of the public sector in the economy has declined proportionally. Actually, the overall impact of public policy on resource allocation has steadily increased since 1940. For example, in oligopolistic industries such as steel, automobiles, and chemicals, the government exercises an influence on output disproportionate to direct expenditures, through the establishment of state corporations which engage in highly effective price leadership.[15] Commercial policy, tax concessions, and numerous other indirect controls have also been widely applied since World War II to alter the pattern of resource allocation without the need for large increases in direct expenditure. The shortage of well-trained civil servants and the limited tax capacity of the system have made indirect controls more or less mandatory as instruments of indicative planning in the short run. These have been relatively successful, since the private sector has demonstrated great flexibility and responsiveness to changing profit expectations and credit availability, both of which have been influenced by public policy.

Because of the government's extensive reliance on investment in the private sector, public expenditures have been kept relatively low, so that the Mexican federal budget has not gone severely out of balance by Latin American standards, except during the immediate postwar period. More recently, public policy has been increasingly successful in permitting growth with price stability, largely because of rural and urban infrastructure expenditures of earlier years which are now beginning to demonstrate their productivity. The revealed preference of Mexican policy makers for a maximum degree of price stability consistent with rapid growth means that the level of public

15. An analysis of the theoretical implications of the use of public enterprises as an instrument of antitrust policy and its illustration in the case of the Mexican steel industry is found in N. Schneider, "Mixed Oligopoly: A Study in the Control of Industry in a Developing Economy" (Ph.D. diss. University of California at Berkeley, 1966).

expenditure may be regarded as a function of the country's joint capacities to (1) tax the private sector, (2) borrow abroad, and (3) channel private savings into public investment through bank and nonbank financial intermediaries. The latter two methods of financing public deficits have become increasingly important since the mid-1950s. Before then, virtually the only source of financing government expenditure was through taxation or increased liquidity. The next section will deal with the level and composition of federal revenues since 1940.

THE COMPOSITION OF FEDERAL REVENUES, 1940–63

The tax structure of a developing country has been shown to depend upon the level and distribution of economic activity itself and particularly upon the relative importance of foreign trade. Harley Hinrichs has shown that the capacity to tax varies from sector to sector in a developing country, with exports and imports being the most easily taxed component of GNP. Accordingly, indirect taxes on foreign trade customarily provide the largest share of government revenue in the early stages of growth. Import substitution policies, as they reduce the traded share of output, tend to lower the government's capacity to tax. All of these observations hold true for Mexico since 1940.[16]

Meanwhile, as the internal market of the economy expands, along with the growth of commercial agriculture and industry, it is likely that direct taxation of income and property will increase in relative importance. The Mexican case illustrates both of these trends, as shown in Table 10.6. Indirect taxes in Mexico declined from 59 percent of total federal income in 1940 to 41 percent in 1963. Import duties, which were between 18 and 20 percent of government revenues before World War II, are now from 13 to 15 percent. Export duties (included by the government under "direct taxes") rose from 9 percent in 1940 to as high as 20 percent in 1955 and fell back to 5 percent in 1963. Indirect taxes on natural resources, reflecting the relative decline in mining production, fell from 7 percent of total revenues in the early 1940s to 2 percent by 1960. Income taxes, on the other hand, rose from 11 percent in 1940 to 42 percent of federal revenues in 1963.

16. For a detailed examination of his approach, involving cross-sectional analysis of a number of countries at various stages of growth, see H. Hinrichs, *A General Theory of Tax Structure Change during Economic Development*, International Tax Program, Harvard Law School (Cambridge, 1966).

Table 10.6: Level and Distribution of Total Federal Revenues, 1940–63
(Millions of current pesos and percentages)

	Total federal receipts		Direct taxes				Indirect taxes						Other income
	(million current pesos)	(percentage)	Sum	Income tax (percentage)	Export revenues (percentage)	Other	Sum	Natural resources	Production & commerce (percentage)	Mercantile revenues (percentage)	Import duties	Other	(percentage)
1940	510	100	21	11	9	1	59	8	24	6	18	3	20
1941	544	100	19	10	8	1	60	7	20	7	23	3	21
1942	631	100	25	12	12	a	55	8	22	7	15	3	21
1943	916	100	36	24	12	a	44	6	19	6	10	3	20
1944	1,082	100	38	28	10	a	47	7	21	6	11	3	16
1945	1,168	100	35	25	10	a	48	6	21	7	12	3	17
1946	1,600	100	31	23	7	1	50	5	18	11	13	3	19
1947	1,728	100	35	28	6	1	50	8	14	10	15	3	16
1948	1,932	100	29	23	5	1	50	9	13	9	17	2	21
1949	2,687	100	40	22	17	1	42	6	13	9	13	2	18
1950	3,057	100	41	25	15	1	42	3	12	11	14	2	17
1951	4,353	100	44	27	15	1	40	5	10	9	14	2	16
1952	4,842	100	45	30	14	1	39	5	11	9	13	2	17
1953	4,315	100	50	26	13	1	42	4	13	10	15	2	17
1954	5,161	100	43	24	18	1	40	3	11	9	15	2	16
1955	7,133	100	49	28	20	1	37	3	11	9	13	2	14
1956	7,981	100	47	31	16	1	36	2	11	9	12	2	16
1957	8,037	100	47	34	13	1	36	1	11	10	12	2	17
1958	8,610	100	44	32	11	1	39	2	11	10	15	2	17
1959	9,053	100	45	34	10	1	45	2	13	11	17	3	20
1960	10,967	100	43	33	9	1	43	2	12	10	16	3	15
1961	11,418	100	44	36	8	1	43	2	13	11	15	3	12
1962	12,829	100	44	37	7	1	43	2	14	11	13	2	13
1963	14,615	100	48	42	5	1	41	2	13	11	13	2	11

a Less than 1 percent.

Sources: Grupo Secretaría de Hacienda, Banco de México (hereafter, Grupo), Estudios sobre Proyecciones, *Manual de estadísticas básicas para análisis y proyecciones del desarrollo económico de México* (July 1964, rev. December 1964), and Annex (August 1965), Tables 6-3 and 6-4, from Secretaría de Hacienda y Credito Público, Dirección de Estudios Hacendarios, based on *Cuenta de la hacienda pública federal.*

The changing structure of the Mexican economy has shifted the tax base away from foreign trade toward internal production. Import substitution has not only reduced the share of commodity exports in GDP; it has also shifted the composition of trade from highly dutiable imports such as luxury consumer goods toward intermediate goods, machinery, and equipment, which tend to receive tax advantages because they are associated with the full employment of domestic resources. Moreover, mineral exports generally contain a larger component of economic rent in value added and can therefore sustain a higher incidence of taxation than manufacturing or commerce. The falling share of mineral exports in total Mexican trade has meant that the share of export duties has declined more than its proportion to the share of exports in total output. Thus the recent pattern of Mexican economic development has served to reduce the traditional source of revenues, in relative terms, and has helped to create the appearance of a regressive tax structure, although tax legislation itself has tended to be progressive.

The government, seeking to encourage private investment, has kept effective rates of taxation of industry fairly low and has maintained the most casual attitude on the auditing of corporate accounts. On the other hand, employees of large corporations and institutions maintaining regular payrolls (from which deductions may conveniently be made) have come to bear a disproportionate share of direct taxation. Since these income recipients constitute a significant portion of the urban middle class, which also receives a large share of the benefits of federal expenditure, the fact that tax incidence falls heavily upon them is somewhat less onerous than would otherwise be the case from the viewpoint of welfare. But it is clear that the effective tax structure, which is very progressive through the middle income groups, becomes highly regressive beyond that point.[17]

The foregoing factors help to explain why, although direct taxes have risen sharply since 1940, they have no more than offset the falling share of indirect taxes in GDP. Accordingly, total revenue as a share of GDP did not rise notably in over two decades. Tax collection is

17. This point is supported statistically in terms of legal rates of taxation in Ifigenia M. de Navarette, "The Tax Structure and the Economic Development of Mexico," *Finances Publiques,* 19, Année 2 (1964). It should be noted that this article maintains that taxes as a share of GNP have increased from 7 percent of GNP in 1940 to 11 percent in 1960 (p. 161). Estimates of gross national product more recent than those obtained by that author would suggest the share to be only 9.5 percent in 1960, using her figures for total taxes.

much more difficult in Latin America than, for example, in northern Europe or the United States, where administrative personnel are more readily available, higher salaries provide less incentive for graft, and society is conditioned to accept a higher incidence of taxation without protest. Still, there is reason to criticize the failure of Mexican tax policy to keep pace with the growing demands for public expenditures associated with the rapid pace of development, urbanization, and social change experienced by Mexico since 1940. Mexico's fiscal performance has been far from adequate to support even the most modest revenue requirements, as revealed by the international comparisons presented above (Table 10.3). While the legal rates of taxation in Mexico are relatively high by international standards, tax laws are not being enforced and their incidence is extremely uneven among the various income earning groups. In the area of foreign trade alone, millions of dollars a year are lost in contraband through willingness of the executive branch of the federal government to permit customs officials a high degree of discretion in the performance of their duties.

One foreign observer of Mexican fiscal policy has suggested that revisions in the tax structure be designed to increase the rate of taxation by more than 50 percent in terms of its 1957 performance.[18] Although such a proposal cannot be taken at face value, it does suggest

18. British economist Nicholas Kaldor, after a short visit to Mexico in 1960, prepared a scathing indictment of the existing tax structure accompanied by proposals for sweeping tax reform. The personal and corporate income tax rates revisions he proposed would have increased federal revenues from 8.1 to 12.6 million pesos (based on 1957 figures), or from 7 to 11 percent of GDP in that year (Table 10.1). He argued in this (suppressed) report that federal revenues should ultimately be increased to from 15 to 16 billion pesos (based on 1957 levels) to permit twice the share of federal expenditures in GDP. The report may be taken as an extreme position, as the following excerpt admits: "I am under no illusion that in the political and social context of Mexico the implementation of these proposals will (*sic*) cause a change that is little short of a social revolution comparable in nature to that caused by the land reform which followed the Revolution in 1910." Nevertheless, Kaldor's report contained much worthwhile analysis of the level, incidence, and implications of existing tax policies. Its call for reform echoed the sentiments of many Mexican economists of high repute. Unfortunately, the report made no proposals for the effective utilization of the increases in revenue that its policies would have provided. The assumption was always implicit that virtually no constraint existed in terms of government absorptive capacity, so that as much as twice the current level of tax revenue might be readily utilized without any major loss in efficiency of public expenditure. Such an assumption can be seriously challenged in terms of the present limitations of the government's administrative apparatus. Ref. Nicholas Kaldor, "Report on Mexican Tax Reform," typescript (1960).

that tax policy has been inadequate to cope with even the normal requirements for increased public expenditure in growth. While a number of improvements in collection have been brought about in recent years and some tax reforms have been instituted to make laws more equitable, the data in Table 10.6 reveal how much remained to be done as of the mid-1960s. One of the results of the fiscal limitations on public expenditure is that Mexico still has one of the highest illiteracy rates and the poorest systems of secondary education in all Latin America. In lieu of an adequate fiscal system the Mexican government has increasingly resorted to the use of monetary policy to channel private savings into public investment. Mexican monetary policy, despite its remarkable success in recent years, is viewed by some officials as a second-best alternative to fiscal reform.

As a larger share of the economy has become monetized and as accounting and reporting procedures have improved in private enterprise, the effectiveness of tax collection has tended to increase as well without major legislative reforms. This is reflected in the rise in income tax shares from 33 to 42 percent of federal revenue since 1960 (Table 10.6). However, it is unlikely that without new legislation the tax structure will become significantly progressive in the near future.

If and when the share of taxation in GDP begins to rise, fiscal efficiency will become increasingly important. This will require a much higher degree of coordination of public revenue and expenditure policy than has existed in the past. Fiscal planning is still in its infancy.[19] The problems of data alone have only begun to be surmounted. Communications among the many branches of government, federal, state, and local, are still rather weak, although some liaison has been established in the context of budgetary planning. As communications within the public sector and between the public and private sectors improve, and as more information about the economy becomes available to policy makers, the efficiency of Mexican planning will undoubtedly increase. One may look forward first to effective budgetary planning of the public sector, and only then to the effective use of tax

19. A number of studies have appeared on fiscal policy and planning, including: Miguel Wionczek, "Incomplete Formal Planning: Mexico," in Hagen, ed., *Planning Economic Development, A Study* (Homewood, Ill.: Richard D. Irwin, 1963); Robert J. Shafer, *Mexico: Mutual Adjustment Planning* (Syracuse: Syracuse University Press, 1966); and Ifigenia M. de Navarrete, *Los incentivos fiscales y el desarrollo económico de México* (Mexico: U.N.A.M., 1967). See also ECLA, *Planning in Latin America*, E/CN.12/772 (2 March 1967); and Comité de los Nueve, Alianza para el Progreso, *Evaluación del plan de acción immediata de México* (August 1964).

and expenditure policy for purposes of stimulating private sector activities and for stabilization in addition of growth.

THE COMPOSITION OF FEDERAL EXPENDITURES, 1940–63

The figures presented above show how public expenditures maintained a relatively low and constant share of GDP. Tax constraints and the desire for monetary stability have been largely responsible for the conservative performance of the public sector. But within a relatively modest total the composition of government expenditures has varied considerably. In Table 10.2 we saw that the planned share of government transfer payments rose from an average of less than 10 percent before 1956 to between 20 and 30 percent between 1956 and 1962. In Table 10.7 *ex post* data indicate that actual transfers were even greater than planned. Transfer payments in this table have been divided between current and capital outlays. The former averaged 10 percent in the 1940s and 20 percent in the 1950s, and the latter (representing the acquisition of real estate and the financing of other sectors in the economy) averaged 9 percent in the 1940s and 15 percent in the 1950s.[20] Meanwhile, administrative expenditures of the federal government have fallen from 60 percent of federal outlays to under 40 percent between 1940 and 1963. On the other hand the share of federal investment in total investment in Mexico has been high, as revealed by Table 10.7. Averaging around 30 percent at the beginning and the end of the period under consideration, the government investment share rose to as high as 40 percent between 1946 and 1955. During the immediate postwar period the government, by conserving on current outlays and especially on transfer payments to households, was able to devote 28 percent of its budget to capital formation. Between 1950 and 1955, capital transfers to private and mixed enterprise averaged an additional 18 percent. We shall see below how this investment was allocated among productive activities. A more detailed analysis of the regional and sectorial pattern of Mexican development expenditures since 1940 indicates that the initial redirection of public expenditure away from current outlays

20. The estimates on which the federal exhaustive expenditure figures on current and capital account in Table 10.1 are based are for budgeted expenditures, while those in Tables 10.7 and 10.8 are for actual expenditures. Hence the two tables are not strictly comparable. It is likely that the data underlying the estimate of exhaustive capital expenditures of the federal government after 1950 (Table 10.1) inadvertently includes some capital transfers as well.

Table 10.7: Level and Distribution of Actual Federal Expenditures, 1940–63
(Average percentages)

	Total federal expenditures		Current expenditures		Transfers			Capital expenditures				
	(million current pesos)	(percentage)	Sum	Administrative expenses	To consumption & investment	Interest on the debt	Unclassified	Sum	Direct physical investment	Acquisition of real estate	Financing of other sectors	Other expenses
1940	552	100	75	62	7	1	4	25	19	a	6	1
1941–45	942	100	68	54	5	3	6	32	25	a	6	1
1946–50	2,147	100	64	45	11	3	4	36	27	a	9	a
1951–55	5,176	100	54	34	14	4	2	46	28	1	17	1
1956–60	9,548	100	62	37	20	4	1	38	24	a	13	1
1961–63	8,992	100	73	39	28	5	1	27	20	a	7	1

a Less than 1 percent.

Note: The figures in this table do not correspond to the subtotals of exhaustive and nonexhaustive expenditures of the federal government used to arrive at total government expenditures in Table 10.1, since the figures above are for realized rather than budgetary expenditures of the federal government.

Source: Grupo, Tables 6-5 and 6-6.

toward capital outlays in the 1940s and early 1950s was largely responsible for the subsequent high and sustained rate of private investment.[21]

The private employment multiplier effect of public investment expenditures almost certainly varied widely from region to region and sector to sector due to the disproportional degree of underutilization of capacity within the economy. This was doubtless also the case for the accelerative impact of public investment, which varied from sector to sector in both magnitude and timing. For example, government investments in dams and irrigation systems had a fairly long gestation period but eventually permitted extremely high rates of return on private investment (over 100 percent per year in some regions of the North and Northwest). Investments in education and technical training, also with a gestation period of several years, did much to break the skilled labor bottlenecks that partially accounted for the relatively low rate of utilization of industrial plant and equipment.[22] While it is not possible to more than hint at these complications in this paper, they serve to illustrate the importance of looking at the sectorial composition of public expenditure as a precondition for disaggregative analysis of the effect of government spending on both stability and growth.

The functional distribution of federal expenditures since 1940 is presented in Table 10.7. It has already been noted that the 1940s and early 1950s were a time of major investment in rural economic infrastructure. This is brought out by the figures, which show the share of expenditures in agriculture, transportation, and communications to be relatively high during this period. Expenditures for the promotion of industry and commerce, on the other hand, expanded from 1946–55, while investment expenditures in education and cultural services have only recently begun to increase in relative importance. One factor that has enabled Mexico to get more development out of its tax dollar than most Latin American countries is the low and declining share of military expenditures in total government outlays. These have fallen from 20 percent to 9 percent of federal expenditure between 1940 and 1963. The general administrative budget has also maintained a low share of total expenditures. This reveals quite clearly how Mexico has avoided the practice prevalent elsewhere in Latin America of using government employment as a means of income redistribution, often

21. Reynolds, *Mexican Economy,* especially chapters 3 to 5.
22. Ibid., chapter 5.

at a considerable sacrifice in terms of productivity. In Mexico the private economy has been relatively more effective in absorbing increases in the urban work force. While many of the recent migrants to the cities initially find it necessary to obtain employment in the service sector at low wages, the rapid and continuous overall rate of growth of the economy has allowed a high degree of vertical mobility for individual workers over the period of their productive life. This means that the composition of low income groups (e.g. domestic service and construction workers) represents a moving population within which there can be considerable optimism about the future. As a result, there has been less political pressure on the government to absorb the unemployed than has existed in such countries as Chile, Argentina, or Brazil. Some credit for this must go to the land redistribution programs which are still in progress. By redistributing underutilized land in small parcels, the government has tended to slow the rate of urbanization. Under the agrarian reform program peasants are able to earn at least a subsistence income in small-scale agriculture, whereas elsewhere in Latin America land reform programs have yet to provide a significant labor absorption function in the rural sector.

Viewing the trend in the distribution of public expenditures, one sees in recent years a definite movement toward health, education, and welfare and away from the promotion of agriculture, industry, and transport and communications. It is apparent that, unless the share of government revenues in GDP increases sharply, government investment in physical (as opposed to human) capital is likely to decline. The ever increasing Mexican population, confronted with outstanding material progress for almost three decades, is now demanding broader participation in the spoils of growth. If these demands are to be met, the share of budget expenditures on social infrastructure as well as transfer payments to households must rise. The only way in which the government will then be able to maintain its extensive share of total domestic investment will be to increase the share of public expenditures in GNP. Otherwise government physical investment expenditures will be eroded by social outlays, and growth will become increasingly dependent upon the private sector. There is little likelihood that increases in net foreign borrowing by the government can be sustained for very much longer, or that the structure of financial intermediaries will accommodate a much larger net transfer of private savings into public investment than presently exists. On the other hand, there is reason to believe that the stage of major public investments in economic infrastructure is passing. Inducements for private investment are now far greater than they were twenty years ago. For that reason there is still considerable excess demand for private investment in Mexico. This suggests that unless new political and social events seriously alter expectations, the private sector might be able to bear a significantly larger share of total investment without serious difficulty.

PUBLIC EXPENDITURE AND ECONOMIC STABILITY

Although the share of public expenditure in aggregate demand has not changed importantly since 1940, year-to-year fluctuations have been considerable. Moreover, changes in the composition of public expenditure have probably had a net disturbing impact on economic stability in Mexico owing to the differing influence of individual components of government spending on the private sector. Nevertheless, the relationship between fiscal policy and full employment is too complex to be adequately handled here. Rather than do that, we shall simply suggest some possible ties between the major components of government expenditure and aggregate demand since 1940. Among the major exogenous disturbing influences in aggregate demand, exports have fallen as a share of GDP since 1940. Moreover, exports have become increasingly diversified and no longer comprise a small number of mineral and agricultural commodities. Tourism and manufactured exports, both of which are far less sensitive to international trade cycles, have greatly increased their share of exports, so that trade is less important as a destabilizing influence on GDP. At the same time the investment share of GDP has risen sharply (from 10 to 20 percent) between 1940 and 1960 (Table 10.8).[23] Whatever investment indicator one uses, the share of total investment in GDP corrected for trend proves to be relatively stable on a year-to-year basis. Nevertheless this is *not* the case for the private and public components of gross investment, as shown in Table 10.9. These shares fluctuate around a downtrend in the relative importance of government investment in total capital formation in Mexico.

23. Table 10.8 reflects the sensitivity of this crucial indicator to various estimating procedures in terms of both its magnitude and its rate of growth. The first column represents the most recent and reasonable estimates of total investment, using the best price deflator obtainable. It should be noted that the real rate of growth of columns 1 and 2 are the same, the differences arising from the conversion into current prices.

Table 10.8: Alternative Measures of Gross Fixed Investment as a Share of Gross Domestic Product

	Gross fixed investment in Mexico			Gross investment as share of gross domestic product			
(1)	(2)	(3)	(4)	(5)	(6)	(7)	(8)
Est. A (Cossío) (Reynolds) 1968	Est. B (Banco de México) 1962	Est. C (Grupo) 1964	Est. D (Vernon) 1963	Est. A/ GDP	Est. B/ GDP	Est. C/ GDP	Est. D/ GDP
	(millions of current pesos)			(percentage)			
1940	702	539	754	793	9.9	7.6	10.6	11.2
1945	1,660	1,486	2,257	2,301	8.4	7.6	11.5	11.7
1950	6,041	4,828	6,041	5,960	14.7	11.8	14.7	14.5
1955	16,674	12,617	11,943[a]	12,560	18.9	14.3	13.5	14.2
1960	33,132	23,226	21,192	21,168	21.3	14.9	13.6	13.6
1962	32,344	24,791	22,552	—[b]	18.0	13.8	12.5	—
1965	[40,843][c]				19.5[c]	—		—

[a] This figure includes government-budgeted, rather than realized, investment.

[b] Dash means data not available.

[c] This figure for gross investment and the corresponding GDP estimate are in 1960 pesos, from memo, Banco de México, Depto. de Estudios Económicos (hereafter, DEE), February 1968.

Sources: Columns 1 and 2 are from Table 10.9. The figures in Estimate A represent the most recent unofficial estimates of DEE (Feb. 1968) using the best available reflators for the underlying indexes as explained in Table 10.9. For that reason this series forms the basis for calculations of investment and the capital stock in the rest of this study. Estimate B is an earlier series of the Banco de México using less accurate (and lower) reflators. Column 3: Estimate C corresponds to Estimate II in DEE, "Alternativos de estimación de la inversión bruta fija en México, 1939–1962," memo by Luis Cossío, 8 May 1965, and is from Grupo, Table 3-1. Grupo prepared this series by summing two independently derived series on (1) public investment (from Dirección de Inversiones Públicas, Secretaría de la Presidencia, México inversión pública federal, 1925–1963 [Mexico, 1964]; Banco de México, Informes Anuales, etc.) and (2) private investment (from Raúl Ortiz Mena et al., El desarrollo económico de México y su capacidad para absorber capital del exterior, Table 14, for years 1939–50; and Nacional Financiera, Dirección de Investigaciones Económicas for the years 1951–62). The private investment figures in Estimate C since 1950 appear to have a strong and increasing negative bias, causing the total investment in Estimate C for 1960 to be 9 percent below Estimate B and 36 percent below Estimate A. Column 4: Estimate D is the total investment figure from Vernon, The Dilemma of Mexico's Development, Table A-3, p. 199. This figure is arrived at similarly to that of Estimate C by summing public and private investment, the latter index taken from Anuarios of the Nacional Financiera. It also suffers from a negative bias in the private investment share and from independently derived and noncomparable components.

The fact that public and private investment move in offsetting directions was at one time taken to suggest that government investment was acting to stabilize the economy following exogenous changes in the level of private expenditure.[24] However, more recent research has produced evidence that reverses the direction of causality, suggesting that it is public expenditure rather than private investment which initially disturbs the level of aggregate demand. Private investment appears to be adjusted by the Central Bank in response to these disturbances through manipulation of the reserve requirements of financial intermediaries.[25]

Several reasons may be suggested for the obviously high degree of fluctuation in government investment expenditures: (1) the degree of decentralization and lack of coordination among the government's operating ministries, (2) the tendency of planned budgets to underestimate revenues, permitting a high degree of discretion in actual expenditure policies,[26] (3) the independent nature of the expenditure criteria of each successive presidential administration, (4) a major shift in the occupational structure of the government bureaucracy every six years, resulting in a time lag between the execution of expenditure proposals and their implementation. Some have gone so

24. This point is made by Raymond Vernon in *The Dilemma of Mexico's Development* (Cambridge: Harvard University Press, 1963). Vernon's analysis points to the need for government expenditures to make up for the lack of private demand and suggests that the political constraints under which that country's major political party operates prevents the government from having sufficient fiscal flexibility to permit adequate full-employment policies.

25. John Koehler, "Information and Policy Making: Mexico" (Ph.D. diss., Yale University, 1968). Koehler's analysis reveals a significant negative correlation between the independent variable private investment (plus exports minus imports) and alternative independent variables (1) public investment plus government consumption, (2) government consumption, (3) government investment, (4) federal government investment, (5) investment of autonomous organisms and state enterprise, and (6) investment of the Federal District government. His data cover the period 1948–65.

26. A detailed analysis of federal budgets and the relationship between stated and actual expenditure policy by presidential administrations since the Revolution is presented in Wilkie, *Mexican Revolution,* part 1. Wilkie has disaggregated the accounts of the federal government in terms of projected and actual budgetary expenditure for economic, social, and administrative activities since 1921. The results are then compared with actual statements of policy by the respective presidents through 1963. The classifications used in his study are different from those above and do not break down expenditures into current and capital or exhaustive and nonexhaustive outlays. Nevertheless they offer useful insights into the economic and social implications of very different presidential administrations.

Table 10.9: Alternative Measures of Gross Fixed Investment and the Share of Direct Government Investment in Mexico, 1939–62

	(1) Total gross fixed investment in Mexico		(3) Government exhaustive investment expenditures in Mexico	(4) Government exhaustive investment plus investment of wholly or partially owned government enterprises	(5) Direct government investment as share of gross investment (3/1 = 5)	(6) Investment of government and government enterprise as share of gross investment (4/1 = 5)
	Est. A	Est. B				
			(millions of current pesos)			*(percentage)*
1939	429	359	159	265	36.9	61.7
1940	702	539	189	336	26.9	47.9
1941	953	717	262	384	27.5	40.3
1942	857	680	275	493	32.1	57.5
1943	825	749	322	522	39.1	63.3
1944	1,183	979	487	724	41.2	61.2
1945	1,660	1,486	561	950	33.8	57.2
1946	2,965	2,442	569	1,130	19.2	38.1
1947	3,797	3,046	820	1,429	21.6	37.6
1948	4,087	3,358	1,050	1,641	25.7	40.2
1949	4,610	4,009	1,141	1,964	24.8	42.6
1950	6,041	4,828	1,392	2,524	23.0	41.8
1951	9,165	6,907	1,561	3,027	17.0	33.0
1952	10,721	8,188	1,870	3,501	17.4	32.7
1953	11,006	8,117	1,642	3,268	14.9	29.7
1954	12,676	10,076	2,156	4,388	16.7	34.1
1955	16,674	12,617	2,189	4,677	13.1	28.0
1956	22,235	16,803	2,344	4,910	10.5	22.1
1957	25,429	19,192	2,946	5,991	11.6	23.6

1958	25,122	18,926	2,933	6,527	11.7	26.0
1959	27,385	19,584	3,207	6,880	11.7	25.1
1960	33,132	23,226	3,175	8,779	9.6	26.5
1961	32,829	24,071	3,178	9,893	9.7	30.1
1962	32,344	24,791	3,496	10,573	10.8	32.7

Sources: Columns 1 and 2 correspond to Estimates III and I, respectively, of Cossío, "Alternativas," Table 17. Both estimates are based on a physical investment index composed of four components: construction and installations, capital goods imports, domestic production of machinery and equipment, and clearing of land. Estimate I, used in earlier published reports of the Banco de México, uses lower reflators than Estimate III for both capital goods imports and the current value of construction activity. Thus the rate of growth of Estimate III in current prices (our A) is considerably higher than that of Estimate I (our B), although the growth rates of the underlying real indexes are the same. The absolute level of investment in Estimate III is higher than in Estimate I since the latter excludes costs of repair, replacement, and reconstruction. It should be noted that still a third estimate of gross investment in current prices based upon the summation of independently derived indexes of private-public investment was used by Vernon, *Mexico's Development*, Table A-3, p. 199, and Chart 3, p. 100. The private investment total in this estimate is from annual reports of the Nacional Financiera. The total thus derived appears seriously to understate the level of investment in 1960 compared with Estimates I and III above. Since the figure for public investment is not different from those used in the present analysis this would suggest that the Nacional Financiera figures severely underestimate the rate of growth of private investment since 1950. The level of investment in 1950 in the Vernon study (5,960) corresponds to that of Estimate A above (6,041), whereas Vernon's figure for 1960 is 21,168, compared to 33,132 above. Column 3 above is from Table 10.1, column 2. Column 4 is the sum of column 3 and Table 10.4, column 2.

far as to suggest that there is a predictable "six-year cycle" in public expenditures which one writer describes as follows:

> In the first year of a six-year presidential term government activity coasts on its previous momentum. The administration takes office in December, but the budget for its first year has already been prepared in September. The outgoing president is reluctant to encumber his successor with large new programs, so this budget will likely be somewhat small. The new administration will be passing time getting organized and planning its particular "style" rather than spending money, so actual first-year expenditures will be low. By the second year, the government will have found its stride and be undertaking its new projects, so expenditures will rise with exceptional speed. For the third, fourth, and fifth years expenditure growth will taper off somewhat. The final year of the administration will be marked by a rush to complete as many of the projects as possible before the end of the term, in part to assure that one's monuments will in fact be finished, in part to give the next president a freer hand.[27]

The hypothesis that the rate of growth of public expenditures is "relatively high from the first to the second year, lower from the second to the fifth, and high again from the fifth to the sixth"[28] seems to be supported by actual expenditure data for the presidential administrations of Cárdenas (1935–40), Ávila Camacho (1941–46), Alemán (1947–52), Ruiz Cortines (1952–58), and López Mateos (1959–64). Years two and three of each term are shown by Koehler to be above the trend line eleven out of twelve times, whereas years four and five are shown to be below the trend nine out of twelve times.[29] These results are sufficient to reject the hypothesis that the two classifications of expenditures are independent and that their observations are distributed randomly in response to random movements in private autonomous expenditures.

Whether or not exogenous changes in public expenditure follow a predictable six-year pattern, one must still explain why private investment outlays appear to be stabilizing. The answer to this lies beyond the realm of fiscal policy. A full discussion of the stabilizing influence of monetary policy through its influence on the rationing

27. Koehler, p. 17; cf. Wilkie, p. 107.
28. Koehler, p. 17.
29. Ibid., pp. 18–21.

of investable funds to the private sector cannot be included in the present essay and is now the subject of a growing literature.[30] We shall only touch briefly on the matter here so as to set fiscal policy in proper historical perspective.

Since 1950 the Central Bank has stabilized the nominal rate of interest in the economy by fixing the discount rate at approximately 10 percent. As the rate of inflation has declined from well over 10 percent to only a few percentage points per annum, the real rate of interest (for those able to obtain investable funds at the official rate) has risen from zero in the early 1950s to 10 to 12 percent in recent years. Despite the rise in real borrowing rates, excess demand for investable funds continues to exist. Credit has therefore been allocated by financial intermediaries to those sectors favored for treatment by the federal government. By regressing the profit share of GDP on lagged investment in the economy as a whole, Koehler roughly estimates the incremental gross rate of return on capital to be "at least 30 percentage points above the possible rate of interest." [31] In view of the fact that effective tax rates as a share of corporate profits are much less than the nominal rate of 40 percent and almost certainly well under 20 percent of gross profits, continuing excess investment demand in the private sector is understandable. Although the marginal rate of return on capital after taxes and risk discounts is undoubtedly well below the average rate, there is little question that the official interest rates have been kept at a below-equilibrium level throughout most of the period under discussion. By pegging the prime borrowing rate and thereby causing excess demand for investable funds, monetary authorities have been able to ration credit by varying the level of deposits that financial intermediaries must maintain in the Central Bank.[32] By adjusting these reserve requirements to changes in the total level of liquidity (bank deposits and foreign exchange reserves) and the price level (wholesale price and cost of living

30. See note 3.
31. Koehler, pp. 36 f.
32. Koehler notes that the marginal reserve ratio rather than the average ratio is varied to prevent banks from having to recall loans.

The reserve regulations have been adjusted more than 30 times since 1950, on occasion to 100 per cent for certain liabilities and institutions. Furthermore, the information on which manipulation of the reserve ratio is based is timely and accurate; the two indicators, the supply of money and *Banco de México* holdings of gold and foreign exchange, are known precisely with negligible lags—28 days at the most in the case of the money supply, immediately in the case of foreign exchange. (p. 39)

indexes), the Central Bank has been able to raise or lower the amount of private investment so as to counteract fluctuations in aggregate demand brought about by government spending and export sales.

Meanwhile the increased price stability enjoyed by the Mexican economy has tended to reduce exchange risk while permitting the real rate of interest to rise well above international prime borrowing rates. Gross foreign lending has accordingly increased rapidly since 1954. This has meant that internal controls on liquidity could potentially have been offset by fluctuations in both short-term and long-term borrowing abroad. As a result, an additional arm of stabilization policy has been government regulation of foreign direct investment and borrowing by government and mixed enterprises abroad. By regulating investment expenditures at home and its own borrowing from abroad the government is now able to exercise a high degree of control over aggregate demand. This has provided a weapon to use in the event that its expenditures act to destabilize the system. Internal stabilization policy has relied not upon fluctuations in the rate of interest but upon direct controls for its effectiveness. In a similar fashion the government's commercial policy has relied primarily on quotas rather than on duties or fluctuations in the exchange rate to bring about external equilibrium in the balance of payments. In both cases the use of direct controls, while generally acknowledged by economists to be inconsistent with allocative efficiency, has served quite well in accomplishing these objectives. It is quite possible that the maintenance of a fixed exchange rate and a fixed rate of return on prime borrowings has improved the expectations of private investors, so that the loss of efficiency which these policies entailed has been more than offset by a higher rate of savings and investment than might otherwise have occurred.

PUBLIC EXPENDITURES AND GROWTH

Although consistent data on government investment are available for the period since 1940, the same is not true for private investment. As a result semiofficial indexes of total investment in the economy have been prepared independently from those of public investment, and they show rather wide deviations one from another, as Tables 10.8 and 10.9 reveal. Because of wide variation in gross investment estimates for Mexico, an assessment of the relative importance of public investment becomes extremely difficult. Before estimates A and

B in Table 10.9 were available, economists concluded that the public share of total investment was steadily rising in the 1950s.[33] On the other hand, more recent estimates of gross investment produce somewhat different conclusions. For example, in Table 10.9 the share of direct government investment in gross investment based on estimate A was 27 percent in 1940, 23 percent in 1950, and 10 percent in 1960. Furthermore, the investment of government and government enterprises as a share of gross investment was 48 percent in 1940, 42 percent in 1950, and 27 percent in 1960. If such calculations had relied only on the earlier figures for gross investment (estimate D), the share of direct investment of government and government enterprises would have been 42 percent in 1940 and would have remained at the same level in 1950 and 1960.

It should be obvious from the foregoing that an unambiguous evaluation of the impact of public investment on growth is yet impossible. This does not diminish the fact that direct government investment continues to play a significant although evidently decreasing role in the expansion of Mexico's capital stock. Meanwhile, the investment of government enterprise has increased its share of gross investment, helping to offset the decline in direct government investment expenditure, particularly between 1955 and 1960 (Table 10.9, column 6).

In addition to the expansion of physical capital, public expenditure on human capital continues to rise. The trend of total government investment in education for selected years since 1925 is presented in Table 10.10. Federal investment in education tripled in the 1940s and increased by six times in the 1950s, illustrating a recent trend toward a much higher share of public investment in human capital than during the earlier postrevolutionary period. The regional pattern of investment in primary education has expanded in rather more balanced fashion than secondary, technical, and higher education, for which there has been an increasing concentration of expenditures in the Federal District and Nuevo León. One writer declares:

33. For example, Vernon used estimate D (Table 10.8) to show the increase in importance of public over private investment during the period. In *The Dilemma of Mexico's Development,* he regarded this as an indication that private investment was not increasing sufficiently to permit sustained growth, and that, as a result, public investment would have to continue to increase its share of total capital formation if growth was to be maintained. He used this as partial evidence for the major conclusion of his book that Mexican policy makers were in a dilemma as to how to finance and administer the necessary increase in the share of public investment.

Table 10.10: Primary Students Registered in Public Schools and Annual Federal
Investment in Education, 1925–60

	Primary students registered in public schools		*Annual federal investment in education*
	(number)	*(1925 = 100)*	*(thousands of 1950 pesos)*
1925	1,034,353	100	4,000
1930	1,367,849	132	7,000
1935	1,817,498	176	8,000
1940	1,994,602	193	9,000
1945	2,705,725	262	14,000
1950	3,026,691	293	29,000
1955	3,936,028	381	48,000
1960	5,401,509	522	191,900[a]

[a] This figure is expressed in thousands of 1960 pesos.

Sources: Registered students: *Anuarios Estadísticos* for selected years. The 1925 figure is for enrollment of all public schools in Mexico. For 1930 and 1935 the total includes enrollment in public kindergarten, primary, secondary and preparatory, normal, and technical public schools. The 1940 and 1945 total includes only kindergarten and primary school enrollment. For 1950, 1955, and 1960, the figures represent the population of primary-school age receiving an education. Investment in education: Totals for the years 1925–50 are from Dirección de Inversiones Públicas, Secretaría de la Presidencia, *México inversión pública federal, 1925–1963*, Table 6, pp. 47–52. The 1960 figure is from ibid., Table 12, p. 119.

In 1960, the Federal District, with only 13.9 percent of the national population, had 53 percent of all people with 12 years of education or more and 56.2 percent of all people with 16 years of education or more. Nuevo León and the District combined, with 17 percent of the national population, had 59.1 percent of the former group, and 62 percent of the latter. Moreover, it is certain that the concentration of educated people in the advanced areas, and particularly in the Federal District, has been a constant feature of the pattern of human resource development in Mexico.[34]

Table 10.10 shows that outlays on education and cultural services (of which investment in education is only a part) have risen from 14 percent of federal expenditures in 1940 to 20 percent in 1963. One independent estimate shows the share of total public and private educational expenditures in GNP for 1962 to be 7 percent, suggesting

34. Charles N. Myers, *Education and National Development in Mexico* (Princeton: Industrial Relations Section, Princeton University, 1965), pp. 111–12.

that a much higher proportion of the cost of education is borne by students and their families in Mexico than in most developed countries.[35]

Estimates by Martin Carnoy of the return to total expenditure on education by year of schooling indicate that the marginal rate rises to a peak in the sixth year, declining gradually by the thirteenth year, and then rising sharply again for years fourteen to sixteen, particularly for those who have completed a university education. These findings differ, for example, from those of the United States, where the marginal rates of return on educational expenditure decline steadily from the eighth grade through the completion of university.[36] Carnoy estimates both the social and private internal rate of return to expenditure on education for 1963 by year of schooling.[37] The social internal rate of return reaches a peak of 37.5 percent for grades five to six, falls steadily to 12.4 percent for years twelve to thirteen, and then rises to 29.5 percent for years fourteen to sixteen. The private internal rate of return is, of course, significantly higher (since it excludes the costs of education borne by the state), rising to 48.6 percent for years five to six, falling to 15.8 percent for years twelve to thirteen, and rising again to 36.7 percent for years fourteen to sixteen. The institutional investment per student year in pesos (1963) is shown to rise sharply in terms of the level of education, from 414 pesos for primary to 2,082 pesos for secondary and 3,720 pesos for university education.

While these rates of return may be biased upward through underestimation of the opportunity cost of schooling to Mexican youngsters,[38] the figures suggest that, in terms of alternative rates of return

35. Martin Carnoy, "The Cost and Return to Schooling in Mexico: A Case Study" (Ph.D. diss., University of Chicago, 1964).

36. The U.S. comparison is from W. Lee Hanson, "Total and Private Rates of Return to Investment in Schooling," *Journal of Political Economy,* 71 (April 1963), as cited in Carnoy, p. 5.

37. These calculations do not include any estimate of the consumption returns or external economies arising from education. The figures remain high even after adjustment for father's occupation (which is highly correlated with years of schooling). Ibid., p. 5.

38. This is already reflected in the estimates, since the peak in return to education is two years earlier in Mexico than in the United States (five to six rather than seven to eight years of schooling). This is because half of the investment costs in Mexico for years seven to eight represent income foregone, whereas this factor is nil in the United States for the same number of years of schooling. The return in Mexico for seven to eight years of education is somewhat less than that of the United States for the same period (23.4 percent

on capital, government expenditures in both primary and secondary education are well made and might even be much higher than at present if fiscal circumstances permitted. This conclusion is supported by U.N. data on educational attainment levels in Latin America as of 1960 (Table 10.11). In that year Mexico ranked among the poorest countries in the hemisphere in terms of the share of population having at least a minimum level of schooling. Seventy-three percent of males and 76 percent of females in Mexico over the age of twenty-five had less than four years of education. While the recent record has been much better than these figures would suggest, they illustrate the backlog of investment remaining to be made in human resources in Mexico. This is true not only for the share of the population in school, or the average number of years of schooling per pupil, but more particularly for the quality of training itself. Standards in the past have been extremely low at all levels. Recent academic reforms, particularly those under the past two presidential administrations, have met with considerable success, despite the opposition of some students and faculty who might suffer personally from higher standards, but much remains to be done.

Since a large share of the benefits from education accrue to society as a whole in the form of external economies, the financing of public expenditures on education is most appropriately accomplished through taxation. But the limitations of Mexico's fiscal system, as described above, have made it necessary to finance additional government investment outlays with domestic and foreign loans from the private sector that require repayment out of profits. This has produced a financial constraint on the nature of government investment expenditure, tending to direct public expenditures toward projects that are most likely to become self-supporting. This works against federal aid to education. Improvement in the effectiveness of taxation would do much to permit an even greater share of GDP to be devoted to public educational expenditures than is now the case. Mass education and improvements in the quality of education may be expected to bring about broader social participation in the benefits of economic growth. A broadening of the capital stock in Mexico to include a greater share of human resources at all levels can do much to redistribute income functionally, while increasing the productivity of nonhuman resources at the same time. This can do much to make

social rate of return for Mexico, 29.2 percent for the United States). Carnoy, p. 81.

growth and social progress coterminous, helping to preserve that political stability which is itself an essential concomitant of sustained growth in Mexico.

The recent pace of Mexican fiscal development has been relatively slow. The share of government spending in gross domestic product has not risen significantly during the past three decades, despite rapid growth in the rest of the economy. Moreover, public demand for goods and services has declined as a share of GDP, while the share of government transfer payments has increased significantly. Hence the characteristic pattern of relatively rapid growth of the public sector in Latin America has not been borne out by the Mexican case. This has been due in part to the failure of taxation to keep pace with structural change. Those sectors of economic activity that have traditionally contributed the largest share of tax revenues have lagged, while tax incentives have been used to stimulate the growth of leading sectors. Meanwhile an ever expanding share of public investment expenditures has had to be financed out of loans from the private sector rather than taxes.

Within the limits described above, Mexico's public expenditure policy has been successful in increasing the rates of capital formation and growth in both agriculture and industry. Public investment has maintained a high and sustained share of total government spending since the late 1930s. Fiscal restraints, particularly in the areas of public administration and defense, have been responsible for this praiseworthy performance. Government investment in power, transportation, and communications provided external economies that stimulated private investment in manufacturing and commerce. In recent years, the government has turned to public education, a hitherto neglected sector, in order to reduce skilled labor bottlenecks that are increasingly responsible for the underutilization of plant and equipment.

Resource allocation in Mexico, while strongly influenced by government spending, has been somewhat distorted in recent years. There is evidence that public expenditure policies served to overemphasize investment in economic infrastructure, plant, and equipment, while neglecting human resources. Because of these policies in the 1940s and early 1950s, Mexico continues to lag behind the rest of Latin America in terms of the quantity as well as the quality of education of its population. The result is a higher physical capital/output ratio

Table 10.11: Distribution of Male and Female Population Twenty-five Years of Age and Over by Educational Attainment in Selected Latin American Countries

Country and year	Male					Female				
	Population 25 years and over (thousands)	Percentage				Population 25 years and over (thousands)	Percentage			
		Less than first level[a]	First level[b]	Second level[c]	Third level[d]		Less than first level[a]	First level[b]	Second level[c]	Third level[d]
Mexico, 1960[e]	5,199	73	24	2.4	1.4	5,285	76	22	1.7	0.3
Argentina, 1947[f]	4,884	37	58	3.6	1.4	4,556	40	55	4.8	0.2
Bolivia, 1950[g,h]	1,110	81	15[i]	3.2[i]	1.0[i]	1,168	88	9.5[i]	2.2[i]	0.1[i]
Brazil, 1950[h]	9,895	78	17[i]	3.2[i]	1.4[i]	9,861	81	15[i]	3.1[i]	0.1[i]
Chile, 1952	1,246	21[j]	56[j]	19[j]	3.4[j]	1,333	26[j]	54[j]	19[j]	1.4[j]
1960	1,457	41	45	12	2.3	1,583	43	46	11	0.9
Colombia, 1951	1,200	55	37	6.0	2.0	1,092	50	44	6.1	0.2
Ecuador, 1950	602	68	27	3.1	1.1	635	76	23	1.5	0.1
1962[k,l]	1,667	64[m]	26[m]	8.1[m]	1.3[m]	—[n]	—	—	—	—
Paraguay, 1950[h]	231	75	23	2.1	0.7	265	83	16	0.8	0.1
Peru, 1961[o]	1,725	26[j]	56[j]	12[j]	3.9	1,835	56[j]	34[j]	7.9[j]	1.4[j]
Uruguay, 1963[p]	711	61[q]	28[q]	9.0[q]	2.2[q]	739	56[q]	32[q]	9.1[q]	0.8[q]
Venezuela, 1950[h]	988	72	24[r]	3.0[r]	1.8[r]	967	80	18[r]	1.7[r]	0.3[r]

[a] In general, persons having completed less than four years or more at the first level of education, including illiterates and persons without formal schooling.

[b] In general, persons having completed four years or more at first level of education but less than four years at second level.

[c] In general, persons having completed four years or more at second level of education but less than four years at third.

[d] In general, persons having completed four years or more at third level of education.

[e] Thirty years and over.

f Twenty years and over.

g Five years and over.

h Excluding tribal or jungle Indian population.

i Including persons having completed an unstated number of years respectively in primary, secondary, and higher education.

j These figures refer to persons who possess respectively: no certificate, primary school certificate, secondary school certificate, higher education degree or diploma.

k Excluding Indian jungle population, data are based on a 3 percent sample of census returns and refer to male and female population.

l Data by level of education are literate persons who are attending or have attended school; illiterate population is included with "Unknown."

m Data refer respectively to persons who have completed four years or more of primary education, six years or more of secondary education, five years or more of higher education.

n Dash means data not available.

o Based on approximately 15 percent sample of census returns. Excluding Indian jungle population estimated at 455,000 in 1960.

p Data are based on a 5 percent sample of census returns.

q Data refer respectively to persons with no schooling or having completed 0–5 years of primary education; 6 years of primary education and 1–3 years of secondary education, first cycle; 4 years of secondary education, first cycle; those who are attending or have attended secondary agricultural or trade school; and those having completed 3 years of higher education, including those who have completed secondary education, second cycle (usually 2 years), or 4 years or more of higher education. "Unknown" includes persons who have attended or are attending military school.

r Including persons having completed an unstated number of years respectively in primary, secondary, and higher education.

Source: U.N. Statistical Office, *Compendium of Social Statistics: 1967,* Statistical Papers Series K, no. 3 (New York, United Nations, 1960), Table 33, pp. 338, 341–42.

and a smaller participation of society in the benefits of growth than would have been true had human capital requirements been responded to earlier. The social and political legacies of this allocative shortcoming remain to be fully appreciated.

The impact of government spending on economic stability has been negative rather than positive in recent years. While raw material exports have decreased their share of GDP along with their influence as disturbances, total government investment has become the most important disturbing element in aggregate demand. Public expenditures have tended to be made independently of the level of private demand, and an unprogressive tax structure has failed to provide built-in stabilizers. Hence the burden of income stabilization policy has fallen on the monetary authorities. In earlier years monetary stabilization policy was not conspicuously successful and Mexican growth was accompanied by general excess demand and high rates of inflation along with the periodic balance of payments crises so characteristic of Latin America. But since the mid-1950s the Central Bank has increasingly been able to exercise a significant influence on the level of private investment spending through manipulation of the reserve requirements of financial intermediaries. As a result, fluctuations in export earnings and government investment have been sustained without serious inflation or prolonged periods of unemployment. Despite this favorable response on the part of monetary authorities to the challenges presented by fiscal shortcomings, there is reason to believe that much remains to be done to bring Mexican fiscal policy up to the level of performance of the economy as a whole.

Comments by R. Albert Berry

This paper comes (perhaps inevitably) to an ambiguous and mixed conclusion as to whether the public sector in Mexico has, in some sense, done a "good job" in the post-1930 period. On the one hand, the author points out that total public expenditures have been small relative to national income in Mexico as compared to most developing countries; on the other hand, he indicates that, of the total expenditures, a relatively high share has been in investment (as opposed to expenditures on defense, administration, etc.) and that much of this investment has been productive and highly complementary with private investment. Such offsetting judgments leave us uncertain as to whether Mexico would have developed faster with a larger government sector; at various times the author indicates that the rate of return to public investment has been quite high, but he makes the same point with respect to private investment, so it is not clear whether increased public investment expenditures at the expense of private investment would have raised the growth rate or not; presumably, if it had been at the expense of consumption, this would have occurred. He does imply that investment in human resources was definitely too small.

The most fascinating conclusions of the paper, it seems to me, are some that do not pertain directly to the question of whether government participation in Mexico was optimal in extent, but rather to the nature of that intervention. Given the "revolutionary" nature of the government, it is surprising that: (1) the government share in general was quite low vis-à-vis other developing countries in relation to GNP; (2) the expenditure on education was particularly low. Both of these conclusions are the opposite of what one might intuitively expect of a presumably revolutionary and socially oriented government. It is possible that part of the lag in the share of government expenditures was due to the very rapid growth of Mexico, with the strength of public demands for various services and so on tending to lag farther behind income than it would have in a slower growing economy. The lack of emphasis on education would seem to have no other explanation than that Mexico's was not a particularly socially oriented government but was rather, as the author has argued in other works, taking advantage of the revolutionary mystique to push an output growth policy with little emphasis on distribution. This is consistent with the fact that the distribution of income in Mexico seems at least as bad as that in the typical Latin American country.

Particularly fascinating hypotheses are implicit in the fact that the low rate of government expenditure seems to have resulted primarily from the government's striking inability to tax. Evidence of the fact that desire to spend has been running well above perceived ability to tax is the increasing share of public investment expenditures that have had to be financed via loans from the private sector. Naturally no government feels that it is easy to tax; but the development in Mexico suggests the possibility that a government by consensus (at least a sort of consensus involving a number of different groups in society), which has characterized the Mexican system, makes it even harder to tax than some other less broadly based government. In any case, the apparent extreme difficulty of taxing constitutes an interesting facet of Mexican development, and one that would warrant further probing.

The study concludes that the impact of government spending on economic stability has been negative. The theory of fluctuating government expenditure as a function of the phase of a given presidency, which underlies this negative impact, is an interesting aspect in itself; of perhaps equal interest is the relative ability the government demonstrated in turning private investment into the stabilizing force in such a way as to prevent the full impact of the fluctuating government expenditures being felt. It would be worth pursuing the question of whether the need to use the private sector as the balancer to keep total investment from fluctuating too severely led to decreased efficiency in the private sector through varying availability of credit, etc.

As we are trying to interpret the reasons for the relatively diminished participation of the government in the Mexican economy in the past, it is difficult to deduce from the paper how successful that government is likely to be in the future in promoting growth and equality. The fact that expenditures on education, while historically very low, have recently expanded very rapidly might lead one to hypothesize that the government is becoming more responsive to the needs of the masses. Do such changes represent a real change in the philosophy of the governing party in Mexico, are they primarily a result of the personalities of presidents and ministers, or precisely what change in the political milieu brings them about? It is this set of possibly unanswerable questions on which this paper throws some light, and on which further work emanating from it would prove extremely useful.

11

Distribution, Growth, and Government Economic Behavior in Peru

BY SHANE HUNT

The original purpose of this study was to set forth, as best as could be done, the means by which policy instruments have been used by the Peruvian government to affect that nation's rate of economic growth. After their initiation, however, papers tend to lead lives of their own, and this one has chosen to broaden itself in one direction and narrow down in another.

It is broader because it could not deal with growth policy alone. Growth is of course a Good Thing, and any government would prefer to foster it rather than to retard it.[1] Nevertheless, the urgency of pursuing other policy goals such as stabilization and distribution frequently leaves a government with few effective instruments left for growth policy. This has generally been the case in Peru, and so the history of growth policy is largely a history of the secondary effects on growth resulting from policies designed with other goals primarily in mind.

Secondary growth effects produced by the pursuit of other policy goals are not necessarily random; in the case of policies for improved distribution, they are more than often unfavorable. Yet the conflict between growth and distribution is not inevitable. It can be avoided

I wish to express my appreciation to members of the seminar of the Research Program in Economic Development at Princeton for their helpful comments. Also, I wish to thank Carol Allen and Robert van Leeuwen for their excellent work as research assistants.

1. Sometimes it is argued that what is important is not growth but development, the difference being that development involves both growth and additional changes that permit a more equitable income distrubution. Growth without development, as a separate policy goal, would therefore seem best defined as growth with unchanging income distrubution, and that is the sense in which I use it in this paper.

by redistributing claims on future income generated by present investment instead of redistributing present income. It can also be avoided by the behavior of the rich; if they love luxury so much that their marginal propensity to save is no higher than anybody else's, then the dilemma disappears.

But in fact, this dilemma of choosing between growth and distribution appears to be very real in Latin America. It seems no accident that the countries which have suffered the most unhappy growth performances in the last twenty years—Argentina, Chile, and Uruguay —are precisely those in which the middle and lower classes have become most powerful politically, most disaffected with the existing social structure and income distribution, and most forceful in demanding distributive change. This close, inverse connection between growth and distribution demands that if policy toward one is to be studied, then policies toward both must be studied. That is the case in this paper.

The paper is narrowed down in that it deals only with budget policy, i.e. the use of taxation and expenditure to achieve combinations of the policy goals already mentioned. This leaves out tremendously important policy fields, such as those dealing with industrial development, public enterprises, and exchange rates. They must be postponed to another paper.

For two reasons, I do not wish to view policy making as a technical problem of correctly turning the handles of instrument variables in order to achieve exogenously determined targets. First, this approach is better suited to policy planning than to the analysis of past policy making, since for the latter one is likely to find the exercise of the instrument as the only evidence suggesting what the target was. Second, the process of choosing targets is very important and should not be left out of consideration. Just as consumer expenditure is determined by the behavior of individuals, as expressed by a consumption function, so is government expenditure and taxation determined by society's behavior, as expressed by the choice of policy targets. Society's preferences, thus filtered through the mechanism of government, are nothing more than a reasonably pacific resolution of the preferences of different competing groups. The policy targets chosen are a reflection of the power of these various groups in the political arena; they are also a major determinant of the net benefit these groups receive from the political process in general and the budgetary process in particular.

Before looking at the taxation and expenditure patterns that have been the result of political struggle over the Peruvian budget, we first look at the political environment itself, as it has been analyzed by various noneconomists. We seek the political origin of the economic behavior embodied in the particular combinations of growth and distribution policies pursued over the years.

POLITICAL ORIGINS OF BUDGET POLICY

Political systems in Latin America run to a pattern, the major features of which are known to every educated layman. It is generally recognized that a small upper class, fully Western, exercises a commanding position in the political process, that a slow-to-emerge middle class is still numerically small and fairly powerless, that an enormous gulf in living standards exists between rich and poor, and that rumblings of unrest within the political system are frequently heard but usually deflected or suppressed. The political system has been described, in a word, as oligarchic.

Oligarchies are relative things, however, since all nations have groups that exercise political power disproportionate to their numbers. With few exceptions, these same groups also maintain much higher living standards than do the less fortunate of the same society. Therefore we must say that the political and social features listed above are merely more characteristic of Latin American political systems than of systems elsewhere in the world.

Moreover, since Latin America has its own diversity, they apply better to some Latin countries than to others. It is generally thought, however, that they apply particularly well to Peru. Nowhere else does the gulf between rich and poor seem greater. There are few other areas in Latin America with poverty comparable to that endured by the peasants of Peru's southern Sierra, but at the same time, in the same country, a century of development in the other half of a dualistic economy has produced great wealth. The gulf seems great in social mobility as well as in income; it is an "often made observation that Peruvian society is rigidly structured and barriers between social classes are unusually difficult to cross—even in comparison with other Latin American countries." [2]

2. Richard Patch, "La Parada, Lima's Market: A Study of Class and Assimilation," *West Coast South America Series*, American Universities Field Staff 14, no. 3 (February 1967), p. 13.

It is this view of society that has led most Peruvian intellectuals to speak of domination, rather than some form of reciprocal accommodation, as the essence of political and economic relationships between classes as well as between nations. Domination, it is argued, is exercised by whites and mestizos over the Indian peasants,[3] and by foreign interests over a small open economy such as Peru's. It is also the essence of relationship between oligarchy and masses. Thus a typical description of Peruvian class structure differentiates between *clase baja, clase media,* and *clase dominante.*[4] Not only is the latter's power emphasized, but its numerical smallness as well. Some make reference to thirty families, some to forty, others to a hundred;[5] nobody has attempted to say with any precision exactly which families are on the list,[6] but the impression of smallness, exclusiveness, and monopolization of power remains strong in both popular and academic minds.[7] A summary assessment of the society of domination is put most bitterly and succinctly by the revolutionary de la Puente: "I think there is not a country in America where infra- and superstructural conditions are so unjust, so rotten, so archaic as in ours." [8]

Of the various forms of domination, the one most extensively studied over the years concerns relations between the national, Spanish-speaking society, represented by white and mestizo, and the Indians. A number of studies document the mechanisms whereby the Indian

3. See Julio Cotler, "The Mechanics of Internal Domination and Social Change in Peru," *Studies in Comparative International Development* 3, no. 12 (1967–68).

4. Jose Matos Mar, "Consideraciones sobre la situación social del Perú," *America Latina* 7, no. 1 (January/March 1964), p. 62. In recent years the most extensive analysis of the concept of domination comes from Francois Perroux, whose intellectual influence in Peru and elsewhere in Latin America is profound. See his *La economía del siglo XX* (Barcelona: Ariel, 1964). One of the few statements of his work that appears in English is "The Domination Effect and Modern Economic Theory," *Social Research,* vol. 17, June 1950.

5. Luis Alberto Sanchez, *El Peru: retrato de un pais adolescente* (Lima: Universidad de San Marcos, 1963), p. 150; Matos Mar, p. 60; Francois Bourricaud, "Structure and Function of the Peruvian Oligarchy," *Studies in Comparative International Development* 2, no. 2 (1966).

6. A rather casual attempt has been made by Carlos Malpica, *Guerra a muerte al latifundismo* (Lima: Ediciones Voz Rebelde, n.d.), part 4.

7. Evidently this is the popular view from within as well as without the oligarchy. Robert Triffin tells the story of attending a large bankers' luncheon in Lima in the 1940s, where he was told, "There are only 100 people in Peru who really matter, of whom 50 are in this room. If we stick together we will be all right."

8. Luis F. de la Puente Uceda, "The Peruvian Revolution: Concepts and Perspectives," *Monthly Review,* 17, no. 6 (November 1965), p. 21.

is excluded from political participation, since he is illiterate and not eligible to vote; from legal redress, since the courts require the use of Spanish; and from economic opportunity.[9] It is quite appropriate that anthropologists and sociologists have focused particularly on this issue, because the assimilation of the Indian into national life remains the overridingly important social problem of the country.

A few years ago it could have been said that the other power relationships to which the term domination is applied were much less well studied. In the case of relationships between oligarchy and masses, however, a spate of recent studies, begun by the work of Bourricaud and continued in a recent publication of the Instituto de Estudios Peruanos, has thrust this aspect of domination to the forefront of interest.[10]

The debate thus stirred up has centered on whether a Peruvian oligarchy really exists. This would be a difficult empirical problem under any circumstances. It is made more difficult in the present context by the absence of any careful attempt at definition of terms. Criteria for separating the confusing variety of social systems into the oligarchic and the nonoligarchic remain obscure.

There are two principal lines of argument suggesting that an oligarchy does not exist. One maintains that even within the closed elitist societies of Latin America there are many competing political groups, and that the traditional aristocracy takes its share of lumps in the domestic political arena.[11] Thus a study of legislative performance can show that the aristocracy loses as many battles as it wins, but the meaning of such a rigorous approach is undermined by the consideration that other groups may bring up only those issues on which they think they have a chance of winning.[12] On the other hand, it is a bit bewildering to assess the elite's strength, and thus whether or not it is an oligarchy, from its performance on unfought political battles. In a less quantitative way, Bourricaud and Favre also give emphasis to the weakness of the elite's power today by stressing the losses of power suffered over the past ten or fifteen years. Thus Bourricaud speaks, somewhat obscurely, of a "shift from absolute to relative

9. E.g. Cotler, "Mechanics of Internal Domination."

10. Bourricaud, *Poder y sociedad en el Perú contemporáneo* (Buenos Aires, Editorial Sur, 1967); Bourricaud et al, *La oligarquia en el Perú* (Lima: Moncloa-Campodónico for the Instituto de Estudios Peruanos, 1969).

11. James Payne, "The Oligarchy Muddle," *World Politics* 20, no. 3 (April 1968), pp. 439–53.

12. Ibid., pp. 449–51.

domination." [13] Without being overly specific, he suggests the shift to be a rather recent phenomenon, caused particularly by the changing role of the armed forces. Favre places the elite's decline at about the same time but associates it with the rise of inexorable pressure for agrarian reform, since he gives particular emphasis to landholding as the basis of oligarchic power.[14]

An entirely different argument against the existence of oligarchy comes from Bravo Bresani, who feels that the upper classes of Peru do not exercise power independently, but instead derive power exclusively from their being the intermediaries of foreign economic interests.[15] Thus landholding per se ceases to be the source of power, since land provides power only if it generates wealth, and this it has done in the past principally by producing crops for export. Bravo's line of reasoning is also followed by Piel, who arrives at a Hobsonian view of imperialism: that the real power lies not with the landowners but with the international financial system, which together with its Peruvian affiliates provides the finance required for export production.[16]

This argument is of enormous practical importance, for at issue is the idea that concentration of domestic power can be understood and combated only by understanding and combating a more fundamental power relationship—the domination of Peru by foreigners. No assessment of the argument seems possible at present, however, until further analysis is directed at evaluating the freedom of maneuver available to domestic elites having economic ties to foreign markets. The thrust of the Bravo-Piel view is that markets, especially world commodity markets, are essentially manipulative rather than impersonal, better formalized by the theory of games than by atomistic models. It is a startling argument to the ears of economists trained in the Anglo-Saxon tradition, but in Latin America it runs far stronger and deeper than does the Marshallian demand curve.[17]

13. Bourricaud, "Structure and function," p. 30.
14. Henri Favre, "El desarrollo y las formas del poder oligárquico en el Perú," in Bourricaud et al, *La oligarquía en el Perú.*
15. Jorge Bravo Bresani, "Mito y realidad de la oligarquía peruana," in *La oligarquía en el Perú.*
16. Jean Piel, "La oligarquía peruana y las estructuras del poder," in *La oligarquía en el Perú,* p. 188.
17. In a famous polemic of the 1920s, this is one point on which Marxist and Catholic traditionalist could agree. See Jose Carlos Mariátegui, *Siete ensayos de interpretación de la realidad peruana,* 13th ed. (Lima: Amauta, 1968),

For this study of public finances, however, the Bravo-Piel argument is not of such importance, except insofar as it suggests that the nation is not a meaningful unit of study. Nevertheless, a fiscal system is nation-specific, and so we have no choice but to deal with that unit of analysis. For our purposes it is enough to know that there is a small group possessing a large share of domestic political power, without needing to know if the ultimate source of that power is domestic or foreign.

But how can one assert the existence of this concentration of power if a methodologically rigorous approach cannot establish its existence? I think one must remain satisfied, for the moment, with the unrigorous, essayist approach of Bourricaud and others. One may supplement this by considering the vast gulf between the commonly held understanding of the requisites for a just society and the legislative accomplishments of any popularly elected administration in recent Peruvian history. A reformist government such as that of Belaunde will chip away where it can, but even its apparent victories such as agrarian reform were easily frustrated through ineffective implementation. This chronic gap between what is widely desired and what is politically feasible is the power of the elite. In Peru the gap has been wide, at least until the present military government came to power, and the elite that maintained the gap has been cohesive on vital issues. As the term is used, therefore, it has been an oligarchy.

Peru's traditional oligarchy is now quite evidently in retreat, however, and by now has perhaps retreated past any reasonably drawn line of demarcation between oligarchic and nonoligarchic systems. The time at which the decline began is not fixed with any certainty at all. While Bourricaud and Favre place the moment somewhere within the last fifteen years, nevertheless the heyday of Peruvian oligarchy was long before that, in the first decades of this century, when the *República Aristocrática* held sway through its political instrument, the Civilista party, and the oligarchy's rule was direct and effective.[18] Peru's political and social history in the past sixty years

---

pp. 80–82, and Victor Andrés Belaunde, *La realidad nacional*, 3d ed. (Lima, 1963), p. 29.

18. Bourricaud, "Structure and function," p. 25, gives the impression that oligarchy *prefers* indirect rule, and that the Civilista period was an aberration. It seems to me rather that indirect rule has been the best that oligarchy could manage during other periods. See Fredrick Pike, *The Modern History of Peru* (New York: Praeger, 1967), pp. 192–200.

is therefore a story of very gradual erosion in oligarchic power, as other groups have developed the leverage to obtain a share of the political system's output.

At the beginning of the century these other groups were exclusively urban; the political system recognized the growing power of urban workers and the middle classes by enacting social legislation, encouraging collective bargaining, and setting the urban beginnings to a national system of public education.[19] Over the decades the process of social mobilization has continued, to the point that in recent years the political system has begun to grant some of its benefits to the Indian peasant, viz. two agrarian reform laws, the earlier law of 1964 being a direct response to the peasants' newly acquired ability in political organization.[20]

Many of the new, challenging groups have relied on mass action and threatened violence as their bargaining tools in the political process.[21] The oligarchy has receded but slowly, however, since in the past it has known that excessive instability would bring the armed forces to the rescue. A few years ago, therefore, Peru was most appropriately described as a military guardianship, where the armed forces permitted the oligarchy to employ "a defensive and delaying tactic which realistically has estimated the possibilities of defeat of the traditional ways but wishes to soften its impact." [22]

This political description of Peru, only a few years old, is already obsolete. The present military government, which took power in October 1968, has assumed an entirely new role for itself. Far from being the traditional defender of oligarchic interests, it represents the triumph of a new, assertive middle class against a weakened oligarchy.

Since this political summary gives particular emphasis to the distribution of political power, it has direct implications for the distributive impact of governmental economic policy. In this case, the thrust of political argument is that power is distributed discontinuously among three groups—oligarchy, Indian peasants, and a middle group which is merely the nonoligarchic, non-Indian residual. If political

19. Jorge Basadre, *Historia de la república del Perú*, 6th ed. (Lima: Editorial Universitaria, 1969), 15, pp. 7–53.

20. Hugo Neira, *Cuzco: tierra y muerte* (Lima, Problemas de Hoy, 1964).

21. James Payne, "Peru: The Politics of Structured Violence," *Journal of Politics* 27, no. 2 (May 1965).

22. Rosendo Gomez, "Peru: The Politics of Military Guardianship," in Martin Needler, ed., *Political Systems of Latin America* (Princeton: Van Nostrand, 1964), p. 300.

power is thus distributed as a three-step function, we should expect the same of economic benefit derived from the budgetary process.[23]

Specifically, taxation and expenditure should reflect oligarchic power by being relatively regressive in upper income ranges, and should reflect domination of the Indian by being relatively regressive in the income range that separates incomes of most Indians from incomes of most mestizos and whites. Moreover, the regression, or weak progression, of the system should be changing over time in the direction of greater progression, but the beginning of such change might be located anywhere between 1900 and 1955.

These expectations about incidence, as well as the earlier description of the distribution of power in the political system, are couched in relative terms, and therefore before examining the Peruvian fiscal system we must say something about patterns of expenditure and taxation in other countries, so that standards of comparison will be at hand.

PATTERNS OF TAXATION AND EXPENDITURE IN DEVELOPING COUNTRIES

Very little work has been done on estimating the incidence of taxation and expenditure in less developed countries. Within Latin America, the few studies to be found have, to my knowledge, all focused exclusively on tax incidence. Carefully done studies in El Salvador and Venezuela both conclude that these tax systems are mildly progressive.[24] A study of Colombia, which dealt only with quartile groups and was therefore quite undifferentiated at the upper end of the income distribution, found tax proportionality but no progression.[25] On the other hand, a more ambitious but looser study by Musgrave showed quite different results: that in all South American countries except Venezuela, families ranking between the 25th and 50th percentiles in income suffered the highest average tax rate. These tax

23. That is, if individuals were arrayed by amount of political power, and if political power could be satisfactorily quantified, a step function would result. If instead the vertical measure were *cumulated* total power, the result would be a political Lorenz curve consisting of three linear segments.

24. Henry Wallich and John Adler, *Public Finance in a Developing Country; El Salvador: A Case Study* (Cambridge: Harvard University Press, 1951), pp. 132–33; Commission to Study the Fiscal System of Venezuela, *The Fiscal System of Venezuela* (Baltimore: Johns Hopkins Press, 1959), p. 40.

25. Joint Tax Program (hereafter, JTP), *Fiscal Survey of Colombia* (Baltimore: Johns Hopkins Press, 1965).

systems therefore seemed to be progressive only below the 25th percentile and regressive over the wide range above it.[26] In the case of Argentina, the conclusion of tax regressiveness was confirmed independently by Herschel.[27]

The redistributive impact of taxation appears more certain in industrial countries, which generally place greater reliance on income taxation. Yet even in the United States, a country that gives particularly strong emphasis to income taxation, incidence studies have shown that progression of the total tax system is weak in both lower and middle income brackets; significant progression is to be found only in the upper brackets.[28]

One concludes that there are probably no tax systems in the Western Hemisphere which are strongly redistributive in either direction. For significant redistributive impact one must look to the expenditure side of government fiscal activity, even though empirical studies are harder to find. The exercise of assigning benefits from government expenditure to various income classes involves such arbitrariness that few have attempted it.[29] No studies come to mind for Latin America; for the United States, the estimates show strongly regressive expenditure favoring the lowest income groups, but also a milder yet still significant redistributive impact running through the full range of income classes.[30]

These studies addressed specifically to questions of incidence are too few in number to permit drawing generalizations about the pattern by which redistribution evolves as countries develop. We may do this indirectly, however, by examining cross-sectional studies that

26. Richard Musgrave, "Estimating the Distribution of the Tax Burden," in Conference on Tax Administration, *Problems of Tax Administration in Latin America,* for the Joint Tax Program (Baltimore, Johns Hopkins Press, 1965), p. 63. The apparent progression in Musgrave's Venezuelan estimate appears erroneous, however, as a result of including taxes on foreign companies in a distribution that pertains only to residents of the country.

27. Ibid, p. 86.

28. George Bishop, "The Tax Burden by Income Class, 1958," *National Tax Journal* 14, no. 1 (March 1961), p. 54.

29. For a brief bibliography, see W. Irwin Gillespie, "Effect of Public Expenditures on the Distribution of Income," in Richard Musgrave, ed., *Essays in Fiscal Federalism* (Washington: The Brookings Institution, 1965), pp. 122–23.

30. Gillespie, p. 162. Also Eugene Schlesinger, Appendix to John Adler, "The Fiscal System, the Distribution of Income, and the Public Welfare," in Kenyon Poole, ed., *Fiscal Policies and the American Economy* (New York: Prentice-Hall, 1951), pp. 418–20.

trace out the differences in expenditure and revenue patterns among countries at different levels of per capita income.[31]

One well-established result, whose significance for distribution and growth is not immediately obvious, is that government revenues and expenditures are *ex post* elastic with respect to GNP. In samples including both developed and less developed countries, elasticities calculated either cross-country or by short time series cluster between 1.2 and 1.3.[32] Expressed as shares of GNP, government expenditures typically rise from about 12 percent to about 20 percent as per capita income increases from $100 to $600.[33]

Although the total is clearly elastic, the identity of the elastic component parts is less clear. Education clearly seems to be one, however. Kuznets calculates from a small sample that education and health expenditures are 3.8 percent of GNP for poor countries and 5.5 percent for rich countries.[34] The approximate correctness of this level is confirmed by Martin and Lewis, and the trend (but not the level) is confirmed by Thorn's regressions.[35] On the other hand, the shares of general government and of development expenditures other than education and health show no evident elasticity; the same is true of total current expenditure less military spending, despite the fact that education and health contribute elastic components to this total.[36]

On the side of revenue, the predominant characteristic of cross-country studies is the relative growth of direct taxes, especially personal and corporate income taxes, and the relative decline of indirect taxes. Hinrichs points out that the direct-indirect tax ratio actually follows a U-shaped curve, with the earliest stages of modernization

31. Alison Martin and W. A. Lewis, "Patterns of Public Revenue and Expenditure," *Manchester School* 24, no. 3 (September 1956); Jeffrey Williamson, "Public Expenditure and Revenue: An International Comparison," *Manchester School* 29, no. 1 (January 1961); Harley Hinrichs, *A General Theory of Tax Structure Change during Economic Development* (Cambridge: Harvard Law School, 1966); Simon Kuznets, "Quantitative Aspects of Economic Growth of Nations: VII. The Share and Structure of Consumption," *Economic Development and Cultural Change* 10 (January 1962), part 2; Richard Thorn, "The Evolution of Public Finances during Economic Development," *Manchester School* 35, no. 1 (January 1967). For a more complete bibliography, see Thorn.
32. Thorn, pp. 36, 41; Williamson, p. 50.
33. Calculated from regression equations in Hinrichs, p. 13; Thorn, p. 40; and Williamson, p. 50. The correspondence between the results from these three sources is only fair.
34. Kuznets, p. 10.
35. Martin and Lewis, p. 218; Thorn, p. 44.
36. Kuznets, pp. 8–9; Martin and Lewis, pp. 205, 209.

having been characterized by the relative decline of traditional direct taxes, particularly land and head taxes, and the rise of indirect taxes on foreign trade.[37] In the world today, however, this earlier stage is largely a matter of economic history. All recent cross-section studies show a strong relation between the share of direct taxes in GNP and per capita income, with elasticities between 1.2 and 1.4.[38] Expressed again in GNP shares, direct taxes run 2 to 4 percent for a country with per capita income of $100, and 6 to 11 percent for a country with a $600 per capita income.[39] Most of this growth is attributable to personal income taxes. Corporate tax shares show some upward trend, but they also show great variability among countries.

Indirect tax shares are only slightly greater for $600 than for $100 countries, about 9.5 percent of GNP in the former and 8.5 percent in the latter.[40] This represents a substantial decline in relative importance in the budget, from about two-thirds of revenues to less than one-half.[41]

It therefore appears that tax systems have been getting more progressive, or less regressive, over time, as individual and business income taxes become increasingly important.[42] The particularly high elasticities of expenditures on education, health, and transfers suggest growing redistributive significance, i.e. regressiveness, on the expenditure side as well.

The growing government share associated with rising per capita income therefore has clear and favorable distributional significance. Its significance for growth is by no means so clear. A growing share has generally been considered good for growth, since it is expected that government's marginal propensity to save will be higher than the private sector's propensity to dissave because of marginal tax increases. As growth proceeds this becomes an increasingly questionable assumption, however, since the high elasticity of direct taxes means that marginal increases in tax collections bear increasingly on saving. Nevertheless, government's commitment to steer expenditure increases into development projects and education is frequently thought suffi-

37. Hinrichs, pp. 73, 101.
38. Thorn, p. 48; Williamson, p. 52.
39. Calculated from regressions in Thorn, p. 48, and Williamson, p. 52. Also Kuznets, p. 8.
40. Kuznets, p. 8; Williamson, p. 52.
41. Williamson, p. 54.
42. This conclusion is not certain, since the relative expansion of direct taxes is partly at the expense of import taxes, which could themselves be quite progressive.

ciently strong to outweigh the negative growth effects of increasing tax progression.

This view cannot be accepted so sanguinely in Latin America. A glance at the expenditure patterns is sufficient to convince that the richer countries do indeed have a larger share of GNP devoted to government expenditure, but that this expenditure runs particularly heavily to transfer payments instead of to investment. Since part of this redistribution is from rich savers to middle class nonsavers, the impact on growth of an expanding government share is probably perverse.

THE INCIDENCE OF TAXATION AND EXPENDITURE IN PERU

Unfortunately nobody has done the careful statistical work that the question of tax incidence in Peru deserves. In fact, the only estimates I have seen are the exceedingly rough ones put together by Musgrave.[43] Rough estimates have their place, of course, and are generally better than nothing, but in this case the dangers of roughness are compounded by the fact that the estimating method used is particularly liable to large error in result caused by small errors in data.[44] Accordingly the conclusion of this procedure, that the Peruvian tax system is regressive, is very much open to question. In fact, some alternative pieces of information run counter to this conclusion.

The first piece of information derives from comparing Musgrave's results for Colombia with those shown in the Joint Tax Program study mentioned previously. Musgrave found a tax structure whose regressivity almost exactly matched the regressive pattern he found for Peru.[45] The result pertained to central government taxes only, but, as Table 11.1 shows, the Joint Tax Program found this same tax system to be progressive.

Two principal differences in assumptions are responsible for this

43. "Distribution of the Tax Burden."
44. Musgrave's method consists of allocating tax payments for each of five taxes to the four quartiles of a distribution of spending units arrayed by size of income. The percentage allocations for each tax are chosen with only a casual empirical foundation and are the same for all South American countries. Next, income is assigned to these same quartiles, by assuming an estimate of Venezuelan income distribution to be applicable to all countries. The ratio of taxes to income is then computed for each quartile. Small errors in assigning either taxes or income to the quartiles can affect the trend of the ratios greatly, and yet both assignments were made most arbitrarily.
45. P. 63.

Table 11.1: Tax Incidence

	I	*II*	*III*	*IV*
		Quartile		
		(in percentages)		
Central government taxes as percentage of income (Musgrave)				
Peru	5.4	12.3	6.6	9.2
Colombia	4.5	12.0	7.7	9.1
Colombian taxes as percentage of income (Joint Tax Program)				
Central government	4.9	5.5	6.7	10.2
All government	10.9	9.4	11.1	12.7
Income distribution				
Venezuela (Musgrave)	5.0	7.0	21.0	67.1
Colombia (JTP)	5.0	12.7	17.1	65.2
Distribution of indirect tax payments				
Internal indirect (Musgrave)	10	25	30	35
Import (Musgrave)	5	20	35	40
Colombian tobacco and liquor (JTP)	15	20	30	35
Colombian gasoline and vehicles (JTP)	7	18	23	53
All other Colombian indirect (JTP)	5	14	23	58
1958 Peruvian indirect taxes				
Musgrave distribution	6.9	21.9	33.1	38.1
JTP distribution	5.9	14.7	23.6	55.8
Peruvian central government taxes as percentage of income				
Musgrave tax allocation with Colombian income distribution	5.4	6.8	8.1	9.5
Musgrave tax allocations, with adjustments for indirect taxes and Colombian income distribution	4.7	4.5	5.9	10.6
Best estimate of tax incidence	19.5	17.4	20.6	16.9
Best estimate of total budget incidence	16.3	15.3	7.6	13.6

Sources: Musgrave, "Distribution of the tax burden," pp. 58–63; JTP, *Fiscal Survey*, pp. 224–27.

completely different result. The first concerns the allocation of income to the four quartiles. Again referring to Table 11.1, we see that there is substantial similarity in the two distributions except for the second quartile, which is little better off than the first quartile in Musgrave's estimate.[46] The second difference lies in the allocation of indirect tax payments, which is done much more regressively in Musgrave's work than in the Joint Tax Program's. If Musgrave's assumptions on these two points are replaced by those of the Joint Tax Program study,

46. The particular allocation of income shown is derived from Musgrave's data on distribution of tax payments and tax burdens for Peru, p. 63.

assessment of the tax system shifts sharply from regression to progression, as Table 11.1 shows.

Moreover, this progressive conclusion probably contains fewer errors, since the Joint Tax Program income distribution by quartiles is probably more accurate and makes a reasonable match to the distribution of indirect tax payments.[47] It is not, however, the best estimate that can be managed, even with the simple adjustments which are all that can be managed here. The other adjustments are all in the direction of greater regressivity, however, so the final estimate is that the tax system shows no progression, but rather exhibits what is best described as wandering proportionality.[48]

We conclude, therefore, that the Peruvian tax system has no noticeable redistributive impact one way or the other. The weakness of the evidence supporting this conclusion should be obvious, however, so much so that the conclusion is best stated negatively: There is no clear evidence of either progression or regression.

If redistributive effect is to be found, therefore, it must be found on the expenditure side of the budget, despite the fact that most types of expenditure defy assignment of benefit to particular groups. Expenditures for general administration, defense, justice, and police are of this nature and must be ignored here, or, what is the same thing, they must be assumed to have their benefits distributed proportional to income. From an a priori standpoint, only social and development expenditures (education, health, agriculture, transport, public works) can be assigned with some confidence, and even here data problems make it impossible to say anything about the grab bag that is public works.

Transport expenditure is probably regressive on balance, i.e. its benefits accrue particularly to the poor, since over the years a large share has been devoted to expanding and improving the national high-

---

47. The frequency distribution of income contained thirty-two separate income bands in the Joint Tax Program study, but only three in the Shoup study from which Musgrave's estimates were derived. The danger of error in the interpolation required for deriving a quartile distribution was therefore less in the former study.

48. These final adjustments are: (1) subtraction of profits of foreign companies from business income tax; (2) assumption that 50 percent of business income tax is passed forward to the consumer, through the ready availability of tariff protection and tax relief for companies or industries in difficulty; (3) use of more comprehensive tax collection totals, including local as well as central government taxes, for 1961 instead of 1958. Banco Central de Reserva (hereafter, BCR), *Cuentas nacionales del Perú 1950–1965* (Lima, 1966), Table 12.

way network, thus making it possible for Indian peasants to migrate to the city and to escape the ages-old domination exercised by mestizos and whites. Expenditure on agriculture could also be regressive, since incomes are lower in the agriculture sector than elsewhere, but in practice the experience of Latin American agricultural programs has been that the power of the few wealthy farmers has permitted them to appropriate most of the benefit.[49] Peru is no exception to this experience, and so the incidence of agricultural expenditure is probably progressive.

For a quantitative assessment of expenditure incidence, however, we must be restricted to a partial estimate involving only education and health, which together accounted for little more than a quarter of government expenditure in 1961. We may concentrate on this portion with some confidence that the other three-quarters of expenditure has an incidence that, like the tax system, shows no obvious departure from proportionality. The benefits of education and health expenditures are treated as transfers received, i.e. negative taxes, in the final row of Table 13.1, which provides an estimate of total budget incidence. This final estimate shows the expenditure advantages gained by urban lower and middle classes, who comprise all of the third and part of the fourth and highest quartile. The public school system functions for them; in 1961 it had not yet been extended greatly to the rural poor, and it is not used by the upper class.[50] As for health expenditures, they are largely located in urban areas, where income levels are higher. The hospitals and clinics built and subsidized are more available to urban residents, while the water and sewage systems provide exclusively urban benefits.

We concluded earlier that the Peruvian tax system, with its absence of strong deviation from proportionality, is not greatly unlike the other systems of the Western Hemisphere. The incidence of expenditure, however, is wholly different from that of the United States, the only other country for which we possess similar estimates. Whereas social expenditures were seen to accrue particularly to the benefit of the poorest sectors in the United States, in Peru the lower half of the income distribution is effectively excluded from such benefits and thus

49. Solon Barraclough, "Agricultural Policy and Land Reform," Conference on Key Problems of Economic Policy in Latin America, University of Chicago, mimeographed (1966), pp. 11–29.

50. In the 1961 census, only 52 percent of the 7–14 age group was enrolled in school.

experiences the high net tax incidence shown in the bottom line of Table 11.1. This is the statistical reflection of the domination of the Indian peasant referred to previously. Hardly any government services are made available to him, but some taxation is levied upon him, particularly the turnover tax and the excises or monopoly prices charged to coca, alcohol, and tobacco.

In making this comparison, the obvious should be emphasized: that in recent years the United States has been painfully knocked into a realization that the extent of redistribution it effects through government expenditure is no cause for smugness. However, in the present instance this condition makes U.S. expenditure incidence all the more interesting as a standard of comparison. It also makes the enormity of the challenge facing Peruvian reformers all the more evident.

While the poor have therefore gained little, neither has great redistributive advantage accrued to the oligarchy. It would be argued by some that common governmental functions such as defense and police should be assigned to the benefit of the oligarchy, since they help preserve a political system possessed of obvious benefit for the oligarchy. This seems too tenuous an assignment in the technical framework that governs studies of incidence, however. Rather it should be considered the achievement of oligarchy that, in a world of tax progression, it has survived with a proportional levy. The price it has paid is assent to fiscal advantage obtained by the new groups diluting oligarchic power.

THE EVOLUTION OF PERUVIAN EXPENDITURE INCIDENCE

Next to be considered is the trend over time in the redistributive impact of the Peruvian budget. Compared to the assessment of incidence in a given year, trend over time can be assessed more accurately and more easily, merely by examining the trend in size and composition of expenditures and revenues. It is here that the cross-country experience of the 1950s will aid in giving perspective to the evolution of Peruvian public finances.

By the standard of these cross-country estimates, we can see that in the 1950s Peru was a country with a small governmental sector. For example, Williamson's regression, dealing with the period 1951–56, predicted a government share of 14.6 percent for a per capita income corresponding to Peru's, but his figure for Peru was only 11 percent.[51] These low levels are confirmed by the data in Table 11.2, which show the Peruvian government sector to have been particularly small throughout the 1940s as well as for most of the 1950s. It was 1952 before the government share (including transfers) rose above

Table 11.2: Growth of Government Expenditure

	Real GNP per capita (1963 prices)	*Government expenditure (incl. transfers) as percentage of GNP (current prices)*	*Government exhaustive expenditure as percentage of GNP*	
			(current prices)	*(1963 prices)*
1942–45	$156	9.8	8.7	9.6
1945–50	164	10.4	9.2	11.9
1950–55	200	12.6	9.9	12.7
1955–60	223	14.6	10.9	12.1
1960–65	261	17.0	11.7	12.1
Expenditure elasticities[a]				
1942–65		2.07[b]	1.56[b]	1.27[c]
1950–65		2.15[b]	1.72[b]	0.99

[a] Equals $(a_1 + 1)$, where calculated from regression of the form $ln\,(G/GNP) = a_0 + a_1\,ln\,(GNP/P)$, so that $G = (e^{a_0}/P^{a_1})\,GNP^{(a_1+1)}$. ($G$ = government expenditure, P = population).
[b] Significantly elastic at 1 percent level.
[c] Significantly elastic at 5 percent level.

Sources: 1950–63: BCR, *Cuentas nacionales del Perú, 1950–1965*, Tables 1, 2, 4, 12. 1964–67: *Cuentas nacionales del Perú, 1950–1967*. 1942–49: author's estimates, based on current price GNP in BCR, *Renta nacional del Perú* (issues of 1947–51) and government expenditure detail in Contraloría General de la República, *Balance y cuenta general de la república* (annual).

12 percent of GNP, and even then this figure was associated with a per capita income of nearly $200, instead of the $100 suggested by cross-country experience.

But how different things were in the 1960s. By the middle of the decade government expenditure had risen to just a shade below 20 percent of GNP, while per capital income was not even half way to $600.[52] A substantial allocative shift had taken place.

51. Williamson, "Public Expenditure and Revenue," pp. 50, 56. Note that his figures pertain to the share of government current expenditure only.
52. In 1965, per capital income is estimated at 280 dollars of 1963 vintage, and the government expenditure share, including transfers, at 19.7 percent. In 1967, the last year for which data are available, the corresponding figures are

This great change in the government's share is reflected in *ex post* elasticities over time that are substantially higher than those of the cross-section studies. As Table 11.2 shows, even without including transfers we get elasticities over 1.5, in place of the 1.2–1.3 range most common in the cross-country studies.

We can never be sure that cross-section studies are accurate predictors of change over time, however. It may be that government expenditure functions, where the observations are countries, exhibit the same upward drift commonly associated with the consumption function, where the observations are individuals. If upward drift is widespread, then many less developed countries must be given credit for improved fiscal capability in the 1960s, but regardless of behavior elsewhere the government of Peru must be given such credit. This capability is important for the redistributive and growth-inducing potential that it represents, but clearly the realization of the potential depends on the political forces determining government economic behavior.

A look at the evolving composition of Peruvian expenditure shows that government's expanding share has indeed been associated with increasing redistributive impact, through the growing importance of education and health expenditure. It will be recalled that the figures of Kuznets, derived largely from 1958, indicated a rise in the GNP share of education and health from 3.8 percent for poor countries to 5.5 percent for rich countries. Peru was one of the poor countries included in Kuznets' sample, and in 1958 its GNP share devoted to education and health was exactly 3.8 percent. This ratio had risen sharply from abysmal levels during the early 1940s, however, and during the 1960s the rise was even more rapid. By 1965 the ratio had risen fully to 6.0 percent, and for education alone it was 5.1 percent. It is here in education that we find most of the explanation for the elastic behavior of total exhaustive expenditures by government. For the 1950–65 period, the elasticity of total exhaustive expenditures is 1.72, but with education removed it drops to 1.18, and is thus not significantly different from 1.0.[53]

It should be noted that this educational expansion is not merely the reflection of an upward drift in expenditure common to all poor countries. Although educational expansion has taken place elsewhere,

---

$363 and 22.3 percent. BCR, *Cuentas nacionales del Perú 1950–1967* (Lima, 1968), Tables 1, 12.

53. The corresponding elasticities for 1942–65 are 1.56 and 1.18.

nevertheless the Peruvian expansion was extraordinary, so that by
1963 its share of GNP devoted to education was exceeded only by
Cuba and Puerto Rico among Latin American countries.[54] Moreover,
this expansion did not proceed independently of the particular administration that was in power; the residuals tabulated in Table 11.3

Table 11.3: Components of Exhaustive Expenditure

	Real GNP per capita (1963 prices)	*Exhaustive expenditure as percentage of current price GNP*			
		Education	Education and health	Defense	Total minus education and defense
1942–45	$156	1.13	1.83	2.46	5.1
1945–50	164	1.67	2.44	2.61	4.9
1950–55	200	1.77	2.60	2.70	5.45
1955–60	223	2.52	3.57	3.17	5.2
1960–65	261	3.60	4.78	2.92	5.2
Expenditure elasticities					
1942–65		2.88[a]		1.37[a]	1.07
1950–65		3.37[a]		1.22	1.13

		Deviations from trend of regressions						
		Education/ GNP		Defense/ GNP		Total ex-haustive minus education and defense/GNP		Education as percentage of total gov't. exhaustive expenditure
Presidency	Period	Pos.	Neg.	Pos.	Neg.	Pos.	Neg.	
Prado	1942–45	1	3	2	2	2	2	13.0
Bustamante	1946–48	3	0	2	1	3	0	18.5
Odría	1949–56	1	7	2	6	4	4	18.4
Prado	1957–62	4	2	4	2	2	4	26.4
Belaunde	1963–65	3	0	0	3	2	1	33.4

[a] Significantly elastic at 1 percent level.

Sources: Same as Table 11.2.

show that the administration of Odría de-emphasized education. The
nature of the de-emphasis is shown more clearly in the figures showing education's share of exhaustive government expenditure. With
every other new presidency, education's share jumped significantly.
Odría did not cut back, but he held the line, even though it made

54. UNESCO, *Statistical Yearbook, 1965,* Table 21.

necessary cutting a year out of the primary school curriculum, thus forcing two cohort groups to compete for admission to secondary schools at the same time.

As the statistics on incidence showed, it is in education that we see most clearly the pressures on the government budget for allocating a greater share of political and economic output to groups newly ar- rived in the political arena. Whether these groups be residents of provincial towns or new migrants to Lima, perhaps their first and strongest demand of government is education for their children.[55] Education is a derived demand, however; the primary demand is for occupational advancement, and so it is that the expansion of educa- tional expenditure under Belaunde had as its purpose the expansion of employment and income for prospective teachers as much as the expansion of educational opportunity for children.

Table 11.4 gives an indication of the different sources of pressure for increasing education expenditures. The growth of government spending on education, expressed in current prices, is divided into four components: increases in the number of public school teachers, in the cost of living, in the average real wage level in the economy, and in the real wage differential existing between teachers and the economy's average. The expansion of the stock of teachers follows a growth path suggested by the pattern of residuals in the previous table; a spurt during the administration of Bustamante (11 percent annu- ally from 1946 to 1948), rather slower growth during Odría (4.4 percent annually from 1949 to 1956), a faster 8.0 percent rate during Prado's administration, and a remarkable 12 percent annual growth in the first years of Belaunde. The growth rates vary by presidency, but within the period of a given presidency the rate does not show systematic variation.

It is quite different in the case of teachers' real wages. The charac- teristic pattern is for real wages to take a big jump with the coming to power of a new administration, either immediately before or imme- diately after the election; but between elections the teacher, and the civil servant in general, is lucky if his money wage merely keeps pace with the cost of living. After an increase of 31 percent in Bustamante's first year, real wages declined so much that two years later teachers

55. William Mangin has pointed this out in the case of residents of Lima *barriadas*. Cf. "Urbanization Case History in Peru," *Architectural Design* 33, no. 8 (August 1963).

Table 11.4: Indexes Relating to Education
(1960 = 100)

	Total number of public school teachers	Total expenditure on education (current prices)	Implicit education price index	Cost of living	Implicit real wage of teachers	Real GNP per capita	Teachers' real wage differential
	(1)	(2)	(3)	(4)	(5)	(6)	(7)
1942	27.3	1.88	6.9	13.21	52.2	66.6	78.4
1943	33.0	2.21	6.7	14.81	45.2	64.6	70.0
1944	34.0	3.44	10.1	16.92	59.7	65.9	90.6
1945	36.8	4.06	11.0	18.80	58.5	66.7	87.7
1946	45.1	7.08	15.7	20.54	76.4	71.3	107.2
1947	51.3	9.32	18.2	27.26	66.8	67.5	99.0
1948	55.7	9.59	17.2	35.2	48.9	63.9	76.5
1949	55.3	13.04	23.6	41.3	57.1	70.4	81.1
1950	56.9	17.44	30.7	47.0	65.3	76.2	85.7
1951	58.4	22.7	38.9	52.4	74.2	82.6	89.8
1952	62.4	25.2	40.4	57.2	70.6	83.5	84.6
1953	63.4	28.1	44.3	60.6	73.1	83.7	87.3
1954	67.9	31.6	46.5	62.2	74.8	90.0	83.1
1955	69.7	35.0	50.2	65.3	76.9	92.4	83.2
1956	74.5	52.3	70.2	68.7	102.2	94.3	108.4
1957	77.5	60.4	77.9	74.9	104.0	92.9	111.9
1958	84.7	75.7	89.4	81.7	109.4	93.5	117.0
1959	90.6	88.5	97.7	91.0	107.4	94.3	113.9
1960	100.0	100.0	100.0	100.0	100.0	100.0	100.0
1961	107.4	129.5	120.6	105.1	114.7	105.1	109.1
1962	114.0	158.8	139.3	108.3	128.6	111.5	115.3
1963	121.2	194.8	160.7	112.4	143.0	112.3	127.3
1964	136.9	241.8	176.6	122.7	143.9	116.8	123.2
1965	152.2	385.1	253.0	143.8	175.9	118.4	148.6

Sources: Column 1: Author's compilation, derived mainly from Ministerio de Edu-cación Pública, *Estadística educativa* and *La educación en el Perú* (Lima, 1967); also *Anuario estadístico del Perú.* Column 2: Author's compilation from *Balance y cuenta general de la república.* Column 4: For 1950–65, BCR, *Cuentas nacionales del Perú, 1950–1965* (Lima, 1966), Table 9. For 1942–49, *Anuario estadístico del Perú.* Column 6: Same as Table 11.2. Columns 3, 5, and 7: derivative from columns 1, 2, 4, and 6.

were worse off than they had been before Bustamante came to power. We see other strong spurts in wages from 1949 to 1951, in 1956, and again in 1961 and 1962.

These election-oriented spurts are testament to the political im-portance of teachers in particular and civil servants in general. Expansion of the stock of teachers and classrooms involves lags and cannot be so neatly timed for the politically sensitive year. Despite the irregularity of wage advances, it is noteworthy that from 1942 to 1956 the long-run trend in teachers' real wages was just the same as for real wages in the whole economy. Since that time, however, the teachers have opened a lead which has widened greatly in the 1960s.

It is in the 1960s that we see their expanding political power quite clearly. Between 1960 and 1965, an expansion of 285 percent in education expenditures is decomposed into a 52 percent increase in the number of teachers, a 44 percent increase in the cost of living, an 18 percent increase in real wages throughout the economy, and a 49 percent increase in the real wage differential between teachers and the general labor force.[56] The increases corresponding to the cost of living and the expansion of real wages elsewhere may be labeled unavoidable, in the medium run if not in the short run; strong pressures to expand expenditure by that amount could be expected under any conceivable circumstances. The remarkable overall expansion of this five-year period is shown in the other two components, an almost equal percentage growth in the number and relative real wage of teachers. The expansion in numbers may be attributed both to parents' demand for education of their children and to university students' demand for places as teachers. It permitted an equal expansion in the total number of students in the system.[57] The equal expansion in relative real wages is attributable exclusively to the political power of teachers, however, and so we must conclude that the expansion of educational expenditure was more a response to demands of teachers than of the families of school children.

Much of this increase originated in the famous Law 15215, which decreed a 100 percent increase in all teachers' salaries, to be provided in four annual steps of 25 percent each, a great expansion of teacher-training facilities, and the guarantee of a job with the government for every graduating teacher. This extraordinary law provoked hardly any opposition when it was introduced in Congress in 1964, so eager

56. That is, $(1.52)(1.44)(1.18)(1.49) = 3.85$. Since the quantum index refers only to teachers rather than to all educational personnel, this assumes that the growth of administrative personnel is proportional to the expansion in the number of teachers. If administrative growth has been more rapid, then the real wage differential growth rate is too high.

57. The number of students in both public and private schools grew by 50 percent during 1960–65. Ministerio de Educación Pública, *La educación en el Perú* (Lima, 1967), p. 51.

were all political parties to look well before so large and influential a block of voters, despite the fact that the fiscal planning required for implementing the law was, to say the least, inadequate. Within two years this fiscal commitment, among others, provoked an economic crisis from which Peru has not yet fully recovered. The last two of the four 25 percent increments were canceled, as was the commitment to hire all graduates of teachers' colleges. In the meantime, however, the expansion of enrollment in the teachers' colleges had proceeded apace, from 4,008 in 1960 to 14,718 in 1965, an increase of 267 percent. By 1967 the government needed fewer than 2,000 new teachers, but the teachers' colleges were graduating 9,000.

It hardly needs saying that in previous decades, particularly before World War II, it was never necessary to make such fiscal commitments in order to secure the support of public school teachers. Comparisons with GNP are not possible for these early years, because GNP estimates begin only in 1942, but it is possible to examine the importance of educational expenditure through the evolving composition of total government expenditure. This is done in Table 11.5,

Table 11.5: Percentage Distribution of Government Expenditure

	General adminis- tration	Armed forces	Justice and police	Educa- tion	Health	Develop- ment	Transfers	Other
1900	28.5	25.1	22.2	2.9	0.7	2.0	9.6	9.0
1905	23.8	35.6	14.3	4.5	2.9	3.3	13.9	1.7
1910	12.5	52.9	11.3	8.1	1.2	2.1	9.4	2.4
1915	18.6	27.4	17.7	10.1	0.7	1.7	16.3	7.4
1920	21.5	23.4	14.6	10.6	5.9	11.0	11.3	1.7
1929	25.8	22.8	14.5	11.7	4.9	8.3	10.9	1.1
1942	19.4	24.7	15.5	10.5	6.4	11.8	11.0	0.6
1945	14.7	26.3	14.8	13.3	7.7	10.9	11.6	0.7
1950	13.3	24.6	15.2	16.0	5.2	14.5	10.6	0.5
1955	11.8	23.8	13.9	14.8	9.4	15.3	10.4	0.6
1960	11.4	21.6	12.1	20.6	8.3	12.1	13.3	0.7
1965	9.6	15.6	12.2	29.4	6.4	16.8	9.3	0.7

Source: Author's compilation, derived from *Balance y cuenta general de la república·*

which gives a long-term perspective of Peruvian budgetary development. From this table we see that the functions of government at the beginning of this century were largely restricted to the maintenance of domestic tranquillity and national defense. The essential change over the course of the decades has been the slow but inexorable expansion of demands for governmental participation in economic and social development. We have already traced that development in the case of education for the period since 1942. We can now see from Table 11.5 that Peru was virtually without a system of national public education in 1900, but that the decade following was a highly important one for educational development, marking the beginning of a commitment to universal public education. At first it applied only to Lima and other accessible coastal areas, but later, in the 1940s, the geographical outward expansion of universal education began in earnest.

It is significant to note that the first important steps toward educational expansion, made between 1900 and 1910, were the handiwork of the quintessential oligarchic government in Peru's history. They came as the result not of immediate pressure from below, but of enlightenment from above. One may reasonably doubt that this enlightenment was motivated by pure charity, however, but rather by a recognition of the likely course of future events. Oligarchic power was built on economic advancement, particularly export development, and this in turn was producing urbanization and social mobilization of the masses. Oligarchic power thus possessed the elements of its own decay, but it is nevertheless to the credit of José Pardo, president of Peru from 1904 to 1908, and other relatively liberal Civilistas like him, that they recognized this and began an early and graceful retreat.

Public health and development expenditures did not acquire a significant share of budgetary allocations until the 1920s, during the eleven-year presidency of Leguía (1919–30). This was a period of big construction activity, financed in part by big foreign loans and devoted largely to national integration and further development of an export economy. Water and sewer systems, hospitals, irrigation works, port works, and, most of all, roads were the newly emphasized responsibilities of government. As mentioned above, many of these types of expenditure probably had an incidence that was not particularly beneficial to the poor. All urban dwellers did benefit from public health investments, however, and perhaps the poorer urban dwellers benefited most. The purely economic investments generally represented a response to the demands of capitalists who required government infrastructure investment complementary to their own private investments. The upsurge in development expenditures during Leguía's period is therefore a statistical manifestation of the historian's view of his presidency: a period of capitalist expansion undertaken by a new group of entrepreneurs who were not well-established members of the old Civilista oligarchy.[58]

Principally through education, therefore, we can see that the expansion of governmental activity was associated with an increasing redistributive impact which may be traced back to the very beginning of this century. Although the first steps in this educational redistribution may be attributed to anticipated rather than actual power possessed by newly emerging beneficiary groups, real power was not far behind. The political power of the urban masses was manifest at least as early as 1912, with the election to the presidency of Guillermo Billinghurst, although it is more obvious in the last twenty years.

It was mentioned earlier that the educational cutback of the relatively conservative administration of Odría illustrates that this particular component of expenditure did not expand independently of presidential administration. In the case of total government expenditure, however, it is surprising how little the overall expansion was influenced by differences in the combinations of political forces that brought successive presidents to power. This is not immediately apparent, if we happen to look at the pattern of residuals which comes from a regression of the expenditure/GNP ratio on real per capita income. The administrations of Bustamante and Belaunde were founded more substantially on the power of emerging middle and lower middle classes, and, as Table 11.6 shows, they have a much higher proportion of positive residuals.

There is some deception in this result, however. A closer look suggests a ratchet effect in government expenditures over the cycle; thus government expenditure is maintained when GNP declines in a recession, causing the ratio to rise, while government expenditure expands with a lag in a boom, causing the ratio to fall at first, then to rise in the boom's later stages as the government's expenditure share surges to a new higher level. This evidence is also summarized in Table 11.6, where the two columns of signs show a remarkable parallelism. The signs tend to be opposite except for the late stages of a boom, when government expenditure also is booming, as in 1955–56 and 1963–65. Thus we conclude that the overall growth in government expenditure has not proceeded independent of the business cy-

58. Jorge Basadre, *Perú; problema y posibilidad* (Lima: F. y E. Rosay, 1931), chapter 8; Pike, *Modern History of Peru,* chapter 8.

Table 11.6: Deviations from Trend

	Real growth in GNP from preceding years (percentage)	*Position in cycle (boom +, recession −)*	*Sign of regression residual*	*Presidency*	*Total residuals for presidency*	
					Pos.	Neg.
1942			−	Prado	2	2
1943	−1.2	−	+			
1944	3.7	−	+			
1945	3.1	−	−			
1946	8.7	+	+	Bustamante	3	0
1947	−3.7	−	+			
1948	−3.6	−	+			
1949	12.3	+	−	Odría	4	4
1950	10.1	+	−			
1951	10.5	+	−			
1952	2.9	−	+			
1953	2.2	−	+			
1954	9.6	+	−			
1955	4.9	+	+			
1956	4.6	+	+			
1957	1.0	−	+	Prado	3	3
1958	3.4	−	+			
1959	3.5	−	+			
1960	9.1	+	−			
1961	8.2	+	−			
1962	9.3	+	−			
1963	3.8	+	+	Belaunde	3	0
1964	6.8	+	+			
1965	4.8	+	+			

Sources: Same as Table 11.2. Dependent variable in regression is $\ln(G/GNP)$, where G is total government expenditures including transfers, and both G and GNP are in current prices.

cle, but it is independent of the political representation of various presidential administrations.

The expansion of government expenditure thus appears inexorable, a fact of political life against which neither an Odría government in Peru nor an Eisenhower government in the United States could do much. Although on the one hand Odría reduced the redistributive significance of expansion by cutting back on education, his alternative emphasis on labor-intensive public works expenditure was certainly not without redistributive impact. Indeed by this emphasis he probably favored still poorer groups: aspiring manual laborers instead of aspiring public school teachers. No government in recent decades has been

able to afford the luxury of throwing away the additional political
advantage to be gained from additional expenditure programs.

THE EVOLUTION OF PERUVIAN TAX INCIDENCE

In similar fashion, we now examine the evolution of tax incidence
over the years. As was the case with total expenditure, the ratio of
total revenue to GNP shows a clear and steady growth over time, and
the *ex post* revenue elasticities, shown in Table 11.7, are a good deal
higher than the 1.2–1.3 range derived from the cross-country stud-

Table 11.7: Growth of Government Revenue
(Revenues expressed as percentage of current price GNP)

	Total revenue	Indirect taxes	Taxes on imports	Excise taxes	Turn-over tax	Direct taxes	Major taxes on income from: Labor	Capital
1942–45	11.2	a	—	0.83	0.17	—	—	—
1945–50	11.6	—	—	0.42	0.27	—	0.65	4.3
1950–55	12.7	6.3	2.8	0.30	0.23	5.8	0.67	3.9
1955–60	13.3	7.4	2.9	0.35	0.46	5.3	0.73	3.0
1960–65	16.0	9.2	3.4	0.29	2.49	6.1	0.72	3.2
Revenue elasticities								
1942–65	1.63[b]			−0.22[b]	5.05[b]			
1950–65	1.82[b]	2.54[b]	2.02[b]	0.86	8.70[b]	1.10	1.02	0.17[c]

[a] Dash indicates data not available.
[b] Significantly different from unitary elasticity at 1 percent level.
[c] Significantly different from unitary elasticity at 5 percent level.

Note: Sources and elasticity formulation same as in Table 11.2.

ies.[59] Also as before, however, we can make no inferences about redistributive impact merely by looking at the trend of the aggregate,
but must instead look directly at the trends of component parts.

Indeed, the recent evolution of revenue structure in Peru is quite
atypical. The first unusual feature we note is that it is the expansion
of indirect taxes, not direct taxes, which has enabled the revenue
system as a whole to be *ex post* elastic. All direct taxes, taken as a
group, have just kept up with GNP growth since 1950, their share
of GNP being a more or less constant 5.5–6 percent. In fact the major

59. Williamson, pp. 50, 52. Thorn, p. 46.

component, consisting of a group of the principal taxes on income from capital, has shown significantly inelastic growth.[60] Although the growth of direct taxes is therefore surprisingly low, their recent level is not; rather by the cross-section standard the level was unusually high in 1950, given the low per capita income which existed, but this same level in 1965 was about average for countries of Peru's 1965 per capita income.

It is important to note, however, that this reasonably high level of direct taxes has not been produced by a widely cast tax-collecting net. While direct taxes have been levied against personal income ever since 1926, they have never attained great fiscal importance, and direct taxes have been, essentially, taxes on businesses, particularly large businesses in the modern sector.

The system of business taxation has given particular emphasis to taxing enterprises engaged in export activities, through failure to allow the real value of all export taxes collected to be offset against regular profits taxes.[61] For this reason I attempted a more accurate assessment of the *ex post* elasticity of taxes on income from capital with respect to real GNP by including the relative size of the export sector in the same equation. The result, for the period 1950–65, is as follows:

$$ln\,(T/GNP) = 6.16 + 1.25\,ln\,(X/GNP) - 1.01\,ln\,(GNP^*/P), \quad (11.1)$$
$$(0.54) \qquad\qquad (0.33)$$

where T = major taxes on income from capital, P = population, and GNP^* = real GNP. Thus, far from being able to explain away the *ex post* inelasticity of taxes on capital income by a possibly declining share of GNP devoted to exports, we find that controlling for the relative size of exports makes the inelasticity even greater and more significant. The sign and significance of the export share coefficient is what one would expect, but the interpretation of it is not certain.

---

60. This group consists of the cedular taxes on business and interest income, the excess profits tax, the tax on retained earnings, the business license tax (*patentes*), the complementary fixed tax that is applied to dividend and interest payments, and all export taxes. Most export tax payments may be credited against liabilities for business income taxes, and so merely represent an advance payment of a profits tax. Those export taxes that cannot be so credited are nevertheless taxes on income, since world market prices are given for a small country and the tax therefore cannot be shifted forward in the short run.

61. For further details, see JTP, *Estudio fiscal del Perú,* chapter 6 (forthcoming).

Although it might indicate the somewhat heavier taxation of the export sector, a more likely explanation is that it serves as a proxy for capital's share. Cycles are transmitted to Peru through its export sector, and a larger export share means prosperity and a high share to capital.[62]

The negative sign of the real GNP variable remains something of a mystery, however. Even supposing that the export share variable controls for cyclical fluctuations in capital's share, we would still expect a secular rise in the share as the modern sector expands. Decline in the ratio of tax base to GNP therefore seems unlikely, but decline in the ratio of tax collections to base is also refuted by prima facie evidence, i.e. the tax rates. The tax rate on commercial and industrial profits has been going up steadily. From a top rate of 10 percent established in 1941, it has risen to 15 percent in 1942, 20 percent in 1947, and 35 percent in 1959. Further change in 1968 did not raise the top rate but raised the lower rates substantially.[63]

There remains only one reason by which this strange sluggishness of profits tax expansion may be explained; it is the continuing erosion of the tax base through special exonerations of continuing taxes and abolition of minor taxes. Most exonerations have come through the Industrial Promotion Law, which has provided generous deductions for reinvested profits and further tax reductions for locating manufacturing establishments outside Lima. Important beneficiaries of this latter provision are mine smelters, none of which were located in Lima before passage of the law.[64] Beyond this, however, not only have mining companies secured the right to special tax provisions, through the Mining Code of 1950, but the most significant new mining venture of the last two decades was undertaken through a special contract containing even more generous terms. Essentially, the Southern Peru Copper Company was accorded the privilege of a special low tax rate until such time as it had recovered its enormous investment in the Toquepala mine. "Recovery" was defined to have taken place when

---

62. The use of capital's share as a less indirect variable was deemed inadvisable, since the ratio does not derive from other data in Peru's national accounts, but rather represents an assumption from which estimates of gross profits are derived.

63. JTP, *Estudio fiscal del Perú,* chapter 2; Ministerio de Hacienda, *La reforma tributaria de 1968* (Lima, 1968), p. 38.

64. See the excellent study by Charles Farnsworth, "The Application and Impact of Tax Incentives for Industrial Promotion in Peru," mimeographed (BCR, 1967).

accumulated profits equaled the original investment, where these profits were calculated *net of depreciation and depletion.*[65]

The lack of emphasis on personal income taxation is another curiosity of the Peruvian tax system. It is well documented that personal income taxes in less developed countries generally have about the same exemption levels and structure of progressivity as do similar taxes in developed countries, but that income levels are so low as to convert an important mass tax in developed countries into something fiscally far less important, levied only on the well-to-do.[66] This situation is acutely and particularly true for Peru. A number of alternative calculations show that personal income tax exemptions, when expressed as a multiple of per capita income, are higher in Peru than in any other South American country.[67]

The problem of excessively high exemption levels could have been solved by inaction, by allowing rising price levels to scale down the real value of exemptions. Unfortunately, pressures to raise these levels have been periodic and irresistible. As Table 11.8 shows, the number of taxpayers was minuscule during the 1950s and early 1960s, and this small number may be expected to decline further, as exemption levels have recently gone shooting up much more rapidly than has average money income. Meanwhile, the cedular tax on wages and salaries was abolished in 1964 and replaced by a stamp tax. This was indeed a curious change. Payments to labor for services rendered are now counted merely as another form of transaction, to be covered by the ubiquitous turnover tax.[68] In place of a 5 percent cedular tax levied with a 30,000 soles exemption (about $1000), there was instituted a 1 percent tax with an exemption of only 2,400 soles annually (about $100). The middle classes, those with 1963 incomes above 30,000 soles annually, were clearly the winners in the important tax changes

65. A public uproar over this contract occurred in 1967, some fourteen years after it first went into effect, and brought about a change in terms.

66. U Tun Wai, "Taxation Problems and Policies of Underdeveloped Countries," *IMF Staff Papers* 9, no. 3 (November 1962), pp. 432–33.

67. Musgrave, pp. 64–65. For example, in 1958 the income of a single person had to be 12 times the national average before he became liable to tax payments, and 14 times before his tax liability rose to 1 percent of his income. The corresponding multiples for a family of four were 26 and 32. The highest corresponding multiples to be found anywhere else in South America were 6, 25, 9, and 17, respectively.

68. Thus we have a part of income taxes masquerading as an indirect tax in our figures. This wage tax amounted to some 7 percent of total turnover taxes in 1967 and is so small a share that its transfer to direct taxes would not greatly affect any of the data or conclusions of this paper.

Table 11.8: Exemptions in Personal Income Tax (Impuesto Complementario de Tasa Progresiva)

	Annual exemptions		Personal income per capita (in soles)	Price index of consumer goods	Number of taxpayers	Taxpayers as percentage of white collar workers
	Single male (in soles)	Family of 4 (in soles)				
1950	S/.12,000	S/.22,800	S/.1586	41.8	5,308	2.0
1961	30,000	66,000	4827	93.5	8,740	2.2
1963	30,000	66,000	5787	100.0	—[a]	—
1964	48,000	114,000	6619	109.2	—	—
1968	98,000[b]	164,000[b]	—	—	—	—
1950	100	100	100	100	—	—
1961	250	289	304	224	—	—
1963	250	289	365	239	—	—
1964	400	500	417	261	—	—
1968	817[b]	719[b]	—	—	—	—

[a] Dash indicates data not available.
[b] Income from labor only.

Sources: Joint Tax Program, *Estudio fiscal del Perú*, chapter 2; Ministerio de Hacienda, *La reforma tributaria de 1968*, pp. 35–36; BCR, *Cuentas nacionales del Perú*, Tables 1, 6, 9, and 11.

of the 1960s. If their income was above 66,000 soles, a family of four gained tax relief on two fronts, as Table 11.8 shows, for their liability was reduced for complementary as well as for cedular taxes.

But rich and poor alike paid substantially more in indirect taxes. As in the case of direct taxes, an unusual evolution over the past fifteen years has produced a tax/GNP ratio much more in line with the experience of other countries. Both $100 and $600 countries, it will be recalled, tended to collect indirect taxes amounting to 8.5–9.5 percent of GNP, and by the 1960s Peru's indirect tax revenues had risen to just that range.

Excise taxes did nothing to contribute to the overall *ex post* elasticity of indirect taxes. These most traditional of internal indirect taxes have never been levied on a wide variety of goods, and the few goods involved are among the least income-elastic. In fact, more than half of the pure excises represented by the appropriate column in Table 11.7 are received from taxes on alcohol alone. In addition to these pure excises, however, the net surpluses of the traditional government monopolies in tobacco, salt, and a few other basic commodities should be considered disguised excises. Most such products are both price and income inelastic, so even if we include them into a broader definition of excise taxes, the resulting aggregate is still strongly inelastic. For example, excises and government monopoly surpluses together averaged some 1.55 percent of GNP in 1942–45 and had declined to 0.63 percent of GNP by 1962–65.

Import taxes were subject to the same process of erosion through exoneration which seems so to have undercut the potential elasticity of taxes on business income, and so it is surprising to see that they were in fact *ex post* elastic during 1950–65. Moreover, this rise in the ratio of import duties to GNP occurred precisely in that period in the 1960s when exonerations from the Industrial Promotion Law were becoming particularly numerous. The cause lay in a series of major tariff increases which occurred at the same time.

These tariff increases were made mostly for revenue purposes, but protection was also an important motive. The 1960–67 period was one of export boom and domestic inflation associated with the luxury of exchange rate stability. Therefore, domestic industry was progressively robbed of protection by diverging price movements; tariff increases helped offset this effect. Moreover, the tariff levels prevalent in the 1950s, while high by worldwide standards, were quite low by the standards of the amazing tariff rates generally prevalent elsewhere in Latin America.[69] A government hard pressed to find new revenue sources found room for maneuver in import taxation, since in Peru as in neighboring countries tariff increases were welcomed and supported by important segments of society as harbingers of prosperity through industrialization.

Over this postwar period, therefore, the dominant trend in incidence of the Peruvian tax system has been toward increased regression (or decreased progression). This is the result of an increased relative importance of indirect taxes and the continued erosion of direct taxes on both individuals and businesses, an evolution that represents a continuing expansion in the power of domestic entrepreneurs and the salaried middle classes.

Looking at revenue structure in a longer perspective, our conclusions must be less certain, but it seems most likely that tendencies toward greater regression in the last twenty years represent a backsliding from a longer-term trend toward somewhat greater progression

69. Santiago Macario calculates the average Peruvian tariff at 22 percent for 1959, as compared to 29 percent for Brazil, 32 percent for Colombia, 38 percent for Chile, and 53 percent for Argentina. See his "Protectionism and Industrialization in Latin America," *Economic Bulletin for Latin America* 9, no. 1 (March 1964), Table 2.

in the tax system. This trend may be traced back as far as 1854, when President Castilla abolished the head tax on Indians, a levy that was clearly the most regressive element in the tax system of colonial Peru. For several decades thereafter, the overwhelmingly important source of revenue was not taxation, but instead the income deriving from Peru's possession of a world guano monopoly. It was only with the collapse of guano revenues in the 1870s that the country was obliged to begin construction of a modern tax system.

The reconstructed tax system relied principally on customs duties supplemented by a few internal excises, and we can see from Table 11.9 that the job had been done by 1900. The system was effective, but regressive. The few direct taxes included in the revenue mix were of trivial importance.

Table 11.9: Percentage Distribution of Government Revenue

	Export taxes	Other profits taxes	Personal income taxes	Import taxes	Turnover taxes	Excise taxes and monopoly revenue	Other revenue
1900	0	2.9	0	59.5	1.6	27.7	8.3
1905	0	3.6	0	50.9	1.4	35.1	8.9
1910	0	4.2	0	49.9	1.2	29.0	15.7
1915	0	5.5	0	28.5	1.4	39.1	25.5
1920	32.6	3.4	0	26.1	0.9	17.7	19.3
1929	7.1	6.2	0.9	30.3	1.8	27.0	26.7
1942	16.0	15.0		11.1	1.5	15.9	40.6
1945	16.5	16.1	5.7	9.0	1.6	11.7	39.4
1950	27.5	13.9	5.4	8.5 (13.0)	2.4	7.0	30.7
1955	11.0	12.3	5.4	18.1 (21.7)	1.5	6.7	41.4
1960	8.9	15.6	5.5	8.5 (19.6)	8.3	5.8	36.2
1965	4.0	10.4	3.5	18.1 (23.9)	19.6	3.6	35.0

Source: Author's compilation, derived from *Balance y cuenta general de la república.* Figures in parentheses are total import taxes, including those collected under various special accounts, as reported by BCR, *Cuentas nacionales del Perú,* Table 13.

The incidence of Peruvian revenue structure did not change greatly between 1900 and the advent of World War I, but thereafter the major changes in taxation were all in the direction of greater progression. First there were export taxes introduced during the war itself, then a regular system of business and personal income taxation, a process begun in 1926 and greatly advanced with the reform and consolidation of income tax laws in 1934. We may calculate crude estimates of the evolution of tax progression merely by repeating the assumptions and calculations of Table 11.1, but using the different revenue structures for various years as they are shown in Table 11.9. These calculations show that the share of major taxes paid by the richest quartile of the population was 51 percent in 1900 and rose to 65 percent in 1920, 70 percent in 1945, and 76 percent in 1950. By 1961, however, this share was back to 62 percent.

The sources of possible error in such calculations are numerous, but perhaps the most obvious is the assumption that the burden of a given tax among quartile groups is constant over time. In the case of import taxes this seems particularly questionable; high transport costs and the low degree of urbanization in 1900 suggest that in fact import tax incidence might have fallen much more heavily on the rich than it does today. If this is the case, the redistributive backsliding of the recent decades may have been sufficient to return the incidence of the Peruvian tax system not just to what it was in 1920, but even to what it was in 1900.

These trends are dangerous for making inferences about the evolution of oligarchic power, however, since the richest 25 percent of the population consists largely of middle class wage earners. The introduction of taxation on exports, business income, and personal income in the second and third decades of this century undoubtedly hurt the oligarchy, but in Peru as in other countries the problems of tax compliance and loophole plugging are so serious that an effective fiscal attack on the oligarchy is evidently a matter not of legislation but of tax administration, a far more difficult challenge. Moreover, legislative attacks on the rich hit even more effectively at the salaried middle classes, the group that now challenges the oligarchy's traditional power most seriously. For this reason, in Peru as in so many other countries, the use of taxation as an instrument for achieving distributive equity has ground to a halt. The theorist's heady talk about making efficiency and equity compatible through more or less competitive markets, lump sum taxation, and redistribution seems applicable only in another world, perhaps somewhere above the clouds.

Meanwhile, back on the Andean earth, we find the long-run redistributive impact of the Peruvian budget lying almost entirely on the side of expenditure, with the expansion of education and public health programs. But an expanding revenue system with unchanging tax incidence does have redistributive significance if it makes possible the expansion of redistributive expenditure, and it is from this viewpoint that a favorable assessment may be given to the most important tax change since 1934. This is the recent development, in the early 1960s, of an effective and significant system of internal indirect taxation.

There remains a further significant tax development which has not yet occurred; this is the transformation of personal income taxes from minor levies on the elite to important levies collected on a mass basis. It took the belt-tightening esprit of total warfare to persuade the American public to permit the income tax this type of transition. Naturally, it cannot be accomplished so quickly without so dramatic an external threat, but it is discouraging to see that in Peru progress seems to have been backwards on this issue. Personal income tax reform must remain the great challenge of Peruvian public finance in the coming decade.

BUDGET POLICY AND GROWTH

In an environment of continuing political conflict over distributive issues, what have Peruvian budget policies been able to contribute to accelerated growth? Part of an answer comes from the first column of Table 11.10, which shows that growth of government investment has kept up with GNP growth, but in very erratic fashion. During periods of fiscal crisis, investment programs are among the expenditure components easiest to cut, so they show marked cyclical instability, with serious slumps in 1954, 1959–60, and 1963. The elasticity of government investment with respect to GNP comes out to something fairly high over the 1950–65 period, somewhat above 1.5, but the instability is sufficiently great to make this calculated result insignificantly different from unitary elasticity.

Table 11.10 also shows that the expenditure shares devoted to fixed investment are about the same in public and private sectors. It might seem surprising that the investment share is not larger in the public sector; certainly economists seem to assume a larger share when they view with evident favor the expansion of government's share of GNP in a developing economy.[70] In fact, in Peru the similarity of

70. The investment share of government is in fact substantially higher in the only other South American country for which data were readily available. This is Uruguay, certainly not a country noted for overzealous investment programs by government, but possessed of a government investment rate of 20.5 percent for 1960–63, as compared to the private sector's rate of only 13.6 percent for the same period. Cf. United Nations Economic Commission for

Table 11.10: Government Investment

	Government fixed investment as percentage of		Private fixed investment as percentage of private consumption plus investment
	GNP	*Total government exhaustive expenditure*	
1950	1.14	13.5	15.8
1951	1.10	11.9	19.8
1952	2.47	23.6	21.0
1953	2.14	19.7	23.3
1954	1.56	16.6	17.5
1955	3.30	29.9	17.3
1956	2.55	21.8	23.2
1957	2.08	19.1	24.5
1958	2.27	20.4	22.3
1959	1.49	14.1	18.4
1960	1.19	12.1	18.8
1961	1.97	17.1	20.5
1962	2.15	18.6	21.5
1963	1.26	11.4	19.8
1964	1.87	14.8	17.0
1965	2.70	19.5	16.4
1950–55	1.95	19.2	19.1
1955–60	2.15	19.6	20.8
1960–65	1.86	15.6	19.0

Source: BCR, *Cuentas nacionales del Perú*, Tables 1, 2, 5.

investment shares is prima facie evidence that the substantial expansion of government's GNP share in the past twenty years has had no significance for the long-run growth rate.

This conclusion is subject to two important qualifications, however. First, it is based on terribly inadequate accounting conventions about what constitutes investment and what constitutes consumption. A far more analytically useful definition of investment would not include durable consumer goods, e.g. residential construction, but would include all productivity-increasing expenditure even if not embodied in material output, e.g. education. If we assume that only half of educational expenditure is properly treated as investment, government investment as a percent of total governmental exhaustive expenditures is changed from something less than 20 percent to something more than 30 percent.

Latin America, *Boletín Estadístico de América Latina* 4, no. 1 (February 1967), p. 245.

The second qualification is that the comparison of Table 11.10, between public and private average rates, does not fully suit our purpose. Marginal investment rates are more suitable, since our analysis concerns the growth consequences of expanding the government sector, not of creating it. However, a comparison of marginal rather than average rates changes our conclusions very little. Government and private sector investment propensities remain the same over the 1950–65 period.[71]

Such comparisons assume implicitly that increases in government expenditure are financed by withdrawing resources proportionally from private investment and consumption, leaving the private investment rate unchanged. Our knowledge of the evolving pattern of government revenue conflicts with this assumption. Despite limited detailed knowledge of sources of saving in the Peruvian private sector, we may be quite certain that the general source is income from capital. Therefore, the surprising inelasticity of tax revenues on income from capital, so unfortunate from a distributive standpoint, is not at all unfortunate from the standpoint of growth. As taxation has become more regressive in recent years, it has shifted more and more away from saving and investment and on to consumption.

These various qualifications therefore give support to the earlier conclusion: the expansion of the government sector, as it has taken place in Peru in the past twenty years, has been good for growth.[72]

TWO FINAL ISSUES

The various results of previous sections need not be restated in conclusion, but two issues touched on at different points in the paper need to be drawn together and summarized. These are the extent to which this budgetary study complements the political studies mentioned

71. The elasticity of investment expenditure with respect to total expenditure, which equals the ratio of marginal to average investment rates, was 0.972 for government and 0.975 for the private sector. However, any one of a number of small definitional changes upsets this equality between marginal rates and shows a somewhat higher rate in the government sector. These changes include increasing the span of years to 1967, using constant price data, regressing first differences, or, most significant of all, redefining investment to include education.

72. Two other factors, not dealt with in this paper, are also important for assessing the desirability of an expanded government sector. The first is possible complementarity between private and public investment, but this represents only one aspect of the second, larger issue: the relative social profitability of public and private investment in Peru.

earlier, and the extent of conflict between policies for growth and policies for distribution.

It will be remembered that the budgetary inferences drawn from the studies of domination were that the fiscal system would be regressive, probably in two discrete jumps at income levels corresponding to the transition from Indian to non-Indian and from masses to oligarchy, but that the degree of regressivity would have diminished over the years. Our statistical results give only partial confirmation to these expectations. We did find that the exclusion of the Indian from expenditure benefit was evident, even dramatic; here indeed was the fiscal manifestation of domination. The domination of masses by oligarchy was not to be seen in expenditure incidence, however, and neither aspect of domination was reflected in the present tax structure, whose wandering proportionality is not very unlike the structure of the United States or any other American country. We are left with a paradox: If an oligarchy has preponderant, dominating power, then why should it not derive greater benefit from the state mechanism which it controls?

There are four possible answers to the paradox. The first and most obvious is simply that an oligarchy does not exist. Unfortunately, this resolution may be little more than a word game; we may well say there is no oligarchy, but we are still left with the impression of nearly every social observer that all kinds of inequalities—income, influence, education—are substantially greater in Peru than in rich countries. It would be foolhardy to discard those impressions on the strength of the statistics in this paper. Nevertheless, these statistics give emphasis to the point that all non-Indian groups receive benefit from the budgetary process and therefore must have power. In this context the use of the loosely defined term domination can be deceptive, since some mechanism of accommodation must exist in a national political environment where all groups have some power, yet are not engaged in civil war.

The second possibility is that a more careful examination of incidence, particularly on the side of expenditure, would reveal progression (favoring the rich) hidden in the crudeness of present estimates. While this outcome cannot be denied, I must confess to a skeptical view of the possibility that more refined studies would change the conclusions radically.

Third, the oligarchy's benefit from governmental action may derive from economic policy measures operating outside the budget, such as those determining exchange rates, exchange freedom, and tariff protection. Although these areas are not covered in this paper, I will hazard an armchair conclusion that here, as in the field of taxation, the oligarchy's triumph is largely the negative one of keeping policies from being turned against it.

That leaves one final explanation, which seems to me the most plausible. It derives from the idea that the oligarchy's favored economic position is created and maintained by its control over natural resources, particularly land, and by its monopoly of contact with the world economy. The oligarchy is the primary beneficiary of capitalism's invasion into a traditional society, and for its purposes it has remained satisfied with a state that is merely permissive, rather than directly augmenting of oligarchic income. To the extent that the state's policies have given direct aid, this has probably occurred mostly in police and judicial administration rather than in economic and budgetary policy.

Viewed in this context, a proportional tax system in a country with income distribution as unequal as Peru's seems a substantial triumph for the upper classes. Furthermore, the triumph is greater than the mere maintenance of proportionality; the tax system has in fact become more regressive in recent decades, at precisely the period when the oligarchy is most evidently in retreat. For reasons described earlier, the oligarchy seems in little danger of attack through increased tax progression. The dangers were increased substantially when the present radical-reformist military government came to power in 1968, but even now, as the antioligarchy attack develops a momentum never before seen in Peruvian history, it is curious to see how lightly regarded tax reform is as a weapon of attack.

To be sure, the secular diminution of oligarchic power may be seen on the expenditure side of the budget, where over the decades the share devoted to educational and social purposes has risen inexorably. This is only one facet of the state's changing role, by which it has slowly become less permissive and more controlling toward the oligarchy. Outside of the budget, this evolution can be traced from the modest beginnings of social legislation in the first decades of this century, through acquiescence to the rising trade union movement and the extension of unionization to coastal farm workers.

With all these various measures, the oligarchy has retained its property and simply has had to mend its ways in labor relations. The direct attack on ownership and uses of property, particularly land, is of more recent vintage. Various measures attempted in the late 1940s were frustrated by ineffective implementation,[73] but today agrarian reform is on the march, and prospects for implentation are decidedly better. It remains to be seen, however, if land is sufficiently important in the oligarchic portfolio to make this the knockout blow Favre suggests it to be.[74]

We next come to the issue of conflict between the goals of growth and distribution. There are indeed several instances in which these goals have come into conflict, with quite opposite outcomes. On the side of taxation, the most obvious and difficult conflict has concerned the severity with which income from capital is to be taxed. In this case growth won over distribution, partly because the growth significance of unequal distribution was obvious and persuasive to policy makers and to public opinion. This is particularly the case with tax exonerations; the entrepreneur who wishes to introduce a new industry to his country, for the small consideration of not having to pay taxes, is a culture hero, and the size of his personal income after taxes does not come to issue.

On the expenditure side, growth and distribution came into conflict on the issue of teachers' salaries, and this time distribution won the day with ease, partly because the growth-promoting alternatives could not be specified. In both of these instances, the "conflict" was an intellectual dilemma which we may view in hindsight. In fact neither of these issues provoked growth-versus-distribution political debates at the time, because the alternatives being decided upon were not clearly stated.

The mechanism by which distribution-motivated expenditure affects growth objectives can be particularly pernicious. In the case of the 1964 education program mentioned previously, it was not a question of reallocating tax revenues away from growth-oriented projects. Rather, there were no tax revenues; distribution expenditure was financed by fiscal deficits which, in their ultimate effect on the economy, did far more damage to growth than one might reasonably have expected from mere tax reallocation. Inflation, balance of payments deficits, exchange speculation, credit tightening on the private sector, and a substantial cutback in private investment, caused partly by

73. For example, a 1947 law intended to improve the lot of sharecroppers resulted principally in their being expelled from the land and replaced by more centralized and capital intensive production.
74. Favre, "El desarrollo y las formas del poder oligárquico."

uncertainty, partly by unavailability of funds, and partly by domestic recession—these have all been the unhappy growth consequences in the last few years of massive, distribution-oriented expenditure programs a few years earlier.

This particular outcome was of course not an efficient one among the feasible set of growth-distribution options. In fact, we have also mentioned several instances of more efficiently chosen programs in which there was essentially no conflict of goals. This was the case, for example, for that portion of expanded educational expenditure that represented the incorporation of new resources into the sector, rather than merely the higher remuneration of already active teachers, and was also within the capacity of the tax system. It was also the case in many other smaller government investment programs, such as those involving road building and settlement in high jungle regions, or systematic assistance to small farmers on the coast.[75]

On the other hand, there are some policy outcomes which have not had favorable results for either growth or distribution. In this class I would put the continued undermining of the personal income tax system. The unfavorable distributional consequences are evident, and it is most unlikely that the beneficiary middle class groups have high marginal savings propensities.

The growth-distribution conflict exists; it crops up time and time again, in different places, under different guises. Its resolution is essentially a political rather than a technical problem, but it should be cause for comfort of technicians to see how random and inefficient some outcomes have been, and how much better served the nation would have been if technicians had done their job of spelling out options and making sure that superior opportunities were not overlooked at the moment of decision.

Comments by Daniel M. Schydlowsky

Shane Hunt offers us a fascinating analysis that goes a long way toward replacing the often heard, simple-minded view of Peru as a

75. For an analysis of four such projects, see Delbert Fitchett, "Investment Strategies in Peruvian Agriculture; Some Recent Experiences in Development Planning," Memorandum RM-4791-AID (Santa Monica, Calif.: The RAND Corporation, June 1966). Also Ralph McLean, "The Effects of Two Penetra-

country governed by a small, self-serving, well-entrenched elite. Instead there emerges the view of a country undergoing dynamic change in its political as well as its economic structure. Hunt's overall conclusion is that in this century Peru's upper class has been gradually losing political power and in addition has become successively diluted with new entrants. He uses fiscal data in a very imaginative way to support this conclusion, and while I agree with it in essence, I believe it worthwhile to bring out some additional points which elaborate the Hunt portrayal in several respects.

THE INCIDENCE OF GOVERNMENT REVENUE AND EXPENDITURE

In a small open economy such as Peru's, it is not possible to arrive at an adequate view of the redistributive effects of government operations without taking into account the very important effect of import duties on relative prices. Indeed, protection to domestic industry against competition from imports amounts to a tax on the users of such import-competing products combined with a subsidy to the respective producers. Neither this implicit tax nor the implicit subsidy appear in the government accounts, yet the production of import-competing commodities amounted in 1963 to 35 percent of the total gross value of production.[1] At a moderate 30 percent average tax subsidy the amount involved in that year is equal to 10 billion soles or approximately 75 percent of total government expenditure in 1963.

While no data is available to estimate directly the distribution of the costs and benefits of this extrabudgetary tax and subsidy, it is possible to get an indirect measure by comparing the relative prices for different commodities in Peru with the corresponding relative prices in the United States and then relate the differences to the household budgets. Table 11.11 shows the relative price in Peru of one dollar's worth of different commodities compared to one dollar's worth of average purchasing power. Assuming that Peruvian domestic prices are all equal to international prices plus or minus the relevant trade

tion Roads Recently Completed in Peru," mimeographed (Woodrow Wilson School, Princeton University, 1969).

1. The following were considered import-competing industries: food, textiles, shoes, clothing, paper, printing and publishing, rubber products, chemicals, petrochemicals, nonmetallic minerals, basic metal industries, metal products, machinery and vehicles, plastics, various manufactures. Data source: Jorge Luis Checkley, "Una tabla de insumo-producto de la economia peruana" (Lima: U.N.M. de San Marcos, 1968).

taxes, these relative prices accurately reflect the results of import protection. Table 11.11 also lists the income elasticities of demand for the various categories, and it is interesting to note that in 1960 higher relative prices were already mildly correlated with higher in-

Table 11.11: Relative Prices and Income Elasticities

Category	Prices June 1960	Income elasticity 1965	Ranks Price	Ranks Elasticity
Meat, poultry	127	0.94	5	15
Fish	84	1.03	18	13
Milk, eggs	108	1.25	10	9
Cereals	90	0.47	15	23
Fruits	138	1.43	2	4
Vegetables	66	0.86	21	18
Sugar	59	0.57	23	22
Fats, oils	70	0.87	19	17
Other foods	89	1.87	16	1
Alcohol beverages	67	0.76	20	20
Other beverages	98	0.84	12	19
Tobacco	45	1.40	24	5
Clothing	110	1.10	9	11
Footwear	108	n.a.	—	—
Textiles	132	1.31	4	7
Rent	111	1.33	8	6
Fuel, light	64	0.69	22	21
Household supplies	106	0.99	11	14
Furniture	94	1.40	13	5
Electrical appliances	108	1.27	10	8
Public transport	121	1.11	6	10
Private transport	67	1.11	20	10
Communications	90	1.50	15	3
Toilet articles	118	1.03	7	13
Drugs & medicines	136	1.04	3	12
Medical services	85	1.04	17	12
Hair dressing	93	1.03	14	13
Domestic services	136	0.89	3	16
Public entertainment	142	1.60	1	2
Books, toys, etc.	128	n.a.	—	—

Spearman Rank Correlation: .565

Sources: "A Measurement of Price Levels and the Purchasing Power of Currencies in Latin America, 1960–62," Tables 11–15, *Economic Bulletin for Latin America* 8, no. 2 (Oct. 1963), p. 195–235; "Long Term Projections of Demand for and Supply of Selected Agricultural Commodities Through 1980," Table 18, Programa de Investigaciones para el Desarrollo, Universidad Agraria, Lima, March 1968.

come elasticity. Presumably this feature has been reinforced in the subsequent tariff reforms. We can therefore conclude that the incidence of higher relative prices is in all probability more extensively borne by the higher income groups of society than by the lower ones. On the revenue side, therefore, this implicit tax appears progressive.

The allocation of the explicit subsidy is much harder to determine since we require to know not only the effective rates of protection implicit in the tariff structure but also the distribution of this protection by size group of income. An educated guess can be hazarded, however, on the basis of several independent pieces of information.

The first of these consists of data on the evolution of the capital/labor ratio and the functional income distribution. Table 11.12 shows the incremental capital/labor ratio declining rather substantially since 1951. This would lead us to expect a decrease in the relative wage rate and an increase in the share of property in domestic income unless

Table 11.12: The Incremental Capital/Labor Ratio

	Gross fixed investment 1963 prices (millions)	Current prices	Depreciation deflator (millions)	1963 prices	Net investment (millions)	Growth population (thousands)	Incremental K/L ratio
1950	7,942	652	34.3	1,901	6,041	n.a.	n.a.
1951	11,227	843	40.4	2,087	9,140	148.8	6.14
1952	12,780	962	42.7	2,253	10,527	149.9	7.02
1953	12,757	995	46.7	2,131	10,626	157.7	6.74
1954	10,230	1,278	50.8	2,516	7,714	172.0	4.48
1955	12,365	1,410	53.8	2,621	9,744	192.9	5.05
1956	14,858	1,552	58.0	2,676	12,182	214.2	5.69
1957	16,220	1,751	62.5	2,802	13,418	231.1	5.81
1958	13,888	2,043	73.4	2,783	11,105	247.5	4.49
1959	10,505	2,377	85.2	2,790	7,715	263.3	2.93
1960	13,682	3,282	89.8	3,655	10,027	278.5	3.60
1961	15,588	3,574	91.2	3,919	11,669	295.0	3.46
1962	17,288	4,121	96.7	4,262	13,026	311.9	4.18
1963	16,391	4,724	100.0	4,724	11,677	326.9	3.57
1964	17,131	5,175	104.7	4,943	12,188	340.0	3.58
1965	19,425	6,370	109.4	5,823	13,602	351.2	3.87
1966	23,755	7,846	114.7	6,840	16,915	352.6	4.80

Note: A correct computation of the incremental K/L ratio would require using labor force figures instead of population. If participation in the labor force has stayed constant or grown, however, the trend shown here is correct.

Source: Banco Central de Reserva del Perú, *Cuentas nacionales del Perú 1950–65, 1950–67,* Tables 1, 6, 7, 9.

the elasticity of substitution of labor for capital were equal to 1.0 or larger, or the import restrictions subsidized labor more than capital, or unemployment increased. On the other hand, we would expect the elasticity of substitution for existing activities to be low since underdevelopment itself implies in part a low structural flexibility and Peru's output at any one time has been to a large extent in extractive and manufacturing industry, where the machine-paced technology allows little substitution.[2] Table 11.13, however, shows that the

Table 11.13: The Share of Property Income
(millions of current soles)

	Rent	Profits	Interest	Foreign factors	Total	Domestic income[a]	Property share
1950	1,115	2,334	153	283	3,885	14,478	26.8
1951	1,291	3,300	184	183	4,958	17,966	27.6
1952	1,462	3,149	238	141	4,990	18,864	26.5
1953	1,612	2,793	234	179	4,818	20,257	23.8
1954	1,702	3,351	288	426	5,767	23,743	24.3
1955	1,867	3,447	399	663	6,376	26,273	24.3
1956	2,013	4,256	459	622	7,350	29,183	25.2
1957	2,300	4,259	600	579	7,738	31,889	24.3
1958	2,591	3,628	662	753	7,634	35,839	21.3
1959	3,062	4,328	603	1,093	9,086	41,793	21.7
1960	3,457	7,378	920	1,391	13,146	48,557	27.1
1961	3,819	7,607	1,094	1,591	14,111	55,278	25.5
1962	4,052	9,633	1,242	1,676	16,603	63,707	26.1
1963	4,253	10,263	1,626	1,809	17,951	69,266	25.9
1964	4,732	12,651	1,651	1,747	20,781	82,925	25.1
1965	5,583	15,709	1,788	1,902	24,982	97,713	25.5
1966	6,144	19,693	2,053	2,767	30,657	115,522	26.5

[a] National income plus payments to foreign factors.

Source: Banco Central de Reserva del Perú, *Cuentas nacionales del Perú 1950–65, 1950–67,* Tables 3, 6.

share of property has stayed around 25 percent (excepting the recession years 1958/59). Additionally, what scattered information is available on the Lima labor market indicates a tightening rather than increased unemployment. Thus we are forced to conclude that the

2. This is confirmed by Clague, who fitted CES production functions to twelve industries and found an elasticity of substitution greater than 1.0 only in textiles. See Christopher K. Clague, "Economic Efficiency in Peru and the U.S.," (Ph.D. diss., Harvard University, 1965), Table 6.1.1.

addition of new productive activities (some of them, tariff-protected, import-substituting ones) led to an *ex post* increase of the aggregate elasticity of substitution. This, in turn, implies a net benefit of protection to labor.

A second element of importance is the effect of tariffs on the import of foreign capital. To the extent that tariff protection induced foreign firms to establish industries that would not otherwise have existed, profits should fall relative to wages, and the tariff structure redistributes income to the lower income groups.

A third element germane to this discussion is the effect of tariff protection on the formation of labor unions. Since labor unions typically form on the basis of industrial labor and tariffs foster import-substituting industrialization, protection probably strengthens the labor union movement. In turn, stronger unions probably mean a higher share for labor of the protection-generated profits. Thus on this count also, protection appears to be redistributive in favor of the poor.

In summary, then, we can conclude that on this wider framework of analysis the Hunt conclusion of neutrality of the fiscal system should be replaced with one of probable progressivity.

THE SIZE OF THE GOVERNMENT SECTOR

In comparing the size of Peru's government sector with that of other countries, it is important to take into account that the relative prices of government services and other components of GNP vary internationally. Of the various studies cited by Hunt, only that of Simon Kuznets adequately considers this problem. As a result, the international comparisons used in the Hunt analysis understate the relative size of the Peruvian government sector.

The importance of standardizing relative prices when making this kind of comparison can be appreciated from Table 11.14, which tabulates the ratio of government consumption expenditures to GDP at domestic and U.S. prices for the nineteen Latin American republics. It will be noted that at U.S. prices the size of the Peruvian government is twice as large as at domestic prices. Furthermore its relative position in the Latin American framework changes from thirteenth to eighth.

The importance of these adjustments can also be seen in the cross-section equations for Latin America tabulated in Table 11.15. The

Table 11.14: The Size of Government in Latin America

| | *Ratio of government consumption to GDP* | |
| | | *At purchasing power parities with Latin* |
	At exchange rates	*American weights*
Argentina	.090	.183
Bolivia	.080	.194
Brazil	.153	.206
Chile	.103	.168
Colombia	.063	.115
Ecuador	.129	.243
Paraguay	.078	.149
Peru	.084	.186
Uruguay	.090	.180
Venezuela	.138	.134
Costa Rica	.119	.208
Dominican Republic	.127	.236
El Salvador	.101	.167
Guatemala	.078	.137
Haiti	.087	.144
Honduras	.098	.194
Mexico	.051	.070
Nicaragua	.083	.132
Panama	.119	.201

Source: Stanley N. Braithwaite, "Comparison of Latin American Real Incomes," Tables 7, 12, Tenth General Conference of the International Association for Research in Income and Wealth (Maynooth, Ireland, 1967).

marginal propensity to spend on government consumption increases by a third, and the elasticities show up as being on opposite sides of unity.

With uniform pricing the Peruvian system also reveals different characteristics in terms of its evolution over time. Table 11.16 shows the results of running the same regressions on data at current prices, constant prices, and U.S. prices. The differences in the results are striking. It is also worth noting that in the Latin American data there appears to be no important correlation between the share of government consumption and per capita income, i.e. the intercepts are not significantly different from zero.

Comparing the Peruvian and Latin American results, we find that at uniform prices (i.e. the same relative prices) Peru has a higher than average share of government consumption, a higher marginal propensity to supply and consume public goods, and a substantially

Table 11.15: The Size of Government Consumption in Latin America:
Cross-section Equations

Marginal propensities:

At exchange rates:

$$G = -41.57 + 0.1168 \text{ GDP} \qquad \bar{R}^2 = .821$$
$$(75.70) \quad (0.01)$$

At purchasing power
parities:

$$G = -4.38 + 0.1580 \text{ GDP} \qquad \bar{R}^2 = .825$$
$$(153.40) \quad (0.02)$$

At exchange rates:

$$G^{\text{p.cap.}} = -9.09 + 0.1314 \text{ GDP}^{\text{p.cap.}} \qquad \bar{R}^2 = .902$$
$$(3.91) \quad (0.01)$$

At purchasing power
parities:

$$G^{\text{p.cap.}} = 1.72 + 0.1650 \text{ GDP}^{\text{p.cap.}} \qquad \bar{R}^2 = .820$$
$$(9.49) \quad (0.02)$$

Elasticities:

At exchange rates:

$$\ln G = -2.36 + 1.0004 \ln \text{GDP} \qquad \bar{R}^2 = .959$$
$$(0.35) \quad (0.05)$$

At purchasing power
parities:

$$\ln G = -1.32 + 0.9368 \ln \text{GDP} \qquad \bar{R}^2 = .954$$
$$(0.36) \quad (0.05)$$

At exchange rates:

$$\ln G^{\text{p.cap.}} = -3.10 + 1.1321 \ln \text{GDP}^{\text{p.cap.}} \qquad \bar{R}^2 = .862$$
$$(0.58) \quad (0.1)$$

At purchasing power
parities:

$$\ln G^{\text{p.cap.}} = -1.6 + 0.9666 \ln \text{GDP}^{\text{p.cap.}} \qquad \bar{R}^2 = .775$$
$$(0.71) \quad (0.12)$$

Note: Standard errors in parentheses.

higher elasticity of the size of the government consumption sector. Furthermore, we have found no relation between the share of Peru's government consumption at uniform prices and the country's per capita income, thus confirming that large government has been extant for quite some time.

All the aforementioned leads to the conclusion that for some years Peru has had a substantially larger government sector than is initially apparent. This, in turn, implies that the "elite" has really had much less power in the early 1950s than is apparent even in the Hunt analysis.

EVOLUTION OF THE FISCAL SYSTEM

Hunt has chosen an unfortunate econometric specification for his general elasticity analysis. His formulation is of the following form[3]

$$\ln \frac{G}{GNP} = a_0 + a_1 \ln \frac{GNP}{P} \qquad (11.2)$$

3. Cf. Hunt, Table 11-2.

Table 11.16: The Size of Government Consumption in Peru

Marginal propensities:

Current domestic prices	$G = -639.96 + 0.1020\,GDP$ (159.59) (0.0027)	$\bar{R}^2 = .993$
Constant (1960 domestic prices	$G = 663.84 + 0.0779\,GDP$ (343.96) (0.006)	$\bar{R}^2 = .942$
Constant (1960) U.S. prices	$G = -51.07 + 0.2009\,GDP$ (41.18) (0.01)	$\bar{R}^2 = .956$

Elasticities:

Current domestic prices	$\ln G = -3.88 + 1.1341 \ln GDP$ (0.43) (0.039)	$\bar{R}^2 = .998$
Constant (1960 domestic prices	$\ln G = -0.668 + 0.8407 \ln GDP$ (0.78) (0.072)	$\bar{R}^2 = .931$
Constant (1960) U.S. prices	$\ln G = -2.33 + 1.0793 \ln GDP$ (0.44) (0.054)	$\bar{R}^2 = .976$

where G stands for government expenditure (or revenue) and P for population. It is not clear whether GNP per capita is in monetary or real terms, but the table leads one to assume the latter.

If we write this specification out fully we obtain:

$$\ln G = a_0 + (a_1 + 1)\ln GNP - a_1 \ln P \qquad (11.3)$$

or

$$\ln G = a_0 + (a_1 + 1)\ln GNP - a_1 \ln P - a_1 \ln \text{prices} \qquad (11.4)$$

whereas the usual elasticity specification is

$$\ln G = a_0^1 + (a_1^1 + 1)\ln GNP. \qquad (11.5)$$

Unfortunately a_1 will only be an unbiased estimator of a_1^1 if GNP is uncorrelated with population (and prices). This is manifestly not the case. We have therefore recomputed the elasticities using the conventional specification and tabulated the results together with the Hunt estimates in Table 11.17. As can readily be appreciated, the results diverge considerably.

The first conclusion that emerges from the new data is that the system has in fact developed in a considerably more balanced fashion than appeared from the Hunt results.

The second point of importance relates to the behavior of the profit tax. On the one hand, the new results assign it an elasticity fairly close to unity although still significantly below it. On the other

Table 11.17: GNP Elasticities of Peruvian Fiscal System, (1950–65)

	Hunt	Conventional[b]	
	Specifications[a]		
	Hunt	*Conventional*[b]	
Total government expenditure	2.15	1.27	(0.03)
Exhaustive expenditure current prices	1.72	1.17	(0.02)
Exhaustive expenditure 1963 prices	0.99	1.00	(0.05)
Total revenue	1.82	1.18	(0.02)
Indirect taxes	2.54	1.34	(0.05)
Taxes on imports	2.02	1.21	(0.07)
Turnover tax	8.70	2.76	(0.23)
Personal income tax	1.02	1.11	(0.05)
Profits tax	0.17	0.82	(0.06)

[a] See text for discussion.
[b] Standard errors in parentheses.

hand, inspection of its yearly yield series (profit tax collections/ accounting profits) show stable cyclical behavior until 1963 and a consistent drop in 1964 to 1966. These observations are confirmed by elasticity computations relating collections to profits: for 1950–63 the result is 0.99 ± 0.05; for 1950–65 it is 0.89 ± 0.05. We conclude therefrom that any tax base erosion that has taken place is of mid-1960s vintage and therefore related not to the mining law but to the industrial promotion exemptions.

The last two points together call into serious question the alleged increased regressivity of the revenue system over the postwar period. Bearing in mind that indirect taxes are themselves somewhat progressive (food and medicine are exempt) and that import duties (budgetary and extrabudgetary) have been getting increasingly progressive, it is very likely that the system on the whole has become more progressive.

On the expenditure side, the results are too aggregative to allow valid new inferences. It should be borne in mind, however, that the results of Hunt's residual analysis may be sensitive to the specification of the elasticity function. More fundamentally, the inference of political attitude from expenditure data requires the assumption of constant productivity of expenditure. This constancy has not been present where expenditure in education is concerned, as illustrated by an incident Hunt himself cites, namely the reduction of the primary school curriculum from six to five years under the Odría government. Although this measure appears directed against the lower classes, it was in fact an expenditure redistribution in their favor: the curricula of the fifth and sixth grades were almost identical, thus the latter had almost no educational productivity.[4] Eliminating sixth grade meant increasing the capacity of the primary school system by 16 percent and lowering the entrance age into the labor force. Lower income groups were the clear beneficiaries of both effects. Adjustment for this productivity difference would probably make Odría look better, but more importantly, it shifts the regression line and raises the real provision of educational services to the nation.

On the expenditure side, then, I believe further analysis would show a greater increase in regressivity over time than portrayed by Hunt.

Putting both sides of the fiscal system together, we can fairly conclude that the postwar evolution has seen an increasing redistributive activity by the government, to the benefit of the lower income groups. Translated to the political plane, this implies a continued erosion of the elite power which Hunt has shown us to have begun early in this century.

BUDGETARY POLICIES AND GROWTH

An adequate assessment of the effect of Peru's fiscal policies on its growth cannot be undertaken without specifying the alternative against which the comparison is made and exploring in depth the various private sector reactions called forth by the policy. Hunt eschews this wide framework at the outset of his paper but later explores one growth effect nevertheless: size of government and public/private savings behavior.

In carrying out the analysis, Hunt suggests very important and valuable adjustments to the conventional way of defining savings and consumption and concludes that the growth of the public sector contributed to increased investment if human capital formation is taken account of.

It is worth pointing out that this conclusion is substantially strengthened if another adjustment is made to national accounting conventions, namely the inclusion of public corporations in the government sector. Such a reclassification leaves the government with a "freely disposable income" resulting from its tax revenues and the operations surplus (or deficit) of the public enterprises (profit and

4. This author belonged to the last class to do fifth and sixth grades, and thus remembers the situation.

Table 11.18: Public and Private Expenditure Behavior

		Private					Public	
Year	Consumption	Fixed investment	Inventories	Total	Independent enterprises	Consumption	Fixed investment	Total
	(1)	(2)	(3)	(4)	(5)	(6)	(7)	(8)
1960	38,405	8,299	2,751	49,455	583	4,776	659	5,435
1961	42,960	9,425	1,930	54,315	1,640	5,938	1,228	7,166
1962	49,538	12,342	1,584	63,464	1,254	6,771	1,545	8,316
1963	57,117	12,018	1,280	70,415	2,100	7,714	993	8,707
1964	66,450	10,809	2,722	79,981	2,805	10,213	1,775	11,988
1965	82,565	13,032	2,160	97,757	3,131	12,542	3,047	15,589
1966	96,723	14,581	4,936	116,240	3,732	14,796	4,250	19,046
1967	111,109	18,841	5,861	135,811	2,866	17,670	5,101	22,771

Ratios

	Private Investment		Public Investment	
	Including Indep. Enterprises $(2+3+5)/(4+5)$	Excluding Indep. Enterprises $(2+3)/4$	Excluding Indep. Enterprises $7/8$	Including Indep. Enterprises $(5+7)/8$
1960	.232	.223	.121	.206
1961	.232	.209	.171	.326
1962	.235	.219	.186	.292
1963	.212	.189	.114	.286
1964	.197	.169	.148	.310
1965	.182	.155	.195	.330
1966	.194	.168	.223	.350
1967	.199	.182	.224	.311

Regression Parameters[a]

Marginal propensities:	.17	.14	.26	.35
Elasticities:	.78	.72	1.39	1.24

[a] equations: $I = a + bE$
$\ln I = a' + b' \ln E$
I = investment; E = expenditure

Source: Banco Central de Reserva del Perú, *Cuentas nacionales del Perú 1950–67*, Tables 2, 5.

depreciation). The private sector, on the other hand, has income equivalent to the conventional definition exclusive of the operations surplus of the public enterprises. The rationale for the reclassification of this item lies, of course, in the nature of the decision making involved. To the extent that these resources are used in a manner directly expressing public policy, they are an integral part of government expenditure. To the extent that they respond to the same incentives as private firms, the converse is true. The importance of the reclassification can be seen from Table 11.18, which tabulates the appropriate information for the period 1960–67.

There is no doubt that Hunt's analysis has been path breaking in bringing analysis and empirical data to bear on the assessment of Peruvian welfare policy. In this comment his conclusions have been amended to yield an appraisal of Peru's policy as *ex post* even more favorable to lower income groups than he portrayed it. Subsequent research will surely amend all these conclusions many times. Students of Peru's development will, however, always remain indebted to Hunt for having opened the field and set a high standard of excellence in its exploration.

PART V: SOME COMPARATIVE STUDIES

12

The Second Postwar Restructuring

BY BENJAMIN I. COHEN AND GUSTAV RANIS

Among the most pervasive of post–World War II phenomena has been the attempt of the less developed countries (LDC's) to try to achieve economic independence to supplement their recently achieved political independence. While it is, of course, hazardous to generalize about the precise nature of this phenomenon, two features seem to recur: one, the typical LDC, even if not newly independent, was formerly subject to a set of colonial economic relationships as far as her previous foreign contacts were concerned; and two, the main instrument for postwar development has been the attempt by LDC governments to achieve a fundamental restructuring of these relationships through their own actions. In short, in place of the nineteenth century colonial package of private capital, trade, know-how, and assured markets, orchestrated mainly by commercial interests in the "mother country," LDC governments now exercise their own judgment on how foreign capital, trade, and technical know-how are best organized and harnessed for national growth and economic independence.

But this effort has followed two very distinct patterns. Immediately after the war and in the first flush of independence many LDC governments attempted to restructure the colonial pattern by taking direct action in a number of markets and across a wide area of public and private activities. We may call this the first postwar restructuring. More recently, however, we have been witnessing what might best be described as an agonizing reappraisal among these governments of the effectiveness of the instruments they have brought to bear. This in turn has led to the gradual attempt in more and more countries to achieve the same basic objectives, but with more efficient tools. We may call this the second postwar restructuring.

The main purpose of this paper is to attempt to gain a fuller understanding of these two restructuring efforts by LDC governments. We proceed by first delineating very briefly the outline of the colonial heritage. Then the immediate postwar effort by LDC governments to change the colonial system is described and evaluated. Next we present a general statement of the second restructuring efforts that have been made over the past five to seven years, especially in the foreign trade sector. The following section cites a number of cases in evidence in selected countries; and the final section tries to draw some tentative conclusions from the evidence presented.

THE COLONIAL HERITAGE

The typical LDC structure inherited from the prewar period consists of three domestic production sectors: a subsistence agricultural sector devoted mainly to food production, a smaller but often vigorously growing agricultural export sector producing minerals or cash crops for the foreign market, and a small trading *cum* services sector providing the financial institutions, services, and overheads to facilitate export sector expansion.[1] The export sector utilizes the reservoir of cheap labor from agriculture—or available through immigration in Ceylon, parts of Africa, the Caribbean—to exploit its climate or raw materials in the form of fiber, tropical foods, or minerals. Inputs into this sector include food produced in the agricultural hinterland and goods and services produced by the commercialized trade *cum* services *cum* industry sector. The output of this sector flows mainly abroad as part of what has been called the colonial pattern, i.e. traditional exports are requited on current account by the importation of some simple incentive consumer goods for the workers being pulled out of agricultural subsistence, plus luxury goods for the entrepreneurial classes. To the extent that they are not consumed or repatriated, the profits from this trading pattern, augmented by new capital flows, provide for the importation of capital goods, which are mainly reinvested in the agricultural export sector or in the overheads and services that support that sector. Historically the role of the foreigner may expand from that of trader to that of entrepreneur, servicing or actually taking over the direction of much of the activity in the export sector. The service sector ministers less

1. Many LDC's, of course, have some industrial activity as well. But typically, except for Latin America, that sector is relatively small in the period under discussion.

and less to the traditional needs of the nobility or the Church and more and more to the needs of the export sector for the services of banking, shipping, insurance, warehousing, and the construction of trade-related social overhead capital (electric power, transportation, housing, etc.). In the case of countries that acquired their political independence relatively early, e.g. in Latin America, there also was some turning to domestic industrial activity before World War II— largely in response to the collapse of export markets during the Great Depression.

The main involvement of the large and virtually stagnant agricultural hinterland during all this is to provide labor and food for the agricultural export sector and in return to receive incentive consumer goods (cloth, kerosene, shoes, radios) directly from abroad. As long as there is anticipation of continuing profitable export opportunities, profits are likely to be reinvested in the service and/or export sector. To the extent that prospects are less bright, profits may be repatriated, but in any case, excepting Latin America in particular, relatively little domestic investment is undertaken that does not bear directly or indirectly on the profitability of traditional production *cum* export activity. While in this fashion the enclave export sector continues to grow in response to the foreign market, the domestic economy experiences little structural change. There is relatively little tendency for the expansion of a domestically oriented industrial sector, little tendency to stimulate major increases in productivity in the domestically oriented agricultural sector, and hence little opportunity for growth of these two sectors in a mutually reinforcing fashion.

THE FIRST POSTWAR RESTRUCTURING

Given this rough sketch of the usual initial conditions, it is clear that the typical post–World War II LDC government would try to gain full control of the critical flows in the economy to ensure that the proceeds of traditional agricultural export sales abroad would not be automatically reinvested for the exclusive benefit of that sector, and that the domestic industrial sector would be given a new order of importance. With little relevant theory to fall back upon and no possibility at all of calling a moratorium on the difficult policy choices that clearly had to be made, most governments of less developed countries responded to the common problem in somewhat similar ways. They saw the issue basically through (early) Prebisch eyes; i.e. with a mixture of concern about unfavorable foreign demand conditions for traditional agricultural exports and a firm belief in the dynamic learning processes associated with the growth of a domestically oriented, import-substituting, modern industrial structure.

Therefore they sought ways and means for the government to intervene to restructure the flow of resources in behalf of long-term national development needs and away from the short-term private profiteers, at home and abroad, associated with the colonial pattern. This meant, first of all, assessing total resource availabilities that could be counted on, both domestic and foreign, the latter in the form of government-to-government aid rather than private commercial investment; and, secondly, deploying these as effectively as possible in pursuit of some overall set of national objectives, e.g. a politically determined minimum growth rate. In this process every LDC government essentially faces the same problem: how to organize most effectively the human and natural resources, actual and potential, of the particular geographic entity under its control, for purposes of growth. In virtually all cases this led to a more or less conscious and more or less formal attempt to plan for economic development, ranging from the simple adding up of ministerial investment budgets to fairly sophisticated five-year plans complete with notions of what the private sector should be asked, induced, or coerced to do.

All such efforts clearly bear the consensus that government can and should provide social and economic overheads, guarantee a minimum of law and order, and establish all the other major so-called basic preconditions of development; but there is much less consensus on either the ideal division of labor between the public and the private sectors in directly productive activities or how to organize the private sector, i.e. how to determine exactly what it should do and whether to induce it or order it to take such actions as are considered socially desirable. Clearly many LDC governments come to these questions with strong ideological convictions as to which industries must be in the public sector; moreover, there is a wide area of choice on how to try to effect "desired" actions in the private sector. In fact there exists a virtually continuous spectrum with respect to each of these dimensions, along which the typical less developed, mixed economy tries to find a comfortable resting place. Neither the law-and-order-only, laissez faire prescription of the textbooks, at one extreme, nor government ownership of all the means of production, at the other, has had real world relevance in the vast majority of the countries with which we are concerned. In practice each country determines the dividing line between the public and private sector in its own unique fashion, considering such elements as the ability or willingness of private capital to come forward, the existence of "critical" industries, the nature of colonial experience with private capital, or other, sometimes ideological, reasons. In spite of some differences in conditions, and larger ones in rhetoric, the differences in actual public/ private mixes have not been startling across LDC's or over time. More interesting is the exercise of real choices between the use of direct and indirect controls to affect actions in what has been left to the private sector, e.g. choices between tariffs and quantitative restrictions; and between the direct allocation of credit in the presence of very low interest rates and its allocation as a consequence of interactions in the credit market; choices between, in short, having government policy essentially work through imperfect markets or attempting to displace these markets.

In the early postwar period, most LDC's opted not only for a relatively expansive definition of what should ideally be in the public sector but also for substantial direct controls over the private sector. Starting with the usual pattern of colonial resource flows and the goal of redirecting the proceeds from traditional exports—plus net foreign capital inflows—into industry and the overheads supporting that industry, the tools most frequently used were exchange controls to siphon off export earnings via the compulsory surrender of foreign exchange and the allocation of import licenses to socially desirable projects in overheads and industry. Domestic credit was similarly rationed out for these purposes at low interest rates. With government budgets typically in deficit and inflationary pressures building up, the resulting increasingly overvalued exchange rates served to subsidize importers and those who were operating the new industrial structure and to penalize agriculture and exporters.

Basic to this decision on the choice of instruments was the feeling that development could now somehow be "ordered" by the same people who had previously succeeded in achieving political change. Underlying it was the fundamental distrust of profits and the private sector, foreign or domestic, because these were somehow associated with and carried the stigma of colonialism which stood to benefit mainly the export enclave and the mother country. Even less developed countries that did not profess to be socialist in orientation were strongly nationalist and provided strong support for any even halfway intelligent autarkic policy.

Moreover, there was in operation a strong identification of industrialization with development. While it is clear that successful growth ultimately means industrialization—in terms of the well-known pressures of demand as well as in terms of an economy's improving skill base—the fact that the causation does not necessarily run from industrialization to successful development was largely ignored. The basic fact that an economy saddled with a large and preponderant agricultural hinterland must somehow devise ways and means of enlisting its support as a fueling device for the industrialization effort was overlooked. Once there was a commitment to controls, coupled with the realization of the difficulty of making decisions relating to large numbers of widely dispersed decision makers in industry or agriculture, the logical conclusion was for the civil service "to do what was feasible," i.e. to allocate resources to the public sector and the large-scale private sector and to neglect would-be claimants outside of this rather narrow magic circle. Also playing a role was the normal lack of understanding or sympathy by an educated, urban-oriented civil service for peasants, accompanied by the overall feeling that anything small-scale, second hand, or labor intensive belonged to a discredited colonial past, and that it is the task of those who build for the future to concentrate on the latest, the most modern, and the most Western techniques and output mixes.

As a consequence of all these factors, much of the postwar expansion in LDC output took place in the large-scale industrial sector in accordance with an import substitution policy with varying degrees of technological complexity—although even here daring jumps to fairly sophisticated production functions were often attempted at an early stage. There is no need to document the details of this import substitution via overvalued exchange rate *cum* exchange controls and deficit financing syndrome. Rapid rates of industrialization could, of course, be achieved in this fashion, but they were purchased at a high price:

1. As we have already noted, the first restructuring tends to discriminate against traditional exports, since a local producer can acquire more local currency by saving a dollar of imports than by earn-

ing a dollar of exports. At the same time little incentive exists for the development of new export industries, while the old may be discriminated against as well.

2. There results a nonoptimal composition of imports for any given level of total imports, since imports are allocated on the basis of bureaucratic decisions rather than by the marketplace.

3. The licensing of imports tends to lead to excess capacity in the economy. While excess capacity is not a logical consequence, it is in fact ubiquitous because a firm's license for imported raw materials is customarily linked to its "rated" capacity, which is usually defined conservatively. A firm does not, therefore, necessarily have the option of expanding output by running a second shift; it must expand its plant. Moreover, in many LDC's a "good year" or two, due say to a windfall in export prices, leads to a temporary relaxation of import controls. Resulting bursts of industrial expansion are then followed by exchange shortages, a return to controls, an inability to provide the necessary raw materials and spare parts, and consequently further idleness of capital stock and an ever more highly inefficient production structure.

4. Import licensing leads to larger than ideal inventories. While licensing gives the government more control than does the marketplace over the level of total imports, individual firms have less certainty about acquiring the amount of imports necessary to achieve the most profitable output level in the next licensing period since profitability is not given much consideration in the allocation of licenses.

5. The control system absorbs the time of a large group of talented people, both those in the government who administer it and those in the private sector who try to get around it. Rewards come from having the power to allocate and receive little slips of paper, not from successful entrepreneurship or efficient management.

6. Import licensing leads to excessively capital-intensive production for those firms lucky enough to get the licenses (this is in addition to the higher capital intensity resulting from the pressures on firms to expand their plants rather than run extra shifts). This undervaluation of imports is coupled with the usual practice of aid donors of emphasizing the financing of the import content of capital projects, and with the preferential tariff treatment normally accorded capital goods.

7. With past output frequently the basis for receiving licenses, it is difficult for new firms to get into the act. Small firms especially are discriminated against since they cannot command the attention of the overworked bureaucracy or compete with large firms in keeping full-time personnel in the capital to watch and influence the allocation of import licenses.

8. When receipt of an import license per se bestows a sizable windfall profit and competition from other domestic producers and imports is strictly controlled, the inducements for static efficient production and for dynamic technological change are minimal.

9. Agriculture is usually neglected, in terms of both the direct attention paid to it and, more importantly, the incentives provided by the price structure. Ultimately this sector, instead of being a major propelling device, turns out to be a major drag on the economy, since it often becomes incapable even of keeping up with population increase, not to speak of freeing workers for industrial growth, without running into food shortages and prematurely rising wages. As the terms of trade turn against industry, imports of food become necessary even in areas that had traditionally been food exporting.

10. The development process is fueled mainly by the reinvestment of industrial profits supplemented by foreign aid. To the extent that any savings are squeezed out of agriculture they are transferred to the large-scale importing and industrialist groups enjoying substantial growth under hothouse conditions.

11. Finally, to round out this description of the normal landscape under the first restructuring, five to ten years after the big push for industrialization has gotten under way, one typically encounters a continuing employment lag—output elasticities of industrial employment of around .3—or high labor productivity on a very small base abetted by an artificially high propensity to import capital-intensive technology in place of the innovative use of indigenous labor.

It is difficult to come up with a quantitative measure of the costs associated with this system. There exists, however, scattered indirect evidence on this point. Based on a sample of ten industries, Anne Krueger estimated that import-substituting industries in Turkey used 20 to 75 lira to save a dollar of imports, and export industries 8 to 14 lira to earn a dollar of exports.[2] In a study of Chile's automobile

2. Anne O. Krueger, "Some Economic Costs of Exchange Control: The Turkish Case," *Journal of Political Economy* 74 (October 1966), Table 3, column 5.

industry, Johnson estimated that about 12 escudos were needed to save a dollar of imports at a time when the official exchange rate was 2 escudos per dollar.[3] Lewis estimated that Pakistani manufactures (mainly import substitutes) received about 40 percent more rupees per dollar than agricultural goods (mainly exports) in the early 1960s.[4]

Such a disequilibrium system soon begins to have its own life and becomes increasingly difficult to abandon. On the one hand, the industrial importing interests become more and more entrenched and accustomed to making large windfall profits. Secondly, not only does the civil service have absolute power but it is able to supplement its income substantially as *sub rosa* payments are required to grease the wheels of progress. Thirdly, emotional residues of the rejected heritage of colonial-type private enterprise often continue to have a stranglehold on the freedom of decision makers, with officials, above all, exercising care to avoid the accusation that they are about to "give away" the country's resources once again—either to foreigners or to domestic profiteers. Perhaps the most vicious of the many LDC vicious circles is the self-fulfilling prophecy of the either absent or antisocial entrepreneur: government policies inhibit private entrepreneurs, thereby leading governments into a more and more active and repressive role. Finally there should be cited the generalized Prebisch-type fears that participation in the world economy is bound to work to the disadvantage of the individual LDC and that it therefore must protect itself via extreme methods of insulation and autarky.

Of course, there exist honest concerns about the dissipation of resources if the control system were ever to be dismantled. Once controls have been instituted and new ones added on top of old ones it becomes increasingly difficult for civil servants—with the best intentions—to know just what would happen if parts of the structure were dismantled. There exist real fears of a complete collapse, with respect to both foreign exchange availabilities and domestic budgetary resources, once the gates are opened to the pressures of the marketplace. Even though there is usually a realization that efficiency may

3. Leland J. Johnson, "Problems of Import Substitution: The Chilean Automobile Industry," *Economic Development and Cultural Change* (January 1967), p. 209.
4. Stephen R. Lewis, Jr., "Effects of Trade Policy on Domestic Relative Prices: Pakistan, 1951–1965," *American Economic Review* 58 (March 1968), Table I.

not be at its highest in the wake of the first restructuring effort, there is also a strong belief that only as long as the situation is physically controlled can the government, in effect, be sure it knows the full weight of the claims on its foreign exchange and financial resources and can thus deal with them effectively.

In short, any arguments for a reversal of the policies of the first postwar restructuring need to be strong enough to overcome substantial resistance. Such a reversal does not, in fact, have a chance unless and until the government concerned, and those aiding it from abroad, become aware of the fact that the costs of these policies, in terms of growth foregone, are not only high but prohibitively so.

Such an awareness has grown considerably in the less developed world during the past half a dozen years or so. Policy makers have been forced to note that per capita income growth in the LDC's as a whole declined from a rate of 2.5 percent during 1950–55 to 1.8 percent in 1955–60, while the annual rate of export earnings declined from 4.2 percent to 2.9 percent. They have been forced to conclude that the dynamic changes expected from a forced draft industrialization program remained on the horizon while agriculture languished and unemployment and underemployment mounted. Increasingly, therefore, two opinions have gained currency in recent years: first, that the "cheap" import substitution possibilities have become exhausted and that the LDC must turn to export promotion instead; and second, that the problem of enlisting the agricultural sector in the domestic development effort must be faced directly and soon.

Most mixed economy LDC's are not able to squeeze out a sufficiently large development effort to be able to disregard a low quality of effort. This sets them off from the Soviet-type economies which, incidentally, are themselves beginning to feel the need to trade quantity for quality. The growing realization that successful development may require a different kind of restructuring usually comes down to a switch in policies by which the government tries to affect private sector actions. In other words, the conventional wisdom about the mainsprings of growth is undergoing gradual amendment, and it is recognized that policies must be altered accordingly. There exists a growing appreciation that the controlled economy syndrome of overvalued exchange rates, import controls, and a highly differentiated credit market, all geared to favoring public, as well as large-scale private, import-substituting industries, has tended to lose for the LDC the chance to harness a large proportion of its economic agents to the development effort. If the scarce energies of officialdom can be freed from patching up an ever more cumbersome and complicated control system, and if the undoubtedly even more precious private energies can be freed from the game of evading these same controls, the entire development effort can be put on a new track. Reassessment of the capacity of the public sector to either manage or directly control widely dispersed activities becomes inevitable—not only in terms of static allocative efficiency, but also, and more importantly, in terms of dynamic participation and innovational behavior patterns.

LDC governments realize that they must continue to try to tap the colonial flows and reorient them, but also that there are alternative, more efficient ways of doing so. While very much remaining at center stage, they are therefore seeking a better orchestration of the large supporting cast in the private sector. Thus, while the restructuring of the colonial pattern remains a major objective, more and more attention is being paid not only to the improved allocation of the imported resources purchased with traditional exports—and supplemented by foreign aid—but also to the aforementioned dynamic aspects involving the incentives and energies of the economy's decision makers, public and private. If agriculture and medium- and small-scale industry are to be mobilized, this cannot be done effectively either by government ownership or by direct controls over resource allocation—if for no other reason than the sheer physical impossibility of reaching the millions of actors concerned. As a consequence, mobilization via policies that work increasingly through the market is gradually coming into vogue in the developing world. This means that the catalytic role of government, rather than its resources capture and reallocation role, is the really critical element.

We intend to analyze in somewhat greater detail the nature of this second post–World War II restructuring effort, especially with respect to the foreign trade dimension. It is well recognized that any liberalization or opening up of the economy to broader participation through the market mechanism requires policy changes in a number of linked and interrelated sectors. The market for credit, for example, is closely linked and complementary to the foreign exchange market. However, while we clearly should not be doctrinaire about which particular sector is likely to be *the* bottleneck sector impeding progress, the foreign trade sector is inevitably high on any priority list, partly because foreign trade often plays a substantial role (up to 25 percent of gross domestic product) and partly, and more importantly, because even in the large, domestically oriented economies, such as India, trade may provide a very important element of residual flexibility for a very tightly constrained economic system. Moreover, it can be said with some assurance that the distortions brought about by misdirected, if well-intentioned, government control policies are usually most flagrant here. It is in any case an empirical fact that real world liberalization efforts in the LDC's have customarily been approached sequentially, sector by sector, with foreign trade—the sector that usually "pinches" the most—receiving early attention.

While the realization that a second restructuring is required to improve performance must be reached by LDC governments themselves, foreign aid can and does help. If aid donors and at least some segments of the aid recipient's decision makers are in agreement on the substance of the argument—e.g. that a more broadly based participation in development is necessary, and specifically, that liberalization of the foreign trade sector would constitute a substantial move in that direction—the basis for the required second restructuring can be laid. The ability to persuade other relevant decision makers of the merits of the case may then make the difference. Just as clearly, imposing a condition on aid without such full prior understanding and agreement on what needs to be done to serve the recipient's own development interests is not only precarious but almost sure to fail.

There are, of course, those who say that even such persuasion may verge on intervention in the recipient country's internal affairs. But unwillingness to intervene on behalf of policy changes that are mutually agreed on as necessary and desirable—even if that agreement is not unanimous—also constitutes intervention, namely on behalf of the status quo. It is not in the interest of the taxpayers of either the donor or the recipient country to support a development program whose effectiveness is undermined by the unwillingness to change policy.

Foreign aid can play three distinct, if related, roles in this context. In the first instance, a certain volume of aid is often required in the political sense to permit a free and open discussion of changes in LDC government policies, for example, those affecting the foreign trade sector. Without such material evidence of intentions to participate in financing the overall development program, it is difficult to raise questions with the recipient on matters of overall government policy. A second use of aid may be in the context of more specific technical assistance or a capital project. For example, an economic advisory team to help determine the precise nature of the policy changes required, or the creation of financial intermediaries to facilitate them, represent ways of bringing to bear the outside resources to eliminate specific bottlenecks on a sector-by-sector basis as needed to implement any agreed-upon restructuring strategy. In the third instance, aid can serve a very important role in putting to rest, or at least allaying, the fears of those who worry about the resource dissipation that might result from a liberalization package. Clearly, the volume of resources required for this third purpose, strictly speaking, does not have to be in addition to the aid needed to obtain a seat at the discussion table or to eliminate bottlenecks from specific projects; but its intent is somewhat different, namely, to provide the assurance that, if there are shortfalls in tax receipts from tariffs or if foreign exchange reserves are threatened by liberalization, additional aid will be available to serve as a shock absorber. These fears may, in fact, be largely psychological since, in the textbook sense, the adoption of any particular policy package, say a shift from quantitative restrictions to tariffs, does not have to imply a larger volume of imports; nor does any particular change in structure have to imply a lower tax intake. But there clearly exist real problems of timing and adjustment and, perhaps even more importantly, reassurance for those those who are taking the political risks inherent in making such changes.

In this fashion less developed countries have increasingly come to the realization, partly on their own and partly with the help of foreign experts, that a change in restructuring policy is needed to improve the quality of the overall growth performance. The first restructuring effort was substantially in error precisely because it failed to set as its goal the full mobilization of the entire economy. The question of what particular changes make sense, especially in the area of foreign trade, still needs to be examined.

THE SECOND POSTWAR RESTRUCTURING

In recent years import liberalization has played an increasingly important role in the attempt to reverse the distortions of past import-substitution policies and to reintroduce some (but not all) of the discarded competitive elements into the developing economy. Most often, this is linked with movement toward a more realistic exchange rate either via a *de jure* or *de facto* devaluation and (possibly) additional effort toward direct export promotion. We will be concerned here mainly with the import liberalization phenomenon, though we recognize that such liberalization is frequently coupled with devaluation as the country tries to move away from its initial disequilibrium position.[5]

One place to start is with a relevant definition of import liberalization. It is quite clear from the sparse literature on the subject—confined mainly to government reports and foreign aid analyses—that there is a good deal of confusion about the precise meaning of the term. Many less developed countries like to think of import liberalization simply as "more imports." Recognizing that excess capacity constitutes a waste of resources—and that more planned imports may imply more foreign assistance—import liberalization is often understood to mean simply more "liberal" import allocations of raw materials and spare parts. Clearly, *ceteris paribus,* any industry operating substantially below capacity is likely to be a very high cost industry; the enhanced ability to bring capacity up to more normal levels will reduce unit costs and permit more of the existing industrial structure to become an efficient contributor to the economy. It should be noted, however, that initial "wrong" decisions on the mix of industrial products and technology are not necessarily solved by more generous current import allocations. If import liberalization means nothing more than adding more wine to leaky bottles, it may not be the most effective way of increasing the competitiveness and efficiency of the developing economy.

A second definition of import liberalization goes beyond the mere notion of "more imports" by emphasizing the partial dismantling of import controls either by broadening quotas or by permitting increased competition in at least some industries for raw materials and spare parts on an open general license (OGL) basis. The former provides more flexibility as to precisely what to procure within broad categories; the latter assures a larger total volume of imported spare parts and raw materials—at a price; both provide substantial benefits in letting the more efficient component of the existing industrial complex obtain bottleneck requirements and thus introduce an important competitive presence into the industrial hothouse. This means that,

5. See C. P. Kindleberger, "Liberal Policies vs. Controls in the Foreign Trade of Developing Countries," AID Discussion Paper no. 14, Office of Program Coordination (April 1967), for a relevant discussion of devaluation. See also Richard N. Cooper's contribution to this volume.

among the (typically) several hundred licensed importers and the existing large-scale claimants to industrial licenses, market pressures begin to have an increasing "bite," and the incentives for enhancing efficiency begin to make themselves increasingly felt.

This is about as far as most of the developing countries seem to like to go, at least initially. Even if there exists a certain conviction about the merits of competitive pressures, it seldom extends to countenancing any real threat to the existing industrial structure from new investors; thus most are willing to permit a dismantling of controls with respect to capital imports, as opposed to raw materials and spare parts, only at a later stage. This, of course, makes difficult the desirable access of potential new entrepreneurs who want to "build a better mousetrap." In some cases, this unwillingness to permit capital goods to be imported on a competitive basis, with all comers, large or small, new or old, participating, reflects the civil service's notion that "liberalization is fine but we must first fill in capacity and be in a position to confine it to the 'priority' industries." In other words, lip service is paid to the notion of enhancing the scope of the market mechanism in allocating resources, while great care continues to be taken to ensure that none of the existing firms is, in fact, hurt. Moreover, intermediate or final consumer goods being simultaneously produced in the country are seldom included. There are many instances, as a consequence, in which the expansion of open general licensing and free lists is accompanied by a growing prohibited or ban list— or prohibitive tariffs based on a "law of similars"—to provide absolute protection when injury can be claimed as a consequence of the importation.

In the next section we shall analyze the experience of a number of specific aid-recipient countries that have attempted some restructuring via import liberalization. While there are many LDC's that have experienced devaluation, there are still only a few even partly documented cases of full devaluation/liberalization packages. One reason for this is the difficulty of establishing whether or how much liberalization has, in fact, occurred. The usual way of ascertaining whether quantitative controls are more or less restrictive is for the investigator to get the feel of the situation by talking to businessmen and officials, but this approach is not very objective. A theoretically preferable way is to measure the discrepancy between domestic market prices of importables and the C.I.F. plus tariff price; any discrepancy can be

attributed to the check on imports imposed by the quantitative restrictions. This approach has the obvious difficulty of requiring reliable price data.

While it would clearly be helpful to have unambiguous criteria
for measuring the success or failure of such restructuring efforts in
different countries, the literature provides little help for assessing an
LDC devaluation that is accompanied by "trade liberalization" and/or
a large inflow of foreign capital. In theory such a devaluation might
not lead to any increase in the general price level even in the short
run for three reasons: (1) the inflow of extra capital will permit a
larger volume of imports, thus offsetting the initial increase in import
price; (2) even if the volume of imports does not immediately increase, domestic prices need not rise if decontrol of imports accom-
panies the devaluation and effects a change in market structure, because the increase in the C.I.F. prices of imports, if not passed on,
simply cuts into the importers' monopoly profits; (3) with time the
economy will certainly operate more efficiently and so produce more
goods with a fixed volume of resources; with money supply and ve-
locity constant, prices may fall.[6] Aside from price changes, another
criterion for evaluating restructuring might be the extent to which
excess capacity is reduced, or exports rise, or savings are affected, as
fiscal charges replace quantitative controls on imports. Kindleberger
has suggested three preconditions for a successful devaluation/liber-
alization package: (1) an elastic supply of foodstuffs, i.e. a good
harvest, (2) an elastic short-run supply of imported raw materials so
that output—especially of export goods—can expand rapidly, and (3)
a political consensus that the policy package is a wise one.[7] This last
factor might be measured by the change in money wage rates following adoption of the package.

Even if most people agreed that a devaluation/liberalization package would make a system economically better off at some distant
point in the future than it would otherwise have been, it is, of course,
also helpful to know how long the transition will take and what the
immediate consequences will be. The countries examined below were
chosen with the hope of illuminating somewhat the preconditions for
success, the measurement of success, and the nature of the transition

6. E. Sohmen, "The Effect of Devaluation on the Price Level," *Quarterly
Journal Economics,* May 1958, pp. 273–83.
7. Kindleberger.

to an improved situation in the wake of the second restructuring effort. With some exceptions the analysis is based on data and observations of 1968 vintage.

SOME CASE STUDIES

Pakistan

Pakistan presented a picture of virtual stagnation during the 1950s. Agricultural production was unable to keep up with population growth; exports, relying almost exclusively on traditional raw jute and cotton, were sluggish and declined through the decade; the only sector that was really forging ahead was large-scale industry, much of it in the public sector Pakistan Industrial Development Corporation, which grew at more than 50 percent annually.

With the beginnings of substantial aid flows in the late 1950s, imports on the average amounted to about 12 percent of GNP, exports to about 6 percent. Domestic savings averaged in the neighborhood of 5 percent. Approximately 50 percent of the First Five-Year Plan (1955–60) development program was financed from abroad. An increasingly overvalued exchange rate behind tight import and exchange controls completed this picture of a rather typical first restructuring effort.

In 1959 the government of Pakistan first began liberalizing its import system by allowing exporters to import an amount equal to a certain fraction (depending on the type of export) of their nontraditional export earnings; the resulting export bonus vouchers could be sold at a premium and used to import any good on a specified bonus list, especially raw materials and spare parts. Thus the scheme amounted to a *de facto* devaluation in the neighborhood of 5 to 10 percent. By 1963 imports under the export bonus scheme amounted to about 7 percent of total private sector imports, which in turn constituted about 70 percent of total imports. Moreover, in mid-1960, an Open General License system was introduced allowing newcomers without previous import records to import for the first time; a system of "repeat licensing" was instituted, with import licenses automatically renewed upon proof of utilization of initial allocations. By the end of 1963 imports entering under the Open General License

8. Philip Thomas, "Import Licensing and Import Liberalization in Pakistan, Critical Evaluation," mimeographed (1965), p. 78. The above description of Pakistan's licensing system draws heavily on Thomas's work.

system accounted for another 14 percent of total private imports.[8] Thus by 1963 about 15 percent of total imports had been liberalized.

In January 1964 four major iron and steel items were placed on a so-called free list (i.e. completely unrestricted imports) and another fifty items were added in July 1964. By the end of 1964 such free list items accounted for 26 percent of total imports and for the bulk of imported raw materials. As goods were placed on the free list, relevant tariffs and other fiscal charges were increased by an average of 13 percent.

With more than 40 percent of total imports liberalized in one way or another, and foreign assistance levels simultaneously increased by substantial amounts, the annual level of imports almost tripled between 1959 and 1964. Single shift capacity in use (based on a survey of sixty-five plants) rose from 53 percent in the second half of 1963 to 76 percent in the second half of 1964 and to 82 percent in the first quarter of 1965;[9] industrial production rose by 12 percent (seasonally adjusted) from the third quarter of 1963 to the first quarter of 1965.

The advent of the 1965 Indo-Pakistan War, combined with the interruption of aid flows and bad harvests, interrupted the liberalization trend and led to a temporary tightening of controls. With the end of hostilities, the decline in budgetary pressures, the resumption of aid, and, most importantly, the return to good harvests (especially during the last couple of years), many additional raw materials, intermediate products, and spare parts were moved from the license to a cash-*cum*-bonus basis (half the import price at par and half at the bonus rate), i.e. approximately 170 percent of par. By 1968 only 20 percent of private imports were still being directly licensed.

Coincident with freer access to imports by new and smaller firms was the government's withdrawal after 1960 from forced procurement at artificially low prices in the major food crops, thus permitting prices to rise, and its concentration instead on a buffer stock stabilization program. With minimum prices guaranteed to producer, price ceilings maintained via the infusion into the market of Public Law 480 fed stocks, and fertilizer subsidies, the terms of trade improved substantially for agriculture; the incentives were "right" for tubewells to be installed, other crop practices to be improved, and substantial

9. Based on an AID survey cited in paper by Walter P. Falcon and Stephen R. Lewis, Jr., "Economic Policy in Pakistan's Second Plan," mimeographed (1966), p. 13.

increases in agricultural productivity to be registered. Perhaps the most notable example of the pervasive effects on improved resource allocation, at least partially attributable to the import liberalization program that began in 1958, was the dramatic rise in private tube-well installations in West Pakistan. Although unforeseen in government plans, 32,000 such private tubewells had been installed by 1965. The pumps required were produced domestically by small engineering firms, using imported pig iron which had not been obtainable in the absence of import liberalization. While other policies made tubewells profitable, import liberalization made them possible. Falcon and Gotsch estimate that "private tubewells accounted for about one-fourth of the total 27 per cent increase in the value of crop output" between 1960/61 and 1964/65.[10] As a consequence of all this, foodgrain production, which had been growing at 1–2 percent annually in 1950–60, spurted ahead to a 4 percent annual clip during 1960–65 and near 5 percent toward the end of that period. Moreover, during the last few years the massive impact of the new "miracle" seeds, Mexican wheat and, though still to a lesser extent, IRRI rice, has swamped all else. West Pakistan wheat production in 1970 is expected to reach 170 percent of 1964–65 levels, and in the East rice production has been growing at better than 5 percent annually. Self-sufficiency is at hand; in fact, fears of oversupply at present price relationships are now making themselves felt. But the drastic improvement of input/output relationships that marked the Green Revolution would not have been possible, certainly not in such a short span of time, in the absence of a more open and restructured economy. Agriculture's terms of trade had been adjusted, fertilizer distribution had moved into private channels, and the water supply had been rendered flexible via import liberalization. In many ways it can thus be said that the agricultural corner had been substantially turned before the new technology assumed major significance; and, more importantly, that it was the very change in policies that permitted the rapid diffusion of that new technology once it arrived.

Moreover, the substantial rise in agricultural productivity provided a fillip to ancillary industries, e.g. the increased demand for pumps led to a general mushrooming of small scale industry in the Punjab. In the small town of Daska, West Pakistan, for example, where there had existed hardly any machine tool production in 1961, by mid-

10. Walter P. Falcon and Carl H. Gotsch, "Agricultural Development in Pakistan: Lessons from the Second-Plan Period," mimeographed (1966), p. 14.

1963 there were 120 machine shops producing diesel engines for tubewell construction.

In this mutually self-reinforcing fashion agricultural surpluses financed the growth of decentralized nonagricultural production activities which in turn provided the physical inputs and the material incentives for further agricultural productivity increase. Moreover, the industrial sector itself began to diversify increasingly. Exports of nontraditional commodities rose by 89 percent between 1959 and 1964, accounting for 60 percent of the total by 1964. This compares with a growth in raw jute and cotton exports of only 21 percent over the same period. The change in aggregate performance, from negligible per capita income increases in the late 1950s to increases in the neighborhood of 3 percent recently, and on what seems to be a sustained basis, is quite remarkable.

Admittedly, it would be foolish to attempt to simply lay this success at the doorstep of liberalization in foreign trade and agriculture. The availability of substantial doses of foreign aid was clearly also of major importance in giving the confidence required to dismantle some of the control structure.

In fact there are some who concluded that

> the immediate consequences of the 1964 actions on industrial output in Pakistan were much more the result of the increase in the level of commodity imports than of any change in their allocation. Given time, the abandonment of licensing procedures would no doubt have brought market forces more effectively into play. As events conspired, however, the trade liberalization measures were one of the casualties of the Indo-Pakistan conflict.[11]

But liberalization and growth have survived that conflict, as well as bad monsoons and interruptions in the subsequent aid flows. The additional financial resources gave the government the ability and, more importantly, the confidence to initiate the second restructuring in the early 1960s. The effects of initial liberalization in helping to make possible the near tripling of the agricultural growth rate and in opening up new vistas for farmers via nonagricultural investment

11. Edward S. Mason, *Economic Development in India and Pakistan* (Harvard Center for International Affairs, 1966), p. 45.

opportunities and incentive consumer goods cannot easily be over-stated. Once these mutually reinforcing growth processes had been begun, the economy's momentum, at least until very recent political events, has apparently been sufficient to carry the economy forward in spite of a number of rather formidable exogenous shocks.

India

India can be said to have adhered somewhat longer to the first re-structuring philosophy than her neighbor on the Subcontinent. How-ever, in June 1966 India devalued the rupee by 58 percent. At the same time selective tariffs were reduced by varying amounts so that the C.I.F. plus tariff rupee price of at least some imports immediately rose by only an estimated 34 percent.[12] On the export side the deval-uation was accompanied by the imposition of export taxes and the abolition of all export subsidies on some traditional exports having the effect that jute manufactures, for example, received a new effec-tive exchange rate only 16 percent higher than the old one. For non-traditional manufactured export items, the government abolished one kind of export subsidy (import entitlements) and introduced in its stead—with some delay—three categories of straight cash subsidies, so that the new effective exchange rate increased from 11 percent (for an item that formerly got a 75 percent import entitlement and now has a 10 percent cash subsidy) to 64 percent (for an item that formerly got a 20 percent import entitlement and now has a 20 per-cent cash subsidy).[13]

Along with the *de jure* devaluation, the tariff changes, the imposi-tion of export taxes, and changes in the form and amount of export subsidies, the Indian government introduced an import liberalization scheme for fifty-nine industries, covering between 70 and 80 percent of the output of the "organized" industrial sector. In these fifty-nine industries import licenses were to be issued "freely" for raw materials and spare parts. Moreover, certain raw materials were placed on

12. Philip S. Thomas, "The 1966 Devaluation and Import Liberalization in India," mimeographed (1966), Table 1.
13. Ibid., Table 2. These effective exchange rates do not take into account the increase in production costs resulting from the higher price of Indian im-ports. For example, the jute industry was granted a subsidy on imported raw jute following devaluation.

open general license, with no restrictions on the amount that could be imported.

This package of policies can clearly be viewed as an effort to move in the direction of the second type of restructuring. The objectives were partly to simplify the previous export subsidy scheme and import control system but also to raise the C.I.F. plus tariff price of imports and then allow the marketplace an increasing role in determining the composition of at least certain kinds of imports, and to enhance the relative profitability of exports over import substitutes.

Based on a survey of 140 industries, one study estimated that in 1964 Indian industry was running at about 82 percent of "desirable" output.[14] But this average figure is heavily influenced by the textiles, basic metals, and food and tobacco industries, which accounted for about 70 percent of manufacturing value added and were operating at over 85 percent of desirable output in 1964. Several other industries were running at much lower levels of desirable output in 1964, e.g. chemicals, 45 percent; metal products, 46 percent; electrical machinery, 50 percent; other machinery, 63 percent; and transport equipment, 64 percent.[15] The devaluation/liberalization package here—though coming much later and accompanied by *de jure* rather than *de facto* devaluation—was intended for similar restructuring purposes.

In assessing the response of the Indian economy to the devaluation/liberalization package we must first of all recognize that imports account for only about 7 percent of GNP and exports for about 4 percent, much lower than in most developing countries. Moreover, we unfortunately cannot easily separate out the overwhelming impact of two consecutive bad monsoons, on the one hand, and a somewhat tardy follow-up on the export subsidy and promotion side, on the other. The bad monsoons led to a substantial rise not only in food prices but also in such agricultural-based exportables as tea, jute manufactures, raw cotton and cotton goods, oil seeds, cashew nuts, tobacco, sugar, and coffee. For example, Indian exports during the year following devaluation were at least 5 percent below the exports

14. National Council of Applied Economic Research, *Under-Utilization of Industrial Capacity* (New Delhi, 1965), p. 8. "Desirable" is based on a judgment of which industries it would be technically feasible to run on two or three shifts daily.
15. Ibid., pp. 53–54.

of the preceding twelve months, with virtually the entire decline of about $76 million accounted for by the drop in exports of the agricultural-based commodities.

At the same time the decline in agricultural income and savings led to an almost Keynesian type of recession in the industrial sector during 1967 and 1968. By June 1967, the index of manufacturing output had risen only 2 percent above its June 1966 level. Thus the failure of manufacturing output to respond convincingly can be said to be in large part due to the same failure of agriculture, quite aside from the statistical fact that agriculture accounts for about half of Indian net domestic product. This failure affected manufacturing via both the supply of raw materials and markets and the provision of the required savings. Add to this the effects of the initial failure to realize that nontraditional exports were really worse off after devaluation because of the simultaneous abolition of the link export system and continued assessment of export taxes on jute goods and tea—and it is not difficult to see why the results of the policy changes were disappointing at first. It should be recalled, however, that the initial policy package was to be part of a two-year program of restructuring, by the end of which all quantitative restrictions, including those on capital goods and excepting only luxuries, were to have been removed. Few of these follow-up steps have, in fact, as yet been taken. In fact, the "indigenous angle clearance" system was never really removed as the "ban list" of prohibited imports was expanded. Thus, while the import regime now provides for more competition at the firm level (if collusion can be avoided) than would obtain under a straight licensing system, the policy package agreed to in principle in 1966 remains far from realization.

On the question of price patterns following the *de jure* devaluation, on the heels of the fairly stable experience of the early 1960s (advances of 3.5 percent per year), the wholesale price index rose by 17 percent in 1964, 7 percent in 1965, 14 percent in 1966, and another 14 percent in 1967. It is, moreover, helpful to isolate agricultural prices if one is to judge the effects of the 1966 package. Between June 1966 and June 1967 wholesale prices rose by 13 percent, as compared to 18 percent during the preceding twelve months. While wholesale food prices rose by 26 percent in this period (as compared to only 19 percent in the preceding twelve months), wholesale prices of industrial raw materials rose by only 2 percent in the year after devaluation (as compared to 29 percent in the year preceding devaluation). The wholesale price index for manufactures rose by 4 percent in the year after devaluation as compared to an 11 percent increase in the year before.

Thus it would seem that devaluation—accompanied by partial liberalization and the virtual doubling of commodity aid—did not lead to markedly higher prices; in fact, given the accident of bad monsoons and some admitted neglect on policy follow-up, it seems very likely that the policy package adopted probably prevented more substantial inflationary pressures. With foodgrain production declining from 89 million metric tons in 1964/65 to 72 million tons in 1965/66, given the benefits of hindsight, the timing of the 1966 policy package could not have been more unfortunate. It is thus fair to hypothesize that the underlying favorable effects of the structural changes of 1966 were virtually completely masked by the happenstance of bad weather. For some time, however, it remained to be seen whether Indian policy makers would reach the same conclusion or whether they would be blinded by the acceleration in the actual level of food prices and poor export performance. Current indications are that, while the pace of further liberalization was clearly curtailed by the initial food shortages of 1965/66 and 1966/67 and the resulting poor overall performance of the economy, the economy now finds itself on a superior set of rails. In 1967/68 the return of a good monsoon was undoubtedly crucial to the record harvest of approximately 100 million metric tons; but even the trend line itself—running through the last good monsoon in 1964/65—seems to be up, due to the introduction of the new seed and fertilizer technology and the essential provision of more adequate price incentives and freer access to imports. The "freeing" of the agricultural sector, in terms of moving both output and input prices closer to equilibrium, had admittedly left much to be desired; restrictions on interstate private trade in foodgrains remain substantially intact, thus providing an artificially low price or disincentive to the most efficient (surplus) regions, and an artificially high price or incentive to the least efficient (deficit) regions. Nevertheless, a beginning was made via the enlargement of food zones in March 1968, and the expectation is that once adequate buffer stocks are built up further liberalizing steps will be taken on food zones, as well as on private fertilizer and seed distribution and on the allocation of agricultural credit.

On the nonagricultural side, not only have most major industries been exempted from industrial licensing requirements since May 1966, but firms have been authorized to diversify production, as long as the new products account for no more than 25 percent of total production and no additional demand for domestic or foreign capital is involved. Industrial output has begun to rise markedly, by 100 percent between 1959/60 and 1964/65; exports, sluggish at first, are now showing a 10 percent increase over last year.[16] It thus seems clear that the 1967 prognosis that "if the momentum achieved in agriculture and foreign exchange policy can be sustained, and if aid continues at least at the levels of the recent past then, provided the monsoons return to normal, near term Indian economic prospects are far brighter than indicated by recent performance." [17] is being justified. It is clearly too early either to crow about the success of India's hesitant second restructuring or to write it off as a failure. It came later than Pakistan's, and thus had not generated the necessary momentum to overcome the adversity of an exogenous natural disaster. While the original gains, e.g. of devaluation, were thus largely eroded, the recent resurgence in agricultural performance and exports—which might validate the claim that favorable structural change has, in fact, occurred—is just now making its appearance.

South Korea

In addition to the normal baggage of problems related to restructuring, Korea was faced with repairing the damages of the partition of the immediate postwar and with the massive destruction of the Korean War and its aftermath. Accordingly, what might be called the reconstruction period lasted until approximately 1960 and was characterized by a large number of government actions over a large area, mainly intended to get the badly mutilated economy back on its feet. Inevitably, such actions were often deficient in overall design and emergency-oriented in character. Moreover, the attempt to drive the necessary resources into the hands of the government brought with it inflationary fiscal policies that defeated the prime developmental

16. This compares with a 3 percent increase in 1965 over 1964 and an actual decline from 1965 to 1966.
17. Kenneth Kaufman, "The Indian Economy: Some Recent History and Near Term Prospects," mimeographed (1967).

purpose of the program by impairing the private sector's willingness and ability to save and invest. In fact, throughout the late 1950s and even in the early 1960s, Korea was racked by substantial inflation in spite of a number of major stabilization efforts assisted by the United States. As long as these efforts were unsuccessful there was little opportunity to restore a sense of predictability to economic relationships and to begin to unleash those forces in the private sector without whose contribution development in the mixed economy is very difficult. Those relatively fine allocative decisions that yield better developmental performance cannot be expected to be made by individual decision makers unless there is some likelihood that contractual obligations will not be swamped by inflation and that entrepreneurial energies will not be diverted into the circumvention of direct controls and the search for a quick financial return.

By 1964 the back of this self-feeding inflationary spiral was finally broken and the government of Korea began to turn its attention to the need for a possible second restructuring of the kind we have previously described. Like others, it determined to deal first with the foreign exchange market before turning to reform in complementary financial markets. Exports normally amount to about 12 percent and imports to about 22 percent of GNP. In May 1964 Korea devalued by at least 50 percent,[18] unified its various rates, and introduced what was supposed to become a floating rate. This floating rate actually settled at 255 won per dollar until early 1965 and moved up to 271 won per dollar by June 1965. Up to 1969 it has fluctuated at around the 285 won per dollar level.

Along with this devaluation, the Korean government gradually liberalized its import control system through a widening of import quotas and the introduction of a partial export retention scheme. In August 1964 a quasi-automatic licensing system was introduced, under which an importer could get automatic approval of import licenses equal in value to 20 percent of his export earnings, sales to U.N. forces in Korea, and gold sales to the Bank of Korea. In November 1964 this was increased to 25 percent as a further stimulus to exports. Additional import liberalization took place in 1965 with an automatic approval system for 1,495 items, discretionary licenses

18. It is difficult to say exactly how much devaluation occurred because Korea had a multiple exchange rate system, ranging from 130 won per dollar to 190 won per dollar. The new rate was set at 255 won per dollar.

for 138 items, and a prohibited list covering 620 items. This meant that almost 75 percent of non-U.S.-aid-financed imports were now on an automatic approval basis.[19] This liberalization trend continued steadily until, by the first half of 1967, 2,984 items were on the automatic approval list, 142 items on the discretionary licensing list, and only 362 items on the prohibited or ban list. In July 1967 a negative list system was adopted, to be further reduced in early 1968, with all other items imported automatically. A reclassification of categories makes it difficult to determine the comparable number of banned commodities (both luxuries and other socially undesirable imports, and products competitive with domestic industry), but indications are that between 80 and 90 percent of actual imports other than those financed by U.S. aid are now admitted on an automatic replenishment basis.[20]

After adoption of the first substantive restructuring package, the wholesale price index of imported goods rose by 29 percent between May 1964 and January 1965 and then remained almost constant. But this price increase was not passed on to other commodities. The total wholesale price index rose by only 2 percent between May 1964 and January 1965; in the twelve months after devaluation wholesale prices rose by only 5 percent, as compared to 42 percent in the year preceding devaluation—this in spite of the fact that the money supply rose by about 23 percent in the year after devaluation as compared to about 10 percent in the previous year. Manufacturing output rose by 20 percent in the twelve months after devaluation compared with 8 percent before. This overall stability in wholesale prices was due in large part to improved agricultural performance at the time of devaluation, permitting decline in wholesale grain prices (by 24 percent between May 1964 and May 1965, as compared to an increase of 77 percent between May 1963 and May 1964).[21] Agricultural output (in constant 1960 prices), in fact, rose by 18 percent in 1964 compared to 6 percent in 1963.

But over the longer haul, especially since agricultural output has

19. *Exchange Restrictions,* IMF Seventeenth Annual Report (1966), p. 335. U.S. aid financed 30 percent of Korean imports in 1964.

20. Ibid. (1967), p. 374

21. This same price pattern occurred in the consumer price index. The Seoul consumer price index for grains fell by 18 percent between May 1964 and May 1965, while the total consumer price index rose by only 8 percent during the same period. In the twelve months prior to evaluation it had risen by 47 percent, with grain prices rising by 96 percent.

not continued to increase at that rate (in fact, there have been difficulties lately, due partly to drought but also to still inadequate price
incentives for cultivators), the curbing of what was once considered
endemic inflation was materially aided by substantial increases in the
volume of imports, from 12 percent of GNP in 1962–64 to 22 percent in 1968. But what is crucial to the story is that most of this increase in imports was financed not by foreign aid but out of the increased export earnings and commercial capital inflows that resulted
from the new policies. Exports that grew at an average annual rate
of less than 15 percent in 1958–62 increased at a truly remarkable
annual clip of 39 percent between 1962–64 and 1967. Once the exchange rate had become more realistic and competitive forces could
make themselves felt, Korea was able to take advantage internationally of her relatively cheap, high quality labor supply. While the Vietnam conflict was certainly helpful in all this, contributing as much as
20 percent of total receipts from goods and services, the marked acceleration in export performance antedates the peak of Vietnam procurement. Moreover, it should be noted that this export boom has
been an unusually balanced one, covering a broad range of commodities, including light manufactures and semimanufactures, and going
mainly to Japan and the United States.

With respect to foreign capital, there has been an equally remarkable inflow of private capital that has more than compensated for the
decline in foreign assistance grants and loans. Private loans totalling
$16 million in 1965 on a disbursement basis jumped to $170 million
in 1966, $266 million in 1967, and between $350 and $400 million
in 1968.

At the same time Korea went further than most contemporary
LDC's in the simultaneous attempt to restructure the complementary
market for credit. In 1965 domestic interest rates were raised to more
realistic levels, thus narrowing the gap between unrealistically low
official rates (at which only established firms and individuals could
hope to borrow—sometimes relending at a large profit) and the as-
tronomically high rates facing the average small borrower in the curb
market. Interest rates on savings deposits were doubled in 1965;
deposits responded by rising from a level of 14.8 billion won at the
end of 1964 to 31.7 billion won at the end of 1965 and 230 billion
won by September 1968. The savings rate, negative in the 1958–62
period and at 5.8 percent of GNP as late as 1962–64, climbed to

13.6 percent during 1968, with increases initially fueled largely by private savings, but with public savings via taxes, beginning to assume a more important role (one-third of total savings by 1968) once the economy was in full swing.

The change in the overall performance of the economy before and after the second restructuring has been little short of spectacular. Real per capita income, rising at 1.5 percent a year during the 1958–62 period, has advanced at an average rate of 6 percent annually between 1962 and 1968, with growth in excess of 10 percent recorded between 1967 and 1968.

Korea has put her abundant, high quality human resources base to good advantage in an export-led—rather than import substitution-dominated—industrialization drive. In that process the juices of domestic innovation and ingenuity, released by permitting the active participation of medium- and small-scale private investors, have begun to flow and have carried the economy forward at a truly remarkable pace. The full participation of the agricultural sector has as yet not been achieved; once this is accomplished—and the government is currently turning its full attention to this problem—there is little reason why Korea should not join the select circle of aid "graduates" who have reached the state of self-sustaining routinized growth.

Ghana

Ghana represents perhaps the most extreme example of what can happen as a consequence of a well-intentioned first restructuring effort. The Nkrumah regime represents a classic case of proceeding on the heady assumption that a newly independent government can do directly in the economic sphere what it had accomplished earlier in the political sphere. The expansion of the public sector, fueled in part by a half-baked socialist ideology, was prodigious, while tight controls were imposed on the shrinking private sector. The goal of the Ghanaian government during the 1950s can be characterized as a big push for large-scale industry, with almost complete disregard for Ghana's comparative advantage internationally. Government deficit financing forced into the hands of the public sector resources used for the construction of scores of government enterprises, in addition to overheads and monuments, while the licensing and control arrangements over the starved private sector became more and more pervasive.

The realization that policies of the immediate postwar were in fact not bringing the desired results came late and less gradually in Ghana than in some other countries. The personal charisma of Nkrumah, Ghana's appeal on the international scene as the first independent black African country, and with its own efforts to walk the pan-African stage, postponed the day of reckoning until 1966, in spite of a truly miserable economic performance. At that time, Ghanaian industry was operating at roughly 35 percent of capacity; its products were selling at from three to four times C.I.F. international prices; unemployment was rising rapidly; and agricultural output was virtually stagnant. The excesses of the Nkrumah regime in terms of the creation of an unusual array of "white elephants" in the field of public monuments, modern factories, and the like pale all other such cases by comparison. But while the realization of the high cost of pursuing these policies came only gradually, the military government that took office in February 1966 came in, in large part, on the basis of a profound dissatisfaction with the economic performance to date.

In July 1967 the first substantial changes in policy, which may be called the beginning of Ghana's second restructuring, were put into effect. They consisted of a 30 percent devaluation of the exchange rate, an equivalent rise in the producer price offered by the cocoa marketing board (to pass on the benefits of devaluation to the producer), and some limited moves in the direction of import liberalization. A small existing open general license category was substantially extended to include most spare parts, chemicals, pig iron, pharmaceuticals, fertilizer, and simple tools, with the expectation that 15 to 20 percent of imports would come in under what amounts to an automatic replenishment scheme. The objective of this package was to reach 55 percent of one-shift industrial capacity by the end of 1967. The Ghanaian authorities, moreover, stated their intention to also liberalize raw materials as soon as the foreign exchange reserves permitted. Their July 1967 policy statement, in fact, pledged "the freeing of trade and payments from all artificial restrictions and controls" as a "firm objective."

Clearly this constituted a small beginning in the right direction. Moreover, the exceptionally good maize harvest during the 1967 calendar year set the stage for a successful devaluation aftermath, enhancing the chances of "making it stick." In fact the November 1967 consumer price index stood at 6 percent below that of a year earlier, indicating that lower food prices had more than offset the impact of some increased import costs caused by the administrative inability to utilize the larger volume of assistance made available by various donors in connection with the adoption of the 1966 policy package. Imports for 1967 were 16 percent below 1966 levels; the 1968 total was only two-thirds of the 1965 level, but the composition had shifted away from capital and consumer goods (from 81 percent to 51 percent of total imports) and toward raw materials (from 16 percent to 32 percent of total imports), thus ensuring a higher utilization of existing plants.

However, in spite of the opportunity that existed, it seems fair to say that the momentum has not been maintained, at least thus far. The bulk of 1967 and 1968 imports has continued to be allocated under an individual license system, with 1,100 registered importers making applications on the conventional basis and any new registrants considered in relation to "their prospective ability to utilize licenses effectively." The shortage of foreign exchange and the difficult debt situation have, in fact, prompted the authorities to reverse some of the tentative early steps toward liberalization. The situation has been further aggravated by Ghana's unwillingness to participate in the United Kingdom devaluation of 1967 and by the unusually heavy rains of 1968, which caused a return to food shortages and a below-normal cocoa crop. The erosion of the initial gains of Ghana's 1966 devaluation became sufficiently pronounced so that minor exports declined in 1967, and only the unexpectedly high international price for cocoa bailed Ghana out the next year.[22]

At the heart of the problem is the fact that the Ghanaian government is not yet really convinced of the basic need for a second restructuring; it continues to think that it can handle the first restructuring effort more efficiently than its corrupt predecessor. Consequently, in spite of much discussion to the contrary, little has been done to sell or abandon the more than sixty major state enterprises, but rather the effort continues to be made to "reorganize" same. Recent policy pronouncements aimed at fostering Ghanaian—as opposed to minority group—participation in retail trade, services, and small-scale industry have made the private sector even more insecure and unwilling to participate. The smaller firms in particular are in difficulty.

With at least 80 percent of imports still very tightly controlled,

22. The picture on minor exports is unclear, since the initial benefits of devaluation were not always passed on to the cultivator by various export marketing boards.

World Bank and other observers conclude that most state enterprises have "more than adequate," and the larger private and joint state-private firms "adequate," raw material imports, with inventories approaching three to four months' supply. On the other hand, many small- and medium-sized firms still do not have adequate imported raw materials and spare parts, and the difficulties in arranging credit undoubtedly play a major role here as well. The import of seventy-nine specified commodities "which are considered to be manufacturable locally in sufficient quantities" continues to be restricted or completely banned. The attitude of a substantial portion of the bureaucracy continues to be one of paying lip service to liberalization and the advantage of making more allocative decisions via the market-place—as amended by indirect controls—just as soon as they feel more comfortable about their (currently nonexistent) foreign exchange reserves. However, it is characteristic of developing countries that difficult decisions have to be made *before* the situation becomes comfortable, that in fact it takes difficult decisions to render the situation comfortable in the first place. While more ample reserves and more dependable aid pipelines are certainly important, it also must be remembered that to wait for a really ideal time to do whatever has been decided is correct might mean to wait for a very long time and, more important, to have lost valuable and often irretrievable advantages in the meantime.

There is, at the same time, some gradually maturing realization that complementary policies in the domestic credit and agricultural sectors can become crucial to the overall restructuring effort. The possibilities of more agricultural credit tied up with a rediscount facility at the Bank of Ghana have been explored. Market price floors for rice and maize were announced for the first time in 1968 in the effort to improve agriculture's terms of trade, putting the government into the business of supporting the private trade rather than displacing it. Due to the bad weather of 1968, these supports have not been tested; moreover, it is unclear whether Ghana has the storage and/or administrative capacity to run a buffer stock operation. Thus here again the follow-through has been lacking to date. The reduction of the discount rate by the Bank of Ghana in early 1968 is a case in point. Intended as a method of increasing bank lending to agriculture and manufacturing, this step had the predictable effect of simply increasing the windfall profits of prime borrowers while leaving the starved medium- and small-scale producers and would-be producers, agricultural as well as industrial, worse off than before. It may well be that only a further deterioration of her economic position will convince Ghana of the need to move seriously ahead with her announced second restructuring effort.

Colombia

Colombian imports normally amount to roughly 12 percent of GNP, exports to about 10 percent. In September 1965 Colombia, a multiple export rate country, devalued the exchange rate relevant for about 75 percent of her imports by 50 percent (from 9 to 13.5 pesos per dollar) and agreed to place at least half of all imports on an automatic license list within six months and 85 percent of all imports within fourteen months.[23] In October 1965 about 20 percent of total import licenses covered goods on the free list; by September 1966 this had increased to about 80 percent of total imports—all at the new rate of 13.5 pesos per dollar. The combination of higher tariff rates and the increased peso costs of given *ad valorem* tariffs (as the import exchange rate depreciated) led to an increase in (nominal) tariffs of over 21 percent in 1966. The initially higher nominal rate for "minor exports" (everything except coffee and petroleum) did not change.

The response of the Colombian economy to these new policies, coupled with generous new aid allocations during this fourteen-month period, is not unambiguously clear. The monthly level of imports rose from $35 million in September 1965 to $71 million in March 1966 (seasonally adjusted) and then fluctuated through November 1966 at a level of about $35 million per month. Total arrivals (seasonally adjusted) were $743 million in the fourteen months after September 1965, as compared to $590 million in the fourteen months before September 1965.

The consumer price index rose by 19 percent (seasonally adjusted) between September 1965 and November 1966, as compared to 7 percent in the preceding fourteen months. Food prices rose by 19 percent (seasonally adjusted) in the fourteen months after September 1965, as compared to 4 percent in the fourteen months preceding September 1965. The rate of inflation clearly accelerated in the

23. The liberalization percentages used in this section exclude imports that are financed by foreign credits for specific projects; such "nonreimbursable" imports account for about 10–15 percent of the total imports.

period after the new devaluation/liberalization policies were initiated.[24] One major contributing reason was the accompanying bad harvest, with agricultural output growing by less than 2 percent in 1965—i.e. less than population growth—as compared to more than 5 percent in both 1964 and 1966. This failure on the part of the agricultural sector to provide a breathing space was undoubtedly decisive in rendering the relatively meager results of the policy package that was adopted. Moreover, devaluation affected the minor exports unfavorably. They rose by 3 percent in 1966, as compared to a 40 percent increase between 1964 and 1965. One might have predicted this slow growth, since the effective exchange rate for imports had fallen substantially while the nominal exchange rate for minor exports had remained at 13.5 pesos since May 1965.[25]

Finally, there was a simultaneous effort to change the internal price relationships or terms of trade between agriculture and nonagriculture. As a consequence, with the money supply expanding at about the same rate as before (16 percent over fourteen months), prices rose more rapidly and, as one might expect, the aggregative performance of real output was not significantly stimulated. While Colombia has no published industrial production index, seasonally adjusted cement production declined by 4 percent in the fourteen months after September 1965, as compared to an increase of 7 percent in the preceding fourteen months; seasonally adjusted electric power output rose by 13 percent in the fourteen months after September 1965, the same rate as in the preceding fourteen months; seasonally adjusted steel production was 13 percent higher in November 1966 than in September 1965, which in turn was 11 percent above the July 1964 level. Unemployment in the capital city of Bogotá was 9.6 percent in September 1966, as compared with 9.7 percent in September 1965 and 7.4 percent in September 1964.[26] We have no

24. The wholesale price index rose by 17 percent (seasonally adjusted) in the fourteen months after September 1965 as compared to 10 percent in the fourteen preceding months.

25. The average effective exchange rate for imports in all of 1966 depreciated by 29 percent, as compared to all of 1965. The average effective exchange rate for minor exports appreciated by 6 percent in all of 1966, as compared to all of 1965. Antonio Urdinoia and Richard Mallon, "Policies to Promote Colombian Exports of Manufactures," mimeographed (1967).

26. These data for Bogotá are from surveys by the Universidad de los Andes, as cited in Robert L. Slighton, *Urban Unemployment in Colombia: Measurement, Characteristics, and Policy Problems* (RAND, January 1968, RM-5393), p. 16.

clear indication on changes in the rate at which industrial capacity was used.

While the evidence on aggregative performance is thus clearly mixed, we can conclude that output rose slightly more rapidly after the second restructuring policies were initiated. In November 1966, however, the experiment was interrupted. Negotiations over new loans between Colombia and the consultative group of national and international aid agencies broke down,[27] and strict controls on all foreign exchange transactions were reimposed. After prolonged negotiations it became clear, however, that the Colombian government had not concluded that the liberalization medicine was inappropriate —only that foreign doctors had been ministering it too publicly— from the view of domestic political feasibility. Consequently, Colombia agreed to a unification of its rates and permitted the rate to depreciate until April 1968, thus accepting a 10 percent devaluation. Import liberalization covering up to 20 percent of total import value was restored by September 1967 and further liberalization was undertaken in 1968. Moreover, to restore the rapid growth of minor exports, tax certificates equal to 15 percent of export value were introduced and other nonfinancial export promotion measures adopted. However, given the bad price experience following the 1965 devaluation, as well as the 1966 confrontation with the community of aid donors, the resumption of liberalization has been gradual and hesitant. Moreover, importers, having been burned more than once, continue to speculate against the reimposition of controls, thus vitiating some of the anticipated beneficial effects of the restructuring package.

The above, admittedly rather cursory, review of a number of liberalization efforts—over an admittedly rather too short period of time —does not lend itself to grand generalizations. Korea, India, and

27. Colombia also failed to meet the September 1966 target for net foreign exchange reserves that would have allowed it to draw the final tranche of its IMF standby. Almost the entire shortfall from the reserve target could be accounted for by a $60 million shortfall from projected export earnings (excluding petroleum), and most of this export shortfall represented coffee exports that were lower than projected. In early 1967 Colombia drew $19 million from the IMF's Compensatory Financing Arrangement, as nonpetroleum exports in 1966 were about $12 million less than the weighted average of actual 1964–66 exports. This seems to be a case where a shortfall from projected exports—as distinct from a shortfall from historical exports—adversely affects a country's development policies. The IBRD's proposed Supplementary Financial Measures is supposed to deal with this type of problem.

Ghana had substantial *de jure* devaluations coupled with gradual import liberalization—more extensive in Korea and India than in Ghana. Colombia had a large devaluation of the import rate coupled with rapid liberalization; and Pakistan gradually devalued *de facto* via the export bonus scheme, accompanied by tariff adjustments and substantial import liberalization. Few of the experiments have run long enough to permit us to report with any certainty on conclusions that might be reached. Some of the countries, e.g. Colombia and Pakistan, were, moreover, interrupted by political crisis or war; others suffered from the overwhelming effect of exogenous shocks that swept all before it, e.g. India. Nevertheless we may be permitted a few tentative observations on the nature of the second restructuring to date and the directions it is likely to take in the future.

First, even at this early stage there is evidence of the possibilities of fundamental changes in economic performance. If we take the Pakistan and Korean examples, which have had the benefit of at least several years of application and where liberalization began to extend to capital goods, as well as raw materials and spare parts, we can note a real turnabout in performance, whether measured in terms of per capita income growth, saving behavior, or export performance.[28] How much of this is due to the higher import levels made possible and how much is due to the restructuring of imports itself is, however, more difficult to establish. The real test of this would be an examination of changes in the industrial production structure, as well as between industry and other sectors. In the short run, changes in the pattern of investment allocation at the margin might have to serve as a proxy. But neither of these two exercises has as yet been carried out.

The extent of "openness" of the economy seems to be of considerable relevance in terms of the potential beneficial impact of any devaluation/liberalization package. *Ceteris paribus,* the linkages between the foreign trade sector and the rest of the economy would

28. For the reader's convenience:

		Pakistan	*Korea*
Growth per capita (average annual)	1955–60	1.2%	1.6%
	1960–65	2.9	3.7
	1965–67	3.4	8.3
Domestic Saving Rate (percentage of GNP)	1958	5.5	−2.5
	1966	9.0	9.2
Export value growth rate (average annual)	1955–60	2.5	−0.8
	1965–67	8.3	39.3

seem to have greater leverage potential in a case like Korea's than in India, where the "trade tail can't be expected to wag the development dog" as vigorously. But it should be noted that the performance of a fairly large, domestically oriented economy like Pakistan can be substantially affected as well.

Second, complementary conditions, especially in the agricultural sector, may be of the utmost importance. In the most successful cases under scrutiny, e.g. Korea and Pakistan, harvests were good and agricultural productivity was increasing substantially at the time the new policies were adopted. This seems essential if the eroding effects of inflation are to be held off and if there is to be time for the restructuring process to gather steam. Changes complementary to devaluation and that reinforce it on the export side—e.g. the levying of export duties for traditional commodities facing an inelastic foreign demand, and the installation of a supplementary direct export promotion machinery, including subsidies—have been characteristic in the attempt to accelerate the usually somewhat delayed response.

Third, there can be little doubt concerning the importance of additional foreign exchange availabilities for the immediate post restructuring period, whether for real or psychological reasons. The replacement of direct controls by indirect ones cannot be achieved overnight. Moreover, officialdom needs the assurance that there will be additional outside help to stem the tide of import demand, as well as to alleviate the impact on the government's budget. But the additional aid and import flows are also directly relevant to the ability to contain the inevitable inflationary pressures that ensue in the wake of such a policy shift. If the higher price of imports associated with the devaluation, especially of industrial raw materials and other imports, is not at least partially offset by the dismantling of controls and the larger volume of imports now made possible, the impact on consumer price indexes with all its consequences would be virtually unavoidable. The chances of ultimate success are much improved if we can have more, as well as better allocated, imports. Such aid—even if given on a government-to-government basis—can be made available to the medium- and small-scale private borrower via production or program loans as well as (if properly liberalized) via two-step loans via development banks.

Fourth, what happens in the way of policy changes in complementary sectors, e.g. agriculture and credit, can be of the greatest importance for the overall success of the second restructuring effort. In Pakistan, for example, the mutual self-reinforcing interaction between agriculture and industry was a central feature of the simultaneous liberalization in the credit and foreign exchange markets which brought private investors out of hiding and into active participation. In Taiwan, a case we have not gone into here since it is relatively well known, import liberalization in 1961 was accompanied by simultaneous policy changes in both agriculture and credit; no wonder that Taiwan is no longer considered to be in need of concessional aid from abroad.

Fifth, especially in the early stages when private sector confidence still hangs precariously in the balance, little is as important as the show of resoluteness and consistency in carrying through with a phased liberalization program. Nothing can be quite as damaging at such a time as hesitation, or a temporary return to restrictionism, in terms of the required total response from the previously disenfranchised economic sectors, whose participation is so essential to final success. Where foreign exchange reserves are low, as in Ghana, and this leads to somewhat half-hearted and ambivalent measures, the private sector is likely to adopt a wait-and-see policy—proving the skeptics right once again.

Finally, it should be clear that our concentration on the dismantling of quantitative controls as part of the restructuring effort gives us only a partial or beginning representation of reality. As is well known, the typical less-developed economy's disequilibrium system can also be maintained by tariff and/or tax/subsidy packages. Ideally, in fact, we should measure the total extent of protection by calculating the effective tariff on various industries, including specific taxes, import surcharges, and deposit requirements, and, in the garden variety of cases in which quantitative restrictions are dominant, using the resulting implicit tariffs (i.e. the percentage difference between domestic and C.I.F. world prices) as the equivalent of the nominal tariff structure. It is however true, in terms of a sequential liberalization effort, that it is the import licensing system that carries the effective "bite" in most actual world cases. Once this bite is removed, tariffs usually become relevant, especially if some of them have been raised in the course of the earlier dismantling of the quantitative restrictions. Not infrequently the tariff pattern that emerges as relevant itself shows no really discernable logical pattern or scientific basis. A policy of high tariffs on finished goods and low or nonexistent tariffs on intermediate goods has frequently led to a very high level of effective protection for domestic producers, which policy, while working through the market mechanism, is still substantially distorting and blunting of competitive pressures. Tariff rationalization is therefore likely to provide the next—and hopefully final—challenge to those who wish to restructure the system along more efficient lines.

As we look into the future, following the dismantling of quantitative restrictions, this will undoubtedly require the evolution of a country-specific tariff policy from which the country must, of course, deviate when necessary. In this connection the confusion between infant industry and revenue objectives of tariffs must be eliminated. In sequential terms, a move toward a uniform tariff rate, perhaps somewhat lower on raw materials and machinery than on finished goods, accompanied by the substitution of excises for tariffs in the luxury good category,[29] may be sensible. This uniform tariff can then be lowered over time, very much in the manner of a gradual withdrawal of temporary preferences. Deviations from uniformity along the way would have to be defended in terms of a continuously convincing, infant industry type of argument, and protective tariffs set in relation to some objective criterion such as domestic value added at world prices.[30] But such considerations take us beyond the scope of the present paper.

Comments by Stephen A. Resnick

Cohen and Ranis have asked the question of what has been done in the past twenty years or so by governments to remedy underdevelopment, and perhaps what has not been done. They have then presented what one might call a revisionist theory of the import substitution or forced industrialization model. I would add to their list of criticisms the creation of "industrial dualism," or the replacement of rural by urban idiocy. I would argue, however, that their paper points to the failure of an appropriate government strategy to

29. See R. McKinnon, "Tariff and Commodity Tax Reform in Korea, mimeographed (1967).
30. This suggestion is made by R. McKinnon, ibid.

rid the country of social and economic barriers to change, not only in terms of not sufficiently increasing intersectorial trade flows and interclass interaction, but also as a critique of government as a very important instrument for change in society. I would further argue that their policy prescription of import liberalization (which I agree is needed; their empirical examples were informative) is an incremental change for incremental planners, while what is really needed is a shock to the underdeveloped country to awaken the population, especially in the rural areas. I question whether the current ruling elites of many countries have the will or desire to accomplish this.

As Shane Hunt indicated in this conference, development is not just an increase in economic growth within an existing social structure; rather it is the modernization of the structure itself to which government policy must turn. If import liberalization is an appropriate development strategy, then it may require an appropriate social system within which it can operate. If, as Cohen and Ranis argue, "more broadly based participation in development is necessary," then to me this argues for an *awakening* of the mass of the population, a *change* in their social psychology, and an all-out war on traditionalism, both private and public. Import liberalization, however, is not a sufficient shock to the underdeveloped country to *engage* the mass of people (especially in the rural areas) into participation in the market economy. Perhaps import liberalization is a necessary beginning in the reduction of market barriers created and abetted by forced industrialization policies, but it is not sufficient to disrupt the barriers to social change or to change the will to change. In fact, for import liberalization to be truly effective, there is a corresponding need for the government to provide the political, social, and economic institutions to allow the respective sectors or classes to respond.

Yet to marshall economic forces in the manner needed is to change the social structure of these societies by disrupting the existing groups and classes, and often this in turn calls for a government revolution. In other words, the existing import substitution policies reflect the existing government preferences, and to change the former implies a change in the latter.

Finally, since the paper touches on U.S. aid, and as nationalism has been referred to in several of these papers, as well as orally, a further brief comment. It is not unreasonable to assume that the relationship between the United States and the underdeveloped world will worsen in the future. Economic development and nationalism often are necessary for each other in the sense that both can change the "atmosphere" of a nation. But the side effects of nationalism often turn out to be anti-West or antiwhite. If what is then needed is a type of government revolution, econometric evidence indicates that the United States will not concur (the United States does not believe in revolutions any more). I suggest that this is a dilemma for AID and for the United States generally.

13

An Assessment of Currency Devaluation in Developing Countries

BY RICHARD N. COOPER

By wide agreement, many less developed countries have overvalued currencies. Yet most countries are reluctant to devalue their currencies even when the signs of overvaluation are unmistakable. A variety of objections are raised to devaluation, but most of them reduce to three basic ones: (1) devaluation will not in fact improve the devaluing country's payments position; (2) devaluation might work if given a chance, but it will unleash forces in the economy that will eventually undercut its benefits and those of other economic policies; and (3) even if devaluation works it will be politically disastrous to those officials who are responsible for undertaking it.

Despite these sources of resistance, currency devaluation has frequently taken place under the pressure of circumstances. These devaluations provide an opportunity to evaluate, at least crudely, the consequences of devaluation and to assess the extent to which the foregoing fears are justified.

This study generalizes from the experience of twenty-four devaluations, involving nineteen different countries. It includes most of the devaluations during the period 1959–66, excluding mainly those involving countries in unusual circumstances, such as Laos and Vietnam. Venezuela was excluded as well because it is a country with a large trade surplus and therefore untypical of less developed countries. Canada, on the other hand, was included because of its large trade deficit and regular importation of capital, making it similar in

This paper was sponsored by the Agency for International Development under its Summer Research Program, but AID bears no responsibility for its contents. I am grateful to MaryAnn Reardon, Malcolm Getz, Stephen Quick, and Mati Lal Pal for research assistance.

that respect to many less developed countries. Iceland and Spain are included since, like many less developed countries, both had multiple currency practices. A few cases of devaluation in the mid-1950s were also included, to enlarge the sample. Availability of data clearly also influenced the selection.

The intent of the study was to examine discrete changes in exchange rates—a "once-and-for-all" change in exchange rate from one level to another, such as is called for under the present international rules governing international payments. This consideration ruled out those cases, such as Chile and Uruguay, where the effective exchange rate has depreciated almost continuously over long periods of time. It might also seem to rule out Argentina and Brazil, where hardly a year has gone by without some change in the effective exchange rate. But these two countries did each have one devaluation that was so far-reaching in character and extensive in amount that they seemed to warrant inclusion here. Canada and Peru had floating exchange rates; but in each case the rate depreciated from one relatively well-defined level to another in the course of a year, so it was thought worthwhile to include them.

The study is subject to four important limitations. First, economic data for less developed countries, while steadily improving, are still very incomplete and are often of poor quality. Second, the data are inevitably after the fact, and they reflect many economic changes other than the devaluation under examination. Much analytical work is required to convert the actual observations into "other things being equal" observations. Only a few crude adjustments to take account of other factors are made here, partly because of inadequacies in the data that would be required to undertake sophisticated adjustments, partly because of the conceptual difficulties involved in such adjustments. Third, the twenty-four cases of devaluation were not studied in any depth. Those well versed in the construction of the statistics from these countries may cringe at the use to which they are occasionally put here; time was not available to explore their construction in the detail required for sophisticated judgments concerning how they can and how they cannot be used legitimately. This study is therefore merely a start on a more thorough cross-sectional investigation of currency devaluations. It is a preliminary report and a tentative agenda for further work, and it is hoped that the generalizations made here will stimulate such work, of which surprisingly little has been undertaken to date. Finally, this study is limited to the period im-

mediately following devaluation, usually one year. The total effects
of devaluation will rarely occur within a year, and even the principal
effects may require well over a year. Nonetheless, what happens
within the year following devaluation is often of overriding political
importance to those responsible for the decision, so the impact effects
of devaluation are of more than passing interest. They have received
too little attention from economists, who generally focus on the nature of the new equilibrium position rather than the characteristics
of the passage.

What follows will be divided into six sections. The first is concerned
with the nature of devaluation. It is followed by sections on the effects of devaluation on the balance of payments, on the terms of
trade, on the level of economic activity, on prices and wages, and on
the political fate of the governments immediately responsible.

NOMINAL AND EFFECTIVE DEVALUATION

Under the rules of the International Monetary Fund, to which all
countries considered here belong, each member country must declare
a fixed par value for its currency, in terms of gold or the U.S. dollar,
which is to be applicable to all current transactions with foreigners. A
currency devaluation involves a specified reduction in the gold or
dollar value of the devaluing country's currency.

Most currency devaluations are not this straightforward. For a
variety of reasons, many less developed countries do not apply a
single, well-defined exchange rate to all current account transactions
with foreigners. Rather, they have a system of multiple rates, the
rates used for a particular transaction depending on the type of
transaction and even sometimes on the foreign country involved in
the transaction. Moreover, a country with a technically unified exchange rate may use import tariffs, export taxes or subsidies, and
direct controls to achieve much the same effects as multiple rates.
Many governments undertake exchange rate adjustment in a piecemeal fashion to achieve an ultimate effect thought to be too dangerous
to be taken all at once.[1] The cases considered here do involve a major

1. For a discussion of the "disequilibrium system" used by many less developed countries, see C. P. Kindleberger, "Liberal Policies vs. Controls in
the Foreign Trade of Developing Countries," AID Discussion Paper no. 14,
1967, published in J. D. Theberge, ed., *Economics of Trade and Development*
(New York: John Wiley & Sons, 1968).

adjustment, however, and therefore exclude some of the more devious exchange adjustments that are nevertheless cumulatively significant.

Where the *de facto* exchange system has become highly complicated, usually under the pressure of accumulating balance of payments difficulties, devaluation is often used as an occasion for tidying up the system as well as for changing the par value of the currency. Thus currency devaluations take a wide variety of forms, and they cannot be handled satisfactorily in any simple, catchall fashion. However, it is possible to distinguish between two broad types of policy change accompanying devaluation: exchange reform and import liberalization.

Exchange reform involves the elimination or virtual elimination of multiple exchange rates and the movement to a unitary rate or something close to it, whether fixed or flexible. The qualification "virtual" is introduced to allow for those cases in which the country retains a separate, less favorable rate for traditional exports of primary products, substituting for an export tax with the purpose either of preventing a deterioration in the country's terms of trade or, more often, of raising revenue and of capturing the windfall profits or rents accruing to producers of traditional products whose supply is thought to be inelastic in the short run.

Import liberalization involves the reduction of quantitative restrictions on the flow of imports: liberalization or elimination of import quotas, relaxation of licensing requirements, and often the reduction or elimination of advance deposits and other impediments to imports. Import liberalization shades from a little to a lot. Both exchange reform and import liberalization can be spread over many months or even years, and this practice has been especially common for import liberalization. In addition, whether or not exchange reform or import liberalization occur, devaluation may be accompanied by a stabilization program, involving restrictive monetary and fiscal action designed to reduce the rate of inflation and help bring external payments directly into balance.

In ten of the twenty-four cases considered here devaluation was associated with extensive exchange reform, and in ten (partially overlapping) cases it was accompanied by moderate to substantial liberalization of imports; both moves complicate the task of assessing the effects of devaluation. Where a change in the parity of a currency was accompanied by a unification of multiple exchange rates or by changes in import tariffs and export subsidies or taxes, the change in the *effective* exchange rates—the amount of local currency that purchasers must actually pay for a dollar's worth of imports and the amount of local currency that an exporter actually receives for a dollar's worth of exports—might be substantially less than the nominal change in the exchange rate and may differ between exports and imports.

Table 13.1 lists the devaluations examined in this study, the month of the devaluation, the extent of the nominal devaluation, and the effective devaluation as it affected merchandise exports and imports, calculated in a manner described in Appendix A. Where the formal

Table 13.1: Nominal and Effective Currency Devaluation
(Percentage change in dollars per unit of local currency)

Country	Time of devaluation	Nominal devaluation[a]	Effective devaluation Exports	Imports
Argentina	Jan. 1959	72	63	61
Brazil	Sep. 1964	66[b]	65[b]	61[b]
Canada	June 1961–May 1962	5	5	10[c]
Colombia	Nov. 1962	26	13	23
Colombia	Sep. 1965	33	6	25
Costa Rica	Sep. 1961	15	14	6
Ecuador	July 1961	17	10	16
Greece	Apr. 1953	50	31	41
Iceland	Feb. 1960	57	54	41
Iceland	Aug. 1961	12	12[d]	11[d]
India	June 1966	37	17	30
Israel	Feb. 1962	40	12[c]	26[c]
Korea	Feb. 1960	23	29	34
Korea	Feb. 1961	50	35	36
Korea	May 1964	49	44	50
Mexico	Apr. 1954	31	28	31
Morocco	Oct. 1959	17	17	12[c]
Pakistan	July 1955	30	28	28
Peru	Jan. 1958–Apr. 1959	31	31	31
Philippines	Jan. 1962	44	14	16
Philippines	Nov. 1965	10	10	0
Spain	July 1959	30	24[d]	26[d]
Tunisia	Sep. 1964	19	20	17
Turkey	Aug. 1958	56	39[d]	39[d]

[a] Parity or principal import rate.
[b] During calendar year 1964.
[c] Includes known changes in import duties and export subsidies.
[d] Effective devaluation calculated for goods and services; the remainder for merchandise only. Figures for Turkey calculated on net exports.

change in par value took place well after a major exchange reform, the nominal change in exchange rate and the indicated date apply to the principal import rate rather than to the par value. In many instances the entries in the table (including some of the dates) should be regarded as approximations rather than exact figures. The effective devaluations, in particular, often cover a period extending some months before or after the month of the nominal devaluation. Moreover, the figures in Table 13.1 may overstate the effective devaluation for several reasons. Where one of the incentives to export is an entitlement to import based on a portion of export earnings, devaluation of the rate applicable to imports, by reducing the profits on importing, will also reduce the incentive to export. Second, tariffs on items important in the cost of living may be temporarily reduced to limit politically sensitive price increases, and such reductions may not be fully reflected in the figures here. Finally, the effective devaluations exclude the effects of removing import quotas.

Several features of the results in Table 13.1 stand out. First, effective devaluation was usually less than nominal devaluation, and often substantially less. The reverse, however, is apparent in a few cases. Second, more often than not effective devaluation for imports was larger than that for exports. Countries that are heavy exporters of foodstuffs and raw materials often imposed an export tax or a less favorable exchange rate on such products when the currency was devalued. Also, several countries subsidized their nontraditional exports after it became clear that the exchange rate was so overvalued as to discourage such exports. The subsidies were removed on realignment of the exchange rate, often to be reintroduced at a later date. Import tariffs, on the other hand, are usually regarded as permanent rather than temporary features of the landscape, and while some special import surcharges were removed at the time of devaluation, the basic tariff level typically remains.

DEVALUATION AND THE BALANCE OF PAYMENTS

Devaluation is normally undertaken to improve the balance of payments, and a devaluation may therefore be judged successful to the extent that it has led to an improvement in the balance of payments. By increasing the profitability of export sales relative to local sales, devaluation should stimulate exports; and by making imports more expensive relative to local goods and services, devaluation should discourage imports. On both counts the balance on goods and services should improve. But a devaluation may have no observed effect on trade, yet still be judged highly successful if it permits numerous controls and subsidies, required at the old exchange rate to prevent a far worse balance than that actually observed, to be eliminated. Moreover, a successful devaluation might actually worsen the balance on goods and services if, in addition to permitting elimination of undesirable balance of payments controls, it induces a larger net inflow of capital from abroad. Such an increased net inflow might result from an inflow of private foreign investment to take advantage of the improved competitive position of the country or from increased inflows of foreign aid for which devaluation and exchange reform were preconditions.

Table 13.2 records the balance of payments before and after devaluation. The first column indicates the balance on goods and services in the year preceding devaluation. Since few less developed countries compile balance of payments data on a quarterly or even semiannual basis, some approximation is required. Whenever the devaluation took place before May, the "preceding year" is the calendar year preceding the year of devaluation; otherwise it is the year of devaluation, except for Korea (1964) and India. Those two countries compile semiannual data, and the record here runs from July through June for them.[2] The change recorded in Table 13.2 is between the preceding year, as defined above, and the year immediately following it. The monetary balance recorded for the two successive years in the last two columns represents the change in net international reserves, defined to include short-term official borrowing abroad and transactions with the International Monetary Fund as well as changes in gross reserves. All entries are measured in terms of dollars, the foreign currency, as is appropriate in assessing a country's balance of payments position; but in a few cases these had to be computed from data reported in local currency.

In fifteen cases the balance on goods and services improved in the year following devaluation. The balance remains negative in most of these cases; that is not surprising, nor does it indicate that devaluation failed to correct the balance of payments position. These countries are all normal importers of capital (although in the year preceding de-

2. In Canada and Peru the exchange rate floated downward steadily for about a year, ending respectively in May 1962 and April 1959. In these two cases the "previous year" is assumed to be 1961 and 1958, respectively.

Table 13.2: Balance of Payments
($ million)

Country	Time of devaluation	Balance on goods and services		Change in capital[a] inflow	Monetary balance	
		Previous Year	Change		Preceding year	Following year
Argentina	Jan. 1959	−256	270	63	−214	119
Brazil	Sept. 1964	26	182	188	72	442
Canada	1961–1962	−839	100	−240	285	146
Colombia	Nov. 1962	−176	30	−14	−44	−29
Colombia	Sept. 1965	−23	−267	176	56	−35
Costa Rica	Sept. 1961	−20	−2	20	−11	7
Ecuador	July 1961	−28	18	8	−14	12
Greece	Apr. 1953	−136	60	−23	19	56
Iceland	Feb. 1960	−13	4	12	−9	6
Iceland	Aug. 1961	5	3	5	12	20
India	June 1966	−1313	−35	54	−29	−10
Israel	Feb. 1962	−450	−33	122	75	164
Korea	Feb. 1960	−228	−34	31	4	1
Korea	Feb. 1961	−262	64	−18	1	47
Korea	May 1964	−320	112	−149	7	−30
Mexico	Apr. 1954	−122	98	−106	−32	−40
Morocco	Oct. 1959	129	−94	119	40	65
Pakistan	July 1955	−21	−21	32	7	18
Peru	1958	−117	78	−47	−13	18
Philippines	Jan. 1962	−161	99	27	−90	36
Philippines	Nov. 1965	38	27	−41	−15	−29
Spain	July 1959	−109	404	−5	66	465
Tunisia	Sept. 1964	−124	−56	68	−15	−3
Turkey	Aug. 1958	−86	−31	−44	73	−2

[a] Including errors and omissions and unilateral transfers.
Note: Columns 2 + 3 = 5 − 4, except for rounding.

Source: International Financial Statistics (I have used various issues and the 1967/68 Supplement of this monthly publication) and *Pakistan Economic Journal*, March 1957.

valuation four countries in fact had current account surpluses, all for rather special reasons) and can be expected to run deficits on goods and services. The point of devaluation is to reduce this deficit to the point at which it can be readily financed by capital imports, not to eliminate it.

In sixteen cases there was an improvement in the net reserve position (monetary balance is positive) in the year following devaluation, and in seventeen cases the monetary balance showed an improvement over the year preceding devaluation. Twelve of these latter cases also involved an improvement in the balance on goods and services. Put another way, in six of the nine cases in which the current account worsened, this was more than compensated for by an increase in net capital inflows. In summary, then, twenty-one of the twenty-four cases showed an improvement in either the current balance or the monetary balance or both. Only Colombia (1965), Korea (1960), and Turkey experienced a worsening in both the current and the monetary balances. The Korean position showed substantial improvement after a second devaluation the following year, however, while Colombia experienced an export boom (excluding coffee) in 1965, our year of devaluation, following a devaluation applicable to nontraditional exports in late 1964. Turkey's exports performed very well following devaluation (see Table 13.4 below), but an extensive liberalization program led to a sharp increase in imports.

On the face of it, this evidence seems to scotch the view that, in general, devaluation will not work. Positions did improve following devaluation. On the other hand, the improvements are not so overwhelming as to allay concern for any particular country, for in three, or seven, or nine of the cases, depending on the criterion used, devaluation did not "work" in the following year. The proportion is substantial enough to give any minister of finance pause. However, other factors, discussed below, contributed to bringing about these *ex post* results.

Before turning to a more analytical interpretation of the effects of devaluation, one further bit of *ex post* evidence may be mentioned. The broad coverage of Table 13.2 is confined (in most cases) to calendar years. For merchandise trade alone, the time period of observation can be geared more accurately to the time of devaluation. Other things being equal, a devaluation should reduce the volume and foreign currency value of imports and increase the volume of exports. Whether it increases or reduces the foreign currency value of exports depends upon domestic supply conditions and world demand conditions regarding the devaluing country's exports. A low world price elasticity of demand for the country's exports combined with fairly elastic supply will lead to a reduction in the value of exports; otherwise the value should increase.

Table 13.3 sets out trade performance over the four quarters preceding devaluation and over the four quarters following the quarter

Table 13.3: Percentage Change in Volume of Merchandise Trade Four Quarters Before and After Devaluation

Country	Time of devaluation	Terminal quarter	Exports		Imports	
			Before	After	Before	After
Argentina	Jan. 1959	IV	25	−15	2	−2
Brazil	Sept. 1964	II	−9	41	−7[a]	−20[a]
Canada	1961–62	I	6	6	9	−6
Colombia	Nov. 1962	III	47	−6	2	1
Colombia	Sept. 1965	II	0	1	−14	23
Costa Rica	Sept. 1961	II	21	8	0	−4
Ecuador	July 1961	II	−17	17	1[a]	−26[a]
Greece	Apr. 1953	I	−13	0	−23	−1
Iceland	Feb. 1960	IV	−2	13	19	−8
Iceland	Aug. 1961	II	−5[a]	40[a]	−17	43
India	June 1966	II	−3	−5	−6	−1
Israel	Feb. 1962	IV	9	24	24	−2
Korea	Feb. 1960	IV	−30[a]	187[a]	70[c]	−7[c]
Korea	Feb. 1961	IV	187[a]	1[a]	−7[c]	28[c]
Korea	May 1964	I	24[a]	38[a]	−10[c]	−7[c]
Mexico	Apr. 1954	I	3	14	17[a]	0[a]
Morocco	Oct. 1959	III	—[d]	12	—	30
Pakistan	July 1955	II	8	−31	—	—
Peru	1958[b]		10	11	−15[a]	−18[a]
Philippines	Jan. 1962	IV	−8	28	9	−12
Philippines	Nov. 1965	III	−12	15	14	2
Spain	July 1959	II	−10[a]	50[a]	−4	−10
Tunisia	Sept. 1964	II	—	—	—	—
Turkey	Aug. 1958	II	−47[a]	62[a]	3[a]	5[a]

[a] Value (in foreign currency).
[b] Before: 1957 to 1958; after: 1958 to 1959.
[c] Dollar value, excluding aid-financed imports.
[d] Dash indicates data not available.

Source: International Financial Statistics.

preceding devaluation. The entries are percentage changes in the volume of exports and imports, or in the dollar value when volume indexes were not available. It can be seen that in fourteen cases imports actually did fall following devaluation, and in several other cases they rose negligibly; exports rose in all but five cases. These developments accord with theoretical expectations for an economy that is not growing and offer further evidence that devaluation had a corrective influence, although in several cases speculation on the prospect of devaluation may also have influenced the results in the indicated directions.

This kind of *post hoc ergo propter hoc* analysis involves serious risk of misinterpretation, however, for trade flows were clearly influenced by factors other than currency devaluation. In particular, it would be inappropriate to credit devaluation with increases in export earnings that merely reflect growth in world demand and that would have taken place without the devaluation. On the other hand, imports may be assumed to rise with domestic income (and with relaxation of import controls), and it would be equally inappropriate to conclude that devaluation had failed on the basis of income-induced increases in imports or increases resulting from import liberalization.

Table 13.4 offers a crude attempt to allow for the effects on exports of the growth in world markets and for the effects on imports of changes in world prices (presumed beyond influence of the devaluing countries) and in domestic demand. Computed exports indicate what each country's merchandise exports would have been in the calendar year following devaluation if it had maintained the same share of the world market (by 3-digit SITC commodity group) that it had in the year preceding devaluation.[3] Computed imports are derived from imports in the calendar year preceding devaluation by applying an income elasticity of demand for imports[4] to the actual growth in each country's real income in the year following devaluation and, where data permitted, by adjusting for changes in the foreign price of imports.

Actual exports in the year following devaluation exceeded computed exports in fourteen instances, and imports were lower than computed imports in fifteen instances. On the assumption that national income did not decline in Cost Rica in the year following devaluation, the trade balance improved over what it would have been otherwise

3. Specifically, $X_j{}^* = \sum_i X_{ij} R_i$, where R_i represents the ratio of total imports of 3-digit commodity group i into the member countries of the Organization for Economic Cooperation and Development in the year following devaluation to those of the preceding year; X_{ij} is the value of exports of i by devaluing country j in the year preceding devaluation; and $X_j{}^*$ is the computed level of exports for j. This formulation automatically allows for any change in world prices of the export products of the devaluing country.

4. Income elasticities of demand for imports were taken from Hollis Chenery and Alan Strout, "Foreign Assistance and Economic Development," *American Economic Review* 56 (September 1966): 712, column b. For Canada, Iceland, and Spain they were computed from import-income relationships in the 1950s. This procedure is obviously only a rough one. More refined analysis would also take into account the impact of devaluation on income.

Table 13.4: Merchandise Exports and Imports
Year Before and After Devaluation
Compared with Computed Values for Year Following
($ million)

| Country | Exports | | | Imports | | | Trade balance | |
| | | After | | | After | | After | |
	Be-fore	Com-puted	Ac-tual	Be-fore	Com-puted	Ac-tual	Com-puted	Ac-tual
Argentina	994	1088	1009	1233	1078ᵃ	933	10	76
Brazil	1430	1411	1595	1263	1304	1096	107	499
Canada	5811	6231	5970	5671	6170ᵃ	5899	61	71
Colombia (1962)	463	494	446	540	559ᵃ	506	−65	−60
Colombia (1965)	537	631	510	454	484ᵃ	674	147	−164
Costa Rica	84	86	93	107	—ᵇ	113	—	−20
Ecuador	127	125	143	94	100ᵃ	85	25	58
Greece	119	131	132	346	398	296	−267	−164
Iceland (1960)	65	74	67	95	104ᵃ	88	−30	−21
Iceland (1961)	71	83	84	75	84ᵃ	89	−1	−5
India	1686	1861	1607	2945	3004	2874	−1143	−1267
Israel	245	258	279	592	643ᵃ	628	−385	−349
Korea (1960)	19	22	31	304	313	344	−291	−313
Korea (1961)	31	30	41	344	362	316	−332	−275
Korea (1964)	87	96	119	560	605ᵃ	404	−509	−285
Mexico	595	623	648	812	901	778	−278	−130
Morocco	329	369	354	326	334	413	35	−59
Pakistan	380	378	340	273	299	417	79	−77
Peru	281	278	312	382	395	318	−117	−6
Philippines (1962)	500	520	556	677	720ᵃ	654	−200	−98
Philippines (1965)	768	844	828	894	944ᵃ	957	−100	−129
Spain	501	529	725	795	832ᵃ	721	−303	4
Tunisia	123	121	121	235	243	248	−122	−127
Turkey	247	246	355	315	336	469	−90	−114

ᵃ Corrected for change in import prices.
ᵇ Dash indicates data not available.

in fifteen of the twenty-four cases, the same showing as that in the second column of Table 13.2.[5]

This calculation makes no allowance for the stimulus to imports from import liberalization. Of the twenty-four devaluations, ten in-

5. Although it is pushing these data further than they can bear, not least because of the differential changes in rates where multiple exchange rates were involved, it is possible to compute the price elasticities implied by the difference between computed and actual exports and imports by using the effective devaluations shown in Table 13.1 (without making allowance, however, for

volved moderate to extensive import liberalization within the following twelve months. Curiously, however, in eight of the ten cases (Table 13.5) the volume of imports *declined* in the four quarters following devaluation. Import liberalization was delayed three to

Table 13.5: Instances of Import Liberalization

Country	Volume of imports (percentage change in four quarters following quarter preceding devaluation)	Change in balance on goods and services ($ million)
Argentina	−2	270
Colombia (1965)	23	−267
Greece	−1	60
Iceland (1960)	−8	4
India	−1	−35
Israel	−2	−33
Korea (1964)	−7	112
Philippines (1962)	−12	99
Spain	−10	404
Turkey	5	−31

Source: Tables 13.2 and 13.3.

twelve months in Iceland (1960), Israel, Korea (1964), Spain, and Turkey, suggesting that the authorities waited to see how the devaluation was going before they dared to relax controls on imports. In Korea, for example, imports rose sharply after the import liberalization of early 1965. Except in Colombia and Turkey, however, it appears that the immediate movement of imports was dominated by the devaluation or by depressions in economic activity rather than by the relaxation of controls over imports.

It should be emphasized again that devaluation cannot normally be expected to have its principal, let alone its sole, effects in the following year. Expansion of exports and substitution for imports will often require new investment, or at a minimum reorganization of existing productive capacity (e.g. changing the pattern of land use). For manufactured goods, new exports may also require the development of foreign markets. All these adjustments take time. What

---

the effects on demand of domestic price increases, i.e. for domestic supply limitations). Where devaluation "worked" (assuring the right signs), these elasticities range from .02 to 1.54 on the export side, and from .08 to .94 on the import side. Significantly, they are all quite low, as would be expected in the period immediately following devaluation.

we have focused on here are therefore merely the impact effects of devaluation. These are the effects, however, that are usually of greatest interest and concern to those politically responsible for decisions to devalue.

DEVALUATION AND THE TERMS OF TRADE

An argument sometimes advanced against currency devaluation is that it will turn the terms of trade against the devaluing country, thereby benefiting the rest of the world at its expense. Worsened terms of trade are not a necessary consequence of devaluation, however, and indeed for a country that is sufficiently small relative both to its foreign sources of supply and to its export markets, the terms of trade will be beyond its influence, hence unchanged by devaluation. All of the countries considered here are "small" in this sense relative to their sources of imports, but not necessarily relative to their export markets: Brazil's coffee prices may influence world coffee prices, Argentina's beef prices may influence world beef prices, and so on. Under these circumstances, devaluation will generally worsen the devaluing country's terms of trade by lowering the (foreign currency) prices received for its exports, the extent of the worsening depending not only on the price elasticity of foreign demand for the country's export products but also on the devaluing country's elasticity of supply of exports—the higher the former and the lower the latter, the less likely will there be a deterioration in the terms of trade.[6]

Table 13.6 indicates the movement in foreign trade prices during the year following seventeen devaluations. The terms of trade deteriorated in eight of these cases and improved in seven. Many of the price movements, however, were unrelated to the devaluations; it can be assumed that changes in dollar import prices and increases in

6. For a country that cannot influence the foreign currency prices of its imports, the devaluation-induced deterioration in terms of trade will be $kh_x/(h_x + e_x)$, where k is the proportional devaluation applicable to exports, h_x is the price elasticity of domestic supply of exports, and e_x is the price elasticity of foreign demand for exports. The terms of trade will remain unchanged if h_x is zero or e_x is infinite; at the other extreme, the terms of trade will worsen by the full amount of the devaluation, k, if e_x is zero or h_x is infinite. This formulation neglects the impact on the terms of trade of devaluation-induced changes in the level of total demand, an effect that is likely to be negligible for the cases considered here, and the impact on export supply of devaluation-induced increases in the prices of imported inputs, an effect that will reduce any deterioration in the terms of trade.

Table 13.6: Change in Foreign Trade Prices and Terms of Trade in Four Quarters
Following Devaluation
(Percentage in dollar prices)

Country	Export prices	Import prices	Terms of trade
Argentina	11	−5	16
Brazil	4	3	1
Canada	−1	. . .[a]	−1
Colombia (1962)	−1	−5	4
Colombia (1965)	1	2	−1
Costa Rica	1	−2	3
Ecuador	−1	—[b]	—
Greece	—	—	−2
Iceland (1960)	2	3[c]	−1
Iceland (1961)	1[c]	−6[c]	7[c]
India	−3	—	—
Israel	. . .	−2	2
Korea (1964)	6	5	1
Morocco	1	3	−2
Philippines (1962)	4	5	−1
Philippines (1965)	−2	3	−5
Spain	−9	−8	−1

[a] Dots indicate no change.
[b] Dash indicates data not available.
[c] Calendar year following devaluation.

Source: International Financial Statistics.

dollar export prices were due to other factors. Dollar export prices
declined in six instances, and these declines might have been brought
about by the devaluations; but in only two cases—India and Spain—
did the decline in export prices exceed 2 percent, and in both of these
the decline was small relative to the devaluation. The general impression conveyed by these data is that the impact of devaluation on
the terms of trade is negligible for most less developed countries. This
result may, of course, have been achieved through actions designed to
prevent a deterioration, such as the imposition of export taxes.
Several countries here did impose taxes on their principal exports of
primary products. But these taxes were imposed primarily to tax
away the windfall profits that otherwise would have accrued to the
producers, often landlords, under circumstances in which the terms
of trade would not have deteriorated. This is obviously the case for
countries (e.g. Costa Rica) so small in the world market that demand for their exports is highly elastic, where the terms of trade

cannot deteriorate; in other cases domestic supply of traditional products (e.g. coffee, beef) is inelastic in the short run, so devaluation would tend to raise domestic prices for these products rather than lower foreign prices.

DEVALUATION AND AGGREGATE DEMAND

Economies have frequently been observed to pause following a currency devaluation, experiencing a slowdown in business activity and a rise in unemployment. These slumps are puzzling at first glance, since a successful devaluation is conventionally regarded as expansionary in its effects, as expenditure is switched from foreign to domestic goods, thereby stimulating domestic business activity. The observed slowdowns may of course be due to developments unrelated to the currency devaluation, such as unusually bad crops. This was an important factor depressing the Indian economy in 1966, and it may also have been a factor following the Colombian devaluation of late 1962. Or the slowdowns may be due to overly stringent monetary and fiscal policies that are undertaken along with devaluation, to assure that the trade balance will improve and to reduce the dangers of a wage-price spiral following devaluation.

The currency devaluation may itself have a direct impact on the level of aggregate demand, however, and that impact will not always be the expansionary one conventionally assumed. This is obviously so when the current account deficit worsens; in that case the public will be spending even more on imports than it receives for exports than before devaluation, and expenditure on domestic goods and services, other things being equal, will decline. A special case of this phenomenon may arise when devaluation is accompanied by import liberalization, with the result that imports absorb a larger amount of domestic purchasing power.

But devaluation may be deflationary—in the relevant sense of reducing total expenditure on domestic goods and services—even when it succeeds in reducing the current account deficit. Following devaluation, domestic spending on imports may increase sharply even though the volume of imports has fallen. This development will occur if the demand for imports is inelastic, in which case devaluation acts much like an excise tax on tobacco or liquor, increasing the price in terms of domestic currency, but not reducing the volume purchased proportionately. Increases in such excise taxes are of course deflationary even though they raise the prices of the products subject to tax. The price elasticities implied in Tables 13.1 and 13.4 suggest that in the short run the demand for imports into less developed countries is quite insensitive to price changes, a fact that should not be surprising given the heavy concentration of raw materials, foodstuffs, and capital goods in their imports. For many less developed countries, those imports potentially competitive with domestic production (implying a relatively high degree of price substitution) have long ago been effectively excluded through tariffs and other policies of import substitution.

The deflationary impact of the increase in domestic currency prices of imports may of course be offset by an increase in incomes arising from sales of exports. But if imports substantially exceed exports even after devaluation, as they typically will for a capital-importing country, the excise-tax effect of devaluation on imports may more than offset increased spending from enlarged incomes in the export sector.[7] This deflationary impact presupposes that at least some of the capital inflow, which after devaluation commands larger amounts of domestic currency, is not immediately spent. The government recipient of a program loan to finance imports, for instance, must sterilize the domestic currency proceeds arising from the sale of foreign exchange, e.g. by retiring public debt held by the central bank. In this respect the monetary and expenditure effects of a devaluation are similar to those of an increase in taxes not paralleled by an increase in government expenditures.

Even when devaluation is deflationary, incomes will not fall if the deflationary impact is more than offset by expansionary fiscal or monetary action. And where policies are endemically expansionary, the deflationary impact of devaluation will be a welcome antidote.[8] But in framing policies to accompany devaluation, the possibility that its direct effect may be deflationary should be given more recognition than it often is, so as to avoid unnecessary deflation.

Table 13.7 indicates four magnitudes influencing aggregate demand in the year following devaluation: changes in the balance on goods and services (measured in domestic currency), in government expenditure on goods and services, in tax revenues, and in the money

7. A more formal analysis of the conditions under which devaluation will be deflationary is given in Appendix B.

8. In at least one case, South Vietnam in 1966, currency devaluation was undertaken specifically *because* of its expected deflationary impact, not to improve the balance of payments.

Table 13.7: Change in Economic Aggregates from Year Preceding Devaluation
(Billions of national currency units)

Country	Balance on goods and services	Government expenditure	Net tax revenues	Government deficit	Money supply[a]
Argentina	10.3	35.2	—[b]	—	51.3
Brazil	.68	1.73	1.87	−.14	3.22
Canada	.09	.59	.93	−.34	.62
Colombia (1962)	−.98	.95	.95	c	1.17
Colombia (1965)	−1.56	1.63	2.08	−.45	1.39
Costa Rica	−.028	.027	.081	−.054	.081
Ecuador	.21	.29	.22	.07	.05
Greece	−.11	.46	1.70	−1.25	2.43
Iceland (1960)	−.19	.36	.42	−.06	.03
Iceland (1961)	.10	.31	.41	−.10	.36
India	−.17	3.83	1.44	2.39	3.12
Israel	−.52	.27	.20	.07	.31
Korea (1960)	−6.0	6.2	6.8	−0.6	.2
Korea (1961)	−4.5	7.9	7.3	0.6	10.1
Korea (1964)	−0.3	15.4	13.1	2.3	14.1
Mexico	.46	1.36	1.16	.20	1.31
Morocco	−.15	.16	—	—	.58
Pakistan	−.38	.27	.37	−.10	.70
Peru	2.2	1.1	1.3	−0.2	1.14
Philippines (1962)	.17	.22	.26	−.04	.29
Philippines (1965)	.81	.23	.14	−.09	.18
Spain	22.7	4.8	9.8	−5.0	1.2
Tunisia	−.025	.015	.018	−.003	.001
Turkey	−1.12	1.35	.95	.40	.61

[a] Twelve months starting with month preceding devaluation.
[b] Dash indicates data not available.
[c] No change.

Source: U.N., *Yearbook of National Accounts Statistics;* and *International Financial Statistics.*

supply. These recorded changes are not entirely "exogenous" determinants of national output and income, since as already noted the level of imports will be influenced by the level of domestic spending as well as by devaluation and other factors, and of course changes in tax revenues will also be influenced by changes in incomes as well as by the new taxes and improved collection that often accompany devaluation. Nonetheless, they give a rough indication of the impact of devaluation on aggregate demand in comparison with that of other factors.

The balance on goods and services when reckoned in domestic currency actually worsened following devaluation in fourteen instances, indicating deflationary pressure on the economy.[9] The worsening of the balance exceeded increases in government expenditure in five instances, thus offsetting additional expansionary pressures from that source; and in thirteen instances the change in the balance plus the change in the government deficit indicate less expansionary pressures than in the year preceding devaluation. It should be noted that the figures in Table 13.7 are in nominal terms, with no allowance for price changes.

The money supply was not allowed to fall in any of these countries in the twelve months following devaluation, although the rise in Korea (1960), Spain, and Tunisia was negligible. Given the emphasis sometimes placed on the need to maintain a tight control over credit to make a devaluation work, it is noteworthy that for these devaluations the relationship between the percentage increase in domestic credit extended by the banking system and the percentage improvement in the balance on goods and services is a very loose one indeed and, if anything, shows a positive correlation (Figure 13.1).

Devaluation can exert a deflationary impact on the economy in two other ways. When currency devaluation redistributes income from those segments of the population with high propensities to spend on domestic goods and services to those with low propensities to spend domestically, e.g. from wages to profits or rents, domestic demand will tend to fall. The low spending group may have a higher propensity to save or it may have a higher propensity to spend on imported goods. In the latter case devaluation-induced redistribution may actually worsen the trade balance as well as causing deflation.

Deflationary redistributions seem to have been important in the declines in economic activity following devaluation in Argentina in 1959 and in Finland in 1957.[10] It is unclear how general this phenomenon is. Typically, real wages do fall following devaluation, and

9. A comparison of column 1 of Table 13.7 with column 2 of Table 13.2 indicates that in five of these fourteen cases—Colombia (1962), Greece, Iceland (1960), and Korea (1961 and 1964)—the balance improved when measured in foreign currency, illustrating the intermediate case, discussed in Appendix B, where devaluation may improve the payments position, yet still be deflationary.

10. See Carlos F. Díaz-Alejandro, *Exchange Rate Devaluation in a Semi-Industrialized Country* (Cambridge: M.I.T. Press, 1965); and Andreas S. Gerakis, "Recession in the Initial Phase of a Stabilization Program: The Experience of Finland," IMF *Staff Papers,* 11 (November 1964): 434–45.

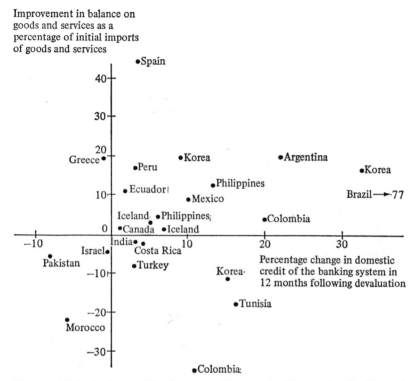

Improvement in balance on
goods and services as a
percentage of initial imports
of goods and services

Figure 13.1: Relationship between Change in Domestic Credit and
Improvement in Current Balance Following a Devaluation

some profits—those in the export and import-competing industries—
certainly rise. Whether this redistribution typically leads to less
spending, however, is more doubtful; investment may be stimulated
by the higher profits. Deflationary redistribution is perhaps most
likely when the principal exports are primary products, when the
elasticity of supply of those products is low in the short run, and
when investment for increased output is not stimulated by higher
profits or rents. As already noted, however, currency devaluation in
these circumstances is often accompanied by the imposition of new
taxes on the exports of primary products, thereby transferring to the
government what would otherwise become higher profits or rents.
These taxes are of course themselves deflationary, except to the extent that the government quickly converts its new revenues into higher
expenditures.

The third source of devaluation-induced deflationary pressure arises from the presence of large private external debt, denominated in foreign currency. Devaluation will increase both the outstanding debt and the debt-servicing burden in terms of domestic currency. The former development may throw some firms and individuals into technical bankruptcy, and the latter will reduce their net earnings. On both counts private investment will be reduced, and indeed if bankruptcy is sufficiently widespread a serious investment slump could develop. This factor is said to have been important in Argentina in 1962, when many firms that had borrowed abroad liberally and at high interest rates for working capital as well as for capital equipment found themselves with sharply increased obligations after the peso was devalued from 83 to 130 per U.S. dollar.[11]

Where external debt is significant, its presence may inhibit the economic authorities from devaluing both for fear of generating bankruptcy and disrupting business and for fear of increasing the real value of the external debt, the latter concern presupposing a deterioration in the terms of trade.

DEVALUATION AND THE WAGE-PRICE SPIRAL

An oft-expressed fear concerning currency devaluation is that it will generate round after round of price and wage increases and that these in turn will nullify the price advantages the devaluation is designed to give to the country's products in domestic and foreign markets. The increase in import prices, it is said, will drive up the cost of living and this will stimulate demands for higher wages, which in turn will raise domestic money costs and hence the cost of living; and so on, in a vicious cycle, ultimately undercutting the gains from devaluation. Furthermore, imported goods may represent important inputs into production for export, and devaluation in this case will directly raise the production costs of exports.

The problem is more complex than this, and the outcome depends in an important way on the dynamics of response by wage earners and businessmen (including farmers) to higher costs and prices. The conditions required for a complete negation of the price effects of de-

11. Roberto Alemann, "Economic Development of Argentina," in Committee for Economic Development, *Economic Development Issues, Latin America* (New York, 1967), p. 51.

valuation are, in fact, quite extreme. Devaluation does, of course, raise domestic prices of imports and export products—that is the mechanism whereby it improves the trade balance—and wages may well respond to the resulting increase in the cost of living,[12] thereby weakening the effects of devaluation. But *nullification* of these effects requires both that wage earners entirely recoup their standard of living through higher wages and that the real value of other income—profits, rents, and taxes—is also maintained.[13] This is simply another way of saying that in order for an improvement to take place in the balance on goods and services, the real expenditure of some segment of the population—wage earners, businessmen, landlords, or government—must fall, and such a decline will ordinarily be achieved only if there is a decline in the real income of some group or groups.[14]

Partial reversal does not exhaust the range of possible outcomes. On the one hand, devaluation may, in fact, result in very little change—or even a reduction—in prices if it is used to replace already existing import controls, subsidies to exports, and other devices to improve the country's payments position. Where imports have previously been restricted by quotas or exchange licensing, devaluation will simply reduce importers' profit margins, acting like a tax on unearned profits generated by the artificial scarcity. Under these circumstances there will be little or no increase in prices, depending on the exact relationship of the devaluation to the scarcity markups already being charged to the consuming public. If devaluation is accompanied by relaxation or removal of the quotas it will increase the degree of competition in the economy, and this in turn may actually lead to a reduction in prices, including prices of domestic goods with

---

12. The discussion usually focuses on increases in the local prices of *imports*. But the local prices of exports will also ordinarily increase, and where exports are staple consumption items, as with beef in Argentina or rice in Southeast Asia, this factor may have a greater effect on the cost of living than the rise in import prices. In 1953 Greece imposed export taxes on cotton, olive oil, and rice to hold down the cost of living.

13. A more formal analysis of this proposition is given in Appendix C.

14. Technically, spending could fall even with the maintenance of real incomes if national hoarding were to rise, an unlikely event except as a result of certain devaluation-induced redistributions of income, discussed in the preceding section.

Total real income need not fall either if there are unemployed resources and output is responsive to devaluation. Even in this case, however, the real incomes of some *initially* employed factors may be expected to fall.

(previously controlled) import content.[15] Furthermore, if monopolistic conditions prevail in the *export* industries, devaluation may
serve to stimulate output without leading to much increase in prices,
by increasing the elasticity of demand facing the exporters.[16]

On the other hand, devaluation may also trigger the release of legal
or conventional restraints on other prices, as when devaluation is
taken as the excuse for raising urban bus fares. Especially under
circumstances of suppressed inflationary demand, there are likely to
be many prices that do not reflect what the market will bear, for fear
of public opprobrium or legal sanctions or even just out of ignorance

15. In partial equilibrium terms, these two points can be illustrated in the
following diagram, which shows the demand schedule for an imported product

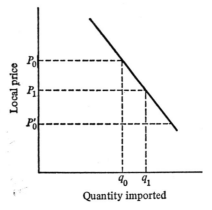

Quantity imported

in the devaluing country. The initial exchange rate would lead to a domestic
price P_o' if the imports were unrestrained, but quotas limit imports to q_o,
permitting the importers to charge a domestic price P_o. A devaluation by less
than $1 - \dfrac{P_o'}{P_o}$ will raise the cost of foreign exchange to importers, e.g. to P_1,
but with local competition it will result in no change in prices charged in local
markets. Quotas hold the quantity of imports at q_o. A devaluation by more
than this amount will raise local prices above P_o, but not by an amount proportional to the devaluation, and will reduce imports. If along with devaluation
import quotas are also removed, and if the devaluation is less than $1 - \dfrac{P_o'}{P_o}$,
local prices will fall to a point like P_1, and imports will increase to q_1. If the
import is an intermediate product, this will lower the prices of competitively
priced finished goods.

16. This last development is said to have been important in Colombia in
both 1962 and 1965. See John Sheahan and Sara Clark, "The Response of
Colombian Exports to Variations in Effective Exchange Rates," Research
Memorandum no. 11, mimeographed (Williamstown, Mass., Williams College,
1967).

or inertia or implied contracts on the part of the sellers of goods and services. Devaluation may provide the occasion for a general reassessment of pricing practices and for recontracting, thus stimulating price increases that could have taken place earlier (and are likely to take place sooner or later) but did not. In this case, domestic costs could rise by more than the amount of the devaluation.

It should be noted that monetary and fiscal policies play a crucial role in determining the extent to which the relative price effects of devaluation are offset by increases in domestic costs. Without monetary expansion to "validate" increased money wages and prices, demand would fall and unemployment would result. The dynamics of response to devaluation thus can influence the ultimate impact of devaluation on the country's trade position. Ideally, devaluation will in the first instance raise local currency prices and hence profits in the export and import-competing industries. This in turn will stimulate those industries to expand, both by hiring additional labor and by increasing investment in capacity (or, in the case of agricultural output, new planting). Labor will be hired away from the nontrade sectors of the economy, possibly with some increase in wages, which the trade sector can afford to pay out of its higher profits, and this will tend to pull up money wages throughout the economy—but as a result of expansion of the foreign trade sector.

An alternative course of events is far less favorable. It arises if the foreign trade sector fails to expand output in response to devaluation, either because of misguided efforts to preserve the status quo or because the gestation period for new investment is longer than the increased profits from devaluation are expected to last. If, then, wage earners respond to increases in the cost of living and to higher profits in the foreign trade sector by demanding, and getting, higher money wages, this will tend to pull up wages throughout the economy. But since profits in the nontrade sectors have not risen (on the contrary, the costs of their import requirements have risen), they can meet the enlarged wage demands only by charging higher prices for their output or by releasing workers. At this point the monetary authorities are confronted with a cruel dilemma: they can maintain tight monetary control, thereby inhibiting price increases but also inducing unemployment; or they can ease up on monetary controls, thereby validating the increases in wages and domestic prices and undercutting the relative price effects of the devaluation. Thus the speed with which output and employment in the trade sector are increased, as compared with the speed with which workers demand and get higher money wages, can be a critical factor in determining the extent to which a devaluation will succeed.

It is difficult to get good evidence on the influence of devaluation on prices and wages, partly because the relevant information is often nonexistent or of poor quality, and partly because movements in wages and prices are influenced by many other factors, such as harvest conditions and productivity growth in the manufacturing sector. Table 13.8 indicates price and wage movements, where data are available, for twelve months from the month preceding the month of devaluation. Price and wage movements beyond that time will, of course, continue to be influenced by the events set in motion by devaluation, but as time progresses other, unrelated factors play an increasingly dominant role. Data are given for the domestic prices of imported goods, the general wholesale price index, the consumer price index, and wages in manufacturing, with data of the first and last type available for only about half the countries. For comparison, the first column shows the extent of devaluation as it should affect the local currency price of imported goods at the port of entry.[17]

The evidence in Table 13.8 clearly suggests that devaluation does lead to an increase in prices, and at least indirectly to an increase in wages, but that increases in the cost of living and in wages are far less than the devaluation—with the notable exception of Colombia in 1962. In no case, however, did the consumer price index decline, and the wholesale price index declined only in Costa Rica. In six instances, the consumer price index increased less in the twelve months following devaluation than it had in the twelve months preceding devaluation, and that relationship also occurred in six instances with wholesale prices, including five cases—Brazil, Ecuador, India, and Korea in 1961 and 1964—common to both groups.

Import liberalization helped to hold down price increases in a number of countries, most notably in Korea (1964), the Philippines, and Spain. But even in the absence of import liberalization, price increases would be moderated to the extent that the higher cost of foreign exchange was absorbed by declines in importers' margins, as they might be if artificial scarcities (e.g. through import quotas or foreign

17. This percentage is related to that in Table 13.1 by the formula $k/(1-k)$, where k is the effective devaluation for imports. The difference arises because the figures in Table 13.1 reckon each exchange rate in terms of dollars per unit of local currency, whereas its reciprocal is relevant for indicating the increase in local currency prices of imports, dollar prices remaining unchanged.

Table 13.8: Price and Wage Increases in the Twelve Months Following Devaluation
(Percentages)

Country	Time of devaluation	Deval- uation[a]	Import prices[b]	Wholesale prices	Consumer prices	Manu- facturing wages
Argentina	Jan. 1959	156	180	115	103	52
Brazil	Sept. 1964	156	—[c]	53	56	49[d]
Canada[e]	1961–62	11	6	3	5	6
Colombia	Nov. 1962	30	33	32	41	37
Colombia	Sept. 1965	33	49	18	20	14
Costa Rica	Sept. 1961	6	3	−1	5	13[d]
Ecuador	July 1961	19	—	2	...[f]	5
Greece	Apr. 1953	69	—	28	22	—
Iceland	Feb. 1960	69	—	6	—	—
Iceland	Aug. 1961	12	—	12	—	—
India	June 1966	43	41	15	13	—
Israel	Feb. 1962	35	—	—	9	10
Korea	Feb. 1960	51	—	15	14	16
Korea	Feb. 1961	56	14	10	...[f]	8
Korea	May 1964	100	36	12	13	18
Mexico	Apr. 1954	45	—	19	17	16
Morocco	Oct. 1959	14	15	16	6	5[d]
Pakistan	July 1955	39	—	—	4	4[d]
Peru[g]	1958	45	—	61	26	11[d]
Philippines	Jan. 1962	19	9	9	6	9
Philippines	Nov. 1965	...[f]	2	5	9	6
Spain	July 1959	35	3	1	1	—
Tunisia	Sept. 1964	20	21	17	11	—
Turkey	Aug. 1958	64	27	25	32	21[d]

[a] $k/(1 - k)$, where k is the effective devaluation for imports shown in Table 13.1.
[b] In local currency.
[c] Dash indicates data not available.
[d] Calendar year.
[e] May 1961 to May 1963.
[f] Dots indicate no change.
[g] Dec. 1957 to Dec. 1959.

Sources: International Financial Statistics, U.N., *Monthly Bulletin of Statistics,* and I.L.O., *Year Book of Labour Statistics.*

exchange licensing) had already led to high local prices for imports. A comparison of the first two columns of Table 13.8 shows that import prices did generally rise less than the amount of effective devaluation, suggesting a sharp drop in importers' margins and reflecting import liberalization where it occurred. But the data on import prices are too fragmentary and the data in both columns are of such uncertain quality that no strong case can be made. It is noteworthy, however, that in eleven instances the wholesale price index rose more sharply than the consumer price index, despite an expectation for the opposite to occur in normal (i.e. nondevaluation) years because of the wage component in consumer prices. This may be due in part to the greater importance of imports in the wholesale price index, but it may also suggest that scarcity markups were trimmed following devaluation. (Where consumer prices rose much more than wholesale prices, as in Colombia in 1962, it suggests that devaluation may have triggered other price increases not directly related to the increased cost of imported goods.)

The hypothesis that markups on imports were sharply reduced following devaluation is further supported by the month-to-month pattern of import prices following devaluation. In the months immediately following devaluation, import prices in local currency rise sharply as importers attempt to pass the full increase in the cost of foreign exchange on to their customers. A peak is reached after two or three months, however, and prices of imported goods fall subsequently for several months, as importers find that the market will not support the higher prices; they had already been extracting scarcity prices before the devaluation, and this limited the extent to which buyers would pay more after devaluation without a sharp drop in supplies. Unfortunately, few countries compile data on the local currency prices of imports, but this time pattern could be observed. among those that do, in Colombia (1965), India, Morocco, Spain, and after the South Vietnamese devaluation of 1966.

Data on wages are sparse and of low quality. Where such data do exist, they indicate an increase in the year following devaluation by rather more than in the preceding. But in nine out of eighteen cases wage increases rose by less than the increase in consumer prices, despite a normal expectation, in a growing economy, for wage increases to exceed increases in the cost of living. Moreover, the wage figures available are for manufacturing, and these probably increased rather more than labor incomes generally, since manufacturing labor is usually better organized and works in a sector (unlike the service sector) that should benefit from devaluation. On only two occasions did wage increases approach (and exceed) the degree of devaluation. Thus it appears that wage increases do not generally undercut the relative price effects of devaluation, and often real wages actually fall.

Prices, like the level of economic activity, are influenced by factors other than devaluation. On the classical view, price level increases are largely determined by changes in the money supply. To hold the price level unchanged following a devaluation would require a fall in prices of nontrade goods and services; and to bring that about would, in most countries, require an unacceptable degree of monetary deflation. Where agricultural output is a significant portion of total output, as it typically is in less developed countries, variations in farm production will also have an important influence on prices. The price level could be held steady in times of poor harvest by sufficiently stringent monetary deflation, but again such deflation is likely to be politically unacceptable.

The combined effects of devaluation, changes in the money supply ($\dot{M}$), and variations in food production ($\dot{F}$) on wholesale ($\dot{W}$) and consumer ($\dot{C}$) prices are indicated in the following cross-sectional regressions, which implicitly assume the same economic structure (e.g. ratio of trade to nontrade sector) for all the twenty-one and nineteen countries included in the two regressions. The variables are all percentage changes, and the standard errors of

$$\dot{W} = 2.83 + \underset{(.14)}{0.32} \left(\frac{k}{1-k}\right) + \underset{(.33)}{0.38} M - \underset{(.39)}{0.70} \dot{F} \qquad R^2 = .59 \quad (13.1)$$

$$\dot{C} = -0.41 + \underset{(.10)}{.42} \left(\frac{k}{1-k}\right) + \underset{(.25)}{0.24} \dot{M} - \underset{(.28)}{0.71} \dot{F} \qquad R^2 = .78 \quad (13.2)$$

the estimated coefficients are in parentheses. The regressions show that *on average* wholesale prices rise by less than a third of the devaluation, with a somewhat greater impact on consumer prices; that increases in the money supply increase prices, but (in a period following devaluation) not by a corresponding amount;[18] and that changes in food production have a substantial impact on both wholesale and consumer prices. In all, over three-quarters of the variation in con-

18. Regressions of prices on changes in the money supply alone resulted in a coefficient close to unity, but with very little of the cross-sectional variation explained.

It should be noted that the standard errors on the estimated coefficients for $\dot{M}$ in both equations and for $\dot{F}$ in the wholesale price equation are rather high, indicating low reliability in the relationship with these two variables. The constant terms are of no consequence on the same grounds.

sumer prices and nearly three-fifths of the variation in wholesale prices could be "explained" by these three variables, although of course this type of evidence is only suggestive, not definitive.

A number of countries hold down the impact of devaluation on consumer prices, and hence presumably also on wages, by subsidizing major items in the cost of living or by imposing price controls. India in 1966 and Korea in its various devaluations maintained price controls, while Colombia in 1965 continued to allow imports of major consumer items to enter at the predevaluation exchange rate for some months following devaluation. When multiple exchange rates are in effect, the latter practice is common. Typically, however, price controls are relaxed and special exchange rates are reduced or removed within a year following devaluation, so that these devices are only partially reflected, if at all, in the observed price changes recorded in Table 13.8.

To sum up, the worst fears concerning wage-price spiraling as a result of devaluation are unfounded. Only Colombia (1962) and possibly Costa Rica represent exceptions, and in the former case a serious decline in food production greatly aggravated the increase in the cost of living. Indeed, harvest fluctuations generally seem to play an important role in determining the cost of living, and devaluations are less likely to be negated by wage increases if they are undertaken in years of good harvest. Finally, real wages fell following devaluation in a majority of the cases considered here—and real wages were undoubtedly reduced from what they otherwise would have been in most of the other cases—a development that is required in the short run if devaluation is to lead to the necessary reallocation of resources to the export and import-competing industries. This does not always imply a long-run reduction in real wages, for where the foreign trade industries are relatively labor intensive, real wages will ultimately be increased by devaluation.

POLITICAL EFFECTS OF DEVALUATION

Even if devaluation works, policy makers may shy away from it on political grounds. National prestige and local pride are frequently factors inhibiting resort to currency devaluation, but an even more important deterrent is the expectation that it will spell political suicide for those responsible for the decision.

A simple test of the political consequences of devaluation is whether the government—in particular the prime minister or president—remained in power during the subsequent twelve months. There are obvious weaknesses with this test. First, a government may have fallen just before devaluation as a result of economic mismanagement or for other reasons, leaving its successor the opportunity to blame the necessity for devaluation on the fallen government. Or a government may have delayed the devaluation to a time which it thought politically safe. Finally and most important, devaluation is often a necessary consequence of economic mismanagement, and it is really the mismanagement, rather than the devaluation, that should be, and often is, the target of political criticism. Thus even when devaluation is in fact the most appropriate remedy, it may be confused with the disease, either by the public or in evaluating the response of the public.

Seven out of the twenty-four governments involved in this study fell in the year following devaluation. In five of these seven cases the political change appears to have been unrelated to the devaluation. The king of Morocco removed his prime minister because of the latter's liberal and modernizing inclinations. General Park's 1961 coup in Korea involved a much broader range of issues than devaluation, although mismanagement of the economy may have contributed to the general dissatisfaction. Costa Rica and Colombia (1965) both experienced orderly changes of government, predictable on past experience even without the devaluations,[19] although economic issues were important in both cases. In the Philippines (1965) President Macapagal was voted out *despite* his attempt to woo the business community through devaluation of the export rate three days before the election.

In both Peru and Ecuador, however, economic mismanagement leading to the necessity for devaluation played a substantial role in the change of government.[20] Economic policy played an important role in the loss of parliamentary strength of the Conservative party in Canada in 1962, but the government held on for more than a

19. In Colombia the presidency alternates between the two leading parties every four years under a 1957 agreement; in Costa Rica quadrennial elections have always led to a change in government since World War II.

20. In Peru the president is chief executive for a term of six years. However, he also appoints a prime minister to preside over the cabinet, which is responsible to the Congress, and President Prado appointed Pedro Beltran as prime minister and minister of finance in July 1959, charging him with straightening out the economic situation.

year. The Congress party in India also lost ground in 1966 over its economic policies. In Israel the devaluation and associated policies led to a hotly debated motion of no confidence, but the government survived it. And in Turkey the coup of 1960 followed strong and widespread dissatisfaction with economic policy, but that change fell outside the arbitrary limit of twelve months set here.

It might be thought that the tactics used in devaluing a currency will influence the chance of political survival, and in particular that resort to piecemeal devaluation may be less of a threat to those in power than a sharp, once-and-for-all change in rate. The nature of this study precludes a careful examination of this possibility, for the observations under consideration all involved fairly substantial changes relative to the periods immediately preceding and following. It is perhaps worth noting, however, that in four of the seven cases in which the government fell, a formal, *de jure* change in parity was involved. Two other cases involved *de facto* changes in a major rate with no change in parity. And Peru had a depreciating flexible exchange rate.

Governments, of course, change even without devaluations, and some standard of comparison is needed to determine whether seven out of twenty-four—29 percent—is a large or a small number of government changes within a twelve-month period. To provide such a comparison, a random sample was chosen from the period 1950–65 of countries that did *not* devalue within a calendar year. In this sample, 14 percent of the governments were changed. It thus appears that currency devaluation, or at least the conditions leading to the necessity for devaluation, roughly doubles the likelihood of loss of power by the government undertaking the devaluation. This chance still remains less than one in three, however, even including changes in government in which devaluation does not seem to have been an issue.

As might be expected, finance ministers fared rather worse than governments: fourteen failed to stay in their jobs during the twelve months following devaluation. Seven of these of course went with their governments, but an additional seven—in Argentina, Colombia (1962), India, Korea (twice), Pakistan, and the Philippines—were ousted or left even when the governments stayed. Again, sometimes the change was not related specifically to devaluation. In March 1963 the entire Colombian cabinet resigned on a political issue, for instance, and Korean ministries were in constant flux throughout this period. A randomly selected control group suggests that seven out of forty finance ministers in nonindustrial countries—18 percent—may be expected to change in a twelve-month period even without devaluation. Thus devaluation seems to increase substantially the possibility that the finance minister of the devaluing country will lose his job; the percentages of finance ministers that were changed in our two samples, one with devaluation and the other without, differ by a factor of three.

CONCLUSIONS

Any conclusions drawn from this examination of two dozen currency devaluations must be highly tentative, for the reasons given earlier. The data are poor. Each country is unique in its economic structure; in its response to sharp changes, such as devaluation brings about; in its domestic price structure; and in its monetary relations with the rest of the world. Wage costs and prices, aggregate demand, and trade flows are all subject to a wide range of influences other than currency devaluation.

Precisely because of these weaknesses, however, generalizations from one or two devaluations are especially hazardous. There is some safety in numbers. Inspection of two dozen cases filters out some of the unique elements that exist in each instance, and provides some assurance against gross error arising from poor data. However, it also requires that the level of explanation and interpretation must be more general and less precise than would be permitted by case studies in depth.

With these qualifications, the following generalizations can be made:

First, currency devaluation seems to be successful, in the sense of improving the balance on goods and services. To be sure, the price elasticities implied by the degree of improvement are quite low, but they are high enough for success. Some of the apparent exceptions to this generalization can be explained by other (possibly related) factors, such as a sharp increase in the inflow of capital following devaluation. Additional foreign aid would permit more generous import licensing, even in the absence of a general import liberalization program; and additional direct investment might raise imports directly. In a few cases, however, devaluation simply failed to have its intended effects. The one-year period used to measure performance of course offers far too little time for the full effects of devaluation, which may require investment in new capacity, to work themselves out. This fact gives greater weight to the high proportion of "successes" in the year following. The first year following devaluation is, however, the period of greatest concern to those responsible for making the decision.

Second, quite apart from monetary and fiscal policies, devaluation itself often initially tends to depress economic activity in the devaluing country, contrary to what has normally been expected. This effect may arise from devaluation-induced shifts in the distribution of income from low to high savers; or it may arise from the large drain on domestic purchasing power created by a rise in the local currency prices of imports, in circumstances in which imports exceed exports and the price elasticity of demand for imports is rather low—both conditions typically found in less developed countries.

Third, devaluations, even large devaluations, do not seem to worsen the devaluing country's terms of trade. Most of the countries considered here apparently account for too small a portion of the world market for devaluation-induced changes in the terms of trade to be a serious consideration.

Fourth, currency devaluation does stimulate increases in local prices of goods and services closely linked with foreign trade; these include export products and local production in competition with imports, as well as imports. It is also accompanied by larger than normal wage increases. But rarely is the increase in wages and other local costs great enough to nullify the effects of devaluation, at least within the following twelve months. Unrelated events, such as bad harvests, can reduce considerably even the long-run benefits from devaluation by contributing to an inordinate rise in the cost of living and hence in wages. This seems to have been a key factor in the instances in which the effects of devaluation were substantially weakened by increases in local costs.

Finally, a decision to devalue does not typically spell political demise for governments that undertake it, but devaluation does seem to be associated with a somewhat higher likelihood of a fall of the government. The chance that a finance minister will lose his job is substantially higher.

No clear-cut recommendations emerge from the study, except that considerable attention should be paid to the economic environment before a decision to devalue is made. The short-run effects of devaluation can be greatly complicated and the long-run effects substantially weakened if it is accompanied by a poor harvest, if it is accompanied by a sudden release of prices that have been hitherto controlled by law or convention, if it is immediately followed by a major wage settlement, or if the public lacks confidence in the ability of the authorities to maintain noninflationary monetary conditions. In all of these cases, induced increases in wages and other costs are made more likely and will reduce the relative price shifts that the devaluation is designed to bring about. A delay in wage response to devaluation is likely to mean a lower overall increase in money wages (but not necessarily in real wages) in the long run.

The price and wage effects of devaluation may be mitigated if import controls are relaxed simultaneously. Historically there has often been a delay of several months or more before import liberalization is undertaken, and by then some of the damage may have been done. Early import liberalization will serve to moderate increases in local prices and, by absorbing more local purchasing power through expenditure on imports, it will also exert some deflationary pressure on the economy.

Finally, however, where analysis suggests that devaluation reinforced by liberalization is likely to exert a strong deflationary impact on the economy, it might be accompanied by relatively early offsetting monetary expansion. Early expansion will help to avoid unnecessary unemployment and excess capacity, and it should thereby forestall the inevitable political demands for economic expansion later. Delayed expansionary policy may come into play just as the devaluation itself is also providing some domestic expansion, and together they may exert undesirable upward pressure on local wages and prices well after the devaluation. However, such "fine tuning" admittedly may not be possible with our still quite imperfect understanding of the dynamics of response to devaluation or to other major policy changes.

APPENDIX A. CALCULATION OF EFFECTIVE DEVALUATION

As noted in the text, the change in a currency's par value does not necessarily imply a corresponding change in the cost to importers of foreign exchange and the local proceeds to exporters arising from their foreign currency sales. Multiple rates may be changed by differing amounts, tariffs may be changed as part of a policy package, certain imports may be subsidized for a period following devaluation, or predevaluation export subsidies may be reduced or removed. The *effective* devaluation for a particular commodity should take into account all of these factors.[1] Unfortunately such calculations would be tedious in their detail for countries with complicated changes in their exchange rates, even if the requisite data were readily available, which they are not. The figures for Greece, India, and Israel, however, reflect such calculations by Eliades, Thomas, and Riemer, respectively.[2]

A simple and expedient, though imperfect, shortcut was adopted here. Where countries record the value of their foreign trade both in foreign and in local currency, an implicit weighted average exchange rate for a given period can be derived from the two sets of figures, where the weights are the value of exports or imports subject to the various exchange rates. The changes in effective rates recorded in Table 13.1 were derived from these average implicit rates on exports and imports, calculated for both the month preceding and the month following the month of devaluation. This procedure should not introduce a downward bias because of devaluation-induced changes in the composition of trade, since these periods are too close to the devaluation for trade composition to be greatly affected by it. But of course the procedure is subject to error where the composition of trade subject to different rates has changed sharply for other reasons. Moreover, this procedure does not in all cases incorporate changes in import duties, for the local currency value of imports may be recorded exclusive of duties. The figure for Canada is adjusted to make allowance for its import surcharges. In a few cases—Brazil, the Philippines (1962), and Spain—the change in multiple rates extended over a period longer than one month, and a correspondingly longer interval has been included here.

Where monthly trade data were not available in both foreign and

1. This notion of effective devaluation differs from another one sometimes used, viz. the nominal devaluation corrected for increases in domestic prices. While correction for increases in domestic prices is important in assessing the incentive effects created by devaluation, especially in countries with rapid price increases, such price increases are treated separately here.

2. Evangelos Ap. Eliades, "Stabilization of the Greek Economy and the 1953 Devaluation of the Drachma," IMF *Staff Papers,* 4 (September 1954); 51–52; Schlomo Riemer, "The Devaluation of the Israel Pound," *Kyklos* 15 (1962), fasc. 3: 657–70; and Philip S. Thomas, "The 1966 Devaluation and Import Liberalization in India," mimeo., Dec. 1966.

domestic currency, or where one series is artificially derived from the other by use of the exchange parity, balance of payments data (in foreign currency) and national accounts data (in local currency) were used instead. This has the twofold disadvantage as compared with the former procedure that balance of payments and national accounts data are typically available only on an annual basis, and the definition of "goods and services" in the two accounts is not always identical. Further errors are thus introduced. Also, for Turkey this technique permitted a calculation only for *net* exports.

Finally, Morocco lacks foreign-currency balance of payments data, so even this technique could not be used, but known reductions in import surcharges are deducted from the nominal devaluation.

APPENDIX B. DEVALUATION AND AGGREGATE DEMAND

Devaluation is normally aimed at improving a country's balance of payments position and especially its balance on goods and services. In assessing its success it is therefore appropriate to focus on the country's earnings and payments in terms of *foreign* currency. But the impact of devaluation on total demand within the devaluing country depends on the resulting increase in receipts for exports and in payments for imports in terms of *domestic* currency, since that is the unit in which incomes are earned and expenditures made.

For a country with a unified exchange rate the relationship between a given balance on goods and services in foreign currency and in domestic currency is $B = rD$, where B is the balance in foreign currency, D is the balance in domestic currency, and r is the exchange rate indicating the foreign currency price of a unit of domestic currency. The change in the foreign currency balance following currency devaluation is then:

$$\Delta B = (r + \Delta r)\Delta D + \Delta r D = r(1 - k)\Delta D - kB \qquad (13.3)$$

Here Δ indicates a change in the variable it precedes, and $k = -\Delta r/r$, the proportionate change in exchange rate (taken to be positive for devaluation).

A devaluation is assumed to be successful if, other things being equal, the balance in terms of foreign currency improves (ΔB is positive). Relationship 13.3 shows that when the devaluing country has an initial deficit on goods and services ($B < 0$), a successful devaluation will *reduce* total demand ($\Delta D < 0$) rather than increase it, as is usually assumed, if improvement in the balance in foreign currency falls short of the initial deficit times the proportionate devaluation (i.e. $\Delta B < -kB$). Even when the improvement is greater than this, the stimulus to aggregate demand will be substantially less than the improvement in the foreign currency balance converted into domestic currency. This is because residents after devaluation must pay more in local currency for a dollar's worth of imports, thereby enlarging the absorption of local purchasing power by the import surplus.

These conditions can be reformulated in terms of price elasticities, measuring the responsiveness of demand and supply of exports and imports to changes in relative prices.[1] On the assumption that the devaluing country is too small to influence the dollar prices of its imports and that the local currency supply price of its exports is unchanged by devaluation, Table 13.9 indicates the range of import demand elasticities for which a small successful devaluation will be deflationary, for various values of export demand elasticities and the ratio of exports to imports.

Table 13.9: Range of Import Demand Elasticity for Which Successful Devaluation
Will be Deflationary

Initial ratio of exports to imports	Elasticity of demand for exports		
	0.5	1.0	1.5
.9	.45–.55	0–.1	—[a]
.8	.40–.60	0–.2	—
.7	.35–.65	0–.3	—
.6	.30–.70	0–.4	0–.10
.5	.25–.75	0–.5	0–.25

[a] Dash indicates no deflationary range.
Note: Table computed for perfectly elastic supply of exports and imports.

If exports face increasing costs, the range of elasticities will be lower than those indicated. The middle area in Figure 13.2 shows the demand elasticity region in which successful devaluation will be de-

---

1. See my "Devaluation and Aggregate Demand in Aid-Receiving Countries," in J. Bhagwati et al., *Trade, Balance of Payments, and Growth,* Papers in International Economics in Honor of C. P. Kindleberger (Cambridge, Mass.: The M.I.T. Press, 1971)

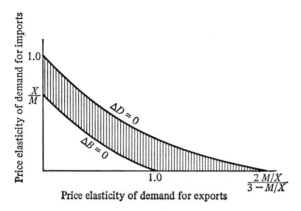

Figure 13.2: Values of Demand Elasticities for a Deflationary
Devaluation

flationary, drawn on the assumptions that the foreign currency prices
of imports are not influenced by devaluation and that the elasticity
of supply of exports is two. On these assumptions, any combination
of demand elasticities in the shaded area will lead to an improvement
in the balance on goods and services in foreign currency but to a
deterioration of the balance in domestic currency, hence to deflationary pressures.

Many less developed countries are likely to satisfy the conditions
under which devaluation will have a negative effect on aggregate demand, at least in the period immediately following devaluation. As
capital-short countries, most of them have continuing deficits on
goods and services, matched by long-term capital inflows. As countries that have pursued policies of import substitution, most of them
have shifted the composition of their imports from finished products
to raw materials, intermediate products, and capital goods, thereby
lowering the price elasticity of demand for imports. Import controls
reinforce this reduction in price sensitivity. Finally, most less developed countries experience supply constraints in the short run, so the
volume of exports cannot be increased substantially until some time
has elapsed. In the short run, the demand elasticity for exports is
also likely to be small. Thus a deflationary impact is likely, although
it may be merely a short-run phenomenon.

Where devaluation is accompanied by trade liberalization, its success should be measured by the improvement over the current balance that would have prevailed with liberalization in absence of the devaluation. By enlarging the hypothetical predevaluation deficit, trade liberalization therefore increases the likelihood that devaluation will be deflationary.

Whether devaluation is in fact deflationary depends also on the nature and treatment of long-term capital inflows. If capital inflows are fixed in terms of local currency (as some private inflows might be), devaluation will reduce foreign currency receipts on capital account, and a "successful" devaluation must improve the balance on goods and services by more than enough to cover this reduction. Such an improvement is more likely to add to aggregate domestic demand. It will necessarily do so if such capital inflows exactly cover the initial trade deficit. This can be seen by modifying relationship 13.3 to include capital inflows K.

$$\Delta(B + K) = r(1 - k)\Delta D - kB - kK \qquad (13.4)$$

If $K = -B$ initially, the last two expressions on the right cancel, and a successful devaluation requires $\Delta D > 0$. But such a devaluation would be undertaken only to build net reserves; continuing capital inflows do not usually cover the current deficit of a devaluing country.

If the capital inflow is fixed in terms of foreign currency, as is likely to be true for foreign aid receipts, at least in the short run, then the earlier analysis holds, except to the extent that the larger domestic currency proceeds from the foreign aid stimulate correspondingly larger domestic expenditures. Thus the budgetary treatment of foreign aid counterpart funds and the closeness of the link between budgetary receipts and government expenditures are important considerations in assessing the impact of devaluation on domestic demand.

For multiple exchange rates and differential changes in rates, the simplicity of relationship 13.3 gives way to more complex relationships, but no new principles are introduced. If the devaluation affecting imports exceeds that for exports, devaluation is more likely to be deflationary, whereas the reverse is true if the devaluation for exports is greater than that applicable to imports.

If before devaluation the central bank is not neutralizing the effects of the balance of payments deficit, the deficit will, of course, be exerting deflationary pressure on the economy as the public pays domestic currency for the purchases of foreign exchange. In that case, devaluation may increase that deflationary pressure under the circumstances indicated above.

APPENDIX C. WAGE-PRICE SPIRALING

Devaluation will typically have secondary repercussions on other costs, thereby weakening—but rarely reversing—the effects of the devaluation on international cost competitiveness. Devaluation may thus stimulate some cost inflation, but the process will normally be self-limiting.

To see this, suppose that the direct and indirect importance of imports, import-competing goods, and exports in the cost of living index is m. A proportionate devaluation by k (measured in terms of dollars per unit of local currency) will, therefore, increase the cost of living index by $\left(\dfrac{k}{1-k}\right)m$, on the assumption that world prices for the devaluing country's imports and exports are unaffected by the devaluation. (If world prices of the country's exports fall, or if the devaluation induces a drop in m, the increase in the cost of living will be correspondingly lower.)

Suppose further that "workers" respond to an increase in the cost of living by demanding a wage increase in proportion p, and suppose that wages account, directly and indirectly, for a fraction w of total domestic costs. Then domestic costs will be increased by an amount $\left(\dfrac{k}{1-k}\right)mpw$. But this will in turn raise the cost of living further, by an amount $\left(\dfrac{k}{1-k}\right)mpw(1-m)$. The induced rise in the cost of living will in turn set off another round of wage increases, and so on, ad infinitum. The ultimate increase in the cost of living, P, will be:

$$P = m\left(\frac{k}{1-k}\right)[1 + pw(1-m) + p^2w^2(1-m)^2 + \ldots]$$

$$= \left(\frac{k}{1-k}\right)\frac{m}{1-pw(1-m)} \quad (13.5)$$

This is an infinite series, but it does not result in an infinite increase in the cost of living so long as $pw(1-m)$ is less than unity. If workers attempt to restore *all* of the loss in real income resulting from devaluation, $p = 1$, and if "workers" include not only wage earners but also salaried persons, businessmen, rentiers, and government enterprises, w may cover the whole of domestic costs ($w = 1$). In this extremely unfavorable case, the only restraint on induced price increases is, ironically, the "import" content (including import-competing goods and exports) of the cost of living, for which by assumption domestic prices are unchanged after the devaluation to a new fixed exchange rate, since they are determined in the world market.

The working out of this ultimate increase in the cost of living will of course take considerable time, and it will not occur before other disturbances—good or bad harvests, changes in world prices, etc.—intervene.

The ultimate increase in *costs* (C) of tradable goods resulting from the devaluation will be:

$$C = \left(\frac{k}{1-k}\right)\left[n + \frac{mpw_x}{1 - pw(1-m)}\right], \tag{13.6}$$

where n is the direct and indirect import content in exports and import-competing goods and w_x is the direct and indirect share of wages in their total (not merely domestic) costs. In general, n will not be the same as m. For simplicity, exports and import-competing goods have been lumped together.

It can be easily shown that so long as p is no greater than unity, C can never exceed the amount of the devaluation, $\frac{k}{1-k}$. But if $p = w = 1$ and $w_x = 1 - n$, the original price relationships between tradable and nontraded goods will be restored, and the devaluation will be thwarted, except insofar as the higher price level induces greater saving. Stated another way, to improve the trade balance, devaluation must cut the real income (strictly, expenditure) of some group, be it workers, capitalists, or government.

Under some circumstances p may exceed unity. This would be the case where some wage or profit increases were overdue but were restrained by law, custom, fear of public opprobrium, or for other reasons. Devaluation may then remove the restraint or provide a publicly acceptable occasion for ignoring it, even though the rise in import prices is not directly involved. Where this is the case, devaluation might actually weaken the devaluing country's relative cost position.

In all cases discussed here, substantial and generalized "wage" increased cannot be sustained without the tacit cooperation of the monetary authorities; they must supply additions to the money supply to support higher price and wage levels. But wage increases may take place initially without this tacit cooperation, thereby confronting the monetary authorities with a painful choice between increasing central bank credit to maintain employment and preserving monetary restraint with the consequence of raising unemployment.

Comments by Carlos F. Díaz Alejandro

The generalizations emerging from Richard Cooper's paper are difficult to challenge. While not surprising, they clearly show that the most exaggerated fears of those opposing devaluation cannot be backed up by substantial experience. But enough negative side effects of devaluation are raised to justify the caution with which economic ministers in developing countries, not to mention those in developed nations, approach changes in the parity value of their currencies. The empirical analysis of the impact of devaluation remains, as the author stresses, in its infancy, and it is not yet clear whether those negative side effects are inevitable.

The key difficulty in empirical studies of devaluation is the separation of its direct and indirect effects from those arising from other economic policies and trends. It is not just a matter of isolating the effects of devaluation from those of other policies adopted simultaneously. Especially for international comparisons, it is also important to establish whether the devaluing country was previously experiencing moderate or fast inflation, for example, and whether that inflation can be characterized as cost-push or demand-pull. Take Figure 13.1 in Cooper's paper, showing little or no correlation between bank credit creation and improvements in the goods and service balance. Changes in credit or money supply in, say, Brazil or Argentina will reflect, among other things, past trends in prices and wages and can hardly be expected to bear the same relationship to the current account balance as money supply changes in India or Tunisia. The comparison may be more relevant if made in terms of deviations from previous trends in credit creation or the money supply. Countries devaluing massively after several years of inflation may do better or worse depending on whether the inflation was due primarily to excess demand, in which case the formula of austerity-*cum*-devaluation may work fast and relatively painlessly, or whether it contained substantial

elements of autonomous cost-push, in which case the negative side effects of that formula may become severe. In short, besides separating
the impact and the long-run effects of devaluation, it may be a useful
next step to consider a typology of devaluations in developing countries, taking account of predevaluation economic trends.

More data on the level and composition of output following devaluation would have been useful. Fears of recession remain a major
obstacle to more flexible exchange rates, and quantification of the
precise extent of recessions would have been interesting. Given Cooper's acceptance of the necessity for real wages to fall if devaluation
is to work, it would have also been useful to see whether investment
rates did in fact increase following devaluation, making up for lower
consumption levels. I suspect they typically do not, at least in the
short run. In fact, a good share of the short-run drop in imports following devaluation may arise from decreases in investments with high
import content, in excess of GNP decreases. If this conjecture is true,
it would imply that the use of an overall income elasticity of demand
in Table 13.4 to compute "normal" imports would yield an over-
estimate for the year following devaluation.

The greater or smaller sacrifices undergone during the short run
following devaluation may or may not be ultimately justified by the
long-run favorable effects of such a policy. Further work in this area
could compare devaluations that have been apparently successful in
the long run (e.g. the devaluations of Mexico in 1954 and Spain in
1959), with those whose long-run success is more doubtful (e.g.
Argentina's 1959 devaluation and Colombia's 1962 one). The comparison will undoubtedy have to go beyond devaluation to take into
account policy packages of which devaluation is only a part. While it
may also get the researcher involved in somewhat amateurish political analysis, potentially it could shed light on the wisdom of different
approaches to the economic engineering of stabilization plans. The
handy excuse that "all depends on the politics of it" may in this area
hide laziness in tracing out the economic leads and lags involved in
stabilization. Researchers should be skeptical of complaints of economic ministers whose plans have gone awry that they have been
"stabbed in the back" by weak-kneed politicians.

Future work should also compare the strategy of massive but in-
frequent devaluations with that of frequent minidevaluations, especially in countries suffering from persistent inflation. Recent Chilean
and Brazilian experience indicates that, given the stubbornness of in-

flationary forces in those countries, the latter policy may involve less risk of severe postdevaluation trauma than the former. Too often the heroics of once-and-for-all large devaluations have been followed by negligible long-run results, leaving in their wake wildly fluctuating relative prices which entrepreneurs cannot take seriously as guides to resource allocation.

There are several points in Cooper's paper with which I am in strong agreement. One is the importance of timing import liberalizations to coincide with devaluation and stabilization plans, especially when foreign aid is readily at hand. Failure to do so can lead to somewhat ridiculous results, such as the unexpected Brazilian current account surpluses following the 1964 devaluation, at a time when that country was supposed to receive massive foreign assistance. Related to this point is Cooper's conclusion on the importance of considering possible unusual deflationary effects of devaluation. Viewed in a longer run perspective, import liberalization can be interpreted as a way to make industry once again part of the trade sector, and as such a potential gainer in future devaluations. In many developing countries industry has become a quasi-home goods sector, as its output prices can be set independently of world market conditions, thanks to prohibitive tariffs and import controls. This status as a quasi–home goods sector explains why industrialists take a dim view of devaluation, which raises their input prices and often shrinks their internal market.

Minimizing the negative short-run impact of devaluation on output and its regressive effects on income distribution may well remain, for noneconomic reasons, necessary conditions for its long-run success. Imaginative policy makers should be able to devise ways of avoiding postdevaluation recessions and glaring inequities in the distribution of the adjustment burden. Cutting back excess demand, even when that has to be coupled with resource reallocation, need not, after all, reduce real output. And devaluations that give extramarginal incentives to producers of exportable and importable goods, who often belong to the wealthiest classes, could also be taken as a good opportunity to revise tax systems in a manner compatible with both greater economic efficiency and a less uneven distribution. Land taxes, for example, could be used more aggressively for this purpose.

14

Public Sector Saving
and Capital Formation

BY LLOYD G. REYNOLDS

The role of physical capital in economic growth was undoubtedly exaggerated in the literature of the 1950s and early 1960s, and an appropriate shift of emphasis has not occurred. On a balanced view, however, capital formation remains *one* important aspect of growth; and the means of financing it are of practical as well as intellectual interest.

Multiyear development plans in the less developed countries usually project a sizable government share in gross capital formation. They also project an ambitious rate of increase in current government revenue and a high marginal savings rate out of revenue. But there has been little systematic study of performance, nor has there been investigation of what happened in the older industrial countries at a comparable stage of development.

Among the questions one would like to answer are the following:

1. What are the *dimensions* of public sector capital formation in the LDC's? Is it typically 25 percent, or 50 percent, or more of total capital formation? It is commonly said that the government's share in today's LDC's is substantially higher than it was in the older economies at a comparable stage of development. Is there evidence to support this opinion?

2. What are the long-term trends in public sector capital formation? Does it typically rise in the early decades of development, then level off, and perhaps eventually decline? Or does it tend to increase continuously? Few of the LDC's have a development record long enough to warrant conclusions on this point. We shall present evidence on trends in some of the older industrial economies; but it cannot be assumed that today's LDC's will follow a similar course.

3. What are the *concrete forms* of government capital formation? When we say infrastructure, or social overhead capital, what do we mean? What is the relative importance of railroads, highways, canals, irrigation works, power facilities, and other uses?

4. What are the major *sources of finance?* Is public sector saving in fact a major source of finance? Is it as large a source as it has been historically in the more developed countries? Is it tending to increase or decrease in importance relative to other sources?

We do not presently have enough data to answer these questions. Fiscal studies in the LDC's have focused on tax structures and the tax revenues of general government. Expenditure analysis, the operation of public corporations, and financial transactions with the private sector have been left in the background. We can only survey the fragments of information that are available, and suggest hypotheses for future study.

Much more material is available on the more developed countries, and this seemed to warrant a section on their experience. In addition to its intrinsic interest, this material permits MDC-LDC comparisons that may be of some significance, and also suggests the kinds of information that should be assembled for the LDC's.

GENERAL CONCEPTS

The Public Sector

The public sector includes: (1) general government at all levels, from the nation to the village, and (2) public enterprises and public corporations operating on a quasi-market basis. In principle, one would like to have comprehensive data for the entire public sector, but this is not always possible. The operations of public corporations are often not reported in any central source, and, short of a special country investigation, one is left with data on general government only. In succeeding sections, we shall try to be clear about when we are speaking of general government and when we are speaking of the entire public sector.

To avoid tedious repetition of standard terms, let us adopt a few conventions. Let GGCF stand for general government capital formation, and PSCF stand for public sector capital formation, including public enterprises and public corporations. Our measures of these, unless otherwise indicated, will be in *gross* terms. Let GDCF stand for gross domestic capital formation. One major concern, then, is with the ratios GGCF/GDCF and PSCF/GDCF.

The GGCF/GDCF ratio is in a sense more significant than the PSCF/GDCF ratio for intercountry comparisons and for appraising trends over time. This is because the range of general government activities is more nearly standardized. The activities carried on by public corporations differ substantially as between, say, France and the United Kingdom, on one hand, and the United States on the other. They also change over time for the same country, as witness the United Kingdom before and after the nationalization program of 1945–50. Thus if we see the PSCF/GDCF ratio rising in a country, this *might* indicate greater investment activity within an unchanged public sector. But it might also be due to increases in the scope of the public sector. Changes in the GGCF/GDCF ratio can be given a clearer interpretation.

The Concept of Capital

A capital expenditure can be defined as an expenditure that will contribute to national output beyond the current accounting period. Construction of public buildings, highways, power plants, irrigation works, and other physical structures is one kind of capital expenditure. But it can be argued that there are at least two other kinds: (1) Expenditures on health, education, on-the-job training, and other things that raise the future productive capacity of the labor force. This "human capital" can be regarded as accumulated and then depreciated over time in the same manner as physical capital. (2) Expenditures that shift the production frontier outward by increasing the output from given inputs. Programs of basic and applied research, and efforts to get research results used in production—for example, by agricultural extension activity—are of this sort.

Many LDC's now use the term "development expenditure" to connote this wider range of activities. The basic distinction in plan documents and government budgets is between development and nondevelopment expenditures. Unfortunately for statistical comparisons, however, the items classed as developmental vary from country to country, often reflecting tactical maneuvering by government agencies.

Whether one uses a narrow or a broad definition of capital formation makes a big difference in the accounting magnitudes. Nancy and Richard Ruggles have recently prepared some interesting estimates on this point for the United States.[1] The U.S. national accounts restrict government capital formation to government construction, all purchases of durable goods being classed as current expenditure. The Ruggles study estimates that, if capital formation is defined to include all durable physical assets, then government capital formation in 1966 (exclusive of military items) amounted to $41.2 billion. Of this total, durable goods accounted for about $17 billion, buildings $9 billion, highways and streets $8 billion, and other structures $7 billion.

The study proceeds to recommend a broader concept of capital, which would include all expenditures having their main impact in time periods beyond the current budget year. On this basis, it is estimated that an additional $40.0 billion, or $81.2 billion in all, should have been counted as government capital formation in 1966. Government expenditures on research and development in this year amounted to about $10 billion, expenditures on education to $20 billion, and "health expenditures of a developmental nature" to another $10 billion. Acceptance of this view (which they extend also to the corporate and household sectors) has drastic implications for the national accounts. The national capital formation rate is much increased, and government capital formation forms more than one-quarter of the total. GNP is increased by the higher capital formation figure and by the fact that the services yielded by past government (and household) capital formation are counted as part of current output.[2]

Tempting as this approach may be, we cannot follow it here for the simple reason of data difficulties. The national accounts prepared by individual countries and compiled and published in the U.N. Yearbook invariably use the narrow or physical concept of capital formation. Shifting to a broader concept would involve, for each country in which one was interested, the same laborious investigation that the Ruggles study makes for the United States. The expenditure accounts

1. Nancy and Richard Ruggles, *The Design of National Accounts* (New York, National Bureau of Economic Research, 1970).
2. The official estimate of GNP in 1966 was $743.3 billion, which the Ruggles estimate revises upward to $903.4 billion. The official capital formation figure of $118.0 billion is revised upward to $308.2 billion by adding: household expenditure on durable goods other than housing, $70.3 billion; government expenditures on durables, $41.2 billion; education, health, research, and other "development expenditures" by government ($40.0 billion), by enterprises ($26.0 billion), and by households ($12.7 billion).

for all levels of government in the country would have to be examined in detail, and specific items sorted into the current and capital (or development) boxes. This we obviously cannot do. It should be remembered, however, that the estimates of government capital formation given below are minimal estimates in that they include only physical structures. Usually, though not invariably, they include only civilian-type physical structures, military expenditure of every type being classed as current consumption.

EXPERIENCE IN MORE DEVELOPED COUNTRIES

We begin with the MDC's, partly because the data for them are more plentiful, partly to provide a background for the later discussion of the LDC's. There is no implication, however, that the future will resemble the past, that the historical experience of the MDC's provides a norm or model to which today's LDC's might be expected to conform. This should remain a completely open question.

The Dimensions of Public Sector Capital Formation

Reliable estimates for most of the MDC's are published annually in their national accounts and reproduced in the U.N. Yearbook of National Accounts Statistics. Key saving and capital formation ratios for fifteen countries over the years 1955–65 are presented in Table 14.1. Note that the GGCF/GDCF ratio is typically of the order of 15 percent. Holland and South Africa, with about 18 percent, are on the high side, while Belgium and the United Kingdom with 11 percent are on the low side. The range is not wide, however, suggesting substantial similarity in government's capital-using role in the advanced industrial countries.

These flow estimates can be compared with stock estimates, i.e. with government's share in ownership of fixed assets. One would not expect the government share to be exactly the same in the two cases. Government capital may be more long-lived on average than private capital, in which case government's share of the depreciated capital stock would exceed its share in gross capital formation. It is interesting, however, that general government's share of national wealth (column 7 of Table 14.1) is typically in the range of 10 to 20 percent.

The picture changes materially when we look at the entire public sector. The median PSCF/GDCF ratio is substantially higher—

Table 14.1: Selected Ratios for Developed Countries, 1955-65
(Percentage)

Country	Capital formation			Saving			Wealth	
	GDCF/ GNP (1)	GGCF/ GDCF (2)	PSCF/ GDCF (3)	GG saving/ Nat'l saving (4)	PS saving/ Nat'l saving (5)	GG saving/ GG revenue (6)	GG wealth/ Nat'l wealth (7)	PS wealth/ Nat'l wealth (8)
Australia	26.7	a	35.3	—	36.6	26.6	—	30
Belgium	19.3	11.1	—	2.6	4.3	1.4	8	14
Canada	24.6	15.5	28.6	19.2	21.2	8.2	13	15
Denmark	20.6	11.9	18.0	38.5	—	17.3	...b	...
France	20.8	12.2	—	29.4	50.7	9.5	22	42
West Germany	25.9	14.3	—	39.4	—	19.9	10	—
Holland	25.9	17.9	33.3	23.6	25.5	13.6	12	18
Italy	22.6	14.1	—	18.5	—	11.2	...	...
Japan	32.5	—	28.7	—	30.2	33.2	16	22
New Zealand	24.4	—	—	—	38.1	20.5	...	...
Norway	30.2	12.4	26.0	44.2	—	20.3	...	...
South Africa	23.4	16.0	40.7	25.7	27.1	20.6	...	...
Sweden	22.9	16.2	39.7	31.0	—	19.9	...	...
United Kingdom	17.0	11.1	42.8	13.3	6.7	4.4	...	13
United States	18.0	14.8	17.1	—	18.8	6.7	11	13

a Dash indicates data not available.
b Dots indicate

Sources: The first six columns were computed from data in the U.N. *Yearbook of National Accounts Statistics, 1955-65.* Each figure is an arithmetic mean of the figures for these eleven years. Data in columns 7 and 8 refer to different years in the period 1950–55 and are derived from Raymond W. Goldsmith, *The National Wealth of the United States in the Postwar Period* (Princeton, Princeton University Press, 1962), p. 99. Only reproducible tangible wealth is included.

around 35 percent—and also more variable from country to country. The variation arises partly from differences in the industrial coverage of public ownership. Thus the United States, with its unusually narrow public sector, stands at the bottom of the range, with a ratio of 17 percent. The United Kingdom, with its much broader public sector, stands at the top of the range.

Long Trends in Public Sector Capital Formation

Few countries prepared national accounts on a current basis before 1940. For earlier periods we are dependent on the efforts of quantitatively minded economists to reconstruct the past from scattered sources. The main pioneer and instigator of this kind of work has been Simon Kuznets. Important contributors include Moses Abramovitz, Noel Butlin, Phyllis Deane, Charles Feinstein, O. J. Firestone, Raymond Goldsmith, W. G. Hoffman, and Henry Rosovsky.

Capital formation estimates covering a century or so are now available for Australia, Canada, Germany, Italy, Japan, Norway, Sweden, the United Kingdom, and the United States. Space limitations prevent a full presentation of this material, but we can comment on the general tenor of the evidence.

The gist of the matter is that there is no single pattern of behavior. The commonest pattern—found in Canada, the United States, the United Kingdom, Norway, and Sweden—is a gradual rise in the PSCF/GDCF ratio throughout the recorded period. For these countries, the post-1945 ratio is at an all-time high, and shows no evidence of decline. In Australia and Japan, however, which had unusually high PSCF/GDCF ratios before 1940, the post-1945 ratios are well *below* those of earlier decades. Finally, in Italy and Germany the PSCF/GDCF ratio, after rising for some decades in the nineteenth century, shows a long-sustained decline and is now at an all-time low. Granted the crudeness of the data, these trends are so divergent as to raise a major problem of explanation and reconciliation.

Let us summarize briefly what seems to have happened in each country.

Canada

Evidence on the GGCF/GDCF ratio is available since 1900, on the PSCF/GDCF ratio only since 1929.[3] The former ratio was only about

3. The basic sources are O. J. Firestone, *Canada's Economic Development,*

7 percent at the turn of the century. It rose sharply from 1900 to 1915, mainly because of heavy federal expenditure on the transcontinental railroads, fell back as this expenditure tapered off, and rose again in the 1920s as the provincial governments embarked on major highway construction programs. From 10 percent in the late 1920s it rose to 11.7 percent in 1950 and 15.5 percent in 1955–65, and the trend seems still to be upward. When publicly owned transport and utility industries are included, the PSCF/GDCF ratio is now close to 30 percent.

United States

The government share of capital formation in the United States is unusually low relative to most other developed countries, but it shows the same acceleration over time observed in Canada. Kuznets's estimates show the government share (on a gross basis, in constant 1929 prices) rising from 4.7 percent for 1869–98 to 8.9 percent for 1899–1928 and 16.3 percent for 1929–55.[4] If military items were included, the acceleration would be even sharper. The government share is also higher on a net than on a gross basis, Kuznets estimated it at 27.6 percent for 1929–55.

United Kingdom

For the United Kingdom, Charles Feinstein of Cambridge University has kindly made available unpublished estimates for the years 1856–1938. These estimates show the public sector share of gross domestic fixed capital formation rising from a bit under 10 percent in the years 1856–75 to about 16 percent in the period 1880–1900, 19 percent in 1900–14, and 28 percent in 1920–38.[5] It will be recalled from Table 14.1 that the PSCF/GDCF ratio for 1955–65 averaged 42.8 percent. This latest rise, of course, is due partly to the extensive nationalization program carried out by the Labor government during

---

1867–1953 (London, Bowes and Bowes, 1958); and Kenneth Buckley, *Capital Formation in Canada, 1896–1930* (Toronto: University of Toronto Press, 1955).

4. Simon Kuznets, *Capital in the American Economy: Its Formation and Financing* (Princeton: Princeton University Press, 1959).

5. The estimates for 1856–1900 are in constant 1900 prices, those for 1900–38 in constant 1938 prices. The series for public sector expenditures covers expenditure by local authorities for the years up to 1919, and from 1920 onward includes also central government and other public sector expenditure. It does not include expenditure by the industries that were nationalized after 1945.

1945–50. But it is not due entirely to that. The Peacock-Wiseman study of government expenditure indicates that even the GGCF/GDCF ratio was somewhat higher in the 1950s than it had been in the 1920s and 1930s.[6] Thus we can conclude that the United Kingdom pattern resembles that for Canada and the United States, showing continued acceleration of the public sector share over the past century.

Sweden

Data on gross fixed investment by sector, over the period 1861–1965, have been assembled as part of a long-term study of economic growth being conducted by the Committee on Economic Growth of the Social Science Research Council (SSRC).[7] The heading "public services" presumably covers most of the public sector, though some investments entered under "transport" may also be public.

The series resembles the United Kingdom series in showing sustained acceleration with no decline up to the present. The public service share of gross investment was 5 percent in 1861–65, about 8 percent in 1865–90, rose to 10 percent in 1890–1900, and stayed near 15 percent in 1900–20. It was a bit above 20 percent in the period 1920–40 and has risen further to the range of 26 to 28 percent in 1950–65. This long-sustained rise probably reflects both some extension of the scope of the public sector and heavier investment in traditional public activities.

Norway

The data for Norway, compiled by J. Bjerke, are not in ideal form for our present purpose.[8] They cover only capital formation by general government, and they show this as a percentage of government expenditure rather than of domestic capital formation. But since Bjerke also estimates the government expenditure/GNP ratio and

6. Alan T. Peacock and Jack Wiseman, *The Growth of Public Expenditure in the United Kingdom* (Princeton: Princeton University Press, 1961).
7. These unpublished data, along with similar data for several other countries, were kindly provided by Moses Abramovitz, who is coordinating the research program. They are subject to further revision before publication, but it seems unlikely that they will change the general tenor of the results.
8. J. Bjerke, "Some Aspects of Long-Term Economic Growth in Norway since 1865," mimeographed (Paper presented to the Sixth European Conference of the International Association for Research in Income and Wealth, Portoroz, Yugoslavia, 1958).

the GDCF/GNP ratio, we can infer what was happening to the GGCF/GDCF ratio.

The estimates cover the period 1865–1956. When we compare the years 1865–80 with the years 1920–40, we notice the following changes: the national capital formation rate has not changed materially; the ratio of government expenditure to GNP has more than doubled; the proportion of government expenditure going into capital formation has remained relatively constant, in the range of 20 to 25 percent. It follows that the GGCF/GDCF ratio must have approximately doubled over this seventy-year period.

In the postwar period, the government expenditure/GNP ratio has risen by about one-third, and the proportion of expenditure going into investment has also risen somewhat. The national capital formation rate, however, has more than doubled. Thus while the GGCF/GNP ratio has continued to rise (it is now about 3 percent, compared with 1 percent in the 1860s), the GGCF/GDCF rate may be somewhat lower today than it was in 1920–40.

Japan

We turn now to the two countries which show a clear decline in the public sector investment share since 1945. The first of these, Japan, is particularly interesting, since Japan is often regarded as a model of successful development under strong government leadership. To Rosovsky's estimates for 1887–1940 we can add Patrick's data for 1952–65, thus coming up almost to the present day.[9]

The government share of capital formation is considerably influenced by the inclusion or exclusion of military items. Military investment was substantial up to 1940. It formed about 20 percent of GDCF in 1890–1910, fell gradually to less than 10 percent during the 1920s, then shot up to 30 percent during the 1930s. All of this was government investment, so that, if it is included, the PSCF/GDCF ratio in some decades was above 50 percent.

Even if military items are excluded, the PSCF/GDCF ratio remains impressive. Rosovsky's estimate for 1887–96 is 24 percent, and one

9. Henry Rosovsky, *Capital Formation in Japan, 1868–1940* (New York, Free Press, 1961); Hugh T. Patrick, "The Financing of the Public Sector in Postwar Japan," in Lawrence Klein and Kazushi Ohkawa, eds., *Economic Growth: The Japanese Experience Since the Meiji Era* (Homewood: Richard D. Irwin, 1968).

can surmise that the ratio was lower than this in the first two decades after the Meiji Restoration. From this level it rose to about 40 percent in the 1900s and, after falling back somewhat from 1915 to 1925, rose again to 40 percent in the early 1930s. In the post-World War II period, the public sector share has fluctuated mostly in the range of 20 to 30 percent. Japan thus seems to conform to one of the possible patterns suggested at the outset: a government capital formation share which rises substantially in the early decades of development, then levels off, and eventually declines.

It should be emphasized that this is merely a *relative* decline, associated with the massive upsurge of private investment during the 1950s and 1960s. In absolute terms, and as a percentage of GNP, public sector investment has continued to rise. In recent years it has been running at about 10 percent of GNP, well above the level in any other of the MDC's. It is also noteworthy that government purchases of capital goods are about equal in size to purchases of current goods and services.

Australia

Noel Butlin's estimates for Australia, which begin in 1861, show a similar acceleration of public sector capital formation for many decades.[10] During 1861–80, the PSCF/GDFC ratio averaged about 40 percent. This rose to 45 percent in the period 1880–1910. After 1910 the PSCF/GDCF ratio exceeded 50 percent rather consistently and averaged 55 percent in the last prewar decade, 1931–39. In the postwar period, however, the ratio has been lower, averaging about 30 percent from 1950–60 and 35 percent from 1955–65.

The Australian data thus conform to the Japanese pattern of a long-sustained rise in the PSCF/GDCF ratio, with a decline appearing only in the post-World War II period. The Australian ratio is also remarkably high, probably the highest for any capitalist country over such a long period. This is associated with the continental scope of the economy and the heavy cost of linking scattered population centers by rail, road, and communications media. Railroad building alone formed more than 40 percent of public sector investment from 1860 to 1920.

10. Noel G. Butlin, *Australian Domestic Product, Investment and Foreign Borrowing, 1861–1938/39* (Cambridge University Press, 1962).

Germany

Data on Germany from 1851 to 1959 have been assembled by W. G. Hoffman.[11] He distributes net investment, in constant 1913 prices, among agriculture, manufacturing, residential construction, public construction, railways, and roads. The last three categories are considered here as public sector. There is probably also some investment of a public utility type under the manufacturing heading, but this cannot be separated out.

If we add the last three headings and then examine the behavior of public sector investment thus defined, we find a pattern different from any encountered previously. The public sector share starts out at about 30 percent in the 1850s, rises to a peak of 36 percent in 1875–79, then declines to a range of 14 to 18 percent from 1885 to 1914. The 1875–79 peak is essentially a peak in railroad building during the 1870s. The subsequent decline represents a falling off of the railroad share of net investment, uncompensated by any appreciable increase in the share of roads and other public construction.

During the interwar period the public sector share remained near 20 percent, except for an abnormal rise in the years 1930–34, reflecting the collapse of private investment during the Great Depression accompanied by a smaller decline in public investment. In the post-1945 period the public sector share has been lower than ever before: 9.8 percent during 1950–54, 13.6 percent during 1955–59. Manufacturing alone absorbed more than 60 percent of net investment during this decade.

In interpreting this material, one must remember that we have probably not caught all of public sector investment in the railways-roads-public construction total. There are also special problems of comparability arising from changes in Germany's borders which may not have been entirely overcome. Allowing for these defects, however, it seems likely that the public sector share of net investment has declined markedly since the 1870s and is now at an all-time low.

Italy

The SSRC study, which covers the period 1861–1964, reports total fixed investment in constant 1938 prices and a sector distribution that

11. W. G. Hoffman, *Das Wachstum der deutschen Wirtschaft seit der mitte des 1910 Jahrhunderts* (Berlin, 1965), p. 143.

includes "public works in the strict sense" and also a larger "public works" figure that comes closer to the public sector concept. Some public sector investment is doubtless contained under other headings, such as housing and industry.

The Italian data resemble the German in that public sector investment was relatively more important before 1900 than it has been since that time. From 1860 to 1900, the public works share of investment was in the range of 20 to 30 percent, while that for public works in the strict sense was 12 to 14 percent. There is a marked drop after 1900 and little change in the percentages from that time to the present. Over the past sixty-five years, the public works share has fluctuated in a range of 10 to 13 percent, while the "strict sense" figure has been consistently 8 to 9 percent.

These percentages are doubtless too low in that they do not include public investment in manufacturing and other areas; but it is unlikely that fuller coverage would disturb the conclusions about long-run trends. The Italian picture seems to correspond to that of an under-developed country making heavy infrastructure investment for several decades, which then declines in relative (though not absolute) importance as private investment takes hold.

It is perhaps unwise to draw any conclusions from such a varied body of material. But a few things can be said:

1. Different countries have characteristically different levels of the PSCF/GDCF ratio, partly reflecting differences in the scope of the public sector. Japan, Australia, and (in recent decades) Sweden and the United Kingdom have relatively high ratios. Canada, the United States, and (in recent decades) West Germany and Italy have considerably lower ratios.

2. The government share in capital formation rises for a prolonged period after accelerated growth gets under way. The data for most countries do not go back far enough for us to observe the beginnings of this process, but they usually do go back far enough to include part of the period in which the government share is still rising. Such an increase is observed in Germany from 1850 to 1880, in Japan from 1890 to 1940, in Australia from 1860 to 1940, and in Norway, Sweden, Canada, the United States, and the United Kingdom right up to the present.

3. The most puzzling question is whether the PSCF/GDCF ratio

tends to level off and perhaps eventually to decline. Seven of the nine countries examined show a sustained rise in this ratio up to 1940, and in five countries the rise has continued in the postwar period. But there is enough variation of behavior to suggest a need for further investigation.

What Does Government Invest In?

Here again our information is richest for Japan and Australia (Tables 14.2 and 14.3). Their experience, plus fragments of information for other countries, suggests several observations:

1. Government capital formation involves predominantly construction rather than durable equipment. Rosovsky's estimates for Japan show construction forming about 80 percent of nonmilitary investment in the public sector during 1887–1900, though this percentage falls gradually to less than 70 percent by the 1930s.

2. Transport and communications have historically been of major importance. In Australia, railroads alone formed more than 40 percent of public investment in the whole period from 1860 to 1920. All forms of transport and communications made up more than half of public sector investment in that era. In Japan, too, railroad construction was a large item, constituting 20 to 30 percent of public sector investment in the period 1900–30. At the height of the railroad building era in Canada from 1905 to 1915, railroad construction made up more than half of all public sector-type construction, and about one-quarter of construction of every sort.

3. In the older economies, however, the transport-communications share, after peaking at different times (1840–70 in Britain, 1870–90 in Australia, 1905–15 in Canada, 1910–20 in Japan), has declined to something like one-quarter to one-third of public sector investment today. Viewed differently, public investment has become considerably more diversified. Areas that have grown in relative importance include housing, schools and hospitals, and urban facilities of every sort (streets, water supply and sewerage, gas and electricity supply, police and fire protection).

4. One should not identify public investment with *central* government investment. In large countries with well-developed systems of state and local government, the bulk of general government invest-

Table 14.2: Government Construction by Purpose, Japan, 1870–1940
(Percentage of total)

	Military (1)	Trans-portation (2)	Buildings (3)	Reparian (4)	Roads and bridges (5)	Other (6)	Public utilities (7)	Agri-culture (8)	Natural disasters (9)	Other (10)	Total
					Public works						
1870–79	4.7	13.0	31.2	16.0	18.3	16.1	—	0.3	—	0.4	100.0
1880–89	9.4	2.4	21.8	24.9	28.2	7.0	—	0.4	1.9	4.0	100.0
1890–99	13.9	7.8	16.3	26.7	21.6	3.2	—	0.5	9.3	0.7	100.0
1900–09	12.3	15.6	22.7	11.1	21.6	6.3	5.9	2.8	1.2	0.5	100.0
1910–19	7.2	24.3	18.6	15.9	14.4	7.4	3.9	4.1	2.0	0.3	100.0
1920–29	2.5	18.2	20.2	9.2	20.4	9.2	3.9	5.7	10.5	0.2	100.0
1930–39	4.9	9.8	14.4	24.5	24.6	8.1	1.9	6.4	5.3	0.1	100.0

Source: Rosovsky, *Capital Formation,* pp. 164–75.

Table 14.3: Public Sector Capital Formation by Purpose, Australia, 1861–1959
(Percentage of total)

	Rail- ways	Roads and bridges	Public buildings	Water and sewerage	Power and commu- nications	Local and semi- govern- mental authorities	Other
1861–70	40.1	19.9	11.3	4.4	1.3	20.6	2.4
1871–80	44.0	18.0	12.2	3.9	2.0	17.6	2.3
1881–90	52.8	12.4	6.9	6.6	1.2	16.5	3.6
1891–1900	40.1	14.8	7.1	8.0	1.6	24.4	4.0
1901–10	41.1	12.7	5.9	10.1	1.7	21.0	7.5
1911–20	40.3	5.9	5.1	9.6	4.2	17.7	7.2
1921–30	27.3	8.2	3.9	9.2	11.7	25.1	14.6
1931–39	19.3	9.4	3.7	10.5	7.5	42.0	7.6
1940–49	10.6	20.5	15.3	7.0	11.7	ᵃ	34.9ᵇ
1950–59	8.8	19.1	14.9	8.4	24.9	ᵃ	23.9ᶜ

ᵃ Not listed separately for these periods.
ᵇ Includes other transport, 5.3; forestry and land development, 5.2; housing, 8.0.
ᶜ Includes other transport, 6.0; forestry and land development, 2.9; housing, 6.6.

Source: Butlin, *Australian Domestic Product.*

ment now occurs at these lower levels. Patrick's Japanese data[12] show the following distribution of government-fixed investment in 1960 (billions of yen):

	Central	Local	Total
General government	155	619	774
Public enterprises	363	136	449
Total	518	755	1,273

In Canada, federal investment exceeded provincial and municipal investment up to 1915, because of the heavy railroad investment already noted. After 1915, however, the lower levels of government pulled ahead. Since 1920, provincial and municipal investment has typically formed 65 to 70 percent of all general government investment (excluding military items).

The British situation is similar to that in Japan. Public enterprises are predominantly national in scope and make up 40 to 50 percent of total public sector investment. On the general government side, however, Peacock and Wiseman report that about four-fifths of all in-

12. Hugh T. Patrick, "Functional Estimates of Japanese Government Expenditures, Fiscal 1952–1963," *Review of Income and Wealth*, September 1967, pp. 231–46.

vestment is made by local authorities. About half of local expenditure on goods and services is capital expenditure. Some 60 percent of local capital expenditures are on housing, the balance on a wide variety of economic and social services.

In the United States, excluding military items and the war years 1941–45, state and local investment has consistently been more than 80 percent of general government investment, rising as high as 95 percent in the decade 1919–28. In the first postwar decade, 1945–55, state and local investment was 77 percent of the total. The states and localities are the main organizers of public capital formation and the main producers of civilian goods.

The Australian data (Table 14.3) do not provide a clear separation between major levels of government. It is significant, however, that the investment share of local and semigovernmental authorities rose from around 20 percent before 1920 to 42 percent during the 1930s.

The predominance of state and local investment in the developed countries may carry implications for the LDC's, where planning of public investment and accumulation of financial resources is often highly centralized at the national level.

Public Sector Saving as a Source of Finance

Some key ratios for the MDC's for the period 1955–65 were summarized in Table 14.1. Where comprehensive information is available on public sector saving, this is shown in column 5, while column 4 shows general government saving only. All figures are in gross terms. A check of the saving columns 4 and 5 against the capital formation columns 2 and 3 provides a rough test of how far the public sector was financing its own capital formation.

Government contributed a substantial part—typically 20 to 40 percent of gross national saving—during this period. Except for Belgium, general government saving consistently exceeded general government capital formation, leaving a surplus for transfers to public corporations or other uses.

When one looks at the public sector as a whole, the picture is more mixed. In a few countries, the public sector saving percentage is higher than the capital formation percentage. But in others the saving percentage is below the capital formation percentage, implying that the public sector was a net borrower. For about half the countries in the table, comprehensive public sector data are not available.

It would be desirable to present saving information for the MDC's over a much longer period in the past. But the basic data are not in such good shape as the capital formation data, and to explore them at all thoroughly would require more space than we have available. We limit ourselves to a few comments, which would probably be sustained by fuller investigation, but which should be regarded here as hypotheses rather than settled conclusions.

1. Different components of the public sector have characteristically different patterns of behavior. Public corporations are typically net borrowers. The fiscal behavior of central government usually differs from that of lower levels of government, though not always in the same way. In the United States, for example, the federal government probably saves little or nothing even on a gross basis. The state and local governments, on the other hand, make substantial gross savings. In Japan these relations are reversed. The central government typically has a substantial surplus over both current and capital expenditures. Local authorities and public corporations, on the other hand, have insufficient revenue to meet their investment requirements. Their investment is financed in large measure by transfers from central government and by borrowing.[13] It would be useful to analyze such intercountry differences in greater detail.

2. Government saving, and particularly central government saving, is much more variable than private saving. Even apart from the abnormality of war periods, a correct response to cyclical fluctuations in private demand implies large year-to-year changes in government's budget position. Since 1945 most of the MDC's have had a consistently high level of aggregate demand, with only brief and mild interruptions, and substantial budget surpluses have been appropriate. This must account in part for the high saving ratios in Table 14.1, which are probably considerably above pre-1945 levels.

3. Scattered data, going back in some cases for a century or so, suggest that the behavior of government saving ratios has paralleled, albeit very roughly, that of government capital formation ratios, as regards both *level* and *trend*. Countries that have had unusually high GGCF/GDCF ratios have tended to have unusually high government saving ratios, and conversely. The extremes may be represented by Japan and the United States. As early as 1900–14, government sav-

13. See on this point Tatsuya Samukawa, "The Public Sector in Financial Flow Statements: Japan's Case," *Review of Income and Wealth,* December 1967, pp. 311–34.

ing in Japan was typically 30 to 40 percent of gross domestic saving, and it has remained relatively high in subsequent decades. In the United States, on the other hand, government saving has typically been less than 10 percent of total saving.

We noted earlier that in most countries the PSCF/GDCF ratio has risen gradually over the past century. It is highly likely that there has been a similar increase in the public sector share of national saving. In Japan, on the other hand, where the PSCF/GDCF ratio has been considerably *lower* since 1950 than in earlier decades, there has been an accompanying decline in the government savings ratio. The government share of gross domestic saving was 30 to 40 percent from 1900 to 1914. During the 1920s it occasionally rose as high as 50 percent. But since 1950 it has fluctuated in the general range of 20 percent.

Such a correspondence in the behavior of capital formation and saving ratios (if it exists) might arise in more than one way and raises interesting problems of interpretation. The first task of research, however, is to test whether the correspondence does exist.

4. Public sector saving typically falls short of investment requirements, so that overall the public sector emerges as a net borrower. For Japan, the Patrick and Samukawa studies show the public sector as a net borrower in most years since 1950. This has clearly been true in the United States, where both federal and state-local indebtedness has risen substantially in the postwar period. Table 14.1 suggests that many (though not all) of the MDC's have been in the same position in recent years.

Evidence before 1940 is less satisfactory because both the saving and investment data are weaker. So we can only hypothesize that public sector saving is usually less than public sector capital formation. Such a finding, if confirmed by further research, should not carry any normative connotation. Private corporations borrow on a substantial scale for fixed investment. There is no a priori reason why public authorities should not do the same.

EXPERIENCE IN LESS DEVELOPED COUNTRIES

We come now to public sector saving and capital formation in the LDC's. Here we cannot rely on the Yearbook of National Accounts Statistics. Most of the LDC's do not even try to complete the savings and capital formation tables in the U.N. system, and the few tables that are published probably contain a considerable margin of error.

A far from exhaustive survey of sources has uncovered three bodies of relevant information: (1) ECAFE has published a study of the size and financing of gross public sector investment in nine Asian countries over the years 1961–66. This was based on detailed examination of individual country accounts and discussions with informed government officials.[14] (2) The studies thus far completed as part of the Economic Growth Center's Country Analysis Program (Argentina, Brazil, Ceylon, Chile, Israel, Mexico, Nigeria, and the United Arab Republic) contain considerable information on the size and composition of public sector capital formation. These data are limited for most countries to the post-1945 period and usually end in the early 1960s.[15] (3) The IMF has made a sample study of the operating results of public corporations in all parts of the world, which permits inferences about typical patterns of capital formation and financing.

The Dimensions of Public Sector Capital Formation

Investment and financing data for the nine ECAFE countries, purportedly covering the entire public sector, are shown in Table 14.4. There is considerable variation among countries in both the GDCF/GNP ratio and the PSCF/GDCF ratio. For about half the countries, the latter ratio falls in a range of 40 to 45 percent. But Thailand, South Korea, and Malaysia, which are private sector oriented, are well below this level. On the other hand India, in which the public sector includes a considerable share of heavy manufacturing, has an unusually high 64 percent.

---

14. U.N. ECAFE, *Economic Bulletin for Asia and the Far East,* September 1968, pp. 10–28.

15. Werner Baer, *Industrialization and Economic Development in Brazil* (Homewood, Ill.: Richard D. Irwin, 1965); Carlos Díaz Alejandro, *Essays on the Economic History of the Argentine Republic* (New Haven: Yale University Press, 1970); Gerald Helleiner, *Peasant Agriculture, Government, and Economic Growth in Nigeria* (Homewood, Ill.: Richard D. Irwin, 1966); Markos Mamalakis, *Growth and Structure of the Chilean Economy: 1840–1968* (New Haven: Yale University Press, forthcoming); Donald Mead, *Growth and Structural Change in the Egyptian Economy* (Homewood, Ill.: Richard D. Irwin, 1967); Howard Pack, *Structural Change and Economic Policy in Israel* (New Haven: Yale University Press, 1971); Clark Reynolds, *The Mexican Economy: Twentieth-Century Structure and Growth* (New Haven: Yale University Press, 1970); Donald Snodgrass, *Ceylon: An Export Economy in Transition* (Homewood, Ill.: Richard D. Irwin, 1966).

Table 14.4: Size and Financing of Gross Public Investment, Selected ECAFE Countries, 1961–66

Country	Total gross investment (percentage of GNP)	Gross public investment (Percentage of GNP)	Gross public investment (Percentage of total investment)	Government saving	Percentage of public sector investment financed by: Domestic borrowing bank	Domestic borrowing nonbank	External aid and other
India	11.7	7.4	63.7	20.0	16.0	29.8	34.2
Pakistan	13.6	5.8	43.0	15.1	9.7	17.0	58.2
Ceylon	14.7	6.8	46.1	8.3	26.2	48.9	16.6
Burma	18.1	8.3	46.0	—	—	—	—
Malaysia	18.7	7.1	37.7	32.0	→ 44.8 ←		23.2
Thailand	21.5	5.8	26.9	44.9	9.0	26.9	19.2[a]
Philippines[b]	—	—	—	—	—	—	—
Taiwan	19.7	8.7	44.4	—	—	—	—
South Korea	15.5	4.9	31.9	12.4	40.7	6.4	40.5

[a] Consists of foreign loans and grants, 30.0 percent; change in cash balance, −10.8 percent.
[b] Financing figures cover 1962–64 only.

Source: ECAFE, Economic Bulletin, pp. 10–27.

Evidence from other countries suggests that these Asian figures are rather high on a world scale. Table 14.5 contains recent data for Argentina, Ceylon, Brazil, and Nigeria, while Tables 14.6 and 14.7 present longer series for Argentina and Mexico. It would seem that

Table 14.5: Government Share of Gross Domestic Capital Formation Selected
Countries and Years
(Percentage of total)

	Argentina	Brazil	Ceylon	Nigeria
1947		15.84		
1948		23.33		
1949		29.41		
1950	28.57	35.11	55.44	
1951	28.57	25.00	45.95	30.42
1952	27.27	26.83	49.98	33.70
1953	29.16	29.39	53.55	33.84
1954	26.92	24.28	55.24	36.08
1955	22.58	23.99	53.62	34.88
1956	18.60	24.78	55.11	33.10
1957	18.64	36.98	48.72	33.09
1958	25.92	40.82	50.53	
1959	22.22	40.83	43.26	
1960	22.02	38.38	45.04	
1961	21.94			
1962				
1963				

Sources: Argentina: Díaz Alejandro, *Essays*, Statistical Appendix, Table 5; Brazil: Baer, *Economic Development*, Appendix 2, pp. 226–27; Ceylon: Snodgrass, *Ceylon* pp. 269–79; Nigeria: Helleiner, *Peasant Agriculture*, Statistical Appendix, p. 410.

in Latin America a "normal" range for the PSCF/GDCF ratio is 25 to 35 percent. Mexico exceeded this level for a time but has fallen back to a range of 25 to 30 percent in recent years. Evidence from Africa is still too fragmentary to warrant any conclusions.

How do PSCF/GDCF ratios in the LDC's compare with those in the MDC's at the present time? Table 14.1 suggests that most of the MDC's fall in a range of 20 to 40 percent. The LDC's, if one excepts India, seem to fall in a range of 25 to 45 percent. The median appears somewhat higher for the LDC's, but better data for more countries would be needed to verify this result.

We saw earlier that in most MDC's the PSCF/GDCF ratio has risen over time and is substantially higher today than it was a century ago. It follows that PSCF/GDCF ratios in the LDC's today are

Table 14.6: Composition of Gross Domestic Absorption, Argentina, 1935–64
(Constant 1935 prices)

| | | | | *Fixed capital formation* | |
	Private consumption	*Public consumption*	*Public construction*	*Private construction*	*Machinery and equipment*	*Total*
1935–38	77.9	10.9	3.0	2.5	4.3	11.2
1939–45	78.9	12.1	2.2	3.1	2.1	9.0
1946–48	73.4	14.5	2.1	3.7	4.9	12.1
1949–51	74.9	13.3	3.1	3.8	3.6	11.8
1952–55	74.8	12.9	2.8	3.7	3.8	12.3
1956–58	74.9	12.4	2.3	3.9	4.4	12.7
1959–61	72.9	12.7	3.1	3.1	6.2	14.4
1962–64	74.3	12.0	2.8	2.9	6.2	13.6

Source: Essays, Díaz, Chapter 5, Table 5.

much above what they were in the MDC's *at a comparable stage of development.* The LDC's are starting out at a (relative) level of public sector investment which most MDC's have reached only recently.

The reasons for this difference include: (1) The scope of the public sector is substantially wider in today's LDC's than it was in the MDC's in the mid-nineteenth century. (2) Foreign funds to finance capital formation now flow mainly through public rather than private channels. (3) Incentives to private investment are frequently weak, partly as a result of government policies. (4) It may be also that private investment is somewhat understated in the national accounts of the LDC's, because of an underestimate of the small and inconspicuous investments by farmers, household enterprises, and other small-scale businesses.

The LDC data do not cover a long enough period to permit conclusions about time trends. In Argentina neither the GDCF/GNP ratio nor the PSCF/GDCF ratio shows any clear trend since the mid-1930s. In Mexico the PSCF/GDCF ratio shows a "bulge" in 1939–45, rising above 60 percent in some years. These years saw a major drive to construct rural infrastructure, particularly roads and irrigation works. From 1935 to 1945 roads and irrigation projects formed almost half of public sector investment. In the ten years after 1945 the PSCF/GDCF ratio fell back gradually to around 25 percent and has remained near that level since. The Mexican experience resembles one standard scenario for economic development—heavy

Table 14.7: Public Sector Investment Ratios, Mexico, 1939–62

	GDCF/GNP	GGCF/GDCF	PSCF/GDCF
1939		36.9	61.7
1940	9.9	26.9	47.9
1941		27.5	40.3
1942		32.1	57.5
1943		39.1	63.3
1944		41.2	61.2
1945	8.4	33.8	57.2
1946		19.2	38.1
1947		21.6	37.6
1948		25.7	40.2
1949		24.8	42.6
1950	14.7	23.0	41.8
1951		17.0	33.0
1952		17.4	32.7
1953		14.9	29.7
1954	18.9	16.7	34.1
1955		13.1	28.0
1956		10.5	22.1
1957		11.6	23.6
1958		11.7	26.0
1959		11.7	25.1
1960	21.3	9.6	26.5
1961		9.7	30.1
1962	18.0	10.8	32.7

Source: C. Reynolds, *Mexican Economy*, Tables 7.8 and 7.9.

infrastructure investment by government, followed by a burst of private investment in manufacturing, agriculture, etc. But twenty-five years is a short slice of history, and comparable evidence from other countries is lacking.

What Does Government Invest In?

Data on the objects of capital expenditure are not readily available and would have to be extracted from national sources. Failing *ex post* data, one can learn something from the *ex ante* allocations contained in national development plans. The limitations of this material are, first, that it usually shows a breakdown of development expenditure rather than of physical capital formation; and second, results do not correspond exactly with plans. There is some tendency for total government investment to fall short of target, while private investment often exceeds the plan figure. The percentage distribution of government investment among sectors, however, is usually not as far off target as the total figure.

Illustrative data for India and Pakistan are shown in Tables 14.8 and 14.9. The largest category is public utility-type investment in

Table 14.8: Sectoral Allocation of Planned Development Outlays, India, 1951-71
(Percentage of total)

Sector	First plan 1951–56	Second plan 1956–61	Third plan 1961–66	Fourth plan 1966–71
Agriculture	15.1	8.9	14.7	16.1
Irrigation	28.1[a]	13.0[a]	8.9	6.6
Large industry	7.6	27.4	20.8	21.5
Village industry		3.2	3.6	3.0
Power			13.8	13.1
Transport and communications	23.6	35.1	20.4	20.1
Education				9.4
Health	25.6[b]	12.4[b]	17.8[b]	7.3
Housing				2.3

[a] Includes irrigation and power.
[b] Includes education, health, housing, and miscellaneous items.

transportation, communications, water supply, and electricity. This usually takes 35 to 40 percent of the development budget. The allocations to industry and agriculture are roughly equal in size and together take another 35 to 40 percent. Finally, 20 percent or so of the budget goes for housing and city planning, education, health and family planning, and other activities.

Allocations differ somewhat from country to country, reflecting characteristics of the economy and national priorities. In Israel, for example, about half the development budget in the years 1953–63 went into "agriculture and national water projects." This reflects the country's limited water supplies and large amounts of potentially irrigable land. Ceylon has attached unusual importance to housing, which was scheduled to take 20 percent of 1959–68 public investment. Mexico has recently made a major drive in education, which doubled its share of the budget between the early 1950s and the early 1960s. As a general rule, however, physical infrastructure investment comes first, followed by manufacturing and agriculture in that order.

The pattern of public investment in today's LDC's is decidedly different from that in the MDC's during the nineteenth century. In

Table 14.9: Sectorial Allocation of Planned Development Outlays, Pakistan, 1955–70
(Percentage of total)

Sector	First plan 1955–60	Second plan 1960–65	Third plan 1965–70
Agriculture	16.0	20.4	13.5
Industry	17.3	12.8	15.3[a]
Water and power	28.8	27.3	24.5
Transport and communications	17.9	18.8	18.3
Education	6.3	6.1	7.9
Health and family planning	3.1	3.0	3.9
Housing	9.2	10.3	8.8
Miscellaneous	1.5	0.6	7.9[b]
Total	100.0	100.0	100.0

[a] Includes fuels and minerals.
[b] Of which the rural works program is 7.2.

that period, agriculture, manufacturing, and housing were not considered proper objects of public expenditure and were left almost entirely to the private sector. Thus public investment was much more heavily concentrated on infrastructure than is true at present. The LDC's are attempting to spread their limited resources over a wider spectrum of activities than that undertaken by their predecessors.

Financing Public Sector Capital Formation

The first obvious source of finance is government saving out of tax revenues. If revenues can be raised as a percentage of national income, and if the percentage of revenues saved can also be increased over time, then general government may be able to finance its own capital formation and even contribute to the capital needs of public enterprises. This is the picture set forth hopefully in most planning documents.

There is considerable doubt, however, whether this expectation is borne out by experience. When we look at the sources of finance for public sector investment in the ECAFE countries (Table 14.4), we note that the contribution of public sector saving is relatively small.[16]

16. It should be noted that the ECAFE study does not include transfers from abroad as part of public sector revenue, i.e. saving is defined as saving out of *domestic* resources. Foreign transfers are shown in Table 14.4 as a separate source of finance.

Only in Thailand and Malaysia does it amount to as much as one-third of the total. Moreover, an examination of year-to-year changes shows that in most countries the contribution of public saving has been declining during the 1960s.

The disappointing performance of public saving is due not so much to failure to raise revenues as to a high rate of increase in public consumption (Table 14.10). Government revenues have been rising at a respectable rate and in most countries form 14 to 20 percent of GNP (the latter figure equaling Sir Arthur Lewis's famous definition of proper fiscal performance). In half the countries of the group, however, current government expenditure has been rising even faster than revenue, so that the saving margin has been shrinking. The main exceptions are Taiwan and South Korea, whose economies have been growing unusually fast, and India, where a war-related, marked rise in tax levels has kept revenue increases somewhat ahead of current expenditure increases.

How, then, are the ambitious capital formation programs of these countries being financed? Looking again at Table 14.4, we see that foreign transfers have been the major source in Pakistan and an important source in several other countries. The largest single source, however, is domestic borrowing, which in most countries has provided something like half of the necessary finance. Some countries (India, Ceylon, Thailand) have been able to mobilize substantial amounts of private saving through postal savings schemes, government insurance systems, and security issues. There has been a growing tendency, however, to resort to borrowing from commercial and central banks. This has been the largest source of finance in the Philippines and a large source in several other countries.

Borrowing is a source of finance in a flow-of-funds sense, as a means of closing the gap in a development program. In real terms, however, an increase in public sector capital formation implies either mobilization of additional real resources or a reduction of private consumption and/or private investment. The real effects will differ with the type of borrowing. Where borrowing represents a transfer of household savings to government, the availability of acceptable government instruments may encourage saving at the expense of consumption. At the same time, there is probably some diversion of funds from private investment, tending to reduce private capital formation. Monetary expansion (at more than the noninflationary rate) may draw some additional resources into use, but this effect is probably

Table 14.10: Government Saving, Selected ECAFE Countries and Years

Country	Govt. saving as percentage of total saving[b]	Savings as percentage of government revenue				Revenue as percentage of GNP 1966		Annual growth rate of government revenue and govt. consumption		
		Period I		Period II		Tax revenue	Total revenue	Period	Government revenue	Government consumption
									(percentage per year)	
	(1)	(2)		(3)		(4)	(5)		(6)	(7)
India	21.4	1954–56	.13	1962–64	.17	12.2	14.6	1956–66	13.2	12.6
Pakistan	7.7	—	—	—	—	—	—	—	—	—
Ceylon	—	1956–58	.25	1964–66	.02	18.2	19.8	1956–66	4.3	5.9
Burma	29.7	1953–55	.24	1961–63	.14	13.7	16.0	1953–63	5.0	7.0
Malaysia	35.8	1960–61	.31	1962–63	.18	16.4	20.8	1960–65	4.8	11.5
Thailand	10.8	1959–61	.16	1964–66	.19	12.0	14.2	1959–66	11.6	10.4
Philippines	2.0	1956–58	.16	1964–66	.02	10.3	10.9	1956–66	9.5	11.2
Taiwan	18.3	1955–57	.05	1963–65	.01	12.4	18.1	1958–63	12.9	10.9
South Korea	9.5	1956–58	.42	1964–66	.11	10.7	13.2	1960–66	21.6	18.5

[a] Usually 1961–66, but slight variation of years from country to country.

Note: Data for general government only.

Source: ECAFE, *Economic Bulletin.*

small in the un-Keynesian world of the LDC's. The main effect is to impose some forced saving on consumers, while at the same time discouraging voluntary private saving.

The impression derived from the ECAFE study is consistent with the evidence contained in the Country Analysis Program studies. Mead reports a surplus of current expenditure over current revenue in the United Arab Republic budget during almost every year of his study, with the deficit growing rapidly from 1954 onward. Helleiner shows the Nigerian budget surplus on current account declining from 1951 onward and falling short of public sector capital formation by progressively larger amounts after 1954. For Ceylon, Snodgrass reports the government surplus on current account declining from 1954 on and becoming negligible or negative after 1958. Díaz reports public sector saving in Argentina as amounting to 25 percent of total gross saving in 1950–52 but falling to only 15 percent by 1959–61. The only deviation from the general pattern is in Mexico, where the government, since 1940, has typically been able to cover its investment, as well as its current expenditures, out of current revenue, and in the early 1960s was running a substantial financial surplus.

Díaz's findings for Argentina, which cover the entire public sector, are worth presenting as an example of method (Table 14.11). An equally meticulous examination of other economies would greatly advance our knowledge of public sector finance in the LDC's. Note that public enterprises in Argentina typically show an overall deficit in their current operations. These enterprise deficits are more than offset by surpluses in the current budget, yielding positive saving for the public sector as a whole. Public sector capital formation, however, typically exceeds public sector saving, leaving a financial deficit to be covered by either borrowings from the private sector, or monetary expansion. The trend of this deficit was upward over the years 1950–63.

These fragments of evidence suggest that: (1) the ratio of public sector saving to public sector capital formation is markedly lower in the LDC's than it has been historically in the MDC's; (2) in most LDC's this ratio is tending to fall over time; (3) an increase in public sector saving is highly desirable—perhaps essential—if public sector capital formation rates are to continue at their present level. Failing this, there is likely to be increasing resort to methods of finance that raise prices, intensify balance of payments difficulties, discourage voluntary saving, and reduce private investment incentives.

Table 14.11: Current Revenues and Expenditures of the Public Sector, Argentina, 1950–63
(Billion pesos at 1960 prices)

	1950	1951	1952	1953	1954	1955	1956	1957	1958	1959	1960	1961	1962	1963
General government (excl. soc. sec.)														
Current revenue	117	125	122	127	131	133	156	149	128	120	155	129	143	139
Current expenditure	96	96	93	104	121	120	104	97	102	81	100	117	118	102
Savings in current account	21	30	29	23	10	13	52	52	26	31	55	62	25	37
Social security system														
Revenues	35	34	32	38	43	43	44	43	32	27	33	38	28	33
Outlays	12	12	13	17	23	28	31	27	29	28	32	41	36	36
Savings in current account	22	22	19	21	20	15	13	17	3	−1	–	−2	−8	−3
Public enterprises														
Enterprises with savings	14	10	13	11	12	9	18	22	15	24	17	16	13	10
Enterprises with deficits	11	14	15	14	16	15	21	26	34	27	18	19	21	17
Net savings of public enterprises	3	−4	−2	−3	−5	−6	−3	−4	−20	−4	−1	−3	−9	−7
Public sector savings	46	48	46	41	25	22	62	65	10	27	54	56	8	27
Expenditure on capital account	58	52	45	47	45	39	38	48	77	49	65	72	59	62
Financial deficit or surplus	−11	−4	1	−6	−20	−17	24	17	−66	−22	−11	−15	−51	−35

Source: Díaz Alejandro, *Essays.*

The Performance of Public Corporations

Our final bit of evidence concerns the financial performance of public corporations. The IMF recently analyzed a sample of sixty-four government-owned corporations in twenty-six countries.[17] Balance sheets and income statements were compiled for each corporation for an average of seven years, mostly within the period 1955–65. Each corporation year was treated as an independent item, yielding some 450 observations. Two other points of method should be noted: (1) All financial items were taken from corporate records except depreciation allowances, for which a standard rate was applied to each type of industry, based on discussions with experts in these fields. (2) To convert data for each corporation to comparable form, incidentally avoiding currency conversion problems, it was necessary to reduce the key financial items to percentages of a base. This would normally be the value of corporate assets. Where investment has been spread over an extended period in the past, however, the current value of assets is somewhat conjectured, particularly in countries with a high rate of inflation. It was decided, therefore, to use as base the "current activity" of the corporation, defined as (current revenue + current expenditure)/2. All figures in Tables 14.12–14.15 are percentages of base in this sense.

The current cash flow of these enterprises, reduced to a percentage of "activity," is shown in Table 14.12. There are substantial differences in performance, by continent and by type of industry. Overall, however, the cash flow amounted to only 8 percent of activity. This fell well short of covering depreciation requirements, which the authors estimated at 24 percent of activity for the group as a whole. Including estimated depreciation in costs, the group showed a current operating *deficit* amounting to 16 percent of activity.

Despite operating losses, public corporations in most industries and areas continue to make large new investments (Table 14.13). Overall, gross investment in the years studied averaged 74 percent of current activity, of which 50 percent was net investment and 24 percent capital replacement. By using estimated capital output ratios, the authors calculate that this level of investment implies an increase

17. Andrew H. Gault and Guiseppe Dutto, "Financial Performance of Government-Owned Corporations in Less Developed Countries," IMF Staff Papers (March 1968).

Table 14.12: Flow-of-Funds Ratios by Area and Industry
(Percentage of activity)

Industry	Europe	Latin America	Africa	Asia	Overall mean
Railways	−20.0	−57.1	18.2	16.6	−13.5
Other transport	−0.5	−3.8	30.2	14.5	10.9
Petroleum	10.1	43.3			33.8
Electricity	27.4	21.0	21.4	37.7	27.2
Communications	24.8	26.7	−27.3	−10.2	5.7
Other industries	−12.4	−6.6	31.7		−6.3
Overall mean	0.7	2.1	19.5	16.4	8.0

Source: IMF Staff Papers, p. 108, Table 3.

of 15 percent per year in output of the corporations studied. This varies substantially, however, by type of industry. The implied rates of annual output increase are 26.4 percent for electricity, 18.5 percent for petroleum, and 0.1 percent for railroad transportation.

The financial position of the public corporations after taking account of investment requirements is shown in Table 14.14. On the average, for each dollar of current activity, the corporations need 66 cents of external funds to meet their investment needs. The situation differs substantially by area and industry, both as regards the size of external financing and the reasons for it. The electricity enterprises need external finance because of their rapid growth rates and high investment requirements. The railways, on the other hand, have low investment requirements but need funds to make up operating deficits.

Table 14.13: Gross Investment Ratios by Area and Industry
(Percentage of activity)

Industry	Europe	Latin America	Africa	Asia	Overall mean
Railways	17.7	32.3	26.8	29.1	27.5
Other transport	14.8	46.3	24.7	19.1	30 1
Petroleum	24.1	70.0	—	—	56.9
Electricity	49.3	114.2	100.9	208.7	129.2
Communications	20.3	51.5	13.8	47.9	37.7
Other industries	162.0	48.5	449.0	—	131.7
Overall mean	80.7	58.4	80.6	91.2	74.3

Source: IMF Staff Papers, p. 111, Table 6.

Table 14.14: Surplus-after-Investment Ratios by Area and Industry
(Percentage of activity)

Industry	Europe	Latin America	Africa	Asia	Overall mean
Railways	−37.7	−89.4	−8.6	−12.5	−41.0
Other transport	−15.3	−50.2	5.5	−4.5	−19.3
Petroleum	−14.0	−26.7	—	—	−23.1
Electricity	−21.9	−93.2	−79.5	−171.1	−102.0
Communications	4.5	−24.9	−41.1	−58.1	−32.0
Other industries	−174.4	−55.1	−417.4	—	−138.1
Overall mean	−80.0	−56.3	−61.1	−74.8	−66.3

Source: IMF Staff Papers, p. 113, Table 8.

One possible source of external funds is transfers from the general government budget. The size of such transfers is shown in Table 14.15. On the average, government transfers provide about half of the necessary external finance. Again, the situation varies markedly by region and industry. Comparison of Tables 14.14 and 14.15 shows that government transfers are very important in Latin America, much less important in Africa. Transfers provide almost all of the funds for the railways and other transport enterprises. But the expanding and profitable electricity corporations are able to get two-thirds of their external funds from other sources, and the petroleum enterprises require no government transfers. The funds not provided by transfers presumably come from bona fide loans from government, other domestic borrowing, or borrowing from the International Bank for Research and Development and other foreign lending institutions.

Table 14.15: Transfers Excluding Loans, from Central Government Budget, by Area
and Industry
(Percentage of activity)

Industry	Europe	Latin America	Africa	Asia	Overall mean
Railways	29.2	90.6	0.6	−0.1	35.3
Other transport	3.3	44.5	−1.5	6.4	17.8
Petroleum	1.3	−1.6	—	—	−0.7
Electricity	1.0	59.6	8.4	56.1	33.7
Communications	−8.1	14.5	42.1	58.0	28.6
Other industries	74.6	45.7	100.6	—	63.3
Overall mean	33.2	42.3	13.4	34.8	32.9

Source: IMF Staff Papers, p. 115, Table 9.

In addition to budget transfers, public corporations usually receive various indirect subsidies, such as tax exemptions, tariff protection, and preferential license treatment.

These findings are obviously subject to errors arising from the nature of the sample, noncomparability in the corporate records used, faulty estimation of depreciation requirements, and other factors. But the errors could scarcely be large enough to alter the general conclusion that "government-owned corporations, rather than serving as a focal point for collecting financial resources for their own investment or for other purposes, have generally placed a financial burden on parent governments." [18]

ISSUES AND HYPOTHESES

The data surveyed above are too frail to support strong conclusions. It does seem that many LDC's are assuming public investment burdens heavier than those borne by the MDC's at a comparable stage of development, with regard to both size and the spectrum of activities included; and they are assuming them despite an inadequate level of public sector saving. Public sector investment is being sustained by large infusions of foreign capital whose continuation on the present scale is by no means assured; by substantial drafts on private saving, which must be somewhat competitive with private investment; and, in some countries, by bank borrowing on a scale that intensifies domestic inflation and balance of payments difficulties.

Our main purpose, however, has not been to draw conclusions but to lay a factual background for future investigation. Among the many possible lines of research, we shall comment briefly on three: the behavior of current government expenditure, the determinants of the PSCF/GDCF ratio, and the economic performance of public corporations.

The Behavior of Current Expenditure

If one is interested in raising the government saving rate to facilitate capital formation, one has to be interested in current expenditure. Given a certain rate of increase in revenues, the saving margin can be widened only by achieving a lower rate of increase in expenditure. We have noted that LDC performance in this respect is quite variable,

18. Ibid., p. 126.

and that in most countries the saving margin seems to be narrowing.

It would be useful, therefore, to analyze the determinants of current expenditure for a substantial cross-section of LDC's. The relevant variables might include:

1. The rate of increase per capita income. The income elasticity of demand for such current services as health and education is probably high in most countries. Thorn's cross-section analysis of countries at all income levels suggests an elasticity of about 1.6 for this category.[19]

2. The rate of increase of the urban population, or of urban population as a percentage of national population. In all countries urban residents consume substantially more public services than rural residents.

3. The extent of military pressure for defense and police expenditures as indicated, say, by the army and police share of the current budget. One could experiment with a dummy variable for presence or absence of a military regime, which might affect the pressure for military spending.

4. The relative wage level of public employees and the rate of increase in this level. In some countries the wages of all "modern sector" workers, including public employees, are well above earnings in traditional activities, and there is often political pressure to widen this gap over time. Some finance ministries feel that they must build into their budgeting a regular increase of, say, 5 percent a year, to take account of this factor.

5. The degree of population pressure, which may generate a demand for overstaffing of government agencies. Output of public services is quite labor intensive, and the rate of increase in government employment may be related more closely to unemployment rates than to increases in the "real" demand for public services.

To the extent that this kind of analysis can explain intercountry differences in performance, it might lay a foundation for policy recommendations.

Government Capital Formation Ratios

What determines the GGCF/GDCF and the PSCF/GDCF ratios? One might hypothesize that these ratios are positively associated with:

1. The GDCF/GNP ratio, serving as a proxy for the economy's

19. Richard S. Thorn, "The Evolution of Public Finances during Economic Development," *Manchester School* 35, no. 1 (January 1967).

stage of development. The hypothesis would be that, in the early decades of development, there is a simultaneous increase in GNP per capita, in the GDCF/GNP ratio, and in the PSCF/GDCF ratio, i.e. PSCF is rising faster than GDCF, which in turn is rising faster than GNP. A difficulty in testing this or any similar hypothesis is that GNP measures in the LDC's are quite unreliable. The "noise" from this source might obscure any actual existing relationship.

2. The availability of finance. There is probably something to the Peacock-Wiseman hypothesis that governments spend what they have, and that as additional resources become available there is an automatic expenditure adjustment. Since the sources of finance for public sector capital formation are diverse and not fully substitutable, one would need to analyze separately such variables as tax revenues as a percentage of GNP, private saving as a percentage of national income, and the availability of foreign capital.

It would be desirable to distinguish central government from lower levels of government as regards both investment behavior and current expenditure analysis. The Peacock-Wiseman hypothesis and other hypotheses about the long-term growth of public expenditure relate mainly to central government. It is a plausible hypothesis that state and local governments, which operate on a more restricted fiscal base, are less responsive than central governments to pressures for increased expenditure.

3. Existence of an effective development planning organization. "Effective" in this connection is synonymous with the ability of the planning group to infiltrate the budget-making process, and more particularly to serve as a proponent of the capital or development budget. Closely related is the training of staff in the various ministries in project preparation, the placing of annual budgets in a framework of multiyear expenditure projections, and a follow-up on project execution. Where these activities are being carried out effectively, one might expect to find both a higher PSCF/GDCF ratio and a more "developmental" emphasis in the current budget.

Our object here is descriptive, not normative. We do not mean to imply that a high PSCF/GDCF ratio is per se a "good thing." The policy objective is presumably to increase *total* saving and investment in the economy and to allocate funds on the basis of prospective return. Efforts to expand public investment may lead to methods of finance that encroach on private saving and reduce private investment more than public investment is increased. They may also lead to displacement of higher yield private projects by lower yield public projects.

Economic Performance of Public Corporations

This is an underinvestigated area, partly because the source materials are scattered. But the fact that public corporations carry out a large part of public sector investment and that they depend heavily on external transfers and borrowing makes careful investigation indispensable to an understanding of the public sector.

Failure to cover full costs is not necessarily an indication of unsatisfactory performance. Losses could result from inadequacies of management and supervision, from overpricing of labor or overstaffing, or from the "political" underpricing of services. On the other hand, systematic use of marginal-cost pricing could also lead to operating losses, and there are well-known welfare arguments in favor of such a policy.

It would seem useful to have case studies of railroads, electricity systems, and other public enterprises in a variety of countries. Starting from theories of optimal enterprise performance—which might themselves need some adaptation to LDC conditions—one could investigate the extent to which operating deficits are inadvertent or deliberate, and whether transfers from the general budget required to cover them represent an efficient use of resources.

This paper has tried to suggest the need for a broad view of public sector operations and for giving expenditure analysis equal billing with tax analysis. Such a reordering of priorities is already apparent in fiscal research in the United States. One may hope that this foreshadows a similar shift of emphasis in work on the less developed countries.

Comments by Howard Pack

Why do governments undertake investment activities? If one considers the types of investment in which they engage, such as roads, irrigation facilities, and electricity-generating plants, it is apparent that none of these really constitutes public goods: that is, potential consumers of the output of these facilities could be excluded from their use if they were unwilling to pay a specified service charge. Of course, from a welfare viewpoint the desirable price might be zero, but nevertheless the potential of exclusion exists. Government capital formation is required not because of the public-good nature of these activities, but as a result of the unwillingness or inability of the private sector to undertake socially desirable activities, for whatever reason. These include the lumpy nature of much overhead capital and the difficulty of finding sufficient private funds; negative attitudes toward foreign investment; the failure of the private sector to perceive potential long-term benefits; and, perhaps most important, the inability of the private sector to appropriate the externalities that may make a project socially desirable but privately profitless, unless unrealistically high prices are charged for the service. On the other hand, even in instances where the private sector may be willing and able to undertake the provision of social overhead capital, political pressures such as those stemming from large-scale unemployment, or a desire to avoid large-scale private enterprise for distributional reasons, may nevertheless lead to public investment; for example, public rather than private ownership of the railroad systems in many Latin American countries has allowed their use as an employer of last resort.

These considerations suggest that the ratio of public sector to total investment will reflect a large set of economic and political factors. One part of Lloyd Reynolds's extremely useful survey of our existing knowledge of the role of government in capital formation focuses on the share of the public sector in total investment (denoted here by i_p). Both time series and cross-section data are presented for developed and less developed countries (LDC's).

For a number of Western countries the data indicate that the government's role in capital formation has been rising continuously, even up to the present. This is a bit surprising, as one might have expected that after the initial burst of public investment in the form of railroads and utilities such activity would have declined.[1] However, we must recognize that i_p may fail to decline simply as the result of prior successful public investment. Thus a successful irrigation program raising agricultural output may result in migration to urban areas and concomitant large expenditures on housing, sewerage, and other urban facilities. Moreover, the continuation of high (even rising) levels

1. There is a question here of changes in the form of ownership, as in the United Kingdom, as well as of the fact that in the United States much of the social overhead was provided by the private sector.

of public investment is probably closely related to changing demands by the private sector. Thus in the United States the high demand for education combined with the postwar baby boom has increased the demand for educational facilities, while the growth of an automobile culture has led to an insatiable desire for more roads. Similarly, increasing income may lead to a growing demand for telephones and a large investment in the communication system. Thus, a constant level of i_p in the developed countries may mask a switch from the dominance of developmental capital, providing mainly intermediate inputs to producers, toward capital that has a very high link with consumption. This suggests that the current LDC's may not be able to reduce their government investment effort even after sustained growth occurs unless there are simultaneous efforts at controlling the composition of final demand.

When we consider the cross-section data for the developed countries there is little systematic variation, say, with per capita income, but rather the ratios reflect, as Reynolds concludes, differences in the conception of the "proper economic functions" of government. The same seems to be true for the LDC's, where i_p ranges from over 60 percent in India to slightly over 20 percent in some Latin American countries. Given the multitude of factors determining i_p one wonders if a cross-section approach as suggested in Reynolds's research agenda is likely to be fruitful. Scatter diagrams relating i_p to a number of variables suggested by Reynolds, such as the tax ratio and private saving ratio, indicate little systematic relationship. Admittedly, in a multiple regression analysis these variables might turn out to be significant. However, recent experience in trying to explain tax ratios suggests that optimism is not warranted with respect to obtaining good cross-section results for relationships for which there are no well-defined behavioral assumptions (as there are in the case of the consumption function).[2] Considerable progress in understanding the budgetary process and the milieu within which it functions will be necessary before meaningful cross-country work can begin. One suspects Reynolds may agree with this evaluation, as his explanation for the rise in Mexico's i_p relies on country-specific structural information rather than on such general economic variables as tax ratios.

2. See for example, H. Hinrichs, "Determinants of Government Revenue Share among Less Developed Countries," *Economic Journal,* September 1965, and the comments by V. Tanzi and C. McCuistron, *Economic Journal,* June 1967.

Moreover in his list of suggested factors influencing this ratio Reynolds includes "the existence of an effective planning organization," a variable not easily quantified but clearly important in determining i_p.

A second area investigated by Reynolds concerns the sectoral allocation of government-fixed investment. This is related to the broader area of the desirable allocation of government-controlled development resources, of which fixed investment constitutes an important component. Although Reynolds infers from admittedly scanty data that the current LDC's invest more in agriculture, manufacturing, and housing than the developed countries did at a similar stage of development, he has not been able to cite systematic studies of the determinants of sectoral patterns of government investment. Critics of existing national development plans have often cited the disproportion between the relative importance of agriculture in the national economy and the resources directed to it in various plans. The Indian plan cited exemplifies this disparity. Thus attention should be focused on the budgetary process and the justification (if any) offered for the neglect of agriculture and the mechanism by which this is transmitted into budgetary decisions. This is an important area of research which may be added to the Reynolds agenda.

Finally, we consider the question of government saving. Reynolds's data indicate increasing difficulty in financing investment programs without resort to domestic or foreign borrowing. But is domestic deficit financing really to be avoided? [3] Presumably a danger inherent in such financing is inflation. However, among the Asian countries considered, most have not experienced serious inflation. Moreover, small government deficits financed by debt issue may serve a useful function by increasing the supply of relatively secure assets or perhaps encouraging the growth of more adequate financial markets. Similarly, bank-financed deficits may increase the money supply in a manner satisfying asset preferences. Or it is conceivable that some amount of Keynesian unemployment is present in some sectors of the economy, and a small deficit may prove beneficial.

This is not to deny that deficit finance may have adverse effects. Rather the point is that the context in which the deficit occurs must

3. Foreign borrowing may present other difficulties connected with the servicing of the debt.
4. For example, investigation of whether government debt, by driving up the interest rate, displaces private investment.

be considered. While some of the relevant framework may be a straightforward adaptation of methods already familiar from Keynesian analysis, systematic exploration of the impact of relatively small deficits on financial market development, the satisfaction of asset preferences, and the response of supply to mild inflation (if it occurs) have yet to be undertaken. Government saving clearly has an important role to perform when private saving is inadequate. Indeed, the recent experience cited by Reynolds suggests that the failure of governments to raise their saving rate may become an important bottleneck to further development. In this area, as in the others discussed above, Reynolds provides an important summary of our existing knowledge and a useful guide to areas of needed further research.

CONTRIBUTORS

R. Albert Berry (Yale University)
Benjamin Cohen (Yale University)
Richard N. Cooper (Yale University)
Carlos R. Díaz-Alejandro (Yale University)
Charles R. Frank, Jr. (Princeton University)
Samuel P. S. Ho (University of British Columbia)
Shane Hunt (Princeton University)
Stephen H. Hymer (New School for Social Research)
James W. Land (Rice University)
Markos Mamalakis (University of Wisconsin-Milwaukee)
Howard Pack (Swarthmore College)
Gustav Ranis (Yale University)
Clark W. Reynolds (Food Research Institute, Stanford University)
Lloyd G. Reynolds (Yale University)
Donald Snodgrass (Development Advisory Service, Malaysia)

COMMENTATORS

R. Albert Berry (Yale University)
Carlos Díaz-Alejandro (Yale University)
Charles R. Frank, Jr. (Princeton University)
Shane Hunt (Princeton University)
Stephen H. Hymer (New School for Social Research)
Van Doorn Ooms (Swarthmore College)
Howard Pack (Swarthmore College)
Hugh T. Patrick (Yale University)
Gustav Ranis (Yale University)
Stephen A. Resnick (Yale University)
Charles R. Rockwell (previously at Yale University)
Daniel M. Schydlowsky (Harvard University)
John Sheahan (Williams College)
Erik Thorbecke (Iowa State University-Ames)

Index

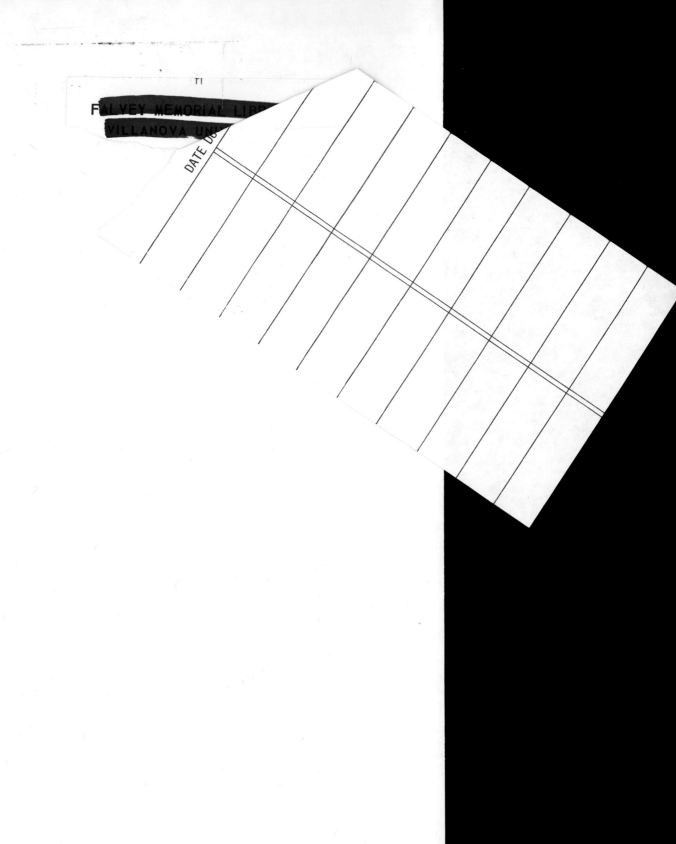